The American Polity

The People and Their Government

The American Polity

The People and Their Government

Everett Carll Ladd

University of Connecticut and
The Roper Center for Public Opinion Research

W · W · Norton & Company

New York London

Copyright © 1985 by W. W. Norton & Company, Inc.

ALL RIGHTS RESERVED.

Published simultaneously in Canada by Penguin Books Canada Ltd, 2801 John Street, Markham, Ontario L3R 1B4.

PRINTED IN THE UNITED STATES OF AMERICA.

The Text of this book is composed in Aster, with display type set in Novarese. Composition by Vail-Ballou. Manufacturing by The Maple-Vail Book Manufacturing Group. Book design by Bernie Klein. Page makeup by Ben Gamit.

FIRST EDITION

Library of Congress Cataloging in Publication Data
Ladd, Everett Carll.
    The American polity.
    1. United States—Politics and government.   I. Title.
JK274.L23   1985   320.973   84–29442

ISBN 0-393-95348-3

W. W. Norton & Company, Inc.,
500 Fifth Avenue, New York, N.Y. 10110

W. W. Norton & Company Ltd.,
37 Great Russell Street, London WC1B 3NU

1 2 3 4 5 6 7 8 9 0

For My Family

We begin our public affections in our families.
No cold relation is a zealous citizen.
                                    —Edmund Burke

Contents in Brief

Contents

Part 5 Public Policy

Preface

In 1987 the United States celebrates the two-hundredth anniversary of its greatest political accomplishment: the writing of the Constitution. The fifty-five delegates to the Constitutional Convention in Philadelphia completed their work on September 17, 1787. On that day, delegate Benjamin Franklin offered his colleagues his assessment of the document they had prepared for submission to the thirteen states.

> I doubt whether any other Convention we can obtain may be able to make a better Constitution. For when you assemble a number of men to have the advantage of their joint wisdom, you inevitably assemble with those men, all their prejudices, their passions, their errors of opinion, their local interests, and their selfish views. From such an Assembly can a perfect production be expected? It therefore astonishes me, Sir, to find this system approaching so near to perfection as it does. . . .

In September 1787, the Constitution and the new government it established were but a beginning experiment, albeit one Franklin felt was full of promise. Now, about to enter its third century, American constitutional democracy is surely no longer experimental. It has been tried and tested, and the soundness of the work done in Philadelphia by Franklin and his fifty-four colleagues continues to astonish us.

I have chosen to call this text *The American Polity*. With the same Greek root as the word politics, polity is a shorter way of saying political system, and the two expressions are used interchangeably throughout this book. But there is reason beyond stylistic convenience for calling this an inquiry into the American polity. The greatest writer on politics in all of antiquity, and one of the most profound theorists of all time, was the Athenian philosopher Aristotle (384 to 322 B.C.) The first to write systematically on democracy as a system of government, Aristotle distinguished between two basic forms of democracy: one involved direct rule by the people, which he thought carried with it great threats to personal liberty and minority rights; the other was based on constitutionalism and the guarantee of individual rights, which he thought held promise of being the best of all government. Aristotle called the latter πολιτεια, or politeia, translated as polity or constitutional government.[1]

The American system of government is a polity in Aristotle's sense of the term: a particular type of democracy established on the principles of constitutionalism and representation, with safeguards for minority rights. It deserves to be studied as something more than a collection of institutions or processes. It is in the meshing of diverse political activities and the interplay of people and their government that we most clearly see what is distinctive about our polity.

Approaching the Study of American Government

I made my debut as a faculty member at the University of Connecticut in the fall of 1964, when Barry Goldwater was waging his spectacularly unsuccessful campaign for the presidency against Lyndon Johnson. The first course I taught was "Poli Sci 173," an introduction to American government. I have taught it about twenty times since then, and it has remained my favorite. The ideas for this text have been shaped by many associations and events, but especially by the still-exciting experience of introducing my own students to the American polity.

Students reading this text have already acquired information on the study of American government and politics from discussions with family and friends, in high school classes, through television, newspapers and magazines, and more. But the subject is a big one, and the ways of examining it are enormously varied. In writing *The American Polity* I have assumed a readership aware of a familiar subject, yet often unclear how the pieces fit together, how the system works. This audience needs a text that provides the store of basic common information about the polity required both for further study and for informed citizenship: detailed information on American political beliefs and values, the primary institutions of government, the form and substance of political participation by individuals and groups, and the major policy commitments and choices the United States has made. But the college student needs something more than these bare essentials. One main reason for writing the text was to attempt to bring greater depth and unity to a subject all too often studied piecemeal. This depth is achieved by providing as backdrops three different perspectives: societal, historical, and cross-national.

[1] *The Politics of Aristotle*, H. Rackham, trans. (Cambridge, Mass.: Harvard University Press, 1977), pp. 206–7.

Societal perspective. Social science has carved up the study of social experience into discrete segments, divided among disciplines like political science, economics, and sociology. This is unavoidable, but society is not so compartmentalized. Those parts of American society that we label "government" influence and in turn are influenced by all of the other parts—components involving the economy; systems of social and cultural values; education and technology; the ethnic, racial, and religious group composition of the population; and many others. For example, in the first twenty-five years following World War II, the median income of all American families doubled in real terms—after controlling for the effects of inflation. This is an economic fact, but who would doubt that it had enormous implications for almost every facet of our society, including political life? The first section of this text looks closely at aspects of American society that are especially important in defining the environment for the country's government, politics, and public policy. In the remaining chapters I keep returning to the many concrete links between the polity and the larger society of which it is a part.

Historical perspective. With so much to discuss about the practice of American government today, the influence of the past can easily be shortchanged. Historical perspective is essential, for two somewhat different reasons. First, contemporary institutions and practices did not suddenly emerge full-grown. We understand them better—whether it is the presidency, political parties, or American welfare policy—by seeing the course they have taken. To ignore the past is to deprive ourselves of an immense amount of comparative experience.

Second, there have been powerful continuities in American political experience. With the drafting of the U.S. Constitution in 1787 and its ratification a year later, a set of political institutions consistent with the country's political beliefs were put in place (see chapters 4, 5, and 6). The persistence of the primary political institutions—the Constitution, the presidency, Congress, the judiciary, the sharing of power by the federal and state governments—over the last two centuries is an extraordinary facet of American political experience. That American presidents have been chosen in fifty consecutive elections from 1789 to the present, sworn in by the same oath to the same Constitution, committed to the same essential political values reflects a measure of stability unmatched anywhere. In this text I frequently draw examples from earlier eras in American life to make more concrete what might otherwise appear as mere assertion that important continuities are everywhere evident in our political system, even in the face of great social and economic change.

Cross-national perspective. Some of the responses the United States has given to enduring problems of policy and governance closely resemble those made by Great Britain, France, West Germany, and the other major industrial democracies. But the American system also reflects its own distinctive institutional arrangements and policy choices. By providing cross-national comparison throughout, I have tried to present our own system in a rounder, more complete and accurate way.

The Ladd Report

The American political parade never stops. Daily newspapers like the *New York Times*, the *Los Angeles Times*, and others, the broadcast networks, and weekly magazines of governmental affairs such as *Congressional Quarterly* and *National Journal*, help us follow the ever-changing course of political events. But the perspective of a political science text, going beyond the headlines and analyzing the dynamics of American society and government, is also important. So that this perspective can be continuously applied to major new developments, I will write a report twice each year, and Norton will make it available without charge to all students who are using *The American Polity* in their course work.

The Ladd Report will analyze important trends and actions in whatever area of government they occur, with specific page references to the text. For example, should a series of new appointments to the U.S. Supreme Court take place in 1985 or 1986 as sitting justices retire, and the Court hands down decisions that depart from earlier ones, *The Ladd Report* will be there to assess these developments in a timely fashion, and to link them with the discussion in chapters 10 ("The Judiciary") and 17 ("Civil Liberties and Civil Rights").

The Plan of the Book

The first two parts of *The American Polity* survey the setting for American political life. Part 1 examines the social setting, including the country's social origins and development, present-day economic trends, and such diverse social attributes of the populace as their ethnic backgrounds and educational attainments. For, in the 1960s and 1970s, the United States moved into a new era in its societal experience, the postindustrial era, with far-reaching implications for government and politics. Part 2 then looks at the central beliefs and values of Americans: the country's ideological tradition, derived from classical liberalism; the expression of this ideology in the basic law, the Constitution; our commitment to and practice of a particular type of democratic government.

We move in Part 3 to a detailed consideration of the principal institutions and arrangements of national government. These include, of course, the Congress, the presidency and executive branch, and the federal courts; but they also include the distinctly American form of governmental interaction, built around *separation of powers, checks and balances,* and *federalism.* Together these arrangements have greatly dispersed power among the states and the three branches of the national government. We see that other democracies have ordered their political institutions quite differently. The strengths and weaknesses of the American system are still debated; that its institutional form exerts enormous influence on every aspect of the country's politics is beyond dispute.

From the organization of government in Part 3, we turn in Part 4 to public opinion, political parties, voting and elections, interest groups, and communications media—the means by which groups participate in politics and government. People do not participate in a political vacuum, but in and through the setting their governmental institutions establish. For example, interest groups are fewer and more centralized in Great Britain than in the United States because governmental decision-making is more centralized there than here. The American system of dispersed power, accruing from separation of powers and federalism, gives interest groups many diverse points of governmental access through which to advance their goals.

Part 5, the last section of the text, is devoted to American public policy in four major sectors: civil liberties and civil rights, political economy, public welfare, and defense and foreign policy. Here again, the positioning of text chapters reflects a logic inhering to the way the political system works or unfolds. National public policy is the product of complex forces that begin with basic characteristics and needs of the society and underlying values and ideological predispositions of the people, that work their way on the institutions of government and through the constraints institutional arrangements impose, and that reflect the push and pull of individual and group participation. Like every other political system, the American polity ultimately expresses itself in the character of the policy choices it makes.

Acknowledgments

Like most other authors, I have always found myself upon completing a book with a long list of debts needing acknowledgment. This is even more the case now as I conclude a comprehensive text to which so many people have contributed so much.

The team of political science reviewers that my publisher, Norton, assembled were extraordinarily painstaking and helpful. My thanks go to Dean Alfange, Jr., University of Massachusetts at Amherst; David Brady, Rice University; Randall L. Calvert, Washington University; James Carter, Sam Houston State University; George Cole, University of Connecticut; M. Margaret Conway, University of Maryland; William Havard, Vanderbilt University; Malcolm Jewell, University of Kentucky; Scott Keeter, Rutgers University; Robert O. Keohane, Brandeis University; Louis W. Koenig, New York University; Fred A.

Kramer, University of Massachusetts at Amherst; Joseph Kruzel, Ohio State University; Robert Lieber, Georgetown University; Paul Light, National Academy of Public Administration; Samuel Long, Pace University; David B. Magleby, Brigham Young University; Thomas Patterson, Syracuse University; Michael B. Preston, University of Illinois; Donald L. Robinson, Smith College; John Schmidhauser, University of Southern California; Charles Tidmarch, Union College; and David Walker, University of Connecticut.

The Study Guide for *The American Polity* has been done thoughtfully and imaginatively by David B. Magleby of Brigham Young University. Margaret Kenski of Pima Community College and Henry Kenski of the University of Arizona have expertly developed the Instructor's Manual and the Test-Item File.

Colleagues in public opinion research have contributed much to this text. In particular, Burns W. Roper of the Roper Organization and Daniel Yankelovich of Yankelovich, Skelly, and White have helped me understand better American attitudes and values. Working closely with my friends at *Public Opinion* magazine during the past seven years has also taught me much—besides being great fun. Seymour Martin Lipset and Ben J. Wattenberg have been coeditors throughout. David R. Gergen was the first managing editor, until January 1981 when he became director of communications in Ronald Reagan's White House staff. William Schambra was the magazine's first deputy managing editor, a position now held by Victoria A. Sackett. Nicola L. Furlan has been the assistant editor. To the current managing editor of *Public Opinion*, Karlyn H. Keene, I owe a debt that almost rivals the one run up by the Reagan administration. Karlyn has read and commented on each chapter, sometimes in two or three succeeding drafts. Her honesty, support, and unfailing good judgment have made this a better book.

My colleagues in the Department of Political Science at the University of Connecticut, and at the Roper Center for Public Opinion Research, have been extraordinarily tolerant and forebearing—especially when I would disappear for large blocks of time to work on the text, only to emerge grumpy and snappish. Ranking high in tolerance and collegial helpfulness are W. Wayne Shannon, G. Donald Ferree, Jr., Marilyn Potter, John Benson, and Lois Timms. Ranking even higher, because her position put her so directly in the line of fire, is my research assistant, Marianne Simonoff. Her care and diligence were sustained throughout the project. Sandra Berriault did a fine job entering much of the text in our trusty word processor. My special thanks and deep appreciation go to my administrative assistant, Lynn A. Zayachkiwsky. Her maturity, thoughtfulness, dependability, and all-round professional competence made it possible for us to keep both the Roper Center and the text more or less on track and on schedule these past two years.

Sometime in 1968 I had the great good fortune of meeting Donald

S. Lamm. He was then a college editor at Norton, and from our discussions came my commitment to write a history of the U.S. party system—published two years later by Norton as *American Political Parties: Social Change and Political Response*. I have worked with him on a number of books since then, and the collaboration has been the most important of my professional life. Now as president of Norton, he has had a big hand in delivering *The American Polity*. As always, his support was valuable and his friendship invaluable.

My many other Norton associations have been strong and positive. Donald Fusting has been my editor on this text, and my respect for his work has deepened over our two years in harness together. Nancy Palmquist did a wonderful job as project editor on the entire manuscript. So, too, did Caroline McKinley, who was responsible for photographs and illustrations.

Authors often close their acknowledgments by recognizing the role played by their families—and for good reason. Not many people go through the experience of writing a book without realizing how much their families have borne the inconveniences and contributed to the joy. *The American Polity* is dedicated to my father and the memory of my mother, to my wife, Cynthia, and our children, Benjamin, Melissa, Corina, and Carll, to Carll's wife, Elizabeth Lovejoy Ladd, and Corina's fiancee, Gerald Moran.

Storrs, Connecticut
December 15, 1984

Part 1 | American Society

1 | The American Polity: Continuity and Change

On May 9, 1831, a twenty-six-year-old French aristocrat completed an arduous voyage to the New World by setting foot in the tiny fishing village of Newport, Rhode Island, where his New York–bound ship had been forced by an unobliging wind. Alexis Charles Henri Clerel de Tocqueville had come ostensibly to study American prisons in order to advise his government on penal reform. But Tocqueville's real intention was to examine "in detail and as scientifically as possible, all the mechanisms of that vast American society which everyone talks of and no one knows." Nine months later, on February 20, 1832, having crisscrossed the United States and interviewed hundreds of Americans—including President Andrew Jackson—Tocqueville sailed for home. It was not until a year-and-a-half later, in the fall of 1833, that Tocqueville began in earnest to write his book. Working quickly, he finished it in just a year. And in January 1835, *De la Democratie en Amerique* was published in Paris. Tocqueville's *Democracy in America* was immediately acclaimed a masterpiece not only in France but also in Great Britain and the United States. Now, 150 years later, it still lays fair claim to being considered the most insightful book ever written about American society and politics.[1]

Tocqueville set out to accomplish two objectives that relate to the

[1]*Democracy in America* is available in several fine English translations and editions. The original Henry Reeve translation, as revised by Francis Bowen, and later further corrected by Phillips Bradley, has been published in paperback in two volumes (New York: Vintage Books, 1958). A one-volume paperback edition contains most of the essential material (New York: New American Library; first published, 1956). For a valuable description of Alexis de Tocqueville, his journey, and his ideas, see George Wilson Pierson, *Tocqueville in America* (Garden City, N.Y.: Doubleday/Anchor Books abridgement, 1959; first published as *Tocqueville and Beaumont in America*, 1938).

Alexis de Tocqueville

study of American government in our own time, and he largely succeeded: to see the system as a whole, and to see where it was headed.

To see the system as a whole. Tocqueville believed that one could not
understand a country's government by looking just at its governmental institutions. There was a strong interaction among (1) the beliefs
and values of a people, (2) their social institutions, and (3) their political system. He thought, for example, that the religious beliefs and
institutions the Pilgrims had brought with them to New England
contributed much to the vigorous democratic practice that took root
long before independence was achieved from the British Crown. The
Pilgrims thought that every individual should have a knowledge of
Scripture, which meant that everyone should be able to read—so
they pioneered in establishing a compulsory system of public education. This helped make citizens more aware and better able to involve
themselves in community life. Believing that each individual was
equal in the eyes of God, the Pilgrims proposed rules, compacts,
and institutions that gave each person a voice in affairs such as
government. Such beliefs were "not merely a religious doctrine,
but . . . corresponded in many points with the most absolute democratic and republican theories," Tocqueville wrote. In New England
"a democracy, more perfect than antiquity had dared to dream of,

*The early Americans
and democracy*

started in full size and panoply from the midst of an ancient feudal society."[2]

This was just one of many linkages involving beliefs, social institutions, and governmental arrangements that Tocqueville described in *Democracy in America*. We cannot understand today's American government and politics unless we recognize that ideas and values, economic perspectives and institutions, the social makeup of the population as defined by ethnicity, education, income, and all such dimensions of American society constantly impinge upon the country's political life.

To see where we are headed and why. Tocqueville lived at a time when Western society was caught up in extraordinary change. The old order based on the principle of aristocracy—in which social position was determined by birth, and a small hereditary elite enjoyed a great disproportion of wealth, social status, and political power—was coming under attack and being replaced, with varying rates of speed from one country to another. The newly ascendant principles were (1) individualism, (2) social equality, and (3) political democracy. *Individualism* involves the idea that society is built around the individual and is obliged to provide him with such rights as life, liberty, and the pursuit of happiness. It also carries with it an emphasis on individual responsibility, and the belief that society advances best by encouraging individual achievement. Tocqueville saw the tide of individualism rising throughout the West.

Individualism and the building of America.

[2]Tocqueville, *Democracy in America*, p. 43.

Social equality and
political democracy

Tocqueville also believed that the increase of *social equality* was irresistible. The aristocracy to which he belonged in France had been humbled by the cry of *égalité* during the French Revolution (begun in 1789); similar currents were sweeping all of Europe. "The gradual development of the principle of equality is, therefore, a Providential fact. It is universal, it is durable, it constantly eludes all human interference, and all events as well as all men contribute to its progress."[3] Social arrangements rooted in the idea that some groups have a permanent claim to superior status, which was the basis of aristocratic society, were collapsing and would never be reestablished. *Political democracy* followed naturally from individualism and social equality. If societies were giving greater recognition to the claims of individuals who had equal rights and deserved an equal chance to work and achieve, political institutions providing for popular sovereignty or rule by the people would have to be devised and extended.

In the 1830s, the world Tocqueville knew was beset by changes that forced societies to come to terms with the great ideas of individualism, equality, and democracy. It was a revolutionary era. Where would it end? The young Frenchman felt that "there is a country in the world where the great social revolution which I am speaking of seems to have nearly reached its natural limits." He meant America. So he came here

> in order to discern its natural consequences, and to find out, if possible, the means of rendering it profitable to mankind. I confess that, in America, I sought more than America; I sought there the image of democracy itself, with its inclinations, its character, its prejudices, and its passions, in order to learn what we have to fear or hope from its progress.[4]

Uniqueness of
American democracy

Still, Tocqueville really did not believe that the progress of individualism, equality, and democracy was going to be the same elsewhere as in the United States. The success of these ideas in America was unique because it was so free of conflict. The revolutionary impact of the ideas occurred

> with ease and quietness; say rather that this country is reaping the fruits of the democratic revolution which we [in Europe] are undergoing, without having had the revolution itself. The emigrants who colonized the shores of America in the beginning of the seventeenth century somehow separated the democratic principle from all the principles which it had to contend with in the old communities of Europe, and transplanted it alone to the New World.[5]

America was founded on revolutionary ideas; but the speed with which these ideas triumphed had in a sense left America a conservative nation,

[3]Ibid., p. 29.
[4]Ibid., p. 36.
[5]Ibid.

American spirit yesterday and today. At right, the 1984 space walk of astronaut Kathryn Sullivan.

one that throughout history would seek to maintain and extend values established at its birth rather than pursue new ones.

Continuity

The political ideals that dominated American life in Tocqueville's day remain ascendant in our own time. They continue to shape the approach of many of the most important political and social movements.

Individualism. The United States is still a polity distinguished by strong currents of individualism. Over the years, the precise claims that individuals make have changed, and so have our views concerning whose rights are insufficiently recognized. Today, for example, the movement for women's rights is stronger and more politically active than in the past. The women's movement is wide-ranging, with a variety of different goals, but underlying it is the basic idea that women are individuals whose claims to the opportunity to achieve personal fulfillment and happiness are the equal of men's. Individualism frames, too, the terms or boundaries of many of the sharpest political disputes in the contemporary United States. What are the rights of individuals accused of crimes, and what measures should law enforcement officials and courts take to ensure them? How are these rights to be balanced against the rights and interests of the rest of the population? Or, in another area, to what extent should abortion be left as a matter of individual choice, rather than proscribed by law? No polity has done more than the U.S. polity to put the individual at the pinnacle of things—or to argue more about which individual rights need greater emphasis.

Equality. In the same way, the egalitarianism that Tocqueville described in the 1830s continues to distinguish the United States in the 1980s. The public's ideal of equality has consistently asserted that each individual must be given an opportunity to strive and to achieve according to his or her efforts and ability, without regard to the individual's social background. It is an ideal that insists on *equality of opportunity*—although emphatically not on *equality of result*. If some individuals work harder or are more able, they should, in the American sense of equality, be permitted to enjoy their rewards. During the Great Depression in the 1930s, public opinion pollsters first asked a sample of the populace whether they thought government should impose limits on how much money people could earn. Even with economic hardship widespread and tensions high, the majority of the populace rejected the idea of income limits. Even the poorest Americans said no to it. This same response is given by Americans today.

Equality of opportunity for everyone is, even with the greatest effort, impossible to achieve fully. And the United States at times has not made the effort at all. The denial of equality of opportunity to black Americans is the most flagrant instance where we have mocked our

Continuity and free expression of political ideas—a 1984 debate between Democratic presidential candidate, Walter Mondale, and Republican president, Ronald Reagan.

The goal of equal opportunity

ideal. But if it has been denied far more than we like to acknowledge, the goal of equal opportunity is nonetheless a powerful force in our national experience. It underlies the many laws national and state governments have enacted to bar discrimination by race, religion, sex, and other such attributes extraneous to individual effort and performance. And it helps account for the enormous positive commitment the United States has made to education, including bringing higher education within the reach of a larger proportion of the population than in any other country. We see the provision of educational opportunity as a primary means by which individuals of diverse backgrounds are given a chance to compete effectively in social and economic life.

Democracy. The third principle that Tocqueville saw shaping the American political system also remains in place: government should rest on popular sovereignty. Over the years, the precise machinery through which citizens choose their political leaders and democratic government functions, has changed in a number of ways, some far from inconsequential. But the commitment to political democracy is as central and vital today as at any time in the past. One aspect of this vitality is a general recognition that the democratic ideal is never fully or finally realized. Throughout U.S. history, there have been recurring movements committed to "political reform," which in virtually all instances has meant making the democratic system operate in closer accord with certain ideal standards.

This holds true today. As we will see in the chapters that follow, debate continues about what steps should be taken to increase the

The war in Vietnam was the focus of national debate for nearly a decade.

Contemporary issues
and democracy

rate of voter turnout in American elections, which now appears low. The issue of campaign finance—the increasing cost of electioneering, where the money now comes from and where it should come from— is a lively one. Reforming the political parties so that they can better perform their representative functions is under continuous debate, especially with regard to the presidential nomination process. Congressional reform—involving such matters as the organization and powers of committees and subcommittees and the influence of interest groups in the legislative process—is seen by many to be critical. The role of the Supreme Court and the rest of the federal judiciary in making public policy prompts heated debate about the proper distribution of power and responsibility among the three branches of government.

The fact that the ideas and ideals of individualism, equality, and democracy still form the underpinnings of the American system and frame the terms of the political debate imparts an extraordinary continuity to our political life. As historian Henry Steele Commager remarked, "Circumstances change profoundly, but the character of the American people has not changed greatly or the nature of the principles of conduct, public and private, to which they subscribe."[6]

SOCIAL CHANGE, THE FORCE BEHIND POLITICS

Sociopolitical periods

For all the persistence of governmental institutions and underlying values, American society has been far from static. Evolving from a tiny farming nation settled on the eastern edge of the North American continent to a highly developed nation spanning the continent and exerting great influence on world affairs, the United States has packed into its 200 years since independence massive changes in technology, economic life, demographic makeup, and more. With these changes, every American political institution has grown and evolved. Not every piece of social change has had a major impact on government and politics, of course, but the accumulated changes have. The components of a social setting are subject to many new developments starting at different times and proceeding at different rates; these changes finally merge to produce a new setting distinct from the preceding one. The idea of a *sociopolitical period* refers to the persistence of underlying social and economic relationships, and their accompanying demands on government, over a span of time. The United States has seen four great sociopolitical periods, each defined not by the

[6]Henry Steele Commager, *Living Ideas in America* (New York: Harper and Brothers, 1951), p. xviii. Also see Daniel Boorstin, *The Genius of American Politics* (Chicago: University of Chicago Press, 1953); idem, *The Americans*, in three volumes: *The Colonial Experience; The Democratic Experience;* and *The National Experience* (New York: Random House, 1958, 1965, and 1973); and Louis M. Hartz, *The Liberal Tradition in America: An Interpretation of American Political Thought Since the Revolution* (New York: Harcourt, Brace, 1955).

Table 1.1
Eras in American Social and Political Development

Sociopolitical period	Approximate time span	Distinctive characteristics
Rural republic	1780s–1860s	A rural and localized society; land-owning farmers are the dominant economic group; government's role is highly limited and centered at the state and local levels.
Industrializing nation	1870s–1920s	An urbanizing society of increasing scale; there is rapid growth of industry and commerce, leading to the ascendancy of corporate business; government's role involves the promotion of industrialization and, subsequently, its regulation.
Industrial state	1930s–1960s	A mature urban, industrial society; complex, integrated industrial economy requiring central management; organized labor becomes a major economic and political interest group; power shifts to the national government, and government's role is greatly expanded.
Postindustrial society	1970s–present	A society of advanced technology, built on a heavy commitment to science and education; the service sector of the economy expands greatly, while manufacturing proportionally declines; older economic interests, including organized labor, lose influence; the proper management of government's role in the political economy becomes the primary domestic issue.

passing of years but by the changing of society (Table 1.1). We are mainly interested here in the last of these, the period in which we are living, but we can better understand the present by seeing the process of change through which American society and government have arrived at it.[7]

An agricultural economy

The rural republic. During the first great social and political period, from the late eighteenth century to just before the beginning of the Civil War, the United States was a pre-industrial society: Land-owning farmers were the dominant group, economically and politically. In 1800 more than four out of every five Americans who worked were farmers, and fifty years later farmers still comprised about two-thirds of the labor force. In 1839, agriculture accounted for nearly 70 percent of the total value of the commodity output of the U.S. economy. Since most people worked in jobs that required little formal or theoretical training, education could be limited to what was required for literacy. Besides, this pre-industrial society could not afford to sustain any substantial portion of its productive-age population in "nonproductive" schooling. The U.S. educational system was a primary-school system: Of the 3.5 million pupils enrolled in 1850, only 20,000 were in grades nine and above; less than 1 percent of the population

[7]These developments are discussed at length in Everett C. Ladd, *American Political Parties: Social Change and Political Reform* (New York: Norton, 1970).

were high-school graduates; and the degrees awarded by all institutions of higher education numbered fewer than 3,000.

The economic activities we identify as "business"—banking, trade, manufacturing—were limited; big business simply did not exist. The Northeast was the center of the country's nascent commerce and manufacturing; in 1850 it accounted for three-fourths of the United States' manufacturing employment, concentrated in industries such as cotton and woolen goods, men's clothing, and shoes.[8] The West of this first period was the "Old West," what we now know as the North Central states. Its economy was mostly agricultural, and wheat and corn were the most important crops.

The South and cotton growing

The American South underwent major social and economic changes in the first half of the nineteenth century. In 1800 it was a land of small farmers. Their egalitarianism was much more characteristic of the South than was the privileged life of the great planters and their slave-based agriculture in areas like tidewater Virginia. But in the early nineteenth century the South's cotton culture became a highly prosperous and expanding enterprise, and slavery an entrenched institution. The most important causes of this transformation were Eli Whitney's invention of the cotton gin, a machine for cleaning cotton; the opening up of extremely rich soil perfectly suited for the cotton culture in Georgia, Alabama, and Mississippi; and, with the peace and renewal of trade which followed the Napoleonic wars in Europe, an enormous market for raw cotton to be used in textile manufacturing. The South produced only 73,000 bales of cotton in 1800, but more than 525,000 bales in 1825, 2.1 million in 1850, and 4.4 million in 1861.[9] The extension of the plantation system made southern society much more highly stratified and increased inequalities of income. Power came to rest with the planter class. The net effect of these changes was to set the South further apart from the rest of the country; differences in political culture, modest at the turn of the century, had become a chasm on the eve of the Civil War.

Transportation and communication

In 1790, 95 percent of all Americans lived on farms or in small villages; the biggest city, Philadelphia, had less than 50,000 inhabitants. Even by 1850, 85 Americans in every 100 were still rural dwellers. This population was scattered over an area which grew through annexations from just under a million square miles in 1790 to 3 million at mid-century. People and goods moved through this vast expanse by waterways, and on land by animal and on foot. There were no railroads until 1830, and in 1850 only the beginnings of the vast railroad network soon to be developed. In communications the first telegraph service (between Baltimore and Washington) did not begin until 1844. There was no integrated national economy, no national

[8]Douglass C. North, *The Economic Growth of the United States, 1790–1860* (New York: Norton, 1966), pp. 115–160.
[9]U.S. Bureau of the Census, *Historical Statistics of the United States: Colonial Times to 1970* (Washington, D.C.: U.S. Government Printing Office, 1975), p. 518.

media of communication; Maine and South Carolina were separated by weeks of arduous travel.

In this highly localized society, "states' rights" had a basic legitimacy which most of us now cannot easily recognize. A large federal government just was not needed in this independent farming society. Federal spending averaged only two dollars per capita each year from the turn of the century through the 1850s. Most governing occurred at the state and local level.

The industrializing nation. In the years from the end of the Civil War in 1865 to the 1920s, the United States became the leading industrial nation, with about one-third of the world's total manufacturing capacity. In the 1860s a clear majority of American workers were in agriculture; but the agricultural labor force began a precipitous relative decline as manufacturing and commerce expanded. By 1920 only about one out of every four workers engaged in farming. Between 1870 and 1920, the number of workers in trade and finance jumped from 830,000 to 8.5 million; in transportation and other public utilities from 640,000 to 4.2 million; and in manufacturing from 2.3 million to 10.9 million.

Growth and centralization

The population of the United States tripled between 1870 and 1920, reaching 106 million. During this period the great cities we know today were built. By 1900, New York City's population had climbed to over 3 million, and New York had taken its place as one of the world's great metropolises. In place of small family farms producing food only for local areas, big corporations drew resources from throughout the country and the world, and serviced national markets. This was the half-century in which all the major electronic media except television developed; telephones first came into use in the 1870s, and by 1920 13.3 million of them were in use in the country. A new transportation network was established, centered on the railroad and the motor car, and the physical mobility of the population was vastly extended. The productive capacities of the economy were enormously expanded by industrialization. Between 1870 and 1920 the gross national product (GNP) of the United States—measuring the value of all goods and services produced—increased in real terms by roughly 800 percent.[10]

Expansion of government

The increases of scale and interdependence that took place in the second period spurred the expansion of government. Regulation of working conditions had made little sense when most Americans were independent farmers; it was a different matter when millions entered the ranks of factory labor. Pure food and drug legislation did not seem imperative when most people lived on farms and consumed what they

[10]These data are from *Historical Statistics of the United States*, p. 231. Describing the increase as 800 percent in *real* terms means controlling for the effects of price changes. In this case, the purchasing power of the dollar in 1929 was used as the base for recalculating the GNP for each year in the span between 1869 and 1931.

produced; the call for such regulation became increasingly insistent with the impersonality of big cities and big business corporations. The industrializing society required much higher investments in education than its agricultural predecessor had; total public expenditures for education grew from just $90 million in 1875 to $558 million in 1913 and $2.2 billion in 1927. The expansion of government services took place mostly at the state and local level; federal expenditures were only moderately higher in the 1870–1920 period (apart from World War I) than they had been before the Civil War, and what increase did take place was largely accounted for by defense, veterans' pensions, and interest on the debt.

The industrial state. The Great Depression, which began in 1929, did not so much create as abruptly signal the emergence of a new sociopolitical setting, the third decisive one in American history. It shifted national attention from one set of concerns to another with unaccustomed speed. Long before the Depression there had been recognition that the further industrial development proceeded and the bigger and more integrated the economy became, the more central economic management and regulation the country would require and the more governmental protection individuals would need. Overall, though, in 1929 the response in American political thought and governmental institutions lagged behind the requirements of the new setting.

Political power in the United States was redistributed after 1929. In the half-century of rapid industrialization, businessmen had

Franklin D. Roosevelt signs into law the Social Security Act of 1935, marking a major shift toward greater governmental responsibility in the lives of Americans.

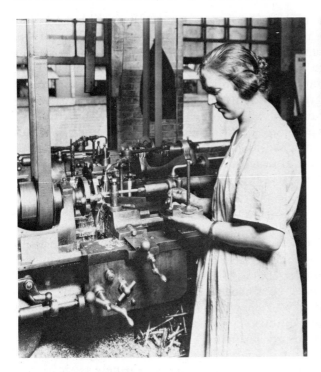

Technology, industrial age and postindustrial, altered the nature of the American workforce.

acquired enormous political influence. They had come to be seen as the architects of prosperity. The country was engaged in a great enterprise, and they were the instruments for its betterment. Then, almost overnight, with the Depression, instead of cheers there were boos and catcalls. Instead of being the custodians of American prosperity, the builders of the American dream, they were presiding over an economic system in unparalleled collapse and appeared powerless to effect a remedy.

Organized labor was one of the principal new claimants for power and recognition in the industrial state. Industrialization had created a large urban working class; but for it to assume real political power it needed effective organization. This was achieved in the ten years after 1935. In the early 1930s just over 10 percent of the nonagricultural work force belonged to labor unions. The general encouragement to unionization given by the administration of Franklin D. Roosevelt, legislation enacted by Congress, and the vigorous initiatives of a new generation of labor leaders produced a surge in membership, which brought it to about 35 percent of the nonagricultural labor force just after World War II. Labor leaders acquired much more economic and political influence than they ever had before.

Rise of organized labor

Prompted by the economic collapse of the 1930s, and more generally by the increased demands of an urban and industrial society, government took on new responsibilities. In 1913 total spending by

New governmental
responsibilities

the national, state, and local governments had been about $33 per person. That figure jumped to $130 per person in 1936, $375 in 1948, and $837 in 1960. Inflation accounted for some of this increase, but much of it was real and reflected government's assumption of a big role in public welfare and economic management. And, responding to the greater integration and interdependence of the society and the national character of many of its problems, the federal government's share of public spending rose above the combined total of the states and municipalities after World War II, the first time this had occurred when the country was at peace. Federal spending has exceeded state and local spending every year since.

Postindustrial society. Today we read about how American politics is changing. By the late 1960s and 1970s, a great variety of changes had come together to define yet another social era, the fourth in the country's history: the postindustrial society. Since American society now differs significantly from that of the New Deal industrial era, the polity could scarcely have remained static.

In the next chapter we review the key transformations that have ushered in the new postindustrial setting and shaped it. And throughout this text we discuss government and politics against the backdrop of the contemporary society—its needs and resources, its group composition and interests, and its social organization.

2 | Postindustrial Society

Historical eras—whether in the life of the planet or of a single country—do not start and stop on a dime. They emerge gradually, with fits and starts and many rough edges. And they disappear the same way, bequeathing all manner of remnants to their successors.

Yet it is evident that the United States as a society has entered a new era over the last quarter-century—a change of immense importance to American politics and government. The present era is often called **postindustrial,** and we will adopt this label. We should not, though, make too much of this shorthand description; more important are the characteristics of this new social era and their implications for social, economic, and political life.

CONTEMPORARY AMERICA: A POSTINDUSTRIAL SOCIETY

The term "postindustrial society" was first introduced by sociologist Daniel Bell.[1] Bell contrasted this era with the preceding era, writing that "industrial society is the coordination of machines and men for the production of goods." Postindustrial society is "organized around knowledge."[2] The key developments defining the postindustrial era are "the exponential growth and branching of science, the rise of a new intellectual technology, the creation of systematic research

---

[1] Bell has noted that the term actually appeared earlier than his first usage of it, with a quite different meaning, in an essay which David Riesman wrote on "Leisure and Work in Postindustrial Society," printed in the compendium *Mass Leisure* (Glencoe, Ill: Free Press, 1958). Bell's most important treatment of postindustrialism may be found in his book *The Coming of Postindustrial Society* (New York: Basic Books, 1973).
[2] Bell, *Coming of Postindustrial Society*, p. 20.

 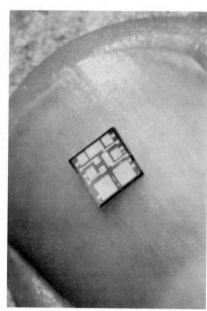

Products of two eras: for the industrial age, it was heavy industry, here, steel; for the post-industrial era, it is the computer industry, here, a microchip so small that a dozen could rest on a thumbnail.

through R & D [research and development] budgets, and . . . the codification of theoretical knowledge."[3]

Other observers have reached similar conclusions. Zbigniew Brzezinski, national security adviser to President Jimmy Carter, sees a new social era "shaped culturally, psychologically, socially, and economically by the impact of technology and electronics—particularly in the area of computers and communications."[4] Similarly, sociologist Amitai Etzioni argues that one social period ended and another began "with the radical transformation of the technologies of communication, knowledge and energy that followed the Second World War. . . ."[5]

Throughout this book, "postindustrial society" refers specifically to the cumulative result of five key developments or sources of social change.

Postindustrialism: five key developments

(1) Advanced technology. Postindustrial America is a society built upon advanced technology. Technology is not a recent phenomenon, but technology built primarily upon abstract and theoretical knowledge *is* new.

(2) The knowledge base. This technology requires an unprecedented commitment to science and education. And it permits an unprecedentedly large proportion of the populace to engage in intellectual rather than manual labor.

[3] Ibid., p. 44.
[4] Zbigniew Brzezinski, *Between Two Ages: America's Role in the Technetronic Era* (New York: Viking Press, 1970), p. 9.
[5] Amitai Etzioni, *The Active Society* (New York: Free Press, 1968), p. vii.

(3) Occupations: The service economy. The occupational makeup of the work force in the postindustrial setting differs from that of the industrial era and earlier times. The white-collar and service sectors grow. Bureaucracy becomes the distinctive work setting.

(4) Mass affluence. Postindustrial America is an affluent society, one where the increase in national wealth, built on technological innovation, has been so substantial as to move the bulk of the populace beyond active concern with matters of subsistence.

(5) New class relationships. The character of social classes and their relationships in the postindustrial era are very different from previous eras. Increased wealth and education, together with a new occupational mix, produce a new class structure.

Let's look more closely at each of these components to better understand recent changes that have altered not just the economy and social relations but also the setting for American political life.

ADVANCED TECHNOLOGY

Technology

Technology is commonly defined as the application of knowledge for practical ends. In this general sense the United States has made serious use of technology from its very inception. In the nineteenth century knowledge about electricity and steam engines was applied with an extraordinary practical impact in manufacturing, transportation, and communication. The country was criss-crossed with rail, telephone, and telegraph lines, and heavy industries like coal and steel were developed. All this contributed to exceptionally large increases in industrial productivity. Manufacturing output climbed by about 1200 percent in the half-century following the Civil War.[6]

From tinkerers to industries

Almost all of the major industries that grew up in the nineteenth and early twentieth centuries—including steel, electrical power, automobiles, and telephone—were "mainly the creation of inventors, inspired and talented tinkerers who were indifferent to science and the fundamental laws underlying their investigations."[7] William Darrah Kelley and Sir Henry Bessemer developed the oxidation process that made it possible to mass-produce steel—even though they were unaware of the emerging science of metallurgy. Thomas Alva Edison did his major work on something he vaguely referred to as "etheric sparks," which resulted in the electric light and otherwise

---

[6] Based on an index of manufacturing production developed by Edwin Frickey, *Production in the United States, 1860–1914* (Cambridge, Mass: Harvard University Press, 1947). The index is reprinted in U.S. Bureau of the Census, *Historical Statistics of the United States,* p. 409.

[7] Bell, *Coming of Postindustrial Society,* p. 20.

Two modes of inven-tion: the great "tinkerer" Thomas A. Edison and a contem-porary designer using computer graphics.

sparked the first electronic revolution—even though he was not sympathetic to the theoretical research being done on electromagnetism.

What distinguishes the technology of postindustrial society is a change in the character of innovation: the sustained application of *theoretical* knowledge for practical ends. Most of the worlds that lay before the "talented tinkerers" have been conquered. Since World War II technological progress has been based directly and explicitly on theoretical knowledge—and thus on the work of the scientific community. From chemicals to computers, from military hardware to agriculture, the dependence on science is now generally acknowledged.

Science Comes of Age

Industry, science, and education

One indication of this dependence is the extent to which business corporations have tied themselves to science and higher education. New industrial complexes have grown up around leading research universities. The development of the computer industry in the "Silicon Valley" near Stanford University in California, and on "Route 128" near the Massachusetts Institute of Technology (MIT), are the most dramatic instances. Many of the leading corporations have become major employers of scientific talent. Bell Laboratories, a unit of American Telephone and Telegraph Company (AT&T) has long employed more Ph.D.s than most research universities—over 3,300 Ph.D.s in 1982. Du Pont, the chemical giant, had 3,350 men and women with doctorates on its payroll in the United States alone in 1984, and many more worked for its foreign subsidiaries. International Business Machines (IBM), the largest computer manufacturer, employs about 2,500 Ph.D.s.

Research and
development (R&D)

There has been a vast increase in the economic resources committed to *research and development* (R&D). The age of the great inventors like Alexander Graham Bell and Thomas Alva Edison, and the gifted implementors of technology like Henry Ford, is in many ways an attractive, even romantic one, involving as it did the solitary individual working with very modest resources in his own garage or tiny laboratory. The practice in postindustrial America contrasts greatly with James Conant's recollection that during World War I, as president of the Americal Chemical Society, he offered the services of the society to Newton D. Baker (then Secretary of War) only to be told that these services would not be needed because the War Department already had a chemist! Conant also described a board headed by Edison, created to help the Navy during World War I, on which Edison placed one physicist because, as he told President Woodrow Wilson, "we ought to have one mathematician fellow in case we have to calculate something out."[8]

However romantic that earlier industrial era seems, it is gone forever. Technological innovation now requires large commitments of resources. Economist John Kenneth Galbraith notes that it cost just $28,500 to produce the first Ford in 1903, compared to $60 million to engineer and tool up for the production of the first Mustang in 1964. And fifteen years later, it cost Ford $3 billion to design, engineer, tool, and market the Escort.

R&D

The growth of R&D

In 1940, all branches of the national government spent just $74 million for research and development. Two decades later, federal R&D expenditures had climbed to $8.7 billion; and in 1983, the national government's R&D spending reached $39.6 billion. (See Table 2.1.)

Table 2.1
Research and Development Expenditures since the 1940s (in millions of dollars)

| | Industrial ⟶ Postindustrial | | | | | |
	1940	1950	1960	1970	1980	1983
All R&D expenditures (government and private)			13,730	26,134	60,222	86,500
Federal government expenditures for R&D	74	1,093	8,746	14,896	29,555	39,625

Source: 1940–50: U.S. Bureau of the Census, *Historical Statistics of the United States: Colonial Times to 1957*, p. 613. 1960: Idem, *Historical Statistics of the United States: Colonial Times to 1970, Bicentennial Edition, Part I*, p. 965. 1970–82: Idem, *Statistical Abstract of the United States, 1982–1983*, p. 593. 1983: U.S. National Science Foundation, *National Patterns of Science and Technology Resources*, 1984.

[8]James Bryant Conant, *Modern Science and Modern Man* (New York: Columbia University Press, 1952), pp. 8–9.

The private sector in the United States expended another $47 billion for R&D in 1983, for a total R&D commitment of over $86 billion. Even when the effects of inflation are taken into account, one finds a growth in R&D from World War II to the present so great as to change the essential character of scientific and technological innovation in the postindustrial age.

THE KNOWLEDGE BASE

Advanced technology, derived from theoretical knowledge, requires a large cadre of scientists and engineers for its continuation and a highly trained and educated labor force for its use. At the same time, by developing machinery to do work once assigned to manual labor and by increasing productivity and national wealth so massively, it has permitted an unprecedented proportion of the population to engage in educational and other intellectual activities.

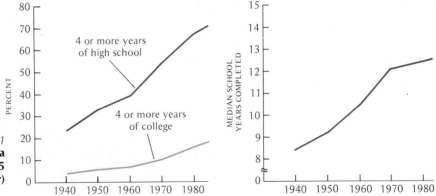

Figure 2.1
Education in America since 1940 (of those 25 years of age and older)

Source: 1940–81: U.S. Bureau of the Census, *Statistical Abstract of the United States, 1978*, p. 143; idem, *Statistical Abstract of the United States, 1984*, p. 144; 1983: idem, *Current Population Surveys*, unpublished data.

The knowledge society   We see the essential character of the *knowledge society* in the U.S.'s commitment to education since World War II. In 1940 just 4.6 percent of the population age 25 and older had graduated from college. But by 1983 the proportion was 18.8 percent, as shown in Figure 2.1. If we look only at the younger segments of the populace—old enough to have completed most or all of their formal education but young enough to reflect the current trends in educational experience—we see an even more dramatic increase. In 1940, only 5.9 percent of those 25 to 29 years of age were college graduates, whereas by 1983 22.8 percent were college graduates—a four-fold increase in four decades.

The American College Explosion

At the turn of this century, there were fewer than 250,000 college students at all levels in all sorts of higher education institutions in the United States. At the onset of World War II, the college student population still numbered fewer than 1.5 million. But between 1960 and 1975, the college population increased by 6.2 million to a total of 9.7 million. Since the mid-1970s (defying many expectations) the number enrolled in higher education institutions has continued to climb. The number of students in degree-credit programs in America's colleges and universities jumped from 9.7 million in 1975 to 12.4 million in 1983 (see Figure 2.2).

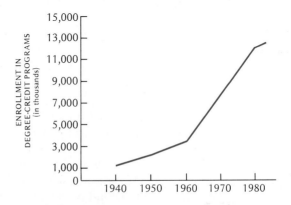

Figure 2.2
The American College Explosion since 1940

Note: Student enrollment figures after 1975 include, but are not limited to, degree-credit candidates. 1980 is academic year 1979–80; 1983 is academic year 1982–83.
Source: U.S. Office of Education Research and Improvement, National Center for Education Statistics, *Digest of Education Statistics* (Washington, D.C.: 1983), and unpublished tabulations. U.S. Bureau of the Census, *Historical Statistics of the United States: Colonial Times to 1970, Bicentennial Edition,* part 1, pp. 382–83.

College enrollments in the U.S. and abroad

Not only are these figures on recent college attendance extraordinary by comparison to earlier periods in U.S. history, but they are impressive when compared to other countries—even the most advanced nations. In 1979, when 11.6 million Americans attended higher education institutions, only 1.2 million West Germans, 1.1 million French, and 800,000 British citizens were enrolled in comparable schools in their respective countries. Those nations have much smaller total populations than the United States, of course, but as Figure 2.3 shows, the percentage of young Americans attending college—about 55 percent in 1979—dwarfs higher education enrollments in any other industrial nation.

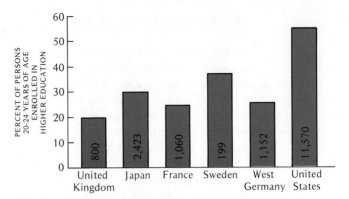

Figure 2.3
Higher Education in Leading Industrial Nations

Source: Organization for Economic Co-operation and Development (OECD), *Educational Statistics in OECD Countries,* 1981, p. 40. World Bank, *World Development Report,* 1980 (New York: Oxford University Press, 1980). Idem, *World Development Report,* 1983, pp. 197, 211. United Nations Education, Scientific, and Cultural Organization (UNESCO), *Statistical Digest* (Paris: UNESCO, 1982), pp. 202, 266, 270, 280, 302, 306. The data are for 1979.

Soaring Expenditures for Education

America's commitment to education has been costly. In 1930, Americans spent roughly $3.4 billion for education, from elementary school through college, public and private. Expenditures climbed only modestly through 1950—but at this point they took off. By 1983, spending for education in the United States had reached $215 billion, as shown in Figure 2.4, $82 billion for higher education and $133 million for elementary and secondary training. Even controlling for inflation, expenditures jumped more than 700 percent between 1950 and 1983.

Americans have borne these heavy financial obligations to education with little complaint. In 1983, the General Social Survey con-

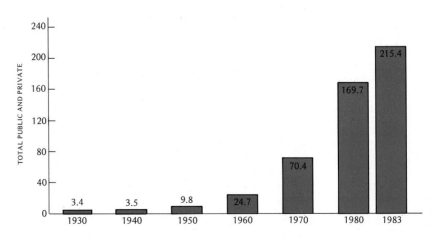

Figure 2.4
Education Expenditures since 1930 (in billions of dollars)

Source: 1930–50: U.S. Bureau of the Census, *Historical Statistics of the United States: Colonial Times to 1970, Bicentennial Edition, Part I,* pp. 373–74, 375, 384. 1960–82: Idem, *Statistical Abstract of the United States, 1982–83,* p. 136.

ducted by the National Opinion Research Center asked a cross-section of the public whether they thought "we're spending too much money, . . . too little money, or about the right amount . . . improving the nation's education system." Sixty-two percent said we were *not spending enough*—this at a time when national expenditures for education were over $200 billion a year! Only 6 percent responded that too much was being expended, while 32 percent said expenditures were at approximately the right level.

Public support for educational spending

As we will see in later chapters, the postindustrial era's emphasis on education has had many political effects. We note in chapter 15, for example, that a more educated populace is less committed to political parties than the publics of earlier eras, and is more independent in its voting. The makeup of interest groups and their political activities similarly reflect the increases in education and the role of knowledge in American life (chapter 13).

OCCUPATIONS: THE SERVICE ECONOMY

In 1790, the first American decennial census found 95 percent of the total work force engaged in agricultural pursuits. As late as 1860, on the eve of the Civil War, a large majority of the work force (roughly three-fifths) was still in agriculture—compared to about one-fifth in non-farm, manual labor jobs and one-fifth in various white-collar and service positions. The rapid industrialization of the late nineteenth and early twentieth centuries changed this ratio dramatically. Millions of Americans left farms and rural areas for factories and the cities. Between 1860 and 1920, the number of Americans engaged in non-farm blue-collar jobs jumped from 2 million to 17 million and neared what was to be its all-time high as a proportion of the total labor force.

Industrialism: from the farm to the factory

After World War II, with the further introduction of machinery into agriculture, the proportion of farmers in the labor force continued to drop—*but so did the proportion of blue-collar workers*. Between 1950 and 1980, the American labor force increased by about 30 million. This was entirely accounted for by the white-collar and service sector, which climbed from about 28 million in 1950 to 64 million in 1980. Today more than two out of three Americans who are gainfully employed work in some form of white-collar or service position, compared to less than three percent in farming and thirty percent in blue-collar and manufacturing positions (see Figure 2.5).

Rise of the white-collar worker

The rapid expansion in the blue-collar and manufacturing work force had been a prime indicator of the growth of the industrial society. The explosion in the number of white-collar and service workers is a distinctive sign of postindustrialism. When in 1956 the number of white-collar workers outnumbered blue-collar workers, it was the first time in the United States or anywhere in the world that the balance had thus shifted.

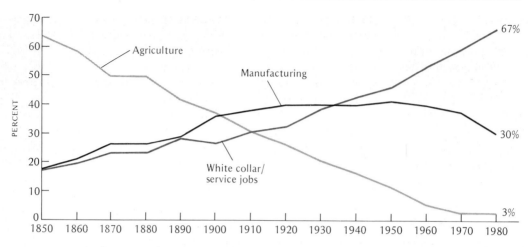

Figure 2.5
**Occupational
Distributions
since 1850** *Note:* Agriculture is composed of farmers, farm laborers/foremen. Manufacturing is composed of craftsmen/foremen, operatives, laborers except farm and mine workers. White collar/service is composed of professional/technical, managers/officials/proprietors, clerical, sales, household, service workers. *Source:* 1850–1970: U.S. Bureau of the Census, *Historical Statistics of the United States: Colonial Times to 1970, Bicentennial Edition, Part I*, pp. 138–9. 1980: idem, *Statistical Abstract of the United States, 1982–83*, p. 386.

Service Workers

Daniel Bell notes that the term "service workers" is an imperfect one because it covers too much ground. It includes those who work as household servants; persons in other personal services such as the operators of beauty shops and retail stores; those in business services like banking and real estate; individuals employed in transportation, communication, and utilities; and those in health, education, research, and government. Bell argues that the growth of the last category has influenced most the development of postindustrial society.[9]

The growth of
government

Nowhere has the increase in service workers been more dramatic over the past three decades than in the government sector. In 1950, American government at all levels—federal state, and local—employed 6.4 million people (excluding those in the military). Over the next three decades, the number of civilian government workers grew by roughly 10 million. While the total work force was expanding by about 80 percent, government employment grew twice as much—by 160 percent. Many bemoan the growth of government; but this increase reflects a generally expanded demand for services—involving health, education, and welfare—that has occurred across postindustrial society. People see government as the best available vehicle for providing many of these services, and so government has expanded. But the demand has been more for government's services than for government per se.

[9]Bell, *Coming of Postindustrial Society*, p. 15.

The American space shuttle and its lab are direct results of federal research and development.

Professional and Technical Employment

The professional and technical work force has increased three times as much as the labor force as a whole. In 1940, 3.9 million Americans were employed in what the Census classifies as professional and technical jobs (teachers, scientists, engineers, etc.); by 1960 the number had jumped to 7.3 million, and by 1980 to 15.6 million. Almost all of the scientific and educational occupations have experienced dramatic increases since World War II. The number of engineers jumped from 297 thousand in 1940 to 1.4 million in 1980—or by roughly 500 percent—while the total work force doubled.

Bureaucracy

Bureaucracy: rationalized administration

A farmer plowing his field symbolized the work setting of the agricultural society. The factory assembly line was the distinctive setting for the industrial society. Bureaucracy is the predominant work setting for the postindustrial era. The term "bureaucracy" has taken on unfavorable connotations in recent years, suggesting large, unresponsive, cumbersome administrative units that deal impersonally with those who turn to them for services. "Well, the government bureaucracy messed that up again." "I wanted to tell the people running Company X what I thought of them, but how can you get anywhere at all with a big bureaucracy like that." But bureaucracy as originally conceived meant something very different. The influential German sociologist Max Weber identified it with "rationalized administration."[10] The management of organizations was advanced,

[10]See, for example, Max Weber, *Economy and Society*, Guenther Roth and Claus Wittich, eds. (New York: Bedminster Press, 1968). Weber's work was composed between 1913 and 1914.

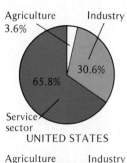

Agriculture 3.6%
Industry 30.6%
65.8%
Service sector
UNITED STATES

Agriculture 6.0%
Industry
49.2% 44.8%
Service sector
WEST GERMANY

Agriculture 8.8%
Industry
55.3% 35.9%
Service sector
FRANCE

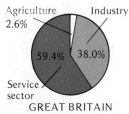

Agriculture 2.6%
Industry
59.4% 38.0%
Service sector
GREAT BRITAIN

Agriculture 5.6%
Industry
62.2% 32.2%
Service sector
SWEDEN

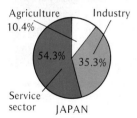

Agriculture 10.4%
Industry
54.3% 35.3%
Service sector
JAPAN

Weber argued, by introducing knowledge of administrative techniques and practice, by striving for imparitiality in the administration of services, and by the general recourse to rationality (rather than subjectivity or personal whim) in organizational management. In this sense, bureaucracy was a great advance over earlier forms of administration.

Today, the principles of rationalized administration have been applied across most large institutions in the United States, from government agencies to large business corporations. The tremendous growth of these bureaucracies has made them, for better or worse, the occupational homes of millions of American workers, and the proportion continues to increase.

Foreign Comparisons

The United States is not alone in having experienced a big increase in the service sector in the postindustrial era. All of the more advanced countries evidence this same trend. But the increase is much greater in the United States. In 1980, when over 65 percent of American workers were in white-collar and service occupations, 49 percent in West Germany, 55 percent in France, and 54 percent in Japan were in these occupations (see Figure 2.6). Looking to the Third World countries, one still finds the majority of workers in agricultural pursuits, a situation parallel to that in the United States early in the nineteenth century.

MASS AFFLUENCE

Throughout human history, people have had to struggle with subsistence needs: taking in enough calories to sustain life, having clothing warm enough to protect against the elements, acquiring basic housing or shelter. Even in more fortunate times and countries where most of the population did not face actual hunger or starvation, the margin over subsistence was always worryingly thin. There might be enough food today, but one could not forget that, as a result of natural disasters, crop failures, or illness, there might not be enough food tomorrow.

Against this backdrop, the economic experience of the contemporary United States is a truly radical one. For the United States is an

Figure 2.6
Labor Force Distributions in the United States and Other Postindustrial Societies
Source: OECD, *Economic Surveys,* 1981, 1982, 1983 (country series).

affluent society in a world that has been dominated by scarcity. The affluence Americans enjoy accrues from a number of conditions, but primarily from the extensive application of technology to economic production. Achieving the present level of national wealth is probably the single most dramatic accomplishment of the postindustrial era.

Poverty and Affluence

Some people resist, even resent, the description of the United States as an affluent society, because to them it suggests a lack of sensitivity to the continued presence of poverty. Surely the affluent society is not one where everyone is wealthy and poverty has been abolished. In the United States in the 1980s, millions of people—just how many is hard to estimate—experience some literal economic deprivation, such as inadequacy of diet or substandard housing. Government statistical data for 1984 showed about 35 million people living below the poverty line—15 percent of the total population.[11] Furthermore, poverty is not just an absolute condition: An important meaning of being poor is having considerably less than most other people. We think of ourselves as poor or deprived when our standard of living is well below the level which has been established as the norm for the society—even if our diet is good, we have enough clothing, and our

Poverty remains a problem, even amidst the wealth of contemporary America.

[11] These data are from U.S. Bureau of the Census, *Money, Income, and Poverty Status of Families and Persons in the United States: 1982* (Washington, D.C.: Government Printing Office, 1983).

needs for shelter are met. Expectations as to economic needs and entitlements will rise at least as fast as the gross national product (GNP)—an economic index that measures the total production of goods and services. Poverty is in part a relative condition.

What Affluence Means

As a description of the condition of a society, **affluence** means something quite precise and limited: It is a situation in which a decisive majority of the population of a country does not face problems related to subsistence, where economic privation is a concern of the few rather than the many. In the quarter-century after World War II, the United States did not abolish poverty or satisfy all economic wants, but it did reach a status where most people did not have to worry about the most basic economic needs.

As late as the end of World War II a majority of the American public had incomes that provided them with only a very narrow margin over subsistence. The median family income in 1947 was just $3,000, and 81 percent of all families earned less than $5,000. Although the dollar would buy more in those days than it will now, these Americans had little left over when essential food, clothing, and shelter were taken care of. Their economic world was bounded by subsistence-type needs.

A Quarter-Century of Growth

Between 1947 and 1973, median family income exactly doubled in real (inflation-controlled) terms. More individual family purchasing power was acquired in this quarter-century than in all preceding years of American history combined. When we remember, too, that at the close of World War II the United States was already a wealthy country by any historical or cross-national comparative standard, the extent of this revolutionary economic change is more sharply etched.

As a result of this big jump in national wealth, Americans have consumed almost twice as much fossil fuel since World War II as they did in all of the preceding years of the nation's existence (a fact which clearly attests to major changes in styles of living, just as it helps explains why an energy crisis developed in the 1970s). The increase of six million in college and university enrollment between 1947 and 1973 is four times the total enrollment in 1940. Expenditures for toys climbed 500 percent in this quarter-century, those for cosmetics by 550 percent. Personal spending for recreation increased 500 percent.

An entire range of consumer goods previously limited to a small elite—if at all available—have come within the grasp of a large segment of the population. In 1947, at the start of the television age, less than one-tenth of one percent of U.S. families (14,000 of them) owned TV sets. But in 1983, 98 percent of all families had television, and

Consumer goods

The dramatic economic growth has brought with it some new problems. For example, the growing demand for oil in the 1960s and 1970s left the U.S. vulnerable to foreign suppliers, as the gas lines of the 1970s remind us.

about 85 percent of them had color television; together they owned 150 million sets. Cereals no longer suffice by being nourishing; they must excite the imagination with delightful shapes, colors, and sounds. Cat foods have come to compete with extravagant claims as to which best titillates the palate of discerning felines. Americans in 1982 owned 8.8 million outboard motors and 12.9 million recreational boats. About 8.5 million Americans traveled abroad in 1982. In matters large and small, sensible and foolish, the range of consumption has been greatly extended in the postindustrial era.

Recent U.S. economic performance

Over the last decade, aspects of America's economic performance have contributed to general economic unease: periodic bouts with high inflation, the successful penetration of American markets by foreign imports such as Japanese automobiles. Yet, despite such apparent problems, the economy still achieved impressive growth over the 1970s. In this decade GNP—measured in terms of dollars of constant purchasing power and adjusted to a per capita basis—increased by 38 percent. As Figure 2.7 shows, this growth rate compares favorably with that of previous decades, although it lags somewhat behind the rate of the 1940s and 1960s.

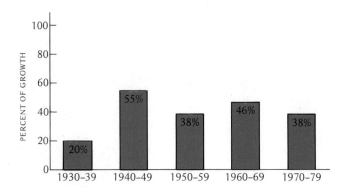

Figure 2.7
Per Capita GNP: Real Growth by Decade since 1930

Source: These percentages have been computed from data published in the *1980 Supplement to Economic Indicators,* for 1970–79; from *Historical Statistics of the United States, Part I,* p. 225, and *Statistical Abstract of the United States, 1980,* p. 440, for the earlier decades.

Income in the United States and Abroad

If the affluence of the United States today is evident when comparison is made to the country's past, it is equally clear when comparison is made to the experience of other countries. According to the calculations made by the highly regarded economists at the Organization for Economic Cooperation and Development (OECD), the United States enjoys a substantial economic edge (measured in terms of the purchasing power of the per capita GNP) over all of the other advanced democracies, Japan included. Between 1970 and 1982, Japan's economy grew faster than the U.S. economy, but the U.S. retained a significant margin in real per capita GNP (Table 2.2). Until recently, it was not possible to compare national income reliably even for countries like the United States and Great Britain; now the OECD measures give a good general picture. Data still are not available that would permit accurate comparisons of income in the economically advanced democracies to that in Communist or Third World countries. The best data we have suggest that the per capita GNP of the Soviet Union is less than half that of the United States, Mexico's just one-eighth as great, India's and China's even lower than Mexico's.

The national wealth of the United States not only gives a distinctive shape to consumption patterns in the country. It also seems to have great influences on many other aspects of social and political life. In following chapters we note the strong support Americans give to their country's political institutions and values, and the stability this imparts. Economic success— which the United States has experienced historically and which has been extended in the postindustrial era—adds legitimacy to political institutions.

World leader in per capita GNP

Social and political effects of national wealth

Table 2.2
National Income Comparisons, 1970 and 1982*

	1970	1982
United States	$4,821	$13,106
West Germany	3,712	10,880
Denmark	3,886	10,968
France	3,464	10,747
Belgium	3,352	10,293
Netherlands	3,633	9,858
Japan	3,066	10,589
Austria	3,034	9,852
United Kingdom	3,291	9,095
Italy	2,895	8,520
Spain	2,294	6,870
Ireland	2,033	6,166
Greece	1,660	5,410
Portugal	1,306	4,552

Source: OECD, National Accounts, vol. 1, Main Aggregates, 1951–1980, p. 86.

*The methodology used by the OECD in deriving the above data involves valuing the goods and services sold in different countries in a common set of international prices. The OECD calls this "purchasing power parities (PPP)." PPPs are international price indexes linking the price levels of different countries. They show how many units of currency are needed in one country to buy the same amount of goods and services which one unit of currency will buy in the other country: for example, how many French francs are needed to buy in France what one U.S. dollar will buy within the United States.

CLASS RELATIONSHIPS

The concept of social class

The concept of **social class** denotes status deriving from the amount of income received as well as the sources of this income: interest earnings from inherited wealth, ownership of a farm, a factory job, and so on. The concept also refers to the social and cultural outlooks that result from income status. For Karl Marx, capitalists were a social class not just because they had relatively large amounts of wealth, but also because of how they derived their money—from their ownership of private industry—and because they shared common interests and outlooks.

Weak class divisions

America's class divisions historically have been relatively weak. Social norms and interests commonly described as middle class have been the common property of many disparate economic groups. In particular, the American working class has never had the coherence and self-consciousness found historically in Europe. And socialism, which developed as a working-class ideology, has always been weak in America (see chapter 4).

Working-Class Consciousness

Still, the United States has not been totally without a politically self-conscious and organized working class. The industrial era—especially the time of Franklin Roosevelt's presidency (1933–45)—stands as its high-water mark. Under the new and greatly expanded government programs of the Roosevelt administration, known as the New Deal, working-class Americans received important recognition and support: legislation guaranteeing the right to organize and bargain collectively; minimum wage legislation; social security benefits; various guarantees of occupational health and safety, and the general humaneness of working conditions. Legislation securing these benefits was not directed exclusively toward urban factory workers, but this group was a principal claimant and beneficiary.

The New Deal and the rise of labor unions

During the New Deal the labor union movement gained strength. The political climate which followed the outbreak of the Great Depression in 1929—including the general encouragement of unionism given by the Roosevelt administration, new supportive legislation, and the vigorous initiatives of a new generation of labor leaders—produced a surge in union membership, from 3.5 million in 1931 to 10 million on the eve of World War II, to more than 14 million when the war ended. This was the heroic age of American labor.

The changing character of the labor movement

In the late 1940s and 1950s, however, union membership as a proportion of the nonagricultural labor force leveled out, and in the 1960s and 1970s it actually declined. In 1955, 33 percent of all workers in nonagricultural pursuits were unionized; but by 1980, the proportion was down to 25 percent. Not only has the American labor movement come to represent a declining proportion of workers, but the sectors where it holds the greatest promise of expansion lie ouside the traditional industrial, blue-collar sector. Government employees have been a big growth area in recent years. Between 1968 and 1980 the membership of the American Federation of State, County, and Municipal Employees (AFSCME) grew from 364,000 to 1,098,000. The American Federation of Teachers (AFT) more than tripled in this time span—from 164,000 to 551,000 members. In October 1973, Albert Shanker (then head of the New York AFT and subsequently the union's national president) was appointed to the national council of the principal national labor federation, the American Federation of Labor–Congress of Industrial Organizations (AFL-CIO), recognition never before extended to someone from other than one of the traditional blue-collar unions.

Economic Gains

If the traditional center of the working class—urban, blue-collar, and trade union—has lost ground numerically, it has also become an established class in contrast to its new claimant status of the New Deal era. Most of the urban working class of the 1930s were economic have-nots; if not poor, they were right on the margin. As such, they supported government-directed efforts to change the economic order. The trade union movement organized this have-not working class and pushed effectively for its economic betterment and security.

Labor's shifting status

In effect, the unions achieved their goals through government intervention and economic growth. The unionized labor force moved up the socioeconomic ladder. For this group, the victory over economic privation was largely won. Much of the working class became middle class. By 1973, the median earnings of families whose head was a skilled manual worker exceeded the national median family income, and in real terms were more than twice what they had been in 1947. In 1981, the median income of skilled blue-collar workers was $25,800, compared to $22,400 for the national family average.[12]

Middle Class, Even Conservative

"The fire has gone out in labor's belly"

The political consequences of drawing a large portion of the working class—especially that represented by labor unions—into what is for all practical purposes lower-middle-class status have been noted for some time now. "The fire has gone out in labor's belly," suggested journalist Stewart Alsop in 1967, because trade unions were no longer representing have-nots. Alsop recalled Franklin Roosevelt's packing Cadillac Square in Detroit with a half-million cheering workers in an

Huge rallies in Cadillac Square, Detroit, marked a high point in the labor movement in the 1930s.

[12] U.S. Bureau of the Census, *Current Population Reports*, Series P–60, No. 96, "Household Money Income in 1973 and Selected Social And Economic Characteristics of Households" (Washington, D.C.: Government Printing Office, 1974), p. 10.

October 1936 rally. He contrasted this to the mere 30,000 who turned out for Democratic President Lyndon Johnson in 1964, when Johnson was at his most popular and his Republican opponent, Barry Goldwater, gave labor its clearest target in many moons. Why then the poor turnout? "The workers who crowded shoulder to shoulder into Cadillac Square to hear Franklin Roosevelt regarded themselves as 'little guys' or 'working stiffs.' . . . The poor, and those who regarded themselves as poor, were in those days a clear majority of the population."[13] Alsop went on to point out that the typical trade unionist in 1964 was simply much better off, absolutely and relatively, than his counterpart had been twenty-five or thirty years earlier. He was more inclined to go boating or camping than participate in solidarity rallies; and he no longer sustained the drive for social change.

George Meany, president of the AFL-CIO from 1952 until his death in 1980, spoke insightfully of the transformation of labor's place in the postindustrial era. In a 1969 interview with the *New York Times*, Meany appeared willing to accept both "middle class" and "conservative" as descriptions of the membership of the labor movement:

George Meany and labor's conservatism

> Labor, to some extent, has become middle class. When you have no property, you don't have anything, you have nothing to lose by these radical actions. But when you become a person who has a home and has property, to some extent you become conservative. And I would say to that extent, labor has become conservative.[14]

A working class which in many ways is middle class and conservative: Yes, that is a distinctive feature of postindustrialism.

New Class Groupings

A new middle class

Another key development affecting class structure has emerged from the extraordinary expansion of higher education since World War II. Most people in the burgeoning college stratum don't fit into the traditional class groupings. They are hardly in working-class jobs: Only six percent hold manual-labor positions of any sort. But neither are they, for the most part, business men and women. Just 25 percent of them are managers or administrators of any kind. Nearly 60 percent of college graduates hold professional and technical jobs.[15] Such positions can be classified as middle class, but it is hard to fit them into traditional theories of class and politics. It does seem that the vast expansion of the college-trained population has fueled a broad

[13] Stewart Alsop, "Can Anyone Beat LBJ?" *Saturday Evening Post*, May 1967, p. 28.
[14] "Excerpts from Interview with Meany on Status of Labor Movement," *New York Times*, August 31, 1969.
[15] These data are derived from three large surveys of the American public conducted in 1980, 1982, and 1983 by the National Opinion Research Center of the University of Chicago (NORC). This ongoing series is known as the "General Social Survey."

transformation of the upper middle class in the United States, from a business-defined and inclined posture to one shaped by intellectual experiences and values. Some observers see the huge college-trained population taking on the properties of an *intelligentsia:* a social class whose distinctive income and occupational status springs from its application of trained intelligence.

In the chapters that follow, we will expand on some of the dimensions of contemporary American society described above. And we will examine their impact on the political life of the country in greater detail.

SUMMARY

Postindustrialism is a term, first introduced by sociologist Daniel Bell, that is now commonly used to describe central features of recent social change in the United States and other developed countries. The U.S. has gradually emerged into its postindustrial era over the last quarter-century.

The postindustrial setting is distinguished by five interrelated developments.

It displays extraordinary technological advances which, for the first time, accrue primarily from the systematic applications of science.

It requires great commitments to the knowledge base. This is especially evident in the rising proportion of the population receiving college training and the big outlays for education at all levels.

Postindustrialism is characterized by the predominant place of the service sector, compared to agriculture and manufacturing. In the U.S. and other advanced countries, white-collar positions have come to far outnumber blue-collar positions.

The achievements of science and technology have produced a level of national wealth in the U.S. that surpasses that of the earlier industrial era as dramatically as the latter surpassed the economic attainments of the agricultural setting.

Finally, social class composition and political behavior in postindustrial America differ from what they were in the preceding period. In particular, the working-class base for trade union activity has eroded, and union members have become more conservative politically. The growing college-trained population scrambles earlier assumptions about class makeup and interests.

3 | The American People

Imagine sitting down with a visiting politician from another country. He wants you to give him some important touchstones for understanding the United States, a nation whose actions affect his own country in so many ways. "What are the American people like?" he asks. "What are some of the most important attributes of this population?" Much could be said. But a few social features stand out, especially when the interest or reference point is primarily political. The educational, occupational, and economic characteristics discussed in the last chapter as contributing to the postindustrial era are part of the answer our visitor should be given. In this chapter, we provide another part.

We should make our visitor aware of the *ethnic and religious make-up* of the country. The United States is unusually diverse ethnically and religiously, and this fact has left its mark on national life. For example, the diversity has been the source of a great deal of social conflict. American political parties historically have been shaped by ethnic tensions and identities. *E pluribus unum*, imprinted on the banner which waves from the eagle's beak in the official seal of the United States, initially suggested the forming of one nation from thirteen sovereign states. But "one, from many" holds more meaning for us today as a description of the continuing political challenge in securing full national citizenship and rights for all the ethnocultural groups that form the American nation.

Our visitor needs to know, too, about American *regionalism.* This is a continent-spanning country. Regions such as the South, New England, the Plains states, and the Pacific Coast have differed greatly in their cultures and economic interests. A great war was fought between 1861 and 1865—the American Civil War—around the powerful sectional issues of states' rights and slavery. Today, regionalism is much less divisive than it was a century ago, but it remains a prominent part of American social and political life.

*The American people,
a diverse people.*

Finally, since the United States has long boasted that it is a land of opportunity, our visitor will want to know something about how this claim has been honored. How much **social mobility** do Americans experience? How fixed or penetrable are class lines? Do Americans believe they have an opportunity to get ahead if they make an effort to do so? Relatedly, how equal or unequal are the economic results, the way income gets distributed?

Social mobility

ETHNOCULTURAL MAKEUP OF THE UNITED STATES

Two key developments in eighteenth-century America were to have lasting impact on national ethnic and religious experiences. One was highly positive, the other a source of national shame. The first was that the United States offered itself as a homeland for those denied religious freedom in their countries of birth. As a practical and symbolic reflection of this commitment, the First Amendment to the U.S. Constitution specifically forbade the establishment of any official religion, proclaiming a policy of governmental neutrality among the many religious sects: "Congress shall make no law respecting an establishment of religion, or prohibiting the free exercise thereof. . . ." At

America offered a home for those who were denied freedom elsewhere or who sought opportunity.

the same time, however, Americans were violating the civil rights and liberties of another group. Through the African slave trade, one-half million blacks were brought to the U.S. against their will. For the most part, they served as slaves in the South's agricultural economy.

Ethnic and religious developments transformed American life in the nineteenth and twentieth centuries. Between 1820 and 1980, more than 50 million immigrants decided to make the United States their home. The greatest wave of immigration took place between 1900 and 1924, when 17.3 million people moved to America—by far the largest migration in any quarter-century in human history.

Eras in American Ethnic Experience

Every period in American history has had its distinctive forms of ethnocultural conflict. The early white settlers of the United States were mostly British Protestants: English, Scottish, and Scotch-Irish. As late as 1830, the white population of 10.5 million was largely of this ethnic and religious background. Also, by this time, there were nearly 2.3 million black inhabitants, most of whom were slaves on southern plantations. Over the next several decades the country's ethnic mix changed significantly as a result of large immigrations from Ireland and Germany. More than 1.3 million people migrated from Ireland, and 1 million from Germany, between 1845 and 1855 alone. Many of these new immigrants were Roman Catholic, and Protestant-Catholic tensions became more pronounced.

The years of rapid industrial development in the late nineteenth and early twentieth centuries saw another major shift in American

The first wave of immigrants

The second wave of immigrants

ethnic makeup. Previously, the country's white population had been mostly North European. The new immigrants, spurred by the labor demands of industrialization, came heavily from central and southern Europe: between 1900 and the outbreak of World War I in 1914, 3.1 million people migrated to the United States from the countries of central Europe, 2.6 million from Russia and the Baltic states, and 3 million from Italy.

Ethnic hostilities and prejudice

America's ethnic growing pains were especially sharp during this period. The contemporary observer is struck by the blatancy of ethnic hostilities and prejudice. In 1921 Vice-President-elect Calvin Coolidge write in a national magazine that "biological laws show us that Nordics [North Europeans] deteriorate when mixed with other races."[1] At about the same time, James J. Davis, who served as secretary of labor under Presidents Harding and Coolidge, proclaimed that old-stock Americans were "the beaver type that built up America, whereas the new immigrants were rat-men trying to tear it down; and obviously rat-men could never become beavers."[2] Such statements by politicians in high office were legion.

The civil rights struggle

After World War II, the United States had to confront its historic discrimination against its black population. Ethnic splits within white America diminished, and the civil rights struggle moved front and center. Racial tensions peaked in the 1950s and 1960s, as major efforts were finally made to extend full citizenship to black Americans. The key policies and actions of this period are discussed in chapter 17.

Latin American immigration

Now in the 1980s the United States is again experiencing a large immigration, this one from Latin American countries, especially Mexico. The story of American ethnic diversity is still being written.

Since the 1920s, when tight curbs were imposed on immigration to the U.S., millions of people have tried to enter undetected. Many have succeeded, but many others have been turned back by guards along the U.S./Mexico border.

[1] Calvin Coolidge, "Whose Country Is This?" *Good Housekeeping* 72 (February 1921), p. 14.
[2] Quoted by Seymour Martin Lipset and Earl Rabb, *The Politics of Unreason: Right Wing Extremism in America, 1790-1970* (New York: Harper and Row), chap. 4.

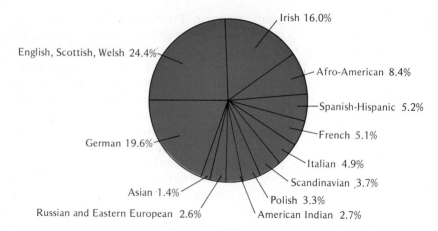

Figure 3.1
National Origin of the American Population*

*In releasing these data, the Bureau of the Census noted that "since multiple ancestry responses are classified in each applicable group, the sum of the ancestry groups is greater than the total number of persons. . . ."
Source: U.S. Bureau of the Census, "Ancestry of the Population by State," *Nineteen-Eighty Census of the Population,* April, 1983, pp. 1–3.

Present Ethnic Makeup

Figure 3.1 shows just how heterogeneous the American populace has become. While people of English, Scottish, and Welsh background are still the largest ethnocultural group in the United States, they are now a distinct minority of the population. In 1980, in a country of 226.5 million, 83 percent were whites, 12 percent blacks, and 5 percent of other stock. Hispanic Americans—6 percent of the population, or more than 13 million people—are not a racial group; a majority classify themselves as whites in Census surveys, but a large minority now describe themselves as "other" (not blacks or whites) when asked their racial identity. Blacks are still a significantly larger proportion of the population in the South than elsewhere in the country; Hispanics are most numerous proportionately in the Southwest.

Religion

The American populace is now roughly 64 percent Protestant, 25 percent Catholic, 2 percent Jewish, and 2 percent of other religions, while 7 percent have no religious preference (see Figure 3.2). Among Protestants, Baptists are by far the largest group, making up about 20 percent of the entire population.

Importance of religious beliefs

Religious beliefs and values remain important to Americans. It used to be thought that when countries become highly developed economically, when large proportions of their populations are college-trained— when they enter their postindustrial eras—the forces of secularization strengthen and religious commitments weaken. The present-day

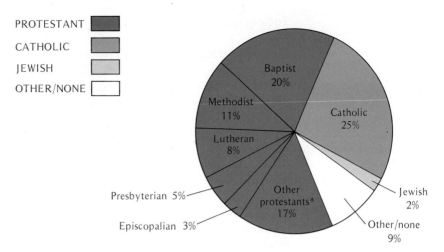

*"Other protestants" includes other, no denomination given, or a nondenominational church.
Source: General Social Surveys, 1980, 1982, 1983; National Opinion Research Center, University of Chicago.

Figure 3.2
Religious Affiliation

United States confounds this view. There has been some decline in church attendance, but Americans still show strong religious attachments. As Figure 3.3 indicates, the proportion of the public stating that their religious beliefs are important to them is much higher in the U.S. than in any other of the highly developed countries. We discuss these findings as part of a more detailed review of American public opinion and values in chapter 12.

Figure 3.3
Importance of Religious Beliefs (self-described), by Country

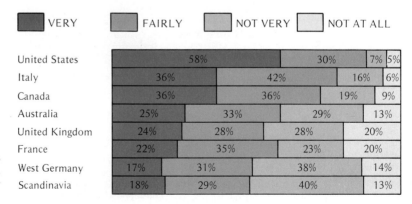

Source: Surveys by the Gallup International Research Institute for the Charles F. Kettering Foundation, 1974–1975, for foreign; Gallup Organization survey of January 20–23, 1978, for U.S.A.
Question: How important to you are your religious beliefs—very important, fairly important, not very important, or not at all important?

Socioeconomic Differences

Many Americans take pride in the ethnic and religious diversity of their country. But they also want a unity in the diversity, part of which involves equality of group access to income, education, and jobs. What is the present performance in this latter regard?

"The melting pot"

Within white America, historic ethnic-group differences in socioeconomic standing have been greatly reduced in recent years. Surveys taken by the University of Chicago's National Opinion Research Center (NORC), show that groups such as Irish Catholics—who in the past were widely subject to discrimination—have advanced greatly in the post–World War II years. The fabled melting pot has eliminated many of the old ethnic differences in socioeconomic status.

Where the "melting pot" failed

Blacks and Hispanics, however, are still in inferior economic positions. The median income for all white families in 1982 was nearly $24,603, but only $13,559 for black families and $16,228 for Hispanics. Even here, though, some movement is occurring. Among married-couple families, the median income for whites was $31,098 in 1982, for blacks $27,279, and for Hispanics $24,353—a significant difference, but one markedly reduced from what had prevailed earlier.[3]

The principal ethnocultural groups of the United States seem to be less dissimilar now than at any point in U.S. history. In Figure 3.4, the political self-description of the members of each group—liberal, middle of the road, conservative—are shown (drawing again upon the NORC survey data). Jews, blacks, and Hispanics, historically associated with relatively liberal political positions, continue to give

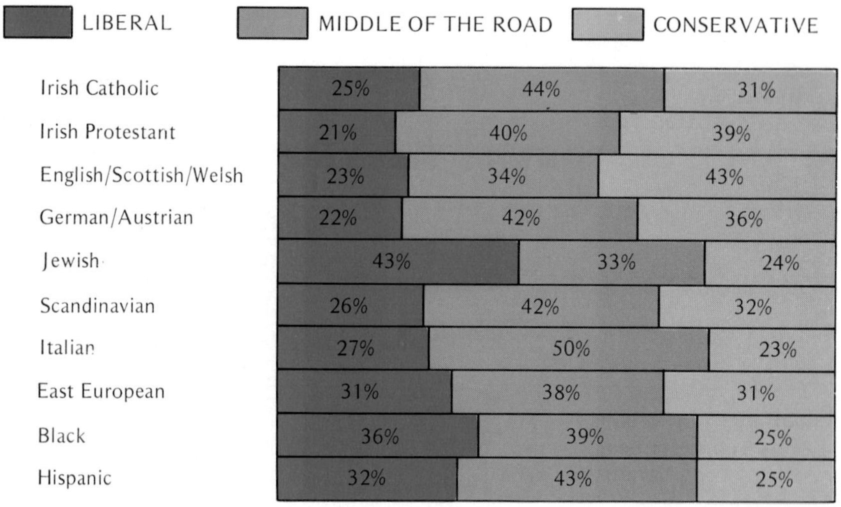

	LIBERAL	MIDDLE OF THE ROAD	CONSERVATIVE
Irish Catholic	25%	44%	31%
Irish Protestant	21%	40%	39%
English/Scottish/Welsh	23%	34%	43%
German/Austrian	22%	42%	36%
Jewish	43%	33%	24%
Scandinavian	26%	42%	32%
Italian	27%	50%	23%
East European	31%	38%	31%
Black	36%	39%	25%
Hispanic	32%	43%	25%

Figure 3.4
How Americans Describe their Political Views, by Ethnocultural Background

Source: General Social Surveys, 1980, 1982, 1983; National Opinion Research Center, University of Chicago.

[3] The *median income* of a group of families is the income exactly in the middle of the range: Half of all families earn more; half less.

more backing to liberalism than do any of the other ethnocultural groups. But, overall, as the various groups have become more alike in socioeconomic position, they have in their political stands as well.

The political cleavage between Protestants and Catholics was a dominant one historically. John F. Kennedy's election as president in 1960, the first Roman Catholic to hold that office, was symbolically important in this context: it signaled the closing of a once great divide. When will a black man or woman be elected president, with comparable symbolism and meaning for American racial experience? National attitudes have changed significantly in this area, making the prospect far less remote than it was even 15 years ago. Jesse Jackson's candidacy for the Democratic presidential nomination in 1984 generated considerable support. Still, Jackson's strong run depended on his overwhelming backing in the black community and drew only a small minority of whites.

REGIONALISM

The major geographic areas of the United States have been fed by different streams of immigration, experienced contrasting economic development, had differing needs, and frequently have been at odds politically. Of the sectional antipathies, that between the Northeast and the South has been the most prominent historically. In the first half of the nineteenth century, the South was rural and agricultural, increasingly committed to one great cash crop, cotton. Unfortunately, slavery was perfectly suited to the flourishing cotton economy; cotton was transformed from a dying institution into one which was aggressively expansionist and vigorously defended by many southern whites. In contrast, the Northeast was the most urban and commercial part of the country. By 1850, it accounted for three-fourths of American manufacturing employment. Because of its seaports, the area was the primary point of arrival for immigrants from Europe, and from its beginnings was the most ethnically diverse part of the country.

Pre–Civil War regional differences

Many of the sectional differences that led to the Civil War persisted after the war. The Northeast industrialized faster than any other part of the United States. The resulting need for labor led to the region's becoming home to a disproportionate number of the newer immigrants of the late nineteenth and early twentieth centuries. While the Northeast was occupied with the ethnic tensions between older and newer immigrants and between Protestants and Catholics, the ethnic politics of the South remained race-dominated, involving a fairly homogeneous white Protestant population on the one hand and blacks on the other. The South remained the most rural and agricultural region. When Franklin Roosevelt took office as president in 1933, the southern states were still decidedly the country's poorest.

Post–Civil War regional differences

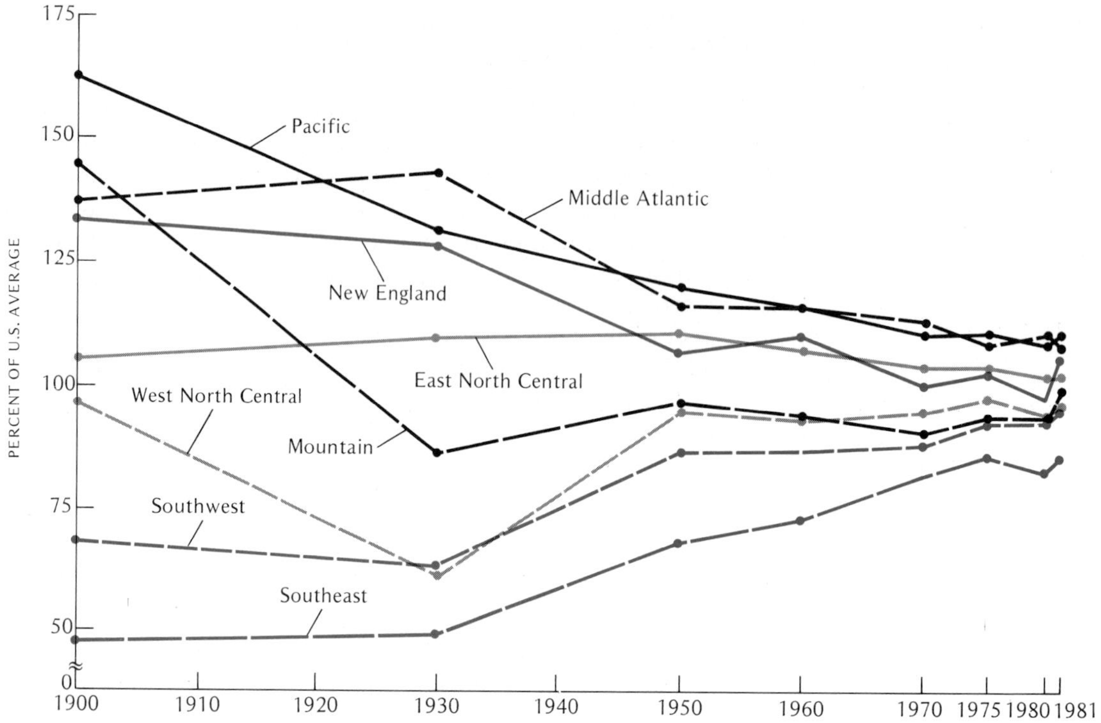

Figure 3.5
Regional Per Capita Income as a Percent of U.S. Average

Source: Regional Growth: Historical Perspective, Advisory Commission on Intergovernmental Relations, June 1980, p. 11. 1981 figures supplied by ACIR.

Sunbelt and Frostbelt

For every generation of Americans up through the 1950s, the Northeast was the "establishment" region. It was seen as the great center of industrial wealth—and was attacked by populist movements in the South and West. Now some would say that things have been turned around. We no longer have the imperial Northeast; the region is now described as a troubled Frostbelt, in a state of decline as it loses people, jobs, and political influence. The South is no longer victimized; it has been redefined as the buoyant Sunbelt. Seemingly, winter-time temperatures have become the decisive feature of American regionalism.

Regional convergence in economic status

This trendy interpretation, however, has the story somewhat twisted. The main economic development is not Frostbelt decline so much as the steady convergence of the regions' economic status. As Figure 3.5 shows, the various sections of the U.S. were vastly unequal at the turn of the century—hardly a desirable situation in terms of national unity. Over the last half-century in the United States, though, per capita income by region has become much more uniform. The Sunbelt states of the South have improved their position vis-à-vis the Northeast and Midwest, but this improvement must be understood

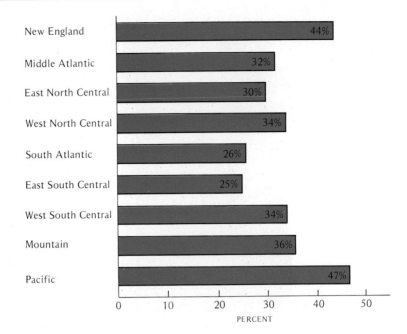

Figure 3.6
Education by Region (percentage of population with at least some college education)

Source: Surveys by the National Opinion Research Center, General Social Surveys, 1977, 1978, 1980, and 1982.

as a reduction of the South's historic economic lag. The southern Sunbelt is still the least affluent part of the country and its population has the nation's lowest education levels (Figure 3.6).

Social and Political Regionalism

Regional convergence in social and political attitudes

In social and political terms, America's regions have also come closer together. Racial attitudes in the southern states still differ from those elsewhere in the country, but not nearly as much as they did three and four decades ago. Sectional differences in party loyalties are now much smaller than they used to be. The trend in political attitudes is toward regional convergence (Figure 3.7). None of this suggests that sectional variations have disappeared or are likely to. Especially on such social questions as abortion, sexual norms, and the role of women, and in the area of religious beliefs, regional differences remain striking. Note in the data presented in Figure 3.8 a pronounced bicoastal liberalism, with New England, the Middle Atlantic, and the Pacific states the most socially liberal, and the heartland South and Midwest decidedly more conservative. Overall, though, American regionalism has lost a lot of its historic divisiveness, as the regions have become more alike socially, economically, and politically.

PARTY IDENTIFICATION

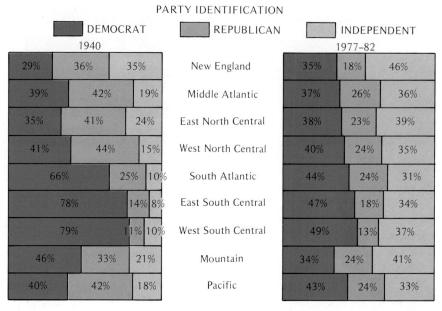

Source: 1940: Survey by the Gallup Organization, July 21–26, 1940. 1977–82: Surveys by the National Opinion Research Center, General Social Surveys, 1977, 1978, 1980, and 1982 (data combined).

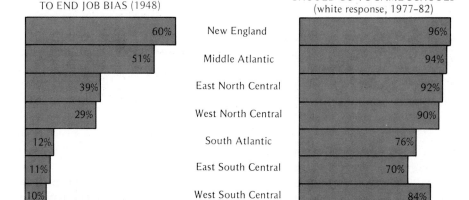

Figure 3.7
Regions Become More Similar

Question: One of Truman's proposals concerns employment practices. How far do you yourself think the federal government should go in requiring employers to hire people without regard to their race, religion, color, or nationality? The percentages shown here are responses for federal government going all the way to end job bias.
Source: Survey by the Gallup Organization, March 5–10, 1946.

Question: Do you think white students and (Negro/black) students should go to the same schools or to separate schools? Data combined for 1977, 1980, and 1982.
Source: Surveys by the National Opinion Research Center, General Social Surveys, 1977, 1980, and 1982.

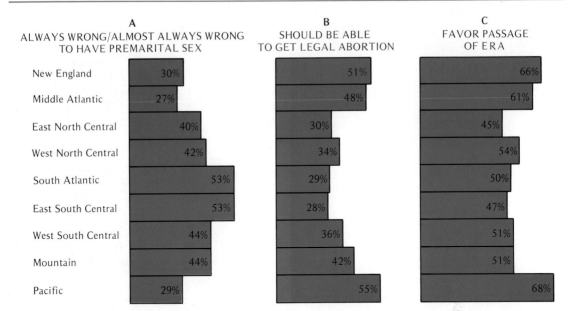

	A ALWAYS WRONG/ALMOST ALWAYS WRONG TO HAVE PREMARITAL SEX	B SHOULD BE ABLE TO GET LEGAL ABORTION	C FAVOR PASSAGE OF ERA
New England	30%	51%	66%
Middle Atlantic	27%	48%	61%
East North Central	40%	30%	45%
West North Central	42%	34%	54%
South Atlantic	53%	29%	50%
East South Central	53%	28%	47%
West South Central	44%	36%	51%
Mountain	44%	42%	51%
Pacific	29%	55%	68%

Figure 3.8
Bicoastal Liberalism

A. *Question:* There's been a lot of discussion about the way morals and attitudes about sex are changing in this country. If a man and a woman have sex relations before marriage, do you think it is always wrong, almost always wrong, wrong only sometimes, or not wrong at all? Data combined for 1977, 1978, and 1982.
Source: Surveys by the National Opinion Research Center, General Social Surveys, 1977, 1978, and 1982.

B. *Question:* Please tell me whether or not *you* think it should be possible for a pregnant woman to obtain a *legal* abortion if . . . the woman wants it for any reason? Data combined for 1977, 1978, 1980, and 1982.
Source: Surveys by the National Opinion Research Center, General Social Surveys, 1977, 1978, 1980, and 1982.

C. *Question:* Do you favor or oppose passage of the Equal Rights Amendment? (Asked of respondents who had heard or read about the Equal Rights Amendment = 83%)
Source: Survey of the Gallup Organization, December 11–14, 1981.

OPPORTUNITY AND MOBILITY

The Horatio Alger story

The sense that the United States has extended opportunities for individual advancement has figured prominently in the nation's experience. Millions of immigrants moved here seeking a better life. The idea that any person can work his or her way up in wealth and status is central to the country's self-image or conception. We see this in American folklore. The name of one nineteenth-century writer of stories for young people has become synonymous with the idea that anyone, no matter how poor, can get ahead through hard work and perseverance. Horatio Alger, who was born in Revere, Massachusetts, in 1832, wrote more than 130 novels which proclaimed the land of

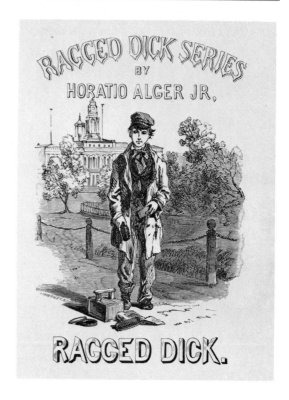

boundless opportunity theme. Today we speak of those who rise spectacularly in social position through personal initiatives as living an Horatio Alger story.

> "There's hope for you Dick if you'll try." "Nobody ever talked to me so before," said Dick. "They just called me Ragged Dick, and told me I'd grow up to be a vagabone (boys who are better educated need not be surprised at Dick's blunders) and come to the gallows."
> "Telling you so won't make it turn out so Dick. If you'll try to be somebody, and grow up into a respectable member of society you will. You may not become rich,—it isn't everybody that becomes rich, you know— but you can obtain a good position, and be respected."[4]

Public opinion and the American Dream

How valid is the claim that the American social system has offered unusual opportunities for individual advancement? We know that a great many Americans believe the claim is true and have stuck with this belief through some rocky times. In 1939, when the United States was still gripped by the effects of the Great Depression, pollster Elmo Roper asked a cross-section of Americans whether they believed "that the great age of economic opportunity and expansion in the U.S. is over, or that American industry can create a comparable expansion and opportunity in the future." Seventy-two percent thought the

[4] Horatio Alger, *Ragged Dick* (New York: Collier, 1962), p. 75.

opportunity was still there, compared to 13 percent who said it was over and 15 percent who were unsure. Sixty-six percent of those *unemployed* said the opportunity remained.[5]

This sense of opportunity persists. In late 1983 a poll taken by ABC News and the *Washington Post* asked whether "it is true in this country that if you work hard, eventually you will get ahead." Seventy-one percent said it was true, including majorities of every economic stratum in the country.[6]

Social Mobility

Another way to approach the question of individual opportunity is to examine objective data on social mobility. Mobility may be measured by comparing people's present income, educational or occupational position with that of their parents. An individual is upwardly mobile when the educational or occupational status he or she acquires is higher than his or her parents'.

Throughout much of history, upward social mobility was very limited. In most aristocratic societies, as a rule, people stayed in the social and economic rank to which they were born, and they worked in the same jobs as their parents. Economic and technological developments of the last two centuries have greatly extended opportunities for upward mobility in countries around the world. Mobility has been especially pronounced in the United States.

The NORC General Social Surveys provide an unusual opportunity to measure precisely the degree of mobility of the American populace. In Table 3.1 individuals are located first by the amount of education they have received and then by the educational experience of their fathers. We see that an exceptionally large proportion of Americans have been upwardly mobile educationally. Among those who today are college graduates, only 33 percent come from families where the father was a college graduate. Two-thirds have more education than their fathers. Of high school graduates, only 5 percent come from families where the father had more than a high school education, while 61 percent are from families where he had less than 12 years of schooling. These data reflect the fact that for each succeeding generation in this century, and especially since World War II, the amount of available education has risen sharply. The old nautical expression, "a rising tide lifts all boats," captures this experience. The educational tide has continued to rise and it has lifted a great many people with it.

In Table 3.2 we see what jobs were held by the parents of Americans who are today in various occupations. Again, this measure reveals an extraordinary amount of occupational mobility, both upward and downward but especially the former.

Upward mobility

Educational and social mobility

[5] Survey by Elmo Roper and Associates for *Fortune* magazine, September 1939.
[6] Survey by ABC News and the *Washington Post*, December 12–18, 1983.

Table 3.1
Educational Mobility
(row percentages)

| | Father's education | | | |
Respondent's education	Less than high school	High school graduate	Some college	College graduate
Less than high school	84	12	3	2
High school graduate	61	29	6	5
Some college	41	31	12	16
College graduate	27	27	13	33

Source: General Social Surveys, 1980, 1982, 1983; The National Opinion Research Center, University of Chicago.

Note: Respondents were asked 2 questions: 1. How much schooling did they have: a. less than high school? b. high school graduate? c. some college? d. college graduate? 2. How much schooling did their fathers have: a.? b.? c.? d.?

Of the respondents who said that they themselves had had less than high school training, 84 percent had fathers (read across) who had less than high school; 12 percent had fathers who were high school graduates; 3 percent had fathers with some college; and only 2 percent had fathers who were college graduates. Of the respondents who said they were high school graduates, 61 percent had fathers (read across) with less than a high school education; 29 percent had fathers who were high school graduates; and 6 percent had fathers with some college.

Follow same order for reading Table 3.2.

Only 20 percent of those in high-status professional and technical jobs today come from families where the father held such a position, and only 47 percent come from families where the father's job was of comparably high status and income—in either the professional or the managerial ranks. Four percent of today's professionals had fathers who worked in clerical or sales jobs, 21 percent in skilled blue-collar positions, 19 percent in unskilled labor, and 9 percent in farming. In sum, while parents' social position influences what positions their children come to hold, many people achieve social status different from their parents. Many are upwardly mobile. The objective data

Occupational mobility

Table 3.2
Occupational Mobility
(row percentages)

| | Father's occupation | | | | | |
Respondent's occupation	Professional/ technical	Managerial/ administrative	Clerical/ sales	Skilled	Unskilled	Farm
Professional/technical	20	27	4	21	19	9
Manager/administrator	11	31	5	21	19	13
Clerical sales	10	21	4	26	29	10
Skilled blue collar	6	11	3	34	28	19
Unskilled blue collar	4	11	3	23	38	22
Farmers	2	8	0	6	4	79

Source: General Social Surveys, 1980, 1982, 1983; National Opinion Research Center, University of Chicago.

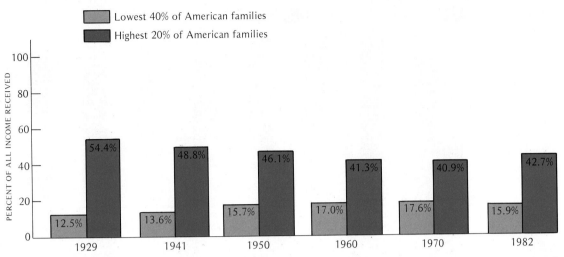

PERCENT OF ALL INCOME RECEIVED

☐ Lowest 40% of American families
■ Highest 20% of American families

Figure 3.9
**Income Distribution since 1929
(percent of all money income received by lowest 40% or highest 20% of American families)**

Source: 1929–55: U.S. Bureau of the Census, *Historical Statistics of the United States: Colonial Times to 1957, Part 2*, p. 166. 1960–78: idem, *Statistical Abstract of the United States, 1980*. 1982: idem, *Current Population Reports*, P-60, #140, Table 4, 1982.

square with what Americans tell pollsters, that they believe they have a good chance to advance through their own initiatives.

What would be the political implications if things were otherwise than we have described—if, for example, most Americans believed that no matter how hard they worked, they were unlikely to advance, and if social mobility were far more limited than it is? It is likely that American institutions would not, in such a circumstance, enjoy the degree of support that they do.

Inequality

Still, if mobility and opportunity are real, they co-exist with a great deal of income inequality. The gap between winners and losers in America's mobility race remains a wide one. The fifth of all families with the highest incomes in 1982 received 42.7 percent of all earnings, while the lowest-paid fifth received only 4.7 percent of national income. Together, the top 40 percent of all families gained over two-thirds of earnings, while the bottom 40 percent received under one-sixth of national income (Figure 3.9).

Since the 1920s and 1930s, the degree of income inequality has diminished somewhat, even as the amount of income available overall has greatly expanded. In 1929, the richest fifth of all families received 54.4 percent of all income; the proportion has since declined significantly, reaching a low of 41 percent in 1965–70. Various government programs, described in chapter 17, have had much to do with this. American social welfare policies have achieved some income redistribution. Whether the amount of income inequality that now

Income inequality

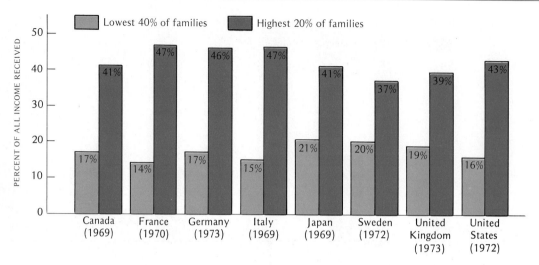

Source: Malcolm Sawyer, "Income Distribution in OECD Countries," *OECD Economic Outlook, Occasional Studies, July 1976.*

Figure 3.10
Income Distributions in Economically Advanced Democracies (distribution of income after taxes)

Income inequality in the U.S. and abroad

prevails is excessive or not is a source of continuing political debate.

How does the United States compare to other advanced democracies in income equality? Such comparisons are tricky, because each country has its own economic measures. Still, economists and statisticians have given us a good general sense of the income picture cross-nationally.[7] Figure 3.10 shows income distributions for the U.S. and other economically advanced democracies. The most striking finding is the broad similarity that prevails from one country to another. The various advanced nations have had vastly different historical experiences. They operate under sharply contrasting political arrangements and types of policies. Yet they distribute income in similar ways. Sweden and Australia rank relatively high in terms of the degree of equality of income distribution, while France and Italy are less equalitarian. The U.S. is closer to France than to Sweden. But the margin of difference from one country to another is hardly massive.

Geographic Mobility

The myth of a "moving-van" America

What we know about social mobility confirms the popular notion that the United States has broadly extended opportunity. But another type of mobility data seems to contradict the commonly held picture: geographic mobility, how much people move from one part of the country to another. Especially since World War II, the impression has grown

[7] For a thoughtful description of some of the problems in cross-national income comparisons, see Malcolm Sawyer, "Income Distribution in OECD Countries," an occasional study in the *OECD Outlook Series* (Paris: The Organization for Economic Cooperation and Development, July 1976), pp. 12–14.

The image of "moving-van America" is much exaggerated, but for some communities it is a reality.

of a moving-van America, where people relocate frenetically, responding partly to wanderlust and partly to job requirements. In fact, the data show that while many people do move around, more tend to stay put. Ninety-one percent of those now residing in the East lived in that region when they were growing up. The figures are almost exactly the same for midwesterners and southerners. While it is true that a higher proportion of those living in the West have come from other parts of the country, even here the data contradict popular folklore that "almost no one now living in the West grew up there." Sixty-seven percent of adult western-state residents lived in that region when they were 16 years old, while 10 percent moved in from the South, 15 percent from the Midwest, and 8 percent from the East.

According to NORC data, 43 percent of all adult Americans live not only in the same state but also in the same city as they did when they were 16 years old. Another 25 percent live in the same state but have moved to a different town. Only 32 percent reside in a different city and state than they did in their high school years.

SUMMARY

Three primary aspects of American social composition have been described in this chapter. Each has helped shape the country's political life.

A series of waves of immigration have made the United States unusually diverse ethnically and religiously. Key to the American political experience has been the task of building a new national identity out of many disparate traditions. Inevitably, ethnic conflict has been prominent in the United States, as the country has moved from one ethnic frontier to another. The split between Protestants and Catholics was once a deep one, but it has long since lost its force. The groups making up white America have become more alike in socioeconomic position and political outlook. In our own time, the oldest of the ethnic cleavages in the country—between whites and blacks—has defined the frontier of ethnic change.

Regional interests and culture have been important parts of the setting for American politics. The greatest political division in U.S. history involved the drastically different sectional interests of the North and South. Today, the big story is regional convergence: In economic position and social outlook, the regions are less dissimilar now than ever before in U.S. history—this despite the hype about the Frostbelt and the Sunbelt.

American social makeup has been influenced by the amount of social mobility that has occurred. A great many people experience movement up and down the social ladder. Class lines are fluid, not fixed. The belief is widely held in the U.S. that opportunity to move ahead is present, if one makes the effort, and this belief is shared by those with low incomes as well as the wealthy. The legitimacy of the political system is thus enhanced.

Our emphasis in chapter 2 was on vast changes in contemporary American economic life that have thrust the country into a new postindustrial era. In this chapter we have extended our description of American society to such matters as the ethnicity and religion of the population, regional interests and outlook, social mobility and the distribution of income. Societies are fairly complex things, and surely a lot more can be said about American society. But the features we have been describing are all extremely important; they are core attributes of the social world we live in.

The setting for politics is formed partly by these central economic and demographic characteristics. But it is also defined by the beliefs and values that people bring to political life. In the next section of this text, our focus shifts to the dominant political beliefs of Americans, and to the ways these beliefs have been expressed in the nation's governmental institutions.

Part 2 | Political Beliefs and Practice

4 | The American Ideology

On Sunday morning, January 4, 1914, American automaker Henry Ford sat in his office in Highland Park, Michigan, with three other Ford Motor Company executives. Ford had called the meeting to discuss employee wages for the coming year. His company's minimum wage was then $2 a day, an amount in line with what American industry was paying. This rate was much lower than present wages, but not as much lower as it appears, because a dollar bought so much more then—a loaf of bread, a bar of Ivory soap, and a pound of sugar each cost about 8 cents, a bed sheet 35 cents, a pair of women's pumps $3.35, and a nine-day all-expense-paid cruise to Bermuda just $46.

Henry Ford told his colleagues that he wanted to raise the minimum wage significantly; he had various calculations of what the company could afford posted on an old blackboard in the office. Charles Sorensen was one executive present with Ford that cold January morning, and years later he wrote a detailed account of the meeting:

> Mr. Ford ... had me transfer figures from the profits column to labor costs—two million, three million, four million dollars. With that daily wage figures rose from minimum of $2 to $2.50 and $3. Ed Martin [another executive present] protested. ... While I stood at the blackboard, John Lee [the fourth Ford executive in the office] commented upon every entry and soon became pretty nasty. It was plain he wasn't trying to understand the idea and thought he might sabotage it by ridiculing it. This didn't sit well with Mr. Ford, who kept telling me to put more figures down—$3.50, $3.75, $4.00, $4.25, and a quarter of a dollar more, then another quarter.
>
> At the end of about four hours, Mr. Ford stepped up to the blackboard. "Stop!" he said. "Stop it, Charlie; it's all settled. Five dollars a day minimum pay and at once."[1]

[1] Charles E. Sorensen, *My Forty Years with Ford* (New York: Norton, 1956), p. 139.

Real wages at Ford increased 150 percent company-wide that day. Henry Ford took arguably the most dramatic step in the entire history of American industry without any pressure from workers; the company was not even unionized. He made his decision over the protests of his fellow Ford executives, who thought it would bankrupt the company. And after word of the pay raise had reverberated across the country and around the world, Ford was denounced by many other business leaders, who believed massive harm would result to all of American business from this "dangerous precedent." Even more startling, as Ford raised wages, he lowered the price of his car, the Model T. Priced at $850 in 1908, the Model T sold at steadily reduced rates until, in 1926, it cost just $295. Why did Ford do it?

Henry Ford offered his own explanation.

> It ought to be the employer's ambition, as leader, to pay better wages than any similar line of business. . . . The best wages that have up to date ever been paid are not nearly as high as they ought to be. . . . We made the change [the $5 day] not merely because we wanted to pay higher wages and thought we could pay them. We wanted to pay these wages so that the business would be on a lasting foundation. We were not distributing anything—we were building for the future.[2]

CAPITALISM, DEMOCRACY, AND THE AMERICAN IDEOLOGY

What Ford did proved to be good business. As prices dropped and wages rose—together with dramatic productivity increases through innovating assembly-line procedures—American workers were able to buy many more cars, Ford cars included. But the $5 day was not just an imaginative economic calculation. Ford took his dramatic step on January 4, 1914, because he maintained that it was the responsibility of American business to "abolish poverty."

In implementing the $5 day, Ford was not revealing moral or intellectual perfection. He was acting out an ideology—with unusual force and insight—that he shared with millions of his countrymen. Henry Ford believed in the idea of ***democratic capitalism.*** America's private-property-based economy existed for something more than making businessmen rich; it existed to make possible an ever-higher standard of living for the general population. It was capitalism committed to democratic and egalitarian ends.

Democratic capitalism

"The idea that everybody can become a capitalist," wrote Leon Samson, a brilliant young American socialist, in 1935, "is an American conception of capitalism. It is [also] a socialist conception of capitalism. Capitalism is, in theory, and in Europe, for the capitalists. . . ." In America, though, it has highly democratic and equalitarian elements, Samson argued, in trying to explain why socialism had failed to make inroads in the United States.

[2] Henry Ford, in collaboration with Samuel Crowther, *My Life and Work* (Garden City, N.Y.: Doubleday, 1923), pp. 117–130, *passim.*

For years Norman Rockwell's cover illustrations for the Saturday Evening Post *depicted one aspect of what it was to be American.*

American capitalism and socialism

Nowhere is capitalism so well advanced [as in the United States]. But one must be careful to distinguish between the development of American capitalism and the *development of the American as capitalist.* For, if one were to examine the underlying aspirations of the American, his real sentiments and moods, it would not be difficult to discover in him trends of the soul that, far from being the traditionally capitalistic trends, are on the contrary tinged with every variety of socialism. Thus, for example, so unmistakable an American as [former President Herbert] Hoover from time to time unburdens himself of the belief that it is the destiny of the American system to abolish poverty. Now, Hoover may not know it but when he talks this way he is simply talking socialism. To "abolish poverty" is a time-honored socialist aim. Who has ever heard a responsible spokesman of European capitalism announce that it is the aim of, let us say, the French or the English "system" to "abolish poverty"?[3]

Henry Ford's decision in 1914 to raise his company's minimum wage from $2 to $5, without any immediate economic pressure to do so, was unusual, even heretical, in the general context of capitalist beliefs and behavior. It was consistent, however, with democratic capitalism—and more generally with the political ideology on which the United States was built.

[3] Leon Samson, "Americanism as Surrogate Socialism," in John H. M. Laslett and Seymour Martin Lipset, eds., *Failure of a Dream?* (Garden City, N.Y.: Anchor Press / Doubleday, 1974), p. 437. Taken from a chapter in Samson's *Toward a United Front* (New York: Farrar and Rinehart, 1935).

THE ROLE OF IDEOLOGY

American politics is sometimes described as nonideological. In one sense this is valid: Conflict between or among competing ideological traditions has been rare in the United States, for reasons we describe later in this chapter. But American politics is highly ideological in another sense: It is shaped and informed, even dominated, by a distinctive set of political beliefs.

Ideology

An *ideology* may be defined as a set of political beliefs and values that are constrained, or tied together. Like a quilt, an ideology is more than the sum of its patches; it is the patches bound together in a specified and ordered arrangement that isn't just a random collection of beliefs but rather a coherent view of the world. It provides answers to such questions as how government should be organized and power distributed, and what political values the society should try to realize.

Political socialization

Socialization. As we grow up, participate in assessing the nation's history and politics in school and with our families, listen to news programs on television, and read books, we are introduced to the underlying political beliefs and values of our society. This is called **political socialization.** Through it, we absorb bits and pieces of the American political ideology.

Most citizens do not spend a lot of time examining political ideas. Political scientist Philip Converse showed two decades ago that most people absorb only portions of formal ideologies. Their beliefs and

preferences are organized loosely, sometimes even illogically.[4] Similarly, in his study of the political beliefs of a group of working-class Americans, Robert E. Lane noted that their views were characterized by "loosely structured and unreflective statements."[5]

There is a big jump from the formal coherence of American ideology, as it gets set forth in books, to the more disjointed political outlook of the average citizen. But even so the links are there. People often do not know precisely where their underlying values come from, so general is the process by which they are introduced to these views. But they are, nonetheless, guided and oriented by the prevailing political ideology. It seeps in through all sorts of openings, and informs the way they view the world.

CLASSICAL LIBERALISM

Classical liberalism

For Americans, the great orienting ideology has always been and still is **liberalism.** We will refer to this ideology as **classical liberalism** to distinguish it from narrower usages of the terms *liberal* and *conservative* in everyday discussion (such as "I am liberal on the question of abortion, but conservative on government spending."). Classical liberalism is a broad political ideology that developed in Europe in the seventeenth and eighteenth centuries. It was brought to the United States by the early settlers and found such fertile soil in America that it crowded out all potential rivals. Classical liberalism became the American creed, the American ideology.

Five elements of American ideology

Five interrelated beliefs or commitments form the core of classical liberalism, and of the American ideology. (1) **Individualism** is the idea that societies and polities exist to fulfill the rights of each individual to "Life, Liberty and the pursuit of Happiness." (2) In order to realize their rights fully, individuals must have **freedom,** the opportunity to make their own choices with a minimum of government restraint. (3) Each individual must have a position of **equality** with other individuals. The intrinsic worth of each person should be seen as equal, and each person deserves an equal opportunity to compete for jobs, income, status, and other social values. (4) One set of goods that all individuals must be permitted to hold are defined by the term **private property.** By acquiring private property, people fulfill deep needs. Private property is a primary way individuals define themselves, protect themselves, and locate their own niche in society. (5) **Democracy** is the appropriate system of political decision-making, because it is the one system based on the sovereignty of individual choice. For individuals to be strong and their rights protected, government must be limited.

[4] Philip Converse, "The Nature of Belief Systems in Mass Publics," in David Apter, ed., *Ideology and Discontent* (New York: Free Press, 1964), pp. 206–61.
[5] Robert E. Lane, *Political Ideology: Why the American Common Man Believes What He Does* (New York: Free Press, 1962).

Building a nation on an ideology. Many nations are established on a common ethnic heritage. But the United States is largely a nation of immigrants, and for it to develop its own unity and identity it needed some other type of cement. Classical liberalism provided it. As the American creed, liberalism has come to define what it means to be an American: adherence to a creed stressing individualism, freedom, equality, private property, and democracy.

Gilbert Chesterton, a distinguished writer and English visitor to the United States in the 1920s noted that much is made of the great American experiment

America founded on a creed

> of a democracy of diverse races, which has been compared to a melting pot. But even that metaphor implies that the pot itself is of a certain shape and a certain substance; a pretty solid substance. The melting pot must not melt. *America is the only nation in the world that is founded on a creed.* That creed is set forth with dogmatic and even theological lucidity in the Declaration of Independence; perhaps the only piece of practical politics that is also theoretical politics and also great literature.[6]

Historian Ralph Barton Perry has made this same point. He argues that "history affords few parallel instances of a state thus abruptly created, and consciously dedicated to a body of ideas whose acceptance constitutes its underlying bond of agreement."[7] Classical lib-

[6] Gilbert K. Chesterton, *What I Saw in America* (New York: Dodd, Mead, 1922), pp. 7–8.
[7] Ralph Barton Perry, *Puritanism and Democracy* (New York: Vanguard Press, 1944), pp. 124–5.

eralism was so securely established in the U.S. that it became the cement holding the society together.

European Origins of Classical Liberalism

European aristocratic society

We can better understand classical liberalism, and what is distinctive about it as the American ideology, by exploring briefly its origins and development in Europe in the seventeenth and eighteenth centuries. Liberalism developed as a protest against the then-dominant values, institutions, and class arrangements of *aristocratic society*. Aristocratic values defended legal and social inequality, special rights, privileges, and obligations of social classes, and arbitrary government as the proper and unalterable nature of things. Each social class had a fixed place in society and had duties and obligations which it had to meet for the well-being of the whole. In the corporal (relating to the human body) analogies so common to ideological defenses of monarchy and aristocracy in Europe, the relationship of the nobility and the peasantry was likened by theorists to that of head and limb. What nonsense it would be to speak of the *equality* of the two! They were naturally different in their abilities, and each had its proper place and function. As the head decides for the human body, so the monarchy and the aristocracy did for the society. Political ideology in every aristocratic society justified permanent subordinate status for most of the populace and their complete exclusion from decision-making.

The middle-class challenge to aristocracy

The ascending middle classes, whose numbers and influence were greatly expanded by the commercial and scientific development that began in seventeenth-century Europe, challenged the aristocratic system. Central to their challenge was a wide-ranging attack on the moral and intellectual foundation of aristocracy. New conceptions developed, for example, of how the human mind functions. The brain was seen as a machine—much like that conceived in the scientific thought of the great seventeenth-century English theorist Sir Isaac Newton. Ideas come from the senses. The job of the brain is to organize the many impressions brought to it. If the brain's input (the sensations from the individual's environment) can be controlled, then the output (the way a person thinks and acts, the type of person he is) can be determined.

Philosophical basis of liberalism

Philosophers then took the argument one step further. The human brain, as a type of Newtonian machine, is approximately the same for all men. The outputs are different only because the inputs vary. John Locke, a seventeenth-century English philosopher, described the brain at birth as an "empty cabinet" a "white paper . . . void of all characters, without any ideas."[8] This is heady stuff. People are

[8] John Locke, *Essay Concerning Human Understanding* (Oxford: Oxford University Press, 1894; first published, 1689).

approximately equal in natural capabilities; they differ in performance only because the environments of some are less good. How, then, can the permanent privilege of the monarchy and the nobility be justified? Aristocrats are simply men blessed with better environments. The intellectual basis of individualism emerged in part from a view of man that attributed his performance to his environment.

The great economic expansion made possible by the commercial revolution of the sixteenth and seventeenth centuries and, a century later, by the industrial revolution, also encouraged individualism. It did so by creating material output great enough to offer people the promise that life could be something more than a struggle for survival. When most people had no prospect of living beyond bare subsistence, no matter how available resources were distributed, they acquiesced to extensive privileges for the few, from which they and their children were formally and permanently excluded. In societies of great scarcity, if any culture is to flourish, it is only by arbitrarily granting privilege to a few. Let the pie dramatically expand—precisely what economic and technological developments began to achieve in the seventeenth and eighteenth centuries—and people outside the hereditary privileged classes will step forward to claim their share. They will come to feel that life owes them something more than perpetual wretchedness.

There was a continuing interaction between events and ideas. The economic stirring of trade, banking, and industry in the seventeenth

New social groupings

and eighteenth centuries created new expectations. Masses of people came to believe that they could change the way they lived and channeled their energies into improving their day-to-day existence. Society became more secularized, and man came to view himself as a sovereign being with rights, not merely duties.

Society became more heterogeneous as economic development produced new social groups. An entrepreneurial middle class existed before the seventeenth century, but now there was a tremendous expansion of this middle class and a proliferation of specialized professional groups. Having arrived at positions of economic importance in the new order, operating from new centers of power which the economy had generated, confident in their ability to understand the world and to participate in it, told by the new ideology that there was no tenable basis for the continuing privilege of the old hereditary ruling class, the middle classes launched their demands for sweeping changes in the character and makeup of the society.

Enter America

The United States was born at the juncture of the revolutionary changes in economic life, science, and political thinking that nurtured liberalism and its sweeping innovations. Liberalism was not made in America; it developed in Europe and was brought to America by the colonists. What made America different from Europe—profoundly different—were the speed and extent of liberalism's triumph here.

In Europe, the aristocratic social structure had been long in existence and was not easily eradicated. For example, those who made the French Revolution in 1789 and the years following never won a complete victory. They succeeded in greatly weakening the aristocracy's grip, of course, but much of the old society survived. Liberalism took root—but as the ideology of one class, the middle class, within a larger society. In the United States, however, the middle class was able to develop without the class awareness and conflict thrust upon its counterparts in Europe. America formed as what historian Louis Hartz called a "fragment society": a piece of seventeenth- and eighteenth-century Europe broken off and transplanted here. The middle-class fragment, separate from the motherland, flourished in the New World without having to confront its natural ideological and class enemies. "A part detaches itself from the whole, the whole fails to renew itself, and the part develops without inhibition."[9]

An ideology unaware of itself. There were political disagreements aplenty among those who created the new American government in the late eighteenth century. But to a striking degree, these disagreements were *within* boundaries set by the liberal tradition. American liberal society—individualistic, committed to personal liberty, democratic, capitalistic, and egalitarian—acquired unity without aristocratic institutions and ideology. "History had already accomplished the ending of the old European order in America," wrote Louis Hartz.[10] A century earlier, historian Alexis de Tocqueville had written: America "is reaping the fruits of the democratic revolution . . . without having had the revolution itself."[11] Ideas that in Europe were clearly identified as part of the distinct ideology of an urban, propertied middle class became in the New World classless.

> There has never been a "liberal movement" or a real "liberal party" in America: We have only had the American Way of Life, a nationalist articulation of John Locke which usually does not know that Locke himself is involved. . . . Ironically, "liberalism" is a stranger in the land of its greatest realization and fulfillment.[12]

The Legacy of Liberalism

The ideas of classical liberalism—with their emphasis on the rights of individuals to political freedom, self-government, private prop-

The margin notes:
Absence of class conflict
The democratic revolution fulfilled

[9] Louis Hartz, *The Founding of New Societies* (New York: Harcourt, Brace, 1964), p. 9.
[10] Louis Hartz, *The Liberal Tradition in America* (New York: Harcourt, Brace, 1955), p. 71.
[11] Alexis de Tocqueville, *Democracy in America* (New York: Vintage Books, 1959; first published, 1835), p. 14.
[12] Hartz, *Liberal Tradition*, p. 11.

erty, and social and economic opportunity—are set forth in the great documents of American political life: the Declaration of Independence, the Constitution, and such great speeches as Lincoln's Gettysburg and Second Inaugural addresses. How much have these ideas really shaped American social and political behavior?

In all societies, ideas taken most seriously have sometimes been ignored or flouted. This is not to make excuses for American shortcomings. We can hardly forget that a number of the men who signed the Declaration of Independence, with its bold insistence that all men are created equal, were themselves owners of slaves. But requiring that an ideology *always* be adhered to before we should take its claims seriously simply dismisses every system of beliefs. Where is the Christian nation that has lived up to the religion's highest claims? Classical liberal ideas, including the emphasis on individual rights, have had great impact on American social and political life, even though the dictates of these ideas have sometimes been ignored.

American Ideological Blindspots

In many ways the deficiencies of American liberalism are outgrowths of the ideology's strength. Liberalism stresses the equality of individuals and the legitimacy of their respective claims for a chance at the good life. Throughout U.S. history, deprived groups—ethnic and religious minorities, and women, among them—have effectively used these values in their fight for equality and recognition. The strength of the liberal creed, together with the extent to which American national identity has been built around it, has provided a means of entry into full citizenship for millions of immigrants. American liberalism often opens rather than closes doors to those previously on the outside.

A certain intolerance. The very strength and unity of the ideology, however, carries with it the basis for a special American form of intolerance. Historian Garry Wills has observed that if there is an American idea, to really be an American "one must adopt this idea wholeheartedly, proclaim it, prove one's devotion to it." There has never been a legislative committee on "un-French activities," or one on "un-English affairs." But the strength of the American creed has allowed the formation of the House of Representatives Committee on Un-American Activities, and this committee's general intolerance in the 1940s and 1950s of dissenting ideas. Over the course of U.S. history Americanism has prompted repeated attempts to uncover political heresy, even to the point of requiring loyalty oaths.[13]

American insularity. "Can a people 'born equal,' " Louis Hartz asks at the close of his study of the American liberal tradition, "ever under-

Adherence to an American creed

---

[13] Garry Wills, *Inventing America* (New York: Vintage Books, 1978), p. xxii.

In the 1950s, the extreme anti-communist campaign led by U.S. Senator Joseph R. McCarthy showed a disregard for civil liberties.

American isolation

stand peoples elsewhere that have to become so? ... Can it ever understand itself?"[14] The American ideological world has been insular. At the outset, it was cut off from the conflicts of the European countries. Over the last two centuries, when countries around the world have been struggling to overthrow aristocratic institutions and traditions, the United States has been an outsider. While generally sympathetic to efforts of other peoples to replace authoritarian regimes with some form of popular government, the United States has been removed from their experiences and problems. American isolationism in the 1920s and 1930s stemmed in part from a sense of the country as being different from the rest of the world and properly separated from its turmoil.

Why No Socialism?

Socialism's evolution in the West

Liberalism's dominance in the United States has precluded certain political solutions and ordained others. This underlying bias shows clearly in America's approach to economic questions. Throughout the Western world, modern economic development—with its historic shift from agricultural to industrial economies—has been full of painful stress and disruptions. Working class movements evolved, with ideologies that are some variant of socialism—protesting the privilege and power of the business class and calling for the common control of the means of production. The United States stands as a striking exception. Socialism has never been strong here. No socialist movement here has ever had serious prospect of winning national power. The

[14] Hartz, *Liberal Tradition*, p. 309.

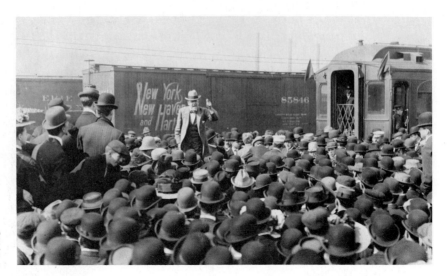

American socialist Eugene V. Debs campaigning in 1912.

electoral high-watermark of the American Socialist party came in 1912, when Eugene Victor Debs picked up 900,000 popular votes for president, six percent of the total vote. No Socialist candidate has ever carried a single state in a national election.

Why no socialism in the United States? In part, because the intense *individualism* derived from liberalism has been resistant to the *collectivism* central to all forms of socialism. Recent public opinion polls have tapped the American commitment to individualism. Respondents were asked in a 1981 poll whether they agreed or disagreed that "there should be a top limit on income so that no one can earn more than $100,000 a year." Seventy-five percent *rejected* such a financial limit on individual opportunity and achievement. Opposed to an income limit were majorities in every income, occupational, and educational group. While a larger proportion of people from wealthy than from poor families opposed the income limit, even those with annual incomes of just $5,000 a year or less rejected it by a margin of 57 to 33 percent. Every asking of this question since the 1930s has produced this same basic result (see Figure 4.1).

Individualism versus collectivism

The egalitarianism of the American ideology has also held back the development of socialism. Leon Samson has argued that Americanism is substitutive socialism. A great appeal of socialism throughout the world has been its emphasis on equality, an emphasis shared by the American creed. When Henry Ford raised his company's minimum wage by 150 percent in 1914, he was expressing an egalitarianism not found in capitalist ideologies of other countries. The American creed's aversion to class rigidity, its impatience with class snobbery, its insistence that a good society is one where people are judged on the basis of what they do rather than on family pedigrees—all these reflect egalitarianism.

American egalitarianism

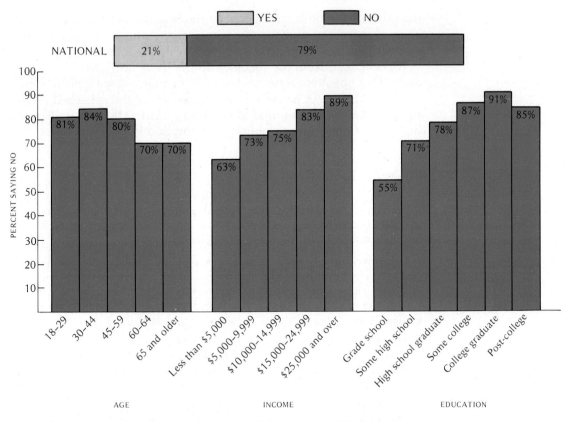

Figure 4.1
Should There Be a Top Limit on Incomes so that No One Can Earn More than $100,000 a Year?

A survey conducted in 1940 by *Fortune* magazine revealed similar objections to the concept of an income ceiling. When asked "Do you think there should be a law limiting the amount of money any individual is allowed to earn in a year?" 74 percent answered "no" and 26 percent answered "yes."
Source: Survey by Civic Service, Inc., March 5–18, 1981.

THE FOUNDATION OF AMERICAN POLITICAL INSTITUTIONS

The ascendancy of liberalism in the United States has had profound influence on American politics. This influence has been strongest in molding the country's political institutions and providing their rationale and legitimacy.

We develop this point in the next chapter, in discussing the origins of the Constitution of the United States and its striking longevity—it will be 200 years old in 1987.

Its strength and endurance stems from the economic success we described in Chapter 2, and the high degree of social mobility noted in Chapter 3. Americans seem generally satisfied with their central institutions and the government established by the Constitution. But the Constitution as the American basic law also owes its strength to

Liberalism and the
Constitution

the faithfulness with which it articulates a dominating national ideology. Liberalism and the Constitution go hand in hand; the latter institutionalizes the central assumptions of the former.

We now turn from the ideology to the basic law built on that ideology. Our objective is not to describe the many specific provisions of the Constitution—Chapters 7 through 11 cover the principal institutions of American national government—but rather to understand better the Constitution's political origins and intellectual roots.

SUMMARY

Americans have strong feelings of national identity and unity. In contrast to other countries whose sense of nation is highly developed, the United States has achieved its identity without ethnic commonality.

The American nation has been built on a political belief system or ideology, *classical liberalism.* Formed out of the social frustrations and political interests of the rising middle classes of seventeenth- and eighteenth-century Europe, liberalism was brought to the New World by the middle-class fragment that settled here.

As it has developed in the U.S., liberalism stresses an individualistic rather than collectivist view of society; *individual rights,* including *political freedom* and *private property rights; equality of opportunity;* and *limited, democratic government.*

Liberalism has been largely unchallenged in the United States. Many groups and individuals have argued that America has denied them their rights under the liberal creed, but few have attacked the legitimacy of the creed itself. Institutions established under American liberalism, such as the Constitution and a private-property-based economy, have drawn strength from the liberal tradition's dominance.

5 | The Constitution

The United States Constitution was written by fifty-five men, representing twelve of thirteen states, who met in constitutional convention in Philadelphia during the spring and summer of 1787. By mid-1788, the new Constitution had been ratified, replacing the Articles of Confederation as the law of the land. A new president and Congress took office under the Constitution in the spring of 1789.

For nearly 200 years in unbroken succession the United States has been governed under a single basic law. In the same span of time France has been governed by ten separate and distinct constitutional orders, including five different republics, two empires, one monarchy, one plebiscitary dictatorship, and one puppet dictatorship installed at Vichy during World War II. The United States has had one constitution and, created under it, one set of governing institutions. The American Constitution of the 1780s is in essence the Constitution of the 1980s. The Constitution was built on the ideological foundation of classical liberalism, and owes much of its staying power to the continuing dominance of liberal ideas.

Over the last two centuries, scores of new nations have come into existence around the world—a global experiment in nation-building filled with hope and achievement, but also with bitter disappointments. The accomplishment of the Constitution's framers is even more impressive when history shows how hard it is to create new constitutional orders that fulfill yearnings for successful self-government rather than dash them.

The building of the new American nation began in the early seventeenth century with European colonization. Nationhood was advanced in the 1770s when thirteen British colonies banded together, declared their independence from the mother country, successfully fought a war of independence, and established a new national government.

Thomas Jefferson's draft of the Declaration of Independence.

But the enterprise of nation-building remained incomplete and uncertain until the Constitution of 1787 was written, ratified, and implemented.

Three related questions need to be answered if we are to understand American constitutional experience and assess properly its legacy. How did the Constitution come to be written, approved, and implemented in the form we know today? Who were the men most responsible for the Constitution and what were their primary political objectives? What are the essential characteristics of the type of government that the Constitution establishes?

AMERICAN EXCEPTIONALISM

In the eighteenth and nineteenth centuries, many Americans came to believe that their country had a "Manifest Destiny." As sociologist Daniel Bell has put it, "not just the idea that a nation had the right to define its own fate, but the conviction of a special virtue of the American people different from anything known in Europe or even, hitherto, in this history of the world."[1] Clinton Rossiter has noted that this belief in a special national place and mission was held by virtually all of the leading American political figures of the "revolutionary generation."[2]

Belief in a national mission

Americans of the late eighteenth century lived, John Adams wrote, in "a time when the greatest law givers of antiquity would have wished to live"; they had before them an opportunity to "establish the wisest and happiest government that human wisdom can contrive."[3] From this sense of unique opportunity flowed a sense of unusual responsibility. "We ... decide forever the fate of Republican government," James Madison told the Constitutional Convention on June 26, 1787.

Where did this highly developed and widely shared view of America as an exceptional society came from? The founders of new institutions often harbor high aspirations. But most members of the revolutionary generation believed deeply that the United States was to be, in the words of Isaiah, "a city ... set on a hill," "a light unto the nations," beckoning through its attainments and example. The United States was established on a large, open territory that was only lightly populated by its original inhabitants, the Indian peoples. There were vistas and promises of a seemingly endless frontier. An abundance of rich land made the U.S. prosperous at the very outset. The ideal of a populace of independent property owners was readily attained. Americans were starting afresh, set apart from European nations.

Constitution as embodiment of liberal ideology

American optimism did not wholly depend on such material good fortune. The American ideology sustained optimism in offering a blueprint for a new and successful society. It specified ideals that were considered at once worthy and attainable. The Constitution embodied the extraordinary breadth of attachment Americans of the 1780s felt to the liberal ideology and their belief that, if only appropriate institutions were put in place, they could maintain national political unity.

TRANSLATING THE LIBERAL CONSENSUS

On July 2, 1776, the Continental Congress—representing thirteen North American colonies—gave its approval to a motion that had been introduced by Richard Henry Lee of Virginia about a month earlier: "That these united colonies are, and of right ought to be free and

---

[1] Daniel Bell, "The End of American Exceptionalism," *The Public Interest*, Fall 1975, p. 199.
[2] Clinton Rossiter, *Alexander Hamilton and the Constitution* (New York: Harcourt, Brace, 1964), p. 17.
[3] C. F. Adams, ed., *The Works of John Adams* (Boston, 1956), vol. IV, p. 200.

Declaration of
Independence

independent states." Assisted by Benjamin Franklin and John Adams, Thomas Jefferson expanded the resolution into the famous Declaration of Independence that was adopted on July 4. Jefferson's Declaration powerfully affirmed the liberal ideal of individual rights made familiar by John Locke and advanced by a century-and-a-half of American experience. (The text of the Declaration is reprinted in the Appendix to this book.)

The War for Independence, which had begun in 1775, was not decided until October 19, 1781, when the British General Charles Cornwallis surrendered his army to General George Washington. With their military band playing "The World Turned Upside Down," 7,000 British troops marched out of Yorktown, Virginia, and laid down their arms. Preliminary articles of peace were signed a year later, on November 30, 1782, and the final treaties were signed at Paris on September 3, 1783. America's *ideological* independence had been achieved long before 1783, however, and was framed around a national commitment to liberal values.

THE ARTICLES OF CONFEDERATION

On July 12, 1776, a committee of the Continental Congress brought in a draft of a proposed constitution. After more than a year of arguing about such questions as how war expenses should be apportioned and voting power allocated among the states, the Congress finally approved the document on November 17, 1777, and submitted it to the thirteen state legislatures for consideration. The **Articles of Confederation,** as this first national constitution was called, were approved by all thirteen states except Maryland by 1779; Maryland ratified the Articles in 1781.

Articles of
Confederation

The Articles of Confederation faithfully reflected American political values of the time. They provided for a national government founded on republican principles—the idea that governmental institutions should be responsive to the will of the people—and distinguished by a commitment to individual liberty achieved through dispersed and limited governmental power. But in some basic structural regards, the government of the Articles of Confederation was flawed.

Weaknesses of the
Articles

The main deficiency stemmed from the states' position as fully sovereign entities that merely ceded certain limited powers to the national government. The sovereign character and equality of the thirteen states was reflected in the manner of their representation in the Continental Congress. Each state, whatever its size, had only one vote; this was cast by delegates appointed by the state legislature. The states were supposed to contribute to the common expenses of the nation—for example, the costs of maintaining a national army—according to the value of their lands. But the national government lacked any means to compel state compliance, and it was always tottering on the brink of bankruptcy.

Continental Congress under the Articles

The impotence of the Continental Congress left the United States singularly ill-equipped to protect its own national interests in dealing with other countries. For instance, the Congress had printed paper money to meet costs of the war with England. Near the war's end, this currency had become virtually worthless in the absence of a national taxing power. The Congress was forced to beg money and supplies from France. After the war, the Congress had to borrow money from bankers in Holland. When it turned to the states for funds as provided in the Articles, or when it sought the power to levy a 5 percent tariff on imports, the states turned this "beggar nation" down. In order to impose a tariff, the unanimous approval of the states was required; in 1781 and again in 1783, at least one state refused.

Inability to raise money

Since Congress did not have the power to levy taxes and could not force the states to use their authority to tax as provided in Article VIII, it was unable to raise enough money for the common defense or general welfare of the United States, Even Revolutionary War debts could not be paid, including salaries owed for military service. Army officers encamped themselves at Newburg, New York, in 1783 and threatened mutiny to force Congress to pay their long-overdue wages. This financial weakness also contributed to the Congress' inability to protect the trans-Alleghany wilderness region. It could not support troops to defend settlers from Indian attacks, nor could it prevent the British and Spanish governments from establishing settlements in these lands.

State currencies

Along with its own financial weakness, the Congress had to contend with states issuing their own currencies. Article IX granted Congress "sole and exclusive right and power of regulating the alloy and value of coin struck by their own authority or by that of the respective states. . . ." But this did not stop states from issuing money. Debtor and creditor factions in various states engaged in bitter struggles. Some states passed laws forcing acceptance of devalued paper currency at its face value; others deferred the collection of debts and prohibited courts from issuing judgments for debts. A former Army captain, Daniel Shays, led a group of armed Massachusetts farmers in an insurrection in 1786, attempting to prevent the county courts from sitting in judgment on debts. The whole system of monetary exchange was in chaos.

Under the Articles of Confederation, the national government was little more than an aspiration. The claim of Article II, that "each state retains its sovereignty, freedom, and independence," was the reality. The provision of Article III that the states "hereby severally enter in a firm league of friendship with each other" fairly described the governmental order.

Signing the Declaration of Independence, painting by John Trumbull.

THE MOVE TO A STRONG NATIONAL GOVERNMENT

As a statement of republican principles embodying an ideal of popular government, the Articles of Confederation were admirable. As a constitution for a workable national government, they were a decided failure. Dissatisfaction with the Articles was not distributed evenly across the populace. American nationalists such as George Washington and Alexander Hamilton were the most profoundly troubled. Merchants in seaport towns felt the weakness of the Articles more acutely than did farmers in the heartlands. Not surprisingly, then, it was those philosophically committed to the idea of a strong, unified nation, encouraged by mercantile interests, who took the lead in efforts to modify the Articles to provide for a stronger national government.

Still, most Americans shared a sense of nation, built around their common political values. Thomas Paine was reflecting this general sentiment when he wrote in his first publication after the peace with Great Britain had been secured, "I ever feel myself hurt when I hear the Union, the great palladium of our liberty and safety, the least irreverently spoken of. . . . Our citizenship in the United States is our national character. Our citizenship in any particular state is only our local distinction."[4] Such views strengthened the hand of the most advanced nationalists, like Washington and Hamilton, who at the time were often called "Continentalists."

Common national values

[4]Thomas Paine, "Thoughts on the Peace, and the Probable Advantages Thereof," *Common Sense*, Philadelphia, April 19, 1783; in William M. Vander Weyde, ed., *The Life and Works of Thomas Paine* (New Rochelle, N.Y.: Thomas Paine National Historical Association, 1925), p. 245.

The biggest barrier to constitutional change grew out of liberalism itself. Americans were suspicious of anything that suggested concentrated governmental power. The Articles of Confederation, whatever their deficiencies, did not create a tyrannical government. Those favoring a new constitutional arrangement had to convince a majority of their fellow citizens that the new government would not be too strong.

Three Who Made a Revolution

George Washington, James Madison, Alexander Hamilton

While many people contributed to the new Constitution, three men played the leading roles: George Washington and James Madison of Virginia, and Alexander Hamilton of New York. Of the three, Washington's involvement was the least intensive and direct, but perhaps the most important. His prestige, as the general who led the fight for independence, was enormous, and his character inspired confidence. The most decisive single factor in the implementation of the Constitution of 1787 was George Washington's total commitment to it. Washington gave essential legitimacy to the effort.

Alexander Hamilton, James Madison, and George Washington.

Madison and Hamilton furnished much of the energy and practical political imagination needed for constitutional reform. As early as September 3, 1780, from Washington's camp at Liberty Pole (now Englewood), New Jersey, Hamilton penned a long letter to James Duane (a member of the New York delegation in the Continental Congress, which included delegates from all the states) indicting the Confederation as "neither fit for war or peace." He proposed correcting the "want of method and energy in administration" by instituting departments with single heads and giving the Congress "complete sovereignty in all that relates to war, peace, trade, finance, and to the

management of foreign affairs."[5] Note the urgency of the call sounded by this 24-year-old statesman:

> The Convention [to reform the national government] should assemble the first of November next. The sooner the better. Our disorders are too violent to admit of a common or lingering remedy. . . . I require them to be vested with plenipotentiary authority that the business may suffer no delay in the execution and may in reality come into effect.

The Annapolis Convention

Hamilton pressed his case over the next seven years. So did James Madison. The two worked in concert in 1782–83 when both were delegates to the Continental Congress. In 1786, they again joined talents and energies at the Annapolis convention, called to discuss the economic difficulties of the states and to "consider how far a uniform system in their commercial regulations may be necessary to their common interest and their permanent harmony." The convention in turn delivered a call to the Congress to appoint delegates "to meet at Philadelphia on the second Monday in May next [1787] to take into Consideration the situation of the United States; to devise such further Provisions as shall appear to them necessary to render the Constitution of the Federal Government adequate to exigencies of the Union; and to report such an Act for that purpose to the United States in Congress Assembled. . . ."[6] The Annapolis convention was a joint triumph for Hamilton and Madison.

Philadelphia, 1787

On May 25, 1787, with 29 men from nine states having arrived at the State House in Philadelphia, the constitutional convention officially opened. By unanimous vote, George Washington was chosen as its president. When it adjourned four months later, the convention had drafted the Constitution of the United States as we know it today.

Delegates to the Convention

The men assembled in Philadelphia were distinguished by extraordinary intellect and achievement. Even Thomas Jefferson called the delegates "demigods"—he himself was representing the new nation in France at the time, and he later took issue with some aspects of the Convention's work. For one thing, the delegates were quite young. Their average age was lower than John F. Kennedy's when he was inaugurated as America's youngest president at age 43. The average age of the 1787 delegates was 42; but, despite their comparative youth, they were both mature and accomplished.

That the delegates shared general beliefs and objectives contributed enormously to their success. Classical liberals, their thinking was infused with new political ideas developed by seventeenth- and eigh-

[5] Harold C. Syrett and Jacob E. Cooke, eds., *The Papers of Alexander Hamilton* (New York and London, 1961), vol. 2, p. 407.
[6] Max Farrand, *The Framers of the Constitution of the United States*, (New Haven: Yale University Press, 1913), p. 10.

Washington presiding at the signing of the Constitution, painting by Thomas Rossiter.

teenth-century European philosophers. The work of the English theorist John Locke (1632–1704) and the French philosopher Montesquieu (1689–1755) were well known to the delegates—the former for his emphasis on individual rights, the latter for his discussion of separation of powers—and influenced the writing of the Constitution.

THE MAKING OF THE CONSTITUTION

The assigned task of the Convention was to revise the Articles of Confederation. But the delegates quickly decided to go beyond their instructions. They would establish an entirely new constitution. On May 30 they voted that "a *national* Government ought to be established," and they proceeded to work out its details.

The delegates agreed at the outset that there should be a *federal* system, composed of state governments and a national government with limited but constitutionally secure powers. While they differed in their assessments of *democracy*, they agreed that ordinary citizens should play a large role in choosing those who would administer their affairs. The delegates believed that ordinary people were capable of actions both sublime and dangerous. A proper constitution should create a setting which would blunt the latter and encourage the former. The delegates shared the liberal distrust of concentrated power, and they created a constitution that would prevent such concentration and thus avoid tyranny.

Alexander Hamilton was a delegate, but his role in the Convention's deliberations was relatively modest. The contributions of Oliver Ellsworth and Roger Sherman of Connecticut, Benjamin Franklin and

A democratic federal government

James Wilson of Pennsylvania, and George Washington as the Convention's presiding officer and unquestioned moral leader were much greater.

The truly decisive intellectual work was done by Madison. His influence and arguments were everywhere: in the Convention debates, in the compromises struck, in the very language of the Constitution. Referring strictly to the work of the Philadelphia Convention—rather than to activities leading up to it or those that followed in securing ratification and implementation—James Madison must be seen as the father of the Constitution.

Powers invested in the national government

The critical question of what powers should be granted to the central government prompted little argument. The national government should be able to levy taxes and regulate both interstate and foreign commerce. It should be able to raise and maintain an army and a navy. Concurrently, the states must be stripped of their powers to issue money, make treaties, and tax imports. Power had to be shifted from the states to the central government.

Representation: the Great Compromise

Over who should control the new government the delegates argued fiercely. The larger states pushed for representation in the national legislature based on population; the smaller states, understandably, wanted to maintain the old system of equal state representation. The **Virginia Plan,** proposed by the larger states, was drafted by Madison and presented to the Convention by Edmund Randolph, Virginia's Governor. The small states backed the **New Jersey Plan,** written by William Paterson, a former New Jersey Attorney General. In mid-July the delegates reached what is known as the **Great Compromise.** Seats in the lower house of the legislature—the House of Representatives—were allocated according to population and filled by popular vote; seats in the upper house—the Senate—were allocated two to each state regardless of size, and filled by vote of the state legislature.

Slavery: the three-fifths compromise

Slavery posed another important argument over control and representation. Southern delegates favored including slaves in the population base that would determine representation in the House of Representatives (although they had no thought of permitting the slaves to vote). In the **three-fifths compromise,** the delegates agreed that "three-fifths of all other Persons" (slaves) would be counted for taxation and representation. Final resolution of the slave trade issue was put off for two decades by the constitutional clause (Article I, section 9) that prevented Congress from outlawing the slave trade until 1808.

Bicameral legislature

Having struck these compromises, the delegates easily resolved their remaining differences. And, on September 17, 1787, they assembled to affix their signatures to the new Constitution. They had provided for a national government with a *bicameral* or two-house legislature, an executive branch headed by a President with broad powers, and a national judiciary consisting of a Supreme Court and such "inferior courts" as Congress might decide to create.

The War Powers Resolution, limiting the powers of the president, was a major topic of debate when President Reagan sent a peace-keeping force to Lebanon.

Key Provisions

The most distinctive feature of the document crafted in Philadelphia is its unremitting attention to the problem of power. The Constitution established a federal system in which authority would be divided between the national and state governments. The formal responsibilities of each would be extensive. Power was then further divided among the three branches of the national government; each was given its own base of authority. An elaborate system of **checks and balances** was established, giving each branch the means to restrain the other two.

Checks and balances

Separation of powers had long been provided for in aristocratic societies among the monarchy, nobility, clergy, and "the commons"—the latter including the rural gentry and urban middle classes. In eighteenth-century England the king had powers distinct and separate from the rest of the nobility—which was represented in the upper chamber of Parliament, the House of Lords—and from the middle classes, which had a base through representation in the lower chamber, the House of Commons.

Separation of powers in England and America

In this aristocratic model, *separation of powers* reflected the divergent claims of the several power centers of the society. But in America after independence, there was no monarchy or aristocracy; here was a middle-class society where "the Commons" was very near the whole of the social order. The classical liberal commitment to a separation of powers expressed itself in a system of independent branches of government each intended to represent the interests of the general public. The president was expected to serve this common interest; so was Congress. The power of "the Commons" itself was to be divided, lest any popular impulse or greedy faction threaten individual claims and minority rights.

In the American Constitution, every basic grant of authority is carefully limited. The president is commander-in-chief of the armed

The veto forces, but it is Congress' power to declare war and "to raise and support armies." The president has broad appointive powers, but his appointments require "the advice and consent" of the Senate. The Congress has the sole constitutional responsibility for enacting all legislation, but the president has a veto over such acts, a veto which can be overridden only by a two-thirds vote of each house. All legislation must be approved in identical form by both houses of the legislature. Never before or since has so sustained an effort been made to provide for governmental authority at once vigorous and checked. The new government would be strong enough to establish a setting where individual intitiatives could flourish, and checked enough so that individual rights would not be violated. The Constitution of the United States is the crowning political testament to these claims of the liberal creed.

James Madison expounded on the liberal theory of power in *Federalist Papers* 10 and 51, written in late 1787.[7] As Madison saw it, spe-

Factions or cial interests necessarily abound in free societies. He called them special interests **factions.** "Liberty is to faction," he wrote, "what air is to fire. . . ." To abolish liberty because it permits the expression of narrow, selfish interests would be as great a folly as "to wish the annihilation of air, which is essential to animal life, because it imparts to fire its destructive agency."

The answer to this dilemma, Madison insisted, is to prevent any individual or interest, or governmental institution, from gaining too much power. In *Federalist Paper* 51, Madison gave the classic liberal answer—the American constitutional answer—to the problem of power.

> But the great security against a gradual concentration [of power] . . . consists in giving to those who administer each department the necessary constitutional means and personal motives to resist encroachment of the others. . . . *Ambition must be made to counteract ambition.* The interest of the man must be connected with the constitutional rights of the place. It may be a reflection on human nature that such devices should be necessary to control the abuses of government. But what is government itself but the greatest of all reflections on human nature? If men were angels, no government would be necessary. If angels were to govern men, neither external or internal controls on government would be necessary. In framing the government which is to be administered by men

---

[7] *The Federalist Papers* is a series of 85 papers written in late 1787 by Madison, Alexander Hamilton, and John Jay, a colleague of Hamilton's from New York, who was to become the first chief justice of the Supreme Court. Their purpose was to help pursuade New York to ratify the Constitution. A very convenient edition of *The Federalist Papers* is that edited by Clinton Rossiter (New York: New American Library, 1961). All references following to *The Federalist Papers* are to this edition.

over men, the great difficulty lies in this: You must first enable the government to control the governed; and in the next place oblige it to control itself.[8]

RATIFICATION

The framers of the Constitution required their handiwork to be ratified by special state conventions. They may have been motivated in this by a desire to bypass the state legislatures, where many members might resent the reductions being made in state authority. But the legislatures could still have blocked ratification by refusing to call for state conventions. Only Rhode Island in fact did so.

The summoning of state ratification conventions prompted a vigorous national debate between those who favored the Constitution—called Federalists since they were endorsing a strong federal union—and the anti-Federalists. In most states the Federalists won easily; remarkable, considering the magnitude of the constitutional change being proposed. Delaware acted first, ratifying the Constitution unanimously on December 7, 1787. A few days later, Pennsylvania followed suit by a two-to-one majority. New Jersey gave unanimous approval on December 18, as did Georgia on January 2, 1788. The vote in Connecticut on January 9, 1788, was 128 to 40 in favor of the Constitution. The Massachusetts vote was the first close one. Delegates approved the Constitution by just 187 to 168 in early February 1788. Maryland endorsed the Constitution overwhelmingly in April, as did South Carolina in May. When New Hampshire ratified on June 21, by a close vote of 57 to 47, the Constitution had received the requisite endorsement of nine of the thirteen states. Virginia followed, also by a close vote, immediately upon New Hampshire, approving the Constitution on June 25.

Three states remained outside the new national union, but only one—New York—was of critical importance, for it was one of the big states, and it separated New England from the states to the South. Opposition in that pivotal state was strong and well-organized, and the anti-federalist faction won 46 of the 65 seats to its convention. Alexander Hamilton was a member of the Federalist minority, however, and his energies on behalf of the Constitution give us a fascinating example of how much effective leadership can mean. Hamilton pleaded, cajoled, and compromised; and more importantly, he offered an intellectually imposing defense of the Federalist position. Through his labors, and aided by the fact that New York looked like a person standing on the pier while the schooner—here, the new government—was sailing away, the New York convention finally voted in favor of ratification on July 26, 1788, by a 30 to 27 margin. The new government was launched—though North Carolina did not ratify until

Federalists versus anti-Federalists

Final ratification

[8] Ibid., p. 322. Emphasis added.

November 1789 and Rhode Island withheld consent to the Constitution until May 1790.[9]

PUTTING THE NEW INSTITUTIONS IN PLACE

Washington elected first president

Legislative elections were held in January and February, 1789. By early April enough Congressmen had completed the journey to New York, the temporary capital, for the government to commence operation. The ballots of the presidential electors were counted in the Senate on April 6. Washington was the unanimous choice for president and, receiving 34 electoral votes, John Adams became vice president. Washington took his oath of office in Federal Hall in New York on April 30, 1789. Fewer than 24 months had elapsed between the convening of the convention in Philadelphia and Washington's inauguration as president under the new Constitution. It had been an extraordinary march along the road of nation-building, and the pace did not slow over the next three years. The task of implementing the new system was as demanding as its writing and ratification had been.

Hamilton, Madison, and Washington again provided the primary leadership. In George Washington the new nation had a president at once strong and cautious. His personal sensitivity to criticism and his high sense of responsibility made him especially careful that no serious error be made that might unsettle the new government. "The eyes of Argos are upon me," he once complained, "and no slip will pass unnoticed."[10] In the eight years of his presidency, no action was more consequential or salutary than his last one: his decision to step down voluntarily after two terms in office. Of all the monuments to successful democratic nation-building, none is more impressive than that of Washington walking away, gladly handing over the responsibilities of office.

The Bill of Rights

James Madison, leader of the House of Representatives, and Alexander Hamilton, first secretary of the Treasury, also played major roles in elaborating the new institutions. Through Madison's leadership, Congress had by September 1789 created the State, Treasury, and War departments, and had passed the Judiciary Act, which established thirteen federal district courts and three circuit courts of appeal. The number of Supreme Court justices was set at six, and Washington named John Jay the first Chief Justice. Again under Madison's leadership, Congress prepared a dozen amendments, ten of which were ratified, guaranteeing what he called the "great rights of mankind." Known since as the ***Bill of Rights,*** these amendments affirmed

---

[9] The story of Hamilton's momentous role in the New York ratifying convention is ably told by Clinton Rossiter, *Alexander Hamilton and the Constitution* (New York: Harcourt, Brace, 1964).

[10] Washington's reference was to the 100-eyed guardian of Io, ancestor of the people of Argos, Greece; the legend is in Homer's *The Illiad* and *The Odyssey*.

Box 5.1
The Bill of Rights

On December 15, 1791, the first ten amendments to the Constitution were ratified. We know them as the Bill of Rights.

Amendment 1: The rights of religion, speech, and assembly.
Amendment 2: The right to bear arms.
Amendment 3: Quartering of soldiers.
Amendment 4: The right to be secure against "unreasonable searches and seizures."
Amendment 5: The right to "due process of law" (including protection against double jeopardy and self-incrimination).
Amendment 6: The right to a speedy trial by an impartial jury.
Amendment 7: The right to a jury trial in common law cases.
Amendment 8: Prohibition of excessive bail and "cruel and unusual punishment."
Amendment 9: The rights of the people are not limited to those enumerated above.
Amendment 10: Powers not delegated to the federal government by the Constitution, or specifically prohibited to the states, are reserved to the states and the people.

the right of trial by jury, barred compelling individuals to testify against themselves in criminal cases, forbade unreasonable searches and seizures, and required that no one "be deprived of life, liberty, or property, without due process of law." The most notable provision was in the first amendment: Congress could make no law infringing freedom of speech, the press, or religion (see Box 5.1).

Hamilton's works were equally notable. As secretary of the Treasury for five years—the second most powerful man in American government—he advanced his consuming commitment to a strong national government. Hamilton was a gifted executive and planner. Recognizing that the new country needed capital to develop its untapped resources, he sought to persuade investors to commit their funds in America. His *Report on the Public Credit* set forth a program securing Congressional approval for funding the existing public debt at the face value of the certificates. The nation's credit could not be secured, he reasoned, unless investors were convinced that the government would honor all obligations in full.

Hamilton and the establishment of a national bank

Hamilton then proposed that Congress charter a national bank to serve as an instrument for collecting and spending tax revenues, and to provide bank notes, which would serve as a badly needed medium of exchange. Congress approved the Bank of the United States, but Washington was urged to veto the legislation by Thomas Jefferson, his secretary of state, and by James Madison, who was a trusted adviser as well. But, Hamilton argued, the provision of Article I, Section 8, giving Congress the authority to pass all laws which shall be "necessary and proper" to carrying out the specific powers enumerated elsewhere in the article must be interpreted broadly. Washington accepted Hamilton's argument and signed the bill. In 1819, the Supreme Court was to explicitly sanction Hamilton's broad construction of the "necessary and proper" clause.

Hamilton's Report on Manufactures

Hamilton rushed ahead. In December 1791 he submitted his *Report on Manufactures*, a bold plan for stimulating American mercantile and industrial development by setting up government tariffs, subsidies, and awards to encourage American manufacturing. While the report as a whole was pigeonholed by Congress, a number of specific tariffs that Hamilton recommended were enacted in 1792.

By the end of 1792, the new government had been firmly established. The American Constitution continues to be a living, evolving instrument which receives definition from precedent and practice; a total of 26 constitutional amendments now exist. But the decisive steps of constitutional nation-building had been taken and implemented, and the major articles of the Constitution are as strongly in force today as in the last years of the eighteenth century.

ASSESSING THE FRAMERS' WORK

Charles Beard's view of the framers' motives

A book appeared in 1913 that for a time greatly influenced many people's thinking about the Constitution. It was Charles A. Beard's *An Economic Interpretation of the Constitution of the United States.* Beard argued that, rather than a document written by public-spirited men for the protection of "life, liberty, and the pursuit of happiness," the Constitution represented the assertion of economic interests of banking, manufacturing, and commerce. Furthermore, he maintained that, instead of extending democracy, the Constitution was imposed to rein in the majority. The Constitution was depicted as the product of a cabal of self-serving "plutocrats" who were fearful of the democratic impulses unleashed after the Revolutionary War. It had to be made to serve popular ends later on under the democratic leadership of leaders like Andrew Jackson, who was president from 1829 to 1837.

Criticism of Beard's view

Was this view of the Constitution's founders justified? Beard's interpretation has been strongly criticized and largely discredited recently, especially by the work of historians R. E. Brown and Forrest MacDonald.[11] Most students now hold a view similar to the prevailing view of nineteenth-century America: while the framers were not above self-interest, they were by no means a narrow, undemocratic economic elite. As historian John Garraty concludes in a recent work,

[11] See R. E. Brown, *Charles Beard and the Constitution* (Princeton N.J.: Princeton University Press, 1956); and Forrest MacDonald, *We the People: The Economic Origins of the Constitution* (Chicago: University of Chicago Press, 1976).

Guarantees of individual liberties have at times brought conflict among competing groups; here, anti-Nazi protesters wave flags in Chicago as American Nazi party members march.

"the closest thing to a general spirit at Philadelphia was a public spirit. To call men like Washington, Franklin, and Madison self-seeking would be utterly absurd."[12]

Political scientist Martin Diamond has discussed the two central values which occupied the revolutionary generation—*liberty* and *democracy*—and how they were treated in the two great documents of the revolutionary era, the Declaration of Independence and the Constitution. The Declaration, Diamond argued, was a bold statement of a principle. It set forth the primacy of liberty as the comprehensive good, the objective against which all political administrations and activity had to be measured.[13] The Constitution set forth the means for the attainment of liberty, a form of government which "had to prove itself adequately instrumental to the securing of liberty." In this pursuit, the Constitution "opted for democracy ... embodying the bold and unprecedented decision to achieve, in so large a country as this, a free society *under the democratic form of government.*"[14]

The Constitution was not a perfect instrument for securing liberty through the machinery of representative democracy. Its most decisive weakness was its failure to ban the undemocratic institution of slavery. Still, the Constitution drafted in 1787 has achieved what Washington hoped for when he said it was to "raise a standard to which the wise and the honest can repair."

[12] John A. Garraty, *The American Nation*, 4th ed. (New York: Harper and Row, 1979), p. 123.
[13] Martin Diamond, "The Declaration and the Constitution: Liberty, Democracy and the Founders," *The Public Interest* (Fall 1975), pp. 46–47.
[14] Ibid.

The Constitution has been seen by many Americans as virtually synonymous with the American nation and its well-being.

In his letter of September 17, 1787, by which he transmitted the Constitution to the Congress for its consideration, Washington penned these words:

> That it will meet the full and entire approbation of every State is not perhaps to be expected; but each will doubtless consider, that had her interests alone been consulted, the consequences might have been particularly disagreeable or injurious to others; that it is liable to as few exceptions as could reasonably have been expected, we hope and believe; that it may promote the lasting welfare of that country so dear to all of us, and secure her freedom and happiness, is our most ardent wish.

That this worthy intention has been substantially realized is the most fitting epitaph we can offer to the work of the Constitution's framers.

THE CONSTITUTION IN AMERICAN GOVERNMENTAL PRACTICE

The story of American constitutionalism did not end in the 1790s. It is still being written today.

The Constitution has continued to evolve and change, in two basic ways. First, it has been formally amended, as provided in Article V (see Box 5.2). And second, court interpretations have imposed important changes in the Constitution. The U.S. Supreme Court is the final arbiter of the Constitution's meaning or requirements in specific cases. Through the Court's interpretations, the Constitution's meaning has been elaborated, enlarged, and updated to meet new conditions. Chapter 10 takes up this critical role of the Supreme Court.

Amendments and judicial interpretation

The Constitution, taken as a whole, provides for a system of government known as **representative democracy.** In the next chapter, we turn to the approach underlying this system and the question of

Box 5.2
*Amendments to the U.S. Constitution
since the Bill of Rights*

Amendment 11 (ratified in 1795): Federal court role in suits against the states.

Amendment 12 (1804): Modified the procedures for electing the president and vice president.

Amendment 13 (1865): Prohibition of slavery.

Amendment 14 (1868): Guaranteed rights of due process and equal protection of the laws, against state infringement.

Amendment 15 (1870): The right to vote cannot be abridged "on account of race, color, or previous condition of servitude."

Amendment 16 (1913): Gave Congress the power to impose an income tax.

Amendment 17 (1913): Provided for the direct popular election of U.S. senators.

Amendment 18 (1919): Prohibited the manufacturing and selling of alcoholic beverages.

Amendment 19 (1920): The right to vote cannot be abridged "on account of sex."

Amendment 20 (1933): Changed the beginning of a president's term to January 20, and of members of Congress to January 3.

Amendment 21 (1933): Repealed prohibition (that is, repealed the 18th amendment).

Amendment 22 (1951): Limited to two the number of terms a president may serve.

Amendment 23 (1961): Gave the vote in presidential elections to residents of the District of Columbia.

Amendment 24 (1964): Prohibited the poll tax in all federal elections.

Amendment 25 (1967): Procedures to be followed in the event of presidential disability, and the line of succession in the case of the president's death.

Amendment 26 (1971): Extended the right to vote in all elections to persons 18 years of age and older.

whether it has functioned as its founders intended, completing our review of basic American political beliefs and practices.

In subsequent chapters, we examine how specific constitutional provisions have shaped the performance of the main governmental institutions—Congress (chapter 7), the presidency (chapter 8), and the courts (chapter 10). We also look at policy implications of various sections of the Constitution, such as how the Bill of Rights has been interpreted to set modern policy in the area of civil liberties and civil rights (chapter 17).

SUMMARY

The *Articles of Confederation* were the first constitution of the new American nation. Ratified in 1779, the Articles were consistent with the prevailing American belief in limited, popular government. But the central government they established was so weak that it could not meet economic or foreign policy needs, or fulfill the emerging sense of nation.

George Washington, James Madison, and Alexander Hamilton gave leadership to the forces seeking to strengthen, or replace, the Articles of Confederation. Their efforts and those of other like-minded politicians culminated in the constitutional convention that met at Philadelphia in the spring and summer of 1787 and drafted a new *Constitution for the United States of America.*

Ratification was completed in 1788 when New York, the last big state to approve, narrowly voted its endorsement. George Washington was sworn in as the first President on April 30, 1789. By the end of 1792, the basic institutions of the new government had been given their practical working form.

The Constitution reflected the basic impulses of the American ideology. Government was to be at once vigorous and restrained. It was to create a climate where individual initiative could flourish and national identity could be expressed, while being so checked and balanced that it could not threaten individual rights.

Authority was divided between national and state governments; and within the former, among the executive, legislative, and judicial branches which were at once independent and mutually dependent. Ambition, as Madison had put it in *Federalist Paper* 51, was made to counteract ambition.

6 | American Democracy

The great British prime minister Winston Churchill once remarked that "democracy is the worst form of government . . . except for all the others." This backhand defense of democracy may well be the most profound defense. Democracy should be judged not by whether it realizes all of its ideals but by the practical yardstick of how its performance compares to that of other systems.

Preference for limited, democratic government is, as we noted in chapter 4, a key part of the American ideology; and the U.S. Constitution has provided a set of such democratic institutions. For many Americans, then, the question of whether democracy is the best form of government involves little debate: "Government by the people" is good, or at least preferable to all other forms of government. Yet if this view seems natural and unassailable to most Americans, it is far from universally accepted. Throughout history most of the world's population have been governed under arrangements decidedly not democratic. Most political theories have defended other constitutional arrangements. Even apart from the argument over the general desirability of democracy, many observers insist that the government of the United States is flawed by democratic standards.

Behind these arguments lies a basic question: What does democracy as a political theory really encompass? Since serious attention to the idea of democratic government goes back twenty-four hundred years, to the Greek city-state of Athens, we might think that the question of democracy's meaning would have long since been resolved to everyone's satisfaction. It has not, however. In this chapter we will take a close look at various conceptions of democracy, especially those common in the United States. We will trace the concept from its Greek origins, through the thinking of the framers of the U.S. Constitution, to present-day perspectives on what democratic government means or requires and different views on America's democratic performance.

WHAT IS DEMOCRACY?

Democracy derives from two Greek roots: *demos*, meaning the people, and *kratis*, meaning authority. During the fifth century B.C., the Greeks, particularly the Athenians, used the term to refer to government by the many, as contrasted to government by the few (oligarchy), or by one person (monarchy). In his famous "Funeral Oration," the Athenian statesman Pericles (495–429 B.C.) declared that "our [Athens'] constitution is named a democracy, because it is in the hands not of the few, but of the many." This idea that ultimate political authority should rest with the general public remains central to all conceptions of democracy.

Aristotle's Idea of Democracy

The first great political theorist to treat democracy coherently as a system of government was Aristotle, an Athenian philosopher who lived between 384 and 322 B.C. He argued that there were three general forms of government—kingship, aristocracy, and constitutional government or "polity"—and three others that were corruptions of the three proper forms: "tyranny corresponding to kingship, oligarchy to aristocracy, and democracy to constitutional government. . . . Tyranny is monarchy ruling in the interest of the monarch, oligarchy government in the interest of the rich, democracy government in the interest of the poor, and none of these forms governs with regard to the profit of the community."[1] In Aristotle's view there were broad interests to be served (what we would call national or public interests). Any regime was degraded when it ignored these interests and instead advanced the selfish claims of one segment of society.

Especially important to our study is the distinction Aristotle made between "democracy" and "constitutional government"; he defined democracy as the perverted form. He was not opposed to popular sovereignty, to regimes based on the consent and participation of the many. He objected only to extreme direct democracy, which lacked a legal structure for protecting minority rights and interests. In short, he defended what we today know as constitutional democracy: majority rule tempered by basic laws which would hold up the ideal of the public interest and protect individual and minority rights.

Aristotle anticipated a question which has occupied many contemporary students of government: What social conditions are necessary

Three forms of government

Democracy vs. constitutional government

---

[1] *Aristotle in Twenty-Three Volumes, XXI Politics*, H. Rackham, trans. (London: Heinemann, 1977), Book III, p. 207.

Aristotle.

for constitutional democracy to flourish? Such a government simply is not possible, he felt, in most social settings. It is impossible when a small elite have great economic privilege while the vast majority have virtually nothing. "Where some own a very great deal of property and others none . . . there comes about either an extreme democracy or an unmixed oligarchy, or a tyranny may result from both of the two extremes, for tyranny springs from both democracy and oligarchy of the most unbridled kind. . . ."[2] Either the few will be successful in preserving their extreme privilege, by resorting to tyrannical rule, or the resentful many will deny minority rights in advancing their claims. What is necessary for constitutional democracy is a large middle class and a fairly even distribution of property.

The importance of a large middle class

[2] Ibid., p. 331.

It is clear therefore that the political community administered by the middle class is the best, and that it is possible for those states to be well governed that are of the kind in which the middle class is numerous . . . for by throwing in its weight it sways the balance and prevents the opposite extremes from coming into existence."[3]

An Idea a Long Time Coming

Aristotle's assessment of democracy in the *Politics* has remarkable range and prescience. And like the experience of his native Athens with a limited form of democratic government, Aristotle's thinking was far in advance of the historical period in which it occurred. One would have to wait two thousand years—until Europe and America in the late seventeenth and eighteenth centuries—to find sustained philosophic inquiry that advanced beyond Aristotle's contribution, and the first successful implementation of democratic ideals.

Liberalism: the right of the individual

As we saw in chapter 4, social and economic changes that began in seventeenth-century Europe nurtured a new set of political ideas and a new view of people and their rights that we know as classical liberalism. The keystone of liberalism is the high value it places on the rights and freedoms of the individual. Democratic government is the natural political expression of liberal individualism, for only democracy gives individuals the power to govern themselves. Once social conditions were such that individualism would flourish, democracy became a practical possibility.

The United States had no monopoly on such social conditions—and no monopoly on governments giving recognition to the claims of individuals. In Britain limits were increasingly placed on the powers of the monarchy and aristocracy in the eighteenth and nineteenth centuries, while at the same time the powers of representatives in Parliament grew. But the requisite social conditions emerged faster and more fully in eighteenth-century America, and so in response did democratic government.

Madison's Idea of Democracy

A plan for democratic institutions

The work of the founders of the new American government of 1787 was a major step in both the theory and practice of democracy. The unique opportunity to establish a national government based on democratic principles in an environment so generally supportive of the enterprise, but with so little precedent in the experience of other countries, forced the founders to confront fundamental issues of democratic theory. In prior examinations of democratic theory, from Aristotle to John Locke to French philosopher Jean-Jacques Rousseau (1712–88), one critical element had been missing: close attention to the practical governmental mechanisms through which constitutional democracy could protect minority rights and achieve social

[3] Ibid.

balance. In 1787 the idea of constitutional democracy was a familiar one, but the actual articulation of the institutions of representative democracy was still in its infancy. The plan for representative institutions developed in *The Federalist Papers* is an important advance in democratic theory.

Madison and Hamilton carried over the basic Aristotlean distinction between democracy and polity, though they referred to the latter as "republicanism." Like Aristotle, the authors of the *Federalist Papers* professed fear of democracy, and understood the term to mean unrestrained government prone to mob rule, disrespectful of minority rights, and incapable of realizing the national interest.

Republicanism

The Federalist Papers argues the case for **republicanism:** as James Madison wrote in *Federalist Paper* 10, "a government in which the scheme of representation takes place. . . ." The people are sovereign, but they cannot and should not govern directly. Representative institutions like legislatures need to be established within a governmental structure of clearly defined and dispersed powers. Through separation of powers and checks and balances, minority rights receive protection, and narrow interests opposed to the general public good are curbed. The framers thought, for example, that some majority passion might sweep through the legislature a law contrary to the basic rights and interests of some minority. But they felt that such checks on the legislative power as the president's veto and the judiciary's power to review and interpret the laws in light of constitutional requirements lessened the chance that minority rights would actually be abused. Through this elaborate process of checks and balances, the public would still remain the ultimate source of all political authority.

Balancing popular sovereignty and individual rights

The representative democracy that the framers of the Constitution sought gave equal weight to *popular sovereignty* and *individual rights*. The former required the selection of political leaders through regularly-held free elections. The latter required mechanisms to stop anyone, even popular majorities, from infringing upon certain rights of citizenship such as those set forth in the Bill of Rights.

MAJORITY RULE VERSUS MINORITY RIGHTS

The American idea of democracy, then, is a system of government equally committed to majority rule and the protection of minority rights. In many instances these two different commitments do not conflict with one another. But sometimes they do. For example, school segregation as practiced before *Brown* v. *Board of Education of Topeka*—the landmark desegregation decision handed down by the U.S. Supreme Court in 1954—seems often to have had majority backing. If we conclude that such segregation denied the claims of American democracy, it is because we believe that majority rule itself is undemocratic when it opposes essential individual rights.

The problem of
majority rule

But which rights are so essential as to be off-limits even to majority will? American constitutional law, as it has developed in decisions of the Supreme Court, addresses this question, and we examine what the Court has said in chapters 10 and 17. But there has never been full agreement among experts in constitutional law, or the public at large, on where the democratic requirement of majority rule must be suspended because the democratic requirement of respect for individual rights requires it.

Prayer in Public Schools

The heated argument over school prayer is a good case in point. Various individuals and groups long opposed what was the common practice of opening the school day with the recitation of a prayer. They argued that it violated the right to full religious freedom guaranteed by the First Amendment to the Constitution. Some students were not in sympathy with the particular religious beliefs expressed by the prayer, and the government (in the form of public school officials) was abridging their freedom of religious choice.

In 1962 the Supreme Court agreed with the challenge to the constitutionality of prayer in public schools, in the case of *Engel* v. *Vitale*, The New York State Board of Regents had recommended to school districts that they adopt a specific nondenominational prayer, to be repeated voluntarily by students at the beginning of each school day. The prayer read: "Almighty God, we acknowledge our dependence upon Thee, and we beg Thy blessings upon us, our parents, our teachers and our country." The school board of the New York community of New Hyde Park adopted this prayer, but it was challenged by the parents of ten pupils in the district. These parents claimed that the prayer was contrary to their religious beliefs and ran counter to the "establishment" clause of the First Amendment: "Congress [and, by application, the states] shall make no law respecting an establishment of religion. . . ."

The school prayer
controversy and
individual rights

Writing for the Supreme Court's majority, Justice Hugo Black ruled that the "constitutional prohibition against laws respecting an establishment of religion must at least mean that in this country it is no part of the business of government to compose official prayers for any group of American people to recite as a part of a religious program carried on by the government." The majority had violated a constitutional guarantee of individual religious freedom. In subsequent cases the Court extended its ruling—for example, by prohibiting the recitation of the Lord's Prayer or other verses from the Bible.

These Court decisions generated strong opposition. Critics argued that the constitutional ban on laws "respecting an establishment of religion" were not meant and should not now be construed to prevent citizens in various communities from deciding that they would like to have a brief prayer at the start of the school day, in which anyone who wanted could choose not to participate. They insisted that school prayer did not abridge a basic constitutional right, and hence the preferences of the majority should be followed.

Public opinion surveys have consistently shown decisive majorities in favor of prayer in schools and in favor of an amendment to the Constitution to overturn the Court's rulings. A 1982 survey by Louis Harris and Associates found that 69 percent backed "a constitutional amendment to allow daily prayer to be recited in classrooms," while just 28 percent opposed such an amendment. According to a July 1983 Gallup Poll, 81 percent of those who had heard of the idea of an amendment permitting school prayer favored it. While the proportions have varied, every national poll conducted over the last two decades has shown a majority wanting to allow the recitation of prayer in public schools.

Amending the Constitution

The efforts to amend the Constitution to permit school prayer first came to a vote in 1966. A majority of U.S. senators voted for such an amendment—but not the two-thirds majority required. Article V of the Constitution contains this provision designed to make it hard for a majority to make changes in the country's basic law: Congress can propose amendments to the Constitution only by two-thirds majorities of both houses, which must then be ratified by at least three-fourths of the states before taking effect.

In 1984 another attempt was made to enact a school prayer amendment, and again the major battle was fought in the Senate. The proposed amendment read:

Proposed school prayer amendment, 1984

> Nothing in this Constitution shall be construed to prohibit individual or group prayer in public schools or other public institutions. No person shall be required by the United States or any state to participate in prayer. Neither the United States nor any state shall compose the words or any prayer to be said in public schools. (Senate Joint Resolution 73.)

In the debate that ensued, lobbying was intense on both sides. Conservative religious groups worked hard for the amendment, and the Reagan administration supported them. The pro-amendment efforts were led in the Senate by Republican Majority Leader Howard Baker, who argued that "our purpose here is to render the state a neutral party in the exercise of religion rather than have the state compel or forbid that exercise." Most of the mainline religious groups—including Methodists, Episcopalians, Lutherans, and Jews—opposed the amendment. Lowell Weicker (Republican of Connecticut) led the fight against the amendment. He maintained that children holding minority religious views would feel uncomfortable participating in a prayer alien to their beliefs and stigmatized if they refused to participate.

The vote in the Senate on March 20, 1984, was a tough one for many senators. Not only did the polls show large majorities in favor of the amendment, but calls and letters from constituents strongly urged enactment. At the same time, senators were sensitive to the rights of minority religious groups. Arlen Specter (Republican of Pennsylvania), who is Jewish, recalled his own experiences as a boy attending elementary school in Wichita, Kansas: how uncomfortable he had felt when Christian prayers were recited at the start of each school day. In the end the Senate decided that school prayer was a case where the claims of minority rights outweighed majority choice. It voted for the amendment 56 to 44—eleven votes short of the two-thirds majority the Constitution requires for constitutional change.

Direct Democracy versus Representative Democracy

Though the framers opted for representative democracy, aspects of the idea of direct democracy have continued to find support in the United States. In the contemporary context, those who advocate more direct democracy want the people to vote or otherwise express themselves directly on major questions of government and policy. Many Americans believe that an extension of direct participation makes the country's democracy purer or more complete. Responding to these views, the United States government has incorporated some of the institutions and practices of direct democracy.

Toward Purer Democracy: The Direct Primary

In the early twentieth century, a new political movement known as **progressivism** gained great strength in many parts of the United States and advanced an ambitious program of political change. The Pro-

Progressive Hiram Johnson campaigning in 1922.

Progressivism

gressives included in their ranks men and women from all classes and sections of the country, but they were especially strong among the growing professional middle classes of the urban Northeast and Midwest. The latter believed that the big-city political party "machines" of the day were often corrupt, beholden to special interests, unenlightened. To purify this "boss-dominated" system, Progressives argued that the people must be given more power to rule directly.

The direct primary

One key reform urged by the Progressives was the **direct primary,** whereby the choice of party nominees is made by rank-and-file party supporters in primary elections, not by party leaders through party conventions and caucuses. The Progressives enjoyed great success in this effort; direct primaries became the dominant instrument for choosing candidates in most parts of the country.

The Referendum and the Initiative

The Progressives also criticized the legislatures of their day as dominated by special interests—like railroads, big corporations, and construction companies wanting contracts for roads and public buildings. They urged that the general public be permitted to vote directly on legislation through **referenda** and **initiatives.** In a referendum, a legislative body certifies a question for presentation to the public in a general ballot; while in an initiative the public, through petitions signed by requisite numbers of voters, requires that policies be put to popular vote. Under the aegis of the Progressives, the referendum and the initiative were widely adopted. South Dakota (1898) was the first state to provide for the initiative.

The referendum

At the local level, referendum democracy flourishes; several thousand measures are presented each year to the voters in school districts, cities, and counties. The public votes directly on appropriations for school buildings, fluoridation of community water supplies, and the siting of waste disposal facilities. Statewide referendum or initiative questions were on the ballot in forty-two states and in the District of Columbia in the November 1982 elections. Just under two hundred propositions were voted on.[4] Colorado voters chose to limit the rate of increase of property taxes, while those in Maine decided to index the state income tax rates to the inflation rate. In Nevada, a 1982 referendum approved the establishment of an office of advocate for utility customers. Nuclear weapons freeze measures carried in California, Massachusetts, Michigan, New Jersey, North Dakota, Oregon, Rhode Island, Wisconsin, and the District of Columbia; a freeze measure was defeated in Arizona.

At the national level, a number of senators and representatives have urged enactment of a voter initiative or amendment to the United

[4]Austin Ranney, "The Year of the Referendum," *Public Opinion*, December/January 1983, pp. 12–13.

VOTE "YES" ON R.I. REFERENDUM #10

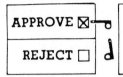

APPROVE ☒

REJECT ☐

Referendum Question #10 on the Rhode Island Ballot
Nov. 2, 1982

"Should the President of the United States propose to the Soviet Union an immediate, mutual, and verifiable freeze on the production and deployment of nuclear weapons and of new systems designed primarily to deliver such weapons as a first step in reducing worldwide levels of nuclear armaments?"

THE FREEZE IS ...   **IMMEDIATE** while negotiations to reduce the number of nuclear weapons go on.
MUTUAL affecting both the United States and the Soviet Union at the same time.
VERIFIABLE by both sides.

VOTE "YES" TO FREEZE THE NUCLEAR ARMS RACE

The R.I. Freeze Campaign
Box 2449
East Side Station
Providence, R.I. 02906

5

States Constitution. Senator Mark Hatfield (Republican of Oregon), a strong advocate, has proposed that the public, through petitions signed by a number of registered voters equal to three percent of the ballots cast in the last presidential election, put on a national ballot any issue except an amendment to the Constitution itself, the calling up of the militia, or a declaration of war. If a majority voted in favor, the initiative measure would become the law of the land without any action by Congress or the President. Hatfield argued that the voter amendment would

The initiative

> be an exercise of the sovereign power of the American people to govern themselves . . . [provide] a concrete means for citizens' participation in the policymaking function of our Government . . . lessen the sense of alienation from their Government felt by millions of Americans . . . enhance the accountability of Government . . . [and] produce an open, educational debate on issues which otherwise might have been inadequately addressed. . . ."5

(Thus far, the initiative amendment has not received the support of either House of Congress.)

There is no simple answer to the question of whether the United States now strikes a proper balance between the direct and representative dimensions of democracy. Yet many leading students of the subject agree that democracy in a complex society makes heavy demands on such intermediary institutions as political parties and legislatures, and on their leadership. Such institutions cannot be bypassed too frequently and still have the capacity to perform the

The problem of "pure" democracy

5 Speech to the U.S. Senate by Senator Mark Hatfield, *Congressional Record*, vol. 125, no. 11 (February 5, 1979).

functions we expect of them as vital intermediaries. While democracy cannot exist if the wishes of the general public are not freely and fully expressed and ultimately followed, succumbing too frequently to temptations to bypass representative institutions—bypass parties through direct primaries, for example, and legislatures through the initiative—may weaken these institutions to the point where they can no longer work effectively. In chapter 15 we discuss this point with specific reference to the American party system.

Size and Representative Institutions

The town meeting

The earliest American institution for direct democracy, the New England town meeting, has declined greatly in practical governing importance. In the town meeting, all adult residents who choose to do so assemble at an appointed time and through majority vote enact a budget and rules bearing on town affairs. When communities were small and much of what government did was concentrated at the local level—as in New England of the seventeenth and eighteenth centuries—the town meeting's direct democracy was an important and practical part of the American system. Today, however, much of government decision-making involves units so large and issues so complex that the idea of all interested citizens assembling to decide them has become impossible. Town meetings are still held in New England, and citizens assemble in communities in all parts of the country to discuss local issues, but representative institutions like school boards and city councils have everywhere become necessary instruments of local government.

HOW DEMOCRATIC IS AMERICAN DEMOCRACY?

Power and democracy

For a nation to be called a democracy, ordinary citizens must have real political power; not only must they be able to vote, but they must be able to exercise ultimate authority over the big decisions of their country's political life. What are these big decisions? How can we know whether the people ultimately make them, or whether political elites—individuals and groups with disproportionate political resources—manage to assume the decisive decision-making roles? The concept of power is one of the most complex political science contends with. Yet for all the analytic difficulties the concept poses, how power is distributed is a matter of great importance to democratic government. At some point power concentrates so substantially in the hands of political elites as to make a mockery of any claim to popular sovereignty. Some observers argue that this has happened in the United States. Others, while denying that this point has been reached, still see extensive power in the hands of elites as a serious problem in American democracy.

Concentration of Resources

Various developments over the last century and a half have produced major concentrations of resources. There were no great fortunes in the United States a hundred and fifty years ago, but now there are enormous accumulations of wealth. Economic units—whether farms, banks, or factories—were generally very small in the 1830s; in the 1980s we have huge national and multinational corporations. The great consolidation of newspapers and magazines into large units that has occurred over the last century had not even begun in the 1830s, and the age of concentrated electronic communication had not even been imagined.

In the 1830s the primary political unit was the local government; now it is the national government. The hundreds to few thousands of citizens in a typical town a century and a half ago had a measure of direct control over government that is simply unattainable in today's far more complex and centralized nation-state.

How have these developments affected political power? Consider the case of an individual who has acquired millions of dollars in personal property as well as the presidency of a big business corporation. If he chooses, he may contribute large sums of money to candidates for elective office. His wealth, and the economic power derived from his position in business, give him a measure of access to political leaders far beyond that of most citizens. A telephone call to a politician from this wealthy corporate leader is likely to have a

Economic power and politics

Former CBS anchorman Walter Cronkite won a high measure of public trust and exerted great influence on American public opinion in the 1960s and 1970s.

much greater impact on policy deliberations than one from the average voter.

But there are many types of politically-important resources other than great wealth. Consider the position of an anchorman for one of the network's evening news programs. He is seen nightly by an audience in the range of 20 to 30 million persons; thus he has communications resources beyond any historic precedent. Political leaders in Congress, the executive office, and state capitals around the country are certainly aware of his capacity to take political messages into millions of households. How likely is it that the anchorman's influence in American political life is roughly equivalent to that of the average citizen?

Many others enjoy disproportionate resources. A president of a big university has much more than the average student at his institution. The head of a major labor union has resources dwarfing those of the typical unionist. The point seems beyond dispute: Politically relevant resources are unevenly distributed; and the economic and technological developments discussed in chapters 1–3 have on balance led to greater concentrations.

What are the implications for democracy of such inequalities? As political scientist Robert Dahl has put it, "In a political system where nearly every adult may vote but where knowledge, wealth, social position, access to officials and other resources are unequally distributed, who actually governs?"[6]

Power Elites

No mature theory of American politics questions that there are **elites:** groups of people who possess disproportionately large amounts of scarce resources and hence power. The fact of disproportionate resources in the hands of special-interest groups requires the constant attention of all who are committed to democratic government. President Dwight Eisenhower, a conservative Republican who had been Commander-in-Chief of allied forces in Europe during World War II—and who was hardly unfriendly to either business or the military—in 1961 warned his fellow citizens to be vigilant against "unwarranted influence . . . by the military-industrial complex."[7] After World War II, as we will discuss in chapter 20, a high level of defense spending became a permanent part of American national government, and interests such as defense contractors and military officials became active and influential lobbyists for their special concerns. Eisenhower saw the dangers this collection of strong, well-organized interests posed for democratic decision-making in the vital area of defense and foreign policy.

The military-industrial complex

[6] Robert Dahl, *Who Governs?* (New Haven, Conn.: Yale University Press, 1961), p. 1.
[7] Eisenhower's "Farewell Address," January 17, 1961.

Marxist critique of
capitalism

Some commentators go well beyond these widely shared concerns and perceptions, however, to the highly debated conclusion that the concentration of power in the hands of elites precludes real democracy in the United States. An extreme case is the argument of contemporary Marxist theorists. Their starting point is the proposition Karl Marx advanced in much of his work in the last century: Power in any society is derived from economic arrangements, and in any capitalist society like the United States the government "is nothing more than a committee for the administration of the consolidated affairs of the bourgeois class as a whole."[8] Building on this perspective, political scientist Michael Parenti states that

> our government represents the privileged few rather than the needy many and that elections, political parties and the right to speak out are seldom effective measures against the influence of corporate wealth. The laws of our polity operate chiefly with undemocratic effect . . . because they are written principally to protect the haves against the claims of the have-nots. . . . Democracy for the few . . . is not a product of the venality of office holders as such but a reflection of how the resources of power are distributed within the entire politico-economic system.[9]

The triangle of power:
business, the military,
and political
leadership

This view is not confined to Marxist scholars. In *The Power Elite*, sociologist C. Wright Mills maintained that America is run by a narrow group of people drawn from three central institutions: leaders of major private business corporations; the heads of the armed services and the defense establishment; and the political leadership of the executive branch of government.[10] For most of American history these units were relatively small and feeble, but after World War II they grew enormously. By the late 1950s, Mills asserted, there was no longer,

> on the one hand, an economy, and on the other hand, a political order containing a military establishment unimportant to politics and to moneymaking. There is a political economy linked in a thousand ways with military institutions and decisions. . . . If there is government intervention in the corporate economy, so is there corporate intervention in the governmental process. In the structural sense, *this triangle of power is the source of the interlocking directorate that is most important for the historical structure of the present.*[11]

Mills's power elite is composed not of isolated groups and individuals but rather of people who have common interests and act together coherently to dominate policy on the major issues of national life.

[8] D. Ryazanoff, ed., *The Communist Manifesto of Karl Marx and Friedrich Engels* (New York: Russell and Russell, 1963), p. 28.
[9] Michael Parenti, *Democracy for the Few* (New York: St. Martin's Press, 1974), p. 2.
[10] C. Wright Mills, *The Power Elite* (New York: Oxford University Press, 1959).
[11] Ibid., pp. 7–8. Emphasis added.

The Liberal Democratic Rebuttal

Constitutional limits on power of elites

Is there a coherent, interacting elite that makes most of the big decisions in the United States, leaving popular sovereignty but an aspiration? Most political scientists don't think so; neither does the general public. The liberal rebuttal to the charge of elite rule must begin with the work of the Constitution's framers, because that work has defined the American system. Those who drafted the Constitution assumed that some interests would inevitably be stronger than others. The task of a properly arranged constitutional democracy, James Madison argued in *Federalist Papers* 10 and 51, was to put limits on what these interests could achieve. He believed that he and his fellow constitution-makers had provided sufficient barriers to any power elite: a large, diverse nation of many contending interests, with government power divided first between the national and state units, and then further divided between legislature, executive, and judiciary. Behind all of this were the people, able to choose their leaders in free elections and thereby to set the general course of public policy.

Pluralism

Fragmentation of power

Most contemporary political observers in the United States think that Madison has been proved right. Political power in the United States is highly fragmented, as interest groups contend within a government structure of dispersed authority. Public policy is the outcome of a highly involved pattern of political bargaining among constantly shifting interest alignments. Sometimes this perspective is called

A state senator periodically meets with his constituents for opinions on current policy.

"pluralist," because it identifies a plurality of competing power centers. The predominant perspective among political scientists is that power is so dispersed at the national level, among the many committees and subcommittees of Congress, federal executive agencies, interest groups, and others, that overall public policy suffers a serious lack of incoherence.[12] The current preoccupation with the fragmentation of the policy process runs almost diametrically against the idea of a coherent power elite able to control public policy.

Some examples undercutting the power-elite theory

To see this argument in action, consider the area of military spending, which was one of Mills' prime examples of a power elite. Big defense contractors certainly interact closely with Defense Department officials and influential congressmen. Typically, though, they do not cooperate but instead fight it out with one another to secure contracts—as when United Technologies Corporation and General Electric battle for contracts to build new jet engines for Air Force planes.

On such foreign policy issues as the U.S. role in Central America or the Middle East, political elites are often sharply divided. For example, some urge a stronger military response to movements in Central America that are seen as threatening U.S. interests and regional stability, while others argue equally strongly that more economic aid to combat poverty, not arms, is the answer. Each faction among the contending elites tries to persuade the public of the rightness of its approach. In these policy debates, it is very hard to see the hand of one strong power elite.

Former New York governor Hugh Carey, campaigning.

[12] Chapters 7, 8, and 9 develop these arguments.

Political action committees, money, and political campaigns

None of this claims that American democracy does not confront continuing problems stemming from the presence of large concentrations of resources in few hands. The whole area of money in politics involves one set of such problems. Various individuals and organizations—including businessmen and large corporations—have extensive financial resources; they also have strong interests in the decisions legislatures and executive agencies make. They try to advance their interests by lobbying, and by making contributions to the campaigns of candidates who support their views or who are in key positions to decide future questions. Through the vehicle of political action committees (PACs), millions of dollars of interest-group money are contributed to campaigns each election year. In chapters 13 and 14 we discuss the role of PACs, the legislation regulating them, and the larger issue of how American elections are, and should be, financed.

Elections and Popular Sovereignty

Critics of American democracy seem consistently insensitive to the role played by popular elections as the decisive instruments for choosing the president, members of Congress, governors, state legislators, mayors, and other political officials. Since the 1960s—when it was finally guaranteed to black Americans—voting has been open to the entire adult populace. While there is concern that voter turnout has not been higher, electoral decision-making is certainly majoritarian. In the presidential election of 1984, 92 million people voted: 53 percent of those of voting age, and 80 percent of those registered to vote.

Voter turnout and the two-party system

Critics have attacked American electioneering and the choice of leaders it provides as mere sham, saying that the Republicans and Democrats are so alike ("Tweedledum and Tweedledee") that voters do not have a real choice of leaders. But this criticism lacks a convincing base. Scores of widely different political parties—Communist, Socialist, Libertarian, and many others—have offered themselves to the American electorate over the past century. If the Democrats and Republicans have won most contests, this seems to reflect general voter satisfaction with the choices these two parties have offered.

THE PUBLIC'S ASSESSMENTS

The people's right to pick leaders and set policies through free elections, the framers believed, would be an adequate final guarantor of popular sovereignty. But are Americans in fact getting the kind of political-economic order that they want? Does the prevailing system correspond to the public's preferences? Consider the way the national economy is organized. Do Americans feel that an unsatisfactory cap-

Public opinion on the
economic system

italist system has been foisted upon them? Would they really prefer some other system? Public opinion surveys—one of the best measures of general sentiment—show clearly that this is not the case. The vast majority of the public endorse the prevailing economic structure. Typically, only ten percent indicate a preference for an economy organized on socialist principles. Ninety percent of those polled in March 1981 by Civic Services agreed that "the private business system in the United States works better than any other system yet devised for industrial countries." Even on the question of nationalizing the oil companies—objects of considerable public resentment as gas and oil prices soared over the 1970s—the public rejects structural change. Only 11 percent told Roper Organization interviewers in December 1979—when prices were near their highest level—that they believed the oil companies should be taken over and operated by the government.[13]

Or consider the imbalances of wealth and earnings the U.S. economy has yielded. Do Americans think these distributions are so unfair as to warrant major changes? In 1940, when the economic privation of the Great Depression was still much in evidence, pollster Elmo Roper asked: "Do you think there should be a law limiting the amount of money any individual is allowed to earn in a year?" Only twenty-four percent said they favored a limit on earnings. And four decades later, in 1981, only twenty percent of respondents nationally felt that "there should be a top limit on incomes so that no one can earn more than $100,000 a year."[14] Americans have real dissatisfactions, including inflation, the level of unemployment, their perceptions of greed and ineptness by business corporations—but they don't favor basic structural change. The American political economy receives fundamental support from the vast majority of the populace, rich and poor, young and old, members of the different ethnic groups, and residents of the various sections of the country. The same is true of other components of the country's social and political organization.

There is the argument that Americans have been brainwashed, or that they display a false consciousness—an inability to distinguish their own true interests, given the "indoctrination" that they have received. There can be no ultimate answer to such a charge. Obviously Americans receive a continuing stream of messages endorsing and defending the basic organization of the economy and the polity. Any democracy, no matter what measure of public support it receives, can be charged with resting on an "induced consent" that fails to

[13] Civic Services, Inc., and the Roper Organization are two among the many survey research organizations polling nationally on a regular basis. Civic Services was founded by Roy Pfautz and has its headquarters in St. Louis, Missouri. The Roper Organization was established by Elmo Roper in the 1930s, which makes it one of the oldest polling firms in the world. Its headquarters are in New York City.

[14] Poll by Elmo Roper for *Fortune* magazine, March 1940; and poll by Civic Services, March 1981.

represent the true interests of its people. Yet the facts suggest otherwise. In a country where there are so many channels of communication and where outspoken criticism of the various institutions is commonplace, the public holds firmly to the judgment that the basic political and economic organization is fundamentally sound.

CONDITIONS NEEDED FOR DEMOCRACY

Is liberal democracy a luxury—something possible in the United Sates, Great Britain, and a small number of economically advanced countries but not readily adaptable to conditions prevailing in much of the world? Many think so. Sociologist Seymour Martin Lipset has argued that a mix of social conditions may be necessary to sustain stable representative democracy. In turn, democracy, once established, serves to further promote and sustain these social conditions. Among the conditions Lipset identifies are a high measure of education and literacy, a vigorous set of voluntary associations, a comparatively high degree of national wealth, a strong national commitment to the principle of equality, and an open class system distinguished by easy movement from one position to another.[15]

The argument that there are social requisites for democracy is not new. Aristotle argued twenty-three centuries ago that a large middle class was essential to a stable polity. Liberal democracy does make heavy demands on social institutions and processes. It requires a public willing and able to participate actively in public affairs, and at the same time willing to accept limits on itself. The public must sustain constitutional guarantees for minorities, including unpopular minorities. Government institutions must be responsive to divergent public demands, while at the same time being reasonably efficient in carrying out their functions. The liberal system must encourage vigorous debate and dissent, without degenerating into political chaos. "In framing a government which is to be administered by men over men," James Madison wrote in *Federalist Paper* 51, "you must first enable the government to control the governed, and in the next place oblige it to control itself."

Democracy in the World Arena

The necessary democratic mix is not easily attained. Looking around the world, we see very few countries that have maintained democratic institutions continuously for a half-century or more. Indeed, there are not many functioning democracies today.

How many are there? The question of whether a given country is

---

[15] Seymour Martin Lipset, "Economic Development and Democracy," in *Political Man* (Garden City, N.Y.: Doubleday, 1960), pp. 45–76.

democratic often cannot be answered with a simple yes or no. Great Britain is unquestionably a democracy, and the People's Republic of China clearly is not. But a number of countries fall in between: they have some democratic attributes, yet in other regards are decidedly not democratic. Sociologist Kenneth A. Bollen has constructed a useful index that incorporates both of the key dimensions of democracy—popular sovereignty and political liberties.[16] Using this index, he classified countries on a scale of 0 to 100; a high score indicates a high measure of democracy. No index of this kind, he acknowledged, is free of conceptual and measurement flaws, but the Bollen measure is still very instructive. By this index, fewer than 30 countries fitted into the range of reasonably strong democracies. Countries one would expect to find in this category were these: the United States, Great Britian, Canada, Sweden, Denmark, Norway, France, Switzerland, West Germany, Austria, Italy, Israel, and Japan. Few countries outside the ranks of the most economically advanced scored high in Bollen's measure.

In those countries like the United States, where the mix of historical experiences, social conditions, and political values are highly supportive of it, liberal democracy flourishes. Even here it is hardly a flawless system or perfectly realized. But democracy squares well with public expectations, especially with the insistence upon protection of individual rights and opportunity for individual participation that distinguishes all of the most economically advanced countries.

SUMMARY

The first conception of democracy was in Athens in the fifth-century B.C.: government by the many rather than by the few . Aristotle enlarged this concept by combining two distinct elements: popularity sovereignty and minority rights. Aristotle chose to call a system that successfully combined these constitutional government or polity. Democracy meant an unrestrained direct democracy or mob rule. The framers of the American Constitution incorporated much of Aristotle's thinking. But they went even further in their specification of a system of carefully engineered representative institutions. What we now call a constitutional or representative democracy the framers called a republic. They believed, like Aristotle, that democracy suggested direct popular government, which was likely to degenerate into mob rule because it lacked institutions able to curb self-seeking interests and assure individual liberty.

Democracy in America is sometimes called liberal democracy. It places equal emphasis on realizing popular sovereignty and protecting individual and minority rights. These two objectives are sometimes in conflict, when majorities take actions that minorities think violate certain of their essential rights as citizens.

[16] Kenneth A. Bollen, "Issues in the Comparative Measure of Political Democracy," *American Sociological Review*, June 1980, pp. 370–90.

The American constitutional tradition holds that majority rule must be superseded in cases where majority actions infringe essential rights of citizenship, such as those articulated in the Bill of Rights. But as the country's experience in the area of civil rights shows, the most fundamental of minority rights have sometimes been denied nonetheless. And thoughtful people necessarily disagree on just which rights or interests are so essential as to be off-limits to majority choice or action.

One criticism of American democracy holds that power is so concentrated in the hands of certain elites as to make impossible the meaningful exercise of popular sovereignty. Defenders of American liberal democratic performance contend, in rebuttal, that the Madisonian system has generally succeeded in preventing great concentrations of power. They agree that some individuals and groups have more of such politically important resources as money, and that concentrations of resources need careful attention and sometimes regulatory remedies—like restrictions on private contributions to candidates for elective office. But they do not agree that political elites have been a unified force opposing majority preferences. They argue that the common pattern finds political elites in competition one with another for general public support. Elections give the public an important resource for determining national leadership and basic policy direction.

Part 3 | Governance

7 | Congress

It was not by chance that the framers devoted the first article of the U.S. Constitution to Congress. They expected the legislature to be the strongest branch of the new government. They also considered it the most important branch, because representative democracy simply could not exist in the absence of an autonomous legislature able to enact laws and accountable ultimately to the people. Much has happened over the past two centuries to alter the operations of Congress and its place in the American governmental system. Today few would consider it the dominant branch. The role of the president and the executive branch has become too great for that. But Congress still plays an enormous and vital part in the country's representative government.

The text of the U.S. Constitution is reprinted in the Appendix to this volume. *Article I, section 8,* enumerates the powers of Congress. "The Congress shall have Power," this section begins, "to lay and collect Taxes . . . to pay the Debts and provide for the common Defense and general Welfare of the United States. . . ." The section then continues through an expansive list of Congress's powers:

> To regulate Commerce with foreign Nations, and among the several States . . . ;
>
> To coin Money [and] regulate the Value thereof . . . ;
>
> To establish post Offices and post Roads;
>
> To declare war . . . ;
>
> To raise and support Armies . . . [and] to provide and maintain a Navy. . . .

The last clause of Section 8 contains the most sweeping grant of legislative power: "To make all Laws which shall be necessary and proper for carrying into Execution the foregoing Powers, and all other Powers vested by this Constitution in the Government of the United States. . . ." Known as the ***"necessary and proper"*** clause, this grant has been deemed sufficient over the last half-century to support any legislative commitment which Congress has wanted to make.

"Necessary and proper" clause

ORGANIZATION OF THE LEGISLATURE

We will first examine Congress' basic organization and institutional form. Its structural independence from the executive—part of the larger scheme of separation of powers—is especially important. We also consider its status as a bicameral, or two-house, legislature, the vast role of its committees and subcommittees, its party organization, staff, and various rules of operation. After we get a good grasp of the institutional form of Congress, we can look at its changing operation and place in American government. The evolution of congressional-presidential interaction is given special attention later in the chapter.

Separation of Powers

The American Congress is charged with representing the public in making laws. In this it resembles other national legislatures, such as the British Parliament, the French National Assembly, and the West German Bundestag and Bundesrat. It differs from them, though, in its constitutional independence from the executive. **Separation of powers** distinguishes all of American government, and certainly the relations of Congress and president.

A majority of the world's democratic governments are *parliamentary* in form, where executive authority is derived from the legisla-

The Capitol, congressional office buildings, and The Supreme Court Building.
1. Hart Senate Office Building.
2. Dirksen Senate Office Building.
3. Russell Senate Office Building.
4. Supreme Court.
5. John Adams Library of Congress.
6. Thomas Jefferson Library of Congress.
7. James Madison Memorial Library of Congress.
8. Cannon House Office Building.
9. Longworth House Office Building.
10. Rayburn House Offfice Building.

ture. In such countries as Australia, Canada, Great Britain, Sweden, West Germany, Italy, India, and Japan, the chief executive official—variously called the prime minister, premier, or chancellor—holds a seat in the national legislature. So do the heads of the principal executive departments, called—together with the prime minister—the cabinet, council of ministers, or, simply, the government. They hold the reins of power in the government because they are the leaders of the legislative majority and are voted into office by the majority coalition.

Parliamentary government and executive power

Under the American scheme, Congress and the president are elected separately, and neither has anything to do with the other's tenure of office (except in the extreme case of impeachment, discussed in chapter 8). Their basic powers and responsibilities are set forth in Articles I and II of the Constitution, and their independence is a fundamental, unchanging feature of American government.

Bicameralism

Within Congress, the idea that power should be divided expresses itself through **bicameralism.** Legislative authority is assigned to two co-equal chambers, the Senate and the House of Representatives. Although two-house legislatures are not uncommon, the U.S. arrangement, where the two chambers share power equally, is rare. In parliamentary systems like Britain, West Germany, and Japan, one house has much more authority than the other. The British House of Commons, for example, elects the government and plays the major role in shaping legislation, while the House of Lords has come to have a distinctly inferior role.

In the United States, the framers provided for two chambers different in size, constituency, and term of office of their members. The House of Representatives, with a membership based on population, was (and is) the larger of the two bodies. In the first and second Congresses it had 65 members, compared to the Senate's 26. Since 1910 House membership has been fixed at 435. Composed of two senators from each state, the Senate had 96 members from 1910 until the late 1950s; when Hawaii and Alaska entered the Union, the total reached the present 100.

Congressional elections

The Constitution stipulates that the House of Representatives must be chosen through direct popular election; members are voted into office from districts of roughly equal population. In contrast, reflecting the federal character of the American union, the Constitution provides equal representation in the Senate for each state, regardless of state populations. Until ratification of the Seventeenth Amendment in 1913, the commitment to different constituencies for the Senate and House also included different election procedures: House members through direct popular ballot, senators by their state legislatures. The Seventeenth Amendment changed the latter provision by requiring direct popular election for the Senate. Regarding term of office, all House members are elected every two years. Senators serve six-year terms, with one-third of them up for election every biennium.

The framers also believed that each chamber should possess its own distinctive legislative character. The House was to be what Madison called "the grand repository of the democratic principle of government."[1] With its short terms and popular election, it was expected to be sensitive to public opinion. At the same time, the House was thought likely to display certain weaknesses common to large, popularly elected legislatures: instability, impulsiveness, unpredictability, inclination to change decisions, and "a short-run view of good public policy." The Senate would be a counterbalance. It would be the source of "a more deliberate, more knowledgeable, longer-run view of good public policy."[2]

Contrasting legislative styles

This sense of contrasting legislative styles is illustrated in a revealing anecdote about the two chambers. Thomas Jefferson had been in France during the Constitutional Convention. Upon returning to the United States, he asked his fellow Virginian George Washington why the latter had agreed to a second chamber, rather than providing for a single-house legislature responsible to the people. "Why," asked Washington, "did you pour that coffee into your saucer?" "To cool it," Jefferson allegedly replied. "Even so," Washington responded, "we pour legislation into the senatorial saucer to cool it." Not all of the framers' expectations have been fulfilled. The Senate is quite capable of acting precipitately, and the House coolly and deliberately. All in all, though, the requirement that both chambers must consider and approve a piece of legislation before it becomes law has remained an important practical element of American legislative practice. As political scientist Richard Fenno observes, while "the framers did not . . . create one precipitate chamber and one stabilizing chamber . . . they did force decisionmaking to move across two separate chambers, however those chambers might be constituted."[3]

Effects of terms of office

Such characteristics of the Senate and House as the former's smaller size, larger constituencies, and less frequent elections have also led the two chambers to operate somewhat differently. For example, Fenno concludes that senators' six-year terms do insulate them a bit from the fluctuating currents of public opinion. Some senators acknowledge the "statesman" proposition: their longer terms make it easier for them to do what they think is right. One senator interviewed by Fenno in the first year of his term observed candidly that "I wouldn't

[1] James Madison, *Notes of Debates in the Federal Convention of 1787* (Athens, Ohio: Ohio University Press, 1976), p. 39.
[2] Richard F. Fenno, Jr., *The United States Senate: A Bicameral Perspective* (Washington, D.C.: AEI for Public Policy Research, 1982), p. 3.
[3] Ibid., p. 5.

have voted against [a piece of legislation] . . . as I did last Saturday if I had to run in a year. The six-year term gives you insurance. Well, not exactly—it gives you a cushion. It gives you some squirming room." Reflecting upon the Senate's 1978 passage of the controversial Panama Canal Treaty, which ceded sovereignty of the Canal back to Panama, another senator doubted that "you would have ever gotten [it] through the House. Not with the election coming up and the mail coming in so heavily against it. The [private] sentiment in the House might not have been any different from what it was in the Senate. But you could never have passed it."[4]

HOUSE AND SENATE RULES

Like other democratic legislatures, Congress has developed various rules and procedures governing the way it handles the flow of legislative business. While the impetus for them has typically been nothing more than the need to establish orderly and expeditious procedures, the rules have sometimes become highly consequential politically as members have learned how to manipulate them for their own particular legislative objectives.

Extended Debate and Filibuster

Filibuster

Because it is much smaller than the House, the Senate is able to operate much more informally. Senate rules afford members greater freedom in floor debate. Senators are permitted to speak as long as they see fit on bills and other legislative issues, whereas the time for House debate is strictly rationed. Frequently, however, senators in the minority on a bill use the extended-debate provision not to air their views fully but to block a vote they know they would lose. The **filibuster** is simply a legislative talkathon, an effort by a minority to hold the floor so long that the majority gives up its effort to secure passage of a bill—because of the press of other business—or at least makes concessions. Senate history is full of instances where determined senators have literally talked bills to death. Southern senators' use of the filibuster to block civil rights legislation in the 1940s and 1950s is the most notable instance, but many different Senate blocs have filibustered for many legislative ends.

Cloture and Unanimous Consent Agreements

Senators are jealous of their individual prerogatives and unwilling to eliminate the extended-debate provision. They have recognized, how-

[4] Quoted in ibid., p. 37. For an insightful study of self-perceived constituency pressures on members of the House of Representatives, see idem, *Home Style: House Members in Their Districts* (Boston: Little, Brown, 1978).

Sometimes filibusters have gone on so long that cots have had to be set up in the Capitol for congressmen.

Cloture

ever, the need to cut off debate in some instances where it was being abused to thwart the majority. The **cloture** rule was first adopted in 1917. In its present form, it permits stopping debate upon the vote of three-fifths of the entire Senate membership—60 votes. When cloture is invoked, the bill must be brought up for final action without more than 100 hours of additional debate.

Unanimous consent

In order to expedite work on legislation, the Senate often dispenses with its time-consuming formal rules and follows privately negotiated agreements submitted to the full chamber for its unanimous approval. These agreements specify the time and procedures of debate on a bill, what parts of it are open to amendment and, sometimes, when the vote on final passage is to take place. **Unanimous consent** means just what it says; such agreements do not come into force if even one senator objects.

House Rules and the Rules Committee

The Rules Committee

With 435 members, the House of Representatives has to be more structured and less individualistic than the Senate. If, for example, it gave its members the right of extended debate, it would literally be paralyzed. One of the ways the House has responded to its need for more formal and restrictive rules of operation has been to empower a powerful committee on procedure.

Before any bill reaches the House floor, it must receive a special order or rule governing the terms of amendment and debate. Issuing these special orders is the task of a committee of the House, the Rules Committee. The rules specify such matters as how long a bill may be debated and how the time for debate is to be apportioned, and what kinds of amendments can be offered. In recent years, rules have become especially complex, requiring in some cases prior notice in the *Congressional Record* (the official report of congressional proceedings) of any amendment to be introduced, the authorization of only certain members to introduce amendments, and so on.

As might be expected, the Rules Committee has often used its procedural control over House business for policy ends—in particular, to block legislation which the committee opposes. For a long period, roughly from the end of World War I until 1970, its independence from House majority leadership made the Rules Committee a potent obstructive force. While in theory the House could always discharge the Committee and bring a bill directly to the floor, it was reluctant to do so, in part because members were not much inclined to cross so influential a body. Over the past decade, however, the obstructiveness of the Rules Committee has been greatly reduced. Still firmly in the role of traffic cop, it has been made to function in a manner much more responsive to the majority party leadership.

Rules Committee's political clout

Suspension Procedures

For speedy handling of noncontroversial legislation, the House has adopted a procedure whereby every Monday and Tuesday members may vote to suspend the rules and consider minor bills—provided that no amendments (provisions added to a bill after it has been introduced) are offered, debate is limited to 40 minutes, and two-thirds approval is required for passage (rather than the usual simple majority). Concerned that some important legislation might slip through even given these restrictions, the Democratic caucus—which is the assembly of all House Democrats—has directed the Speaker to remove from consideration any bills requiring the expenditure of more than $100 million in one year. The Speaker is the chief presiding officer of the House. He is also the leader of the majority party, and is elected by that majority to his post.

Suspension of rules

Discharge Petitions

To dislodge a bill stalled in a House committee for more than 30 days following referral, the discharge rule allows the House to remove the committee from jurisdiction upon the petition of at least 218 members—a House majority. The petition is then placed on the discharge calendar; if the discharge petition is supported by a majority when it is called up for a vote, the bill being discharged is brought to the floor for immediate consideration.

Discharge petitions

THE COMMITTEE SYSTEM

An army, the old adage has it, moves on its stomach. Its food supply determines its capacity to advance. In much the same way, it may be said that Congress moves on its committees. The legislative process in Congress is very much a committee process. Congressional committees play such an important role in large part because of congressional workload. American government does much more today than it did in the nineteenth century. More complicated pieces of legislation must be conceived, drafted, debated, and enacted. The numbers of bills introduced and laws enacted tell part of the story. Just 207 bills were introduced in the eighth Congress, which sat between 1803 and 1805; 111 were passed. By contrast, 11,490 bills and joint resolutions were introduced in the ninety-seventh Congress (1981–1983), and approximately 700 measures were enacted into law. Total federal spending provided for by Congress in 1803 was less than $8 million; in fiscal year 1984, federal spending stood at $854 billion.

One congressional response to these increasing demands has been longer sessions. In the early nineteenth century, Congress met for only short periods each year: after fall harvesting and before spring planting. Many members were farmers, and their needs had to be accommodated. Even as late as World War I, Congress was in session only nine months out of every twenty-four. Today, however, the national legislature is in nearly continuous session, punctuated by fairly short recesses for vacation, campaigns, and district work. A more important response to the growth of legislative business has been to do most of the work in committees. A chamber of 435 representatives, or 100 senators, operating as a committee of the whole for the consideration of legislation, cannot begin to cope with the volume and variety of the contemporary legislative agenda.

Larger workload, expanding committees

The dominant role of committees in the American legislative process cannot be explained solely by the amount of work to be done, however. The British Parliament also enacts a lot of complex legislation, but it has far fewer committees than Congress, and more importantly, it relies on them much less for the conduct of its affairs. The reason for this is the tight party discipline that prevails in Parliament, leaving no room for strong autonomous committees. The government, consisting of the majority-party leadership, dominates the legislative process. It certainly does not want, and has not permitted, strong legislative committees to develop; the latter would only undermine the government's control.[5]

Parliamentary government and committees

As a general rule, the stronger the political parties are in a legislature, and the tighter the control they maintain, the weaker committees are. In the U.S. Congress, party discipline and control are weak, and the committees are very strong.

---

[5] S. A. Walkland, "Committees in the British House of Commons," in John D. Lees and Malcome Shaw, eds., *Committees in Legislatures: A Comparative Analysis* (Durham, N.C.: Duke University Press, 1979), p. 256.

Types of Committees

Congress has four principal types of committees: 1) *standing*, 2) *select* or *special*, 3) *joint*, and 4) *conference*. Together with their many sub-committees, the **standing committees** of Congress are where most of the work of legislating takes place. They are called "standing" because they are permanent units with continuing membership and staff. Among the 16 standing committees of the Senate are Agriculture, Nutrition and Forestry; Appropriations; Armed Services; Energy and Natural Resources; Finance; Foreign Relations; and Judiciary. House standing committees (of which there are 22) include Appropriations; Armed Services; Banking, Finance, and Urban Affairs; Budget; Education and Labor; Public Works and Transportation; Rules; and Ways and Means (counterpart to the Senate Finance Committee and concerned with taxation). Every bill introduced into either house is referred to a standing committee responsible for the policy area in which it falls. The committee (and its relevant subcommittee) have the power to amend the measure as they see fit, and to delay action or speed it on its way. The committees sift through the immense volume of legislation introduced each session, work out compromises, and try to hammer out workable legislation.

Select and special committees are of two main varieties: those established for the purpose of investigating problems and reporting on them to the parent chamber, as in the case of the House Select Committee on Aging and the Senate Select Committee on Intelligence; and those with membership from one party only, set up to perform party functions. Among the latter are the National Republican Senatorial Committee, which dispenses campaign funds to Republican Senate candidates, and the House Democratic Steering and Policy Committee, which acts as a kind of executive committee of the Democratic caucus and nominates Democrats for election by the caucus to the various standing committees when vacancies occur. In the ninety-eighth Congress (1983–1985), there were twelve select and special committees in the House of Representatives, nine in the Senate.

Joint committees serve as coordinating vehicles within the bicameral legislature, drawing their membership from both the House and Senate. In recent decades, they have been used largely for congressional oversight (discussed later in this chapter) and policy exploration. Joint committees have functioned in such areas as atomic energy, defense production, and the reduction of federal expenditures. There were four joint committees of the ninety-eighth Congress, the most important of which were the Joint Committee on Taxation and the Joint Economic Committee.

Conference committees grow out of the requirement that every bill must pass the House and Senate in exactly the same form before it can become law. They adjust differences between the two chambers. Conference committees are set up to deal only with specific pieces of legislation; they have no life beyond the measures for which they were

[margin notes:] Standing committees / Select and special committees / Joint committees / Conference committees

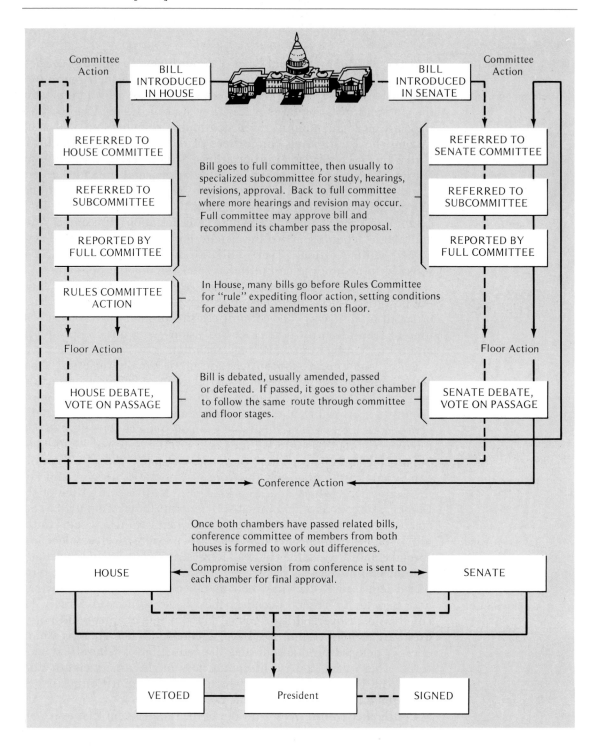

Committee Action

BILL INTRODUCED IN HOUSE

BILL INTRODUCED IN SENATE

Committee Action

REFERRED TO HOUSE COMMITTEE

REFERRED TO SENATE COMMITTEE

Bill goes to full committee, then usually to specialized subcommittee for study, hearings, revisions, approval. Back to full committee where more hearings and revision may occur. Full committee may approve bill and recommend its chamber pass the proposal.

REFERRED TO SUBCOMMITTEE

REFERRED TO SUBCOMMITTEE

REPORTED BY FULL COMMITTEE

REPORTED BY FULL COMMITTEE

RULES COMMITTEE ACTION

In House, many bills go before Rules Committee for "rule" expediting floor action, setting conditions for debate and amendments on floor.

Floor Action

Floor Action

HOUSE DEBATE, VOTE ON PASSAGE

Bill is debated, usually amended, passed or defeated. If passed, it goes to other chamber to follow the same route through committee and floor stages.

SENATE DEBATE, VOTE ON PASSAGE

Conference Action

Once both chambers have passed related bills, conference committee of members from both houses is formed to work out differences.

HOUSE

Compromise version from conference is sent to each chamber for final approval.

SENATE

VETOED

President

SIGNED

Source: *Congressional Quarterly Guide to Current American Government,* Fall 1983 (Washington, D.C.: CQ, Inc., 1983), p. 145.

Figure 7.1
How a Bill Becomes Law
This graphic shows the most typical way in which proposed legislation is enacted into law. There are more complicated, as well as simpler, routes, and most bills never become law. Bills must be passed by both houses in identical form before they can be sent to the president. The path of a House bill is traced by a solid line, that of a Senate bill by a broken line. In practice most bills begin as similar proposals in both houses.

convened. When the House and Senate conferees agree upon a report, they submit it for approval to the full chambers, and it must be accepted or rejected without amendment. When both houses accept a conference report, the measure is passed and sent to the president for signing. If either chamber rejects a conference report, however, the bill is returned to the same or to a newly constituted conference committee. Conferees are supposed to consider only those portions of bills on which the two chambers disagree, and when the differences are modest, the conferees' discretion is in fact quite limited. But when the House and Senate versions differ more drastically, conference committees have much greater discretion and sometimes produce legislation at variance from what either chamber had envisioned. To curb runaway conference committees, the Legislative Reorganization Act of 1970 required them to supply the full chambers with statements on the reasoning behind their recommendations and the policy effects. This act also stipulated that conference committee reports could not be officially considered until at least three days after they were presented—when, hopefully, some members had found time to review the reports.

THE AGE OF SUBCOMMITTEES

House and Senate committees have long had subcommittees, for the very same reason that the parent chambers themselves first established committees: to break the business of legislating into units of manageable size. Given the increasing volume and complexity of legislation, recourse to specialized subcommittees was unavoidable. For example, the House Appropriations Committee—charged with reporting spending bills for every area of federal activity—has 13 subcommittees. Each subcommittee handles appropriations in one relatively manageable sector: agriculture, defense, transportation, and so on. (Figure 7.1 shows the place of subcommittees in the legislative process.)

While the number of subcommittees has increased, especially in the House, where the count grew from 83 in the eighty-fourth Congress (1955–1957) to 130 during the ninety-eighth (1983–1985), having gone as high as 151 in the ninety-fourth (1975–77), the big change has come in subcommittee autonomy. In the half-century or so from World War I until 1970, both the House and Senate permitted their affairs to be dominated by very strong and independent committee chairmen—congressional "barons" they were often called. These chairmen acquired and maintained their positions through **seniority:** a time-honored and rarely violated practice where the most senior member of the majority party on a committee was appointed chairman. Virtually impervious to removal no matter how arbitrary their conduct, the chairmen exercised broad control over committee business. They determined when committee meetings would take place, whether or when specific bills would be considered, what jurisdiction subcommittees would be assigned, what staff would be appointed, and so on. Subcommittees were then firmly under the thumb of any parent committee chairman who chose to exercise the powers available to him. In the early 1970s, however, a vast redistribution of power occurred in Congress, especially in the House of Representatives. Authority was taken away from the "barons" and redistributed among rank-and-file members. Known as **spreading the action,** this internal democratization has had wide ramifications; one major result is subcommittee autonomy.

A New Bill of Rights

In January 1973 a committee of the House Democratic caucus, chaired by Julia Butler Hansen of Washington, recommended a plan which came to be known as the "Subcommittee Bill of Rights." It freed subcommittees from the control of the parent committee chairmen. Each subcommittee's jurisdiction is now determined by all the majority party members of the parent committee and is not easily altered. Bills are automatically referred to the appropriate subcommittees in accord with the established jurisdiction. Subcommittees meet when they choose and subcommittee chairmen select subcommittee staff. Members of the majority party (in the House, this has been the Democrats continuously since 1955) bid in order of seniority for vacant subcommittee chairmanships, and are approved by a caucus of all parent committee Democrats. In short, committee chairmen can no longer appoint the subcommittee chairmen, "stack" subcommittee membership, or otherwise control the latter's work.

Spreading the action has been carried further. Under other provisions approved by the House Democratic caucus, no member can chair more than one subcommittee. No member can fill a second subcommittee vacancy before every other Democrat, submitting his claim in order of seniority, has gained one. In December 1976 the Democratic caucus ruled that no chairman of a full committee could chair a subcommittee on another committee; and in 1978 it decreed that upon reelection a Democratic representative could retain only one subcommittee membership—rather than two as was previously the case—before newly elected members could put in their bids.[6]

The House of Representatives had 22 standing committees and 130

Margin notes:

Seniority and spreading the action

Subcommittee autonomy

Subcommittee reform

---

[6] James L. Sundquist, *The Decline and Resurgence of Congress* (Washington, D.C.: Brookings Institution, 1981), p. 382. The subcommittee movement received an initial boost from the *Legislative Reform Act of 1946* which, among other things, reduced the number of standing committees from 43 to 19. As Roger Davidson and Walter Oleszek observe in *Congress Against Itself* (Bloomington, Ind.: Indiana University Press), many of the discarded committees became subcommittees of the now-larger remaining committees (p. 47).

subcommittees during the ninety-eighth Congress; the Senate, 16 standing committees with 103 subcommittees. Counting special, select, and joint committees, Congress had a grand total of roughly 300 separate committees. The old back-bencher's dream of "every member a chairman" had come remarkably close to being realized. Over half of all House Democrats had a chairmanship in the ninety-eighth Congress; in the smaller Senate the proportion of majority Republicans holding chairmanships was much higher.

STAFFING CONGRESS

Over the past two decades, congressional staff has greatly expanded. Like the increase in subcommittees, the staff explosion has come in part as a response to greater demands of legislative business. The big staff expansion also reflects a successful search for independence. Congressional analyst Allen Schick notes that staff is the currency permitting congressmen to gain greater expertise and hence independence for the legislature from the executive branch, and for rank-and-file members from committee chairmen and other congressional leaders.[7]

Members' Staff

Figure 7.2
Personal Staffs of House and Senate Members since 1930

The greatest expansion has occurred among aides employed in the service of individual congressmen. Members' staffs tripled in size between 1957 and 1977 in both the House and Senate (Figure 7.2). Congressmen have put many of their new assistants to work back in their legislative districts. At present over 2,700 are so assigned—an

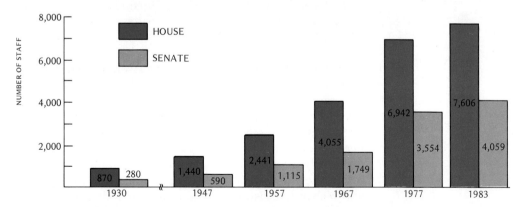

Source: Norman J. Ornstein *et al., Vital Statistics on Congress, 1984–85* ed. (Washington, D.C.: AEI, 1984), p. 121.

[7] Allen Schick, "The Staff of Independence: Why Congress Employs More but Legislates Less," paper presented at the White Burkett Miller Center for Public Affairs, University of Virginia, October 1980, p. 13.

average of 6 or 7 per congressman. Members have found this useful in serving their constituents' needs for help in dealing with government, and useful as well as a little electoral machine made available to them year-round at public expense.

Committee Staff and Congressional Agency Staff

The number of assistants assigned to committees also grew over the 1960s and 1970s. Committee staffs reached their high point in 1979: roughly 2,000 for the select, special, and standing committees of the House, and 1,400 for the Senate committees. Between 1979 and 1983, however, House committee staffs leveled off, and Senate committee staffs were reduced by almost one-sixth. The cut on the Senate side occurred as the Republicans took control of the Senate in 1981 for the first time in a quarter-century and proceeded to fulfill their pledge to scale back committee staffing. In 1983 there was a slight increase in both House and Senate committee staff.

Congressional research agencies

The four major research agencies of Congress—the General Accounting Office (GAO), the Library of Congress, the Congressional Budget Office (CBO), and the Office of Technology Assessment (OTA)— employ more than 10,000 additional staff members. Perhaps three-fourths of this total are not really congressional staff in anything more than a technical sense. The Library of Congress performs a general service in maintaining and making available to scholars the world's largest research library collection; only its Congressional Research Service works directly for Congress. And the GAO is a small army of auditors and accountants overseeing all federal spending. Figuring in cleaning and maintenance people, and the Capitol Police Force, congressional staff numbers more than 31,000. Of these, fewer than 20,000 acually work on legislative business.

Legislatures Abroad

Legislative staff

No other national legislature staffs itself so lavishly. The Canadian parliament comes closest, and it employs only about one-tenth as many assistants as Congress.[8] The contrast between Congress and Great Britain's Parliament is even more striking. House of Commons committees are not staffed at all on a full-time basis; a pool of clerks, perhaps 20 in all, are assigned on an ad hoc basis to perform clerical tasks only. In 1979, each member of Parliament (MP) received a personal allowance of (in dollar equivalents) just $7,500 for secretarial and research assistance—about one-fortieth of what was provided at that time to a member of the U.S. House of Representatives.[9]

[8] Michael Malbin, *Unelected Representatives: Congressional Staff and the Future of Representative Government* (New York: Basic Books, 1980), p. 10.
[9] *British Political Facts* (Strathclyde, Scotland: The Centre for the Study of Public Policy, University of Strathclyde, 1979).

The Cost of Legislating

Expense allowances

Each member of the U.S. House of Representatives in 1983 received a personal allowance of $367,000 for staff support and between $89,000 and $280,000 for other office expenses, depending on certain contingencies such as the distance of his district from Washington. On the Senate side, each senator received between $850,000 and $1,500,000 for staff salaries, the precise amount determined by the size of the state he represented. In addition he was given extensive allowances for postage, travel, telephone, office furnishings, and the rental of office space in his home state. Whereas the total cost of operating Congress in 1955 was about $70 million, the price tag had climbed to $1.5 billion by 1983.[10]

PARTY ORGANIZATION

The Speaker

Those members of Congress who are Democrats, and those who are Republicans, vote as solid blocs against each other on all issues involving the partisan organization of the House and Senate. For example, majority-party members in the House always vote together and elect their leader to the office of *Speaker*—the chief presiding officer. Whichever party has a majority in each house names the chairmen of all the standing committees and subcommittees, and allocates to itself a majority of committee seats. Republicans and Democrats in both houses also establish their own party leadership bodies, shown in Figure 7.3.

Lack of party cohesion

Partisan discipline and coherence does not, however, extend beyond the divvying up of "the spoils of office." On the substance of policy, the Democratic and Republican parties in Congress cannot hold together. The observation of political scientist E. E. Schattschneider, made 35 years ago, remains a valid description of the lack of party cohesion in Congress:

> The roll calls in the House and Senate show that party votes are relatively rare. On difficult questions, usually the most important questions, party lines are apt to break badly, and a straight party vote, aligning one party against the other, is the exception rather than the rule. . . . Often both parties split into approximately equal halves. . . . At other times one party votes as a unit but is joined by a substantial fraction of the other. Finally, a predominant portion of one party may be opposed by a predominant portion of the other party, while minorities, more or less numerous, on each side cross party lines to join their opponents . . .

[10] These data are from Roger H. Davidson and Walter J. Oleszek, *Congress and Its Members* (Washington, D.C.: Congressional Quarterly Press, 1981), p. 241; and *Vital Statistics on Congress, 1984–1985 Edition* (Washington, D.C.: AEI, 1984), pp. 120–46, passim; *Statistical Abstract of the United States, 1984*, p. 322.

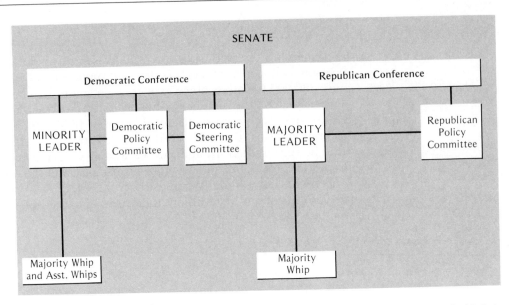

SENATE

Democratic Conference

Republican Conference

MINORITY LEADER

Democratic Policy Committee

Democratic Steering Committee

MAJORITY LEADER

Republican Policy Committee

Majority Whip and Asst. Whips

Majority Whip

Figure 7.3
Party Organization in Congress

[overall] the roll calls demonstrate that the *parties are unable to hold their lines in a controversial public issue when the pressure is on.*[11]

Recent congressional voting bears out Schattschneider's generalization. In the first session of the ninety-eighth Congress (1983), only 51 percent of all recorded votes were what *Congressional Quarterly (CQ)* called "party unity" votes. And, it should be noted, *CQ*'s standards for such votes reflect the general lack of cohesion in the congressional parties. A "party unity" vote is one where at least a bare majority of Democrats oppose a bare majority of Republicans. If *CQ* were to impose a more demanding standard, such as 90 percent or more of Democrats voting against a comparable majority of Republicans, the proportion of votes qualifying as "party unity" would shrink to a mere handful. The modest levels of "party unity" voting in recent Congresses are shown in Figure 7.4. *CQ* also computes "party unity" scores for congressional Democrats and Republicans. These indicate what percentage of all contested roll calls the average member votes with his party's majority against a majority of the other party. In 1983, the composite party unity score for congressional Democrats was 76 percent, for Republicans 74 percent. Both of these figures are actually on the high side of recent congressional experience, reflecting the relatively high degree of partisan feeling generated by the Reagan administration programs. Looking back over the preceding decade, the Republicans' party unity score dropped as low as 62 percent in 1974, while the Democrats' low was 63 percent, also in 1974.

These scores are composite averages. The Democrats' score of 76 percent in 1983 means that on the average in contested votes, 76 percent of all Democrats were on one side of a question while 24 percent

[11] E. E. Schattschneider, *Party Government* (New York: Rinehart, 1942), pp. 130–32.

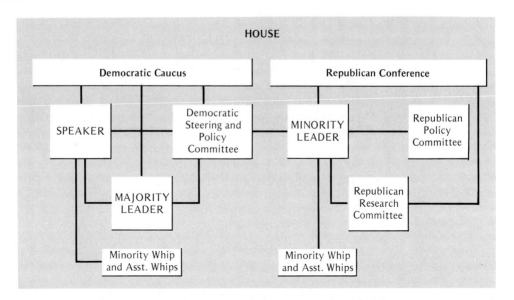

Figure 7.3 (continued) were on the opposite side. Such a substantial partisan disunity has important consequences: for one, the party in Congress with a nominal majority often loses, even on the most important votes. In the first two years of the Reagan administration (1981–82), when the core of the president's domestic program was being acted upon, House Democrats had 242 seats to the Republicans' 192. But even this 50-seat majority proved insufficient to prevent the party from losing many of the major showdown votes. The more conservative Democrats frequently crossed party lines and voted with the president.

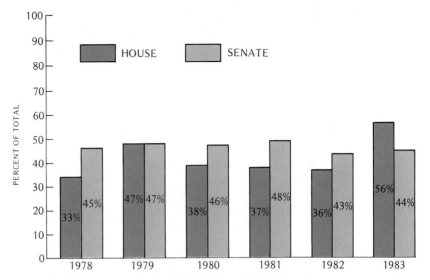

Figure 7.4
"Party Unity" Voting in Congress since 1978 (in percent)

Source: Congressional Quarterly, December 31, 1983, p. 2790. Party unity votes, as defined by CQ, are "recorded votes in the Senate and House that split the parties, a majority of voting Democrats opposing a majority of voting Republicans."

In chapter 15 we discuss the reasons why American political parties are much less disciplined and cohesive than are their counterparts in other democracies. As noted, in most democracies the government—the prime minister and the cabinet—are members of the legislature and are voted into their executive posts by the legislative majority. Were Conservative MPs in the British House of Commons to cross party lines and vote with the opposition Labor party they would, in the parliamentary tradition, be declaring "no confidence" in the Conservative government and would remove it from office. The very structure of legislative-executive relations in a parliamentary system strongly encourages party unity. But the opposite applies in the American system, given separation of powers. The president holds office for a fixed term, independent of Congress. His tenure is unaffected by how congressmen vote. Party leaders try to exert pressure, of course, and they can appeal to feelings of party loyalty. But there are no compelling structural incentives for party-line voting.

THE COMPOSITION OF CONGRESS

Requirements for office

The Constitution sets only three requirements for congressional membership: 1) Before taking office, senators and representatives must have been citizens of the United States for at least nine and seven years, respectively; 2) a senator must be at least 30 years of age and a representative at least 25 years; and 3) each member must be an inhabitant of that state in which he shall be chosen. Not surprisingly, though, the membership of Congress has a much more distinctive cast than these general and nonrestrictive standards dictate.

Party Membership

Partisan ties are surely the most important entrance requirements. Although political party organizations are relatively weak in the United States compared to other democracies, and many Americans now hold their party loyalties very lightly, one still does not, with rare exception, gain election to Congress without a strong party connection— and, specifically, without ties to the Democratic or Republican parties. The largest group of senators and representatives to come to office in the past half-century unattached to either of the two major parties were the 17 elected in 1936. No Congress since World War II has had more than three members who were not Democrats or Republicans. Every congressman and senator elected in 1984 belonged to one of the two major parties.

Since the New Deal realignment made them the majority party more than a half-century ago, the Democrats have dominated Congress with a consistency unequaled by any other party in American history. Of the last 27 Congresses (from the seventy-third chosen in

1932 to the ninety-ninth elected in 1984) only two had Republican majorities in both House and Senate—the eightieth, elected just after World War II, and the eighty-third, which came in with Dwight Eisenhower's first-term victory in 1952. The Democrats have had majorities, usually very large ones, in the House of Representatives for all but four years since 1930. When the GOP ("Grand Old Party," as the Republicans came to be called in the late nineteenth century) gained control of the Senate in Ronald Reagan's big 1980 victory, and retained it in 1982 and 1984, these were only their third, fourth, and fifth upper-chamber successes since 1932. The box score for the last 27 Congresses shows a lopsided electoral game: 22 Congresses with the Democrats controlling both houses, two with the Republicans controlling both, and these with split-party control. The early 1980s are the closest the Republicans have come to a "congressional era" since the Great Depression. Their Senate majorities from 1981 through 1986 represent the only time in 50 years that they have controlled either house of the national legislature for three consecutive terms.

Social and Religious Background

Congressmen generally look like members of a national political elite. They are more highly educated than the public at large, come dispro-portionately from a few prestigious occupations, and are far above average in wealth. Virtually every senator and congressman has a college degree. A majority have done some form of graduate work, with law school training by far the most common. In 1983, 200 House members and 61 senators listed their previous occupation as law-yer.[12] In the same year, 138 in the House and 29 in the Senate had been businessmen or bankers. Education was third, with 43 represen-tatives and 12 senators having been teachers, professors, or educa-tional administrators. No other occupational background even approached law, business, and education. Agriculture now runs a dis-tant fourth. Early in the twentieth century, the Senate acquired a reputation as a club for millionaires. Its present composition does little to dispute that status. About a third of all senators are now millionaires—a position they emphatically did not derive from their relatively modest senatorial salaries of (in 1984) $72,200. House members are generally of upper-middle-class standing; only 30 or so are millionaires.

The religious makeup of congressmen differs significantly from that of the general public. But this is not unusual for a group of national leaders, for certain denominations are generally stronger among high-status groups. Of all senators and representatives in 1983, 26 percent were Catholics, roughly the proportion of Catholics in the general

---

[12] *Vital Statistics on Congress, 1984–1985 Edition*, pp. 21, 24.

populace. But Episcopalians and Presbyterians—small denominations in the country, with members of notably high social status—had large numbers of congressional adherents; while the biggest Protestant denomination nationally, the Baptists, had relatively few adherents in Congress. Twelve percent of the members of both houses in 1983 listed themselves as Episcopalians, 11 percent as Presbyterians, and only 9 percent as Baptists. Seven percent were Jewish.[13] Every Congress in American history has been composed disproportionately of white males. In recent years, though, the number of women and blacks has been edging upward. In the elections of 1982, 21 blacks won election to the House of Representatives—the highest number ever. All of them are Democrats. Similarly, the 21 women elected to House seats in 1982, together with the two returning senators who are women, are the most ever. Women in the ninety-eighth Congress were evenly divided between the two parties: twelve were Democratic representatives, nine were Republican representatives, and two were Republican senators (see Table 7.1).

Table 7.1
Women and Blacks in Congress since 1917

	Women		Blacks	
Congress	*D*	*R*	*D*	*R*
65th (1917)	—	1	—	—
70th (1927)	2	3	—	—
75th (1937)	6	1	1	—
80th (1947)	3	5	2	—
85th (1957)	9	7	3	—
90th (1967)	5	6	6	1
95th (1977)	13	5	16	1
98th (1983)	12	11	21	—

Source: U.S. Bureau of the Census, *Statistical Abstract of the United States, 1984,* p. 258; idem, "The Social and Economic Status of the Black Population in the United States: An Historical View, 1790–1978," *Current Population Reports,* series P-23, no. 80, 1979, p. 154; M. Christopher, *Black Americans in Congress* (New York: Crowell, 1976), pp. 309–11.

THE CHANGING CONGRESS

Today's Congress is the product of nearly two hundred years of evolution and change. While its formal position in the American constitutional scheme is essentially the same now as it was in 1789, its role in the dynamic process of policy-making is very different. Congressional-presidential relations have seen important shifts, and Congress's internal distribution of power has changed as well.

[13] These data have been adapted from *Vital Statistics on Congress, 1984–1985 Edition,* pp. 28–29.

Early Legislative Predominance

Through much of the first century after independence, Congress was the dominant branch of U.S. government. This status was in accord with the preferences of most Americans. Their experience with the British Crown and governors of the colonies had engendered among them a strong mistrust of executive authority. After independence, this mistrust expressed itself in state constitutions which "produced what was tantamount to legislative omnipotence."[14] The national government under the Articles of Confederation really made no provision at all for executive authority.

Congress at the center

The new constitution drafted in 1787 was a highly conscious effort to end government-by-the-legislature and provide for a coherent, active, countervailing executive authority. Yet even the Constitution's framers expected Congress to dominate the new governmental system. And following the first 15 years or so under the Constitution—when the great Federalist leaders in President George Washington's cabinet, and subsequently President Thomas Jefferson and his aides, provided relatively strong executive leadership—Congress did in fact become the governmental fulcrum.

The Congressional Caucus

At the beginning of the nineteenth century, the House of Representatives was the more prominent of the two legislative chambers. Most legislation in the early years originated there rather than in the Senate. House leadership was especially strong under Henry Clay, who served as Speaker for three separate terms: 1811–14, 1815–20, and 1823–25. Clay dominated the House caucus of the Democratic-Republican party—the assembly of all members of that party in the lower chamber—while the caucus was the most influential element of American government. Up until the 1820s, the caucus picked the ruling Democratic-Republican party's presidential candidates: Thomas Jefferson in 1804, James Madison in 1808 and 1812, and James Monroe in 1816. The president was in effect the nominee of a party system centered in the House of Representatives.

Henry Clay and the House caucus

Indicative of the standing of Congress in general, and of the House in particular, is the career of John Quincy Adams of Massachusetts, the son of the second president and himself the sixth president (1825–29). After losing his bid for a second presidential term, Adams ran for the House, won, and went on to play an active and distinctive part in House affairs. Today, we simply cannot imagine a president seeking election to the House of Representatives following his term as chief executive.

John Quincy Adams in Congress

[14]Charles C. Thach, Jr., *The Creation of the Presidency, 1775–1789: A Study in Constitutional History* (Baltimore, Md.: John Hopkins University Press, 1969), p. 34.

Henry Clay holding sway over the House.

The Senate Giants

By the 1830s the balance of strong leadership had shifted from the House to the Senate. Henry Clay's decision in 1831 to run for a Senate seat is symbolic. The Senate's smaller membership and longer term of office proved attractive to nationally aspiring leaders. In addition, the election of senators by the state legislatures gradually led to the most important state party leaders becoming senators. With such political muscle, the Senate's stature grew. From the time of Andrew Jackson up to the Civil War, Senate giants like Clay of Kentucky, Daniel Webster of Massachusetts, and John Calhoun of South Carolina were the most prominent American politicians.

Andrew Johnson and Congress

The Civil War changed the legislative-executive balance temporarily by putting a premium on presidential leadership. But with the end of the war and the assassination of President Lincoln in 1865, the era of congressional ascendancy resumed with a passion. Finally in control of both houses of Congress, the so-called "Radical Republicans" moved quickly to impose their own vision of Reconstruction on the defeated South. The House impeached President Andrew Johnson in 1867, and the Senate almost got the two-thirds majority needed to convict him and remove him from office. (Johnson's impeachment will be discussed in detail in chapter 8.)

Age of strong party leadership

While Johnson's successors managed to stabilize the powers of the presidency, the predominance of Congress was largely unchallenged for the rest of the century. A young political scientist, Woodrow Wilson, voiced this reality in the title of his classic work, *Congressional Government*, published in 1885. Wilson noted that "the business of the President, occasionally great, is usually not much above routine. Most of the time it is mere administration, mere obedience to directions from the masters of policy, the Standing Committees [of Congress]."[15] Over the 1880s and 1890s, however, power shifted within the Congress as strong party leadership developed in both House and Senate. This gave the country its only era of legislature-based party government. There were two stages to this development.

The Ascendancy of the Speaker

The Speaker as "boss"

In the first, the Speaker of the House of Representatives managed to accumulate an impressive array of prerogatives. By the time Thomas B. Reed held the post in 1889–91 and 1895–99, the office had assumed such governmental authority that the Speaker was likened to a prime minister. This ascendancy was short-lived. Even in their heyday, strong Speakers like Reed and his successor, Joseph Cannon, were burdened with such nicknames as "Boss" and "Czar." Reformers in both parties had a potent weapon with which to attack them: appeal to a populace inclined to view strong party leadership as undemocratic. In 1910, a House revolt against Cannon greatly weakened the Speaker's authority.

The Caucus and its Power

There was one final attempt at disciplined party government, this time with the caucus of House Democrats as the instrument of con-

SPEAKER REED KNOWS HIS BUSINESS.
From the *World* (New York).

[15] Woodrow Wilson, *Congressional Government* (New York: Houghton-Mifflin, 1913; first published 1885), pp. 253–54.

*Speaker of the House
Joseph Cannon.*

The battle over
the caucus

King Caucus

trol. In 1911, the caucus directed Democrats on various committees not to report any legislation other than that submitted by the leadership "unless hereafter directed by this Caucus."[16] Two years before, the caucus had adopted a rule whereby a two-thirds vote in caucus would subsequently bind all party members. When a bill came up for a vote members were expected to vote as the party caucus instructed them. Violation resulted in the loss of such party entitlements as committee assignments. A similar rule applied in the Senate.

The outcry against government-by-caucus built up quickly. Republicans were outraged because the domination of the Democratic caucus left them with little influence. Reformers thought "King Caucus" was as objectionable as the Speaker's control had been. The Secretary to the National Voters' League, established in 1913 by prominent proponents of congressional reform, charged that the Democrats had not abolished "Cannonism"—referring to the regime of Speaker Joseph Cannon—but only disguised it. A minority still ran Congress, now through the caucus rather than the office of Speaker.[17]

Democrats fought back in defense of the caucus with some of the most coherent arguments for party government ever heard in the American legislature. Democratic Speaker Champ Clark of Missouri argued that

> responsibility rests upon the majority, and we shrink not from acknowledging our responsibility to the country and of acting accordingly. . . .

[16] Wilder H. Haines, "The Congressional Caucus of Today," *American Political Science Review* 9 (November 1915):697*n*.
[17] Lynn Haines, *Your Congress* (National Voters' League, 1915), pp. 67, 76–77.

We intend to place our ideas upon the statute books on the great questions now pressing for solution. . . . We must have organization in order to enact the will of the people into law, and we have got it. . . .[18]

But soon even Democrats joined in the attack on the caucus system. For a party member to be required by a binding caucus vote to back a bill that he disagreed with was unworthy of the Congress of the United States, Senator Gilbert Hitchcock of Nebraska argued in 1913. "Like all caucuses, I believe the fact to be that our Democratic caucus degenerated into a political machine."[19] Outside Congress the attack was even stronger. "King Caucus" was dethroned, never to be restored.

Leadership Shifts to the Presidency

By 1915 the brief American experiment with congressional party government had been abandoned. In the absence of central party leadership, power flowed back to the committees and to the chairmen, who dominated committee action. At the same time an equally momentous shift was propelling policy initiative away from the legislature altogether and to the presidency. Whereas government-by-the-legislature prevailed throughout most of the nineteenth century, government-by-the-president has been the rule in much of the twentieth century.

Power shifts to the president

Why did initiative and leadership shift from Congress to the president? One factor was the growth of an industrial economy, which required an expansion of federal regulation and management. Theodore Roosevelt, a Republican who served as president from 1901 to 1909, was the first to recognize and articulate the growing public feeling that stronger presidential leadership was needed to handle the greater demands on government. He argued that "it was not only his [the president's] right but his duty to do anything that the needs of the nation demanded unless such action was forbidden by the Constitution or by the laws. . . ."[20]

Presidential responsibility

Although the Republican presidents of the 1920s were less assertive than either Theodore Roosevelt or Democrat Woodrow Wilson, they could not escape responsibility when things went sour. Herbert Hoover, rather than Congress, received most of the blame for the Great Depression and for the perceived inadequacy of government's response to it. And the subsequent success of Franklin Roosevelt in providing vigorous leadership to combat problems of the Depression solidified the public's inclination to look to the presidency rather than to the legislature.

---

[18]*Congressional Record*, September 24, 1913, pp. 51, 57–59.
[19]*Congressional Record*, August 29, 1913, pp. 38, 58–59.
[20]Theodore Roosevelt, *An Autobiography* (New York: Scribners, 1925; first published, 1913), p. 357.

The Great Depression produced widespread hardship—including the spread of shanty towns, nicknamed "Hoovervilles," outside many large cities.

After 1933, Congress found it increasingly necessary to confer responsibilities upon the executive branch. Given the commitment to greater governmental management of the economy and provision for public welfare, there was little alternative; a legislature can't manage complex programs. It was inevitable that the Congress would lose ground to the presidency as big (executive) government developed in this century. It was by no means inevitable, however, that executive growth would be uncritically endorsed and the presidency depicted in heroic terms. In the three decades or so after 1935, a mythology developed around the presidency. The president came to be seen as the great engine of democracy, "a kind of magnificent lion who can roam widely and do great deeds."[21]

A House of Misrepresentatives?

The other side of the coin was a growing inclination to disparage Congress. If the president was the engine that drove American government along its necessary course, Congress was the brakes, capriciously applied so as to make the journey fitful and incomplete. James McGregor Burns argued that Congress was so organized as to make coherent majority action exceedingly difficult.

> Even if majority support has been won for a program, organized minorities in either house can exploit the frailties of congressional organization and procedure to thwart the majority. Each chamber has an absolute veto on the other. In the Senate a band of dissidents can scuttle the program; even one determined senator can greatly dilute it.[22]

[21] Clinton Rossiter, *The American Presidency*, rev. ed. (New York: New American Library, 1960), p. 84.
[22] James MacGregor Burns, *Congress on Trial* (New York: Harper & Brothers, 1954), p. 123.

The great danger in all this was "legislative paralysis," the inability to mount needed governmental action except through sporadic bursts of successful presidential intiative. In Burns's critique, Congress was nothing short of the "House of Misrepresentatives."

In the Congresses of 1935–1965, with the absence of strong party leadership, power was fragmented, and the formulation of coherent policy often did depend upon executive initiatives. The dominant voice of the committee chairmen, who held their posts through seniority, not because they were loyal to the national party programs, detracted from Congress's representativeness. Still, the critique of Congress, like the accompanying cult of the presidency, lacked balance. If Congress was sometimes a roadblock to new policy initiatives, that was broadly in accord with explicit constitutional intent. In providing for separation of powers and checks and balances, the framers intentionally sided with barriers to precipitous governmental action. Supporters of the programs of activist presidents like Franklin Roosevelt and John Kennedy had reason to criticize congressional resistance, but those who opposed these presidential initiatives had equal reason to applaud the restraints Congress imposed. And Congress often did cooperate with presidents to produce an enormous amount of legislation during the New Deal and in succeeding decades. Congressional action was not nearly as slow, reactive, or conservative as its critics of the 1930s, '40s, and '50s suggested.

> **Congress and the constitutional system**

THE CONTEMPORARY CONGRESS

By 1965, Americans had for several decades been given a picture by the press and other commentary of the presidency as the repository of boldness and vision, and Congress of recalcitrance and conservatism. There was enough truth to these assertions to give them credibility, but there were also enough flaws in them to invite a powerful rebuttal in subsequent years. Four developments in 1965–75 changed presidential-congressional relations and the prevailing view of them. First, Congress was gripped by a new surge of political individualism. It has always been an institution where the individual member has been given much power and independence. But in the 1960s it experienced new demands by members that changed its internal operation and made it far more assertive vis-à-vis the president. Second, the idea that a strong president was good for the nation was shaken by a stream of events that came in rapid succession, especially the Vietnam War. Third, belief that presidential initiative was synonymous with liberal-progressive government was upset as the United States entered an era of aggressively conservative presidents. Suddenly, Congress became the progressive branch. And fourth, there was Watergate. The Watergate scandal gave the cult of the virtuous presidency a hard kick in its solar plexus, and for a time knocked most of

> **Congressional resurgence**

the air out of it. The temporary weakening of the presidency—with Richard Nixon forced to resign from office, Gerald Ford left to pick up the pieces, and Jimmy Carter desperate to project a new model of presidential comportment—gave Congress an extraordinary opportunity to reassert itself.

Congressional Individualism

Political individualism—the antithesis of party regularity and cohesion—has been both a cause and an effect of the weakness of political party organizations in the U.S. The new wave of political individualism of the 1960s was heightened by the communications media. Television, a personality-emphasizing institution, became the dominant medium of mass communication in the 1950s and 1960s. From this and other structural changes a new type of congressman gradually emerged: more assertive and less inclined to defer to leadership, whether in Congress or the executive branch.[23]

Three recent elections (1958, 1964, 1974) are especially important in the conversion of Congress because they brought in large numbers of Democratic newcomers. The Democrats have been the party in which changed outlooks and expectations have had the greatest actual impact—especially since, as the majority, they have had the power to implement new practices. Democrats gained 51 House seats in the elections of 1958, a year in which the country was gripped by the worst recession since World War II. In 1964, when Republican presidential nominee Barry Goldwater was buried electorally by Lyndon Johnson, Republicans lost 37 seats in the House. And in the election following the Watergate scandal (1974), House Democrats picked up a whopping 52 seats. These three big Democratic "freshman classes," generated a new assertiveness. They also pushed for shifts in the balance of power in Congress itself, especially in the House of Representatives, by spreading the action widely among all Democratic members. From roughly the end of World War I until the late 1960s, the majority party member who had served longest on a committee automatically became its chairman and was virtually assured of retaining that post as long as he remained in Congress. But in the late 1960s and early 1970s the seniority system was modified, with provision that the Democratic caucus could displace chairmen who proved insufficiently responsive to the membership. As noted earlier, the power and autonomy of the subcommittees was greatly extended and the number of subcommittees increased. The staff available to individual members and to legislative committees was also greatly expanded.

Political individualism

Democrats and congressional reform

---

[23] In discussing "the forces fueling the individualistic tone of the present-day Congress," Thomas E. Mann puts the case bluntly: "As far as elections are concerned, senators and representatives are in business for themselves. . . . They are political entrepreneurs . . . seizing opportunities, generating resources, responding to pressures. . . ." Thomas E. Mann, "Elections and Change in Congress," in Thomas E. Mann and Norman J. Ornstein, eds., *The New Congress* (Washington, D.C.: American Enterprise Institute, 1981), p. 53.

Television has brought congressmen directly to the public through such programs as CNN's Relations *where citizens can call in and ask their congressmen specific questions on the air.*

Through these and other means, power was distributed more widely among the rank-and-file of the majority party, and, to a much lesser degree, among the minority party as well.

Some Effects of Strong Presidents

A strong president and Vietnam

America's involvement in Vietnam was a political watershed for the country. The loss of life which the war exacted, its staggering material cost, the domestic protests it engendered, and the government's seeming inability to achieve a satisfactory resolution shook and divided the nation. For liberal Democrats, this was especially painful, since it was an activist liberal Democratic president, Lyndon Johnson, who led the country into heavy involvement in the Vietnam fighting. Many Democrats changed their thinking about the virtues of bold executive leadership.

Strong presidents and conservatism

If Vietnam attested to the fact that strong presidents could serve ends that many deemed ill-advised, conservative activists like Richard Nixon and Ronald Reagan have taught many liberals that the "great engine of democracy" could be a strong force against their policy interests. In 1965 liberals could look back on 32 years of a presidency dominated by liberal Democrats, with Dwight Eisenhower's eight years merely a "breath-catching" interlude. In 1985, though, they looked back on the 32 years since Eisenhower's election as a period when Republicans dominated the presidency—a hold broken only by the eight years of the Kennedy and Johnson administrations and, somewhat dubiously from a liberal perspective, the four years of Jimmy Carter.

The House Judiciary Committee during the televised Watergate hearings.

The Watergate Scandal

Watergate and the presidency

The errors of judgment and the betrayal of responsibility by a president and many of his closest aides—what Watergate has come to mean for many—capped off widespread disillusionment with presidential power, which had been growing since the mid-1960s. While most Americans still esteemed the office and looked to it for leadership, the presidency was stripped of the sometimes uncritical reverence that had enveloped it since the 1930s. In August 1974, few Americans would describe the president as "a kind of magnificent lion who can roam widely and do great deeds." The lion was caught lying and drummed out of office by a Congress responsive to public sentiment. Suddenly, separation of powers was looking a lot better than it had a decade earlier.

LEGISLATIVE RESURGENCE

Three areas of congressional reassertion

Picture a legislature composed of ever more assertive and individualistic politicians, who concluded with increasing frustration that they had relinquished too much authority and initiative to the executive. Then picture them occupying a branch of government constitutionally independent of the executive and co-equal to it. Finally, picture them suddenly liberated from the myth that their executive-branch rivals had a corner on political wisdom and virtue. "I seen my opportunities and I took 'em," the eminent Democratic politician from New York, "Boss" George Washington Plunkett of Tammany Hall, offered as his political epitaph earlier in this century.[24] Watergate presented Congress with such an opportunity. The result was congressional resurgence. Three areas where Congress reasserted itself are especially important. One involves the **power of the purse,** especially the congressional efforts to develop a national budget more coherently. A second is the great expansion of **legislative oversight** over the departments and agencies of the executive branch. The third, related to oversight, involves expanded congressional use of the **legislative veto** as part of an effort to ensure that executive-agency actions conform to legislative wishes.

The Congressional Budget and Impoundment Control Act of 1974

Power of the purse

One important aim of Congress in its resurgence of the 1970s was to recapture its **power of the purse.** The immediate target was the Nixon administration's sweeping use of **impoundment**—holding back funds which Congress had appropriated for various stated purposes in its regular budgetary actions.

Impoundment

Impoundment. This practice developed early in the twentieth century for a specific purpose, and with Congress' blessings. After 1921, the Bureau of the Budget (now the Office of Management and Budget) established the practice of apportioning appropriated funds to the various federal departments in quarterly installments. In so doing it sometimes discovered that more dollars were available than were needed to meet the statutory purpose, and it placed these in reserve—a type of impoundment of excess funds. Congress welcomed this practice and gave it formal recognition in a 1950 law. When Richard Nixon took office in 1969 he found himself under another more specific congressional directive bearing on impoundment. Congress had instructed the president in a 1968 measure to trim some $6 billion from the spending it had approved so as to bring revenues and expenditures into greater balance. "We have appropriated more than we should have," Congress in effect said to the president. "You find places to cut $6 billion."

Nixon's use of impoundment

Building on this base, Nixon asserted a broad authority to impound funds. He believed that spending under the "Great Society" programs of the Johnson administration had surged out of control, and he saw impoundment a means of achieving cuts beyond what he could persuade a profligate Congress to make. Speaking for the administration, then deputy director of the Office of Management and Budget (OMB) Caspar Weinberger argued that the president's constitutional responsibility to "take care that the laws be faithfully executed"

[24] See William Riordan, *Plunkett of Tammany Hall,* (New York: E. P. Dutton, 1963), p. 3. The Society of Tammany, known as Tammany Hall, was a fraternal organization that controlled the New York Democratic party from roughly the middle of the nineteenth century until the middle of this century.

sometimes necessitated impounding appropriated funds. The president, said Weinberger, must look beyond individual appropriations acts to all laws he is supposed to execute—including laws that place a ceiling on the national debt. When the intentions of different statutes conflict, as when appropriations' measures call for spending in excess of revenues, contrary to debt limitation statutes, the president may try to reconcile the conflicting requirements through impoundment.

Behind such rhetoric, a power-play of breathtaking proportions was being attempted. For the first time a president was asserting the general right to scuttle programs that had been duly enacted into law, by preventing funds appropriated for them from being expended. For example, in 1972 Nixon eliminated a whole series of Department of Agriculture programs and cut some $9 billion from funds appropriated for the Environmental Protection Agency. Had this sweeping use of impoundment been sustained, the nature of executive-legislative relations and separation of powers would have been significantly altered. The fact that the Nixon administration even entertained its expansive claims on impoundment showed how far presidential assertiveness and congressional retreat had proceeded.

Fiscal incoherence. As the battle over impoundment waged, many congressmen were occupied with another budget-linked problem, this one of long duration: How could greater coherence be brought to the whole budgetary process? As things stood, the taxing and spending halves of the program the president presented to Congress were assigned to different committees in both the House and Senate and acted on independently. On the spending side, a number of separate **appropriations bills** (bills allocating funding for programs and agencies) were enacted each session, each handled by a different appropriations subcommittee and considered by Congress independently of one another. Beyond this, a growing proportion of governmental expenditures were outside the control of the appropriations committees altogether, having been mandated by "backdoor spending" provisions included in legislation written by various standing committees.[25] How could priorities be determined and the overall impact of individual spending decisions on the total budget be properly assessed and controlled? The United States didn't have a fiscal policy, one commentator noted, only "a fiscal result."[26]

Financially, the left hand did not know what the right hand was doing. As a result, many in Congress concluded in the late 1960s and early 1970s that much more was wrong than the president's challenging them through impoundment. Representative Al Ullman of Ore-

The budgetary process in Congress

Need for reform

[25] "Backdoor spending" as used in Congress refers to expenditures beyond the control of the appropriations committees, such as social security payments, farm price support payments, and pensions paid to retired government employees.
[26] Edwin L. Dale, Jr., *New York Times*, June 15, 1975.

Congress plays an important role in economic policy, and the chairmen of the principal committees concerned with fiscal policy matter are centers of attention. Here, Robert Dole, at the time chairman of the Senate Finance Committee holds a news conference. Senator Dole was elected Senate majority leader in December 1984.

gon, the most senior Democrat on the House Ways and Means Committee, lamented that

> the only place where a budget is put together is the Office of Management and Budget downtown. When they send their recommendations to us we go through a few motions of raising or lowering the spending requests, but we have lost the capacity to decide our own priorities. Until we can devise a vehicle for putting those non-appropriated funds in the same basket and coming up with an overall limitation we have not faced up to the issue at all.[27]

The budget act. Congress finally acted to remedy this situation and passed the Congressional Budget and Impoundment Control Act in June 1974. It was signed into law by Richard Nixon just four weeks before he left office. The administration had already given up on impoundment as a tactic in the face of adverse court decisions, and most of the impounded appropriations had been released.

Congressional Budget and Impoundment Act

Under the budget and impoundment act, the president may only propose to Congress that it cancel or defer spending previously authorized. In cases where the president simply proposes deferring expenditures to some future time, the act stipulates that his action stands unless either house votes to overrule him. But when the president seeks to terminate a program provided by statute or hold back funds for reasons of fiscal policy, his initiative is cancelled unless a bill explicitly rescinding the original appropriation is enacted within 45 days. On matters of impoundment, the president proposes and Congress disposes. Since 1974, the two branches have settled fairly comfortably into the roles which the budget act prescribes.

[27] *Congressional Record*, October 10, 1972, pp. 34600–602.

The new budget process. The other part of the 1974 legislation imposes a new organization on congressional budget-making. A budget committee in each house, together with staff of the Congressional Budget Office (CBO)—all established by the 1974 Act—arrive at recommendations on the basic outlines of fiscal policy. The budget committees and the CBO are supposed to consider such questions as how large a deficit is desirable or permissible given the state of the economy, and what taxing and spending measures are consistent with this target. Then, according to the plan, they specify spending levels for all major programs—national defense, agriculture, health, and welfare—taking into account recommendations from the standing committees that consider legislation in each of these areas. The budget committee recommendations are reviewed by House and Senate and, as modified, go into the first annual budget resolution in May. The resolution recommends overall federal spending levels and sets financial guidelines. Each substantive committee, whether Agriculture, Education and Labor, or Foreign Affairs, is given an expenditures target that it is supposed to observe as it takes up the bills that come to it.

In September, the House and Senate budget committees report a second resolution that reflects the May commitments along with new judgments on national economic needs. If the spending decisions Congress made during the spring and summer exceed the total provided by the September resolution, budgetary discipline can be imposed through a reconciliation process. Under reconciliation, Congress can direct the standing committees to report bills that either raise revenues or cut spending.[28] In effect, the budget committees have emerged in the role of fiscal watchdogs within Congress. They are an institutional voice for restraint against the continuing demands for new programs and increased spending coming from the substantive committees.

In 1981, the Reagan administration and its congressional allies made heavy use of the reconciliation provisions of the budget act in a novel way, as part of their efforts to get major cuts in government spending approved by Congress. The budget act envisioned reconciliation occurring at the end of the budget process to bring spending into accord with the targets set by the second budget resolution. In 1981 the administration succeeded in getting Congress to employ reconciliation at the beginning of the budget process, to make reductions in existing programs. In May and June, following dramatic battles, budget resolutions were passed that contained reconciliation instructions requiring House and Senate committees to make cuts of some $36 billion.

Marginal notes: Budget committees and the CBO · Budget reconciliation · Presidential use of reconciliation

[28] A detailed account of the new budget process in Congress can be found in Allen Schick, *Congress and Money* (Washington, D.C.: The Urban Institute, 1980). See also James P. Pfiffner, *The President, the Budget, and Congress: Impoundment and the 1974 Budget Act* (Boulder, Colo.: Westview Press, 1979); and Roger H. Davidson and Walter J. Oleszek, *Congress and Its Members* (Washington, D.C.: Congressional Quarterly Press, 1981), chap. 11.

The process provided by the Congressional Budget and Impoundment Control Act of 1974 is now rooted in congressional practice. The new process is hardly a panacea, but few members want to go back to the pre-1974 arrangements. The budget committees and the CBO have won generally high marks, and Congress can now attack the problems of budget-making a bit more coherently.

Legislative Oversight

The 1974 Budget Act is an instance where congressional resurgence is generally applauded. But developments in the area of legislative oversight have met with a decidedly mixed reaction. **Legislative oversight** is an attempt by Congress to supervise the vast executive establishment set up to administer laws it has enacted. Prior to the 1930s, when the national government was small, oversight was a fairly easy matter. Today, government is so large and does so much that effective oversight has become difficult to manage.

During the 1970s, Congress began placing much more emphasis on oversight. It broadened the spending oversight functions of the General Accounting Office (GAO). The GAO made twice as many reports on executive branch activities in 1976–80 as it had in 1966–70. More importantly, Congress extended the number and independence of its subcommittees and greatly expanded their staffs. One result was more time for oversight hearings and related meetings. In addition, Congress began routinely adding onto legislation the requirement that executive agencies notify the appropriate committee(s) before promulgating program changes, so that the committees could call hearings if they chose and bring their influence to bear, perhaps taking steps to reverse the agency actions. Such legislative stipulations typically provide for a waiting period of 30 to 60 days between the time the agency notifies the committee(s) and the time its administrative action is due to take effect.

The right to know. Congress also began asserting a near-absolute right to information as part of its oversight functions. An amendment to the 1974 foreign aid bill required that all covert actions of the Central Intelligence Agency be reported "in a timely fashion" to the "appropriate committees" of Congress. Cabinet members and other agency heads were required to furnish information Congress wanted, under threat of being cited for contempt if they refused.

In December 1982, for example, a contempt citation was issued against Anne M. Burford, then Administrator of the Environmental Protection Agency (EPA), for refusing to turn over documents concerning EPA enforcement of the 1980 "Superfund" hazardous waste cleanup law to the House Public Works Committee and the House Energy and Commerce Oversight Subcommittee, as requested. Acting on instructions from President Reagan and the Justice Department, Burford had claimed executive privilege, alleging that disclosure

<table>
<tr><td>Legislative oversight</td></tr>
<tr><td>EPA and the right to know</td></tr>
</table>

of contents would jeopardize the outcome of EPA lawsuits then in progress.[29] It was only after a year and a half of charges and counter-charges by Congress and the Reagan Administration that contempt charges against Mrs. Burford were dropped.

Presidents and their executive department subordinates have come to feel, not surprisingly, that congressional oversight has expanded beyond reasonable limits. And more neutral observers agree that at times the new congressional demands are burdensome. During one nine-month period, between October 1981 and July 1982, for example, EPA officials were called upon to appear before congressional committees more that 70 times.[30] In one extreme case, early in 1979, Secretary of Energy James Schlesinger had to make twelve appearances before congressional committees in less than two months—most of them briefing sessions where he gave "updated answers" to queries he had previously answered.[31] Other officials of the Energy Department had to appear at almost 100 hearings in just over a month—in part because so many different committees and subcommittes have jurisdiction over various facets of energy policy. Even some people on the legislative side think things went too far. The staff director of one oversight subcommittee of Congress told of "chasing down" the chairman of a regulatory commission while "seven other committees were doing the same thing. . . . He was up there four days a week for six weeks in a row. You can't run an agency and have to do that. . . . I felt we truly were beleaguering an executive . . . to such an extent that he just couldn't get his job done."[32]

> Overuse of congressional oversight?

The Legislative Veto

The *legislative or congressional veto* provision was first employed in a 1932 law. President Herbert Hoover was authorized to reorganize agencies by executive order, but it was further required that each such order be transmitted to Congress, where it could be disapproved by either house within 60 days. This provision turned the usual legislative-executive relationship upside down: The president was allowed to write the equivalent of law, but Congress could subsequently veto (reject) what he had written.

> Congress and the legislative veto

In recent years, Congress has turned increasingly to the legislative veto, because it has found the provision useful in meeting two somewhat contrary objectives: giving the president and executive agencies the authority to act, and keeping Congress very much in the picture, able to overturn executive actions. By 1980, 200 laws containing more than 250 legislative veto provisions were on the books. One-third of all of these were enacted after 1975.

[29] *Congressional Quarterly*, December 18, 1982, p. 3077.
[30] Ibid., July 31, 1982, p. 1827.
[31] P. Smith, "Mandatory Limits Eyed on Thermostat Settings," *Washington Post*, March 13, 1979, p. A5.
[32] Quoted in Sundquist, *Decline and Resurgence*, p. 338.

Some examples:

(1) *War Powers Resolution* (1973). Absent a declaration of war, the president may be directed by concurrent resolution (passed by both houses, but not requiring the president's signature) to remove U.S. armed forces engaged in hostilities abroad.

(2) *Department of Defense Appropriation Authorization Act* (1974). National defense contracts obligating the U.S. for any amount over $25,000,000 may be disapproved by the resolution of either house.

(3) *Naval Petroleum Reserves Act* (1976). The president's extension of the production period for naval oil reserves may be vetoed by resolution of either house.

(4) *Omnibus Budget Reconciliation Act* (1981). Secretary of Education's schedule of expected family contributions for Pell Grant recipients may be rejected by resolution of either house; Secretary of Transportation's plan for the sale of government's common stock in the rail system may be vetoed by concurrent resolution.

Types of legislative vetoes. Congressional veto provisions varied in the ease with which they permitted Congress to overrule agency actions. From the president's standpoint, the least objectionable type of veto was one where both houses had to concur before the executive action was disallowed. But one-house vetoes were more common, where, if either the House or Senate said no, the executive initiative was dead. In some cases, the one-house veto was delegated to one or more committees of one chamber, or to a subcommittee. In 1979, Congress even gave one of its agencies, the Office of Technology Assessment, power to veto the design of research for a study the Veterans' Administration was making—which is getting pretty far into the detail of executive agency actions.

One- or two-house vetoes

It isn't surprising that presidents haven't liked Congress' increasing recourse to the legislative veto, even though they have recognized in many instances that Congress would not have given them authority to act at all unless it retained a ready means of blocking the action. President Jimmy Carter reflected general presidential sentiment when he argued in 1978 that legislative vetoes were "intrusive devices that infringe on the Executive's constitutional duty to faithfully execute the laws."[33] Heavy use of the veto involves Congress in the day-to-day practice of rule-making, something which is properly the domain of executive agencies.

With the argument between president and Congress over the legislative veto unresolved, the U.S. Supreme Court entered the dispute, through its ruling in the case of *Naturalization Service v. Chadha* (1983). This case began back in 1974 when Jagdish Rai Chadha, a Kenyan East Indian who had overstayed his student visa, won a verdict from

[33] Jimmy Carter, "Message to the Congress," June, 1978, in *Public Papers of the Presidents of the United States—Jimmy Carter, 1978* (Washington, D.C.: Office of the Federal Register, National Archives and Records Service, 1979), book 1, p. 1147.

The Court's challenge to legislative veto

the Immigration and Naturalization Service (INS) suspending his deportation. A year later, though, the House of Representatives exercised the one-house veto that had been written into an immigration act, and overturned the INS action. Under the veto, Chadha had to be deported after all, even though INS had decided he could stay in the U.S. Chadha appealed to INS and to the federal courts, in a complicated legal battle. A U.S. Court of Appeals agreed with Chadha's contention that the legislative veto provision of the immigration act was unconstitutional, in violation of separation of powers. The Supreme Court upheld the Appeals Court ruling. Six of the nine Justices felt that Congress had overstepped unconstitutionally into the executive branch's domain and had skirted the requirements of bicameralism. Writing for the majority, Chief Justice Warren Burger concluded: "To accomplish what has been attempted by one House of Congress in this case requires action in conformity with the express procedures of the Constitution's prescription for legislative action: passage by a majority of both Houses and presentment to the President."[34]

Despite the *Chadha* ruling, however, the veto issue is still alive. Congress wrote 17 separate veto provisions into five laws in the first four months after the ruling was handed down. "There is still some degree of uncertainty as to whether certain formulations of legislative vetoes would withstand Supreme Court scrutiny," House counsel concluded. The fate of the legislative veto remains uncertain.

THE TWO CONGRESSES

Congress performs two very different functions: that of *lawmaker* and that of *representative assembly*.[35] As lawmaker it is charged with passing the laws which the United States requires to address its various public problems. As a representative assembly it responds to very different needs. Composed of 535 senators and representatives, each with his own electoral interests, Congress must hear and respond to the claims of diverse constituencies. And the sum total of these claims may not always be consistent with the requirements of sound public policy for the nation.

Two Roles, Two Records

Recognition of these different, sometimes opposing, legislative functions came a long time ago, in the early days of legislatures in Europe. On November 3, 1774, the great British politician and philosopher,

[34] Immigration and Naturalization Service v. Jagdish Rai Chadha et al., *United States Law Week*, June 21, 1983, p. 4918.
[35] Davidson and Oleszek, "Introduction: The Two Congresses," in *Congress and Its Members*, pp. 5–11.

Edmund Burke, described the constituent-oriented British Parliament as "a congress of ambassadors from different and hostile interests, which interests each must maintain, as an agent and advocate, against other agents and advocates." Then Burke set forth the idea of the same Parliament as lawmaker for the nation, "a deliberative assembly of one nation, with one interest, that of the whole—where not local purposes, not local prejudices, ought to guide, but the general good, resulting from the general reason of the whole."[36]

Congress as representative assembly

Any assessment of Congress should not lose sight of its different functions. In the opinion of many observers, Congress is doing very well as a representative assembly—as well as or better than at any point in its history. As a lawmaking institution the same Congress receives criticism and concern from inside its own ranks as well as from without. Its very success in one role contributes to its difficulties in the other.

Resources for Representation

Congress is exceptionally well tooled to function as a representative assembly. The 435 House districts are at last of the same population size. The right to vote in congressional and other elections has been extended to all citizens. The extreme inequalities in the power of individual members in past Congresses has been greatly reduced. Staff resources now available to Congress permit individual members to respond to constituency interests more fully than ever.

Public opinion and Congress

Americans seem to appreciate the successful adaptation of Congress as a representative chamber. Public opinion polls have regularly asked respondents how good a job they think their congressional representatives are doing. Without exception in recent years, congressmen have received high marks. At the same time, however, the public gives low marks to Congress as a policy-making institution. In Harris surveys, for example, only 20 percent of the public say they have a "great deal of confidence" in the leadership provided by Congress.[37] The public thinks the Congress of individual reprsentatives is performing well, while it sees the Congress as a policy institution doing poorly.

Opportunities for Interest Groups

Many of the steps that have added to the representative capacities of Congress have been highly disintegrative to Congress as a whole. Power is fragmented, and coherent national policy-making hard to achieve.

[36] Edmund Burke, "Speech to Electors at Bristol," in *Burke's Politics*, Ross J. S. Hoffman and Paul Levack, eds. (New York: Knopf, 1949), p. 116.
[37] In 1975, for example, 13 percent said they had a great deal of confidence of Congress; in 1978 the proportion was 10 percent; in 1980, 18 percent, and in 1983, 20 percent. Surveys by Louis Harris and Associates, the latest October 5–9, 1983.

Interest groups and
subcommittees

One result has been to strengthen the hand of interest groups. Groups are now able to take their cases directly to individual congressmen, without any party mediation, and establish close working ties with the subcommittee(s) in their areas of interest. Politically active interest groups are a necessary and proper part of a free society. Given the far-flung activities of modern government, it was unavoidable that there would be a proliferation of organized special interests. But in the current era, these special interests have been permitted to operate upon a highly individualistic, fractured Congress—giving them excessive influence.

The problem of the contemporary Congress is not that it is unresponsive. But what Edmund Burke two centuries ago called the "interest . . . of the whole—where not local purposes . . . ought to guide, but the general good . . ." has sometimes been poorly served.

Congressional Reform

Changes needed to correct this problem have been hard to achieve and almost certainly will continue to be so. While the fragmentation of power in Congress is widely deplored, even among many congressmen themselves, it generally serves the electoral and representation needs of individual congressmen. Why should a congressman who has his own subcommittee and a large staff, which can be employed to help his electoral fortunes and to advance legislation which he or his constituents favor, surrender these resources? To function better as a lawmaking body, Congress needs more discipline, a defined hierarchy, and leaders who can bargain with the executive branch and with interest groups, and then commit the Congress to the best overall mix of programmatic responses. But discipline, hierarchy, and leadership are not the best prerequisites for a representative assembly. And they do not coincide with the electoral needs and career expectations of today's legislator.

Congress as lawmaker

Some of the congressional reforms of the last two decades have responded effectively to the demands on Congress as a lawmaker for the nation. Perhaps the most notable achievement is the Budget Act of 1974, which addresses the need for Congress to respond more coherently to national budgeting. But most of the changes Congress embraced over the 1960s and 1970s reflected its needs as a representative assembly and the interests of its individual members. As Congress has changed, the imbalance between its representative and lawmaking functions has become more pronounced.

SUMMARY

Congress differs from other democratic legislatures in two important regards. One involves separation of powers. In the American scheme—though not in the more common parliamentary arrangement—the legislature and the executive are separate institutions. It is possible, and common, for the two to be controlled by different parties. The two branches must work together if American government is to function, but the Constitution makes them co-equal and independent.

Also setting Congress apart is the extent to which power is dispersed within it. Committees and subcommittees are strong, central party leadership weak. Nowhere in the democratic world is the individual legislator so independent—and so powerful.

For a brief time in the late nineteenth and early twentieth centuries, Congress experienced strong party organization and discipline; this was gone by 1915. Over the last two decades, power has been even more widely dispersed among the membership, as the perogatives of the once-dominant committee chairmen have been cut back, the number of subcommittees expanded and their independence buttressed, members' staff increased, and more.

In recent years Congress has experienced a resurgence, in part the product of external events and in part of its own making. The idea that strong presidential leadership is the "great engine of democracy," so widely held from the time of Franklin Roosevelt through the mid-1960s, was shaken by a stream of events, the most important of which were Vietnam and Watergate.

As this shift of assessment occurred, Congress began asserting itself more vigorously. It passed important new legislation dealing with natonal budget-making. It applied its oversight powers so extensively that even some neutral observers thought it sometimes overreached its constitutional boundaries. It took a little-used provision, the legislative veto, and applied it routinely as a convenient means of blocking executive agency actions that it disagreed with—even matters like a ruling of the Immigration and Naturalization Service that suspended the deportation of Jagdish Rai Chadha. The Supreme Court ruled in Chadha's case that Congress was using the legislative veto unconstitutionally to get around the requirements of bicameralism and separation of powers. Despite this ruling, however, the future of the veto remains uncertain. Congress has shown no inclination to abandon it.

Congress functions both as a representative assembly and as a national lawmaker. While each is vitally important, these roles do not necessarily get along very well together. Over the last two decades, a series of reforms have strengthened the legislature's capacity to perform its representative functions. But some of these reforms have also had a disintegrative effect, strengthening the position of the individual representative at the expense of the capacity for central leadership—and the capability of legislating effectively for the naton.

8 | The Presidency

A few days before his assassination in November 1963, President John F. Kennedy penned a personal note to political historian Clinton Rossiter, commenting on Rossiter's book on the presidency. Rossiter had introduced his study with a quotation from Shakespeare's *Macbeth*. The Scottish general, about to seize his country's throne, relates to his "first lady" a dream in which "Methought I heard a voice cry 'Sleep no more!' " Rossiter felt this a fitting commentary on a prime feature of the American presidency: the enormous demands placed on the office.[1]

Kennedy wrote that, while that quotation was apt, he believed there was an even better one in Shakespeare's *King Henry IV, Part 1*. Glendower boasts that "I can call spirits from the vasty deep." Hostpur replies:

> Why, so can I, or so can any man;
> but will they come when you do call for them?

For Kennedy, it was the gap between the calling and the coming, between the large amount a president seeks to accomplish and the little he can accomplish, that best characterizes the position of this democratic chief executive.

In the first part of this chapter, we examine the key structural features of the American presidency. We will see that the limitations on presidential power are indeed impressive. The framers sought to avoid the possibility of presidential dictatorship, and in this worthy aim they have been proved successful. But in the process they created a

---

[1] Clinton Rossiter, *The American Presidency* (New York: New American Library; 2d rev. ed., 1960). The *Macbeth* quotation is from Act II, scene II.

*President John F.
Kennedy.*

presidency that is better able to "call spirits from the vasty deep" of American public policy than to ensure that these spirits will answer and be moved.

In the second section of the chapter we turn to a description of what a modern president does, of the many different roles and responsibilities we have thrust upon his office. The president wears many hats, from party leader to formulator of legislative programs, from commander-in-chief of the armed forces to administrator-in-chief of the executive branch. It is not easy to find someone who can do all of this well. A president cannot be expected to do all of it alone, of course. In the third section we review the institutional presidency, the collection of aides and offices that now comprise the Executive Office of the President. Then we turn to a subject always present in discussions of the American presidency: the nature of presidential power, how it is realized, and how adequate it is when set against what we expect presidents to accomplish. We conclude the chapter with a discussion of what Americans think about the presidency as an office, and how they assess the performance of recent presidents.

WHAT KIND OF A CHIEF EXECUTIVE?

In their constitutional definition of the essential powers and character of the presidency, the framers were breaking new ground. Nowhere in 1787 was there a prototype for the national executive they had in mind. During the nearly two centuries since Article II of the Constitution was drafted, the American presidency has remained a unique office, one where executive authority has been organized and articulated differently from any of America's sister democracies.

A REPUBLICAN EXECUTIVE

The nature of the presidency

We saw in chapters 5 and 6 that the political ideals that guided the Constitution's framers, derived from European political thought of the seventeenth and eighteenth centuries, were called "republican"—emphasizing both popular sovereignty and individual liberty. This meant in part that political institutions would no longer have a class and hereditary base but would instead gain their legitimacy from their reliance on the popular will. The American presidency was set up to be consistent with the enlightened expectations of the times. The president would not resemble a king—not even a limited monarch favored by so many European thinkers of that time. He would be elected for a fixed term of four years, with re-election possible; any native-born citizen (or citizen at the time of the Constitution's adoption) of at least 35 years of age would be eligible to stand for office. These provisions represented a monumental break from the hereditary, aristocratic practice that still prevailed in Europe.

At the same time the framers were fearful of unrestrained democracy and of the possibility that the American chief executive might be too inclined to appeal to popular passions in ways harmful to minority rights. They sought to insulate the office by having the public participate in presidential selection only indirectly. Their chosen mechanism was the ***electoral college.*** As it turned out, the framers made two mistakes, one mechanical, the other philosophical—and both had to be corrected before the presidency as we know it emerged.

The electoral college

Article II provided that each state should appoint, "in such Manner as the Legislature thereof may direct, a Number of Electors, equal to the whole number of Senators and Representatives to which the state may be entitled in the Congress. . . ." These electors would meet in their respective states on a day designated by Congress and cast their votes for president. Any eligible person receiving an absolute majority of the votes cast would be declared president. If no one received a majority, the House of Representatives—with each state delegation having a single vote—would select the president from among the five contenders with the highest number of electoral votes.

A Mechanical Failure

Almost immediately, the electoral college arrangement malfunctioned. The procedures did not distinguish between electoral votes cast for president and those cast for vice president. In the election of 1800, Thomas Jefferson of Virginia, the presidential choice of the new Democratic-Republican party, and Aaron Burr of New York, Jefferson's vice presidential running mate, each received the same number (73) of electoral votes. Everyone knew that Burr's 73 votes were for vice president, but they were not so designated. Something of a constitutional crisis resulted. The election was thrown into the House of Representatives, with an inevitable invitation for political chicanery given to the anti-Jefferson opposition. And the overly ambitious Burr sought to take advantage of this unforeseen opportunity to engineer his own election as president.

The electoral college crisis

Jefferson did prevail, but it was evident there was a defect needing immediate remedy. The 12th Amendment was proposed by Congress on December 9, 1803, and was declared ratified on September 25, 1804, when the legislatures of 13 of the 17 states (the required 75 percent) had approved it. The amendment provided that the electors would cast separate and distinct ballots for president and vice president.

A Philosophical Failure

The framers had an incomplete appreciation of the powerful democratic forces stirring in the new nation. As a key public office, the presidency had to reflect the democratic temper of American society. And it was in fact quickly democratized, without changing a word in the Constitution, through the agency of the developing party system. There were two steps through which the emerging political parties took over the electoral college procedures and converted them into a means for ratifying popular preferences for president. The first came as early as 1796, as selection of presidential electors in the state legislatures became a party contest between the Federalists and the Democratic-Republicans. The people voted one party or the other into majority status in the respective state assemblies, and these legislative majorities then picked electors pledged to vote for their parties' presidential nominees.

Party contest for electors

The second step was taken about three decades later, and involved picking presidential electors not by state legislatures but through direct popular balloting. More and more states made this changeover in the 1820s and 1830s. The election of 1824—finally decided in the House of Representatives in favor of John Quincy Adams—saw the beginnings of popular presidential electoral contests in 18 of the 24 states. Still, only 360,000 popular votes were cast nationally, and in so pivotal a state as New York the issue was wholly decided within the legislature. Four years later the popular vote jumped to 1,150,000, in a country where the voting-age male population was about 2,400,000. And by 1832, when Democrat Andrew Jackson won reelection over Henry Clay, candidate of the opposition National Republicans, presidential elections had been virtually transformed into the contest we know today: Eligible voters in each state went to the polls on election day and cast ballots for their choice for president by picking a slate of electors publicly pledged to him.

Popular balloting for electors

This democratization of the presidency strengthened the office. James Sterling Young has observed that

> nomination and election by popular acclaim [gave] the presidency the stature of popular spokesmanship and an independent electoral strength which was convertible, on occasion, to bargaining advantages over Congress. . . . In a nation pervasively mistrustful of government, democracy, and democracy alone, [converted] a figure of authority into a personage of national influence.[2]

AN INDEPENDENT EXECUTIVE

Powers of the president

The framers, influenced by their classical liberal preference for dispersed power, provided for an executive branch separate from the legislature and independent of it for its tenure in office. To ensure its independence, the executive had to have powers conferred directly by the Constitution, not by another branch of government. Section 2 of Article II made the president commander-in-chief of the armed forces, established his power to make treaties and to appoint ambassadors, federal court judges, and "all other Officers of the United States." Other constitutional provisions gave the president an explicit legislative role through the veto power (Article I, section 7), and conferred upon him sweeping administrative responsibilities in that "he shall take Care that the Laws be faithfully executed" (Article II, section 3).

A CHECKED AND BALANCED EXECUTIVE

But if the president was to be constitutionally independent of the other branches, especially the legislature, he was to be subject to restraints by them lest he get too strong. Every basic constitutional grant of authority to the president is constitutionally limited. The president is commander-in-chief of the armed forces, but it is within Congress' power to declare war and "to raise and support Armies." He has broad appointive powers, but his appointments require "the Advice and Consent" of the Senate. He has the power, in the conduct of foreign affairs, to make treaties, but the Senate's consent is required before the treaties come into force. The president stands at the helm of the ship of state and supervises the execution of all the laws of the United States—a formidable grant of authority, made even more formidable in the modern era by vast increases in the scope of legislation—but Congress determines what these laws shall provide, and may repeal them at any time.

[2] James Sterling Young, *The Washington Community, 1800–1828* (New York: Harcourt, Brace, 1966), p. 253.

Ambivalence and Power

Separation of powers

The presidency is a highly visible example of American ambivalence about political authority. Compared to other democratic heads of government, the U.S. president has on one hand a uniquely expansive grant of political power. He holds nothing less than the executive power of the United States, conferred directly by the people through popular elections rather than indirectly, as in parliamentary systems, through the partisan balance prevailing in the national legislature. On the other hand, the president's constitutional powers must be shared with the legislative and judicial branches, which are formally independent of him. Congress may defer to him for a time, especially if he is seen to be skillful and vigorous and enjoying strong public support. Never in U.S. history, however, has there been any prolonged period when the system of checks and balances did not operate with the full force of the original constitutional intent—to rein in assertive presidents. Even so capable a president as Franklin D. Roosevelt—with his popularity at its height following his 1936 landslide victory over Alfred Landon—encountered strong resistance from a Congress that his own party dominated.

FDR and Court-Packing

FDR was reelected for a second term in November 1936 by one of the largest margins in American history: He trounced his Republican opponent, Governor Alfred Landon of Kansas, by almost two to one (63.5 percent to 36.5 percent) in the major party vote. FDR's Democratic party won overwhelming majorities in Congress, leading the Republicans 331 seats to 89 in the House of Representatives and 76 to 16 in the Senate. The New Deal received widespread acclaim as a successful new approach to national problems. It is not surprising, then, that Roosevelt—frustrated by the Supreme Court's actions in declaring unconstitutional such primary legislation of his administration's first years as the National Industrial Recovery Act, the Agricultural Adjustment Act, the Railroad Retirement Act, and legislation establishing the Tennessee Valley Authority—decided in early 1937 that he had an unequivocal mandate to end the Court's "obstructionism."

The court-packing plan

Just after the congressional session began in 1937, Roosevelt asked Congress to approve a reorganization act for the Court that would add a new justice whenever one of the sitting justices reached the age of seventy and did not retire. No one doubted that FDR's objective was not to increase efficiency but to obtain new seats on the Court that could be filled with pro-New Deal justices. The celebrated **court-packing** plan was launched. The plan failed spectacularly. Roosevelt's bill was voted down by a Senate controlled by the Democrats

There was a lot of editorial comment on FDR's courtpacking plan of 1936.

by nearly 5 to 1. Reviewing the president's humiliating defeat, Rexford Guy Tugwell, a Roosevelt assistant, noted that "the Congress had been annoyed during the last several years by the taunt that it was merely a 'rubber stamp' for the president. . . . There was a disposition to show Franklin that the Congress was still an independent body in spite of the president's popularity."[3]

FDR ultimately lost the court-packing battle because the populace—including those segments most supportive of him—was firmly committed to the independence of the three branches with their constitutionally sanctioned capacity to check one another. Though it disagreed with the Court on issues involving the New Deal, the public was unwilling to endorse the president's attempt to short-circuit checks and balances. Only 33 percent of those polled in late February and early March 1937 wanted Congress to pass Roosevelt's plan to reorganize the Supreme Court.

Checks and Balances in Action

How well has the constitutional system of checks and balances held up in recent years? Some observers expected it to be rendered somewhat obsolete by sweeping economic and technological change. Consider the impact of new technology on decision-making in foreign affairs. The Constitution states that the declaration of war falls to Congress. In the early nineteenth century the mobility of armed forces was limited to the speed a ship could sail or a horse could run. Weap-

Changing technological constraints

[3] Rexford Guy Tugwell, *FDR: Architect of an Era* (New York: Macmillan, 1967), p. 168.

onry was no more advanced than gunpowder. So the constitutional check on presidential direction of the armed forces seemed reasonable and worked much as the framers intended. Difficulties with England involving the freedom of American shipping led Congress to begin debating in 1810 whether to declare war. This debate went on for more than two years before Congress finally declared war on England in June 1812. By the middle of the twentieth century, though, communication, transportation, and weapons technology had drastically accelerated the timetable of war. Vast permanent military establishments had acquired the capacity to wreak massive destruction in a matter of hours. Now the president's command position as head of the armed forces—when he could claim to act on behalf of vital national interests—had become dominant.

War Powers Resolution

1973 War Powers Resolution

Just when the president's power seemed greatest, Congress reasserted its checks. While congressional resurgence in the late 1960s and 1970s was evident in all areas, it was especially strong in foreign affairs. In 1973 Congress, traumatized by the long, costly, and deeply divisive war in Vietnam, passed the **War Powers Resolution** to reassert legislative limits over executive action in military intervention. The resolution provides that the president can commit American armed forces only when one of three conditions prevails: 1) following a formal declaration of war by Congress; 2) when Congress has given some specific statutory authorization; or 3) in the case of an attack on the country or its military units, or otherwise in the face of a threat to the lives of American citizens. This measure became law over the veto of President Richard Nixon, who argued in his veto message that

American soldiers in Vietnam.

the resolution "seriously undermines this nation's ability to act decisively and convincingly in times of international crisis." Presidents Ford, Carter, and Reagan have also attacked the resolution as an infringement on the executive's constitutional powers as commander-in-chief.

More neutral assessments have found that Congress' action seems to be an attempt not to curb the president's constitutional role, but rather to assert the constitutional role of Congress in the context of modern conditions. The War Powers Resolution acknowledges the need for broad and independent presidential initiative in the use of American military force. It recognizes the obvious imperatives of present-day technology—that if the United States is attacked, the president must immediately commit the country to the extent he concludes is required by circumstances, even if this means outright war. But when the president must act quickly in the absence of specific congressional authorization, he immediately reports to Congress the reasons for his actions and secures legislative approval for their continuation over any prolonged period.

Congressional check on the presidency

Impeachment

In another area, congressional resurgence has extended even to invoking the most extreme of all legislative checks on the chief executive: removing him from office. We have seen that the framers wanted the president to be independent of Congress for his election and tenure in office. But they envisioned the need, in an extreme case, for removing an executive who grossly violated his oath. They provided in section 4 of Article II that the president (and other "civil Officers of the United States") shall be dismissed if impeached and then convicted of "Treason, Bribery, and other High Crimes and Misdemeanors." Such removal has not been undertaken lightly. Impeachment proceedings have been advanced in Congress against only two presidents: Andrew Johnson in 1868, and Richard Nixon in 1974. The **impeachment** process has two stages. The House of Representatives formally brings charges—which is what impeachment means. If it votes to impeach, the president (or other officer) is then tried by the Senate. "When the President of the United States is tried," Article I, section 3 stipulates, "the Chief Justice [of the U.S. Supreme Court] shall preside: And no person shall be convicted without the concurrence of two thirds of the Members present."

Impeachment

The impeachment of Andrew Johnson. Only one president has ever been formally impeached by the House and tried by the Senate. Andrew Johnson of Tennessee succeeded Abraham Lincoln as president in 1865, upon the latter's assassination, and almost immediately got into deep political trouble. Johnson had been put on the ticket in 1864 as part of the effort to reach out in reconciliation to the South; Johnson was

The impeachment of Andrew Johnson

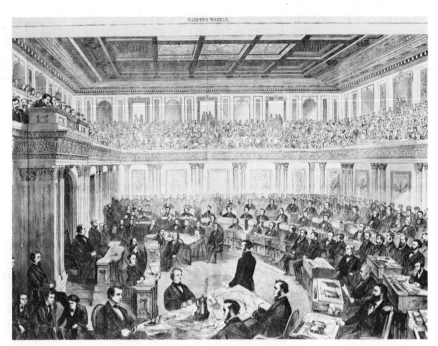

HARPER'S WEEKLY.

The impeachment trial of President Andrew Johnson.

a southerner who opposed secession. But he was not a Republican—instead, he was a (pro-) "War Democrat"—so he began his presidency on the wrong foot with the highly partisan Republican majority in Congress. Passions were very high following the long and costly Civil War. Any president, even Lincoln, would have been hard-pressed to control these passions as he charted policies for postwar Reconstruction. Johnson lacked the necessary skills, and his rupture with congressional Republicans deepened. Most historians do not believe that Johnson was in fact guilty of "high crimes and misdemeanors"—bad policy choices and inept political management would seem the harshest charges that could be sustained—but he was impeached by the House on February 24, 1868. The vote was unanimous.

With Chief Justice Salmon P. Chase presiding, Johnson's Senate trial opened in March 1868. After about two months of often bitter argument, votes were taken on May 16 and 26. A majority voted to convict, but not the two-thirds majority required by the Constitution. By the narrowest of margins (35 for conviction, 19 against) Andrew Johnson was left in office to serve out the remainder of his term.

Richard Nixon and Watergate. Richard Nixon, the only other president subjected to impeachment proceedings, was never actually impeached—and hence never tried in the Senate. But he is the only president forced from office by these constitutional provisions. Richard Nixon resigned as president on August 9, 1974, when it was clear that he had lost the public backing needed to govern, and that the House would impeach him if he did not resign. Few Americans—and

Richard Nixon's resignation

Richard Nixon waves farewell to his staff after resigning the office of president.

Nixon and Watergate

neither the president's friends nor his congressional opponents—wanted the agony of a Senate trial.

The events leading to Nixon's resignation are now referred to by the single word "Watergate." But the scandal that forced him from office grew from a complex of developments.[4] The actual Watergate incident was the June 17, 1972, break-in at the offices of the Democratic National Committee (DNC), located in a Washington commercial and residential complex known as the Watergate. Notwithstanding denial by the president himself, the burglary—undertaken for the purpose of political espionage—was subsequently linked to Nixon's campaign organization, the Committee to Re-elect the President, and to White House aides. Although the incident did not materially affect the outcome of the 1972 elections (Nixon won by a 23 percent margin), the subsequent disclosures of a conspiracy to cover up the crime implicated the president and many of his staff and campaign officials. Through the efforts of federal district court judge John J. Sirica, who presided over the initial trial of the men who broke into the DNC offices, congressional investigators, enterprising journalists, and others, the president's complicity in the Watergate cover-up was brought out with increasing clarity over 1973 and early 1974. The final blow was the discovery of tape recordings, made on Nixon's initiative, of

[4]*Congressional Quarterly*'s two-volume account *Watergate: Chronology of a Crisis* (Washington, D.C.: Congressional Quarterly, 1973) is especially helpful because it brings together all of the basic events, testimony, etc.

conversations in his office that showed his certain knowledge of the cover-up efforts. This revelation of presidential lying and obstruction led to a storm of public protest that culminated in Nixon's resignation on August 9.

Watergate was more than a break-in and cover-up. It was a product of the intense passions and protests of the Vietnam War period, and the feeling among administration officials that they were under siege politically. It reflected, too, a decade of presidential aggrandizement, where the traditional sense of presidential restraint was violated by increasingly assertive—one might say arrogant—behavior. The framers had decided against any ceremonial titles for the president; the occupant would simply be addressed as "Mr. President." But in the 1960s and early 1970s that sense of democratic proportion had been lost. Painful though the process was, Watergate and congressional resurgence helped bring it back.

End of an era of presidential aggrandizement

A VIGOROUS ONE-PERSON EXECUTIVE

Models of a strong executive

Popular feeling in the 1780s and 1790s that the presidency must not in any way resemble the British monarchy was strong and emotional, After all, a war had been fought and won to free the colonies from the absolute tyranny of a king. For most Americans, King George III was the model of a strong executive—and this model was not a comforting one when the new Constitution proposed to build up the executive power. The framers were acutely sensitive to this climate and did not want to advance anything that resembled monarchy.

George Washington's vision of the presidency

But the framers were convinced that the country needed more vigorous executive leadership than it had under the Articles of Confederation. The resolution of this tension in favor of a powerful but checked executive was a tribute to George Washington, who was almost universally expected to be the first occupant of the office. Washington favored a strong executive and worked hard to gain approval for it. The deep respect most Americans had for his character proved decisively important. Pierce Butler of South Carolina, a Convention delegate who was among those most skeptical about the wisdom of a strong executive, later argued that the president's authority would not have been drawn so expansively "had not many of the members cast their eyes toward General Washington as president; and shaped their ideas of the Powers to be given a president *by their opinions of his virtue.*"[5] Washington passionately rejected casting the president as a kind of monarch, and the delegates as well as their countrymen trusted him.

There was good reason for this trust. Washington's aversion to monarchy and his deep commitment to republican institutions was

---

[5] Farrand, ed., *Records of the Federal Convention of 1787*, 3:302. Emphasis added.

eloquently expressed in a passage from a letter he wrote on August 1, 1786, to John Jay of New York:

> What astounding changes a few years are capable of producing. I am told that even respectable characters speak of a monarchical form of government without horror. From thinking proceeds speaking; thence to acting is often but a single step. But how irrevocable and tremendous! What a triumph for the advocates of despotism to find that we are incapable of governing ourselves, and that systems founded on the basis of equal liberty are merely ideal and fallacious! Would to God that wise measures be taken in time to avert the consequences we have but too much reason to apprehend.[6]

There was a second critical factor that swung the Convention behind a strong presidency: the delegates' commitment to the liberal ideal of checked and balanced power. For the same reason that the Convention initially insisted that the legislature have powers to rein in the executive and the judiciary, it came to agree with the "presidentialists" who argued that the executive must have enough authority to check the legislature. James Madison of Virginia, the delegate who most reflected the Convention's mainstream, moved over the course of the debates in Philadelphia to back a strong president as a barrier to congressional autocracy.[7]

Presidential check on Congress

DUTIES OF THE PRESIDENT

Presidents and their aides sometimes unburden themselves on how demanding the job of president really is. (This always seems a bit curious, since they have worked so hard to get the chance to assume the burden.) Indeed, the responsibilities of a modern president are so numerous and diverse that it has become virtually certain that no occupant of the office will ever perform all of them well. Box 8.1 shows some of the principal dimensions of the president's job as it has evolved over two centuries of American political experience.

Responsibilities

All the president's roles continue to be very real and very demanding. As the only government official elected from a national constituency, the president commands media attention in articulating broad public wants and needs. Since the New Deal, Americans have believed that the president plays the largest part in the national government's prime responsibility to intervene in the economy to restore, maintain, or extend economic well-being. The president not only serves as

Chief of state

[6] Jared Sparks, ed., *The Writings of George Washington, Being His Correspondence, Addresses, Messages, and Other Papers, Official and Private* 9 (Boston: Hillard, Odiorne, and Metcalf and Hillard Gray, 1835), pp. 187–89.
[7] Ibid., 3:35.

> ### Box 8.1
> #### *Presidential Responsibilities*
>
> *Chief of State:* The president is the ceremonial head of the American government.
>
> *Chief Executive:* To the president falls the Constitutional charge to "take care that the laws be faithfully executed."
>
> *Commander in Chief:* He controls and directs the American armed forces.
>
> *Chief Diplomat:* He has prime responsibility for the conduct of U.S. foreign policy.
>
> *Chief Legislator:* The president is expected to play a large role "guiding Congress in much of its law-making activity."
>
> *Chief of Party:* He has a partisan role as the leader of his political party.
>
> *Voice of the People:* He is "the leading formulator and expounder of public opinion in the United States."
>
> *Protector of Peace:* In the face of challenges, domestic as much as foreign, the president is expected to promote national security and tranquillity.
>
> *Manager of Prosperity:* The president is now expected "to foster and promote free competitive enterprise, to avoid economic fluctuations . . . and to maintain employment, production, and purchasing power," in the words of the Employment Act of 1946.
>
> *World Leader:* More than just chief diplomat of the U.S., he has broad responsibilities for the Western alliance and for international affairs globally.
>
> *Source:* Rossiter, *American Presidency*, pp. 16–40, *passim.*

the head of government, but also as chief of state: the ceremonial head of the nation. (While prime ministers are the head of government in parliamentary democracies, officials who do not bear significant governmental responsibilities, such as the British monarch, are chief of state.)

Commander-in-chief The president is head of the U.S. military establishment—a force currently consisting of 2.4 million men and women and a vast array of advanced weapons. Given the economic, technological, and military strength of the United States, the president's utterances and actions in foreign policy impact greatly on the world community. The president is responsible for the security of the country. When a serious crisis threatens American lives and interests—whether the disabling aftermath of a hurricane on the Gulf Coast or the prospect of war in the Middle East—he is expected to take calming or restorative action. Rather than sitting back in the Oval Office waiting for Congress to act, the president must formulate a comprehensive set of programs, present them to the Congress, and lobby actively for their

*Presidential authoriza-
tion is needed for the
launch of American
bombers and missiles
in the event of a
national emergency; a
military attaché always
carries the black brief-
case containing the
necessary codes for
detonation.*

enactment. In many of his leadership roles he is expected to tran-
scend narrow partisanship. Yet both his allies and his opponents expect
him to uphold the philosophy and electoral interests of the political
party on whose platform he was elected. (A platform is an agenda of
the party's goals and programs as adopted every four years by the
national nominating conventions of each party.)

Public Relations

Just as the president has an extraordinary array of responsibilities,
so he needs an extraordinary array of skills. First and foremost, he
External political skills   must have the **external political skills** required to win the nomination of a major political party and ultimately a national election.

Campaigner. The candidate must be able to move among his fellow
citizens and convince them to support him over other able and ambitious politicians. He must be able to speak effectively to small groups
of businessmen to whom he turns for campaign contributions, to public
rallies in city squares, and to national audiences linked by the crucial
medium of television. He must have the stamina and the will to criss-
cross the country in the extended campaigns that have come to distinguish American presidential politics. The formal campaign in 1984
began with the Iowa caucuses on February 20 and continued through
the general election of November 6. The campaigns of out-of-power
contenders, like Democrats Walter Mondale, Gary Hart, and Jesse

*President Reagan—
"The Great
Communicator."*

Jackson, began at least a year earlier.[8] And what seemingly trivial campaign failures may be sufficient to do in a serious contender! Democratic Senator Edmund Muskie was the favorite for his party's presidential nomination in 1972 until he reacted emotionally, on camera, to a personal attack while campaigning for the New Hampshire primary. Muskie's campaign never recovered from what many considered a sign of weakness: "crying in the snow at Manchester." He was soon out of the race as a presidential candidate.

Communicator. Presidents need highly developed external political skills once in office as much as they did when campaigning. To maintain his popular standing and advance his programs, a president uses appearances at conventions of various interest groups, press conferences, and televised speeches. Friend and foe alike have dubbed President Ronald Reagan the "Great Communicator" for his highly developed skills in using the medium of television.

[8] What is being described here is the campaign activity required by the regular processes of presidential selection. One recent president did achieve his office without ever having entered himself in a presidential campaign. Gerald Ford was nominated for vice president by Richard Nixon on October 12, 1974, following the resignation of Spiro Agnew, and he was duly confirmed by both houses of Congress as provided for in the 25th Amendment. When Nixon resigned on August 9, 1974, Ford assumed the presidency in the regular constitutional succession. It was not until 1976, when he successfully sought the Republican nomination for another term and ran unsuccessfully against Democrat Jimmy Carter, that Ford was at last himself a principal in a presidential contest.

Working with Other Politicians

Internal political skills

Internal political skills are no less vital to presidential success. The president is the most important—though only one—member of the political leadership community in the United States. On a daily basis, he must interact with fellow leaders—senators, governors, heads of labor unions and major business corporations—to try to persuade them to follow his lead. Political scientist Richard Neustadt has noted that any president's success in advancing his programs and interests depends in large measure upon "the residual impressions of tenacity and skill" that he conveys to the leadership community. Even a president whose popular standing is high will have trouble leading effectively if his professional reputation is low.[9]

Dwight Eisenhower, fresh from his decisive victory in 1956, backslid and equivocated, convincing a large proportion of political Washington that he lacked the skill and determination to set a coherent course for either his party or the country in domestic affairs. "Ike's" general popularity was high but his professional reputation was low. Two years later, Neustadt argues, the situation was reversed. The Democrats had scored big gains in the recession-dominated congressional elections of 1958, and Eisenhower's popularity with the public had dropped. But through skillful and determined action on behalf of his programs, the president in 1959 greatly improved his professional reputation.

The internal political skills required to impress the political community are sometimes quite different from the external skills needed to move the public at large. Strength, determination, steadfastness, the capacity to fight hard for one's policies without personalizing the disagreements, and the sense of when and how to compromise to achieve the largest possible portion of one's program objectives are especially valued by politicians. They are critical to a president.

Administrative Skills

The president is a politician, but he is also an executive—and his leadership is likely to suffer seriously if he does not possess a high measure of administrative skill. The executive branch is a huge enterprise: 2.8 million civilian employees were involved in the expenditure of more than $854 billion in fiscal year 1984 (October 1983–September 1984). The president need have, and can have, little to do with the day-to-day running of the branch, but he is ultimately accountable for overseeing and guiding a business so large that it dwarfs corporate giants like Exxon, IBM, and General Motors. (The

[9] Richard E. Neustadt, *Presidential Power* (New York: Wiley, 1980), pp. 47–48.

Box 8.2
One political scientist's tongue-in-cheek "job advertisement" for a modern-day president

Wanted—Chief Executive for Large, Troubled Public Enterprise

Must be dignified and capable of personifying the aspirations of all elements in a diverse and extremely heterogeneous organization. Must be a successful manager, capable of supervising several million employees, most of whom cannot be directly rewarded or punished. All employees except personal staff will also work for a rival employer. Must be skilled in diplomacy and have good knowledge of world affairs. Should be up on military matters as well. Must be capable of program development for entire enterprise. Job performance will be reviewed after four years, at which time applicant's record will be compared with the promises of numerous aspirants for his position. Applicant must be skilled in economics. A premium will be placed on ability to deal with complex fiscal, monetary, and regulatory matters. Should be good at maintaining alliances with other large public enterprises who do not always share common purposes. Applicant must have power drive but pleasant personality, a good sense of humor, and must be flexible and open to criticism. Must be trustworthy but shrewd. Must be a good speaker and skilled at press relations. Boundless energy is a must. . . . There is no certain deadline [for applicant], but early application is helpful, since the board will have to be convinced that the above qualifications are met.

Source: W. Wayne Shannon, "As If Politics Were About Government: Presidential Selection from a Governance Perspective," paper presented to the New England Political Science Association, March 1980.

sizes of various government departments are compared with those of the largest private U.S. businesses in the next chapter, Figure 9.1.)

President as manager

Managing complex organizations has long been thought to involve special abilities and training. Schools of business administration each year turn out thousands of graduates with advanced training in corporate management. Yet little thought seems to be given to the skills needed to manage the most challenging of all executive positions, the American presidency. It is almost as if we are confident that the necessary skills will automatically materialize. Of course the president has no shortage of experts ready to advise him on the proper organization and operation of the executive branch. And his personal staff—the White House Office—includes hundreds of managers. But it is misleading to insist that a president does not need to be a skilled manager because he can hire outstanding managerial talent. Even choosing compatible, responsible, and able subordinates demands exceptional administrative skill.

Policy Skills

Policy judgment

In our chief executive we expect a composite leader: the president as CEO and the president as politician. Yet even this demanding mix is of no value without the crucial skill: **policy judgment.** The president must not only do "it" well but must determine what "it" is that needs to be done. He establishes the policies for which his political and managerial talents are employed, and is the final judge on policy direction. He does not need to be expert in every program area—he has a large staff to assist in his administration's programs—but he must choose wisely in the substance and politics of policy if his administration is to succeed.

FDR's success at policy-making

We remember Franklin D. Roosevelt as a great president in large part because his New Deal policies were an effective response to national needs in the 1930s. Although, of course, some of the individual programs were flawed, the overall policy direction that FDR imposed looks good through the eyes of history. This is what we hope for in the policy approach of every president—that when the immediate emotions, partisan and otherwise, are past, his approach will have addressed ably the country's most pressing needs.

Leadership: The Whole Is Greater than the Sum of Its Parts

In geometry the whole is always precisely equal to the sum of its parts; in social experience it is usually more or less. At its best, presidential leadership moves the nation as far as possible in the directions the public favors, by means that are acceptable given prevailing values and institutional requirements. While the product of a successful synthesis is easily perceived, how to achieve it through individual leadership skills is not readily understood or achieved.

Washington and presidential leadership

The record of the country's first president, George Washington, attests to the complex character of the leadership synthesis. Washington was not an outstanding public orator. Neither was he at ease in bargaining and compromising with his fellow politicians. He displayed no special administrative skills. By conventional standards he was not a brilliant man—although he was intelligent—and he possessed no unusual sophistication in addressing the policy issues of his day. Yet Washington was widely acclaimed by his contemporaries, and by later generations, as a great political leader.

One reason for Washington's success was simply that he was in the right place at the right time. He was a respected and experienced military man from Virginia, still young enough to lead at the time (1775) that the second Continental Congress was looking for a southern commander-in-chief to give national balance to its largely New England army. At the end of the war with Great Britain, Washington, the victorious general, was considered a national hero. This strengthened his reputation as president. He was a man of personal force,

Charles Wilson Peale's portrait of George Washington.

magnetism, and unquestioned integrity. But, above all, Washington's political judgment on the big questions of his day proved right. He saw the necessity of giving the squabbling states a coherent national government, and he worked consistently for the nation against powerful state and regional pressures. He believed that national unity was the prime need of his time, and he devoted his presidency to its realization. Washington appreciated the importance of establishing the legitimacy of the infant republic's political institutions and he repeatedly acted in ways of great practical importance to the building of this legitimacy—as in his decision to withdraw from the presidency in 1796 while he was still in good health, letting the process of orderly democratic succession work.[10]

Overall, George Washington practiced politics with energy and intelligence for the lofty ends of national unity and democratic legitimacy. The mix of personality, reputation, formal leadership skills, and transcendent good judgment that enabled him to succeed (historian James Thomas Flexner described him as "the indispensable man" in early American nation-building) is not easily captured by presidential job descriptions or analyses.

[10] See Seymour Martin Lipset's insightful account of "Washington's role [in] the institutionalization of legal-rational authority in the early United States," *The First New Nation* (Garden City, N.Y.: Anchor Doubleday, 1967), p. 25. For a more general discussion of Washington's role in the political life of late eighteenth-century America, see James Thomas Flexner, *Washington: The Indispensable Man* (Boston: Little, Brown, 1969).

THE INSTITUTIONAL PRESIDENCY

"The president needs help." This was the conclusion of the Committee on Administrative Management, appointed by President Franklin Roosevelt in 1936. The scope of presidential responsibility had become such, the committee felt, that it was necessary to enlarge and formalize the president's staff support. Acting on the committee's recommendations, Roosevelt in 1939 established the Executive Office of the President (EOP). The key units in the EOP were the White House Office, comprising the president's immediate staff, and the Bureau of the Budget (now the Office of Management and Budget—OMB), the executive's agency for budget-making and review created by Congress in 1921.

An elaborate staff structure

This was the beginning of the **institutional presidency**, built around an elaborate staff structure. The total of White House assistants to President Herbert Hoover had been just 26 in 1930, and annual expenditures for this staff were under $1 million. Even figuring in other executive branch help, such as the Bureau of the Budget, Hoover's assistants numbered under 100. Of course, it wasn't until 1857 that public funds were appropriated by Congress at all to pay even the salary of a private secretary to the president. The size of Herbert Hoover's staff still seems extremely modest against the backdrop of the vast increases of the past half-century. EOP personnel in the years immediately after FDR's 1939 executive order totaled roughly 300; by the time of Dwight Eisenhower's presidency in the 1950s it had climbed to 600. In 1970, with Richard Nixon in the White House, EOP personnel had increased to some 2,000, when a leveling-out and then a modest reduction finally occurred. In Ronald Reagan's administration, the EOP has had 1,600 to 1,700 employees.

The White House Office

It is as true today as it was in 1937 that the president needs help. It is not at all clear, however, just how that help is best provided or what changes would be most useful. In the 1930s, more help meant more people. But the corps of advisers and assistants has become so large that more people are no longer the answer to how to provide the president with the help he needs.

In fact, many experts believe that the White House staff should be further reduced. This was the first recommendation of a panel of the National Academy of Public Administration, established in 1978 to assess the organization of the institutional presidency. The staff should be structured, the panel argued, to serve the immediate and personal needs of the president, not to duplicate the expertise of the cabinet departments.[11] (Cabinet departments will be discussed in more detail in chapter 9.)

Organizing the White House staff. How well any group of staff members actually serve their executive is determined, of course, by the intelligence, experience, personality characteristics, and energy they bring to their jobs. But when staff size increases beyond a handful, organization comes into play. How his White House Office is organized to perform the tasks placed upon it helps determine the success any president enjoys.

Organizational styles

Some presidents want to interact regularly with many different aides. They resist rigid hierarchy in their staff. Stephen Hess refers to this style of staff organization as "circular."[12] As practiced by Franklin Roosevelt, Lyndon Johnson, and Jimmy Carter, the circular mode has a number of senior assistants reporting directly to the president. Other presidents, such as Dwight Eisenhower and Richard Nixon, have been comfortable with a more hierarchical arrangement that places larger coordinating and integrating responsibilities upon a chief of staff. H. R. Haldeman, Nixon's chief of staff until the Watergate scandal forced his resignation, was often criticized for using an authoritarian approach in running the White House and barring the door to the president. But two senior Nixon aides, speechwriter (now *New York Times* columnist) William Safire and National Security Adviser (later Secretary of State) Henry Kissinger, have reported that Haldeman was only performing ably the role Nixon set for him. The president wanted time for solitary contemplation and he wanted to be shielded from staff intrusions.[13]

Reagan's staff

Ronald Reagan's staff arrangements don't neatly fit either the circular or hierarchical models, but they have been closer to the former. In Reagan's first term, Chief of Staff James Baker had great influence, but a few other senior staff—especially long-time California associates Edwin Meese and Michael Deaver—played important roles and had direct access to the president. Reagan wanted some clear hierarchy, yet he wanted to avoid designation of one clearly ascendant staff chief.

Demands on staff. There can be no one right way to arrange the White House staff, because each staff must meet a president's individual style of work. There are, however, some enduring demands on staff

[11] *A Presidency for the 1980s,* a report by a Panel of the National Academy of Public Administration (Washington, D.C.: National Academy of Public Administration, 1980), p. 17.
[12] Stephen Hess, *Organizing the Presidency* (Washington, D.C.: Brookings Institute, 1976), p. 3.
[13] William Safire, *Before the Fall* (Garden City, N.Y.: Doubleday, 1975); and Henry Kissinger, *The White House Years* (Boston: Little, Brown, 1979).

organization. Because presidential time is a scarce commodity, staff arrangements must be such that items needing the president's attention get it—in the best form for his action—while other items are carefully kept away. Staff must permit the president to work most efficiently, leave him accessible to officials who need to see him (and whom he needs to see) but not let him be overwhelmed by intrusions, bring him the questions he *must* decide (but not every question he *could* decide). Then, when the president has chosen a course, an effective staff helps him sail it with as little expenditure of his time as possible.

Naturally, all this is easier said than done. For, while staff are supposed to serve the president's interests, they inevitably also have and serve their own. Every presidency suffers because key White House aides become absorbed in individual pursuits of power and recognition. "No conceivable staffing arrangements will meet all his needs," wrote presidential scholar Hugh Heclo, "and yet every arrangement carries the potential of submerging his interests into those of his helpers and their machinery."[14] The rarefied atmosphere of the White House poses problems for the proper functioning and, in a sense, mental health of the staff who dwell therein. The West Wing of the White House—where the Oval Office and facilities for senior presidential aides are located—is the physical center of the American political universe. Even an occasional visitor to the West Wing cannot fail to detect the air of restrained excitement. It is easy for staff to let this go to their heads, or to succumb to the pressure-cooker atmosphere.

Power, especially the ultimate singularity of power, gives the White House its distinctive atmosphere and style. In Congress, formal constitutional authority always rests in many hands; in the White House, it rests in one pair of hands. George Reedy, a long-time aide to President Lyndon Johnson, notes: "In the Senate no course stands the remotest chance of adoption unless a minimum of fifty-one egotistical men are persuaded of its wisdom. . . ." At the other end of Pennsylvania Avenue, a course carries the day when, and only when, it has the approval of one man. "The life of the White House," says Reedy, "is the life of a court."[15] There is, then, great pressure on staff members to behave like courtiers, to court the favor of the president as the source of whatever power staff members possess. Any aide known to have the president's support or approval is strong; any aide denied access or approbation is weak. In such a setting it takes unusual strength of character to tell a president he is wrong. Having staff mature enough and confident enough to do this is important for the well-being of the nation.

Staff strains and pursuits

At the center of power

[14] Hugh Heclo, "The Changing Presidential Office," in Arnold J. Miltsner, ed., *Politics and the Oval Office* (San Francisco: Institute for Contemporary Studies, 1981), p. 163.
[15] George E. Reedy, *The Twilight of the Presidency* (New York: New American Library, 1970), pp. xi, 17–18.

THE EXECUTIVE OFFICE OF THE PRESIDENT

Figure 8.1
The Executive Office of the President
Year in parenthesis represents date when office received formal statutory recognition. Omitted from staff figures are approximately 100 employees performing household management and similar tasks. Staff size figures are for 1983–84.

The personal staff of the White House are the most visible part of the institutional presidency. They are, however, only one unit out of ten in a presidential staff structure, called the Executive Office of the President (EOP), that employs over 1,600 people and costs roughly $110 million to operate (in 1984). Figure 8.1 shows the various units of the EOP, when each was formally established, and the number of staff within it. All EOP agencies report directly to the president, and the top officers of each are appointed by him. But, unlike senior staff of the White House Office, the heads of a number of other EOP units must receive Senate confirmation—including the three members of the Council of Economic Advisers, the Director of the Office of Management and Budget, and the Special Representative for Trade Negotiation. And, while the president has considerable discretion in reorganizing the EOP, many of its units outside the White House operate under the specifications of statutes enacted by Congress. The Council of Economic Advisers, for example, functions under the terms of the Employment Act of 1946; and the National Security Council (NSC), under the National Security Act of 1947.

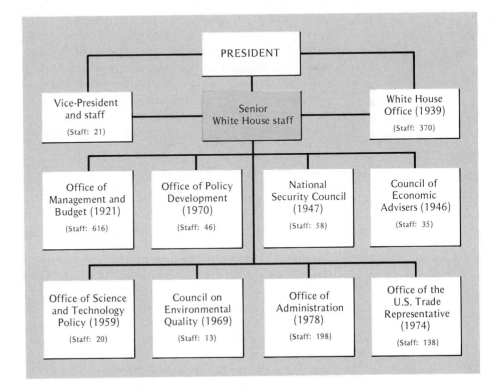

National Security Council

National Security
Council

The NSC has four statutory members: the president, the vice-president, the secretary of state, and the secretary of defense. In addition, the director of the Central Intelligence Agency and the chairman of the Joint Chiefs of Staff are statutory advisers. NSC staff are under the direction of the Assistant to the President for National Security Affairs. The role of the council and its staff is purely advisory. The president calls upon them as he sees fit in formulating and managing American foreign policy.

Office of Management and Budget

Office of Management
and Budget

The OMB is the largest agency in the Executive Office of the President, successor to the Bureau of the Budget established in 1921. Its 600 staff members help the president accomplish his political objectives in formulating and administering the budget, reviewing the organizational structure and management procedures of the entire executive branch, developing regulatory reform proposals, and assessing program objectives. When a president is trying to achieve major governmental change, he is likely to lean even more upon the staff resources of the OMB. Ronald Reagan has relied heavily on OMB Director David Stockman and the OMB staff for the often highly detailed and technical work required by the administration's budget-cutting objectives. The decision to cut the budget was political, but only the OMB had the skills and experience to implement the cuts.

The OMB and NSC, along with the White House Office, are the most important units of the Executive Office of the President. Their functions, as well as those of other units, are discussed further in chapter 9.

THE VICE PRESIDENT

It is doubtful that any political office in the United States has been the subject of as many jokes as the vice presidency. Benjamin Franklin did not like the idea of a vice presidency to begin with, and he suggested that the holder of the office should be addressed as "His Superfluous Majesty." In declining a vice presidential nomination by the Whig party in the middle of the nineteenth century, Senator Daniel Webster of Massachusetts said that "he did not propose to be buried until he was already dead." Thomas Marshall, who served for eight years as Woodrow Wilson's vice president, gave us the classic vice presidential joke: "Once there were two brothers. One ran away to sea; the other was elected vice president. And nothing was ever heard of either of them again." (Marshall was perhaps best known for his wit. He created another classic line when he whispered during a

Senate debate over which he was presiding that "what the country *really* needs is a good five-cent cigar.")

Succession

It was the country's first vice president, John Adams, who provided the most perceptive summation of the office: "I am nothing, but I may be everything." A vice president's constitutional powers are feeble: he presides over the Senate (when he wants to) and casts the deciding vote if the Senate is deadlocked (which rarely happens); that is all. But he is, in the constitutional sense, "a heartbeat away from the presidency." Article II provides that "in Case of the Removal of the President from Office, or of his Death, Resignation, or Inability to discharge the Powers and Duties of the said Office, the Same shall devolve on the Vice President. . . ." Thirteen of the nation's forty presidents first served as vice presidents; nine of the presidents succeeded to the presidency upon the death or (in one instance) resignation of an incumbent.

Assistant to the President

Since the vice president has no signficant constitutional powers, except the constitutional role of standing first in the line of succession, he is wholly dependent upon the president for his assignments. Historically such assignments have been extremely modest. No vice presi-

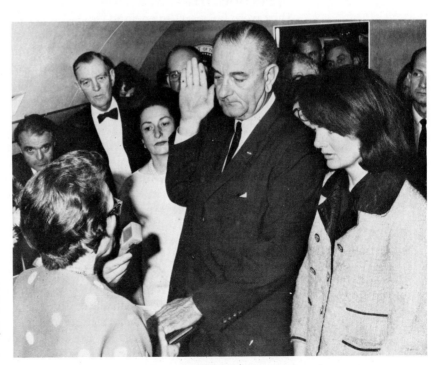

Vice President Lyndon Johnson is sworn in as president immediately following the assassination of President Kennedy.

dent through Alben Barkley (who served under Harry Truman from 1949 to 1953) was given major governmental or political responsibilities. The reasons for this are clear. Vice presidential candidates have often been chosen for political and geographic balance on a ticket. As we saw, Lincoln picked Andrew Johnson of Tennessee as his running mate in 1864 because he wanted a pro-union southern Democrat to strengthen a broad unionist appeal. New York liberal Franklin Roosevelt wanted Texas conservative John Nance Garner for ticket balance in the 1932 presidential race. Thus chosen, vice presidents rarely became friends and confidants of their presidents, and they lost out to more trusted assistants in contests for the president's ear.

Expanding vice presidential responsibility

But over the last three decades the picture of vice presidential weakness has substantially altered. Without any single dramatic development, a new consensus has taken form. The enormity of presidential responsibilities, together with the substantial possibility that a vice president will succeed to them, requires that individuals not be chosen as vice presidential candidates unless they are presidential material. It follows that presidents should not toss their vice presidents into ceremonial oblivion, but should assign them real responsibilities so that they will be prepared to take on presidential duties if necessary. As presidents have begun to act on this strong, if informal, consensus, they have come to find that active, well-informed vice presidents are handy to have around.

The first notable departure occurred with Eisenhower and Nixon in the 1950s. The two men were not close, personally or politically; they were far apart in age and experience. Eisenhower had decidedly ambivalent feelings about his vice president and seriously considered dropping him from the ticket in both 1952 and 1956. Despite this, the president's strong inclination to delegate responsibility and his lack of interest in Republican party affairs led him to assign his vice president major political tasks. Nixon was also picked to represent the United States on highly visible and important foreign trips. Richard Nixon entered the vice presidency in 1953 as a quite junior Republican politician from California; he left in 1961 as the most prominent Republican (after the retiring Eisenhower), and a man who had come within a whisker of winning election in his own right against Democrat John F. Kennedy in November 1960. Kennedy's choice of Lyndon Johnson as his vice presidential running mate in 1960, and Gerald Ford's designation of Nelson Rockefeller as vice president in 1974, were also important steps in the rise of the office. Johnson and Rockefeller were powerful, strong-willed figures. Their willingness to accept the vice presidency was symbolically important. Kennedy never really trusted Johnson politically, and Ford could not make the use of Rockefeller that he wanted to because Republican conservatives so disliked the former New York governor. But no office that held political forces like Lyndon Johnson and Nelson Rockefeller could really be described as "His Superfluous Majesty."

Vice President George Bush debates Democratic vice presidential candidate Geraldine Ferraro during the 1984 presidential campaign.

The Vice Presidency Today

Jimmy Carter and Ronald Reagan completed a seemingly permanent elevation of vice presidential responsibilities. Both made their vice presidents—Walter Mondale and George Bush, respectively—close associates and confidants, movers in the inner circles of administration affairs—even though neither president–vice president team had been close prior to their election. A new imperative is working. Presidents now need able and informed vice presidents. Vice presidents know that their role now requires them to function as loyal assistants to their presidents. Mondale won Carter's complete trust and confidence. Bush became a close political friend and associate of Reagan.

PRESIDENTIAL POWER

Power of persuasion

Richard Neustadt, a former presidential assistant, argues that the power of the presidency gets depicted too much in terms of formal authority and not enough in terms of persuasion.[16] A president is strong or weak, succeeds or fails in his governing tasks, on the basis of whether he can convince the many political groups and offices with whom he must deal "that what the White House wants of them is what they ought to do for their sake and on their authority." In part Neustadt is describing political life under separation of powers. A president's entire legislative program lies beyond his formal powers of com-

[16] Neustadt, *Presidential Power*, pp. 26–43.

mand. He has resources to persuade Congress to enact his policies, but he has few means to force legislators to enact them. Democracy limits cases of command and stresses the need for consent. In the extreme case where the consent of the governed is lost totally, a president's constitutional command powers become an empty shell. As we saw in the months just before the Watergate scandal forced his resignation, Richard Nixon retained the formal authority of the presidency but he was without the capacity to persuade. His most basic, practical power had slipped away.

Is Persuasion Enough?

The constitutional command powers of an American president are not very great when placed against his diverse responsibilities and the nation's high expectations of his performance. If a president cannot secure broad approval for his initiatives among the public at large and in the political leadership community—especially in Congress—his position is weak. Whenever the country has had effective presidential "rulership," James Young observes, it has received it "within a constitutional framework [that was] deliberately *designed to make rulership difficult.*"[17]

Executive-legislative deadlock?

Some maintain that the U.S. is too dependent on having a president able to move by persuasion. At certain times, when a politically adroit president enjoys high popularity, the system responds effectively. But all too often the president's persuasive resources are insufficient to overcome the fragmentation and disarray inherent in the American separation of powers. Lloyd Cutler, who served as counsel to President Carter in 1979 and 1980, argued while his chief was still in office that the formal institutional resources for executive leadership were so insufficient that the Carter presidency could not succeed. "In parliamentary terms, one might say that under the U.S. Constitution it is not now feasible to 'form a government.' . . . The separation of powers between the legislative and executive branches, whatever its merits in 1793, has become a structure that almost guarantees stalemate today."[18] The presidency is still what President Theodore Roosevelt once called a "bully pulpit." Unfortunately, Cutler wrote, no recent president has been able to get his programs through Congress in anything approaching coherent form. The United States, he suggests, needs to go to a parliamentary type of government to end this executive-legislative deadlock.

Contradictory Judgments

There is reason to be skeptical about such judgments. Any time political institutions manage to sustain strong popular support over a span

[17] Young, *Washington Community*, p. 252. Emphasis added.
[18] Lloyd N. Cutler, "To Form a Government," *Foreign Affairs*, Fall 1980, p. 127.

President John F. Kennedy at his Inaugural Ball on January 20, 1961.

of two hundred years, the presumption should be that they are doing something right, at least in the thinking of those governed by them. The American public has shown little dissatisfaction with the constitutional limits on the presidency. And there is no agreement among experts as to whether the U.S. has a problem with regard to presidential power and, if so, what it is. The presidency of John F. Kennedy in the beginning of the 1960s was hailed by many experts as "Camelot." The vigorous young executive had an office through which he could make good things happen. Arthur Schlesinger, Jr., noted in 1965 that Kennedy's presidency was based on the belief that

> the Chief Executive . . . must be "the vital center of action in our whole scheme of government." The nature of the office demanded that the President place himself in the very thick of the fight . . . [that he] be prepared to exercise the fullest powers of his office—all that are specified and some that are not.[19]

The presidency was strong, and it was good that it was strong.

Following Kennedy's assassination, however, the activist president who was his successor used his office to lead the United States into a war that saw an American army of half a million men engaged in a

[19] Arthur M. Schlesinger, Jr., *A Thousand Days* (Boston: Houghton Mifflin, 1965), p. 120.

A strong presidency or
a weak presidency?

small Asian country. The Vietnam War lasted twice as long as any previous military conflict in which the United States had been involved and claimed more American lives than any conflict other than the Civil War and World War II, and it prompted massive dissent at home. Vietnam dominated Lyndon Johnson's administration and that of his successor, Richard Nixon. Watergate followed almost immediately upon Vietnam. Now many of the same commentators who had proclaimed and endorsed a strong presidency denounced the presidency as bloated in its powers, imperial in its bearing and style, and dangerously open to personal abuses of power. The presidency was strong—but there was trouble in its strength.[20]

Enter Jimmy Carter. He banished "Hail to the Chief" as the president's song and donned his cardigan for low-key chats with the public. In matters of far greater substance, especially the conduct of U.S. foreign policy, he wanted a more restricted role for the president and for the nation. Quickly, though, events such as the seizure of the U.S. Embassy in Iran and the holding of its staff as hostages for fourteen months came to be seen as dramatic signs of the Carter administration's weakness and the decline of American power. The presidency was now weak—and it was bad that it was weak.

Changing lessons on
presidential power

These oscillations must have had an impact on the people who saw them, even on presidents. Having seen the glorifications of a strong presidency, might not Lyndon Johnson and Richard Nixon have been encouraged to think that greater assertiveness on their part was really in the national interest? Having been warned repeatedly of the dangers of an "imperial" presidency, might not Jimmy Carter have drawn back more than he should and otherwise would have from the assertion of executive leadership? Lloyd Cutler formulated his arguments about presidential weakness against the backdrop of the Carter presidency. After Reagan succeeded Carter, however, the situation seemed almost immediately to change. The new administration won support, even in the Democratic-controlled House of Representatives, for substantial portions of its foreign, defense, and domestic programs. The new president seemed amply able to set the tone and direction for American national government. Indeed, discussion shifted to whether a Reagan revolution was altering basic governmental commitments developed over the preceding decades.

The presidency is an office of which much is expected in the American governmental system. It has fairly modest and much-checked formal powers, but great resources for political leadership by persuasion. Different presidents have employed the power of persuasion for contrasting ends, in constantly shifting political circumstances. There is as yet no consensus as to whether the president's powers and institutional position should be changed, much less as to a particular set of changes to be obtained.

---

[20] See idem., *The Imperial Presidency* (New York: Popular Library, 1973), p. 359.

ASSESSING PRESIDENTS

Presidents' reputations have undergone some startling changes. No president is all good or all bad, of course; each reveals a mix of positive and negative attributes. At any given time, one facet of a president's performance is emphasized; later it may be a quite different facet. Assessments of Herbert Hoover, the country's thirtieth president, reflect this pattern of sharp interpretative shifts over time. Until the Great Depression, Hoover was widely considered a humanitarian, an outstanding organizer and doer, and a progressive Republican. His work in organizing relief help to avert starvation in Belgium after World War I earned him international acclaim on both organizational and humanitarian grounds. The election of 1928 was not, at the time, viewed as a contest between a Republican conservative (Hoover) and a Democratic liberal (New York Governor Alfred E. Smith), but rather as one between two moderate progressives; many observers thought Hoover's credentials as a progressive were better than Smith's.

Herbert Hoover: a reassessment

Then came the Great Depression and President Hoover's responses to it. A new picture of Hoover emerged: of a very conservative, insensitive man who was a failure at managing the great economic crisis. Over the last 15 to 20 years, however, the picture has again changed. Students of Hoover's presidency have adopted a far more complimentary view of his political commitments and performance. One study published in 1975 declares Hoover to be a "forgotten progressive." "There is a good deal of talk today about a 'new' Hoover. Dis-

President Herbert Hoover.

parate political groups ranging from the far right to the far left think they are rediscovering him, because his progressive philosophy contained ideas whose time has finally arrived."[21]

Both the positive and the negative judgments of Hoover were correct in part. He was a progressive man of great managerial talent. His administration's response to the Great Depression was by no means only short-sighted and conservative. But Hoover did find it hard to recognize the immense impact of the Depression on the thinking of his fellow citizens, and his response to criticism was to "hunker down" and to emphasize less humanitarian aspects of his political approach. Not surprisingly, as Joan Hoff Wilson points out, the prevailing judgment during the Depression and its immediate aftermath filtered out the positive dimensions of Hoover's work, while interpretations since the 1960s have seen it through a different, less critical filter.

Dwight Eisenhower's presidency has also prompted striking shifts of interpretation. General Eisenhower came to the presidency a hero of the American effort in World War II. As president, however, his lack of a bold domestic policy and his view that the presidency was to be used sparingly rather than vigorously invited criticism, especially from those who expected the president to be a doer of great deeds along the model of FDR. But, recently, Eisenhower's strengths are again being emphasized in something of an "Eisenhower revival." His refusal to be pushed into military action in Vietnam appears far more commendable after the sad experience of that war.[22] His modest judgments on the possibilities of governmental action appear sounder after a long spell of governmental activism than they did before. That Eisenhower had a coherent sense of leadership—which, while very different from FDR's, is impressive in its own right—has come to be better appreciated by leading students of his presidency:

An Eisenhower revival

> On reexamination, Eisenhower's approach to presidential leadership emerges as distinctive and consciously thought-out, rather than an unfortunate example of artless drift. . . . When carefully explicated, this approach promises to add significantly to the repertoire of assumptions about how the expanded modern presidency can be conducted.[23]

Personality and the presidency

What is the conclusion to be drawn from all this—that if one waits long enough one will see almost any reputation rise and fall, and all judgments are unreliable? Of course not. But one should beware of facile generalizations which praise or damn. There is no easy judgment about a president's vice or virtue; most American chiefs of state have had some of both.

[21] Joan Hoff Wilson, *Herbert Hoover: Forgotten Progressive* (Boston: Little, Brown, 1975), p. 269.
[22] See Louis W. Koenig, *The Chief Executive*, 4th ed. (New York: Harcourt Brace, 1981), p. 349.
[23] Fred I. Greenstein, "Eisenhower as an Activist President: A Look at New Evidence," *Political Science Quarterly*, Winter 1979–80, p. 596; and *idem, The Hidden-Hand Presidency: Eisenhower as Leader* (New York: Basic Books, 1982).

President Dwight Eisenhower.

Presidential Character

Not only do conclusions about the merits of a particular presidency change over time; so do judgments about what we should look for in a prospective president. In the 1930s, 1940s, and 1950s little emphasis was placed on the requisite personality traits of a potential president. If pressed, one would have conceded that certain types of personalities were better suited to the office, more likely to give the country the performance it wanted. But personality did not seem a critical factor. Neither Roosevelt, Truman, or Eisenhower—the three men who occupied the presidency between 1933 and 1961—raised any serious concern about personality.

In succession during the 1960s and early 1970s, however, the U.S. had two presidents whose personalities raised concern among many people. Lyndon Johnson and Richard Nixon seemed too driven, too aggressive, too inclined to view as hostile the political world with which they had to deal. Personality emerged as a more important variable than it had been for assessing potential presidents. Political scientist James David Barber gave more systematic emphasis to these general concerns in his book *The Presidential Character.* Barber described Johnson and Nixon as "active-negative" personality types. The active-negative "seems ambitious, striving upward, power-seeking. His stance toward the environment is aggressive and he has a persistent problem in managing his aggressive feelings. . . . Life is a hard struggle to achieve and hold power, hardened by the condemnation of a perfectionist conscience."[24] Barber argued that "active-negatives" can be identified before they get to the presidency, and that it is important to do so because their presidencies are likely to be deeply troubling for the nation. Others are less confident that we know enough to practice political psychology successfully, except in extreme cases.

The Public's Ratings

Sometimes the public revises its assessment of presidents. When in office, for example, Harry Truman was not popular.[25] Truman's public-opinion ratings for his entire presidency were the lowest of any chief executive over the last half-century (although Nixon's marks were very low at the time of Watergate, as were Carter's throughout much of his last two years in office). Now, however, the public gives Truman quite high marks, partly in response to the generally favorable literature that has appeared on the Truman presidency. When Gallup asked, in late 1979, "Of all the presidents we have had, who do you wish were president today?" Truman received more mentions than any other president except Kennedy and Franklin Roosevelt.[26]

Figure 8.2

Public Answers to the Question: Please Tell Me whether You Agree or Disagree with the Following Statements about the Presidency

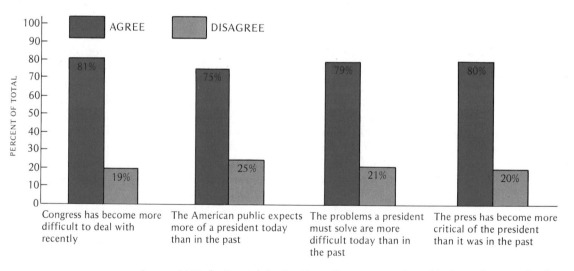

Source: "Attitudes Toward the Presidency," a survey conducted in December 1979 by the Gallup Organization for the Corporation for Public Broadcasting.

[24] James David Barber, *The Presidential Character* (Englewood Cliffs, N.J.: Prentice-Hall, 1977), pp. 12–13.
[25] The Gallup Poll has measured presidential popularity since the days of FDR, using the question, "Do you approve of the way [the president's name] is handling his job as president?"
[26] "Attitudes Toward the Presidency," a survey conducted in December 1979 by the Gallup Organization for the Corporation for Public Broadcasting.

Americans are not reluctant to criticize presidents for inadequate performance in office, but at the same time they recognize that the job has become extremely demanding. By large margins, the public thinks that Congress has become more difficult to deal with, that the communications media are more critical of presidents than they used to be, that the problems presidents are expected to solve have become increasingly complicated, and that the public itself may now be too demanding (see Figure 8.2). People want their presidents to set high standards, but they do not expect them to be persons without faults or immune to the problems that affect others. A Gallup poll late in 1979 found that large majorities would not object strongly if their presidents swore, or had seen a psychiatrist, or had been divorced (see Table 8.1).

Table 8.1
Personal Expectations about the President (in percent)

	Object strongly	Not object strongly	Don't know
If he smoked marijuana occasionally	70	27	3
If he told ethnic or racial jokes in private	43	54	3
If he were not a member of a church	38	59	3
If he uses tranquilizers occasionally	36	60	4
If he uses profane language in private	33	65	2
If he had seen a psychiatrist	30	65	5
If he wore blue jeans occasionally in the oval office	21	77	2
If he were divorced	17	79	4
If he had a cocktail before dinner each night	14	84	2

Question: I am going to read a number of statements that could describe a person. Please tell me whether or not you would object strongly to each statement if it were true about a president.

Source: "Attitudes Toward the Presidency," a survey conducted in December 1979 by the Gallup Organization for the Corporation on Public Broadcasting.

Survey of recent presidential performance

Americans are sophisticated critics of their presidents. Louis Harris and Associates conducted a poll in July 1983, in which people were queried: "I'd like to ask you about the last nine presidents of the United States. Please keep in mind Roosevelt, Truman, Eisenhower, Kennedy, Johnson, Nixon, Ford, Carter, and Reagan. If you had to choose one, which president do you think . . . was best on domestic affairs?" Respondents were then asked to rate presidents in other areas. They answered that Roosevelt and Kennedy were best on domestic matters, and Nixon on foreign affairs; that Kennedy most inspired confidence; that Nixon set the lowest moral standards; and that Carter was least able to get things done (Table 8.2). The survey shows a pub-

Table 8.2
Americans Rate Their Presidents (in percent)

	FDR	HST	DDE	JFK	LBJ	RMN	GRF	JEC	RWR
Best on domestic affairs	22	8	7	27	6	4	3	5	6
Best in foreign affairs	14	9	9	21	1	25	2	6	4
Least able to get things done	1	2	5	4	9	11	15	35	7
Most inspired confidence	23	8	8	40	1	2	2	3	6
Set the lowest moral standards	3	2	2	10	7	46	2	4	5

Question: "I'd like to ask you about the last nine presidents of the United States. Please keep in mind Roosevelt, Truman, Eisenhower, Kennedy, Johnson, Nixon, Ford, Carter, and Reagan. If you had to choose one, which president do you think [read each item] . . . was best on domestic affairs . . . was best in foreign affairs . . . was least able to get things done . . . most inspired confidence in the White House. . . ." Sample size was 1,252.

Source: Survey by Louis Harris and Associates, July 14–18, 1983.

lic that makes more complex judgments about presidents, rather than assigning them to two bins labeled "good" and "bad."

SUMMARY

The framers had contrasting objectives in mind when they designed the presidency. They wanted to end the extreme executive weakness that distinguished government under the Articles of Confederation. But they also wanted the president so checked and balanced that he could not rule arbitrarily.

As the contemporary presidency attests, they succeeded to a large degree in these pursuits. The singularity of the office—the Constitution vests "the executive power of the United States" in one individual, the president—adds greatly to its visibility and persuasive force. But the president remains subject to great constitutional restraints, the most basic one being separation of powers: Every law the executive administers, every dollar it spends, requires the action of a separate and very independent branch of government, the Congress.

Many different types of responsibilities have been put on American presidents by the Constitution and modern political necessity. The president is at once party leader and ceremonial chief of state, manager of domestic prosperity and leader of the Western alliance, administrator-in-chief, commander-in-chief, and legislator-in-chief. Sometimes his plate seems to get a little too full.

To accomplish all the different things expected of him, a president would have to possess a truly amazing collection of skills. He would have to be a great communicator and campaigner, an adroit politician among politicians, a consummate administrator, a great conceptualizer of policy—and comprising all these and more, a great democratic leader. Perhaps it isn't too surprising that we don't always quite get everything in one individual.

Of course, the president gets a lot of help. Formalized in 1939, the Executive Office of the President (EOP) is composed of a series of staff agencies. At the center is the White House Office, consisting of senior presidential assistants and other staff. The Office of Management and Budget and the National Security Council are two other pivotal units of the EOP.

No one argues that presidential staffs suffer from any lack of numbers. But getting them to function coherently and efficiently on behalf of presidential objectives is always hard. Often derided in the past as mere standby equipment, the vice presidency seems to have emerged as the source of high-level presidential assistance.

Some observers worry that the formal powers and institutional resources of the presidency are insufficient, when set against the demands placed on the office. Policy stalemate or incoherence, resulting from the executive–legislative separation, is the greatest concern. But over the last quarter-century, assessments of presidential power have undergone great fluctuations, under changing political circumstances and types of presidential leadership. There is now nothing approaching general agreement on any type of institutional change.

Assessments of presidents, by experts and the public, have undergone quite striking shifts over time. Performance that looks deficient by standards elevated by the experience of one generation, often looks better against the backdrop of another generation's problems. The things we worry about or look for most in potential presidents also change. For those who lived through the years of Vietnam and Watergate, a president's personality or character has come to be seen as of national importance.

9 | The Executive Branch and the Bureaucracy

The administration of modern government is a vast and complex undertaking. In this chapter we examine the departments, agencies, and staff of the executive branch of American government, their historic development and current operations. We also focus on some of the persisting problems that confront the administration of the federal executive. At one level, the work of federal agencies is tangible and well understood. Much of it is a part of the day-to-day life of virtually the entire population. We see the administration of the federal government as it delivers our mail, collects taxes, distributes Social Security benefits to millions of citizens, regulates the distribution of new drugs or medicines, and operates a far-flung defense establishment in which about thirty million Americans who are now living have served and in which more than two million are now on active duty.

PERCEPTIONS OF THE BUREAUCRACY

Still, the actual workings of the executive branch are surrounded by myth and confusion. As we saw in chapter 2, people often have vague and diverse perceptions of the term we use to describe governmental administration: "bureaucracy." To the German social theorist Max Weber, the bureaucratic model of organization was distinguished by its large size, the presence of clear hierarchy, the formalization of rules and procedures, the systematic maintenance of records, and the employment of a full-time appointed staff who perform specified duties

"Miles of files" is a common image of the Federal bureaucracy.

using bodies of professional or technical knowledge.[1] In this sense, bureaucracy is a scientific concept. But it is also a highly disputed description frequently overladen with derogatory meanings. As Charles Goodsell observed, "The employee of bureaucracy, that 'lowly bureaucrat,' is seen as lazy or snarling, or both. The office occupied by this pariah is viewed as bungling or inhuman, or both. The overall edifice of bureaucracy is pictured as overstaffed, inflexible, unresponsive, and power-hungry, all at once."[2]

Americans often protest that the administration of their national government has become too big, self-serving, unresponsive, inefficient, and intrusive. Daniel Katz and his colleagues found in a large national survey that the majority of Americans—often an overwhelming majority—feel that there is excessive duplication of governmental services, that officials are unwilling to take responsibility, that those who gain most from government offices are the people running them, and that much of the money appropriated for public assistance never gets to the people who need it.[3] Yet the very same study found that, when asked about their *personal experiences* in seeking

[1] H. H. Gerth and C. Wright Mills, *From Max Weber* (New York: Oxford University Press, 1946), pp. 196–99.
[2] Charles T. Goodsell, *The Case for Bureaucracy* (Chatham, N.J.: Chatham House Publishers, 1983), p. 2.
[3] Daniel Katz, Barbara Gutek, Robert Kahn, and Eugenia Barton, *Bureaucratic Encounters* (Ann Arbor, Mich.: Institute for Social Research, 1975), p. 136. The survey referred to was conducted by the Survey Research Center of the University of Michigan in April and May of 1973, but numerous other studies conducted over the past 10 to 15 years have arrived at similar findings.

governmental services, a large majority of the people were satisfied with the way the agencies responded to their problems: they were treated fairly, the bureaucrats gave them the time they needed, government's response was efficient, and, most important, thanks to governmental service agencies their problems got solved.[4] Widespread approval arising from personal contacts and experience coexists with widespread criticism of governmental performance in general—depending on how the issue is posed.

Myths about Bureaucratic Growth

Confusion abounds even about objective facts of recent governmental experience. First, widespread growth of the federal bureaucracy is often discussed as a kind of unquestioned truth. Actually, from the mid-1950s through the early 1980s, when the total civilian labor force in the United States jumped from 65 million to 110 million—an increase of roughly 70 percent—the number of civilian employees of the federal government climbed by less than half a million—from 2.4 million in 1955 to 2.9 million in 1983—an increase of about 20 percent. Second, complaints about the federal bureaucracy are much more common than those about local government bureaucracy. But in 1984 local governments employed more than three times as many people as the federal government and accounted for the vast majority of the recent increase in governmental workers. Washington and its environs are thought of as the citadel of the big federal bureaucracy, but, though the principal offices of the national government are located there, only 12 percent of federal employees work in the Washington area.

Every four years Americans elect a president, vested with "the executive Power . . . of the United States of America." The executive branch, however, is much more than the president and those he appoints to top posts in his administration. The executive branch has broad responsibilities requiring thousands of officials in activities ranging from the most routine program administration to making far-reaching policy decisions. Executive departments and agencies are expected to administer faithfully laws Congress has passed, and in many though not all cases are supposed to reflect policy directions established, within the law, by the president and the department heads he appoints. They are not, however, passive instruments of congressional and presidential intent. Neither is there some simple and direct translation of those intents into policy. Instead, the many units of the executive branch and the personnel comprising them respond to the president and to Congress, to interest-group and constituency demands, and to norms and interests that originate within the bureaucracy itself. How is the federal government of the United States organized to execute its many programs and provide all the services expected of it?

Executive branch responsibilities

[4]Ibid., pp. 121–22.

EVOLUTION OF THE EXECUTIVE BRANCH

For all the present scale of the executive branch of the national government, the constitutional foundations for it are modest. Article II states that the president "shall nominate, and by and with the advice and consent of the Senate, shall appoint ambassadors, other public ministers and consuls, judges of the Supreme Court, and all other officers of the United States, whose appointments . . . shall be established by law. . . ." It further stipulates that Congress may "vest the appointment of such inferior offices, as they think proper, in the President alone . . . or in the heads of departments." Every federal department and agency has come into existence through simple legislation enacted by Congress, and each may be reorganized or eliminated at any time in the same way.

Birth of executive departments

When the first Congress convened in 1789, its members agreed that several executive departments should be established and that each should be headed by a single official—appointed, as the Constitution required, by the president with the Senate's advice and consent. The departments of State, Treasury, and War (the latter renamed and reorganized in 1947 as the Department of Defense) were set up in 1789, as was the office of Attorney General (now the Justice Department). The Post Office Department was also created in 1789, but its present-day successor, the U.S. Postal Service, is no longer a department of cabinet rank.

Only four of the present thirteen executive-branch departments—State, Treasury, Defense, and Justice—can trace their lineage all the way back to Washington's presidency. Four others—Interior, Agriculture, Labor, and Commerce—were established in the late nineteenth and early twentieth centuries. The remaining five departments have been established since 1950: Health, Education, and Welfare (HEW) in 1953; Housing and Urban Development (HUD) in 1965; Transportation in 1966; Energy in 1977; and Education in 1979. The last of these came into being when the old Office of Education was separated from HEW and given independent departmental status. HEW was at the same time renamed and recast as the Department of Health and Human Services (HHS).

Early Executive-Branch Activity

The first federal employees

The earliest executive offices were restricted to the minimum number of areas—finance, foreign policy, defense, postal service, and law. They also had very limited duties and needed few employees. For example, the State Department at the outset had only 9 staff members besides the Secretary! A quarter-century after the Constitution was ratified, federal employees numbered just over 4,800. Of these, only 500 or so worked in Washington; most were scattered in towns around the country providing the one service that required many workers—

Table 9.1

Civilian Employees of the
Federal Government, 1816–1983

Year	Total number of employees	Number employed in the Washington, D.C. area
1816	4,837	535
1821	6,914	603
1831	11,491	666
1841	18,038	1,014
1851	26,274	1,533
1861	36,672	2,199
1871	51,020	6,222
1881	100,020	13,124
1891	157,442	20,834
1901	239,476	28,044
1911	395,905	39,782
1921	561,142	82,416
1931	609,746	76,303
1941	1,437,682	190,588
1951	2,482,666	265,980
1961	2,435,804	246,266
1971	2,874,166	322,969
1981	2,858,742	350,516
1983	2,379,840	353,361

Source: United States Bureau of the Census, *Historical Statistics of the United States, Colonial Times to 1970*, Bicentennial ed., Part 2; pp. 1102–03; U.S. Office of Personnel Management, Workforce Analysis and Statistics Division, monthly releases, latest that of October 1983.

delivering the mail. By 1816 there were over 3,200 U.S. post offices; as the country grew, so did the number of post offices, reaching about 30,000 in 1871. Total federal employment climbed gradually from about 4,800 in 1816 to 51,000 in 1871, and most of this growth was accounted for by the postal service (Table 9.1).

Department of Defense

In our own time the largest executive department—indeed, the largest single employer in the country—is the Department of Defense (DOD). DOD employed just over three million Americans in 1984, including more than 2 million active-duty military personnel, and 1 million directly hired civilian workers. Compared to this, the American armed services were tiny throughout most of the country's history. Total military personnel numbered just 7,000 in 1801, 21,000 in 1840, 28,000 on the eve of the Civil War, and 42,000 in 1871 (when postwar demobilization had been completed).[5]

[5] Students interested in more detailed information on the size of the national government in general, and of the military branches in particular, over the country's history are referred to two publications of the U.S. Bureau of the Census: *Historical Statistics of the United States: Colonial Times to 1970*, bicentennial ed., 2 vols. (Washington, D.C.: U.S. Government Printing Office, 1975); and *Statistical Abstract of the United States*, published annually by the Government Printing Office. The growth of the American armed services each year from 1789 to 1970 is shown on pages 1141–43, part 2, of *Historical Statistics*.

Government as a Promoter of Interests

After the Civil War new federal agencies and programs were established with the intent of promoting the special interests of various segments of the population. Lawrence Dodd and Richard Schott have noted that

> whereas the original departments had been built around specific federal functions—the War Department for national defense, State for the conduct of foreign relations, and so on—the latter half of the nineteenth century witnessed the creation of certain offices, bureaus, and departments of the federal government around group interests. Farming, the largest occupation in its day, secured recognition with the establishment of a Department of Agriculture that gained full cabinet status in 1889. Education interests got a foothold with the creation of a Bureau of Education (1869) in the Interior Department, forerunner of the Office of Education. The emergence of organized labor, whose ranks were swelled by the industrial revolution, led to the creation of the Department of Labor in 1888. Not far behind were small business and commercial interests that helped secure the establishment of a Department of Commerce in 1903 (actually a joint Department of Commerce and Labor until 1913).[6]

These "clientele-oriented departments" for the most part were originally intended not to subsidize or regulate but to promote—for example, by collecting and disseminating relevant statistical information and supporting research.

One of the new agencies was, however, a major provider of cash benefits. After the Civil War, the leading veterans' organization, the Grand Army of the Republic (GAR), was fabulously successful in persuading Congress to establish and then liberalize veterans' pensions; the Pension Office (within the Department of the Interior) administered these benefits. In 1891 the Commissioner of Pensions could claim that his was "the largest executive bureau in the world." It had over 6,000 staff members, supplemented by thousands of local physicians paid on a fee basis. Over 40 percent of the entire national government budget in the early 1890s was devoted to veterans' pensions and other benefits. Political scientist James Q. Wilson notes that in the Pension Office

Federal agencies and group interests

> the pattern of bureaucratic clientelism was set in a way later to become a familiar feature of the governmental landscape—a subsidy was initially provided . . . to a group that was powerfully benefited and had few or disorganized opponents; the beneficiaries were organized to supervise the administration and ensure the funding of the program; the law authorizing the program, first passed because it seemed the right thing to do, was left intact or even expanded because politically it became the only thing to do.[7]

[6] Lawrence C. Dodd and Richard L. Schott, *Congress and the Administrative State* (New York: Wiley, 1979), p. 27.
[7] James Q. Wilson, "The Rise of the Bureaucratic State," in Francis E. Rourke, ed., *Bureaucratic Power in National Politics*, 3d ed. (Boston: Little, Brown, 1978), p. 64.

Governmental Regulation

Another important group of federal agencies and commissions involved in economic regulation began to evolve in the late nineteenth century, many of them outside the major cabinet-level departments. While the U.S. has had less governmental ownership of economic enterprises than most other democratic countries, and has attempted less central economic planning, it has extended governmental regulation of the economy further than most democracies. The government tries to realize various public objectives in the economic arena by regulating what private businesses do.

Interstate Commerce Commission

The first major federal regulatory commission was the Interstate Commerce Commission (ICC), set up under the Interstate Commerce Act of 1887. The ICC was given responsibility for regulating carriers, initially railroads and shipping lines, that transported products cross-country. Not surprisingly, the need for such sustained national regulation was first felt after the Civil War as the industrial economy developed and its parts became vastly more interdependent.

The Interstate Commerce Act and the Sherman Anti-Trust Act (1890) were the most important pieces of legislation in the first round of federal regulatory expansion. In a second round, between 1906 and 1915, key legislation included the Food and Drug Act (1906), the Fed-

Many complain about government regulation.

A "camel" truck designed by government committee

eral Trade Commission Act (1914), and the Clayton Act (1914) which, like the Sherman Act before it, was an anti-trust law. In a third wave during the 1930s, a host of new regulatory statutes were passed, including the Communications Act (1934), the Securities Exchange Act (1934), the National Labor Relations Act (1935), and the Civil Aeronautics Act (1938). The latest round came in the late 1960s and early 1970s with passage of consumer protection and environmental legislation, including the Truth-in-Lending Act (1968), the Clean Air Act (1970), and the Clean Water Act (1972). A great variety of agencies and commissions have been created to administer these laws, such as the Federal Trade Commission (1914), the Federal Communications Commission (1934), the National Labor Relations Board (1935), and the Environmental Protection Agency (1970).

Regulatory legislation

Growth of the Executive Branch

The departments and agencies of the federal executive have expanded in every era of U.S. history as the business of government has in some way been enlarged. By any measure, however, the greatest growth has occurred over the last half-century. If the measure is the *number* of government employees, the time of maximum growth was the 1930s and 1940s. During these decades, total federal personnel increased by more than 400 percent—from about 600,000 when Franklin Roosevelt took office in 1933 to roughly 2.5 million in 1953 when Republican Dwight Eisenhower ended the Democrats' 20-year control of the executive (Table 9.1). On the other hand, if the measure of federal growth is *expenditures*, the time of greatest increase has been the last 20 years. Federal expenditures climbed from $118 billion in 1965 to $850 billion in fiscal year 1984.

Today, we see as one end product of this expansion the prominent presence of governmental agencies, especially federal agencies, among the largest organizations in the country. Ranked by their expenditures (in the case of government) or by their sales (for business corporations), the three largest organizations in the United States are all executive branch agencies: the Departments of Health and Human Services, Defense, and Treasury. Exxon surpassed all other private corporations, but its total sales in 1982 were only about 40 percent as great as the expenditures of HHS. Expenditures by the two largest state governments, California and New York, were comparable to the sales of the largest companies (Figure 9.1).

Size of federal agencies

Comparing the number of employees, one comes to much the same conclusion. In 1982, the Defense Department and the American Telephone and Telegraph Company (before divestiture) were the two largest civilian employers, each with approximately one million workers. But DOD far outranked AT&T when its military personnel were included. Whichever measure is used, about half of the largest organizations in the U.S. are governmental and half private.

Figure 9.1 **The Largest Governmental and Industrial Organizations (by dollars of corporate sales or governmental outlays, or by number of employees, for the year 1982)**

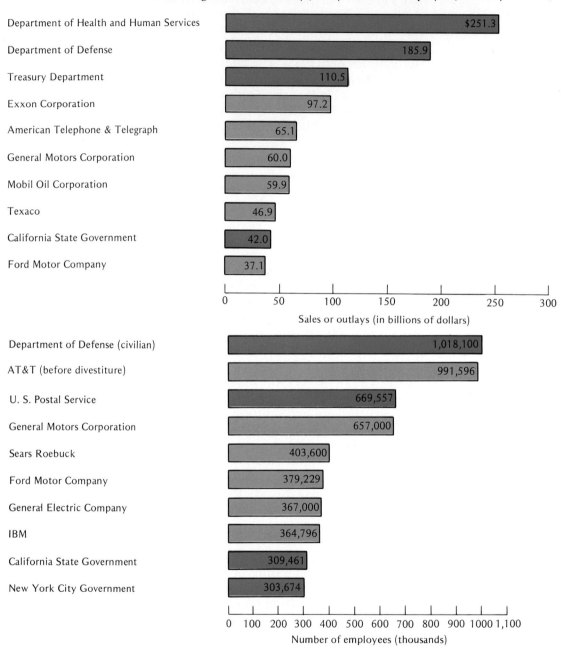

Source: *Fortune*, May 2, 1983, pp. 228–29, June 13, 1983, pp. 154–73; *Budget of the United States Government, Fiscal Year, 1984*, p. 9-4; U.S. Postal Service; U.S. Senate Committee on Governmental Affairs, *Organization of Federal Executive Depts. and Agencies, 1983*; U.S. Department of Commerce, Bureau of the Census; State of California, Dept. of Finance, Administrative Services Unit; State of New York, Dept. of Employment; State of Texas, Dept. of Employment; N.Y.C. Government, OMB.

THE FEDERAL EXECUTIVE TODAY

The principal departments, agencies, and commissions of the federal executive branch are shown in Figure 9.2. Thirteen of them—the executive departments—are shown to outrank all other agencies. This position reflects an interesting mix of status considerations, historical experience, and practical political reality.

Cabinet Rank

The meaning of cabinet rank

The heads of these thirteen departments, each of whom holds the title of secretary, collectively form the president's cabinet, and their departments are described as "of *cabinet* rank."[8] In the American system, the cabinet lacks any constitutional or even statutory base. In contrast to parliamentary systems, where the cabinet collectively exercises governmental authority, in the U.S. it has no clear governing role. Presidents often work closely with individual cabinet officers, of course, but rarely with the cabinet collectively. Cabinet rank is simply a symbolic affirmation of importance within the executive hierarchy.

From where does this importance stem? As the director of the then Bureau of the Budget stated in 1961 when he testified on a bill that would establish a new executive department,

> Departmental status is reserved for those agencies which (1) administer a wide range of programs directed toward a common purpose of national importance; and (2) are concerned with policies and programs requiring frequent and positive presidential direction and representation at the highest levels of Government.[9]

Departmental status and cabinet rank symbolize basic national commitments and a breadth of policy responsibilities beyond what obtains in the case of other agencies. The breadth of their policy responsibilities and their elevated status do not mean, though, that the cabinet departments are in all cases the largest executive-branch units, in either overall budget or number of employees. The U.S. Postal Service and the Veterans Administration (VA)—neither of which has department status—each has more employees than any cabinet department other than Defense. And, as Table 9.2 indicates, the VA, the Postal Service, and the Office of Personnel Management have bigger annual budgets than eight of the thirteen departments.

---

[8] A few other officials, such as the U.S. ambassador to the United Nations, also hold cabinet rank.
[9] Statement of David E. Bell, June 21, 1961.

Figure 9.2 **The Executive Branch**

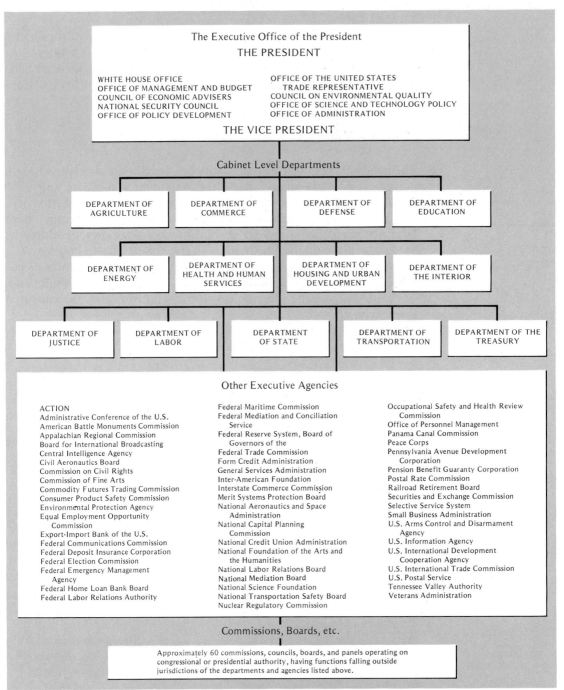

Source: United States Government Manual, 1984/85, p. 816.

Table 9.2
Federal Expenditures by Agency

Departments and Agencies (cabinet departments are capitalized)	Outlays (billions of dollars)
HEALTH AND HUMAN SERVICES	$276.6
DEFENSE	207.9
TREASURY	116.4
AGRICULTURE	46.4
LABOR	38.1
Veterans Administration	24.8
Postal Service	22.8
Office of Personnel Management	21.3
TRANSPORTATION	20.6
HOUSING AND URBAN DEVELOPMENT	15.3
EDUCATION	14.6
ENERGY	8.4
National Aeronautics & Space Administration	6.7
Tennessee Valley Authority (TVA)	4.9
INTERIOR	4.6
Environmental Protection Agency	4.3
Railroad Retirement Board	4.0
JUSTICE	2.8
STATE	2.3
COMMERCE	1.9
President: Executive office & directly appropriated funds	5.6
Legislative and judicial branches	2.2
Other agencies	10.3

The above figures represent actual 1983 outlays, with the exception of the Postal Service and the TVA, for which only 1982 figures are provided. In these last two cases, totals reflect expenditure of nongovernmental as well as governmental revenues. Both the Postal Service and the TVA are largely self-financing (purchase of stamps, sale of electrical power).

Source: Executive Office of the President, OMB, Budget of the U.S. Government, FY 1985, pp. (8-179), (9-5).

Independent Agencies

Another group of agencies, such as the Central Intelligence Agency (CIA), the Veterans Administration, the Environmental Protection Agency (EPA), and the General Services Administration, are referred to as "independent," which means simply "outside the executive departments." Many of them are in no sense independent of presidential direction. The director of the CIA and the administrator of the EPA are subordinate to the president in the same way as the secretaries of State and Transportation.

Some of the **independent agencies,** however, really have been insulated from presidential direction. The U.S. Postal Service is a case in

EPA workers inspecting chemical waste dumps.

Independent agencies

point. In urging that the Post Office Department be reorganized as an independent, noncabinet Postal Service, President Richard Nixon argued that efficiency would be served by freeing the agency "from direct control by the president, the Bureau of the Budget, and the Congress," and relatedly from partisan political pressure. The Postal Service now has the independence Nixon recommended. It is headed by an eleven-person board of governors, appointed by the president with Senate confirmation. The governors serve nine-year overlapping terms. The administrative head of the Postal Service, the Postmaster General, is appointed by and responsible to this board of governors—*not the president.* Although the Postal Service must submit a budget annually to the Office of Management and Budget, the OMB has no authority to modify it. And there is no requirement that the budget be transmitted to Congress. The Postal Service is now self-financing, and it can borrow money and sell bonds as it sees fit, as long as its total indebtedness does not exceed $10 billion.

Foundations and Institutes

A number of **foundations** and **institutes** have been established in the executive branch to promote science and scholarship. The first to be established, the Smithsonian Institution, is now a century-and-a-half old. James Smithson of England bequeathed his entire estate to the United States, to establish in Washington an institution "for the increase and diffusion of knowledge. . . ." Federal subsidies followed.

But only after World War II did the federal government's investment in science and the arts became massive, with the establishment of the National Science Foundation, the National Institutes of Health (and its many components such as the National Cancer Institute and the National Heart Institute), and most recently, the National Endowment for the Arts and the National Endowment for the Humanities.

In all of these cases it was felt that a degree of agency insulation from regular political direction was in order. The oldest of the federal scientific establishments, the Smithsonian has the greatest autonomy. Its business is conducted by a board of regents which consists of the vice president, the chief justice of the Supreme Court, three members of the Senate, three members of the House of Representatives, and six others appointed by joint resolution of the Congress. The chief executive officer of the institution is chosen by this highly independent board. When the National Science Foundation was established in 1947 to provide federal funding for scientific research, especially at the nation's colleges and universities, the scientific community worked hard to achieve for the new facility a high measure of independence from political interference. The aim was to create a kind of university structure within the executive branch, and this was substantially realized. Policy-making authority resides in a 24-person National Science Board, appointed for six-year terms by the president, with the advice and consent of the Senate.

The Smithsonian and the National Science Foundation

Independent Regulatory Commissions

Another large group of federal agencies, the **independent regulatory commissions,** were set up with the idea that they should be insulated from regular presidential leadership and political direction. As noted, the first of these was the Interstate Commerce Commission, established in 1887 to regulate such carriers as railroads and shipping lines engaged in interstate commerce. Eleven others have subsequently been created.[10] Economic regulation is not the exclusive province of the independent commissions—various bureaus in the regular departments, such as the Food and Drug Administration (FDA) within Health and Human Services, and the Occupational Safety and Health Administration (OSHA) in the Labor Department, play prominent regulatory roles—but the commissions are key regulatory bodies.

In contrast to most of the important executive departments and agencies, the regulatory commissions are headed by boards rather than single executives. By law these boards must be bipartisan. The

[10]They are the Civil Aeronautics Board, the Commodity Futures Trading Commission, the Consumer Product Safety Commission, the Federal Communications Commission, the Federal Energy Regulatory Commission, the Board of Governors of the Federal Reserve System, the Federal Maritime Commission, the Federal Trade Commission, the National Labor Relations Board, the Nuclear Regulatory Commission, and the Securities and Exchange Commission.

FDA inspectors dump milk contaminated by cancer-causing substances in the feed given to cattle.

Regulatory
commission structure

commissioners' terms are long (5 years or more) and overlapping, and commissioners may be dismissed by the president only for "inefficiency, neglect of duty, or malfeasance in office." Commissioners cannot be fired simply because the president doesn't like their views. The president still has influence over regulatory commission policies. He appoints commissioners and designates commission chairmen. Even with long overlapping terms, a president usually gets to see his appointees established as a majority on each regulatory body; he is certain to do so if he enters his second term. The requirement of bipartisanship in commission membership is of little consequence; a Republican president can always pick conservative Democrats, and a Democratic president liberal Republicans. Nonetheless, the commission structure is a barrier to presidential influence and direction in major areas of federal economic policy. This was the original intent. It continues to spark strong criticism, however, from those who insist that an unacceptable incoherence of national economic policy is encouraged through this system. We discuss this issue in chapter 18.

The departments, agencies, and commissions have extraordinarily diverse program responsibilities—far more than we can treat here. In chapters 17 through 20, the policy roles of many of the executive agencies are discussed further.

THE BUREAU

The **bureau** is the basic unit of federal administration. The word "bureaucracy" was coined in eighteenth-century France, a neologism formed from the French word for a place where officials worked (the bureau) and a suffix derived from the Greek word for "rule." The root meaning of bureaucracy connotes "rule by officialdom." The *Dictionary of the French Academy* defined "bureaucratie" in 1798 as "power, influence of the heads and staff of governmental bureaux."[11] In subsequent usage, "bureaucracy" has lost some of its original stress on "rule," but the idea of appointed officials organized around an administrative office is still central to most modern conceptions of bureaucracy.

Nature of bureaus

Today, bureaus are the administrative organization set up to actually operate the various programs of the executive departments—as in the Bureau of the Census of the Department of Commerce. The same type of administrative structure is sometimes called an "office" (the Office of Surface Mining Reclamation and Enforcement of the Department of Interior), an "administration" (the Food and Drug Administration of the Department of Health and Human Services), or a "service" (the Internal Revenue Service of the Department of the Treasury). James Fesler notes that "these operating units are so important in federal administration that one could regard the executive branch as literally a 'bureaucracy'—that is, a government by bureaus—and could treat the departmental and presidential levels merely as superstructure."[12] Most of the executive departments are really collections of bureaus. Some bureaus are older than the departments in which they are now located. The Bureau of Land Management was established in 1812, thirteen years before the Interior Department of which it is now a part, was formed. And five bureaus are actually larger (in number of employees) than the Departments of State, Labor, Energy, Housing and Urban Development, and Education. (These are the Social Security Administration, the Internal Revenue Service, the Public Health Service, the Forest Service, and the Army Corps of Engineers—for civil functions.)

Department of Agriculture's organization

To understand the scope of federal government activities and the kinds of programs and services the government provides, we must look beneath the "umbrella" departments to the constituent bureaus, offices, administrations, and services. Figure 9.3 shows the operating structure of the Department of Agriculture—a middle-sized executive department. More than twenty services (bureaus) run the department's wide-ranging programs. A number of these services are huge governmental agencies. For example, the Farmers Home Administra-

---

[11] Martin Albrow, *Bureaucracy* (New York: Praeger, 1970), p. 17.
[12] Fesler, *Public Administration*, p. 45.

Figure 9.3 **United States Department of Agriculture**

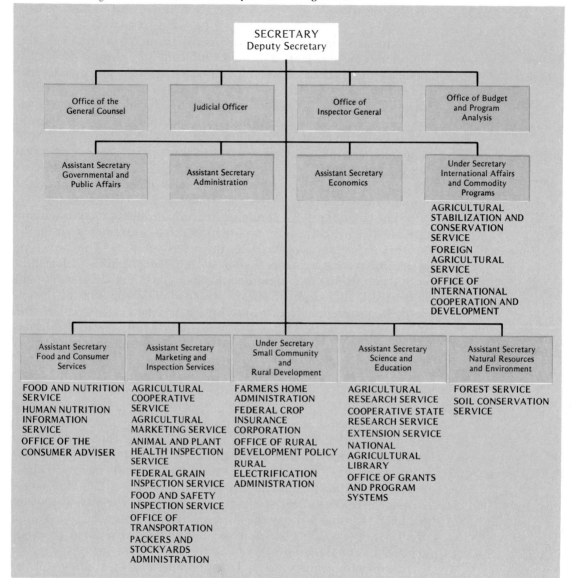

Source: The United States Government Manual, 1984/85, p. 823.

tion, established to provide credit for people in rural areas unable to obtain credit at reasonable rates elsewhere, makes loans to low-income persons to buy houses in the open country, to farm owners and operators for land conservation purposes, to those wanting to repair farm homes and service buildings, to young people (ages 10–21) who want "to establish and operate income-producing enterprises of modest size," and many others. In 1984 the Farmers Home Administration employed 16,500 people and expended roughly $4.7 billion.

The main federal bureaus, with their large, on-going program activities, have naturally become focal points for interest groups and, in turn, look to interest groups to help protect and maintain themselves. And congressmen serving on the committees and sub-committees with jurisdiction over the programs which bureaus manage have come to take a close interest in bureau affairs. A complex and important set of policy systems has gradually emerged in the federal executive, with the bureau typically at the center. As we look more closely at these systems, we will draw our examples primarily from the Department of Agriculture (USDA) and agricultural programs, although much the same relationships apply to many other client-oriented departments, such as Labor, Commerce, Energy, and Transportation.

Bureaus and the federal government

The Bureau: Hub of Federal Policy

A president is elected, and upon taking office he appoints a group of political executives to give direction to his administration's programs. The formal authority of these executives, and their political influence deriving from the mandate the voters gave the president, are substantial. But many observers stress the limits rather than the extent of their power. For the president and his cabinet secretaries often have less enduring roles in federal programs than do the heads of governmental bureaus. The former come and go; the latter seem to go on forever.

Transience of political appointees

A president may serve one term, two at most. The people he appoints to administer the executive departments on average have even shorter terms. For example, from 1960 through 1972, about 40 percent of all cabinet secretaries served under 24 months; over 50 percent of all undersecretaries and assistant secretaries held their posts two years or less.[13] "The single most obvious characteristic of Washington's political appointees," political scientist Hugh Heclo observes, "is their transience."[14] Among the political executives of the federal government, everything seems to be constantly in flux. They have come to government from all corners of national life. Many of them have had little or no contact with one another prior to receiving their presidential appointments. They must try to master exceedingly complex jobs in short periods of time and in the context of almost entirely new teams of executives.

Durability of bureau roles

The political direction coming to the bureau from the president, and the cabinet secretary or assistant secretary, is short-term and episodic. In contrast, the relationship between the bureau and the political interests which have a stake in its programs endures. This contrast between the transience of political executives and the durability of the policy environments in which they must work tells us

[13] Arch Patton, "Government's Revolving Door," *Business Week*, September 22, 1973, p. 12.
[14] Hugh Heclo, *A Government of Strangers* (Washington, D.C.: Brookings Institution, 1977). p. 103.

much about why practical control over programs resides to such a large degree in the bureaus and with the political interests organized around them. The strength and durability of bureaus' role in federal policy results, too, from the mutually supporting nature of their ties to interest groups. When two different organisms are associated in a manner of mutual benefit, biologists call their relationship "symbiosis." In this sense, the association of bureaus and interest groups is a symbiotic one.

Interest Groups and Bureaus

Consider the Rural Electrification Administration (REA) within the USDA. It delivers important services to rural dwellers—organized through the National Rural Electric Cooperative Association—such as helping rural electric and telephone utilities obtain financing through loans and loan guarantees. In turn, the Rural Electric Cooperative Association has served as a personal lobby for the REA, lobbying congressmen on behalf of the REA's programs and budget. Political scientist Theodore Lowi notes that a principal agricultural interest group, the American Farm Bureau Federation, has had a similar connection with the Extension Service of the Agriculture Department throughout its entire history.[15] And Harold Seidman, who served as assistant director of the Bureau of the Budget from 1964 to 1968, observes, "Each of the agencies dispensing federal largess has its personal lobby: the Corps of Engineers has the Rivers and Harbors Congress; the Bureau of Reclamation, the National Reclamation Association; the Soil Conservation Service, the National Association of Soil and Water Conservation Districts."[16]

The interest group/bureau connection Some depict these ties as grubby and self-serving. But the matter is considerably more complicated. A federal program like rural electrification began with a clear and respectable need: it cost much more to extend electric and telephone service to remote rural areas than to cities and towns, because wires had to be strung across miles of isolated and sparsely settled territory to reach a few paying customers. The REA stepped into the breach by providing the funding. It is neither surprising nor troubling that the bureau and the interests it served established a firm and mutually supporting association. Once enough of these ties have been established, however, the position of the cabinet secretary and assistant secretaries becomes very weak, because they find it hard to control the bureaus' policy commitments. Furthermore, the line between legitimate interest in extending needed services, and the narrow interest of group/agency self-advancement, is both blurred and easily crossed.

The symbiotic nature of the ties between bureaus and interest groups has led some to question conventional descriptions of group power.

[15] Theodore J. Lowi, *The End of Liberalism* (New York: Norton, 1979), p. 72.
[16] Seidman, *Politics, Position and Power*, p. 164.

Rural Electrification Administration linemen at work.

In many cases we have been describing, it would be misleading to suggest that a powerful interest group has muscled its way in and forced government to do its bidding. Rather, the agency and the interest group have compatible objectives and need each other.

Congress and Bureaus

Just as the associations of interest groups and bureaus are often enduring, so are those of congressional leadership and bureaus. As we saw in chapter 7, power in the U.S. Congress is highly fragmented, distributed across an elaborate system of nearly 300 committees and subcommittees. Each executive agency bureau falls within the jurisdiction of one or several subcommittees that develop legislation defining bureau programs and provide funding for them. A subcommittee chairman usually pays close attention to the work of "his bureau" because he may care deeply about it, because it matters to his constitutents, and/or because he thereby gains power. Here again is symbiosis. Congressmen and bureau administrators need and use each other. And the permanence of their ties and interaction, coupled with the transience of cabinet secretaries and other senior political executives, further encourages the remarkable fragmentation of executive authority.

Congressional ties to bureaus

Congressmen do not have formal grants of administrative responsibility, but they often play large roles in guiding agency programs. In fact, a congressman's reach over executive-branch programs sometimes far exceeds that of cabinet secretaries. For example, Representative Jamie Whitten of Mississippi, chairman of the House Appropriations Committee and, as well, chairman of the Appropriations Subcommittee on Agriculture, Rural Development, and Related Agencies, has been called the "permanent secretary of Agriculture." Over the last quarter-century, a time when the Democrats have continuously controlled the House of Representatives, Whitten's say in agricultural programs has been immense.

The Life of the Bureau Chief

The administrators who head federal bureaus are responsible not just to their executive superiors—the cabinet secretaries and the president. In a very real sense they are also responsible unofficially to congressional committee leaders and to influential interest groups. This means that bureau chiefs have a confusing mix of "masters"— but also that they can attain a striking degree of political autonomy. If astute and inclined to play one master against another, a bureau chief can achieve a measure of longevity and program control that does not exist in the administration of other democratic governments. Within our pluralistic government, bureaus are not merely administrative units, but also the focal points of a system of dispersed power. Bureau chiefs are typically policy-makers, not merely administrators of policies others make.

Bureaucratic autonomy

Once in place, the bureau–subcommittee–interest group triangle becomes a familiar and comfortable policy environment for its participants. And they will resist attempts at reorganization. Committee leaders often don't like change because it might disrupt their established channels of oversight and influence. Interest groups fear that new arrangements might weaken their claims. And bureau chiefs find their own autonomy and influence enhanced by established and enduring congressional and group ties. Many efforts at change initiated by presidents and cabinet secretaries have crashed against these "iron triangles." Figure 9.4 shows a current triangle.

"Iron triangles"

Change is made especially difficult by the fact that the triangular-interactions often involve intensely held inside interests and weak or diffuse outside concerns. For example, a program of agricultural price supports—maintaining farm prices at levels deemed fair to farmers— may benefit only a small group of farmers at the expense of a large group of consumers. But the interests of the former are intense while those of the latter are by comparison weak and disjointed. It isn't always this way, though. Sometimes outside interests can become strong enough to overturn established policy systems. One recent example has to do with the public's concern over the environment. By 1970 environmental interests had gained enough political muscle to get Congress to establish the Environmental Protection Agency (EPA). The EPA assumed authority in a variety of areas that had been under the jurisdiction of old-line departments. For instance, it took over the regulation of pesticides that had formerly been lodged with

Agency programs and the public interest

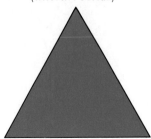

Agricultural Stabilization and Conservation Service,
Price Support and Loan Division,
Peanuts and Tobacco Section, U.S. Department of Agriculture
(executive bureau)

Figure 9.4
A Modern Iron Triangle

Tobacco Growers
(interest group)

House Committee on Agriculture,
House Subcommittee on Tobacco
and Peanuts
(Congress)

a bureau in the Department of Agriculture. Firms manufacturing pesticides felt more comfortable with their ties to the USDA and resisted the shift. But the environmental lobby succeeded in severing the old interest group-bureau bond.[17] Today environmental groups look upon the various offices or bureaus of the EPA as their own, much as agricultural interest groups have for a long time viewed the USDA as their own.

The Public Interest

This description of interest-group ties to bureaus does not give us much help in determining whether the resultant programs are legitimate ones, as judged by the standard of the public interest. Interest groups invariably claim that the programs they favor serve larger national ends, not just their own interests, and often they sincerely believe they do. Different groups will inevitably construe the public interest in different ways. The fact that an interest group strongly backs a program does not mean that the program is bad. What is clear is that American public-policy formation, built as it is around a multiplicity of interest-group, bureau, and congressional committee interrelations, is remarkably fragmented.

The bureau: the hub
of policy-making

As Figure 9.5 suggests, the federal bureau is frequently the hub of a set of interactions involving 1) *administration leadership,* 2) *congressional leadership* (usually defined at the committee or subcommittee levels), 3) *inside group interests,* and 4) *outside interests.* The strength of any one part will vary from one program area to another and may shift over time. For example, a politically popular president and an effective cabinet secretary may well be able to build upon public sup-

[17] Peter Woll, *American Bureaucracy,* 2d ed. (New York: Norton, 1977), p. 104.

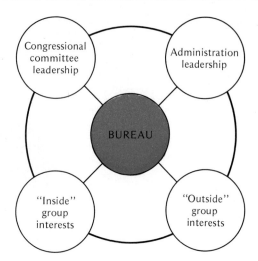

Figure 9.5
The Policy Wheel in Executive Organization

port for change to override the preferences of inside interests and established congressional committee preferences. Conversely, a strong subcommittee chairman, especially if he is operating in conjunction with well-organized inside interests and in the absence of sustained opposing efforts by the president, may be able to push bureau activities decisively in a direction that he favors. Inside interests—such as those of farm groups in USDA programs—are often highly influential, but they may be overriden by the growth of outside interests. While their relative strength varies from case to case, the component parts of the policy wheel seem to be constants. And viewed from the perspective of executive branch organization and operation, the bureau is typically the focal point of the policy wheel.

THE PRESIDENT AND THE BUREAUCRACY

The Constitution gives the president "the executive Power . . . of the United States of America." But how is that power to be exercised over a federal executive establishment as complex and fragmented as the one we have been describing? One part of the answer involves the president's formal authority over his subordinates.

The Power to Hire and Fire

Removing political executives

A great variety of statutes and political traditions now define the president's appointive and removal authority. With regard to appointments, the president picks the political executives who head the executive departments and agencies, with or without the requirement of Senate confirmation, depending upon the office. Department secretaries (and assistant secretaries, etc.) and regulatory commission board members require Senate confirmation, while members of the White House staff who serve as personal presidential advisers do not.

With regard to dismissals, the rule worked out in 1789 still generally applies. The question then before Congress and Washington's administration was: Should the Senate's "advice and consent" be required for dismissing political executives as well as appointing them? Or should the president have the sole right of removal? George Washington favored the latter and, with the Constitution silent on the issue, narrowly persuaded Congress to support him. Today, a president still may remove most of the political executives he appoints without any statutory restriction. There are some key exceptions—the biggest involving commissioners of the independent regulatory agencies, who can be fired only for malperformance or malfeasance in office. Note that this summary of presidential power applies only to *political executives* (and other assistants), numbering about 8,000. Under legislation enacted by Congress, neither the president nor his political appointees can hire or fire most of the 2.8 million executive-branch employees, who are career staff working under the provisions of a civil service system, as discussed later in the chapter.

Executive recruitment

Even filling 8,000 posts within the president's appointment authority is a chore for any new administration. No president or small group of presidential assistants knows 8,000 people prepared to leave their present jobs and serve ably in diverse posts throughout the executive branch. Recent presidents have set up quite elaborate recruitment efforts, but the results have still often been disappointing. For certain positions the problem is not choosing among a number of worthy candidates but rather encouraging able people to leave jobs in the private sector—where they receive higher salaries and much greater security and privacy—and come to Washington.

Every new administration is besieged by people wanting political appointments. A great many political leaders and groups are involved in successful presidential campaigns, and after an election many of them invariably press their own candidates for administration posts. Some of these candidates are admirably qualified, others decidedly unsuited. Many are never chosen. Back in the nineteenth century, one disappointed appointment-seeker took his revenge by shooting President James Garfield. Garfield lingered two and a half months after the shooting, dying on September 19, 1881. He had actively served only four months as chief executive.

The Executive Schedule

Of the 8,000 positions open to presidential appointment, perhaps 700 are of major importance to agency and program direction. These include cabinet secretaries and other agency heads, and second-level political executives, such as deputy secretaries and assistant secretaries. Occupants of these posts are appointed by the president to positions within a job classification scheme known as the **Executive Schedule.** The Executive Schedule has five levels, each with established compensation (the Executive Schedule pay rates). Box 9.1 shows which jobs fit into which levels of the schedule.

Box 9.1
The Executive Schedule

Level 1: The heads of executive departments, like the Secretary of State, the Secretary of Defense, and the Secretary of Transportation.

Level 2: The heads of major agencies, of the Executive Office of the President, such as the Office of Management and Budget; the heads of large independent agencies including the National Aeronautics and Space Administration, the Central Intelligence Agency, the Veterans Administration, and the Federal Reserve.

Level 3: The heads of other independent agencies, such as the General Services Administration and the Small Business Administration; commissioners of the major regulatory agencies, including the Interstate Commerce Commission and the Federal Trade Commission; the heads of government corporations, such as the Federal Deposit Insurance Corporation and the Tennessee Valley Authority; the directors of scientific foundations, such as the National Science Foundation; the heads of important administrations or bureaus within executive departments, such as the director of the Federal Bureau of Investigation and the Comptroller of the Currency.

Level 4: The heads of smaller independent agencies like the Selective Service System, the Equal Employment Opportunity Commission, the St. Lawrence Seaway Development Corporation; the chiefs of important bureaus within the executive departments.

Level 5: The heads of minor agencies like the Renegotiation Board and the Foreign Claims Settlement Commission; the directors and deputy directors of other constituent units within executive departments and agencies.

Source: Adapted from Seidman, *Politics, Position, and Power*, pp. 243–44.

Presidential Control Over the Bureaucracy

Presidents and their cabinet secretaries often complain that they lack sufficient control over the executive-branch bureaucracy. But they are referring to only a very small segment of the 2.8 million people who work for executive agencies. As we have seen, the president appoints the top political administrators and can fire them if they fail to do his bidding. The bulk of federal workers, however, do not play policy roles at all. They issue Social Security checks, deliver the mail, process tax returns, and more. These jobs are vital to government, but presidents don't seek greater control over them. The majority of these positions are handled through a civil service system, described below.

Presidents' concern over bureaucratic unresponsiveness revolves around fewer than 10,000 officials who play important policy

Career officials

roles but who are not subject to presidential appointment or dismissal authority. These are career officials, who are subject to civil service hiring, promotion, and firing provisions. At the bureau level, virtually all key officials, the bureau chief included, are career officials. Presidents and cabinet secretaries come and go; senior career officials usually stay much longer. Their greater longevity and dominant place in the bureaus—which have such large policy-making roles—give career bureaucrats great influence.

Any president, elected by the people and wanting to implement his programs, is bound to feel some frustration when he encounters bureaucratic resistance. Presidents and their political appointees often express frustration that career officials don't fully support administration policies and even try to sabotage them. Sometimes, amidst mutual complaints and recriminations, pitched battles break out between the two sides.

The Reagan Administration and the EPA: A Case Study

The political furor surrounding the Environmental Protection Agency in 1982 and 1983 illustrates this executive-branch warfare. The Reagan administration came into office committed to cutting back what it deemed excessive and unproductive federal regulation in environmental programs. The Democratic majority in Congress, the environmental lobby, and many senior career EPA administrators generally opposed the Reagan proposals. In the ensuing struggle, the political appointees at the EPA, including Agency Administrator Anne Burford, came under attack for not faithfully executing various pieces of environmental legislation. Much of the criticism and evidence of violations by the EPA officials originated within the agency bureaucracy. In March 1983, with charges flying, Burford and most of her political associates at EPA resigned. This *Washington Post* news release reported the immediate aftermath:

> At the EPA's offices in Waterside Mall, dozens of career employees found cause for celebration. . . . Downstairs in the shopping mall, Harry's Liquor, Wine and Cheese sold 8 cases of champagne and 6 ounces of Russian cavier to the General Counsel's Office [at the EPA].[18]

Commenting on the bitterness and tensions, journalist Dick Kirschten wrote that "as top presidential appointees fled the Environmental Protection Agency (EPA) in rout last month, the permanent staff acted as though it had been liberated from an army of occupation."[19]

[18] *Washington Post*, March 26, 1983, p. 23.
[19] Dick Kirschten, "Administration Using Carter-Era Reform to Manipulate the Levers of Government," *National Journal*, April 9, 1983, p. 732.

Nixon and the Bureaucracy: A Case Study

Perhaps the most dramatic instance of tension between political executives and career officials came during Richard Nixon's tenure in office. The tension stemmed from the suspicion, even animosity, that some in the political leadership of the Nixon administration felt toward the career bureaucracy—feelings which seem to have been reciprocated. In a manual prepared by White House staff, Nixon appointees were warned that the career service was stacked against the administration: "Because of the rape of the career service by the Kennedy and Johnson Administrations ... this Administration has been left a legacy of finding disloyalty and obstruction at high levels while those incumbents rest comfortably on career civil service status."[20] The anger extended to the president himself, as is evident from these comments of his captured by his White House taping system and released following the Watergate investigation:

> "You've got to get us some discipline George [then OMB Director George Schultz]. You've got to get it, and the only way you get it, is when a bureaucrat thumbs his nose, were going to get him. . . . They've got to know, that if they do it, something's going to happen to them, where anything can happen. I know the Civil Service pressure. But you can do a lot there. There are many unpleasant places where Civil Service people can be sent. We just don't have any discipline in government. That's our trouble. . . . So whatever you—well, maybe he is in the regional office. Fine. Demote him or send him to the Guam regional office. There's a way. Get him the hell out.[21]

In a February 1971 news conference, the president publicly described his opponents in the federal bureaucracy as "dug-in establishmentarians fighting for the status quo."[22] And in an interview later that year, he told reporter Howard K. Smith that "I think it is repugnant to the American system that only the bureaucratic elite at the top of the heap in Washington [believes it] knows what is best for the people. . . ."[23]

Nixon's distrust of career federal administrators seems excessive, but it was not entirely misplaced. When Nixon entered the White House, Democrats far outnumbered Republicans among top career executives of the federal government. Many of the administrators

Nixon and the bureaucracy

[20] This document has been included in the Report of the Select Senate Committee on Presidential Campaign Activities, *Executive Session Hearings*, "Watergate and Related Activities," 93d Cong., 2d sess., Washington, D.C.: 1973, 19:9,006.

[21] Tape of Meeting held April 19, 1971. A transcript was published in the *New York Times*, July 20, 1974, p. 14.

[22] Richard M. Nixon, news conference, February 17, 1971, printed in *Public Papers of the Presidents, 1971* (Washington, D.C.: Government Printing Office, 1972), p. 167.

[23] Howard K. Smith interview of Richard M. Nixon; the text may be found in *Public Papers of the Presidents, 1971*, p. 463.

brought in under Democratic presidents Kennedy and Johnson had real disagreements with Nixon's programs.[24] To secure greater White House control over the executive branch, the Nixon administration tried a number of things. In his 1971 State of the Union message, Nixon proposed merging eight existing domestic departments into four new superagencies: the Departments of National Resources, Human Resources, Economic Affairs, and Community Development. Congress would not go along. But immediately after his November 1972 victory, the president moved ahead anyway. He named four cabinet members—the secretaries of Treasury, Agriculture, HEW, and HUD—as *presidential counselors*. By making them White House office staff as well as cabinet officers, he gave them functional responsibilities over economic affairs, natural resources, human resources, and community development, respectively. At the same time, he appointed trusted political staff to positions throughout the executive branch "in direct charge of the major program bureaucracies of domestic government."[25] By manipulating the civil service personnel system, his administration also sought to change the partisan makeup and policy commitments of the most senior levels of the career service.

Nixon's attempts to achieve central political direction over the sprawling federal administration soon got sidetracked as his administration was engulfed by Watergate. Fighting for survival, it lacked both the energy and the political clout required to follow through on its struggle with the bureaucracy. But were Nixon's ideas for change well-conceived? On the one hand, the idea of an independent civil service pursuing its managerial tasks according to politically neutral standards of professional competence remains an attractive one. Nixon's efforts to "take over" the bureaucracy were a frontal challenge to that ideal.

On the other hand, as Richard Cole and David Caputo have observed, the ideal of a neutral bureaucracy had not been realized.[26] As the activities of the national government expanded, the bureaucracy found itself with greater policy discretion—and frequently behaved as partisans of various programs, not neutral administrators. The idea that a greater measure of direction over executive-branch policy-making should reside with those given a popular mandate—the president and the political executives whom he appoints—finds strong support in both prevailing concepts of public administration and democratic theory.

The unique attempt of the Nixon administration as well as the more modest efforts of every modern president stem from a persisting

The plan to reorganize executive departments

The ideal of a neutral bureaucracy

---

[24] Joel D. Aberbach and Burt A. Rockman, "Clashing Beliefs Within the Executive Branch," *American Political Science Review* 70 (June 1976):456–68.
[25] Richard P. Nathan, *The Plot That Failed* (New York: Wiley, 1975), pp. 61–62.
[26] Richard L. Cole and David A. Caputo, "Presidential Control of the Senior Civil Service," *American Political Science Review*, June 1979, p. 394.

problem: how to manage the federal bureaucracy, with its extensive discretionary powers, in the interest of such competing ends as political responsiveness, national policy coherence, and administrative effectiveness?

ORGANIZATION OF THE FEDERAL CIVIL SERVICE

As we noted, the struggle of successive administrations against bureaucratic opposition to their programs focuses on only a small number of fairly senior career administrators. Most federal civil workers have little or nothing to do with designing or directing governmental programs. This distinction becomes evident when we look at the tasks most civil servants perform. Roughly a half-million workers, one-fifth of the full-time federal civilian labor force, are in blue-collar jobs (including nearly 10,000 painters, 5,000 cooks, 13,000 sheet-metal workers, and 16,000 pipe fitters). In 1981, there were 69 wind-tunnel mechanics, 172 cemetery caretakers, 149 stevedores (dock-workers), and 348 sign painters. While such jobs are important to federal agencies, they are hardly what presidents have in mind when they worry about a recalcitrant bureaucracy.

Similarly, most of the nearly 2 million full-time white-collar workers in the executive branch have responsibilities little related to policy-setting. Secretaries are the largest single white-collar group: some 86,000 in 1981. There were more than 35,000 nurses, 30,000

Figure 9.6
Full-Time Civilian Employees of the Federal Government by Selected Occupational Categories (with examples of professions within each category)

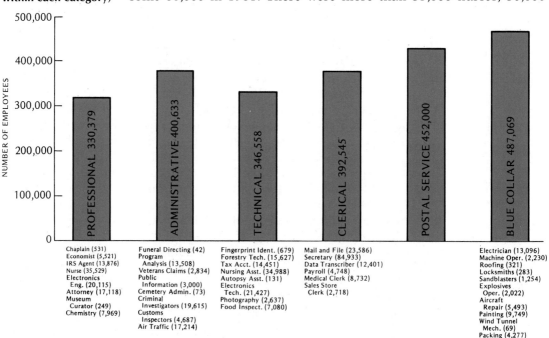

Source: Office of Personnel Management, *Occupations of Federal White-Collar and Blue-Collar Workers,* October 31, 1981.

computer specialists, and 17,000 air traffic controllers. The government employed over 500 historians, 3,300 psychologists, 1,700 microbiologists, and 2,500 pharmacists. Among its professional workers were 16,000 civil engineers, 8,000 chemists, and 4,500 map-makers. Of its administrative personnel, 4,700 were customs inspectors, 5,000 were loan specialists, and 73 were cemetery administrators. Its technical employees included nearly 16,000 forestry technicians, 2,600 photographers, 2,900 dental assistants, and 7,000 food inspectors. (See Figure 9.6.)

Problems in hiring and firing federal employees

While these employees may not be the focus of policy concerns, they pose other problems relating to effective personnel management. Many of these problems are long-standing and not peculiar to government; in part, at least, they arise in any large bureaucracy. How, for example, can one organize a personnel management system to prevent workers being fired for the wrong reasons, such as personal animosity and favoritism, while permitting them to be disciplined, even dismissed, for the right ones, such as incompetent performance? How can one grant agencies flexibility in hiring, so that they can exercise their informed judgment and get the best people for the available jobs, without inviting "old-boy cronyism" and other abuses?

Civil Service and the Merit System

The merit system

Over 90 percent of all federal civilian workers are now covered under some kind of **merit system.** What is meant by a merit system? Basically, the term has been closely linked in the U.S. with civil service, referring to procedures for the appointment of civil servants on the basis of competitive examinations rather than political sponsorship.

Civil service merit systems came into being in the late nineteenth century to replace the so-called spoils system, under which each administration had a free hand to hire and fire virtually all federal workers: "To the victor, the spoils." The initial idea of a merit-system alternative was largely negative, focusing on the importance of keeping political influence out of appointments and promotions.

Reforming the civil service

The Pendleton Civil Service Act of 1883 was the first important piece of reform legislation at the federal level in the U.S. Borrowing heavily from the practices of the British civil service of the time, the Pendleton Act required competitive examinations for federal appointments, guaranteed tenure of office (assuming competent performance), and required civil service workers to be politically neutral (not to use their posts to advance party goals or to discriminate on a partisan basis). Initially only about 10 percent of the federal work force was covered by Pendleton Act provisions, but the proportion grew steadily. Today, more than nine out of ten federal workers are covered by a merit system. Later legislation, especially the Hatch Acts of 1939 and 1940, extended protection of the civil service by barring on-the-job political pressure. The Hatch Act of 1939 placed severe restrictions on practically all political activities of federal employees except voting; the Hatch Act of 1940 extended coverage to state and local government workers whose jobs were funded in whole or in part by the federal government. The specific intent of this legislation was to prevent political executives from putting the squeeze on their subordinates within the bureaucracy. Since it would be difficult to differentiate "friendly persuasion" from subtle forms of coercion, even voluntary political work by government employees was banned.

The largest merit system today, encompassing 1.7 million workers, is administered by the government's central personnel agency, the Office of Personnel Management (OPM). The OPM was established in 1978 as one of two successor agencies to the old Civil Service Commission. By law, a number of agencies are outside the OPM-run civil service, including the U.S. Postal Service and its 660,000 employees. Other "excepted" agencies are the Federal Bureau of Investigation, the intelligence agencies, the Foreign Service of the State Department, and the Tennessee Valley Authority. All of these operate their own independent merit systems.

Getting a Civil Service Job

Staffing the federal bureaucracy first involves calculating the personnel requirements of the departments and agencies. With passage of the Civil Service Reform Act of 1978, such planning became the responsibility of the OPM. The OPM announces examinations designed to measure applicants' qualifications for various openings, processes applications, and administers the tests. Some exams are narrowly fitted to specific positions; others are of the "broad-band" variety—

Civil service
examinations

that is, designed to certify applicants for a range of different posts in government. The Professional and Administrative Career Examination (PACE)—an important "broad-band" example—is used to certify college graduates and college seniors for an extensive assortment of entry-level administrative and professional positions. The PACE recruits for two civil service grade levels, GS-5 and GS-7.

Actually, many candidates for civil service jobs never take a written test. Middle-level and upper-level positions in the civil service (GS grade levels 9–18) require the "unassembled" examination, which isn't an examination at all. Each candidate submits a statement that describes his or her relevant educational background and other pertinent training or experience, and lists persons, such as previous employers and teachers, who could be contacted for informed evaluations. What the candidate submits for these senior professional and managerial jobs in the government is exactly what he or she would for a comparable position in a university or a private business corporation.

Why call it an "examination"? The elusive goal is a type of objective certification that removes any opportunity for bias on the part of those doing the hiring. But no one has been able to devise satisfactory written examinations for many complex professional and managerial positions. Those who know what such posts require must assess candidates in terms of training and experience and arrive at the best judgment as to who are most qualified. Yet the greater the need for judgment, the greater the opportunity for bias or favoritism. One interesting indication of the quest for objectivity is that the *curriculum vitae* submitted by candidates for upper civil service positions are actually "graded" with numeric scores.

Veterans in the Civil Service

Probably the most substantial denial of the merit principle in the federal civil service system is extraneous to the examination process. All veterans of the armed services who sustained a service-related disability get 10-point bonuses added to their examination scores; all other veterans get 5 points (except for those who entered the military after 1976 and served only in peacetime). In addition to their 10-point bonuses, disabled veterans are placed at the head of the eligible register for all openings except scientific and professional positions at GS-9 and above. This means that they must be put on the list for hiring ahead of nonveterans, even those with much higher examination scores.

Veterans' preferences

Veterans' preferences don't end there. Normal civil service procedure requires the OPM to send an agency a list of three certified candidates for an opening, leaving the agency free to pick from the list the individual it considers most qualified. But when a veteran appears on a list ahead of a nonveteran, the agency *must* pick him unless it

gets the OPM's approval not to do so. Not surprisingly, veterans' organizations pay close attention, keeping the pressure on. At the other end of the employment process, when an agency is required to cut back on its work force ("reduction in force" or rif), the law states that veterans cannot be riffed before nonveterans in the same type and grade of work. Often veterans are retained while nonveterans with greater seniority are laid off.

The preferences accorded veterans in the civil service seriously challenge the merit system. Of course, veterans' preference provisions were put in not with merit in mind, but rather as an additional recognition of those who served in their country's defense. But another big problem arises: few women are veterans. Thus women are rather systematically excluded from the preferential treatment the veterans' bonus confers. How should this problem be addressed?

The Carter Proposals

The 1978 Civil Service Reform Act

In 1978 President Jimmy Carter attempted to find a solution. In his proposals for the Civil Service Reform Act, Carter endorsed a number of reductions in veterans' preferences. Among them, veterans would receive preference in governmental appointments only for a limited time after their discharge, rather than for life. Women's groups strongly backed these changes, but in the end the veterans' groups won out. The act was passed without most of the proposed reductions in preferential treatment for veterans.

Dismissing Civil Service Workers

Another dilemma presents itself when questions of dismissing workers arise. Civil service arrangements were implemented in large part to preclude the political favoritism of the spoils system. One way was to make it hard to fire people by requiring that a "preponderance of evidence" establish an employee's unacceptable performance before he or she could be dismissed. Anything less than that, it was felt, would make it too easy for supervisors to continue political favoritism by simply claiming that work was deficient. Strong federal employees' unions now add their weight as well to the side of protecting employees' rights.

But the same civil service regulations and union pressure that make it hard to dismiss employees for such illegitimate reasons as political preference also make it hard to fire lazy, unreliable, or insufficiently competent workers. Leonard Reed argues that "for many fine and capable civil servants, the acceptance of the incompetent and the slacker affects their own attitudes and performance. For federal executives the invulnerability of the unproductive worker makes a mockery of the whole concept of efficient management."[27]

Anecdotes about this problem abound. A classic example of the perils a supervisor may encounter if he tries to dismiss an employee is recounted by the former head of the Office of Personnel Management, Alan Campbell. The supervisor in question was trying to justify the dismissal of an employee

Difficulty of firing incompetent workers

> whose repeated absences from her duty station placed undue pressures on her co-workers. The supervisor spent 21 months preparing documentation and conferring with personnel officers, and finally succeeded in building his case. However, at the end of that time, the supervisor received a poor performance rating from his superiors for the neglect of his other duties. Had the employee appealed the case might yet be unresolved.[28]

Commenting on this case, James Fesler notes that it is even more difficult to bring about the dismissal of a worker who tries but who is simply incapable of performing his job competently.[29]

The American public concurs that incentives and sanctions for government workers are inadequate, and that federal workers' output often lags behind that in the private sector.[30] But in all this, we should be on the watch for exaggeration. Many politicians, journalists, and other commentators have long enjoyed getting in their criticisms of

[27] Leonard Reed, "Firing a Federal Employee: The Impossible Dream," in Charles Peters and Michael Nelson, eds., *The Culture of Bureaucracy*, (New York: Holt, Rinehart and Winston, 1979), p. 208.
[28] Alan K. Campbell, "Civil Service Reform as a Remedy for Bureaucratic Ills," in Carol H. Weiss and Alan H. Barton, eds., *Making Bureaucracies Work* (Beverly Hills: Sage Publications, 1980), pp. 161–62.
[29] Fesler, *Public Administration*, p. 107.
[30] For example, a national survey conducted by the Roper Organization in November 1981 found 60 percent of the opinion that government employees work "less hard . . . [than] people in comparable jobs in private industry." Only 5 percent thought they generally work harder, and 31 percent saw little difference between the two. The distributions were about the same on the question of whether government workers are more or less likely to come up with new ideas, or to be recognized for good ideas when they have them.

"Of All the Dirty Tricks! I Thought That Was Just Another Campaign Promise"

"overprotected, inefficient bureaucrats." Over the last decade, 5,000 to 6,000 workers who had been on their jobs beyond the probationary period have been dismissed for cause each year, and many others have been induced by their superiors to retire from government service. Still, undoubtedly, the federal civil service has erred on the side of job protection.

Dismissals and the 1978 Civil Service Reform Act

To try to correct the imbalance, the 1978 Civil Service Reform Act gave greater authority to agency heads in matters of dismissals, and streamlined discharge and demotion procedures. Now when an employee is dismissed for unacceptable performance and appeals to the Merit Systems Protection Board, the dismissal will be upheld if supported by "substantial evidence" rather than "a preponderance of evidence."

Has the 1978 reform made much difference? One study found that the number of workers fired actually declined from 1978 to 1980. But, in presenting these data, the authors note that "the issue should not be simply whether more people are fired but whether supervisors and managers deal appropriately with problem employees."[31] It is too soon to tell if modest, long-term gains will result from the 1978 legislation.

[31] Carolyn Ban, Edie Goldenberg, and Toni Marzotto, "Firing the Unproductive Employee: Will Civil Service Reform Make a Difference?" *Review of Public Personnel Administration*, 2 (Spring 1982):97, 98.

THE SENIOR EXECUTIVE SERVICE

Executive Schedule
and General Schedule

Most career administrators with significant policy responsibilities have been brought into an arm of the civil service known as the Senior Executive Service (SES). Established by the 1978 Civil Service Reform Act, the SES includes about 8,500 executives in the three highest General Schedule (GS) grades of federal employment and in Levels IV and V of the Executive Schedule. (There are 18 grades in all in the General Schedule; the Executive Schedule covers top government executives not under the General Schedule.) At least 90 percent of the SES must be senior career civil servants; the rest can be noncareer appointees.

Mobility and Neutral Competence

The civil service reformers who pushed for the SES wanted a corps of senior career administrators not locked into particular bureaus and programs. Rather than being tied to specific positions, members of the SES are supposed to constitute a mobile pool of top managerial talent, available for assignment where needed in the executive branch.

The idea of neutral
competence

A second, related goal was to provide the executive branch with a staff of skilled career managers who see themselves and, in turn, are seen by presidents and political appointees as sources of neutral competence rather than program advocacy. It should be possible, civil service reformers have long thought, to create in the U.S. a cadre of skilled, experienced career officials able and willing to serve any properly constituted administration, and in turn trusted and relied upon by administrations with contrasting political goals. The SES should not be merely skilled administrative "hired guns." "Just tell us what to do, boss" is not the desired end. Civil servants take an oath to uphold the Constitution, and out of this commitment grows a defensible basis for making judgments independent from those of the political executives of the day. Beyond this, senior administrators have a responsibility to argue back to their political superiors (even if they ultimately acquiesce), for their experience and understanding must be brought into play: "S.E.S. personnel should embody the 'institutional memory' that has so often rescued political leadership from disastrous adventures."[32]

Woodrow Wilson on
bureaucracy

Early in his career as a political scientist, Woodrow Wilson gave expression to the idea of larger ends and interests to be served by public administrators.

> The question for us is, how shall our series of governments within governments be so administered that it shall always be to the interest of the

[32] John A. Rohr, "Ethics for the Senior Executive Service," *Administration and Society* 12 (August 1980):211.

public officer to serve, not his superior alone, but the community also with the best efforts of his talents and the soberest service of his conscience? How shall such service be made to his commonest interest by contributing abundantly to his sustenance, to his dearest interest by furthering his ambition, and to his highest interest by advancing his honor and establishing his character? And how shall all this be done alike for the local part and the national whole?[33]

The ideal SES, then, would be prepared to serve ably different groups of political executives, accepting their claims to political leadership. In this way, the Constitution's grant of executive power to the president and his appointees would be honored, and with it the democratic requirement that the people should be the ultimate arbiters of policy through those whom they elect. At the same time a higher ethic of administration would be interposed, predicated on enduring standards for sound constitutional government.

The ideal senior bureaucracy

The British Experience

Students of American public administration have long felt that some nations—among them, Great Britain—have done a better job than the U.S. in producing cadres of senior career officials with a high *esprit de corps* and a reputation for neutral competence in the service of shifting political executives. In Britain, the civil service's "administrative class" of about 7,500 officials assists cabinet ministers in all facets of governing: providing them with information about what is happening within their departments, identifying alternate courses of action, and translating the policy goals of the party in power into concrete programs and legislation. The ideal of neutral competence figures prominently in the work of the senior British civil service, for once a policy is determined by a minister or by the cabinet, career administrators are supposed to execute it loyally even when they personally disagree with it. As one British administrator put it: "The soul of the service is the loyalty with which we execute ordained error."[34]

Britain: a history of bureaucratic neutrality

Some observers maintain that the British model has been over-idealized.[35] Even if this is so, the American sense of how the British civil service operates contributed a great deal to the development of the SES and the conception of how it should operate.

Politicization

Earlier we described the bitter recrimination and bureaucratic warfare that in recent decades has sometimes developed between presi-

[33] Woodrow Wilson, "The Study of Administration," *Political Science Quarterly*, June 1887; reprinted in *Political Science Quarterly*, 56 (December 1941):505.
[34] As quoted in Ian Gilmour, *The Body Politic* (London: Hutchinson, 1969), p. 198.
[35] Norton Long's brief discussion of this is perceptive. "The S.E.S. and the Public Interest," *Public Administration Review*, 41 (May/June 1981):306–7.

dents and their political appointees on one side, and senior career administrators on the other. In pushing for the SES, Carter administration officials, especially civil service head Alan Campbell, hoped that it might make for a more constructive relationship.

Presidential attempts
to politicize the
bureaucracy

In the 1960s and early 1970s presidents seeking a stronger hand on the bureaucracy had increased the number of political appointees in executive agencies. As new layers were added, a kind of bureaucratization of political leadership occurred. At the same time, in response to both presidential quests for greater control and defiance by career officials, there was an increased politicization of the bureaucracy.[36] Everyone lost. While the numbers of political executives increased, they remained few compared to the career civil servants; and their restricted tenure of office greatly limited their practical ability to assert the desired control. Career officials were subjected to increased criticism and to heightened efforts at manipulation. And the recriminations and tensions involving political executives and career officials detracted from the mutual confidence and assistance both groups require to work effectively.

The only satisfactory way out of this corner lies in building a corps of senior career officials dedicated to the ideal of neutral competence employed on behalf of the current political leadership and constrained by a lively sense of responsibility to larger long-term needs of government.

> Since political appointees cannot get by on self-help alone, one of the greatest contributions to political leadership would be a well-organized, higher career service distributed across the executive branch. In fact, no reasonable alternatives exist, for in a day-to-day sense only bureaucrats can control the bureaucracy.[37]

Is the SES the answer?

Whether the still-new SES will fulfill these expectations remains to be seen. Still, as Norton Long points out, "this is the first time the country has been willing to recognize a Senior Executive Service whose neutral competence could be a major public resource. That recognition, if broadened and deepened, may well prove a significant institutional advance."[38]

SUMMARY

Over the last two centuries, a vast governmental system has evolved to administer American national government. The executive branch now includes over 100 cabinet departments, independent agencies, regulatory commissions, foundations, boards, and related organizations, and employs about 2.8 million men and women in civilian service.

[36] Heclo, *Government of Strangers*, especially pp. 64–81.
[37] Heclo, *Government of Strangers*, p. 234.
[38] Long, "S.E.S. and the Public Interest," p. 306.

The executive agencies with the broadest policy mandates and the greatest prestige are the thirteen departments with cabinet rank. Four of them trace their lineage back to the beginning of George Washington's first administration: State; Treasury; Defense (originally the War Department); and Justice (originally the office of the Attorney General). The other nine departments are, in the order in which they were established: Interior; Agriculture; Commerce; Labor; Health and Human Services; Housing and Urban Development; Transportation; Energy; and Education.

The Constitution vests executive authority in the president, but effective presidential direction of the sprawling executive branch is not easily achieved. While the president appoints the heads of the various executive agencies and their principal deputies (with the Senate's advice and consent), and may remove most of these officials without congressional action, Congress plays an active role in executive-branch management. One reason why congressional influence is so great involves the strength and independence of the bureaus, the main units of program responsibility and administration. Headed typically by senior career civil servants, bureaus are tied not just to the departments and agencies of which they are a part, but also to the congressional committees that legislate the substance of their programs and appropriate their budgets.

Sometimes bitter battles have broken out between presidents and their political appointees on one hand, and senior career administrators in the various executive agency bureaus on the other hand, as presidents have sought to exercise greater policy control and direction over the bureaucracy. In an effort to break the cycle of conflict and recrimination, the Carter administration proposed, and Congress enacted, the 1978 Civil Service Reform Act. One portion of this Act establishes the Senior Executive Service, comprised of about 8,500 senior career administrators. These officials of the permanent government would be less tied to specific bureaus and programs and more a source of much-needed neutral competence in executive branch administration.

Apart from the issue of political direction and responsiveness, personnel management for the civil service involves classic public administration problems. How can one preclude civil servants being fired because of political favoritism, while permitting them to be dismissed for such proper reasons as incompetent performance? Federal employement has acquired the reputation for erring excessively on the side of job security—a reputation it seems to have earned.

Other problems confronting the federal civil service stem from contrasting objectives in its staffing practices: providing preferential treatment for veterans on one hand while trying to assure that government jobs will be open to all on the basis of merit rather than favoritism on the other.

10 | The Judiciary

The United States Supreme Court, and American courts generally, have exercised great political power. One noted student of the judiciary, Robert G. McCloskey, considers the Supreme Court "the most powerful court known to history." Observers from other countries "have never ceased to be amazed at the part played by the nine judges in national affairs. . . ."[1] This judgment invites little disagreement today. But it would certainly have surprised the framers of the Constitution, who thought the judiciary would be decidedly the weakest of the three branches of government. The president, Alexander Hamilton argued, has a major grant of power as commander-in-chief of the armed forces, while Congress holds

> the power of the purse and as well makes all the laws by which the country is governed. The judiciary, on the contrary, has no influence over either the sword or the purse . . . and can take no active resolution whatever. It may truly be said to have neither *force* or *will* but merely judgment; and must ultimately depend upon the aid of the executive arm even for the efficacy of its judgments.[2]

As it has turned out, Hamilton underestimated the importance of a power the American courts do have, the power *to say what the law is*. Congress enacts legislation, the president signs it into law, and the executive agencies administer it. But the courts, and ultimately the U.S. Supreme Court, decide what the law actually means or requires. This power extends even to the determination of what the "higher

---

[1] Robert G. McCloskey, *The American Supreme Court* (Chicago: University of Chicago Press, 1960), p. 225.
[2] Alexander Hamilton, *Federalist Paper* No. 78.

The Supreme Court, 1984. From left to right: Standing, John Paul Stevens, Lewis Powell, William Rehnquist, Sandra Day O'Connor; Seated, Thurgood Marshall, William Brennan, Chief Justice Warren Burger, Byron White, Harry Blackmun.

law" of the Constitution stipulates. This elemental grant of political power has assumed breathtaking proportions over the course of American history. As Charles Evans Hughes—Chief Justice of the Supreme Court from 1930 to 1941—observed in 1916: "We are under a Constitution, but *the Constitution is what the judges say it is*, and the judiciary is the safeguard of our liberty. . . ."[3]

In the first section of this chapter we look at the courts as key political institutions in the U.S., and consider how they perform their special kind of political decision-making. Then we examine the organization of the court system, including the relationship of the state and federal courts and the jurisdiction of each. How judges get selected and the composition of the highest federal courts is taken up next. In the final section of the chapter we review public opinion on the courts: how Americans assess judicial performance.

COURTS AS POLITICAL INSTITUTIONS

Constitutional powers of the courts

The primary political responsibilities of the federal courts are not explicitly spelled out in the Constitution; only the general framework for them is provided. Article III assigns "the judicial power of the United States" to the Supreme Court and a system of lower federal courts. Article VI stipulates that "this Constitution, and the Laws of the United States which shall be made in Pursuance thereof . . . shall be the supreme Law of the Land; and the Judges in every State shall

[3] Charles Evans Hughes, *Addresses* (New York: Putnam, 1916), p. 185. Emphasis added.

be bound thereby, any Thing in the Constitution or Laws of any State to the Contrary notwithstanding." This latter provision has been critical to the political development and role of the federal courts. For, if the supremacy of the Constitution were to be more than a pious wish, there had to be a final arbiter of what the Constitution required. Here, the framers looked to the Supreme Court.

Judicial Review

The practice of *judicial review*—whereby an independent judicial branch reviews and gives final construction to legislative and executive acts and determines their constitutionality—is key to the courts' political role. As it has developed in the U.S., judicial review is exercised by state as well as federal courts, although the Supreme Court makes final binding determination of whether legislation is consistent with the Constitution.

A distinction must be made between judicial review of laws enacted by Congress and those enacted by state legislatures. The framers saw the Supreme Court playing umpire in the federal system, striking down state legislation that clashed with the requirements of national law. Alexander Hamilton argued in *Federalist Paper* 22 that true national government would be impossible if each state court system could separately decide what the Constitution and federal legislation require. It is essential "to establish one court paramount to the rest, possessing a general superintendence and authorized to settle and declare in the last resort a uniform rule of civil justice." Section 25 of the Judiciary Act of 1789 (enacted by a Congress of which many of the framers were members) explicitly conferred upon the Court authority to review state court decisions involving state actions in which a federal claim was raised.

On the issue of the Court's striking down acts of Congress, however, the historical record is more ambiguous. Some framers argued strongly for this power, as Hamilton did forcefully in *Federalist Paper* 78: "There is no position which depends on clearer principles than that every act of a delegated authority, contrary to the tenor of the commission under which it is exercised, is void. No legislative act, therefore, contrary to the Constitution, can be valid." But who is to decide if an act contradicts the Constitution? Shouldn't Congress itself be the judge? Hamilton was adamant that this was not intended.

Supreme Court: federal system umpire

Judging constitutionality

> It is far more rational to suppose that the courts were designed to be an intermediate body between the people and the legislature in order, among other things, to keep the latter within the limits assigned to their authority. The interpretation of the laws is the proper and peculiar province of the courts. A constitution is, in fact, and must be regarded by the judges as, a fundamental law. It therefore belongs to them to ascertain its meaning as well as the meaning of any particular act proceeding from the legislative body.

Marbury v. *Madison.* A decade and a half after the Constitution was ratified, Supreme Court Chief Justice John Marshall echoed Hamilton's argument:

> The Constitution is either a superior paramount law, unchangeable by ordinary means, or it is on a level with ordinary legislative acts. . . . If the former part of the alternative be true, then a legislative act contrary to the Constitution is not law. . . . It is, emphatically, the province and duty of the judicial department, to say what the law is.

Marshall concluded that "a law repugnant to the Constitution is void; and that courts, as well as other departments, are bound by that instrument."

Marbury v. Madison

The case in which Marshall delivered this momentous ruling was *Marbury* v. *Madison*, decided in 1803. William Marbury had been an official in the administration of President John Adams. Along with more than fifty of his fellow Federalists, he was nominated and confirmed for a federal judgeship just before Adams left office in March 1801. Final work on Marbury's commission was completed so late, however, that it did not get delivered before Thomas Jefferson and his new administration took office. Angered by the attempt to stack the federal judiciary with so many Federalists, Jefferson ordered that Marbury's commission (and others similarly not delivered) be held back. Marbury took his case to the Supreme Court, seeking an order requiring the Jefferson administration to give him his appointment.

John Marshall had been secretary of state in Adams' administration, and it was actually his oversight that had led to Marbury's commission not being delivered. By the time the Supreme Court heard Marbury's appeal, Marshall was chief justice. The case seemed to present him with a no-win dilemma. If the Court issued the order Marbury wanted, Jefferson and his secretary of state, James Madison, would certainly ignore it. The Court had no means to enforce compliance. And, as a new institution trying to establish itself, the Court might suffer permanent damage from such a precedent. But if it did not issue the order, the Court would be seen to be caving in to Jefferson's point of view.

An historic ruling on constitutionality

In the ruling for a unanimous Court, Marshall found a way to escape this dilemma and expand upon the Court's authority. Since the president had signed the commissions and the secretary of state had recorded them, the appointments were in order. The Jefferson administration was wrong in not releasing them to Marbury and his colleagues. Having thus rebuked Jefferson and Madison, Marshall turned to the question of whether the Supreme Court had the authority to issue the order Marbury wanted—and he concluded that it did not. He held that a minor provision of the Judiciary Act of 1789 under which Marbury had sought remedy had added unconstitutionally to the Court's original jurisdiction and had to be struck down. Thus was the Court's power to declare an act of Congress unconstitutional first formally enunciated.

In subsequent years, the Hamilton-Marshall position on judicial review triumphed completely. But it was by no means generally accepted at the time. Sheldon Goldman found that, insofar as judicial review of congressional acts was considered at all by most framers, it was endorsed only in a narrow form: as a means whereby flagrant violations of the Constitution by Congress or the president could be declared void.[4] It would be a weapon in reserve, to be used rarely as a check in extreme cases, not the expansive power it has in fact become.

Extending judicial review. Since its beginnings, the U.S. Supreme Court has held over 900 state acts to be unconstitutional, and has voided more than 120 federal statutes in whole or in part.[5] Up until the Civil War, only two congressional acts had been held unconstitutional; the rate of such findings increased substantially in the later nineteenth century and has increased even more in the twentieth century. Four-fifths of all federal statutes (or portions thereof) struck down by the Court have been voided since 1900.

Judicial review and
civil liberties

Since the late 1930s, national legislation found unconstitutional has been concentrated in one area—*civil liberties and civil rights.* Of the 40 provisions of federal law struck down between 1943 and 1979, "all but two [were voided] because they infringed certain personal rights and liberties safeguarded under the Constitution."[6] For example, in *Afroyim* v. *Rusk* (1967), the Court declared unconstitutional a section of the Nationality Act of 1940 which stripped American citizens of their citizenship if they voted in a foreign election; the Court held that under section 1 of the Fourteenth Amendment Congress lacked the constitutional authority to enact any legislation denying Americans their citizenship without their express consent. And in two companion cases (cases at the same time and similarly decided), *Blount* v. *Rizzi* and *United States* v. *The Book Bin* (1971), statutes authorizing the Post Office Department to cut off service to mail-order houses dealing in pornography were struck down as unconstitutional violations of First Amendment guarantees of freedom of expression.

Judicial review abroad. Comparable powers of judicial review are by no means commonly held by courts in other democracies. In Great Britain the constitutional doctrine of the supremacy of Parliament means that the courts may not strike down any law which the legislature has enacted. In France, only a circumscribed power resembling judicial review exists, and it resides not in the courts but in the Constitutional Council (which includes a number of ranking political officials, among them all living past presidents of France). Private

---

[4] Sheldon Goldman, *Constitutional Law and Supreme Court Decision-Making* (New York: Harper and Row, 1982), p. 12.
[5] Congressional Research Service, *Constitution of the United State of America, Analysis and Interpretation* (1980 supplement), Senate Document 96-64, 1982; and Henry J. Abraham, *The Judicial Process* (New York: Oxford University Press, 1980), pp. 304–10.
[6] Abraham, *Judicial Process*, p. 297.

individuals cannot challenge a law's constitutionality; only the president, the premier, the heads of the two houses of the legislature, or a group of at least 60 members of the legislature by petition may do so.

Other countries have developed certain aspects of judicial review, but not the full-blown form one sees in the U.S. In West Germany no ordinary court is permitted to decide constitutional questions in the course of litigation. A Federal Constitutional Court has wide-reaching powers to decide all controversies involving the meaning of the German Basic Law (the country's constitution). In Canada and a handful of other countries, most of which have federal systems of government, the ordinary courts exercise judicial review much as in the United States. For example, in Canada authority to declare acts of Parliament void clearly does not flow from English common law—Canada's legal heritage—which recognizes the principle of parliamentary supremacy, and the Canadian Constitution says nothing at all about judicial review power. Nonetheless, through continuing use judicial review has developed into an unwritten rule, "a binding convention of our [Canadian] Constitution."[7] The roots of judicial review in Canada can be "traced to pragmatic considerations flowing implicitly from the principle of federalism. . . ." With their separate state or provincial governments, federal systems need some central body able to decide when state actions contradict national legislation. The regular courts have assumed this role in a number of former British colonies, including Canada and Australia.

Judicial Policy-Making

The American courts' power of judicial review is one resource in a more general capacity to make policy. When the Supreme Court holds that an act which Congress has passed and the president has signed violates the Constitution and hence cannot be enforced, it obviously is setting national policy. But rulings on constitutionality are not the only or even the most important instrument for judicial policy-making. Most of the work of the courts does not involve constitutional adjudication, but rather the interpretation of ordinary legislation.

Whenever a legislature enacts a law, it makes policy; but the scope of these policy initiatives varies widely. There is a vast difference between the public policy implications of a new parking ordinance and sweeping Social Security legislation. Similarly, a court's policy role is much more limited when it applies a specific drunk-driving law than when it interprets an act setting complex new environmental goals and requirements. As a general rule, the narrower the scope of a law and the more precisely and unambiguously its terms are prescribed, the less policy discretion courts have. The wider the sub-

[7] Richard J. Van Loon and Michael S. Whittington, *The Canadian Political System* (Toronto: McGraw-Hill Ryerson, 1981), p. 179.

Supreme Court decisions have often sparked protests.

stantive reach of a law, and the more expansive the goals it proclaims, the greater are the court's policy powers stemming from interpretation.

Politics and the law. A distinction is sometimes made between "playing politics" and "interpreting the law." In this view, "politics" is a natural part of the life of the legislative and executive branches, but not of courts. Courts are supposed to be objective in their rulings. Americans expect—and often get—a high measure of impartiality from their courts. The tradition of an independent and impartial judiciary means that a person brought to court on a criminal or civil matter should not have his case determined by his political persuasion— whether Democratic, Republican, Socialist, Libertarian, or any other. Blacks as well as whites, the poor as well as the wealthy, women as well as men, lonely outsiders as well as "pillars of the community" are entitled to "equal justice under the law." That this ideal has sometimes been denied does not discount it. It posits a norm that has been extraordinarily influential over the conduct of judges, jurors, and other legal officials.

But in another sense the federal judiciary is as political a branch of government as the legislature and executive. The bench is not organized in an explicitly partisan manner, but party ties are not absent. Every American president has been guided by partisan considerations in appointing federal judges. Democratic presidents have regularly given over 90 percent of their appointments to fellow Democrats; Republican presidents have been similarly partial to members of their party. Judges often have strong political preferences and values, and indeed have often been active in partisan politics prior to their court

The political nature of the judiciary

appointments. Especially when the complex character of statutes gives judges great discretion in interpreting them, the program preferences and values that judges bring to the bench become evident.

The whole idea of the judiciary as a distinct branch within a government of separated powers posits a fundamental political role. The first three articles of the U.S. Constitution are devoted to the *three principal political branches of national government*. Making public policy for a nation is in the largest sense a political act. Whenever they make policy—whenever they interpret any but the most narrowly defined statutes—courts act politically.

Making Policy by Deciding Cases

Opinion of the court

The courts are a special type of political institution, bound by a set of norms and practices distinct from those of all other governmental units. They make policy within a structure and tradition that exerts great influence over the results. The best way to get a sense of the special properties of judicial policy-making is to examine decisions rendered by the U.S. Supreme Court. A court makes policy by deciding *cases in law*. An **opinion of the court** entails the resolution of a particular policy dispute presented in a case brought before it. As the highest court in the land, the Supreme Court usually hears cases of only substantial national policy importance.

The Supreme Court and political philosophy

Decisions of the Supreme Court are an unusual blend of practical political action and political philosophy. The latter comes into play so prominently because the Court's influence depends in significant part upon its success in convincing other actors—the president, members of Congress, lower-court judges, lawyers, and, to some extent, the public at large—of the intellectual soundness of its legal interpretations. When the law in question is the Constitution itself, the Court expounds on the most fundamental values of the American polity. Through Court decisions, concrete disputes get resolved but, at the same time, large philosophic questions are consciously explored. Because the Court is often divided, and one or more judges in the minority issue dissenting opinions, the argument gets joined directly and, on occasion, with great force.

Brown v. *Board of Education of Topeka* (1954)

Three key Supreme Court decisions of the last several decades illustrate concretely aspects of the reach of judicial decision-making in important areas of contemporary public policy. Together these rulings provide a good sense of how much the Court can accomplish, and how it is sometimes uniquely situated to act decisively when the other branches cannot act.

The first of these three cases is probably the single most important Supreme Court decision of recent years. In **Brown v. Board of Edu-**

cation of Topeka (1954), the Court signaled a vast shift of national policy in race relations. *Brown* and its companion cases came to the Supreme Court as specific challenges to what was then the general southern and border state practice of maintaining two separate public school systems: one for whites and one for blacks. At issue was the requirement of section 1 of the Fourteenth Amendment: "No state shall . . . deny to any person within its jurisdiction the equal protection of the laws." Did the prevailing segregation of black students deny them equal protection mandated by the Fourteenth Amendment? Box 10.1 gives excerpts from the Court's decision.[8]

When Congress passes a statute treating a central question of national policy, the objective set forth in the statute is not always promptly and harmoniously achieved. So it is with Supreme Court decisions. *Brown* was immediately engulfed in intense controversy. At once hailed by some for signaling the demise of the "separate but equal" doctrine instituted in 1896, it was vigorously denounced by others as a usurpation of state prerogatives. In March 1956, 101 of the 128 members of Congress from 11 southern and border states issued a tract that labeled the *Brown* decision "a clear abuse of judicial power" and applauded states intending to "resist enforced integration by any means."[9] Massive resistance in many southern states followed for years after.

Nonetheless, when Chief Justice Earl Warren, speaking for a unanimous Court, concluded, "We have now announced that such segregation is a denial of equal protection of the laws," the nation was launched on a new policy course that would entail major changes in educational programs by local, state, and national government. Narrowly construed, separation of powers and checks and balances envision a situation where the excesses of one branch are curbed by another. In a more general sense, this constitutional doctrine allows for the failure of one part of government in discharging its constitutional duties to be corrected by another part of government not subject to the same political constraints. The work of the Supreme Court in *Brown* shows this process at its best. By the 1950s, many Americans believed that the presence of segregated schools throughout the South grossly denied the constitutional claim to equal rights for all citizens. But opinion among the white majority in southern states was such that local government would not act to end segregation. Congress had ample legislative authority to act, but the near-unanimous opposition of

Segregation and the Fourteenth Amendment

Brown: the success of checks and balances

---

[8] References to Court decisions are written in a distinctive format. For example, the citation for the *Brown* decision often appears as follows: 347 U.S. 483; 98 L. Ed. 873 (1954). "U.S." stands for *United States Supreme Court Reports;* "L. Ed." refers to *Lawyers' Edition.* These are two separate publications—the first by the U.S. Government Printing Office, the second by a private publishing company—which print the complete text of every Court decision. The first number is always the volume in on which the opinion is located; the second number is the page on which the opinion begins.

[9] U.S. Congress, Senate, "Declaration of Constitutional Principles," *Congressional Record* #102 (March 12, 1956):4460.

Facts. Five cases originating in the states of Kansas, South Carolina, Virginia, and Delaware, and in the District of Columbia, came to the Supreme Court for reargument on June 8, 1953. All involved challenges to the constitutionality of racial segregation in public schools. In each, black schoolchildren through counsel sought admission to community schools to which they had been denied access. The lead case involved a suit by Oliver Brown to require the Board of Education of Topeka, Kansas, to admit his eight-year-old daughter Linda to a then all-white public school only five blocks from her home.

Decision. In a unanimous opinion the Court held that the segregation which the plaintiffs complained of violated the guarantee of equal protection of the laws under the Fourteenth Amendment to the U.S. Constitution. Mr. Chief Justice Warren, delivering the opinion of the Court, said in part:

> ... Today, education is perhaps the most important function of state and local governments. In these days, it is doubtful that any child may reasonably be expected to succeed in life if he is denied the opportunity of an education. Such an opportunity, where the state has undertaken to provide it, is a right which must be made available to all on equal terms.

> We come then to the question presented: Does segregation of children in public schools solely on the basis of race, even though the physical facilities and other "tangible" factors may be equal, deprive the children of the minority group of equal educational opportunities? We believe that it does. ... To separate them [children in grade and high schools] from others of similar age and qualifications solely because of their race generates a feeling of inferiority as to their status in the community that may affect their hearts and minds in a way unlikely ever to be undone. The effect of this separation on their educational opportunities was well stated by a finding in the Kansas case by a court which nevertheless felt compelled to rule against the Negro plaintiffs: "Segregation of white and colored children in public schools has a detrimental effect upon the colored children. The impact is greater when it has the sanction of the law; for the policy of separating the races is usually interpreted as denoting the inferiority of the Negro group. A sense of inferiority affects the motivation of a child to learn. Segregation with the sanction of law, therefore, has a tendency to [retard] the educational and mental development of Negro children and to deprive them of some of the benefits they would receive in a racial[ly] integrated school system. We conclude that in the field of public education the doctrine of "separate but equal" has no place. Separate educational facilities are inherently unequal. Therefore, we hold that the plaintiffs and others similarly situated for whom the actions have been brought are, by reason of the segregation complained of, deprived of the equal protection of the laws guaranteed by the Fourteenth Amendment. ...

Linda Brown speaks at the University of Kansas on civil rights nearly thirty years after the famous Brown school desegregation decision.

southern congressmen, many of whom held positions of great authority in the congressional committee system, was sufficient to block legislation. Of all the units of government in a position to act, only the Supreme Court was sufficiently insulated from such political pressures to take corrective steps.

Baker v. Carr (1962)

Legislative apportionment

The school desegregation decisions are by no means the only occasion when the Court has moved to correct an abuse that other units of government had authority to handle but for various political reasons did not. **Legislative apportionment** provides another important recent instance. The right to vote is one of the most basic elements of democratic citizenship. But achieving a system that guarantees the ideal of "one person, one vote" can be difficult. A great variety of political devices have been used to curtail the full exercise of this right, one of the most common involving juggling the size and boundaries of legislative districts so that some people's votes carry more weight than others.'

The idea that legislative districts should be of approximately equal population size—except in the U.S. Senate, which provides equal representation for each state—has been widely endorsed as general electoral policy. In practice, however, legislative districts in states around the country were often wildly disproportionate in size prior to 1962. As cities grew, residents of small towns and rural areas, fearful of the rising political power of their urban brethren, defended provisions that gave their areas over-representation.

Apportionment in Connecticut is an instructive example (see Figure 10.1). The Connecticut Constitution of 1818 stipulated that all towns already incorporated were entitled to two representatives in the lower house of the state legislature, but that towns established after that date would be entitled to only one.[10] This was changed slightly in 1955, when all towns with populations of at least 5,000 were given two representatives. Yet in 1960 an extraordinary situation existed: Hartford, with over 160,000 inhabitants, had only two representatives, while the old colonial town of Union, with just 383 residents, also had two![11] Under this apportionment scheme, the small

Apportionment in Connecticut

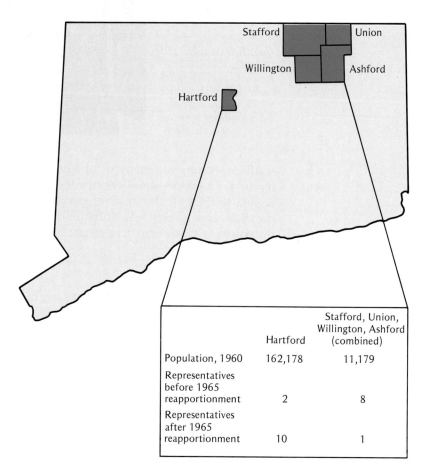

Figure 10.1
Apportionment in Connecticut Before and After Reapportionment of 1965

	Hartford	Stafford, Union, Willington, Ashford (combined)
Population, 1960	162,178	11,179
Representatives before 1965 reapportionment	2	8
Representatives after 1965 reapportionment	10	1

[10] David M. Roth, *Connecticut: A History* (New York: Norton, 1979), p. 113.
[11] *State of Connecticut, Register and Manual, 1960*, pp. 198, 272.

towns controlled the legislature and their representatives blocked any effort to reapportion. The large urban and suburban areas favored reapportionment, but they were too underrepresented to achieve it.

Court challenges. Inevitably, voters victimized by legislative malapportionment in U.S. House of Representatives districts and state legislative districts looked to the courts for redress. For a long time, though, the judiciary preferred not to meddle in legislative apportionment on the grounds that it was the exclusive province of a co-equal branch of government. For example, the Supreme Court ruled in *Colgrove* v. *Green* (1946) that the "times, places and manner of holding elections" provision of Article I, section 4, of the U.S. Constitution gave Congress the authority to assure equitable representation in U.S. House districts; hence, it was up to Congress, or the state legislatures, to take care of any imbalances. "Whether Congress faithfully discharges its duty or not, the subject has been committed to the exclusive control of Congress."

Colgrove v. *Green*

In the landmark case of **Baker v. Carr** (1962), however, the Court abandoned its long-standing reservations and jumped into the political thicket. Speaking for a 6–2 Court majority, Justice William Brennan rejected the earlier view that apportionment presents a political question for which there were no appropriate judicial responses. The inequitability of legislative districts, Brennan held, can properly be subjected to judicial standards under the equal protection clause of the Fourteenth Amendment. Justice Tom Clark wrote a concurring opinion which probably reflected the underlying motivation of the Court's majority most faithfully. (Justices write concurring opinions when they agree with the basic decision of the court but want to further explain their own reasons for reaching the judgment.) Justice Clark conceded that "although I find the Tennessee apportionment statute offends the Equal Protection Clause, I would not consider intervention by this Court in so delicate a field if there were any other relief available to the people of Tennessee."

Baker v. *Carr*

In the flurry of cases which followed *Baker,* the Court enlarged upon and implemented its new policy. In *Wesberry* v. *Sanders* (1963), Justice Hugo Black, speaking for the majority, held that ". . . the command of Article I, section 2, that representatives be chosen 'by the people of the several states' means that as nearly as is practicable, one man's vote in a congressional election is to be worth as much as anothers." And in *Reynolds* v. *Sims* (1964), Chief Justice Earl Warren for the majority held that

Wesberry v. *Sanders*

Reynolds v. *Sims*

> the right of suffrage can be denied by a debasement of suffrage or dilution of the weight of a citizen's vote just as effectively as by wholly prohibiting the free exercise of the franchise. . . . Legislators represent people, not trees or acres. Legislators are elected by voters, not farms or cities or economic interests. . . . The Equal Protection clause requires that the seats in both houses of a bicameral state legislature must be apportioned on a population basis.

Implementing the
Baker decision

While *Baker* and other apportionment decisions produced more than a little grumbling among legislators and other politicians, compliance followed swiftly. In contrast to *Brown*, where powerful interests continued for many years to try to subvert or at least restrict the decision, *Baker* and the rulings subsequent to it were immediately fulfilled. This occurred in part because legislative apportionment simply did not generate the passions of race relations. In part, too, it occurred because the means of enforcement or execution were more straightforward. The courts could simply block elections under legislative apportionment schemes that did not meet the standards of population equality. In a few years, the Supreme Court brought about a fundamental shift in national policy on legislative apportionment at the local, state, and national levels.

Roe v. *Wade* (1973)

Sometimes when it makes public policy, the Court enjoys the good fortune of being on the side of the angels. *Brown* and *Baker* are cases in point. Whatever judgments prevailed in the past, few people would now argue that a state's maintenance of a rigidly segregated school system is other then a clear denial of equal protection under the law. The Court articulated an emerging national consensus on a matter of basic democratic practice. But in many other instances, the Court finds itself in the middle of an argument on which thoughtful men and women entertain sharply divergent views—and continue to long after the Court's judgment has been rendered. In such cases, the Court gets enmeshed in unresolved—sometimes unresolvable—political argument. Its decisions affect policy but fail to convince substantial segments of the populace on what policy should be.

A good illustration is **Roe v. Wade** (1973), the Court's much-discussed and much-criticized decision on abortion. Justice Harry Blackmun delivered the opinion for a 7–2 Court majority in *Roe*, striking down a Texas statute that had made abortion a state crime if performed for reasons other than saving the life of the mother. Similar statutes long on the books in a majority of other states were invalidated through the application of this decision.

Blackmun's majority opinion emphasized the core right of privacy:

> This right of privacy, whether it be founded in the Fourteenth Amendment's concept of personal liberty and restrictions upon state action, as we feel it is, or, as the district court determined in the Ninth Amendment's reservation of rights to the people, is broad enough to encompass a women's decision whether or not to terminate her pregnancy.

At the same time, Blackmun's opinion explicitly recognized the constitutional basis for *some* substantial state regulation of abortion. It rejected "Jane Roe's" (not the real name of the Texas woman bringing the suit) argument "that the woman's right is absolute and that

Court ruling on
abortion

she is entitled to terminate her pregnancy at whatever time, in whatever way, and for whatever reason she alone chooses." It held that "a state may properly assert some important interests in safeguarding health, in maintaining medical standards, and in protecting potential life."

In its effort to reconcile the right of a woman to have an abortion if she wants with "important state interests in regulation," the Court introduced the much-debated "trimester" standard, which broke pregnancy into three distinct terms and outlined the permissible restrictions which a state may impose in each one. In the first three months of pregnancy, the Court held, the decision to have an abortion must be left entirely to a woman and her physician, although the state can forbid abortions by non-physicians. During the second trimester, the state may regulate abortion but only in ways reasonably related to maternal health. And during the final three months of pregnancy, the state can if it chooses forbid all abortions except those necessary to save the mother's life.

The Court's decision in *Roe*, which has set national policy on abortion, illustrates the difficulty in locating clear *constitutional* guidelines for many contemporary disputes. The Constitution simply does not say anything that applies unambiguously to state regulation of abortion, and judges are of necessity thrown back on their own values and their sense of what is good public policy. In such cases, those on the losing side of the issue usually charge the Court majority with improper "judicial legislation": finding a controlling constitutional standard where one does not exist. The dissenting opinions in *Roe* by Justices William Rehnquist and Byron White echoed this criticism. The decision, Justice Rehnquist wrote, "partakes more of judicial legislation than it does of the determination of intent of the drafters of the Fourteenth Amendment." In his notably truculent dissent, Justice White found

> nothing in the language or history of the Constitution to support the Court's judgment. The Court simply fashions and announces a new constitutional right for pregnant mothers and, with scarcely any reason or authority for its action, invests that right with sufficient substance to override most existing state abortion statutes.

Without attempting any judgment on the merits of these charges in *Roe* v. *Wade*, one can note that continuing concern over "judicial legislation" is a nearly unavoidable result of the expansive policy role America has given its courts as an independent branch of government empowered to say what the law is. If the Supreme Court is to have broad interpretive authority with regard to the claims of the Constitution and laws made under it, it will inevitably exercise that authority in cases where there is no emerging or achieved national consensus and where the relevant constitutional stipulations admit differing interpretations. When in such cases the Court overrules the statutory judgment of a legislative majority, critics are bound to cry foul.

Sidenotes:
"Trimester" standard

No clear constitutional guidelines

Power of "judicial legislation"

Recent Developments in Judicial Intervention

Expansion of judicial intervention

In their constitutional role of saying what the law is, American courts have been heavily involved in policy formation throughout the country's history. But over the last two decades there has been a significant broadening of judicial intervention—and this has generated intense controversy. "Today no action of government seems complete without litigation," judicial scholar Martin Shapiro writes.

> Our newspapers tell us of judges who forbid the transfer of air-force squadrons from one base to another, delay multi-million construction projects, intervene in complex negotiations between public employers and their employees, oversee the operation of railroads, and decide the location of schools. . . . Judges now joyously try their hand at everything from the engineering of atomic reactors to the validation of I.Q. tests. They run school districts, do regional land use planning, redesign welfare programs, and calculate energy needs. . . . Today there seems to be no public policy issue, no matter how massive, complex, or technical that some judge somewhere has not felt fully capable of deciding, aided only by the standard processes of litigation.[12]

Judicial intervention in agency management

Departing from past practice, many federal district courts and some state courts are now inclined to become directly involved in the daily management of major public agencies: prisons, mental hospitals, facilities for the elderly, local school systems. In *Wyatt* v. *Stickney* (1972), federal district judge Frank M. Johnson found "intolerable and deplorable" conditions prevailing in Alabama's largest state mental health facility. The court held that, as a matter of due process under the Fourteenth Amendment, hospital inmates "unquestionably have a constitutional right to receive such individual treatment as will give each of them a realistic opportunity to be cured or to improve his or her mental condition. . . ." In support of this finding, the court set forth detailed constitutional standards of care and treatment. Similarly, in *Hamilton* v. *Schiro* (1970), federal district judge Herbert W. Christenberry ordered the mayor of New Orleans to "immediately implement" directives for the reform of New Orleans prisons: providing specified medical and dental services, constructing a new hospital, guaranteeing "adequate security for medical personnel to facilitate the needs of the medical program," maintaining a year-round recreational program, building an indoor recreation area, and limiting the number of prisoners in the main facility.

Judicial administrators

To achieve such sweeping changes in the programs and administrative practices of executive agencies, courts frequently appoint special administrators. In *Hamilton* v. *Schiro*, Judge Christenberry

---

[12] Martin Shapiro, "Judicial Activism," in Seymour Martin Lipset, ed., *The Third Century: America as a Post-Industrial Society* (Chicago: University of Chicago Press, 1979), p. 125.

Only a decade ago, the court ruled in O'Connor v. Donaldson *that nondangerous individuals could not be involuntarily committed to a state mental hospital if they were capable of surviving safely in freedom by themselves or with the help of others. Kenneth Donaldson, who initiated the suit, was thus set free after being confined in a state mental hospital for fourteen years.*

appointed a "master" to investigate New Orleans prison conditions; he subsequently transformed the master's findings into a decree and then continued to hold jurisdiction until the reforms were implemented. In *Gates* v. *Collier* (1972), federal district judge Elbert P. Tuttle placed the Mississippi state penitentiary under the direct supervision of a "monitor," who was instructed to examine the prison's records, review the way management was operating the prison, and report his findings to the court.

The cost of implementing court decisions

Court-directed reforms of state and municipal institutions to meet "conditions-of-confinement" and "right-to-treatment" standards often require major public expenditures. "More often than not, this has been accomplished by leveraged judicial threat...."[13] For example, in *Hamilton* v. *Love* (1971), the federal judge warned that

> if the state cannot obtain the resources to detain persons awaiting trial in accordance with minimum constitutional standards, then the state will not be permitted to detain such persons.... This court, of course, cannot require the voters to make available the resources needed by public officials to meet constitutional standards, but it can and must direct the release of persons held under conditions which violate their constitutional rights....

If the state did not appropriate the money which the judge considered necessary, he would order it to turn loose persons accused of serious crimes. In a 1978 ruling, another federal judge ordered Rhode Island's maximum security prison closed within the space of one year, the period of time he thought adequate to build a satisfactory replacement.

One important source of the courts' new activism is a general

[13] Robert S. Gilmour, "Agency Administration by Judiciary," *Southern Review of Public Administration,* 6 (Spring 1982):26.

Courts in an age of bigger government

expansion of the perceived responsibilities of government. In discussing Congress and the presidency, we have seen how these institutions have grown in the modern period as they have taken on a host of new tasks pursuant to public well-being. Americans expect a broader range of governmental services and protections than they did in the past. Like other political leaders, judges have responded—sometimes wisely, sometimes foolishly—to these increased expectations and demands. As the courts have become involved in a wider range of policy questions, groups have organized to participate more effectively in this judicial setting. There has been a major expansion of public advocacy law centers. At the beginning of the 1960s only one such center existed in the United States: the National Association for the Advancement of Colored People's Legal Defense Fund. During the 1960s and 1970s, however, law centers for public advocacy, receiving government or foundation aid, "were established in almost every field of social policy—welfare, education, housing, health, environment—and for almost every group of potential clients. . . ."[14] The growth of such centers and staff with the resources to litigate on behalf of policy interests has naturally heightened demands on the courts.

Problems with Increased Judicial Intervention

The development of a more activist judicial branch is a natural response to changes in American society and politics. But it is not problem-free. One problem is that the courts are not responsible, as legislators or executives are, for the costs of their actions. A court ordering school busing does not have to find the money to pay for it; one that blocks the construction of a new power-generating facility does not have to find the electricity to meet future needs.

Rights versus interests

A related problem involves the increased difficulty in adjusting priorities and finding compromises when interests get expressed as basic legal rights. Martin Shapiro cites the issue of handicapped persons obtaining public transportation. When such a question is brought before the executive and legislative branches, decision-makers can argue about whether expending millions of dollars on bus lifts and subway elevators is merited, considering the benefits that would accrue from alternate uses of the same funds. However, "once a court declares that the handicapped have a right to equal access to public transportation, then the money must be spent even if the cost-benefit ratio is insane." Shapiro maintains that courts too often use the language of *rights* rather than *interests;* and the more court intervention expands, the harder political compromise and adjustment becomes, "for they [the courts] are always demanding that the particular interests that they choose to prefer at the moment be given absolute priority over all of the other interests at play."[15]

[14] Nathan Glazer, "Towards an Imperial Judiciary?" *Public Interest,* 41 (1975):116.
[15] Shapiro, "Judicial Activism," p. 130.

Judicial Self-Restraint

Supreme Court justices have long grappled with the issue of how activist the Court should be, and where lines should be drawn in the American system of separation of powers. Some judges have made a strong philosophic commitment to judicial deference to the acts of popularly elected legislatures and executives, an approach sometimes called "judicial self-restraint." Early in this century, Justice Oliver Wendell Holmes, Jr., was a notable proponent of self-restraint; this commitment peppered his eloquent dissents and other remarks. Justice Holmes once said to his 61-year old colleague Justice Harlan Stone: "Young man, about 75 years ago I learned that I was not God. And so, when the people ... want to do something I can't find anything in the Constitution expressly forbidding them to do, I say, whether I like it or not, 'Godammit, let 'em do it.' "[16] On another occasion, he remarked to John W. Davis, who was the Democratic party's presidential nominee in 1924, "Of course I know, and every other sensible man knows, that the Sherman law [the Sherman Anti-Trust Act of 1890] is damned nonsense, but if my country wants to go to hell, I am here to help it."[17]

More recently, Justice Felix Frankfurter, who served on the Supreme Court from 1939 until his retirement in 1962, was the most eloquent and consistent proponent of self-restraint. In a system that gives a nonelective, life-tenured court expansive policy authority stemming from constitutional and statutory interpretation, there is a constant temptation, Frankfurter felt, for judges to transform themselves into a super-legislature or super-executive. Separation of powers, he believed, requires mutual forbearance by the executive, legislature, and judiciary. For the Court, such forbearance means a general willingness to confine its overturning of legislative and executive acts to instances where truly basic rights are engaged. Thus in his dissent in *Trop* v. *Dulles* (1958), Frankfurter observed that

> it is not easy to stand aloof and allow want of wisdom to prevail, to disregard one's own strongly held views of what is wise in the conduct of affairs but ... [the Court] must observe a fastidious regard for limitations on its own power, and this precludes the Court's giving effect to its own notions of what is wise or politic.

THE COURT SYSTEM OF THE UNITED STATES

American federalism, which we discuss in detail in the next chapter, posits two distinct levels of government: national and state (with local government a subdivision of state). This federal structure extends into

Oliver Wendell Holmes, Jr., and judicial self-restraint

Felix Frankfurter on separation of powers

[16] Abraham, *Judicial Process*, p. 373.
[17] As told by Francis Biddle, *Justice Holmes, Natural Law and the Supreme Court* (New York: Macmillan, 1961), p. 9.

the judiciary. Two distinct sets of courts operate in the U.S.: federal courts exist side by side with courts established by the fifty states. In the pages that follow, we will examine the organization of this dual court system. We will also consider the important question of ***jurisdiction:*** which cases originate in the federal courts and which in the state courts. The country's highest judicial authority, the Supreme Court of the United States, is at the apex of the dual court system; by deciding appeals from both the highest state courts and lower federal courts, it establishes necessary uniformity in national law and legal practices.

Jurisdiction

Federal Courts

The basic national court structure includes the ***U.S. district courts,*** which function as trial courts or courts of original jurisdiction (where a case is first tried); the ***U.S. courts of appeals,*** which are the lower federal appellate courts (hearing appeals of decisions rendered in lower courts); and, of course, the ***U.S. Supreme Court.*** In 1983, there were 95 district courts, with about 515 judges, and 11 U.S. courts of appeals, with 132 judges. The Supreme Court is composed of 9 justices, including the chief justice of the United States.

National court structure

Evolution of the federal court system. The Judiciary Act of 1789 created 13 federal district courts, with a district judge assigned to each. The act also provided for three federal ***circuit courts,*** with one district judge and two Supreme Court justices riding each circuit to hear appeals. While bills were introduced from time to time over the next 90 years to create separate circuit courts of appeals with resident judges and substantial jurisdictions, none were enacted until 1891. Lawrence Friedman describes the long political argument over creating federal courts of appeals as "one of the most enduring political struggles in American political history."[18] The Circuit Court of Appeals Act of 1891 at last established a new tier of courts to hear most of the appeals growing out of district court actions.

Courts of appeal

In 1903, Congress created ***special three-judge U.S. district courts*** to consider suits filed by the Attorney General under the Sherman Anti-Trust Act or the Inter-State Commerce Act. These special district courts were made up of two judges from the court of appeals and one judge from the district court in the area. Appeals from these three-judge courts would go directly to the U.S. Supreme Court. In 1910 the Mann-Elkins Act additionally empowered these special courts to hear cases brought by private individuals involving the constitutionality of state or federal statutes, and to issue injunctions to block enforcement of the challenged statutes. The heavy volume of civil rights

District courts

[18] Lawrence M. Friedman, *A History of American Law* (New York: Touchstone Books, 1973), p. 120.

litigation after 1960 included a large increase in petitions brought to the three-judge district courts, as civil rights groups challenged the constitutionality of various state laws governing race relations.

Other changes during the 1920s brought the federal court system to the basic form we know today. Following extensive lobbying by **Reorganization of** the American Bar Association and the urgings of Chief Justice Wil- **federal courts** liam Howard Taft, Congress further expanded the jurisdiction of the federal courts, and strengthened their administration by authorizing the Chief Justice to assign federal judges to temporary duty anywhere in the system, and creating the Conference of Senior Circuit Judges (later named the Judicial Conference), which would meet annually to discuss common judicial administrative problems.

Present organization. Figure 10.2 shows the present organization of the federal courts. Along with the district courts, courts of appeals, special three-judge district courts, and the Supreme Court, there are a number of other specialized courts. The Federal Court Improvement Act of 1982 established a twelve-judge **U.S. Court of Appeals** *Figure 10.2* **for the Federal Circuit,** merging two special courts of long standing. **Federal Judicial** The new court has exclusive jurisdiction over appeals from district **Organization** courts of decisions involving patent rights, as well as appeals from

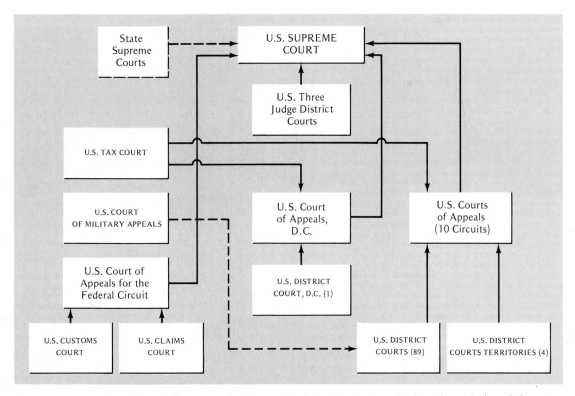

Source: Adapted from Ball, *Courts and Politics,* p. 74. The arrows show the direction of appeals through the system.

the Merit System Protection Board and Boards of Contract Appeals. It also has exclusive jurisdiction in international trade, and acts as an appeals court in cases involving claims against the U.S. government.

Another special federal court is the **U.S. Claims Court:** a trial court handling claims against federal agencies arising out of governmental contracts. The **U.S. Customs Court** consists of a chief judge and eight associate judges. Congress created it to hear cases involving rulings by U.S. customs collectors. It serves as the trial court for disputes between private citizens (and business corporations) and the government over the amount of customs duties, the value of imported goods, and decisions to exclude certain merchandise from the country. The **U.S. Tax Court,** made up of a chief judge and fifteen associate judges, was originally part of the executive branch under the Internal Revenue Service. Congress transformed it into a specialized court in 1969 under its taxing powers granted by Article I, section 8, of the Constitution. The Tax Court is still a quasi-administrative agency, independent of the Internal Revenue Service, rather than a court in the traditional sense. Its jurisdiction includes taxpayers' challenges to IRS rulings. The last specialized federal court is the **U.S. Court of Military Appeals.** Composed of three civilian judges, it reviews all appeals from military court-martials.

Margin note: Special federal courts

State Courts

For all the scope of the federal courts, the state courts handle the majority of the country's judicial business. Each state determines the shape of its court system, either through provisions written into its constitution or through simple legislation. This has resulted in considerable variation from one state to another in how judges are selected and the courts arranged. Still, by looking at the structure of the California court system, we get a sense of some common patterns and distinctions. (See Figure 10.3.)

Municipal courts. At the lowest rung of the California judicial hierarchy are the municipal courts. State legislation authorizes each county board of supervisors to divide its county into judicial districts. The municipal courts have original trial jurisdiction in cases involving minor crimes and in all civil cases where the amount involved is $15,000 or less. These courts also have small-claims jurisdiction in cases like disputes between tenants and landlords for amounts not exceeding $750. In 1981, about 6.7 million cases, over 90 percent of the California total, were handled by the municipal courts—including about 5.2 million traffic cases (other than parking violations). The municipal court judges in California are elected for six-year terms on nonpartisan ballots by voters in the judicial districts.

Margin note: Municipal courts

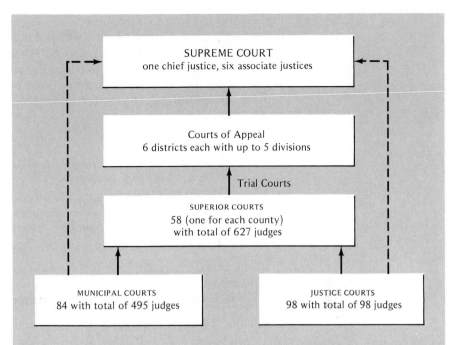

Figure 10.3
California State Court Organization

Source: "The California Judicial System," summary prepared by the Administrative Office of the Courts, the staff agency of the Judicial Council of California, March 1981.

Superior courts. At the next rung of the California hierarchy are the superior courts. As trial courts of general jurisdiction, they have original trial jurisdiction in all cases except those assigned to the municipal courts—including trial jurisdiction for more serious crimes like armed robbery and murder, and for civil cases involving dollar amounts in excess of $15,000. The superior courts handle probate (wills and estates) and juvenile matters (involving persons 16 years and younger). Each of the 58 California counties has at least one superior court. Judges are elected for six-year terms on a nonpartisan ballot.

State superior courts

Courts of appeal. The courts of appeal are California's intermediate courts of review and carry the main load of appellate work. They have appellate jurisdiction wherever superior courts have original trial jurisdiction. When an appeal is taken from a superior court decision, it is heard by a court of appeal. The state of California is divided into six appellate districts. Its judges are elected on a nonpartisan ballot for twelve-year terms.

State courts of appeal

The state supreme court. At the top of the hierarchy is the California supreme court, the state's highest appeals court. Its broad power of review enables it to pass on important legal issues and maintain uniformity in the law across the various state judicial districts. Members

State supreme court

of the supreme court are appointed by the governor and must be confirmed by a state commission on judicial appointments. After confirmation a judge serves until the next gubernatorial election, when he must run, unopposed, on a nonpartisan ballot; the public simply votes yes or no on the judge's appointment. As with the courts of appeal, supreme court judges are elected for twelve-year terms.

Jurisdiction

What determines which cases are heard by which courts? Part of the answer may be found in Article IV, section 2, of the U.S. Constitution, which permits federal court jurisdiction in "all cases, in law and equity" that meet one of two sets of standards—involving either the subject matter of the case or the character of the parties to the suit. Under the first standard, federal courts have jurisdiction in

First standard of jurisdiction

1) cases arising under the U.S. Constitution, a federal law, or a treaty;
2) cases involving admiralty and maritime laws.

Under the second standard, federal jurisdiction is granted when

Federal jurisdiction

3) the U.S. government is a party to the suit;
4) one or more state governments is a party;
5) the controversy is between citizens of different states;
6) a case involves an ambassador or some other official representative of a foreign country;
7) a case arises between citizens of the same state because of a dispute involving land grants claimed under titles of two or more states.

When the federal courts have jurisdiction, cases typically originate in the U.S. district courts. Congress has given the district courts only original jurisdiction; they are the "workhorse" trial courts where the cases and controversies are first heard. The U.S. courts of appeals and the Supreme Court have only limited original jurisdiction; most of the cases reaching them do so on appeal.

Concurrent and exclusive jurisdiction

Article III, section 2, sets the outer limits of federal court jurisdiction, but nothing in the Constitution prevents Congress from assigning certain portions of this jurisdiction to state courts, on a concurrent or even on a exclusive basis. **Concurrent jurisdiction** means that a case may originate in either a state or a federal court; **exclusive jurisdiction** means it is assigned exclusively to one or the other. For example, Congress has provided that if the dollar amount in civil suits involving citizens of different states exceeds $10,000, the case may be tried in either a federal district court or a state court. Otherwise, exclusive jurisdiction is granted to the state courts. This provision was enacted to reduce the federal court workload. U.S. district courts have the sole power to hear all proceedings in bankruptcy. This exclusive federal jurisdiction accounts for a substantial portion of the district courts' workload: there were 528,000 bankruptcy filings in 1982 alone. In addition, Congress has granted exclusive original jurisdiction to the federal courts in all prosecutions for violation of federal criminal laws.

In most instances where a case arises under a state law, exclusive original jurisdiction is held by the trial courts of that state. Appeals may be brought, though, from the highest state courts to the U.S. Supreme Court when a substantial federal question is raised. And challenges to state laws on the grounds they violate the U.S. Constitution or federal statutes may in some instances be initiated in the special three-judge federal district courts.

How Cases Reach the U.S. Supreme Court

Congress determines the jurisdiction of the U.S. courts of appeal. Essentially two kinds of cases have been given to these appellate courts to review and decide: appeals from federal district court rulings and reviews of decisions of federal administrative boards and commissions. In the latter, the appeals courts exercise a form of original jurisdiction, in the sense that appeals of many administrative agency rulings first enter the judicial system at this level.

Limited original jurisdiction of the Supreme Court

The original jurisdiction of the U.S. Supreme Court—where it is the first court to hear a case—is very limited. Cases taken up by the Court under its original jurisdiction have averaged less than one a year. The vast majority of cases reaching the Supreme Court come on appeal from other courts, specifically from the highest state courts, the three-judge federal district courts, and the U.S. courts of appeals. The Constitution gives Congress broad power to determine the Supreme Court's appellate jurisdiction; Congress has in turn given the Supreme Court great discretion to decide which cases it will devote its scarcest resource—time—to hearing.

Writ of certiorari

Certiorari. Most cases that the Court reviews come to it through one of two procedures. The first involves the **writ of certiorari:** an order to a court whose decision is under challenge to send the records of the case to a higher court so that the latter may review the decision. One of the parties to a lower-court decision petitions the higher court to issue the writ. Legislation enacted by Congress in 1925 gave the Supreme Court power to grant or deny writs of certiorari at its own discretion. As Howard Ball notes, through this authority "the justices of the Supreme Court carefully select a very small percentage of petitions to the Court for review on the merits. In order for the Court to take the case, it must—in the estimation of the sitting justices—be a controversy of major proportions."[19] At least four of the nine justices must agree in order for a writ of certiorari to be issued.

Right of appeal

Appeal. The second main avenue to Supreme Court review is by the legal right of ***appeal.*** The Supreme Court must accept cases on *appeal* when 1) the highest court of a state declares a federal law or a portion of it to be unconstitutional, 2) the highest court of a state upholds state law when it is challenged on the grounds that it violates the U.S. Constitution or an act of Congress, 3) a U.S. court of appeals holds a section of a state constitution or a state statute unconstitutional, and 4) a lower federal court declares an act of Congress unconstitutional and the U.S. government is a party to the suit. Appeals may also be brought directly to the Supreme Court from the three-judge district courts—but the Court in practice rejects many of these cases "for lack of a substantial federal question."

Special Procedures in Court Action

The Supreme Court has evolved a number of rules and procedures bearing on what sorts of cases it will hear. One of the most important is the insistence that the Court will intervene only when there is a definite case or controversy involving bona fide adversaries. The Court will not issue advisory opinions. It will not hear contrived cases developed merely to test a law. This limits, of course, the Court's control over the timing and the form of various issues brought to it.

Standing to sue

Standing. For a party to bring a suit he must have standing. This means he must show that he has sustained or is threatened with real injury.[20] A famous finding of lack of standing involved Dr. Wilder Tileston, a Connecticut physician who wanted to challenge his state's legislation preventing "the use of drugs or instruments to prevent conception, and the giving of assistance or counsel in their use." The U.S. Supreme Court held that

> no question is raised in the record with respect to the definition of [Dr. Tileston's] liberty or property in contravention of the Fourteenth Amendment. . . . [Hence] the appeal must be dismissed on the ground that appellant has no standing to litigate the constitutional question which the record presents. . . .[21]

In a subsequent case, Estelle Griswold, executive director of the Planned Parenthood League of Connecticut, and Dr. C. Lee Buxton, medical director of a center which the league operated, were convicted of violating the same Connecticut statute and fined $100 each.

[19] Howard Ball, *Courts and Politics: The Federal Judicial System* (Englewood Cliffs, N.J.: Prentice-Hall, 1980), p. 108.
[20] See Caren Orren, "Standing to Sue: Interest Group Influence in the Federal Courts," *American Political Science Review,* 70 (1976):723.
[21] *Tileston* v. *Ullman,* 318 U.S. 44 (1943).

The Vietnam Veterans of America brought a class-action suit against chemical companies which manufactured a herbicide, nicknamed Agent Orange, that was sprayed in Vietnam. In 1984, a federal court announced a settlement in the veterans' favor.

Personally affected or injured, they had standing. The Court granted their appeal, made on the grounds that the law violated their Fourteenth Amendment rights. In *Griswold* v. *Connecticut* (1965) the Court declared Connecticut's birth control statute unconstitutional.

Class-action suits

Class-action suits. A class-action suit is one filed by an individual on behalf of himself and perhaps many hundreds or thousands of others allegedly wronged in the same fashion. The petitioner in a class-action suit must show unequivocally that he is a member of the affected class and not simply someone sympathetic to it. Among the well-known instances of successful class-action suits are the school desegregation cases of 1954, which were initiated on behalf of all pupils affected by the prevailing educational segregation in the school districts under challenge. In a number of cases in the 1970s, the Supreme Court narrowed the availability of the class-action challenge by stipulating that a person bringing such a suit must notify all the members of the "class" potentially benefiting and must bear the costs of notification.[22] Personal injury and more than nominal involvement with others for whom a legal challenge is mounted have been significant facets of the rule of standing.

[22] See, for example, *Eisan* v. *Karlyle and Jacqueline*, 416 U.S. 979 (1974).

Justiciability

Justiciability. Another important limitation which the courts have imposed on their intervention in policy disputes involves **justiciability.** At issue here is not whether an individual has standing to sue, but whether courts are institutionally suited to providing remedies in the particular type of case. Political scientist Sheldon Goldman identified several central questions that bear upon justiciability:

> Is there something that a court can do for a plaintiff assuming that the plaintiff is in the legal right? Is the dispute moot (no longer a dispute)? Is the subject matter of the dispute one that is essentially a political question best resolved by the political branches of government? Is the subject amenable to judicial resolution?[23]

Rules to maintain separation of powers

At first glance, arguing whether a litigant has standing to sue, or whether a particular controversy is justiciable, may seem simply an abstract preoccupation of the legal profession. In fact, these judicial standards are important factors defining the special kind of political role American courts play. If every significant political issue were considered justiciable, and if every interested person could bring suit, the federal courts would be handling the entire range of political controversies dealt with by the executive and legislative branches. Judicial rules such as those involving standing and judiciability are an expression of judicial respect for separation of powers.

Administration of the Federal Courts

Do courts perform too many tasks?

We have come to expect that those who direct government agencies will favor developments that increase their agencies' workload and responsibilities. More work can mean more staff and bigger budgets, and the opportunity for greater influence. Interestingly enough, leading officials of the judicial branch take the opposite position. Supreme Court Chief Justice Warren Burger has argued forcefully in recent years that courts in general—but especially federal courts—now perform tasks they need not. The answer, he maintains, is not primarily more staff—although he thinks additional judges are needed—but going outside traditional judge-directed proceedings altogether (more informal conciliation efforts now being tried in many states), and delegating functions to lower courts.

Proposed National Court of Appeals

Looking to state courts, Justice Burger has questioned whether judges are needed initially to preside over probate matters (involving wills and estates), to resolve child custody cases, or to handle divorces. Regarding federal courts, he has expressed doubts that judges are required at the outset to administer bankrupt estates "when only a small proportion of these cases involve contested issues requiring judicial decision, and when these cases can readily be referred to a federal judge." He has strongly urged getting the federal courts out

[23] Goldman, *Constitutional Law*, p. 8.

of "diversity of citizenship" cases: "How long must we wait to keep out of federal courts an automobile intersection collision which reaches federal courts simply because one driver lives in Newark and the other in New York? Or one in Virginia and one across the Potomac in Washington?"[24] Along with a number of other justices and legal scholars, Justice Burger has endorsed the idea of a **National Court of Appeals.** This intermediate court, between the Supreme Court and the existing U.S. courts of appeals, would have jurisdiction over appeals referred to it by the Supreme Court and would be able to decline review unless the Supreme Court specifically directed it to decide the case. If created, the National Court of Appeals would relieve the Supreme Court of some of its present workload, while still providing a single high national court review.[25]

A litigation explosion. These efforts to trim judicial responsibility must be seen against a vast increase in recent years in the number of disputes brought to the courts for resolution. Justice Burger noted that in the first year his predecessor, Earl Warren, was chief justice (1953), the Supreme Court had 1,312 case filings and issued 65 signed opinions plus 19 *per curiam* opinions (rulings issued by the court without lengthy supporting argument). In the Court's term that ended in July 1982, it had 4,422 new filings, plus 889 carried over from the preceding term, for a total of 5,311. The Court issued 141 signed and 10 *per curiam* opinions. Justice Burger worries that the Court cannot maintain proper quality in its decisions, given the current workload.[26]

Increase in judicial caseloads

The entire legal system has been challenged by extraordinary increases in cases. In 1982, 238,874 new cases were filed in federal district courts—a twelve percent increase over the preceding year. More than 206,000 civil cases were filed in U.S. district courts—nearly double the number filed in 1975. And 28,000 appeals were brought to the U.S. courts of appeals, up from less than 17,000 in 1975 and 7,000 in 1965. Federal court organization has slowly changed in response to these heightened demands. District court judges are now provided with a variety of assistants; along with stenographers, court reporters, bailiffs, and law clerks, they are assigned professional court administrators and United States magistrates. The professional court administrators take from the judges much of the burden of overseeing the courts' increasingly complex administrative machinery. Under the Federal Magistrates Act of 1968, judges were permitted to appoint magistrates (for eight- and four-year terms of office) to assist in processing court caseloads. In 1981, magistrates handled over 300,000

[24] Remarks of Chief Justice Warren E. Burger at the Arthur T. Vanderbilt dinner, sponsored by New York University and the Institute of Judicial Administration, New York City, November 18, 1982.
[25] Warren E. Burger, "1982 Year-End Report on the Judiciary," report released annually by the Office of the Chief Justice, p. 3.
[26] Remarks of Justice Burger, at the Vanderbilt dinner.

separate court proceedings—including trial jurisdiction in 95,000 misdemeanor cases, bail proceedings, issuance of arrest warrants, and other preliminary proceedings in criminal cases.

More than any previous Chief Justice, Warren Burger has concerned himself with the administrative requirements of the court system. He has attended to the interrelationship of state and federal courts, working through such bodies as the Conference of Chief Justices—which includes chief justices from all fifty state supreme courts—the National Center for State Courts, and the Institute for Court Management. He has led efforts to strengthen the operations of the federal judicial system through an active chairmanship of the Judicial Conference of the United States. The conference includes federal judges from the eleven U.S. circuits and from specialized federal courts such as the Court of Claims. This emphasis on the administrative needs of the courts will be even more important in the future as the workload of the judiciary increases further. We are accustomed to thinking of executive-branch agencies as complex bureaucratic organizations; the same perspective is needed toward the courts.

Warren Burger and court administration

SELECTION OF JUDGES

Just as the courts are a special type of political institution, so judges are a special type of politician. The political side of judgeships extends throughout the process by which they are selected for the bench. As Joseph C. Goulden observed, "judges are of political, not divine, origin...."[27] What is the political process through which judges reach the bench?

Judges in State Courts

Election is the predominant means by which state court judges are chosen. Judges sometimes run on partisan tickets, as in West Virginia and Illinois. More commonly, they run without party labels, the system used in California, Washington, and Michigan. In still other states one finds variants of the selection process that applies to federal judges: the governor appoints or nominates, and the state legislature then consents or elects. This is the procedure in Connecticut, Massachusetts, Maine, and Delaware. The Northeast is the only part of the country where some form of popular election of judges has not become the rule.

Federal Judges

Article III of the U.S. Constitution says little about judicial selection. It provides only that judges of the Supreme Court and of the lower

[27] Joseph C. Goulden, *The Bench Warmers* (New York: Weybright and Talley, 1974), p. 23.

courts "shall hold their offices during good behavior"—that is, for life terms. Article II, section 2, stipulates that the president shall have the power to nominate, and with the "advice and consent of the Senate" to appoint "ambassadors, other public ministers and consuls, judges of the Supreme Court, and all other officers of the United States. . . ."

The formal process for selecting federal judges seems straightforward. The president proposes a candidate and submits his name to the Senate; if the Senate concurs by majority vote, the president's nominee is confirmed and takes office. But as it has evolved over two centuries, the process is considerably more complicated than the constitutional form might suggest. Different practices apply in selecting federal district judges, judges of the courts of appeals, and justices of the Supreme Court.

District-court appointments. The constitutional requirement that the Senate approve judicial nominees, coupled with the fact that district judges serve jurisdictions within individual states, has led to the informal but powerful practice of **senatorial courtesy** in district-court appointments. Once a nomination has been sent to the Senate, it is given to the Senate Judiciary Committee. The Judiciary chairman routinely sends out what are known as "blue slips." These are forms that alert the senators from the nominee's home state and ask for their opinions and information concerning the nomination.

In effect, through the blue slip the Judiciary Committee asks the senators whether the president's nominee is acceptable. If a senator receiving the blue slip is of the same party as the president, his failure to return it with a statement of endorsement is taken under senatorial courtesy as a veto of the nominee. The willingness of the Senate to grant de facto veto power to senators of the president's party from the nominee's state is a form of mutual back-scratching. By following the practice, a senator knows that when a nominee from his own state is submitted, his brethren will grant him this same courtesy—more precisely, this same power. When the senators from the nominee's state are not of the president's party, this right of veto does not apply. This reflects political realism, for to require a president to consult senators of the other party with the same care and diligence with which he consults senators of his own party would upset the normal sense of political fairness.

The Senate's willingness to veto a nominee who does not receive proper home-state clearance is rarely tested, because a system of prior consultation has developed. Before the nomination is ever submitted, negotiations take place between the senators from a prospective nominee's state and the attorney general or deputy attorney general representing the administration. The extent to which Justice Department officials will defer to the home-state senators' wishes depends upon instructions from the president. Presidents Eisenhower and Kennedy made it clear that their Justice Department subordinates

Margin notes:
Senatorial courtesy

De facto veto power over district court nominees

Prior consultation

were authorized to negotiate for the best possible nominees. Lyndon Johnson was willing to defer to the preferences of the home-state senators as long as the individuals they recommended were not clearly unacceptable to him. The only absolute in this process is that a nomination will surely fail if the home-state senator or senators of the president's party strongly oppose it.

ABA evaluations

Independently of the above process, candidates for district-court appointments are informally investigated by the Justice Department; their names are then given to the Standing Committee on Federal Judiciary of the American Bar Association. The committee ranks these nominees on a scale: "exceptionally well qualified," "well qualified," "qualified," or "not qualified." At early stages in the review process, the ABA Committee provides the Justice Department with information on what is likely to be the rating of the leading contenders; poor preliminary ratings may be the basis for eliminating candidates from further consideration.[28] Nominees are sometimes approved, however, even when they receive "not qualified" ABA ratings. This may reflect the clout of the nominee's home-state senators. Or it may reflect doubts about the ABA's standards in particular cases. For example, the ABA committee will not approve anyone who has reached the age of sixty-four—a standard many senators do not generally accept.

Courts-of-appeal appointments. President Jimmy Carter changed the procedures for choosing nominees to the U.S. courts of appeals.

Courts of appeal appointments

Through an executive order he established the United States Circuit Judge Nominating Commission to make recommendations for nominations based on merit. Working through panels that it set up for each of the eleven circuits, the commission forwarded to the president the names of persons deemed most qualified on the basis of "character, experience, ability, and commitment to equal justice under law." Since the president first determined the composition of the panels and then chose the court nominees from the lists presented to him, his role remained decisive. President Ronald Reagan disbanded the Circuit Judge Nominating Commission, returning to the pre-Carter selection procedures, with senators and others recommending candidates to the Justice Department.

Supreme Court appointments. Since the Supreme Court has national jurisdiction, the tradition of senatorial courtesy has never applied to

Supreme Court appointments

nominations to it. The president makes nominations with broad national policy considerations in mind, and traditionally the Senate has granted him considerable leeway. This does not mean that the president's nominations always have smooth sailing in the Senate. In

---

[28] See Sheldon Goldman and Thomas P. Jahnige, *The Federal Courts as a Political System*, 2d ed. (New York: Harper and Row, 1976), pp. 49–50. For a review of Reagan administration practices in selecting federal judges, see Goldman, "Reagan's Judicial Appointments at Midterm," *Judicature* 66 (March 1983):342.

the nineteenth century, about one out of every three nominations failed; in the twentieth, about one in nine.[29] The last two presidential nominees to be rejected were Clement Haynsworth and Harrold Carswell, nominees of President Richard Nixon in 1969 and 1970, respectively. These rejections resulted in part from political tensions as a conservative Republican president confronted a more liberal Democratic Senate. But other considerations proved decisive. In the case of Harrold Carswell in particular, hearings conducted by the Senate's Judiciary Committee revealed an individual with dubious qualifications for so high a judicial appointment.

Routes to the Judiciary: Backgrounds of Federal-Court Appointees

Federal court appointments throughout U.S. history, including those to the Supreme Court, have typically gone to members of the president's party. Even when presidents reach across party lines for nominations—as Richard Nixon did when he chose Lewis F. Powell, Jr., of Virginia for a Supreme Court opening in 1971—they usually pick individuals of a philosophic bent similar to their own. While nominally a Democrat, Powell's conservatism was compatible with the views of the president who picked him. In this century, only three presidents have given more than 10 percent of their judicial appointments to individuals outside their own parties, none more than 20 percent.

Partisan and policy considerations in court appointments

Presidents appoint to the bench fellow partisans and people who, as best they can determine, hold compatible policy perspectives. They also frequently send other political signals in making their appointments. Jimmy Carter appointed women and ethnic minorities to the federal judiciary in greater numbers than any other president. (Carter had unusual opportunities to reconfigure the federal bench because Congress created 152 new federal judgeships in 1978.) He had pledged to make the federal judiciary more diverse and pluralistic with regard to ethnicity and sex. As Table 10.1 shows, he succeeded. About 14 percent of Carter's appointees to U.S. district courts were women, compared to just 1.6 percent of Johnson's, .6 percent of Nixon's, 1.9 percent of Ford's, and 4.3 percent of Reagan's (in his first two years in office). In all, Carter appointed 40 women, 38 blacks, and 16 Hispanics to the federal bench.

Political considerations

Informal political criteria also guide presidents in their Supreme Court appointments. For example, nominations have at times served to recognize social groups that had been excluded from full participation in American social and political life. President Lyndon Johnson finally broke the color bar when he appointed Thurgood Marshall to the Supreme Court in 1967; President Ronald Reagan broke a similar barrier in 1981 when he appointed Sandra Day O'Connor the first female Supreme Court justice.

[29] Goulden, *Constitutional Law*, p. 19.

Table 10.1
Judicial Appointments of Recent Presidents by Sex and
Ethnicity (in percent)

	Women	Blacks	Hispanics
	U.S. Courts of Appeal		
Johnson	2.5	5.0	*
Nixon	0	0	*
Ford	0	0	*
Carter	19.6	16.1	3.6
Reagan	0	5.3	0
	U.S. District Courts		
Johnson	1.6	4.1	2.5
Nixon	0.6	3.4	1.1
Ford	1.9	5.8	1.9
Carter	14.4	13.9	6.8
Reagan	4.3	0	2.9

*Data not available.

Source: Johnson, Nixon, and Ford: Sheldon Goldman, ''Carter's Judicial Appointments: A Lasting Legacy,'' *Judicature* 64, 8 (March 1981): 344–55. Carter and Reagan: *Congressional Quarterly* 41, 2 (January 15, 1983): 83; based on figures from the Justice Department. Reagan's appointments refer only to the years 1981, 1982.

Current Supreme
Court appointees

The current Supreme Court is composed of five justices whose party background prior to appointment was at least nominally Republican, and four who were Democrats. Among the current sitting justices, one was appointed by Dwight Eisenhower, one by John Kennedy, one by Lyndon Johnson, four by Richard Nixon, one by Gerald Ford, and one by Ronald Reagan (see Table 10.2). Justices Rehnquist and O'Connor, together with Chief Justice Burger, are the most consistently conservative in their court decisions, while Justices Brennan and Marshall are the most consistently liberal.

Table 10.2
Members of the U.S. Supreme Court, 1984

Name	Year of birth	State appointment from	President who appointed	Party background	Judicial oath taken
Burger, Warren E.	1907	Va.	Nixon	R	6/23/69
Brennan, William Joseph, Jr.	1906	N.J.	Eisenhower	D	10/16/56
White, Byron Raymond	1917	Colo.	Kennedy	D	4/16/62
Marshall, Thurgood	1908	N.Y.	Johnson	D	10/2/67
Blackmun, Harry A.	1908	Minn.	Nixon	R	6/9/70
Powell, Lewis Franklin, Jr.	1907	Va.	Nixon	D	1/7/72
Rehnquist, William Hubbs	1924	Ariz.	Nixon	R	1/7/72
Stevens, John Paul	1920	Ill.	Ford	R	12/19/75
O'Connor, Sandra Day	1930	Ariz.	Reagan	R	9/25/81

PUBLIC OPINION AND THE COURTS

In many regards, Americans give their courts high marks. When asked whether various individuals and groups "tend to act more in their own self-interest or more in the public interest," the public felt that federal court judges acted more in the public interest than did newsmen, doctors, cabinet officers, other government officials, members of Congress, labor leaders, or business executives (Figure 10.4). The public also believes that judges deal fairly with all groups in the population. It rejects the view that judges too often allow their personal beliefs and political opinions to enter into their rulings, or that they have assumed too much power. Americans are for the most part not unhappy with the big decisions handed down by federal courts. For all the furor which followed *Roe* v. *Wade,* only 28 percent of the public said they disagreed with the Court's ruling.[30] The public also accepts the basic thrust of the Court's leading civil rights decisions.

Yet, for all of this general approval, the last fifteen years have seen growing public unease directed at "the courts." The unease has one clear, overriding source or cause: anger over the rising incidence of crime (Figure 10.5). Studies have shown that public fears and concerns about crime have risen significantly, and they include the sense that the courts have failed to do their part in seeing to it that the guilty are properly punished. The concern does not distinguish between

Public criticism of judicial leniency toward criminals

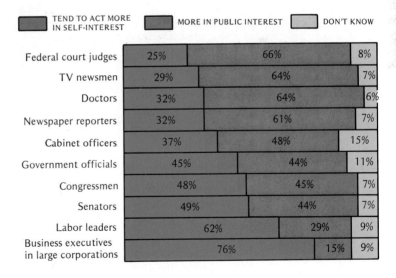

Figure 10.4
Americans Evaluate the Court System. What the problem isn't: Judges are most selfless

Question: Do you think most people in the group tend to act more in their own self-interest?
Source: Survey by the Roper Organization (Roper Report 81-8), August 15–22, 1981.

[30] Poll taken by CBS News and the *New York Times,* March 1982.

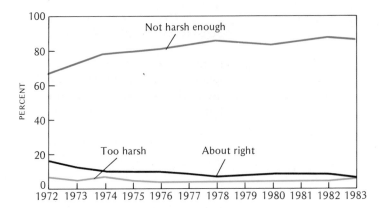

Figure 10.5
What the problem is: Public wants tougher penalties for criminals

Question: In general, do you think the courts in this area deal too harshly or not harshly enough with criminals?
Source: Surveys by the NORC, University of Chicago, taken in the spring of the years shown.

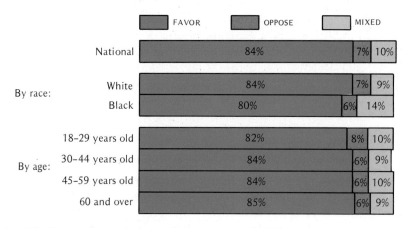

Question: Would you tell me whether on balance you would be more in favor of or more opposed to . . . harsher prison sentences for those convicted of crimes.
Source: Survey by the Roper Organization (Roper Report 84-2), January 7–21, 1984.

state and federal courts. Nor is the Supreme Court especially criticized; no one decision arouses massive resentment. Americans simply think judges have been too lenient with criminals. Two-thirds of the public disapprove of the way the criminal courts are doing their job.[31] In 1972, 66 percent of the public said the courts have not "dealt harshly enough with criminals"; the proportion rose to 79 percent in 1975 and 85 percent in 1983.[32] In 1983 only 4 percent described the courts as "too harsh" in their treatment of criminals, and only 6 percent thought they treated criminals with the appropriate severity.

[31] Poll taken by the *Los Angeles Times,* January 1981.
[32] Polls taken by the National Opinion Research Center, "General Social Surveys," Spring 1983.

Another survey showed that 84 percent of the public favored harsher prison sentences for persons convicted of crimes.[33] In chapter 17 we will look more closely at some court rulings bearing on the rights of persons accused of crimes that have helped spur these reactions. Concern about crime and judicial handling of it has eroded what is otherwise strong public backing for the courts and their performance in the American system of divided governmental powers.

SUMMARY

The framers of the U.S. Constitution provided for a system of federal courts as a third separate branch of the national government. Together with a set of lower federal courts, the Supreme Court was made the repository of "the judicial power of the United States." Above all, the courts were given the power to say what the law is.

The courts are in many ways weak institutions, compared to legislatures and executives. In Alexander Hamilton's words, they are without the powers of the purse and the sword. But the authority to say what the law is has proved a formidable one. One facet of it is *judicial review*, the power to review acts of legislatures and actions of executive officials to determine whether they are in conformity with the Constitution, and to declare them void if they are held not to be.

The framers believed that American federalism required federal courts to exercise judicial review over state legislative actions; otherwise there could be no uniform and respected national law. The Supreme Court would be the umpire of the federal system.

Whether the framers believed that judicial review should extend to declaring unconstitutional acts of a co-equal branch of national government is less clear. Hamilton asserted strongly that judicial review of acts of Congress was essential. Most of those who drafted the Constitution apparently gave little thought to this question, and expected that if the courts were to invalidate congressional acts they would do so only when there was the clearest violation of constitutional requirements.

In interpreting constitutional provisions or statutes, courts make law as surely as legislatures do. Furthermore, federal courts are now often heavily involved in administrative matters. This growing intervention has prompted criticism, including the charge of "judicial legislation"—that judges are too inclined to discover constitutional or statutory provisions mandating what are in fact their own political views and values. But every branch of government is now activist compared to times past, partly in response to increased public demands for governmental efforts to redress all manner of problems.

The fact that courts are political institutions that make policy does not mean that there is nothing special about how they enter the policy process. Courts operate within a context defined by a limiting set of judicial rules and standards. Real cases or controversies in law, involving appellants who have

[33] Poll taken by the Roper Organization, January 7–21, 1984.

suffered injury that is appropriately redressed through judicial action, are the prime vehicle for judicial action. Separation of powers requires that the courts follow procedures distinct from those governing political executives and legislatures.

The United States has a dual court system, with federal and state courts existing side by side and sometimes sharing jurisdiction. *Concurrent jurisdiction* means that a case may originate in either a state or a federal court; *exclusive jurisdiction* means it is assigned exclusively to one or the other. When a case arises under a state law, exclusive original jurisdiction usually belongs to the trial courts of that state. However, appeals may be brought from the highest state courts to the U.S. Supreme Court when a substantial federal question is raised.

The process for selecting judges varies greatly from one court to another. The majority of state-court judges are elected, commonly on nonpartisan ballots. All federal justices are appointed by the president, with the Senate's advice and consent.

For appointments to the federal district courts, the practice of *senatorial courtesy* is followed: the Senate will not confirm the president's choice unless that individual is acceptable to the senators of the president's party from the state in which the judge would sit. Presidential appointments to the Supreme Court are scrutinized, instead, in terms of broad national policy considerations and whether the requisite level of judicial competence has been met.

11 | Federalism

The precise character of the American federal system has been argued about endlessly since 1787, but its essential features are generally recognized and agreed upon. Under **federalism**, power is constitutionally assigned both to a central government and to governments of the states making up the American union. Each is given constitutional protection against the intrusions of the other. Within a complex and continually evolving set of constraints, the national and state governments share some functions and exercise others independently.

The first government of the United States, under the Articles of Confederation, was *confederal* in form. The states possessed virtually all governmental power; they had simply joined one another in what the Articles accurately called "a firm league of friendship." As we saw in chapter 5, the constitutional reformers of 1787 thought that the national government under the Articles was too weak and dependent. But they did not want to go to the opposite extreme and create a *unitary* form, where authority was vested exclusively in a central government. The constitution that the framers proposed was neither confederal nor unitary but rather, as James Madison observed in *Federalist Paper* 39, "a composition of both." Formal authority would be shared by the national and the state governments.

Writing in *Federalist Paper* 51, Madison argued the case for federalism as one element in a scheme of divided power.

> In the compound republic of America, the power surrendered by the people is first divided between two distinct governments [the national and the state] and then the portion allotted to each subdivided among distinct and separate departments. Hence the double security arises to the rights of the people.

Federalism would help promote a protective clash of interests within the institutions of government. This clash is still much in evidence, but so is an opposite reaction it has made necessary: A system of government predicated on dispersion of authority and competition among constituent units cannot function well in the absence of continuing effort by these units to cooperate. The business of the American government just does not get done unless the three branches of the national government and those of the states work together in their environment of widely shared responsibilities.

Federalism: An Enduring American Innovation

The prospects for American federalism have sometimes seemed in doubt. At the time of the Civil War, the question was whether a national federal union could and would endure. More recently the question has been whether the states can or should survive as important actors in the American governmental scene. Commenting on what many thought was the states' poor performance during the Great Depression, political scientist Luther Gulick asserted that "the American state is finished. I do not predict that the states will go, but affirm that they have gone."[1] Today, some observers argue that the dispersion of power and decentralization inherent in federalism are anachronistic, given the interdependence of the society and the national character of so many of its problems in the postindustrial era.

Each time it has been counted out, however, the federal system has recovered and shown its strength and resiliency. It remains one of America's most striking political inventions. Political scientist Samuel Beer noted that "at Philadelphia in 1787, it is generally recognized, the Americans invented federalism. . . ."[2] Martin Diamond called it "the most important contribution made by the American founders to the art of government. . . ."[3] And in an eloquent opinion penned in 1971, Supreme Court Justice Hugo Black asserted that " 'our federalism' . . . occupies a highly important place in our nation's history and its future. . . ."[4]

Endurance of federalism

Historical antecedents. In developing federalism, the American framers could draw on some earlier political thought. In the seventeenth century, German theorists who dealt with questions of law and government were especially interested in arrangements through which the territories making up the German Empire could retain their sep-

---

[1] Luther H. Gulick, "Reorganization of the State," *Civil Engineering*, August 1933, p. 420.
[2] Samuel H. Beer, "Federalism, Nationalism, and Democracy in America," *American Political Science Review* 72 (1978):11.
[3] Martin Diamond, *"The Federalist* on Federalism: 'Neither a National Nor a Federal Constitution, But a Composition of Both,' " *Yale Law Journal* 86, 6 (May 1977):1273.
[4] *Younger v. Harris*, 401 U.S. 37 (1971).

arate existence while the Empire would be able to perform its appropriate central functions. The works of Johannes Althusius and Ludolph Hugo are the most impressive. But this German thought and governmental practice were so remote from the American experience of the eighteenth century that it is doubtful they actually exerted much influence. English and French schools of political philosophy, on which the framers drew so heavily, wholly ignored issues of federalism. A new governmental form really was invented at Philadelphia in 1787, in response to two inescapable elements of American political thinking of the time: there should be a strong national union under a government with substantial authority, and the states should continue to have major political roles and power.

Federalism abroad

The invention is exported. American federalism has since proved attractive to other nations and their constitution-makers. Today, approximately twenty countries have federal systems. No exact figure can be cited because, while some governments are unquestionably federal, others are only partially so. And, while most federal governments are in democratic nations, a few are in countries that are not democratic. Communist Yugoslavia has a lively federalism, and the Soviet Union has some federal features. Over a third of the present federal systems came into being following the breakup of Britain's colonial empire. Besides the United States—Canada, Australia, India, Pakistan, Malaysia, and Nigeria have federal governments.[5] On the European continent, the Federal Republic of Germany (West Germany) is true to its name. And Switzerland's well-established federal government has had a long and interesting constitutional development.[6] Box 11.1 provides a closer look at federalism in the United States' northern neighbor, Canada.

THE CONSTITUTIONAL BASE OF AMERICAN FEDERALISM

American federalism has been highly dynamic and changing. But the Constitution clearly spells out its basic structure. Constitutional provisions on federalism can be usefully divided into five categories: those relating to the powers of the states, the powers of the national government, restrictions on states, federal guarantees to states, and interstate relations.

---

[5] William H. Riker, *Federalism: Origin, Operation, Significance* (Boston: Little, Brown, 1964), p. 25.
[6] According to Daniel Elazar, 18 countries have federal forms of government: Argentina, Australia, Austria, Brazil, Canada, Czechoslovakia, the Federal Republic of Germany, India, Malaysia, Mexico, Nigeria, Pakistan, Switzerland, the United States, the Soviet Union, the United Arab Emirates, Venezuela, and Yugoslavia. See Daniel Elazar, "State Constitutional Design in the United States and Other Federal Systems," *Publius: The Journal of Federalism* 12 (Winter 1982):8.

Box 11.1
Federalism in Canada

Canada was created as a federal union by the British North America Act of 1867. Four English colonies—New Brunswick, Nova Scotia, Quebec, and Ontario—were united under one government. Though allied to the British Crown, Canada was given a significant measure of self-government. A parliamentary system of government was established, with a two-house legislature and a cabinet responsible to the lower house, following the British model. Seats in the upper house or Senate were apportioned equally among Quebec, Ontario, and the Maritimes—according to the "federal principle"—while seats in the lower house, the House of Commons, were distributed by population.

The founders of Canadian federalism borrowed from the U.S. model, but they modified it considerably. One particular "defect" they sought to remedy was "overdecentralization," a condition which in 1867 they blamed for the American Civil War. Since they thought the U.S. Constitution had erred by vesting too much residual power in the states, the Canadians turned things around and vested these powers in the central government.

Interestingly enough, however, while the American system subsequently became increasingly more centralized, Canada moved toward greater decentralization. Actual practice confounded the constitutional intent. Whereas nationalism triumphed in the U.S. after the Civil War, and citizens considered themselves Americans first and state residents a distant second, in Canada no such strong national feeling developed.

One factor holding back a full sense of national identity was the historic rivalry and animosity between English-speaking Canadians centered in the province of Ontario, and French-speaking Canadians concentrated in the province of Quebec. Another was the striking economic disparities among Canada's provinces. Per capita income in the oil-rich province of Alberta is about four times higher than in the poorest province, Prince Edward Island. These income disparities are roughly twice as great as those between the poorest and the richest American states. Together, the ethnic-linguistic and the economic divisions have presented a formidable challenge to Canadian unity.

Powers of the States

Article I, section 3, of the Constitution establishes the upper house of the national legislature, the Senate, as the federal chamber. Seats are apportioned to represent the states as equal units. Each has two U.S.

senators (California with 24.7 million residents in 1982 and Alaska with just 438,000). Today this is the only instance in American legislative representation where districts of unequal size are still sanctioned, as constitutionally they must be.

Article II, section 1, delineates a state role in the selection of the president. Each state chooses, in a manner determined by its legislature, a number of presidential electors equal to the number of senators and representatives the state has in the U.S. Congress. Every state now picks its electors in the same fashion, through a direct popular vote organized by the political parties, in which the slate of electors pledged to the candidate who gets the most votes is chosen. But at different times in U.S. history states have used a variety of procedures in picking electors.

Selection of the president

Article V provides for a formal state role in amending the Constitution, by establishing two different procedures, both of which involve state governments directly. In the first, after Congress by a two-thirds vote has proposed amendments to the Constitution, the amendments are submitted to the state legislatures; at least three-fourths of the legislatures must ratify them before they can take effect. In the second, which has never been tried but often discussed, legislatures of two-thirds of the states may call for a convention to propose amendments. As in the first procedure, the amendments would still have to be ratified by three-fourths of the state legislatures (or state conventions) before becoming law.

Amending the Constitution

Probably the most discussed constitutional provision relating to the powers of the states is in the *Tenth Amendment:* "The powers not delegated to the United States by the Constitution, nor prohibited by it to the States, are reserved to the States respectively, or to the people." The Supreme Court has given different constructions to these words at different times in U.S. history. For much of the nineteenth and into the early twentieth century, the Court interpreted the amendment as an important statement of states' rights and residual powers. From the 1930s through the 1960s, however, the Court generally backed assertions of national authority and gave the Tenth Amendment little weight. For example, in the landmark case of *United States* v. *Darby* (1941), it broadly construed Congress' powers under the commerce clause of Article I, and dismissed the Tenth Amendment as but stating "a truism that all is retained which has not been surrendered." Over the last decade the Court has seemed unsure how much weight it wanted to place on the Tenth Amendment. Its most dramatic ruling came in *National League of Cities* v. *Usery* (1976), when it struck down the amendments to the Fair Labor Standards Act that Congress had enacted two years earlier. These amendments extended to state and local government employees federal minimum-wage and maximum-hour requirements that previously had been applied only to employees engaged in interstate commerce. In the majority opin-

The Tenth Amendment

The Nebraska legislative chamber—the only unicameral state legislature in the country.

ion, Justice William Rehnquist argued that

> This Court has never doubted that there are limits upon the power of Congress to override state sovereignty. . . . One undoubted attribute of state sovereignty is the states' power to determine the wages which shall be paid to those whom they employ to carry out their governmental functions.

Tilting toward a broader interpretation of the Tenth Amendment, Justice Rehnquist reiterated and strengthened an earlier Court finding that the amendment "expressly declares the constitutional policy that Congress may not exercise power in a fashion that impairs the states' integrity or their ability to function effectively in a federal system. . . ."

Powers of the National Government

The most formidable statement of the powers of the national government comes in *Article I, section 8*. After a long enumeration of what Congress can do—borrow money, raise armies, declare war, regulate commerce, advance science and the arts—section 8 declares that "the Congress shall have power . . . to make all laws which shall be necessary and proper for carrying into execution the foregoing powers, and all other powers vested by this Constitution in the government of the United States, or in any department or officer thereof." This sweeping grant has supported a generally expanding set of federal government functions and responsibilities. *Article VI* establishes the Constitution and the laws made under it as "the supreme law of the

The reach of Congress' power

The United States House of Representatives.

land," and requires state judges to uphold these provisions, "anything in the Constitution or Laws of any State to the Contrary notwithstanding."

Restrictions on States

The Constitution in a number of instances tells the states things they cannot do. The biggest set of prohibitions comes in *Article I, section 10*. No state can make treaties with foreign countries, issue currency, grant titles of or nobility, or pass any "bill of attainder," "ex post facto law," or any law "impairing the obligation of contracts"; and without the consent of Congress no state can tax imports or exports or keep military forces in time of peace.

Five amendments to the Constitution, all enacted after the Civil War, add other important prohibitions on state action. The *Thirteenth Amendment* was directed against the southern states and forbade slavery. Coming on its heels and also passed with the South in mind, but with language that has had much broader applicability, the *Fourteenth Amendment* asserts that no state "shall abridge the privileges or immunities of citizens of the United States; nor shall any State deprive any person of life, liberty, or property, without due process of law; nor deny to any person within its jurisdiction the equal protection of the laws." As we saw in chapter 10, a stream of important Supreme Court cases have arisen under these expansive terms.

The *Fifteenth Amendment* requires that no state deny to its citizens the right to vote "on account of race, color, or previous condition of servitude." In the *Nineteenth Amendment*, ratified in 1920, states were prohibited from denying the vote on the basis of sex. And the *Twenty-*

Limits of states' powers

sixth Amendment, which became law in 1971, brought the legal voting age down to 18 all across the country by stipulating that the right of citizens who are 18 years or older to vote shall not be denied by any state "on account of age."

Federal Guarantees to States

States are given a number of guarantees under the Constitution. According to *Article I, section 8,* all taxes that Congress levies must be uniform in their rates and other provisions for all states; no state may be taxed discriminatorily. *Article IV, section 3,* provides that no new state shall be brought into the Union from territory of one or more existing states without the express consent of the concerned state legislatures as well as the approval of Congress. In *Article IV, section 4,* the national government guarantees each state a republican form of government, protection against invasion, and, when the state requests it, federal assistance against domestic violence. Presidents have mobilized the National Guard and even used regular army troops to maintain calm and order in the states. *Article V* stipulates that the Constitution cannot be amended to deprive states of equal representation in the U.S. Senate.

National Guardsmen are often sent to aid flood victims.

Interstate Relations

The last of the constitutional provisions on federalism bears on the relations of one state to another. *Article IV, section 1*, stipulates that "full faith and credit" shall be given by every state to the laws and actions of every other state. The next section of this article provides that a state is bound to apprehend and extradite a person formally accused or convicted of violating the felony laws (those covering more serious crimes) of another state. It also asserts that each state shall grant the "privileges and immunities" given its own citizens to those of every other state—a provision presumably inserted to assure that a resident of, say, Virginia would not be discriminated against by the police or other governmental officials when traveling or doing business in New York or South Carolina. This may seem quaint today, but it was a natural enough concern in 1787.

This is the federal framework that the Constitution establishes. Both the national government and those of the states are given expansive governmental mandates. Both are told there are things they cannot do. The national government is pledged to assure the states some basic protections, and the states in turn to honor each other's laws. This structure has been broad enough to permit a great deal of change in federal-state relations, but precise enough to maintain federalism over two centuries of extraordinary social and political transformations.

EVOLUTION OF AMERICAN FEDERALISM

Most of what was done by American government in the country's early years was accomplished at the state and local level. Education was exclusively a local affair, and law enforcement very nearly so. The federal government played a significant role in national defense, of course. In domestic affairs it promoted such internal improvements as building roads and canals needed to move people and goods around the nation. But that was about all. Before the Civil War the states were clearly the dominant actors in most domestic affairs.

The Early Years: States' Rights

States were understandably jealous of their prerogatives, and elaborate formulations of states' rights flourished. One example is the doctrine of **nullification**, whose main proponent was South Carolinian John C. Calhoun. Calhoun held that the Union was composed of *sovereign states* that did not surrender sovereignty upon entering it. As a condition of its sovereignty, a state retained the right to review the actions and laws of the central government and, if need be, to declare

Nullification

President Jefferson Davis (seated facing) General Robert E. Lee, and the Cabinet of the Confederate States of America.

them "null and void." Like claims of other states' rights, nullification has been associated with the South and its struggle to maintain slavery. But interestingly enough, the doctrine was first advanced in New England on behalf of economic interests, not racial issues.

Secession. If a state believed the demands of the Union were incompatible with its own interests and sovereignty, according to those who advocated the right of secession, it could pull out of the Union altogether. This is, of course, the ultimate expression of the idea of states' rights. Eleven southern states exercised in 1861 what they saw as their right of secession, and the American Civil War began.

Secession

Dual federalism. Nullification and secession were always considered extreme positions, but the idea of dual federalism was widely supported in pre–Civil War America. It presupposed a very clear line between national and state governments. Both were sovereign, but the states had the larger sphere of action. Dual federalism stressed the *reserved powers* of the states compared to the limited mandate of the national government.

Dual federalism

Nationalist assertions: the Marshall Court. In this environment where states rights had broad appeal, one of the most consistent advocates of a broader national role was John Marshall, chief justice of the Supreme Court from 1801 to 1835. Marshall managed to win some victories for his nationalist perspective; his ruling in *McCulloch* v. *Maryland* (1819) is the most celebrated.

In 1791 Congress created the Bank of the United States to hold and dispense federal funds and perform other monetary functions. Though

McCulloch v. *Maryland*

the Constitution says nothing explicitly about Congress' power to create corporations like the bank, the bank's constitutionality was not contested in the courts before its charter expired in 1811. A second bank was chartered in 1816, but it proved politically unpopular, partly because it competed with state banks. Maryland passed legislation imposing a heavy tax on bank notes issued by the Bank of the United States. McCulloch, a cashier of the bank's Baltimore branch, issued notes without paying the required tax, thus setting the case in motion.

The reach of the "necessary and proper" clause

In the opinion of the Court, the Constitution and the laws enacted under it by the government of the United States form the supreme law of the land and cannot be infringed or countermanded by any state. Among the powers enumerated in Article I, section 8, there was no mention of establishing a bank or creating any other corporation. But neither was there anything prohibiting such action. The Constitution, Marshall insisted, clearly provided for a variety of actions not expressly mentioned when it stipulated at the end of section 8 that Congress shall be able to enact "all laws which shall be necessary and proper for carrying into execution the foregoing powers. . . ." Establishing a national bank was a legitimate congressional act under the "necessary and proper" clause.

> We admit, as all must admit, that the powers of the government are limited, and that its limits are not to be transcended. But we think the sound construction of the Constitution must allow to the national legislature that discretion, with respect to the means by which the powers it confers are to be carried into execution, which will enable that body to perform the high duties assigned to it. . . . Let the end be legitimate, let it be within the scope of the Constitution, and all means are appropriate, which are plainly adapted to that end, which are not prohibited, but consist with the letter and spirit of the Constitution, are constitutional. . . .[7]

Despite such ringing language, however, Judge Henry Friendly has noted, "the use made of these powers through the first century of our history under the Constitution was restrained."[8]

The Civil War and Its Aftermath

Decline of extreme states' rights

The Civil War was a momentous event in the life of the country. Few political institutions came out of the ordeal unchanged; federalism was no exception. After the war the federal union was put back together again with most prewar elements intact. But in one striking shift, extreme states' rights doctrines like nullification and secession had been scuttled once and for all by the Confederate Army's surrender at Appomattox Courthouse on April 9, 1865. Since then, politicians have from time to time insisted upon their states' sovereign right to

[7] *McCulloch* v. *Maryland*, 17 U.S. 316 (1819).
[8] Henry J. Friendly, "Federalism: A Foreword," *Yale Law Journal* 86 (May 1977):1020.

pursue certain interests against federal standards—as many southern politicians did when confronted by new civil rights laws and rulings in the 1950s and 1960s. But after 1865, few Americans took seriously the idea that a state could declare national government acts "null and void" or withdraw from the Union.

Constitutional change. More generally, the Civil War was a watershed in American federal relations. The Thirteenth, Fourteenth, and Fifteenth Amendments to the Constitution were enacted following the war; of these the Fourteenth is especially important. "Although these Amendments were doubtless intended primarily to safeguard the rights of the newly emancipated Negroes," Judge Friendly observed,

Importance of the Fourteenth Amendment

> Mr. Justice Miller's prophecy that this would be their sole effect turned out to be an exceedingly poor one. In time the due process and equal protection clauses of the 14th Amendment would vest the federal judiciary, particularly the Supreme Court, with a roving authority to invalidate state statutes. . . .[9]

Technology and the economy. Other changes led to an expansion of the national government's role. One was the transformation of the country beginning in the second half of the nineteenth century under the impetus of developments in technology and the economy. The U.S. shifted from a rural, localized country to an industrial, interconnected society. Between 1870 and 1920, America's population tripled, reaching 106 million. The great cities were built—in this half-century New York grew from 942,292 to 5,620,048, Chicago from 298,977 to 2,701,705. Huge industrial and financial institutions were established. In place of an economy of small family farms producing foodstuffs for immediate areas, there was one dominated by big corporations drawing resources from the entire country (indeed, the world) and servicing national markets. A new communications technology made reports of activity in one sector the immediate property of the entire nation. This was the half-century in which all major electronic media except television were developed. The number of telephones in the United States grew from 3,000 in 1876 to 340,000 in 1885, 4.1 million in 1905, and 13.3 million in 1920. A new transportation network was established, centered on the railroad and the motorcar. Miles of railroad track in operation increased from 8,800 in 1850 to 82,000 in 1880 and to 406,000 in 1920.

Effects of new technology

Regulation. With all these forces increasing the scale of enterprises and drawing the parts of the country closer together, demands for greater national-government involvement became more insistent. The

[9] Ibid., p. 1021. The court opinion of Justice Miller to which Friendly refers came in the *Slaughterhouse Cases,* 83 U.S. 36 (1873).

Regulatory legislation

new federal regulatory legislation of the late nineteenth and early twentieth centuries, discussed in chapter 9, was one result. Pure food and drug legislation, for example, didn't seem important when most people lived on farms and consumed largely what they produced; but it became necessary in an age of large cities and big impersonal corporations.

This new national economic regulation was, however, only the first stirring, a hint of things to come. Federal spending remained modest. Outside of defense, veterans' pensions, and interest on the national debt, spending rose very little. Most governmental expenditures were still at the state and local levels.

The New Deal Years

"If the War between the States was a watershed," Judge Friendly observed, "the New Deal was a tidal wave."[10] Signs of major federal expansion were first evident in the years immediately following World War I. In 1926, with Calvin Coolidge, a conservative Republican, in the White House, federal per capita spending was nearly four times as high as a decade earlier under Woodrow Wilson, a progressive Democrat. The level of governmental activity in the United States has always reflected the demands of the social setting much more than the specific programs of the incumbent administration. The big jump in spending after World War I came because the country was entering a new sociopolitical era, one that posed much greater demands on national programs. Urban, industrial society required more governmental regulation and public assistance than the rural, localized, agricultural society that preceded it.

Extending national government functions

Under President Franklin D. Roosevelt after 1933, the managerial and welfare functions of the national government were greatly extended. New regulatory bodies such as the Securities and Exchange Commission (SEC) were established to watch over various sectors of the economy—in the case of the SEC, to protect investors and the stock market through orderly procedures in securities exchange. The national government also intervened on behalf of groups that found it hard to compete without assistance. For example, the National Labor Relations Act (the Wagner Act) was passed in 1935 to aid trade unions by making it unlawful for an employer to interfere with workers' rights to organize and bargain collectively.

Welfare and prosperity. The national government also assumed welfare functions previously handled informally through private channels, by state and local agencies, or not at all. In 1934 Roosevelt told Congress that the American people demanded "some safeguard against misfortunes which cannot be wholly eliminated in this man-made

[10] Ibid., p. 1023.

world of ours." And in 1935 the Social Security Act was passed. Two of the most important new national programs encompassed by the Social Security legislation were unemployment compensation and retirement benefits. More generally, the national government declared that henceforth it would be responsible for smoothing out business cycles, preventing excessive unemployment, promoting economic growth—in short, for maintaining and extending prosperity.

In response to all these new functions, federal expenditures again increased sharply. Between 1925 and 1941, federal per capita spending jumped 400 percent. And, reflecting a pronounced tilt toward the national government, combined state and local spending dropped below federal spending during World War II and stayed below it when peace returned—for the first time in American history.

Interdependence. During the New Deal and extending into the 1940s and 1950s, a major transformation of American government took place through the steadily increasing scale and interdependence of the various parts and sectors of the society—technological, economic, and political. Public problems assumed a more national character, and the national government grew in response, both absolutely and relative to the states.

Cooperative federalism. With this, there was a shift from dual federalism to cooperative federalism. The relative independence or autonomy of the different levels of government under the dual federal perspective of the nineteenth century has sometimes been compared to a layer cake—each governmental layer was supposed to be sepa-

Federal, state, and local government cooperation at work in industrial development.

rate and distinct from the others. In contrast, the increasing governmental interdependence which developed during the New Deal and the decades following suggested a marble cake: functions swirled and mixed together. American government had become more complex and the various powers and functions of the nation and the states more interconnected.[11] By midcentury the venerable institution of federalism had become a vast engine of intermeshing parts.

FEDERALISM IN THE MODERN ERA

Modern technology and governmental centralization

The term ***cooperative federalism*** describes the enlarged federal role and heightened intergovernmental sharing of responsibilities that had evolved by the middle of this century. The arrangements and assumptions of cooperative federalism itself were again quickly altered in the face of a new host of centralizing movements. And once more, technology was a principal cause. Throughout American history, technological development has brought society closer together, making its members more interdependent; thus government has had to play a bigger role. In the postindustrial era, as we noted in chapter 2, advances in communications, particularly television, have made it possible for Americans in northern Maine, in the industrial heartland of the Midwest, in the rural South, and in the suburban sprawl of southern California, to hear the same news, watch the same entertainment programs, see the same products advertised, and in general to share in a remarkably national cultural life. Further integration of the economy has exerted similar centralizing pressures. In response, studies of public opinion and popular culture have shown, state and regional variations in outlook have diminished and a more uniform national pattern has emerged.[12]

National Rights

Expanding national rights and responsibilities

Another factor affecting American federalism has been an enlarged sense of national rights and responsibilities. In 1913, the journalist and Progressive theorist Herbert Croly drew a distinction between "the national idea" and "the provincial idea," noting that the two impulses have given rise to conflicting pressures throughout U.S. history. At the time the Constitution was ratified, Alexander Hamilton

[11] Morton Grodzins, *The American System: A New View of Government in the United States*, (Chicago: Rand McNally, 1966).
[12] The Roper Center for Public Opinion Research has made extensive comparisons of state and regional differences in opinion and values, documenting the weakening of regional variations. See *Public Opinion*, February/March 1983, pp. 21–33. This is not to suggest that American social and political attitudes are now homogeneous from coast to coast. Significant differences growing out of contrasting historical experience, ethnic makeup, and economic interests of the states and regions persist. But over the last two decades the movement has been toward more nationally uniform outlooks.

was the most forceful and imaginative proponent of the idea of nation, and Thomas Jefferson the most eloquent defender of states' rights. When the Civil War was fought partly over these contending claims, Abraham Lincoln gave the idea of nation this ringing affirmation: "The Union is older than any of the states and, in fact, it created them as states. . . . The Union, and not themselves separately, procured their independence and their liberty. . . . The Union gave each of them whatever of independence and liberty it has." A protracted argument over the respective claims of the nation and the states goes on. During the past quarter-century, the balance has shifted toward claimants for national rights, lending greater legitimacy to initiatives of the national government.

National challenge to racial discrimination

Beginning in the 1950s, strong assertions of the rights and claims of national citizenship successfully challenged the racial discrimination that was the South's historical legacy. By the 1960s national opinion had moved to the point where major changes in race relations were required. Of course, the traditions and institutions that had consigned black Americans to second-class citizenship throughout the southern states were not produced by federalism. But the nature of a federal system, which gives considerable latitude to the states in policy choice, permitted discriminatory racial practices to be perpetuated with the force of state law. The attack on segregation became, in a sense, an attack on federalism. When southern governors like Orval Faubus in Arkansas and George Wallace in Alabama proclaimed their states' rights to continue to discriminate against blacks, they helped undermine the claim to legitimacy of the larger concept of states' rights which underlies federalism itself. Writing about federalism in 1975, William Riker observed that in the century after the Civil War

> the main beneficiaries have undoubtedly been southern whites, who could use their power to control state governments to make policy on blacks that negated the national policy. . . . Clearly . . . in the United States, the main effect of federalism since the Civil War has been to perpetuate racism.[13]

States' Rights under Attack

The erosion of state power

Even if Riker erred in so sweeping an indictment, the lessons of the 1950s and 1960s seemed to be that the people talking the loudest about the importance of states' rights were those who took issue with the basic American value of equality. Surely this validated the expansion of national governmental authority and initiative not just in race relations but across the broad spectrum of public policy. As the claims of national citizenship have grown stronger, and the practical role of

[13] William Riker, "Federalism," in *Handbook of Political Science*, vol. 5, Fred I. Greenstein and Nelson W. Polsby, eds. (Reading, Mass.: Addison-Wesley, 1975), p. 154.

In 1963, Governor George Wallace defied the federal government ruling that blacks must be allowed to enroll in the state university, and blocked entrance to the University of Alabama.

the national government has been greatly enlarged, the states have been left in an awkward position. Just what is their role and legitimacy? If the states are not sovereign but simply administrative units of the national government with changing roles in an evolving political process, why should one worry about pushing them aside if national approaches seem more productive? "Federalism came to be seen as a passing phase in the developmental process. . . ."[14] The governmental enterprises of the fifty states, with their 8.5 million full-time employees (in 1980) and myriad departments and functions could scarcely be ignored. But prevailing theory could and did accord them a fairly feeble, largely administrative status.

A Tide of National Legislation

The volume of new national legislation testified to the erosion of the states' position. One big thrust came in civil rights. But it was by no means confined to this area. There was extensive new federal legislation on behalf of public safety and well-being, utilizing the "commerce" power—Article I, section 8, of the Constitution gives Congress power "to regulate Commerce . . . among the several states. . . ." Probably the most far-reaching new statute was the Occupational Safety and Health Act (OSHA) of 1970. Other legislation included the National Traffic and Motor Vehicle Safety Act of 1966, the Highway Safety Act of 1966, the Natural Gas Pipeline Safety Act of 1968, the

[14]David R. Beam, Timothy J. Conlin, and David B. Walker, "Government in Three Dimensions: Implications of a Changing Federalism for Political Science," paper presented at the 1982 Annual Meeting of the American Political Science Association, Denver, Colo., September 2–5, 1982.

The National Governors Association meets each year to discuss the effects of federal actions on the states.

Federal Coal Mine Health and Safety Act of 1969, the Port and Waterways Safety Act of 1972, the Federal Railroad Safety Act of 1970, the Consumer Product Safety Act of 1972, the Motor Vehicle and School Bus Safety Amendments of 1974, and the Highway Safety Act of 1976.[15] These laws provided national standards and enforcement in the various areas their titles suggest.

In other policy areas the legislative surge was also strong. Protection of borrowers and consumers was extended by the Consumer Credit Protection Act of 1968, the Fair Credit Billing Act of 1974, the Real Estate Settlement Procedures Act of 1974, the Equal Credit Opportunity Act of 1974, the Home Mortgage Disclosure Act of 1975, and the Consumer Leasing Act of 1976. Another major series of laws were enacted placing the national government firmly behind efforts to protect the environment. Notable here were the National Environmental Policy Act of 1969, the Water Quality Improvement Act of 1970, the Clean Air Amendments of 1970, the Noise Control Act of 1972, the Federal Environmental Pesticide Act of 1972, and the Deep Water Port Act of 1974. The list goes on and on in almost every sector of public policy. The change was not incremental; it was a massive increase which qualitatively altered the national government's role. Let the end be legitimate, Congress was saying, and legislation on almost any conceivable subject is permitted, even required.

New areas of governmental concern

Growth of national power was further enhanced by a series of Supreme Court decisions—in their own way as consequential as the new legislation. In a long series of cases, the Court selectively incorporated key provisions of the first eight amendments to the Consti-

Supreme Court decisions bolstered national power

[15] For a fine review of these manifold federal interventions and their impact on the federal system, see Henry J. Friendly, "Federalism: A Foreword," *Yale Law Journal* 86 (May 1977): 1025–27.

tution within the due process clause of the Fourteenth Amendment, thus making them applicable to the states. (See chapter 17 for a full discussion of selective incorporation.) Following *Monroe* v. *Pape* (1961), the long-ignored civil rights acts of the Civil War Reconstruction period were employed not only to prevent racial discrimination but to address many other alleged denials of constitutional rights: for example, those involving inmates of state prisons.

> In carrying out this mission, federal courts have felt authorized to take on an enormous degree of supervision of the operations of state prisons and mental institutions and to impose affirmative obligations on the states. One federal court, in an effort to obtain minority representation, has ordered the complete remodeling of a city government.[16]

These judicial initiatives were discussed in chapter 10.

Grants-in-Aid

In some cases the national government addresses problems by authorizing its agencies to spend money directly to deal with them. In many instances, however, reflecting the large presence of the states and municipalities in the American governing system, federal funds are given to states and municipalities in the form of *federal grants-in-aid*, with various stipulations on how they are to be spent.

Before the Great Depression, Congress made grant funds available to the states for only a few clearly national functions such as building "post roads"—so called because the original rationale for a roadway system connecting all parts of the country was to service a national postal service mandated by the Constitution. During the Depression, a variety of new grant programs were added to cover additional services including welfare, employment assistance, public health care, public housing, and school lunches. From the end of World War II up until the 1960s, still other programs were established providing grants for airports, hospitals, urban renewal, and library services. When John F. Kennedy took office in 1961, some 44 federal grant programs were in place.

The growth of federal grant programs

Major increases. Extensive new grant programs were enacted in the 1960s and 1970s. Congress passed legislation through which revenues raised nationally were made available to states and cities to clean up the environment, provide health benefits for the elderly poor, make loans and grants to college students, establish or enlarge urban transportation systems, combat crime, get rid of slums, and extend a host of other services.

Some authorities conclude that about 500 federal grant programs

---

[16] Ibid, p. 1028. The case involving city government to which Friendly refers is *Bolden* v. *City of Mobile,* 423 F.Supp. 384 (1976).

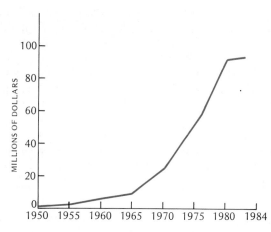
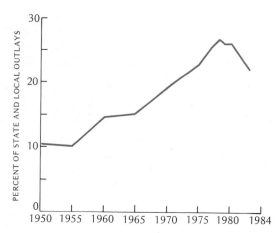

Figure 11.1
Trend of Federal Grant-in-Aid Outlays since 1950

Source: Office of Management and Budget, *Special Analyses: Budget of the United States Government* FY 1985, p. H-16.

were providing aid to state and local governments when Ronald Reagan took office in January 1981; others put the total even higher. Calculations made by the Office of Management and Budget (OMB) show 361 grant programs in 1981. The complexity of much of the legislation, and the fact that it is possible to count different program activities in different ways, account for the discrepancy in estimates. But it is clear that a huge increase in federal grants-in-aid had occurred in the preceding quarter-century. In 1955, as Figure 11.1 shows, federal grants totaled approximately $3.2 billion and provided about 10 percent of the total amount expended by state and local governments. A decade later, these grants had risen to $11 billion and accounted for 15 percent of state and local expenditures. By 1980, federal grants to state and local governments had reached $91 billion and were providing 26 percent of all funds spent by states and municipalities. In the 20 years between 1957 and 1977, grants-in-aid doubled in real terms—that is, controlling for inflation—every five years and increased overall by an extraordinary 700 percent.[17]

Grants for health services. The largest number of federal grant programs operate in the health-care area, and Medicaid is the biggest of these programs. By the end of the 1970s the national government was shouldering roughly one-third of the nation's health-care bills—an outlay representing more than $900 per person annually. Beyond this fiscal burden, the national government exercised broad influence over the entire health-care industry. It regulated the construction of health-care facilities, had a voice in the distribution of doctors and other

Medicaid and Medicare

[17] G. R. Stephens and G. W. Olsen, *Pass-Through Federal Aid and Interlevel Finance in the American Federal System, 1957–1977*, vol. 1, a report prepared for the National Science Foundation, Washington, D.C., August 1979.

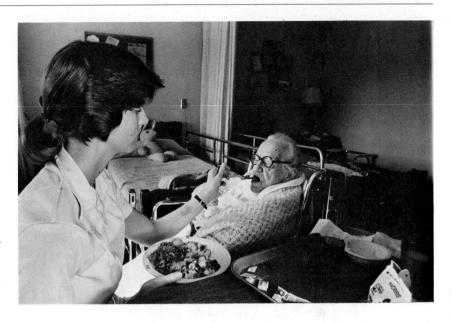

Medicare, a program of health insurance for the elderly, is run wholly by the federal government.

health-care professionals through various manpower programs, and, in effect, regulated health-care prices through its Medicare and Medicaid reimbursement plans. *Medicare*, first enacted in 1965, is a wholly federally funded health insurance plan for the elderly, financed through the Social Security system. *Medicaid*, passed three years later, is a welfare program for persons of limited financial means. Medicaid is financed through general revenues, not through the Social Security payroll tax. Federal grants for Medicaid are made to the states, which in turn supplement them with their own appropriations; in 1981, federal Medicaid grants totaled $15 billion.

The Reagan Reversal

Cuts in grant programs

The steady growth of federal grants to the states over the late 1950s, 1960s, and 1970s was halted by the Reagan administration in the early 1980s. Seeking curbs on domestic spending, the administration cut back on what it considered unnecessary grants-in-aid. Many smaller grant programs were eliminated and others were consolidated. Overall, according to OMB figures, there were 259 grant programs in 1984, compared to 361 three years earlier. Cuts were also made in some programs that were continued. For example, energy conservation grants had totaled $515 million in 1981; three years later, expenditures were down to $280 million. Grants to the states for sewage treatment system construction had been $4.1 billion in 1981, but were reduced to $2.4 billion in 1984. Total spending under federal grants leveled out in terms of actual dollars and fell substantially both as a percentage of the gross national product and as a proportion of all state and local government spending. In 1978 26.8 percent of state

Table 11.1

Selected Programs of Federal Grants to State and Local Governments, 1984

Function, Agency, Program	Outlays (millions of dollars)
Energy	
Energy conservation grants (Commerce Dept.)	$ 280
Natural Resources and Environment	
Sewerage treatment system construction grants (EPA)	2,430
Agriculture	
Extension service	334
Commodity Credit Corporation (food donations)	1,580
Transportation	
Federal aid highways (trust fund)	13,777
Mass transportation capital fund	1,250
Formula grants	2,389
Community and Regional Development	
Community development grants (HUD)	3,468
Urban development action grants (HUD)	440
Rental rehabilitation grants (HUD)	300
Education, Training, Employment, and Social Services	
Social services block grant (HHS)	2,675
Human development services (HHS)	1,771
Family social services (HHS)	659
Basic state grants (job training) (Labor Dept.)	4,919
Federal-state employment service (Labor Dept.)	1,445
Vocational and adult education (Education Dept.)	824
Compensatory education for the disadvantaged (Education Dept.)	3,475
Education for the handicapped (Education Dept.)	1,095
Rehabilitation and handicapped research (Education Dept.)	1,004
Health	
Alcohol, drug abuse, and mental health administration (HHS)	462
Medicaid (HHS)	20,674
Income Security	
Child nutrition programs (USDA)	3,396
Special supplemental food programs (USDA)	1,264
Assistance payments program, AFDC (HHS)	7,686
Low-income home energy assistance (HHS)	1,873
Subsidized housing programs (HUD)	9,913
Payments for operation of low-income housing projects (HUD)	1,031
Unemployment trust fund, training, and employment (Labor Dept.)	1,889
General-purpose fiscal assistance	
Payments to states under Mineral Leasing Act (Interior Dept.)	715
General revenue sharing (Treasury Dept.)	4,567
Federal payment to the District of Columbia (Treasury Dept.)	486

Source: Executive Office of the President, OMB, *Special Analyses: Budget of the United States Government, FY 1985,* Table H-27.

and local expenditures were supported by federal grants; by fiscal year 1983 the proportion had dropped five points to 21.8 percent.

The overall reductions occurred even though some grant programs increased substantially. As a result of rising health-care costs, grants to the states for Medicaid jumped from $17.8 billion in 1981 to $20.7 billion in fiscal year 1984. Federal aid for highway construction rose from $7.8 billion in 1981 to $13.8 billion in 1984. Table 11.1 shows spending under the largest grant programs in the 1984 fiscal year.

Increase in Medicaid grants

Types of Grants

The national government's grants-in-aid to state and local governments are of four broad types: 1) *categorical grants,* 2) *project grants,* 3) *block grants,* and 4) *revenue sharing.* Before considering the differences among these types, we should note that in the real world the distinctions are often not as sharp as they appear on paper. The lines separating certain categorical grants from block grants often blur, as do those between block grants and revenue sharing.

Categorical grants. This is the original type of federal grant to the states. Funds are provided for a particular category of services. Each state wishing to participate in a categorical grant program is required to put up some of its own funds to match the federal monies, agree to establish agencies to spend the funds, submit plans to a federal agency in advance of receiving support, permit national officials to inspect the completed work, and place all state and local officials who administer the grant under a merit system. Congress determines the purposes for which states receive funds under categorical grant programs, but the state governments have a voice in how these programs are carried out. Grants for highway construction are categorical; so are assistance payments under Aid to Families with Dependent Children (AFDC.)

Categorical grants

Project grants. Many of the new programs established in the 1960s and 1970s did not distribute monies to the states under the fixed formulas of the older categorical grants but rather provided variable grants to projects. Under the project grant programs, agencies prepare proposals and submit them to the nearest regional office of the federal agency administering the program. Nongovernmental agencies—private, nonprofit human service organizations—as well as state and city governments are commonly permitted to receive these grants, and in fact became major recipients. The argument for project grants was that they enabled Congress to target funds with greater precision and to find the agency best suited to providing a needed service. Their widespread use in the 1960s and 1970s—for such programs as bilingual education, the prevention and control of juvenile delinquency, combating drug abuse, and assistance for the handicapped—reflected

Project grants

Some federal programs provide funds to state government and community educational programs.

feelings that state and local government agencies were often insufficiently sensitive to the needs of minorities and the disadvantaged and had to be gotten around. In the 1980s the Reagan administration made a special effort to trim project grant programs, arguing that they undercut the place of the states and municipalities in the federal system.

Block grants. The growth in the 1960s and early 1970s of categorical and project grant programs prompted complaints by state and municipal officials. The latter argued that they were strangled in paperwork and red tape and that they did not have sufficient voice in determining how federal funds were being expended. They pressed for *block grants*—grants to state and local governments for services in broad program areas. Block grants may be used at the discretion of state and local officials, as long as certain general requirements are met. In the 1970s and early 1980s, Congress consolidated a great number of categorical and project grant programs in such areas as public health, manpower training, vocational assistance, and community development into more comprehensive block grants. The Reagan administration has strongly favored block grants, arguing that the greater discretion they give state and local governments in determining how funds should be spent accords with a proper view of federalism. Moreover, the administration has taken something of a hands-off approach with respect to enforcing those terms and restrictions that Congress has written into block grants. It has given the states the greatest possible flexibility under these programs. Some observers complain that enforcement has been too lax.

Block grants

Revenue sharing. In response to demands of state and local officials for greater discretion and flexibility in federal grants, the Nixon administration pushed for a program of general revenue sharing, and Congress enacted the program in 1972. It has provided several billion dollars each year to state governments and to 38,000 local governmental units—cities, townships, and counties. Revenue sharing is the system of federal granting with the fewest strings. The only limits—common to the other types of grants as well—are that funds may not be used to support programs which discriminate against any person because of race, color, national origin, sex, age, religion, or physical handicap. Otherwise the states and municipalities may use their revenue-sharing monies as they see fit, for whatever activities they choose. Block grants are restricted to particular program areas; revenue sharing has no such restrictions. Not surprisingly, revenue sharing is the most attractive to state and local governmental officials, since it gives them the greatest discretion. But it has never been especially popular in Congress, which sees the program restricting its voice in determining what activities will benefit from federal largesse. The Reagan administration likes revenue sharing in principle, but, because of its effort to hold federal spending down, it has opposed the increases in revenue sharing wanted by the states. Political compromises have fixed appropriations for revenue sharing at about $4.5 billion a year.

Revenue sharing

Project grants stand at one end of the spectrum, revenue sharing at the other. State and local governments get federal money in project grants, but they are required to use these funds for specific programs and often have to compete for funds with nongovernmental agencies. Under revenue sharing, the taxing resources of the federal government are, in effect, put at the disposal of the states and municipalities through essentially unrestricted grants. Figure 11.2 summarizes the relationship of the four principal types of grants in terms of their breadth of focus and the degree of discretion they give state and local officials.

Overload of the Federal System

The two major political parties have long been at odds over the expanding role of federal government. Many Democrats have favored greater use of the resources of the central government in meeting national needs. In contrast, Republicans have tried to restrict what they consider to be excessive growth of government in general, and excessive nationalization of governmental authority in particular—a process they think has left the states and municipalities diminished.

The work of the ACIR. This continuing partisan quarrel tends to blur another quite different development: growing agreement among federal/state relations experts on where the problems lie in contemporary American federalism and what needs to be done about them.

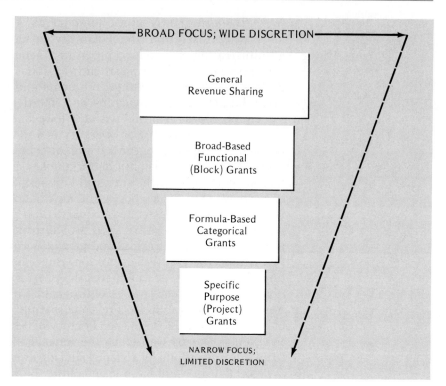

Figure 11.2
Breadth of Focus and Degree of State Discretion in Grant Programs

Reflecting this informed consensus is the work of the *Advisory Commission on Intergovernmental Relations* (ACIR): an advisory organization established by congressional act in 1957, representing city, county, state, and national government officials.

The ACIR has identified a number of trends in intergovernmental relations which it thinks have had unfortunate consequences. Among these, it cites the confusion and red tape that accompanied the proliferation of federal grant programs and the extent to which federal rules and regulations have come to dominate so many areas that historically have been considered the states' domain. It also points to the increasing intervention of the federal courts in various intergovernmental questions.[18]

Above all, the ACIR has argued, the problem of contemporary federalism involves a failure to sort out which governmental functions should be performed at the national level and which can be better handled by the states and municipalities.

Sorting out state and national roles

> The Commission believes . . . that this permits the national government to avoid some of its most basic domestic governmental responsibilities, while cluttering up its agenda with issues that more properly belong on

[18] See, for example, Carl W. Stenberg, "Federalism in Transition: 1959–1979," in the ACIR's *Intergovernmental Perspective* 6 (Winter 1980):8.

that of a municipal or county council, a school board, or a state legislature.[19]

The ACIR thinks that the federal government should assume full financial responsibility for those programs "which are aimed at meeting basic human needs," such as Aid to Families with Dependent Children, Medicaid, and housing assistance. (The present mixed federal and state administration and financing of these programs is described in chapter 19.) Hundreds of smaller project and categorical grant programs should be phased out, leaving the states and cities to finance activities and make program decisions in these areas.

More national responsibility? Some observers do not agree with the ACIR's conclusion that the intergovernmental system has experienced too much centralization. They concede that some administrative problems developed, such as too much paperwork and too many petty regulations, but they think these problems can be resolved. On the bigger question, they remain champions of an expanding national government role. Richard Nathan, a former government official who has written widely on the federal system, defends strong centralization of responsibility on the grounds that "people and jobs move in a free society, and people are concerned that financing and public services be equitable regardless of where people might live."[20] Only the national government is equipped to respond to the demands of an increasingly nationalized society. Still, many experts on American federalism, including the ACIR, think that the balance did swing too far during the sixties and seventies, away from recognition of a discrete and viable state role.

Managing the expanding national government role

The Reagan Proposals for a New Federalism

In his State of the Union Address on January 26, 1982, Ronald Reagan made federalism—once dubbed the "dismal swamp" of intergovernmental relations—the centerpiece for a sweeping set of proposals. He urged a "new day" for federalism, depicting his plan as "a program to make government again accountable to the people . . . accomplishing a realignment that will end the cumbersome administration and spiraling costs at the federal level." The Reagan proposals reflected partisan rhetoric, but some thoughtful consideration as well.

One part of the president's new federalism program as proposed in 1982 provided for a complete federal takeover of Medicaid (what the ACIR had urged), but specified an end to federal involvement in AFDC

[19] *An Agenda for American Federalism: Restoring Confidence and Competence*, Advisory Commission on Intergovernmental Relations, Washington, D.C., 1981, pp. 107–8.
[20] Richard Nathan, "No to Block Grants for Welfare," *Commonsense*, Winter 1980, p. 10.

and Food Stamps (contrary to the ACIR's recommendation). All Medicaid costs would be assumed by the national government, while all Food Stamps and AFDC costs would be borne by the states. The transition to this new arrangement would begin with the establishment of a trust fund into which would go revenues from existing federal excise taxes, including the Oil-Windfall Profits tax, taxes on tobacco, alcohol, and telephones, and a portion of the tax on gasoline. Trust fund revenues were estimated at $28 billion for fiscal year 1984, and these funds would be disseminated to the states. States would draw on the trust fund in amounts proportional to the support they had received from the grant programs being phased out. After 1987, according to the administration's proposal, the trust fund would gradually be reduced, with state tax resources substituted for the federal funds being lost.

The administration's proposals were the beginning, not the end, of what will be a protracted debate. The proposals were soon joined by

Resorting federal-state responsibilities

two other major proposals: one put forward by various state government interest groups, and the other by Senator David Durenberger of Minnesota. Both called for bigger federal financial commitments than Reagan had suggested. Negotiations opened on the three plans, with the idea that the administration would eventually transmit broadly supported legislation to Congress. Early on in these negotiations, the White House tentatively accepted the argument advanced by the National Governors' Association that the Food Stamp program be retained as federal.[21] Later in 1982, however, negotiations on the president's new federalism proposals broke down and no major action was taken. One reason for this was the political tension that resulted from mixing together two different sets of objectives. The Reagan administration sought simultaneously to reduce federal domestic spending overall and to sort out in a different way the mix of federal-state responsibilities. An effective rearrangement might well be incompatible with reducing spending. The sorting out proposed by the ACIR would increase, not decrease, federal spending. Richard Williamson, who had been assistant to the president for intergovernmental affairs, acknowledged this.

> I think it was a strategic error to put the federalism initiative on the table at the same time we were trying to get cuts out of a budget that had already suffered. It poisoned the well for the federalism discussion because the mayors and governors were so concerned they were going to be left holding the bag with a recession coming on.[22]

---

[21] For a thoughtful discussion of these "new federalism" proposals, see Albert J. Davis and S. Kenneth Howard, "Perspectives on a 'New Day' for Federalism," *Intergovernmental Perspective* 8 (Spring 1982):9–21.

[22] 1983 interview with Richard Williamson: Juan Williams, "Failed 'New Federalism' Reveals the Wages of Power," *Washington Post*, June 12, 1983, p. 12.

In 1983 and 1984, discussion of new federalism issues was put on the back burner, largely because no solution was found to the deadlock of 1982. But important changes in the actual practice of federal-state relations proceeded apace. As noted, state governments were given greater discretion under the block-grant setup pushed by the Reagan administration and as a result of the reduction in regulations and administrative oversight for many federal domestic programs. Two leading students of contemporary federalism argue that this has contributed to a "resurgence in the role of state governments."[23] Furthermore, they maintain, the recent gain in state influence is unlikely to be reversed.

> Unless federal taxes are raised well above the level necessary to close the budget gap, which seems unlikely, the federal government does not have the fiscal flexibility to reverse this flow of influence and responsibility to the states. . . . The federal government is pulling away from domestic and social programs, the state governments have taken on added duties and importance.

The Equity Issue

One important issue in American federalism that we have not yet discussed involves the question of equity. States vary in the wealth they have available for meeting various service needs, and there is a general conviction that the national government should do something to reduce these differences. But just what should it do? How much should it equalize state financial resources?

State tax capacity

Several formulas have been developed to measure interstate economic variation. Figure 11.3 shows one index that measures the states' "tax capacity," which is calculated by estimating the amount of revenue that each state would generate if all of them used identical tax rates. Estimated tax capacities vary only because of differences in underlying state resources—and these are quite substantial. Oil- and mineral-rich states like Alaska, Wyoming, Texas, Oklahoma, and Louisiana are at the high end of this tax-capacity index. At the low end are states that lack such natural resources and are not highly industrialized: Mississippi, Alabama, South Carolina, Tennessee, and Maine. Texas' per capita tax capacity is roughly twice Mississippi's.

Equalizing states' resources

No system for new national-state relations will be found acceptable if it does not provide in some measure for fiscal equalization among states of unequal resources. At the present time, most fiscal assistance to state and local governments—in the form of categorical or block grants—achieves some equalization through allocation formulas sensitive to states' fiscal status. For example, under Medicaid and

[23]Richard P. Nathan and Fred C. Doolittle, "Reagan's Surprising Domestic Achievement," *Wall Street Journal*, September 18, 1984.

Figure 11.3 **Tax Capacity of the fifty States**

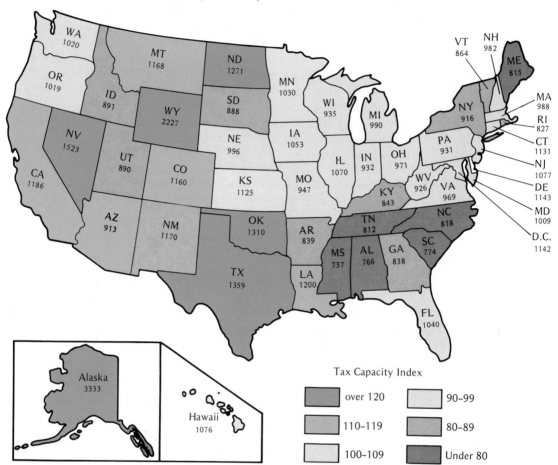

Tax capacity per capita measures a state's underlying economic resources. The tax capacity index is formed by dividing each state's per capita income by the U.S. average, and multiplying by 100. Alaska's tax capacity looks greater than that of the other states, but this is misleading. Per capita income in Alaska is high—but so are prices for goods and services. For example, costs of food "at home for a week" range in Alaska from 35% to 143% higher than the U.S. average, as reported in *The Alaskan Statistical Review* of 1980.
Source: ACIR, *1981 Tax Capacity of the Fifty States,* September, 1983, pp. 8–9.

AFDC, states with low per capita income receive more funds proportionally than high-income states. But the overall impact of existing grants in terms of equalization is modest. Any major restructuring of program responsibilities of the national and state governments will have to confront a basic question: How much should state resources be equalized through a national grant formula?[24]

[24] For a discussion of state tax capacity and equalization formulas, see Robert B. Lucke, "Rich States–Poor States: Inequalities in Our Federal System," *Intergovernmental Perspective* 8 (Spring 1982):22–28.

THE FUTURE OF FEDERALISM

The states still play an imposing role in American governmental relations, one bequeathed them by the Constitution and reinforced by centuries of practical governmental experience. The place of the states is enhanced, too, by their considerable political muscle. As Samuel Beer noted, in a country with 80,000 governments embracing 500,000 elected persons, there is built-in a powerful intergovernmental lobby on behalf of federalism.[25] Thousands of state and local government officials have an active interest in keeping their units of government active and viable.

Freedom

There is, as well, an impressive intellectual case for federalism. It includes arguments involving *freedom, pluralism, experimentation,* and *manageability.* The linkage of federalism to the maintenance of freedom can be traced back to the *Federalist Papers.* We have seen that Madison and Hamilton integrated the principle of the separation of powers with the idea of federalism to produce what they believed would be a watertight defense of freedom.[26] Other countries such as Great Britain have achieved high levels of political and social freedom without such dispersion of governmental authority. But the many Americans still hold to the classical liberal belief that divided power as promoted by federalism helps guard against any unit of the government becoming too strong.

Pluralism

Pluralism. A related defense of federalism posits the idea that the diverse needs of a heterogeneous population scattered over a big territory can best be served by a multi-level government. While various public opinion studies of recent years have shown that many citizens have a greater awareness of national officials and programs than of the state and local counterparts, the public-at-large still finds the system of semi-autonomous states useful in the articulation of local needs and interests. Even the strongest proponents of national citizenship agree that there are some areas where local choice should prevail. Few voices are heard, for example on behalf of a national school system.

Experimentation

Experimentation. There seems to be some merit in a governmental system that gives states room to experiment with programs reflecting their contrasting needs and interests. Many states have pioneered social programs long before the national government acted on them. The state of New York introduced minimum-wage, maximum-hour, and child-labor legislation decades before it was achieved nationally. If

[25] Samuel H. Beer, "The Adoption of General Revenue Sharing: A Case Study in Public Sector Politics," *Public Policy* 24 (Spring 1976):129.
[26] See, especially, James Madison, *Federalist Paper* 51.

The federal government was guided by New York's pioneering statutes regarding child labor.

describing them as "laboratories of federalism" seems extravagant, the states have in fact experimented productively with many programs and policies. "It is one of the happy incidents of the federal system," Supreme Court Justice Louis Brandeis wrote in 1932, "that a single courageous state may, if its citizens choose, serve as a laboratory, and try novel experiments without risk to the rest of the country."[27]

Manageability. Finally, Americans have indicated, when asked in public opinion surveys, that they see benefits in the more manageable size of state and local government. Because the United States has become so nationalized and operates through such vast institutions, the federal system's constitutional assurance of a role for governments closer to the people is especially attractive. One recent survey showed that 53 percent of the public believed the national government has acquired too much influence, while only 33 percent made this judgment about state government and just 20 percent about local government.[28] In this same poll, 54 percent described local government as "responsive

Manageability

[27] *New State Ice Co.* v. *Liebmann*, 285 U.S. 262, 311 (1932), Justice Brandeis dissenting.
[28] Survey conducted by the Roper Center for Public Opinion Research, with field work done nationally by the Roper Organization, November 1981. Data available through the Roper Center, University of Connecticut.

to peoples' needs"; only 34 percent assessed the national government this way.

In the mid-1970s, the states' role in the American governmental system seemed to some to be in permanent and irreversible decline. Centralizing impulses of the postindustrial era appeared to have robbed the states of much of their political vitality. Today, however, one finds greater appreciation of the part states still have to play. This part is different from what it was in the nineteenth century, when the society was far less interdependent than it is now and demands for national action much weaker. Adaptation of American federalism to the social and political requirements of the late twentieth century will present a continuing challenge, especially in sorting out those areas which demand national solutions from those where state direction and variety should be encouraged. But adaptation need not mean deterioration or decay. Though different, the future of our federalism seems likely to be no less dynamic than its past.

New roles for state and national government

SUMMARY

Federalism was invented by the framers of the U.S. Constitution in 1787 to meet two contrasting objectives to which many Americans were committed: achieving a strong national union and preserving the states as important political units. *Federalism* is a system of government in which formal authority is shared by the national and the state governments. Today, about 20 countries have some form of federal system.

Federalism has a detailed and explicit base in provisions of the U.S. Constitution. Various articles and amendments specify the powers of the states and of the national government, impose restrictions on the states and extend guarantees to them, and treat interstate relations.

As American society has evolved, so has the federal system. In the localized society of the early nineteenth century, the states were the most important governmental units, and doctrines of states' rights flourished—including extreme ones like those proclaiming the right of nullification and secession.

After the Civil War established beyond all debate the permanence of the federal union, and as industrialization and technological development tied the country closer together and made it more interdependent, the role of the national government gradually expanded. Each subsequent stage of socioeconomic development produced greater political centralization.

By the mid-1970s, many observers wondered if the erosion of state authority had proceeded so far that the states had been permanently consigned to a mere administrative role. Through an expanding set of categorical and project grant programs, the federal government was providing the states and municipalities with ever-larger portions of their financial resources—reaching a high of 26.8 percent in 1978—and subjecting them to more and more restrictions and regulations.

The last decade has seen some important reversals of these trends. Pressures on federal resources have led to a substantial decline in the proportion of state and local funding coming from Washington, and the states have asserted greater administrative flexibility through block grants and revenue sharing. The very scale of national institutions has made the more manageable size of state governments seem more attractive.

Work has begun on the difficult task of sorting out those functions which in the contemporary setting require a national approach from those for which state and local control is both possible and desirable. Underlying this shoring up of federalism in a changing polity has been the vitality of the basic constitutional design of the American federal system.

Part 4 | Participation

12 | Public Opinion

In no country today, not even the most dictatorial, can the general public's views on government and policy be wholly ignored. In the United States and other democracies, however, public opinion is given special weight and attention. Democracy endows it with a moral or ethical status. Democratic government simply does not exist if citizens' preferences on the many questions of public policy are not respected.

Despite this emphasis, the precise role that public opinion *should* play, and that it *does* play, in democratic government is not entirely straightforward. Consider, for example, the question of how fully governmental actions ought to reflect public preferences. If it is clear that the people favor something, should government do it? Our answer is likely to be: "Often, but not always." If a large majority favored laws denying members of a political minority the right to express themselves, and if elected officials responded to this clear public preference by passing such legislation, who would call this a sign of healthy democracy? Attention to individual freedom and minority rights is as much a part of our sense of democracy as majority rule.

PUBLIC OPINION AND DEMOCRATIC GOVERNMENT

Political scientist V. O. Key defined public opinion as "those opinions held by private persons which governments find it prudent to heed."[1] Government acts on an issue when it is understood to be of public rather than purely private consequence—and public opinion involves

---

[1]V. O. Key, Jr., *Public Opinion and American Democracy* (New York: Knopf, 1961), p. 14.

preferences and perspectives on public issues. We amend Key's definition slightly: **Public opinion** is the aggregate of citizens' personal opinions on questions considered part of public as opposed to private life. All of the preferences, hopes, fears, aspirations that people hold do not necessarily comprise public opinion, because many of them involve strictly private choice. The color a person prefers in a house, the type of music one likes best, the college one wants his or her children to attend are not public issues; there isn't public opinion on Beethoven and Billy Joel, although there are certainly musical tastes that can be measured.

Distinctions are often made among *opinions*, *attitudes*, and *values*. **Opinions** connote less deeply rooted judgments on current policies, leaders, and events. "What is your opinion on the president's trip to

China?" Political **attitudes** suggest more fundamental perspectives on enduring social and political questions, such as attitudes toward race relations. **Values** are people's ideals and the commitments they make, involving religious beliefs, standards for interpersonal relations, moral and ethical judgments. All three comprise public opinion in the term's broadest sense. In this chapter we will not try to distinguish among these components when we refer to public opinion in one substantive area or another.

Opinions, attitudes, and values

The Debate over Role

We noted in chapter 6 the continuing argument between proponents of direct and representative democracy. The former favor measures that enhance the public's direct determination of policy, while the latter stress the need to strengthen the role and performance of representative institutions. This general debate spills over into contrasting expectations for public opinion.

Expanding the role of public opinion. In *The American Commonwealth*, English theorist James Bryce saw the role of public opinion gradually advancing through a series of stages, "from its unconscious and passive into its conscious and active condition." He foresaw the possibility of a new stage, not then realized,

Rule by public opinion

> if the will of the majority of the citizens were to become ascertainable at all times, and without the need of its passing through a body of representatives, possibly even without the need of voting machinery at all. . . . [When this happens] popular government would have been pushed so far as almost to dispense with, or at any rate to anticipate, the legal modes in which the majority speaks its will at the polling booths. . . . To such a condition of things the phrase, "Rule of public opinion," might be most properly applied, for public opinion would not only reign but govern.[2]

The advent of scientific public opinion polling in the 1930s was seen by some observers to make possible the ultimate evolution of public opinion's role envisioned by Bryce. Did not the polls permit "the will of the majority of citizens . . . to become ascertainable at all times"? The most important figure in the founding and early development of public opinion polling, George H. Gallup, clearly thought so. The polls, he argued, "can make this a truer democracy."[3] Anything that enlarges the sway of public opinion over governmental decision-making is desirable.

[2] James Bryce, *The American Commonwealth* (New York: Macmillan, 1916), vol. II, pp. 261–62.
[3] George H. Gallup, "Polls and the Political Process—Past, Present, and Future," *Public Opinion Quarterly*, Winter 1965, p. 549. See, too, George Gallup and Saul Forbes Rae, *The Pulse of Democracy: The Public Opinion Poll and How it Works* (Westport, Ct.: Greenwood Press, 1968; first published 1940).

A critique of
public opinion

The danger of "rule by public opinion." **Others** rejected the direct democrats' expectations for public opinion as simplistic and unattainable. The distinguished journalist Walter Lippmann, in *The Phantom Public,* offered one of the strongest rebuttals over a half-century ago. The populace is poorly equipped in its level of information and interest for what "rule by public opinion" suggests. Mass publics just don't involve themselves in the details of policies and legislation, only in broad questions of ends and means. They are perfectly capable of passing judgment on the general objectives and approach of a governmental program, and they are competent to decide which party or candidate is best able to carry out the program. But this is where their role stops. As Lippmann saw it, democratic theory had created much confusion through its overstated definition of the proper role of the public and public opinion. Thus democracy

> has never developed an education for the public. . . . It has, in fact, aimed not at making good citizens but at making a mass of amateur executives. It has not taught the child how to act as a member of the public. It has merely given him a hasty, incomplete taste of what he might have to know if he meddled in everything. The result is a bewildered public and a mass of insufficiently trained officials.[4]

Can Public Opinion Be Manipulated?

Other issues enter the debate over the proper role of public opinion: Are people's political opinions basically their own, reflective of their true inner values and interests, or are they in some sense manufactured for them by powerful interests?

The helpless public. **Many** theorists have insisted that mass publics are all too easily manipulated, and the image of an ill-informed and emotional populace, preyed upon by demagogues, has often been invoked. The success that dictators Benito Mussolini and Adolf Hitler had in the 1920s and 1930s in rallying many of their countrymen behind anti-democratic, expansionist, and racist appeals added to such fears. European theorists of that time, such as Gustave Le Bon and Robert Michels, argued that the "common man" was just too susceptible to demagoguery for democracy to work well, if at all.[5] In Europe in the early days of democratic experience, conservative theorists were the most likely to express foreboding about the ease with which the masses could be pursuaded to support bad leaders and bad policies—not surprising since traditional conservatism had been uncomfortable with the idea of democracy in all of its forms. But in our own day, the left as well as the right expresses fears about manufactured public opinion.

[4] Walter Lippmann, *The Phantom Public* (New York: Harcourt, Brace, 1925), pp. 61–108 *passim*, pp. 144–45, 147–49.
[5] See Gustave LeBon, *The Crowd* (New York: Penguin, 1977; first published 1919); and Robert Michels, *Political Parties* (New York: Dover, 1959; first published in English, 1915).

False consciousness. Some theorists invoke the idea of "false consciousness," in which the public is seen as manipulated into views that are not really its own. Marxist theorist Herbert Marcuse argued, for example, that the great wealth of the contemporary United States has enabled it to smother discontent in a blanket of affluence and in effect buy consent to policies that elites favor. The "establishment" has succeeded in imposing on the public an outlook that serves its own needs.

Is public opinion a farce?

> We are again confronted with one of the most vexing aspects of advanced industrial civilization: the rational character of its irrationality. Its productivity and efficiency, its capacity to increase and spread comforts, to turn waste into need, and destruction into construction, the extent to which this civilization transforms the object world into an extension of man's mind and body makes the very notion of alienation questionable. The people recognize themselves in their commodities; they find their soul in their automobile, hi-fi set, split-level home, kitchen equipment. The very mechanism which ties the individual to his society has changed, and social control is anchored in the new needs which it has produced.[6]

Of course, if one wants to belittle a democratic society, it is convenient to argue that the public opinion to which it professes such respect and obedience is basically a farce, the product of elitist manipulations. But many commentators in many different settings have raised questions about how authentic public opinion really is. In present-day America it isn't just critics of democracy who portray the public as easily manipulated. This assessment underlies the perspectives of many in the advertising and public relations professions (although they profess no unease about it). Advertising theorists insist that improvements in their techniques, together with new communications technology and vast commitments of financial resources, permit the engineering of public acceptance of products, institutions, and ideas.

Selling the candidate. From the claim that consumer tastes and product preferences can be induced, it was not a very great step to the conclusion that political tastes can also be shaped by advertising.

"Advertising" candidates

Over the last two decades, a small army of advertising people, media specialists, and other campaign consultants have assumed a dramatically enlarged role in American electioneering, around the basic premise that techniques that sell soap can sell candidates and causes. V. O. Key observed:

> Propagandists and advertising men encouraged the acceptance of the most exaggerated estimates of their powers. Given enough money, they could sell soap, cigarettes, policies, presidential candidates. . . . Eventually the image of public opinion as an irresistible giant yielded to the

[6] Herbert Marcuse, *One Dimensional Man* (Boston: Beacon Press, 1964), pp. xii–xiii, 7–9 *passim.*

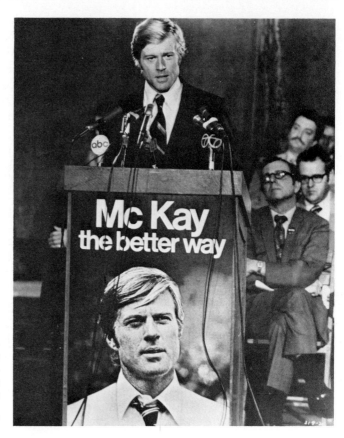

The film, The Candidate, *portrayed the "selling" of a candidate, who after his election, says to his campaign manager, "what do I do now?"*

image of the all-powerful opinion manipulators, engineers of consent and molders of mass opinion.[7]

The idea that "selling is selling" is now commonly expressed. A veteran political consultant, who had been "selling" candidates for many years, decided he would like a change of pace and secured a senior post in a large advertising agency specializing in consumer products.

> When I first spoke to them, they were a little concerned that perhaps my background in marketing candidates was not just right for the new post selling . . . [a well-known consumer product]. But as we talked, they saw that I was right, that there really isn't any difference. If you are good at selling, what difference does it make if you are promoting a candidate or a soft drink?[8]

Political advertisers—called "political consultants"—insist that public consent to candidates can quite easily be engineered, assuming that the "sponsor" (i.e., the candidate) cooperates. When his candidate loses a race, the consultant often complains that "he just

[7] Key, *Public Opinion,* p. 6.
[8] Personal communication to the author, July 1, 1983.

wouldn't do what we told him to do." Political consultants also argue that manipulating political opinion is no less reputable than manipulating consumer tastes. Media consultant Michael Kaye makes the latter claim unashamedly: "If I sell a car, I am not a bad guy. The minute you add one ingredient, the politician, all of a sudden it becomes distasteful or wrong. I am still waiting for someone to say why it is wrong. Why is it wrong to sell politicians?"[9]

Debate over marketing candidates

Some politicians have long had an answer to Kaye's question. Adlai Stevenson, twice Democratic party candidate for president (in 1952 and 1956), remarked that "the idea that you can merchandise candidates for high office like breakfast cereal is the ultimate indignity to the democratic process." Democracy assumes—more, requires—the presence of public opinion that reflects the people's needs and interests, not those of advertising hucksters. But does public opinion live up to its democratic billing?

We do not ask whether public opinion can ever be fooled or manipulated; of course it can be. Over a century ago Abraham Lincoln told a visitor to the White House that "you may fool all the people some of the time; you can even fool some of the people all the time. [But] you can't fool all the people all the time." Lincoln's whimsically put but serious point is the same one that occupies us here. In the pages that follow, we explore what is known about American public opinion to learn whether it still meets Lincoln's expectation. We will see how general properties and overall patterns bear on the argument whether public opinion is authentic and autonomous or the plaything of those who would manipulate it for their own ends.

PROPERTIES OF PUBLIC OPINION

Survey research, described later in the chapter, has revealed much about the properties of American public opinion. Public opinion undoubtedly has certain common characteristics in all or most countries, but its patterns are also shaped by the contrasting social, economic, and political experience of different nations. What we see in the United States reflects the country's two hundred years under one set of democratic institutions, the absence of sharp class polarization, the levels of public education and communication, and other formative elements.

An Informed Public?

On first review, survey research seems to raise serious doubts about whether Americans know enough about the various questions of pub-

[9] Michael Kaye, quoted in Larry J. Sabato, *The Rise of Political Consultants* (New York: Basic Books, 1981), p. 321.

lic affairs to play the part democratic theory assigns them. A cursory examination of poll data reveals extraordinary lack of interest and unawareness, even on basic facts of political life. This finding lends support to those who argue that mass publics can readily be manipulated because they know so little about issues they are supposed to decide.

Lack of knowledge about leaders

A national poll taken by the Roper Organization in 1975 showed that only 36 percent of adult citizens could identify their two home-state U.S. senators.[10] This same poll presented respondents with a list of prominent politicians and asked whether "you feel you know a lot about, or feel you know a fair amount about, or very little about, or have never heard of" each of them. A quarter of those surveyed said they had never heard of, or knew little about, Gerald Ford—the incumbent president! When it came to such highly visible senators as Democrat John Glenn and Republican Howard Baker, the proportion professing little or no knowledge became much higher: 63 percent in the case of the much-celebrated former astronaut from Ohio, and 83 percent for the Republican Senate leader from Tennessee. In a 1981 NBC News/Associated Press poll, 44 percent claimed never to have heard of Speaker of the House Thomas P. O'Neill, and 72 percent not to have heard of Defense Secretary Caspar Weinberger. In late 1982, only two of the Democratic hopefuls for the party's 1984 presidential nomination were known by as many as half the adult population.[11]

Inattention to policy specifics

Looking at levels of factual information about important political events and programs, we see even more unawareness. In November 1982, only a third of adults polled had even a slight sense of the size of the current federal deficit—that is, could give an estimate within a hundred billion dollars. Yet the size of the deficit was a hot issue. When asked in fall 1981 which country, the United States or the Soviet Union, is a member of the NATO alliance, only 47 percent correctly identified the United States.[12] Since America had taken the lead in forming the North Atlantic Treaty Organization with its European allies after World War II, and the NATO pact remained the most important of all U.S. alliances, the fact that less than half felt confident enough to pick the U.S. over the U.S.S.R. as a NATO member is fairly startling.

[10] Poll taken by the Roper Organization, December 6–13, 1975.
[11] These data are from a Gallup poll of December 10–13, 1982. Respondents were given a list of presidential hopefuls and asked, "Now, will you please tell me which of these persons you know something about?" Fifty-nine percent said they knew something about former Senator and Vice President Walter Mondale, and 50 percent about Senator Glenn. None of the rest were known to more than small minorities.
[12] These data are from a poll taken by ABC News/*Washington Post*, October 14–18, 1981. The question asked was: "One of these two nations, the United States or the Soviet Union, is a member of what is known as the NATO alliance. Do you happen to know which country that is, or are you not sure? Forty-seven percent said the United States, 2 percent the Soviet Union, while 50 percent were not sure.

A cautionary note on
direct democracy

As we will see, rushing from findings like these to the conclusion that meaningful public opinion does not exist is unjustified. But there is doubt about the wisdom of submitting every important policy issue to a referendum vote. Many Americans lack basic factual information, even with high levels of education and plentiful political communication. We should also be cautious about claims like "82 percent of Americans favor" this or that program. Often the public does not have enough information and awareness to justify them. In 1978 and 1979, for example, there was lively debate concerning the SALT II negotiations: the second round of the strategic arms limitation talks. The culmination of SALT II was a draft treaty, reached by United States and Soviet negotiators, which limited each country to a maximum of 2,250 long-range nuclear missiles and bombers. The treaty was not ratified by the Senate. But during the long debate over its wisdom, politicians often cited poll findings on what the American people wanted done. Proponents seized on the results of a number of well-respected surveys that showed overwhelming majorities favoring ratification.

Yet, in the fall of 1979, when the CBS News/*New York Times* poll asked not only "Do you think the Senate should vote for or against [the treaty], but also "or don't you know enough about it to have an opinion?" 55 percent said they did not know enough about it. In January 1979, a CBS News/*New York Times* poll found that only 23 percent of respondents nationally could correctly identify the United States and the Soviet Union as the two countries "involved in the SALT treaty—the treaty that would limit strategic nuclear weapons." It was misleading to suggest that there was a clear body of public opinion on the issue of ratification.

How Stable and Structured Is Public Opinion?

Consider two hypothetical individuals. The first eats, sleeps, and breathes politics. He devours the *New York Times* and other leading newspapers, and closely follows virtually every major issue. When asked his views on a particular program, he answers confidently, because he has reached his conclusions through a painstaking accumulation of pertinent facts. His opinions have a bedrock firmness. The second individual, in contrast, pays little attention to the intricacies of governmental programs and political arguments. He gives the daily newspapers only a cursory glance, except on the sports pages. When asked his views on a program, his answers are more a spur-of-the moment reaction than a considered judgment. If individuals of the latter type predominate, public opinion on many governmental questions may be highly unstable.

An influential study by political scientist Philip E. Converse addressed this subject. Converse concluded that the amount of political information people have goes far toward determining the struc-

Fluctuations of
opinion responses

ture, constraint, and stability of their beliefs. Without much factual information, the beliefs of large segments of the populace bounce around wildly over time. Between 1956 and 1960, the Institute for Social Research at the University of Michigan posed the same questions to the same people on three separate occasions, asking their views on issues such as school desegregation, federal aid to education, foreign aid, and federal housing. Many respondents moved from one side to the other on these questions in successive interviews. After closely examining this pattern, Converse concluded that most of the movement was not true opinion change but rather the result of respondents answering in essentially a random fashion. Only a distinct minority had something close to hard-core opinions. "For the remainder of the population, response sequences over time are statistically random."[13]

If this is true, it carries substantial implications for the role of public opinion in democratic government. Giving great weight to the clear, considered preferences of the people is supported by everyone sympathetic to democracy. But should views that are virtually "statistically random" be accorded such weight? If the public really knows little about most policy disputes—even those that have been extensively discussed—and if the opinions it expresses are very lightly held, why should politicians or anyone else pay attention to them?

Sharper divisions
in the 1960s

Philip Converse's work stimulated further research on the subject. Several investigations concluded that Converse's findings held up only for a particular period in time: the 1950s. During the mid- to late 1960s, these studies concluded, the relatively issue-less politics of the Eisenhower years gave way to heated divisions over civil rights, Vietnam, and social issues. When the political parties and their nominees began taking distinct positions on such divisive issues, they imparted to voters ideological cues that had been lacking in the previous decade. This led to more constrained public responses.[14]

General Values versus Program Specifics

Another type of public opinion research yields conclusions very different from Converse's or even those of his critics. It focuses on the overall patterns of responses Americans give. These turn out to be remarkably stable and predictable. The Gallup Organization has polled American opinion continuously since the mid-1930s, rarely missing

[13] Philip E. Converse, "The Nature of Belief Systems in Mass Publics," in David Apter, ed., *Ideology and Discontent* (New York: Free Press, 1964), p. 242.

[14] For studies concluding that Converse's findings were time-bound and not reflective of the pattern that appeared in the 1960s, see Norman Nie and Kristi Andersen, "Mass Belief Systems Revisited: Political Change and Attitude Structure," *Journal of Politics*, August 1974, pp. 541–91; John C. Pierce and Douglas D. Rose, "Non-Attitudes and American Public Opinion: The Examination of a Thesis," *American Political Science Review*, June 1974, pp. 626–49; and Norman H. Nie, Sidney Verba, and John R. Petrocik, *The Changing American Voter* (Cambridge, Mass: Harvard University Press, 1976), especially chap. 7.

so much as a month. Gallup asks questions on foreign policy, the role of government, many different domestic programs, a wide range of social issues from abortion to race relations, and more. The findings in each of these areas at all times shows a clear, persisting structure in what people are saying. Through all the changes in political events and circumstances, Americans make basic distinctions and express general preferences that in the aggregate don't look random or uninformed.

Strong underlying public values

The basic source of this contradiction in assessments of public opinion can be traced to a central distinction that democratic theory has long made: Mass publics can hold underlying values and express broad preferences coherently, even while they are inattentive to much of the detail of governmental programs and policies. As we have seen, Walter Lippmann took it as evident that the public is unlikely to initiate specific programs or immerse itself in their detailed specifications. But it can choose perfectly well between contrasting approaches presented to it by political leaders. Political scientist Harwood Childs argued that

> the general public is especially competent, probably more competent than any other group—elitist, expert, or otherwise—to determine the basic ends of public policy. . . . On the other hand, the general public is not competent to determine the best means for attaining specific goals, to answer technical questions, to prescribe remedies for political, social, and economic ills, and to deal with specialized issues far removed from the everyday experience and understanding of the people. . . .[15]

Elmo Roper was one of the founders of modern public opinion research. In 1942 he reviewed what he had learned from his first decade of survey investigations.

> I believe that a great many of us make two mistakes in our judgment of the common man. *We overestimate the amount of information he has; we underestimate his intelligence.* I know that during my eight years of asking the common man questions about what he thinks and what he wants I have often been surprised and disappointed to discover that he has less information then we think he should have about some question we consider vital. But I have more often been surprised and elated to discover that, despite his lack of information, the common man's native intelligence generally brings him to a sound conclusion.[16]

Public inattention to program specifics

Roper's commentary may seem to wax a bit sentimental: in effect, "underneath all that ignorance, there beats a heart of pure gold." But it states the wisdom of the distinction orthodox democratic theory has made between the public's role, and that of leaders and activists, in the process of democratic government. Most people do not have responsibility for writing laws or otherwise determining the specific

---

[15] Harwood Childs, *Public Opinion: Nature, Formation and Role* (Princeton, N.J.: Van Nostrand, 1965), p. 350.
[16] Elmo Roper, "So the Blind Shall Not Lead," *Fortune*, February 1942, p. 102. Emphasis added.

shape of programs, and they clearly do not pay much attention to programs at such a level. While we might wish that schools would do a better job of giving students information on government or that more people would spend more time deepening their knowledge, this is a different matter than whether the public can play the role specified by democratic theory: determining what Harwood Childs called "the basic ends of public policy." A populace may be quite attentive to those ends, and notably clear and consistent in its specifications on them, without having much factual knowledge of program details. One cannot account for the findings of a half-century of public opinion research in the U.S. without granting that great coherence in underlying attitudes and values coexists with great inattentiveness and confusion on the details of policy.

Public Opinion on Foreign Affairs: A Case Study

Public ambivalence on foreign policy

By looking closely at public opinion in selected policy areas, we can get a clearer understanding of its stability and underlying structure. In foreign affairs and defense, for example, it is not hard to find proof that many people do not pay much attention to policy details. But it also becomes apparent that Americans have coherent values and expectations that guide their assessments of leaders and events, and that these views have been remarkably consistent for a very long period of time. Since World War II, Americans have accepted the need for their country to exert sustained international leadership. The "we can go it alone" isolationism which shaped U.S. defense and foreign policy for much of the country's history collapsed after 1941. Distrustful of the Soviet Union, Americans have insisted over the past four decades that their country's defenses be at least the equal of the U.S.S.R.'s, and they have backed up this view by supporting high defense expenditures. At the same time, the public has rejected a strident or bellicose foreign policy, and it has always been reluctant to see American troops committed to foreign wars. It has wanted policy to walk the line between strength and stridency. All steps that can reasonably be taken to relax tensions between the United States and the Soviet Union (and other countries) should be taken, but not those that would weaken the U.S. military position and leave it vulnerable to external threats.

Each component of the above outline of public opinion is deeply rooted, and the public has shown that it is prepared to make sacrifices or accept consequences in seeing it carried out. For example, since World War II the U.S. has maintained a large and expensive military establishment. (See chapter 20 for a detailed description of the national defense commitment.) In fiscal year 1984 alone, defense outlays stood at $231 billion, while veterans' benefits claimed another $26 billion. Against this backdrop, pollsters have asked national samples of Americans whether they think the country is spending too much,

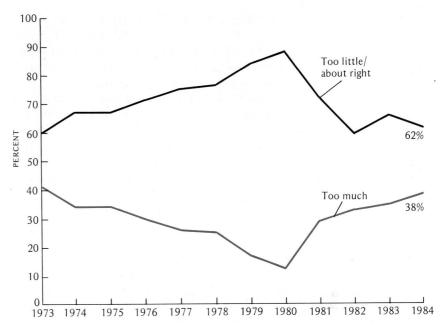

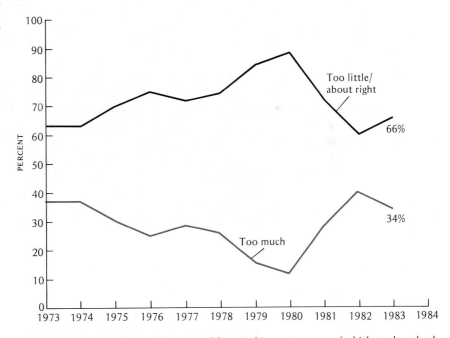

Figure 12.1

Is the U.S. Spending Too Much on Defense?: Two Polls, Two Results

Question: **A:** "We are faced with many problems in this country, none of which can be solved easily or inexpensively. I'm going to name some of these problems, and for each one I'd like you to tell me whether you think we're spending too much money on it, too little money, or about the right amount."

Question: **B:** "Turning now to the business of the country—we are faced with many problems in this country, none of which can be solved easily or inexpensively. I'm going to name some of these problems, and for each one I'd like you to tell me whether you think we're spending too much money on it, too little money, or about the right amount—the military, armaments and defense?"

Source: **A:** Survey by the National Opinion Research Center, General Social Surveys, conducted in the spring of each year shown.

Source: **B:** Survey by the Roper Organization, conducted in December of each year shown.

the right amount, or too little on defense. With only a few exceptions—at the height of the Vietnam War—every time this question has been asked, a majority of the populace has maintained that U.S. military expenditures were either at about the right level or lower than they should be (see Figure 12.1).

Public opinion on defense spending

Figure 12.1 is based on surveys taken by the National Opinion Research Center (NORC) of the University of Chicago and on surveys by the Roper Organization. Each of these two leading survey facilities uses its own methodology, but the pattern of public responses is basically the same. During the Carter administration, for instance, both surveys found growing unease about the adequacy of U.S. military preparedness and growing support for increased military spending. The proportion of the public wanting defense cuts fell steadily, reaching a low of just 12 percent in 1980, Carter's last year in office. Then, as the Reagan administration pushed for bigger military budgets, those wanting defense cuts climbed—although support for high levels of spending remained strong. In December 1983, Roper found 66 percent in favor of maintaining or increasing the current expenditure level; in January 1984, using a similar question, a CBS News/*New York Times* poll found the proportion at 77 percent; an NBC News poll put it at 72 percent. These various surveys found a stable and consistent set of opinions, belying any suggestion of "statistical randomness."

Public Opinion and Inherent Personal Values

Tocqueville on the stability of public opinion

The further one probes, the more one sees a public that holds firmly to core values and assessments in each area of public policy. One may agree or disagree with the wisdom of the public's positions, of course. But one cannot dismiss them as flighty, erratic, or greatly susceptible to manipulation. A century and a half ago, the great French social theorist Alexis de Tocqueville commented on the great stability, even obdurateness, of American public opinion in holding to a basic course defined by some enduring values:

> I hear it said that it is in the nature and habit of democracies to be constantly changing their opinions and feelings. This may be true of small democratic nations, like those of the ancient world, in which the whole community can be assembled in a public place and then excited at will by an orator. But I saw nothing of the kind among the great democratic people that dwells upon the opposite shores of the Atlantic Ocean. *What struck me in the United States was the difficulty of shaking the majority in an opinion once conceived of.* . . . [The public] is engaged in infinitely varying the consequences of known principles . . . rather than in seeking for new principles.[17]

[17] Alexis de Tocqueville, *Democracy in America* (New York: Vintage Books, 1958), vol. 2, pp. 271–72. Emphasis added.

Public Opinion on Social Issues: A Case Study

Recent empirical research bears out Tocqueville's shrewd assessment: The public stays with and elaborates a few basic commitments, and resists being moved in new directions. Changes occur through "infinitely varying the consequences of known principles . . . rather than in seeking for new principles." Core values are not replaced or rejected; they are applied in a different way to new claims.

One of the most powerful sets of American values, we noted in chapter 4, involves individualism. A high moral claim is granted to arguments on behalf of extending individual rights and opportunities. In recent decades, this value has been applied to groups and interests somewhat different from those of the past. Women's views of their position in American society, for example, have been undergoing important changes. "What about our rights and interests as individuals?" many women are now asking. The value of individualism is not new, but this application of it is. The American public has had to adjust to a new status for women, and hence men, in the home, the workplace, and other social settings. One can chart this adaptation through public opinion as roles more in accord with current expectations of individualism gradually receive wider acceptance. Elect a woman president? In 1937, when Gallup first asked a

Individualism extended: the changing view of women in politics

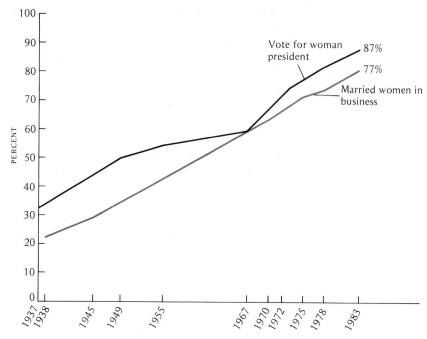

Figure 12.2
**A Changing Role for
Women**

Question: Would you vote for a woman for president if she qualified in every other respect? (1937). If the party whose candidate you most often supported nominated a woman for president of the United States, would you vote for her if she seemed qualified for the job? (1949, 1955). If your party nominated a woman for president, would you vote for her if she were qualified for the job? (1967–83).
Question: Do you approve of a married woman earning money in business or industry if she has a husband capable of supporting her? (1938, 1970). Do you think married women whose husbands make enough to support them should or should not be allowed to hold jobs if they want to? (1945). Do you approve or disapprove of a married woman earning money in business or industry if she has a husband capable of supporting her? (1972–83).
Source: Woman president: Surveys by American Institute of Public Opinion (Gallup) 1937–71; National Opinion Research Center, General Social Surveys, 1972–83.
Married woman in business: Surveys by American Institute of Public Opinion (Gallup) 1938, 1970; Roper Organization for *Fortune,* 1945; National Opinion Research Center, General Social Surveys, 1972–83.

sample of the public nationally whether they would vote for a qualified woman for president if their party nominated one, only 32 percent said they would. Since then, the proportion has steadily increased: to 50 percent in 1949, 59 percent in 1967, and 87 percent in 1983. There is a clear and predictable structure to the change, shown in Figure 12.2, as the old emphasis on individual rights and opportunities gets redefined and reapplied.

Ambivalence of Opinions

Sometimes when one looks closely at public opinion on an important issue, it appears at first as though people can't make up their minds what they want done. They seem to be pushing for opposing things. For example, on the question of government's place in American life, the public has said repeatedly over the last decade that it thinks gov-

Public ambivalence
on the role of
government

ernment, especially at the national level, has become too big, too powerful, and too costly. But at the same time, the citizenry looks to government for help in resolving virtually every public problem it faces: Government should take vigorous action to make sure prices don't rise and to assure that there are jobs for all who want to work. Government should guarantee low-cost medical care. Government should not reduce expenditures—if anything, should increase them—for schools, recreation, police, national defense, environmental protection, and aid to the needy.

What are we expected to do? politicians sometimes ask incredulously. Voters are fickle and erratic. Public opinion is a poor guide to policy action because it is so often on both sides of the fence. Americans *do* have mixed minds about contemporary government. Those who are flatly pro-government or anti-government are rare; most people make conflicting assesments. These responses, though, do not seem to be an immature desire to have one's cake and eat it too. They show a realistic *ambivalence*—holding opposing values and assessments—that has emerged, almost inevitably, from a variety of historical and contemporary experiences.

This ambivalence follows naturally from the joining of legacies from America's ideological past with some contemporary developments. It is often assumed that the American tradition is anti-state, but this isn't so. The founders of the American republic were an unusual breed

*"I often have an urge these days to stand up and
be counted, but I don't know what for."*

philosophically: strongly committed to the state and architects of a new national union under the Constitution, but also certain that a government unchecked would usurp and tyrannize. This mix of pro- and anti-government perspectives taught the public to revere coherent and active national government, and at the same time to be vigilant against governmental abuse. Americans began their modern political experience without an ideological tradition wholeheartedly for or against the state.

Recent experience has enlarged the scope and meaning of this legacy. During the New Deal, the national government assumed new responsibilities and won general approbation for its performance in meeting them. When the society grew markedly richer in the post–World War II years, popular expectations of what should be achieved in both the private and the governmental sectors rose. Americans came to expect more leisure time, more consumer goods, higher standards of living and, as well, more governmental service in protecting the environment, extending educational opportunities, helping those in need, assuring adequate income in old age and retirement, and more. Without any profound bias either for or against the state, large majorities of the public saw the government's role in achieving a fuller life inextricably scrambled with the various private roles. For them, the proper questions were "Is it practicable?" and "Does it work?"

Heightened expectations after the New Deal

The other side of this nonideological posture toward the state has involved a readiness to criticize government whenever its actions seemed not to work or advance a better life. Over the 1960s and 1970s, as it began doing so much more, American government presented a much bigger target for criticism. None of this suggests a lack of coherence in public thinking on the role of government. The dualism mirrors the position in which American society finds itself. The idea of a division of labor that is at the core of representative government seems to be reinforced by these findings of ambivalence in public attitudes: It is the task of those who head the institutions of government to strike an appropriate balance between the contending public impulses.

Nuclear Freeze: A Case Study of Ambivalent Public Opinion

The ambivalence in attitudes toward government is evident in other policy areas, such as the debate over whether a nuclear freeze should be enacted—involving a halt to the testing, production, and installation of more nuclear weapons. Whenever pollsters have asked whether the U.S. should agree to a nuclear freeze with the Soviet Union, the answer has been an overwhelming yes. A CBS News/*New York Times* poll of May 1982 found 72 percent favoring a freeze, compared to only 21 percent opposed and 7 percent of no opinion. But when this poll posed additional questions on the freeze, it revealed a complex mix of colliding values. What if a freeze resulted in the Soviet Union's having somewhat greater nuclear strength than the U.S.? Would you

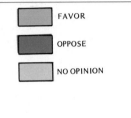

FAVOR

OPPOSE

NO OPINION

Figure 12.3
Public Opinion on the Nuclear Freeze

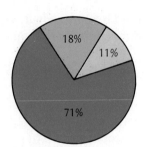

18%

11%

71%

What if either the United States or the Soviet Union could cheat on the number of its nuclear weapons without being detected by the other side, would you favor or oppose such a nuclear freeze?

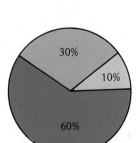

30%

10%

60%

What if a nuclear freeze would result in the Soviet Union having somewhat greater nuclear strength than the United States, would you favor or oppose such a freeze?

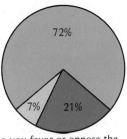

72%

7%   21%

Do you favor or oppose the United States agreeing to a nuclear freeze with the Soviet Union—that is, putting a stop to the testing, production, and installation of additional nuclear weapons by both sides?

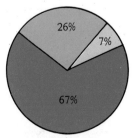

26%

7%

67%

What if in order to get the Soviet Union to agree to freeze its nuclear weapons the United States would have to freeze its weapons first, would you favor or oppose such a nuclear freeze?

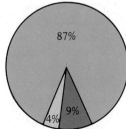

87%

4%   9%

What if a nuclear freeze would result in the United States and the Soviet Union having about an equal amount of nuclear strength, would you favor or oppose such a nuclear freeze?

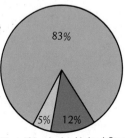

83%

5%   12%

What if both the United States and the Soviet Union could catch the other country if it were cheating on the agreement, would you favor or oppose such a nuclear freeze?

Source: CBS News / *New York Times* survey, May 19–23, 1982.

still favor it? Only 30 percent said they would. What if the U.S. had to freeze its weapons development first in order to get the Soviet Union to enter into an agreement? Would you then be in favor? Only 26 percent would. (See Figure 12.3.)

Americans have clear goals in this area: They want to reduce international tension and, specifically, the risk of nuclear war. But they are concerned about Soviet behavior and do not think their country's defense should be diminished. There is no *single* opinion on the freeze issue; the public has more than one value it wants served.

STUDYING PUBLIC OPINION: POLLING AND ITS INFLUENCE

Public opinion, we have said, is the sum of citizens' personal views—opinions, attitudes, and values—on public issues. It gets expressed in many ways. People write letters to newspapers, hold rallies, cast votes on election day. But increasingly over the last half-century, public opinion has been expressed through polls conducted among representative samples of the populace. The idea that public opinion is what polls say it is represents quite a leap from earlier conceptions. Public opinion used to be seen as an almost mysterious force, a swelling up of popular feelings on this issue or that. Now it is practically a statistical exercise: "67 percent of Americans believe . . . while 24 percent think that . . . and 9 percent are undecided."

Reliance of public opinion polls

Polls can be wrong. They can yield misleading pictures of what the public's thinking is—for reasons we will discuss in the pages that follow. But they came to be relied upon, once their techniques were perfected, because all other outlets or expressions of public opinion were so open to the possibility that they have left out large numbers of people. Letters to the editor and rallies are notorious in this regard; they reflect some people's opinions, of course, but whose? How faithful a slice are they of the total body of public thinking? Even if expressions of opinion that require active effort, like attending a march to protest some governmental action, should receive more weight because the effort suggests greater commitment, the fact is that such expressions are partial rather than complete. The views of more activist segments of the population may not accord with majority sentiment.

Systematic polling: the dominant tool of opinion measurement

Opinion polling can claim to be truly democratic. Samples are drawn so as to represent all groups and classes in proportion to their actual size in the entire population. Questions can be framed more or less neutrally and precisely, and everyone's answers fairly recorded. Polling offers a more objective means of gauging public opinion. As a result, systematic polling has become the dominant tool for opinion measurement. An assortment of groups and institutions, including the communications media, politicians, business corporations, and other interest groups have concluded that opinion polling is useful enough to them to justify spending large sums of money on it. The polling industry has become a big one, and it plays a large part in contemporary politics. Polls have become a staple of political assessment and commentary in every advanced industrial democracy.

Polling and the Social Sciences

Public opinion surveys are an instrument of social science research. Political scientists and sociologists, in particular, have found surveys a means of measuring more efficiently and reliably many topics central to their disciplines. For example, political scientists utilize opinion surveys to study voting decisions. They use them to examine the makeup of political party coalitions: which groups back which party, with what strength and what regularity, for what objectives. Sociologists employ carefully designed surveys to measure such phenomena as ethnic and religious prejudice. The academic study of public opinion is now almost wholly dependent upon the opinion survey method.

Polling and the Media

Measured in terms of the total number of polls conducted and the financial support for them, scholarly research is a small part of polling, however. It is dwarfed by other uses. Increasingly over the last two decades, communications media have found polls extremely useful in news reporting. They employ surveys to forecast election outcomes and to explain why people voted as they did. They track public sentiment on a broad assortment of current issues, as part of their regular news coverage. The surveys taken by CBS in conjunction with the *New York Times*, ABC News together with the *Washington Post*, NBC News, and the *Los Angeles Times* are not only media-sponsored but media-managed efforts conducted in-house by their own staffs. Many local newspapers and television stations also sponsor polls.

Polling and Campaigns

The requirements of news reporting and social science research differ; both of these in turn are different from the directly political uses of polls. Today it is rare when a candidate for major office does not commission polls to assess what voters want and how well his campaign is registering. Presidential candidates routinely set up large polling operations that conduct surveys almost daily during the campaign. Pollsters have become important campaign strategists, working hand in hand with media experts and other consultants in planning all aspects of campaigns. Candidates are not the only political actors using polls. Interest groups sponsor surveys on subjects of political importance to them and then introduce results into political debate, often to demonstrate that the people really endorse what the group is urging. The American Medical Association (AMA) is one interest group that makes heavy use of polls in its lobbying efforts. Polls have become widely used political weapons. In recent lobbying on environmental issues, for example, both sides have emphasized poll findings in their efforts to set the terms of the debate favorable to what they want done.

How Polling Developed

"Must I drink the whole bottle," Belgian mathematician Adolphe Quetelet once asked, "in order to judge the quality of the wine?" If the answer were yes, wine tasting would be a quite different art. A small sample is sufficient to judge, providing it has all of the important characteristics of the larger unit. This principle of sampling is

---

Box 12.1

How Polls Are Taken

Of a number of books and manuals available on public opinion polling, among the best is Charles W. Roll and Albert H. Cantril's, *Polls: Their Use and Misuse* (Cabin John, Md.: Seven Locks Press, 1980). Here, very briefly, are some of the "nuts and bolts."

Polling by mail, telephone, and in person. The least expensive type of polling is the mail questionnaire. And in some instances, especially where one needs to pose a lengthy and complex set of questions to a very interested group within the population, data gathering by mail can be very effective. But most of the time this approach yields unacceptably low returns of completed questionnaries, and it is very slow.

The pioneering survey research organizations in the United States began their work almost exclusively with in-person interviewing; Gallup and Roper still do much of their interviewing in respondents' homes. The advantage of this form is the opportunity it presents a skillful interviewer to establish rapport with respondents. Many people seem to be more willing to explore controversial subjects in a thoughtfully conducted in-person interview than over the telephone.

But telephone interviewing is taking over the industry. It is faster and cheaper than in-person interviewing. Over 97 percent of all households in America now have telephones, so the old argument that telephone interviewing leaves out large numbers of less affluent people no longer applies. Survey organizations are finding that, especially in the high-crime sections of cities, refusal rates are lower when interviewing is done by telephone rather than in person. The ABC News/*Washington Post*, CBS New/*New York Times*, NBC News, and *Los Angeles Times* polls are all conducted exclusively by telephone.

Drawing a sample. In the early years of U.S. polling, samples of the population were drawn largely through the *quota* method. (Quota sampling is still common outside the United States.) In this type of sampling, census information is utilized to find the distribution of the population by such relevant attributes as age, education, income, and region. A frame is then designed so that the makeup of the interviews conducted matches the overall population distributions. Interviewers are instructed as to how many respondents they are to

today employed by researchers in many fields. When marine biologists chart the chemical properties of a bay, they cannot submit all of it to laboratory analysis, nor do they collect samples wherever they feel like it. They draw portions of the water from different spots throughout the area, at different depths, using procedures so that their samples reflect the range of properties of the entire bay. Sampling in public opinion research follows this same general idea. (See Box 12.1 on "How Polls are Taken.")

get in the various specified categories: so many men and women, so many people 18 to 29 years of age, etc. This approach is quite efficient, but it has major drawbacks and has largely been abandoned in the United States. Chief among the drawbacks is the fact that the interviewer makes the decision which individuals are to be interviewed. The element of randomness is lost. And various forms of bias creep in. Anyone who has ever been out with interviewers working on quota samples has heard such statements as "Oh, I'm not going to interview *him*, he looks so grouchy."

Probability sampling. U.S. survey firms now rely on sampling procedures that make use of probability principles. The idea behind them is to give every individual an equal or known chance of falling into the sample. One common approach is to divide the population into categories on the basis of the size and location of the places people live. Particular areas (such as city blocks) are then chosen on a systematic or random basis. So many interviews are assigned for each block, selecting every *n*th household. People are interviewed solely because the place they live is within an area included in the sample.

Random-digit dialing (RDD). This approach applies the theory of probability sampling to telephone interviewing. A survey firm obtains from the telephone company a tape of information on the working three-digit prefixes (called COCs, for central office codes) in telephone numbers and the assigned banks of the latter four digits. COCs are then selected at random, and a number of interviews to be completed is assigned to each COC—depending on how many working residential numbers there are within it. Random-digit numbers are then generated for each COC or prefix. Calls are continued until the desired number of interview completions is achieved.

Sampling error. Statisticians know how to calculate what the chances are that a sample will be representative of the population. "Sampling error" refers to the extent to which the results in a sample can be expected to differ from the results that would have been obtained if everyone in a population had been interviewed. *Sampling error* encompasses only a small fraction of possible *survey error*. Inaccurate poll results can stem from bad question-wording, poor interviewing, sloppy sampling, and many other sources. Sampling error per se is exclusively statistical. The laws of probability can result in samples that are unrepresentative of the total population.

The *Literary Digest* and the Birth of Systematic Polling

One event a half-century ago dramatized the basic premises of sampling applied to the study of public opinion, and helped change the course of opinion research: the famous *"Literary Digest* fiasco" of 1936. The *Literary Digest* was a large-circulation magazine with articles on topics of general interest: economic, cultural, political, and so on. As early as 1895, it began collecting the names of prospective subscribers as part of its general efforts to increase circulation, and its mailing list rapidly grew to include millions of names. In 1920 the magazine's editors first hit upon the idea of using these lists as a base from which to test political sentiment. By 1928 the *Digest* was conducting a presidential poll in which 18 million ballots were distributed through their mailing lists. Those receiving ballots were asked to check off their choice for president and return their "vote" to the magazine. The *Digest* tabulated them and printed the results at intervals during the campaign. It showed the grand total in its last issue before the election.

Over several elections, the *Literary Digest* poll results corresponded remarkably closely to actual election results—and its prestige naturally rose. In 1928, for example, the poll predicted a victory for Republican Herbert Hoover with 63 percent of the popular vote; Hoover won the election with 59 percent. Four years later, the *Digest* poll indicated that the Democratic candidate, Franklin Roosevelt, would win handily, and he did. The final poll results in 1932 were within 1.5 percent of the actual vote distribution. In 1936, however, the poll fell on its face—and in such a dramatic fashion that the magazine itself was discredited. All during the 1936 campaign, the *Digest* issued reports on the return of its mailed ballots showing Republican Alfred Landon well ahead of incumbent Franklin Roosevelt. The *Digest's* final report, based on nearly 2.4 million ballots, pointed to a resounding Landon victory. Republicans were shown carrying 32 states with a total of 370 electoral votes, and winning 54 percent of the popular vote. In the actual balloting on November 5, however, Roosevelt won 61 percent of the popular vote and 523 of the 531 electoral votes. Landon was buried under the biggest landslide in American political history. Why the *Digest* poll failed became a topic of intense discussion.

The Digest's miscalculation

In fact, the *Literary Digest's* failure was predicted well in advance of the election, and its source was explained by George Gallup and a number of others who were founding public opinion research in the U.S. on the basis of new sampling procedures. As Gallup pointed out, while the 2.4 million returned ballots seemed an impressive number, they could be no more reliable than the sampling frame from which they were drawn: the magazine's mailing list. And that list was skewed toward the middle and upper middle class. In the 1936 election, where class lines were relatively sharp, and lower- and working-class voters much more supportive of Roosevelt than those in the middle class,

Sampling bias and imbalance

FINAL RETURNS OF THE MAMMOTH NATION-WIDE PR

The cover of the Literary Digest *announcing the "final returns of the mammoth nation-wide presidential poll."*

the bias of the *Digest*'s sample was immense. Another problem was that the magazine mailed out over 20 million ballots but received back just over 10 percent of them; it had no way of determining whether those taking the trouble to "vote" were even a cross-section of those receiving the ballots, much less of the entire American electorate. And the *Digest*'s method of polling was insensitive to opinion shifts occurring at later stages of the race, because it provided for only one mailing during the campaign.

Advent of scientific surveys

For many who followed the *Literary Digest* fiasco, perhaps the most striking thing was the contrast between the immense, cumbersome efforts of the magazine and the lean, efficient new scientific surveys pioneered by Gallup, Elmo Roper, and Archibald Crossley. Whereas the *Digest* "surveyed" millions, the new polling methods sampled only a few thousand. But because the latter could achieve samples that corresponded at least roughly to the makeup of the entire population, they were dramatically more successful. The "little" Gallup poll was largely right, while the huge *Literary Digest* effort was so embarrassingly wrong—a juxtaposition that brought the new age of polling in with a bang. As George Gallup and Saul Forbes Rae were to observe later:

One fundamental lesson became clear in the 1936 election: the heart of the problem of obtaining an accurate measure of public opinion lay in the cross-section, and no mere accumulation of ballots could hope to eliminate the error that sprang from a biased sample.[18]

Problems in Opinion Polling

The major breakthrough in sampling made by Gallup and Roper in 1936 forever changed the way public opinion is measured. Later work by statisticians improved upon the sampling techniques, but the underlying principles had been sound. Today, the problem with polls generally has little to do with the way samples of respondents are drawn from the total population. But the polls' performance is not problem-free.

Is opinion research scientific?

Polling experts are often asked whether opinion research is really scientific. Modern-day polling certainly draws upon scientific knowledge, especially on how to draw samples which reliably reflect attributes of the entire population. Scientists do use survey findings in their research, just as they use many other types of data. But polling as such is not a science; it is a set of techniques, informed by science, that are utilized for a great variety of purposes. Some of these uses are problem-causing. Yet even when opinion surveys are used in the most dispassionate and carefully designed types of research, they may still yield invalid results. The methods of science do not always yield reliable knowledge. For many different reasons, ranging from weaknesses of theory to problems in the data collection, inaccurate pictures sometimes emerge from polling. Poll findings should not be accepted uncritically.

Swift Results from a Slow Machine

One set of problems arises from the incompatibility of survey research methods with some of the needs of journalism. The *press*, meaning all mass communications media, must work quickly in order to do its mandated job, to bring the story promptly to the audience. From this basic requirement, speed and timeliness have become highly regarded values. But to do its job, polling must typically move slowly; time is required to frame questions properly, pretest and refine them, do the field work, transform the resulting data to computer-readable form, and perform careful analysis of them. The results of opinion polling on issues of consequence also typically require extensive, time-consuming explanation and exposition.

News media must often move quickly in their canvass of political events, and a great variety of developments vie for press attention. Given this competition for media time and space, public opinion on, for example, the SALT II treaty or the fighting in Central America can rarely expect to receive as much as 90 seconds of television news-

[18] George Gallup and Saul Forbes Rae, *The Pulse of Democracy* (Westport, Conn: Greenwood Press, 1968; first published in 1940), pp. 54–55.

cast or 500 words in a newspaper article. An obvious problem arises when such accounts cannot begin to properly explicate the subject. In such cases—which are common, not exceptional—"tight editing" equals "gross oversimplification."

Good news reporting has focus and arrives at relatively clear and unambiguous conclusions. In contrast, good opinion research typically reveals such characteristics of public thinking as tentativeness, ambivalence, and lack of information or awareness. The journalist wants crisp answers to such questions as: Is the United States public becoming more conservative? Has the taxpayers' revolt run its course? Do Americans want to see a tougher line taken against the Soviet Union? Do they support government policy in El Salvador? Frequently, though, results of the best survey research aren't consistent with journalists' needs. Conclusions emerging from polling on the various issues often fail to sustain the focused conclusion that is the staple of good news reporting. Today, with the press so heavily involved in the financial sponsorship and even the actual management of polls, there are powerful incentives to act as though poll findings are typically newsworthy. Law professor Michael Wheeler maintains that "the most flagrant error of the press is the common practice of reporting polls as if each American holds a firm opinion on every topic."[19]

Announcing outcome. One specific problem in television's use of polls has prompted heated debate and some recent legislative action. Over the last decade television news has made increasingly heavy use of a type of survey known as the "exit poll." Samples of precincts are drawn—around a state, or the entire country—that together yield a cross-section of the electorate. Interviewers are then positioned outside the selected precincts, and they ask each voter, immediately after he has cast his ballot, to fill out a short questionnaire on how he voted and why. The results are rapidly tallied and fed into a computer. Even while votes are still being cast, tallies are available, based on the samples, which point to the likely overall results. All three of the major commercial television networks use exit polling extensively.

The first protests appeared in November 1976, when the networks described the emerging results in various states while some people were still voting. The criticism of exit polling swelled in 1980, especially on the West Coast, where because of the time difference voting continues three hours or so after the polls have closed in the East. Voters in states like Washington and California heard on their car radios while driving home from work, and in many cases while driving to the voting stations, that the election was in effect all over, with Ronald Reagan well on his way to a resounding victory. Exit polls were not the only source of data on which the network news staffs made their early projections, but they were an important source.

Focused conclusions

Growth of exit polls

Protest over exit polls

[19] Michael Wheeler, "Reining in Horse-Race Journalism," *Public Opinion,* February/March 1980, p. 42.

Was harm done to the electoral process? Were some people discouraged from voting by the news that their candidate seemingly had the race all sewed up, or had been beaten? Several studies that sought firm answers suggested that the impact was probably negligible, but these studies were not conclusive. Protests mounted. The networks replied that it was their duty to report the races as completely as possible, and that exit polling was an important tool in their coverage.

Against this backdrop, two western states took action. Washington and Hawaii passed laws which effectively banned exit polling within their borders. The Washington statute, passed in 1983, makes it a misdemeanor punishable by imprisonment of up to 90 days or a fine of $1,000 for any person "on the day of any primary, general or special election . . . within a polling place, or in any public area within three hundred feet [thereof, to] conduct any exit poll or public opinion poll with voters." The three networks, together with the *New York Times*, immediately challenged the statue in federal district court, charging that the state of Washington was violating their First Amendment rights of speech and the press, and that it would strangle research that is of great value in better understanding American elections. The district court has ruled against the networks, upholding the state of Washington's statute.[20] Almost certainly, the Supreme Court will hear the case eventually.

Laws against exit polls (margin note)

Political Distortions

Problems resulting from polling appear even greater when one looks at its uses in the rough-and-tumble world of American politics. Politicians and interest-group officials have learned that polls can be impressive weapons. In a democracy, it is always comforting to be able to demonstrate that "the people agree with the position I am taking." To this end, poll findings are employed, often highly selectively, on behalf of various interests. Many consumers of politically biased poll reports probably have a hard time distinguishing between them and valid information on public opinion.

One striking illustration of politically motivated distortion of survey findings came in testimony that pollster Louis Harris gave on October 15, 1981, to the Subcommittee on Health and Environment of the U.S. House of Representatives. The message that Harris delivered, drawing on surveys that his organization had conducted, was that any effort by Congress to modify the Clean Air Act—which was up for review—would meet the strongest possible public condemnation. The Clean Air Act is one of the most important pieces of national environmental legislation, and some of its provisions have been the subject of heated debate. We discuss the act in chapter 13.

The political use of polls (margin note)

[20] Declaratory judgment by Judge Jack E. Tanner, July 11, 1984, in the case of *The Daily Herald Co. v. Munro.*

In his response to Democrat John Dingell of Michigan concerning the Clean Air Act, Harris stated:

> I am saying to you just as clear as can be that clean air happens to be one of the sacred cows of the American people, and the suspicion is afoot, however you slice it, that there are interests in the business community and among Republicans and some Democrats who want to keelhaul that legislation. And the people are saying: "Watch out. We will have your hide if you do it."[21]

Harris was testifying at the request of Democrats, other than Dingell, who opposed changes in the act.

Inaccurate interpretations of polls

Harris' surveys and those of other organizations did indeed show widespread public backing for the goal of a clean environment. But these data did not suggest that there was any clear public opinion on the specifics of the Clean Air Act. Indeed, survey research had established that most people knew almost nothing about specific provisions of the act—as is the case with most such legislation. Mr. Harris' suggestion that Americans were insisting passionately that Congress make no changes in the act was inaccurate. A perfectly valid expression of political values or preference was being offered in the guise of scientific poll results.

Bias in survey questions

In many cases, political interests assert themselves in polling by framing questions in such a way as to strongly encourage the desired political answer. Consider the following survey question on public reactions to the much-publicized pollution of the Love Canal in upstate New York:

> As you know, residents near the Love Canal, in the Niagara Falls, New York area, were reported to have stillbirths, cancer, deformed children, and chromosome damage as a result of the dumping of hazardous chemical wastes. The people who live near the Love Canal want to move out and are suing the chemical company there and the federal government for $3 billion for damages done to them. How serious a problem do you think the dumping of toxic chemicals is in the country today—very serious, only somewhat serious, or hardly serious at all?[22]

The only remarkable finding was that, after so obviously biased and leading an introduction, there were still some people (7 percent of the total) who answered "hardly serious at all." The question set out to make the case, and it determined what the answers would be.

Such biased approaches are all too common. In October 1982, in a poll ostensibly taken to determine American attitudes toward Israel and the Palestinian question following Israel's invasion of Lebanon, the question was asked of those who said they thought Israel was

---

[21] For further discussion of the Harris testimony and public opinion data on environmental issues, see Everett Ladd, "Clearing the Air: Public Opinion and Public Policy on the Environment," *Public Opinion* (February/March 1982), pp. 16–20.

[22] Survey by Louis Harris and Associates, June 1980.

justified in its actions:

> If you knew that during the ceasefire between Israel and the PLO from July 1981 to June 1982, the PLO observed the ceasefire and launched no rocket attacks while Israeli bombing caused the deaths of almost 100 people, would you still feel that Israel was justified in invading Lebanon?[23]

Aided by so obviously prejudicial a lead, this question found what its sponsors wanted, that about half of those who had indicated support for Israel's action shifted their stand.

The Difficult Task of Question-Wording

All survey research, to the extent it tries to understand the public's thinking rather than provide ammunition to advance a cause, confronts a perplexing set of challenges in the area of question-wording. When misleading results accrue from surveys, deficiencies in question form and language are now the principal source of the problem.

Technical problems. Some survey items inadvertently pose two separate questions within one, making it impossible to know what **Double-barreled questions** respondents are actually answering: "Please tell me whether you agree or disagree with the following statement: It is important that the federal deficit be substantially reduced and that spending for national defense be cut below the president's proposal." This is called a "double-barrelled" question. Even if the first part of this statement were

[23] Survey by Decision-Making Information for the Institute for Arab Studies, October 1982.

separated to stand by itself, there would still be an easily recognizable problem: "It is important that the federal deficit be substantially reduced" poses a variant of the old "motherhood and apple pie" factor. Who is going to declare himself against it? Everyone wants to reduce the federal deficit; the problem comes in finding a way to accomplish the objective with the least harm to other values. Those who design poll questions are also aware that the range of alternatives presented to respondents must not be put too narrowly or otherwise unrealistically. Example: "What should be the United States' response to the war in El Salvador: sending American soldiers to aid the Salvadoran government, or staying completely out of the situation?" We know from well-designed questions that many people favor another alternative: helping the Salvadoran government in ways short of committing American troops. The point is that a great many problems in question design have been detected. The polling literature has given helpful guidance in avoiding these pitfalls.

Ambivalence and low levels of information. Other problems are trickier to handle. It is especially difficult to frame questions on subjects where the level of relevant information among the general public is low.

> One very real difficulty with interpreting opinion data from surveys is that since many people are responding to questions to which they have not given much previous thought, their replies can vary with even subtle differences in the way the question is worded.[24]

On abstract policy issues, as we have seen, the public's opinions often haven't taken clear form. How questions are worded helps determine the apparent majority position. That problem is compounded when the public has mixed feelings on an issue being investigated.

Question wording presents only minimal problems for the experienced survey research specialist when:

When polling is easy

1) the level of relevant information among respondents is high;
2) the public has focused on the issue in the context of an actual decision;
3) the choice presented is not complex;
4) the issue is not distinguished by major public ambivalence.

A common instance where the above conditions apply is asking respondents how they plan to vote late in a campaign, when the candidates of both parties are well known and the decision is a real one for most respondents because they will actually be making it shortly in the polling booth.

When the opposite of all of these elements apply, however—when the information level is low, opinions have not crystallized, the question is highly complex, and many people are ambivalent—even the most sensitive approach to question-wording can yield unreliable

[24] Robert S. Erikson, Norman R. Luttbeg, and Kent L. Tedin, *American Public Opinion* (New York: Wiley, 1980), p. 29.

results. Any version of the question is likely to produce findings significantly different from other equally valid and informed questions. The latter conditions can be found in varying degrees in polling on virtually every complicated policy issue. The deeper one probes, the tougher the problem appears.

When polling is hard

> The prevailing model underlying the discipline of survey research is that of the single opinion. A person holds an opinion, which he communicates to an interviewer. When he is influenced to change his mind, he replaces his former opinion with another one. This model has the virtue of great simplicity, but it makes no sense, because conflicting and contradictory opinions may be held simultaneously and because they constantly jostle one another for dominance.[25]

The very design of the structured public opinion survey may be incapable of dealing with the complexity of opinion, given the mix of contrasting values and expectations that vie one with another for priority in our thinking on issues.

Bogart's conclusion is not that opinion research is incapable of yielding useful knowledge. Instead, he gives greater force to the caution that "the mechanics of survey research, like any other human enterprise, are subject to a substantial range of error. . . ." Survey questions are like the blind men before the elephant—each reaches out trying to grasp and comprehend something it really cannot see.

Solutions to Polling Problems

As polls become more widely used, those of us who "consume" them need to become "smarter shoppers." Governmental legislation restricting polling doesn't seem to offer a satisfactory solution, because polling appears to fall well within the bounds of free inquiry, which the U.S. Constitution mandates, and because much useful information is gathered from polls. The answers, then, must involve more knowledge about polls and wiser use of them.

More information needed about polls

Journalists need to learn more about polls. Courses on public opinion research that are specially tailored to the needs of the press are already being developed. Journalists also need ready access to larger bodies of polling information. Is a particular question biased or otherwise defective? It is becoming possible for journalists to plug into data banks that contain large numbers of related questions, and this should stimulate more informed press coverage.

Higher standards needed in polling

Citizens who read poll results need to be more sensitive to the distortions that can arise from polling. The cautions contained in this chapter are a starting point. Organizations of responsible polling organizations try to set higher standards for their profession, and these efforts need to be supplemented. The National Council on Public Polls

[25] Leo Bogart, *Silent Politics: Polls and the Awareness of Public Opinion* (New York: Wiley-Interscience, 1972), p. 17.

(NCPP) and the American Association for Public Opinion Research (AAPOR) already do important "self-policing" with regard to professional standards. They need to do more, especially to publicize problems inherent in question form and wording, the area of greatest deficiency in opinion research.

HOW AMERICANS VIEW THEIR SOCIETY

Some of the most important aspects of a country's public opinion involve views not of issues and events but of the country itself. How confident are a people in their social and political institutions, and in their values? How satisfied or dissatisfied are they with the way their leaders have managed governmental affairs?

A Crisis of Confidence?

This dimension of public thinking has loomed large in the United States over the last 15 to 20 years because of the abundant evidence of national self-dissatisfaction. This dissatisfaction has been noted by many different observers, including our recent presidents. On July 15, 1979, President Jimmy Carter addressed the public on the theme that many citizens had lost confidence in themselves and their country's future. The result was a severe challenge to the very fabric of American democracy. The threat, the president argued,

> is nearly invisible in ordinary ways. It is a crisis of confidence. It is a crisis that strikes at the very heart and soul and spirit of our national will. We can see this crisis in the growing doubt about the meaning of our own lives and in the loss of a unity of purpose for our nation. The erosion of our confidence in the future is threatening to destroy the social and political fabric of America.

After the bitter experiences of the long Vietnam War, after soaring energy prices and double-digit inflation, after the Watergate scandal and a heightened sense of the frailties of government, many other Americans worried that the public had become less certain about the country and the ideas and institutions on which it was founded. Some noted academic observers concluded, in effect, that history had at last caught up with the United States. In 1975 Daniel Bell saw a long-term loss of faith by Americans in their country's future.[26]

Many opinion polls taken between 1965 and 1980 did indicate a big drop in national self-confidence. During the Vietnam years, according to Harris polls, American began expressing markedly diminished confidence in the "people in charge of running" the various central

Drop in national self-confidence

[26] Daniel Bell, "The End of American Exceptionalism," *The Public Interest*, Fall 1975, pp. 197–98.

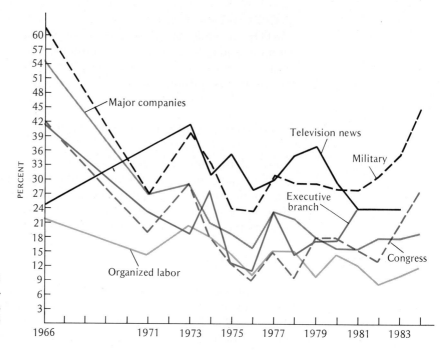

Figure 12.4
Confidence in the Leadership of Central U.S. Institutions, 1966–83

Question: "As far as people in charge of running [read list] are concerned, would you say you have a great deal of confidence, only some confidence, or hardly any confidence at all in them?"
Source: Surveys by Louis Harris and Associates, 1966–78; ABC News / Louis Harris and Associates, 1979 and 1980; Louis Harris and Associates, 1981 through November 9–14, 1984.

institutions of the society. As Figure 12.4 shows, however, in recent years there has been some recovery. In the late fall of 1984, according to Harris, 19 percent of the public felt a "great deal of confidence" in the way major corporations were run, 28 percent in television news, and 28 percent in the leadership of Congress.

Over the 1960s and 1970s, according to surveys conducted by the Institute for Social Research of the University of Michigan, large majorities of Americans came to see their political leadership as insufficiently competent and sensitive to the public interest. In 1958 only 18 percent of respondents agreed that "the government is run by a few big interests looking out for themselves," but by 1980 the proportion had soared to 77 percent. Though it dropped in 1983, it still remained an uncomfortably high 66 percent (Figure 12.5). In 1958, just 25 percent maintained that the national government cannot regularly be trusted to do what is right, while in 1982, 66 percent maintained this. The proportion of Michigan survey respondents who said they believed that "quite a few [of the people running the government] don't seem to know what they are doing" stood at 28 percent in 1964, jumped to 45 percent in 1970, climbed further to 52 percent in 1976, and crested at 63 percent in 1980.

Dissatisfaction with government performance

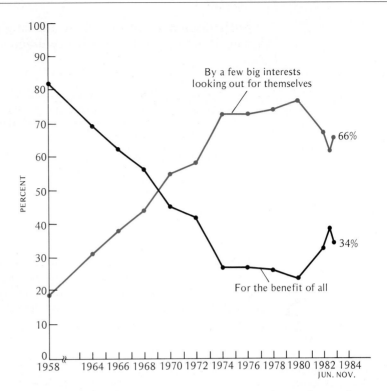

Figure 12.5
Is the Government Run for the Benefit of All or by a Few Big Interests Looking Out for Themselves?

Source: Surveys by the Center for Political Studies of the Institute for Social Research, University of Michigan Election Studies, 1958–82; *New York Times,* June 13–18, 1983, and November 18–22, 1983.

What Is the Public Saying?

Underlying faith in the American system

If the populace intended literally all of the criticisms that these various poll findings suggest, then a severe blow was struck to American confidence and self-esteem over the 1960s and 1970s. All along, though, other measures advised against a literal reading. For example, polling data suggested that the people had not changed their basic conception of the nation or their commitment to it, but rather that they were simply angry about aspects of leadership performance and were looking for ways to let this be known. A May 1975 Yankelovich survey that found nearly three-fifths of Americans claiming their country was in "deep and serious trouble," also discovered that 82 percent professed confidence that in the future "our country will be strong and prosperous." And 80 percent believed that the "American way of life" was superior to that of any other country. For all their complaints about the behavior of private business corporations, 94 percent agreed that "we must be ready to make sacrifices if necessary" to preserve the "free enterprise system."[27]

[27] Survey by Yankelovich, Skelly, and White, May 14–22, 1975.

Such discrepant results show the importance of distinguishing among different levels—and hence different results—of public criticism:

	Level	Result
Mood:	Dissatisfaction with leaders and their performance	Public wants its leaders to ⟶ "do a lot better."
Confidence:	Loss of confidence in basic institutions and processes	Public is receptive to ⟶ significant institutional change.
Legitimacy:	A crisis of legitimacy	Public looks for a new ⟶ structure to the social and political order.

After the buffeting the country took in the 1960s and 1970s, it would have been surprising if the public mood were not testy. This need not mean, however, that the public had lost confidence in the country's central institutions and certainly not that the system had lost its basic claim to loyalty and legitimacy.

Figure 12.6
Comparing America to Other Countries

Question: Earlier on in American history, many people around the world thought the United States was the very best place in the world to live. Do you think it still is, or not?
Source: Survey by Civic Service, Inc., March 5–18, 1981

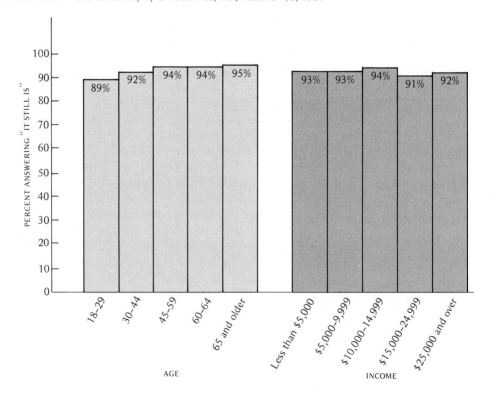

Strong Foundations

Powerful confirmation that basic confidence remained, even in the face of considerable dissatisfaction with current performance, was shown by questions administered in 1981 to a national sample. "How proud are you to be an American?" Seventy-eight percent of respondents nationally described themselves as "extremely proud," only 2 percent as "not proud at all." "Do you think the United States has a special role to play in the world today, or is it pretty much like other countries?" This latest testing of the "manifest destiny" idea found 80 percent insisting that the country occupied a special place, while only 15 percent thought it was "just another country." Nine respondents in every ten said they believed that "the U.S. [is] the very best place in the world to live." (See Figure 12.6.) And 56 percent maintained that the best is still ahead for the United States, whereas only 35 percent felt "the country has already seen the best times we are going to." It is unlikely that these questions would have elicited a much more supportive response at any point in the past.

Broad backing. Just as striking are the answers of various demographic groups. The proposition that "the U.S. [is] the very best place in the world to live" was endorsed by 88 percent of those aged 18 to

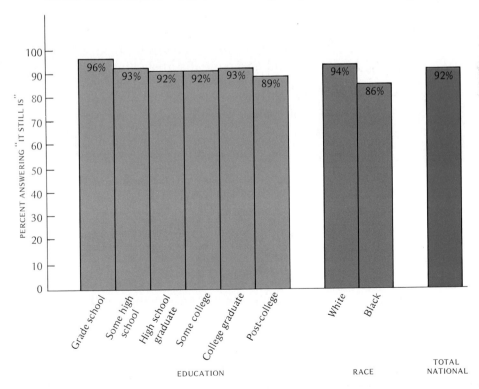

29 and 95 percent of those 65 and over, by 96 percent of grade-school-educated Americans and 88 percent of those with advanced degrees, by 95 percent of Republicans and 92 percent of Democrats, by 89 percent in the Northeast and 94 percent in the Southwest, by 93 percent of those earning less than $5,000 a year and 92 percent with family incomes of $25,000 and higher, and by 94 percent of whites and 86 percent of blacks. This optimistic sense of nation extends with essential uniformity through every identifiable group in the population.

Attitudes of black Americans

The responses of black Americans are especially striking. If any group has ample reason for deep dissatisfaction, it is the country's black population. Nowhere in American national experience have the central tenets of the nation been so ignored and mocked as in racial discrimination—from slavery to the legacy of discrimination which persists today. Yet 76 percent of black respondents nationally stated that they thought the United States had a special role to play in the world; 86 percent said the U.S. is the best place in the world to live; and 64 percent were "extremely proud" to be Americans (29 percent said "somewhat proud" and only 5 percent "not proud at all").

Other surveys have shown strong popular support for all aspects of the basic design of the American social, economic, and political institutions. The public's behavior seems consistent, too, with the interpretation that the dissatisfactions noted earlier were limited largely to current performance and did not indicate an erosion of institutional confidence or a withdrawal of public support for the system.

Satisfaction among Americans. In an effort to explain why the political and economic dissatisfactions of the last two decades have not done more to shake underlying confidence, Daniel Yankelovich noted the high degree of satisfaction Americans have consistently shown in their private lives.

> When people were asked about their private and personal lives, the same overwhelming 90% majority stated that everything was going very well indeed . . . , that they were optimistic about their futures . . . , and that, on the whole, they were satisfied with their lot. . . . In 1975, eight out of ten American families reported that they were doing quite well personally. . . . In the midst of the worst economic setback since the 1930s, a majority of families expressed keen satisfaction with such crucial aspects of their private lives as their confidence in handling personal problems, the pleasures and cohesiveness of family life, the enjoyment they get out of life, their ability to derive from life what they feel they are entitled to, and their progress in getting ahead and achieving success. . . .[28]

So long as the citizenry manifests this level of personal satisfaction and optimism, Yankelovich concluded, "political stability will be sustained and *ressentiment* will be kept at bay."

[28] Daniel Yankelovich, "The Status of *Ressentiment* in America," *Social Research*, Winter 1975, pp. 767–68.

The nation is the ideology. An additional factor restricting the scope and impact of the confidence gap is the nature of Americans' attachment to their country. We noted in chapter 4 Leon Samson's point that America is a nation built on an ideology.[29] The U.S. was established around a pervasive, almost monolithic commitment to classical liberal ideas—individualism, freedom, equality, and democracy. Reflecting these persisting beliefs, the central social and political institutions of the country have shown an extraordinary staying power—and the longer they have lasted, the more natural and legitimate they have seemed. The "regime" (meaning the Constitution and the institutions established under it), the ideology (classical liberalism cum "Americanism"), and the "country" were all established at the same time. Today most Americans don't distinguish one from the other; there has been an extraordinary fusion of the three.

This particular character of American nationalism extracts its price. If the country and the regime are almost one, failures involving the latter are especially painful. For most Americans, the Watergate scandal was not so much a partisan as a national calamity. The country's honor was seen as involved far more than would be the case in, say, France with alleged transgressions by a Fifth Republic president.

Yet the very fusion that causes the pain serves to limit the damage. One can easily condemn a regime which is distinct from the nation; but that is not possible in the American fusion of the two. When things go wrong in the American regime, the public ultimately blames the leaders, not the ideology and the institutions. The presidency is sound, if only individual presidents would do better. The private business system is estimable, if only business leaders would guide it more effectively. And so on. This helps explain the otherwise curious contradiction in public confidence over the last twenty years: Americans profess to be mad as hell, but the behavioral consequences appear to have been slight. While there has been real dissatisfaction, which the polls have picked up, it has been largely confined to a criticism of leadership performance. Confidence in the central institutions themselves has been little affected. The public has not felt any real need for institutional change.

> The problem is more with leadership than the system

Slumps and Winning Streaks

Political scientist Jack Citrin has noted the strength of the American system's ideological underpinnings. What happened in the late 1960s and 1970s was simply that the U.S. experienced a long "losing streak."

> Political systems, like baseball teams, have slumps and winning streaks. Having recently endured a succession of losing seasons, Americans boo

[29] Leon Samson, "Americanism as Surrogate Socialism," in John H. Laslett and Seymour Martin Lipset, eds., *Failure of a Dream?* (New York: Doubleday, 1974), p. 426. Samson's essay was first published in *Toward a United Front* (New York: Farrar and Rinehart, 1935).

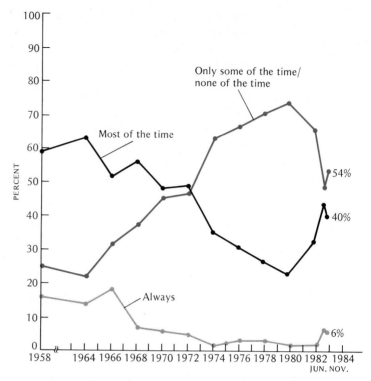

Figure 12.7
Do you Trust the Government to Do What Is Right?

Question: How much of the time do you think you can trust the government in Washington to do what is right—just about always, most of the time, or only some of the time?
Source: Surveys by the Center for Political Studies of the Institute for Social Research, University of Michigan Election Studies, 1958–82; *New York Times,* June 13–18, 1983, and November 18–22, 1983.

the home team when it takes the field. But fans are often fickle; victories quickly elicit cheers. And to most fans what matters is whether the home team wins or loses, not how it plays the game. According to this analysis, a modest "winning streak" and, perhaps, some new names in the lineup may be sufficient to raise the level of trust in government.[30]

Recent poll findings seem to bear out Citrin's only partly whimsical analogy. As divisive and dispiriting events like the Watergate scandal and the Vietnam War have faded, trust in government has recovered—although not to the levels professed in the 1950s and 1960s (Figure 12.7). More generally, confidence in the nation's direction and performance has climbed. As Figure 12.8 shows, in May 1980 only 21 percent of Americans interviewed by Yankelovich, Skelly, and White said that things in the U.S. were going very well or fairly well. By December 1983, however, the proportion had risen quite dramatically to 60 percent.

[30] Jack Citrin, "Comment: The Political Relevance of Trust in Government," *American Political Science Review,* September 1984, p. 987.

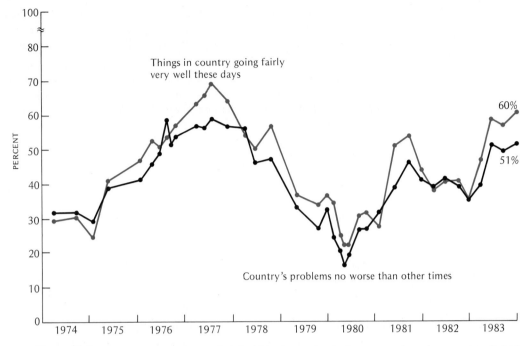

Figure 12.8

How Are Things Going in the Country Today?

Question: How do you feel that things are going in the country these days—very well, fairly well, pretty badly or very badly?

Question: In commenting on how things are going in the country, some people tell us that the problems we face are no worse than at any other time in recent years. Others say the country is really in deep and serious trouble today. Which comes closest to your own feelings—the fact that: Problems are no worse than at other times. . . . The country is in deep and serious trouble. . . .

Source: Surveys by *Time* / Yankelovich, Skelly, and White, latest that of December 6–8, 1983.

Americans are, in Citrin's metaphor, very demanding fans. They expect their home team to have a strong winning record. The record of the 1970s was below national expectations. Now the fans see some improvement. We can be sure, though, that in the future they will not hesitate to shout again, "Fire the manager!" if another slump ensues.

SUMMARY

Public opinion is assigned a critical role in a democracy. Government by the people, democracy, must mean government responsive to the public's preferences for leaders and policies, or it is a sham.

Questions have been raised from a variety of perspectives as to whether public opinion can meet democracy's requirements. Many oservers have argued that the mass public is insufficiently informed about and attentive to the issues on which its judgment is supposed to be controlling. Critics have portrayed the public as too easily manipulated by demagogic leaders. In the U.S., some charge, the "establishment" has succeeded in imposing on the people outlooks that serve its, not their, needs. Arguments made by advertising and public relations theorists in a way back up the critics, through their stress on how easily consent to candidates and causes can be engineered.

Opinion research in the U.S. does reveal a public strikingly inattentive to the details of even the most consequential and controversial policies. This suggests a potential for manipulation. But the research also indicates great stability and coherence in the public's underlying *attitudes* and *values*. Americans show themselves perfectly capable of making the distinctions needed to determine what Harwood Childs called "the basic ends of public policy," and of pursuing these logically and clearly. There is a persisting structure to American opinion that belies the picture of a populace helpless before the "engineers of consent."

To observe that the public holds strongly to basic values is not to assert that its preferences are always clear or readily followed. People are frequently ambivalent—committed at one and the same time to opposing or competing goals. They think that contemporary government is too big, too powerful, and too costly, and they would like to see it reined in. But they also look to government for help in solving a great variety of problems, and don't think there is any alternative to an expansive role for the state. Such pushes and pulls of contending values dominate American public opinion.

The public's ambivalent responses pose some tricky measurement problems for opinion research. It is no easy task to frame questions so as to give proper weight to the contending objectives people so often bring to complex policy issues. In general, problems related to question design contribute more to deficiencies in opinion research than any other factor.

Pioneered a half-century ago by George Gallup and Elmo Roper, systematic polling has become the dominant tool for opinion measurement. A wide assortment of groups and institutions—including academic social scientists, the press, politicians, business and other interest groups—all find polling valuable in their work. But each makes its own special use of poll information, very different from those of the others. Journalists look to polls as sources of news, whereas political interest groups want poll findings that buttress their positions or help them chart strategies. Given the varied uses, the maxim *caveat emptor* is very much in order: the buyer or consumer of poll reports should be wary.

Some of the key aspects of American public opinion involve views of the country itself. In the late 1960s and 1970s, a great many indicators, including opinion polls, suggested that there had been an alarming drop in national self-confidence. But close examination showed that the populace had not changed their basic sense of the nation or commitment to it. Instead, they were troubled about leadership performance and were anxious to let that be known. "Political systems," Jack Citrin observed, "like baseball teams, have slumps and winning streaks," and the U.S. had been in a slump. In the 1980s, the fans seem less restless but no less demanding.

13 | Interest Groups

An ***interest group*** is a body of people acting in an organized fashion to advance shared political interests. It is the pursuit of shared interests that provides the impetus for organization. It is the presence of organization that transforms an interest into an interest group. And it is the political character of the interests—the attention to governmental action and public policy—that makes certain organized groups function at times as interest groups or ***lobbies.***

Lobbying encompasses the various efforts of interest groups to influence governmental decisions, especially legislative votes. Lobbyists are those who represent interest groups before governmental agencies. The term "lobby" came into use in seventeenth-century England, when a large anteroom near the House of Commons was referred to as the "lobby." Those who approached members of Parliament, trying to persuade them to vote a certain way, were lobbying. The existence of political interests and their organized pursuit of various policies are a central part of American political life. In this chapter we look closely at interest groups: their historical presence, their resources, the ways they influence policy today, and their impact on the quality and character of American democracy.

A Nation of Joiners

After visiting the United States in the 1830s, Alexis de Tocqueville wrote that "in no country in the world has the principle of association been more successfully used or applied to a greater multitude of objects than in America." Americans were a nation of joiners. Tocqueville explained this propensity, interestingly, in terms of

Senator Daniel Patrick Moynihan speaking at a rally held by an interest group in New York.

individualism:

> The citizen of the United States is taught from infancy to rely upon his own exertions in order to resist the evils and the difficulties of life; he looks upon the social authority with an eye of mistrust and anxiety, and he claims its assistance only when he is unable to do without it. . . .

Joining together with other like-minded persons to attack common problems expresses a sense of individual responsibility and self-confidence:

High levels of participation

> If a stoppage occurs in a thoroughfare and the circulation of vehicles is hindered, the neighbors immediately form themselves into a deliberative body; and this extemporaneous assembly gives rise to an executive power which remedies the inconvenience before anybody has thought of recurring to a pre-existing authority superior to that of the persons immediately concerned. . . . In the United States associations are established to promote the public safety, commerce, industry, morality, and religion. There is no end which the human will despairs of attaining through the combined power of individuals united into a society.[1]

A Nation of Interest Groups

Tocqueville's observation still applies. This general proclivity for forming private associations to meet public needs extends to the pursuit of political interests. The variety of interest groups in the United

[1] Tocqueville, *Democracy in America*, vol. 1, p. 198.

States ranges from strictly local associations, such as small-town chambers of commerce (which try among other things to influence town councils on off-street parking or zoning regulations) all the way to massive national associations like the American Federation of Labor and Congress of Industrial Organizations (AFL-CIO), the principal U.S. labor union federation, and the National Association of Manufacturers (NAM), a preeminent industry association comprising over 13,000 companies. Every conceivable issue before the American polity at the national, state, and local levels has a distinct set of interest groups and associations trying to shape policy on it.

Number and diversity of interest groups

How many interest groups are there in the United States? No one can say precisely. While some groups are exclusively political and required by law to register as lobbyists (see below) and hence can be counted, many other groups intervene only sporadically in political affairs and never register. They often don't even think of themselves as interest groups, even though they sometimes work actively for political goals. For example, the 336,000 individual churches and parishes in the United States, with a total membership of 135,000,000, exist primarily for religious and social purposes. But on occasion, these churches and their national denominational organizations try to influence public policy, often on social questions such as abortion, school prayer, and the death penalty. Churches are also at times outspoken on questions of national defense and foreign policy, such as the development of nuclear weapons.

Business interests

Virtually every large business corporation in the United States and many small businesses have strong legislative interests. General Motors and Boeing Aircraft are affected by governmental actions in many ways: Each gets government contracts, is subjected to a welter of federal and state regulations, pays taxes, has a big stake in international trade policy. Are most businesses interest groups? Sometimes, and to some extent. Business firms exist for many purposes and objectives other than those political, but at times they function as interest groups as they try to influence what government does.

TYPES OF INTEREST GROUPS

The Federal Regulation of Lobbying Act, passed in 1946, requires that groups attempting to influence legislation before Congress register and report the amount they expend in lobbying efforts. This legislation is full of loopholes and it contains almost no enforcement provisions. Any organization that really prefers not to register finds it easy to avoid doing so. But the law states an obligation that many groups heed. The roster of those registered gives a sense of the extent and diversity of interest groups nationally.

More than 3,000 groups are registered. Among them are major business associations, such as the Business Roundtable and National

Association of Manufacturers; individual corporations, from American Express to Phillips Petroleum to the Kellogg Company; trade and professional associations, including the American Petroleum Institute, the American Meat Institute, the Electronic Industries Association, the National Education Association, and the American Medical Association; trade unions such as the American Federation of State, County, and Municipal Employees AFL-CIO, and the Amalgamated Clothing and Textile Workers' Union AFL-CIO; and a wide variety of organizations known as citizens' groups, among them the National Rifle Association, the National Clean Air Coalition, the Sierra Club, and the Religious Coalition for Abortion Rights.

Registration of lobbyists

These registered interest groups are only the tip of the iceberg. There are, for example, some 6,000 national trade and professional associations alone, and virtually every one of them has policy interests. The asbestos industry has five trade associations. Nine associations represent brewers. There are four trade associations for china tableware and four for chocolate. The trucking industry has approximately fifty trade associations. About ten associations promote the interests of businesses that produce and sell wine. More than 4,000 individual business corporations retain representatives in Washington, D.C. The Nation's capital has also become[2] "the leading headquarters city . . .

[2] Robert H. Salisbury, with John P. Heinz, Edward O. Laumann, and Robert L. Nelson, "Soaking and Poking Among the Movers and Shakers: Quantitative Ethnography Along the K Street Corridor," paper presented at the annual meeting of the American Political Science Association, Washington, D.C., August 30–September 2, 1984. *See also National Trade and Professional Associations of the United States, and Labor Unions,* 19th ed. (Washington, D.C.: Columbia Books, 1984).

with some 29 percent of all national non-profit associations head-quartered there in 1981. . . ."

State and local groups

Interest groups operate at the state and local levels as well. In Connecticut, for example, where groups and their representatives are required to report to a State Ethics Commission, some 400 individuals were registered as lobbyists in 1984, representing about 350 groups and associations. Many organzations that try to influence policy nationally have state affiliates which, quite independently, pursue state policy objectives. The AFL-CIO is a national interest group, but there are fifty state AFL-CIO units which have their own staffs and their own state-related legislative agendas. All in all, the interest-group world in the United States is massive. Tens of thousands of individuals and groups expend hundreds of millions of dollars each year in efforts to shape public policy. Little wonder that House of Representatives Speaker Thomas P. O'Neill remarked with exasperation that "everybody in America has a lobby."

The Most Common and Durable Source of Faction

The sheer volume of interest groups does not mean, however, that all the different kinds of interests in the country are more or less equally engaged in interest-group activity. Some interests are disproportionately represented. James Madison saw the pattern two centuries ago. In *Federalist* Paper 10, he wrote that while every type of political interest gets mobilized in a democracy,

The economic basis of interest-group activity

> the most common and durable source of factions has been the various and unequal distribution of property. Those who hold and those who are without property have ever formed distinct interests in society. Those who are creditors, and those who are debtors, fall under a like discrimination. A landed interest, a manufacturing interest, a mercantile interest, a monied interest, with many lesser interests, grow up of necessity in civilized nations, and divide them into different classes, actuated by different sentiments and views.

The prime source of organized interests, then, is economic status. Interest groups spring up to represent claims of different sectors in the economy (Madison listed farming, manufacturing, trade, and banking as the most important) and the interests of economic "haves" and "have-nots." The consuming conflict of America in the 1780s was not between rich and poor. It was among farm interests in different parts of the country, and between farm interests and the mercantile and monied interests concentrated along the northeastern seaboard. When he wrote *Federalist Paper* 10, Madison had just spent a decade absorbed in the struggle of these various regionally organized economic interests. The Constitutional Convention of 1787 itself had to mediate the contending claims of representatives of the different economic sectors.

Is this Madisonian interpretation of interest-group organization and conflict valid today? The answer must be a qualified yes. The United States has seen an extraordinary array of contending groups and interests throughout its history. Groups defined by ethnic and cultural interests (blacks and whites, old-stock immigrants and newer arrivals, Protestants and Catholics, Christians and Jews) have often been centrally involved in the struggle. Still, the lion's share of interest-group activity has involved economic interests, with the horizontal or sector split far more prominent than the vertical or haves-versus-have-nots split. We see this today when we look at interest-group activity in Washington. In 1983 more than 1,300 separate interest groups were involved in new registrations with the Clerk of the U.S. House of Representatives and the Secretary of the Senate, under the terms of the Federal Regulation of Lobbying Act. Their overwhelmingly economic bias is evident. As Table 13.1 indicates, 54 percent of

The continuing prominence of economic interests

Table 13.1
Lobby Registrations Filed with U.S. House of Representatives by Type of Group, 1983 (in percent)

Business corporations	54
Trade associations	25
Labor unions	2
State and local governments	4
Citizens' groups	6
Other	9
Total	1,375 registrations

Source: Data compiled from *Congressional Quarterly,* weekly reports of April 23, May 14, June 18, July 16, August 27, October 15, November 26, December 17, December 24, 1983, and February 18, 1984.

all new registrants were business corporations and another 25 percent trade associations. Adding in the 2 percent that were labor unions, we see that over four-fifths of all groups registering or reregistering as lobbyists in 1983 had predominantly economic objectives. Although this list suggests something of a vertical dimension, the representation is overwhelmingly horizontal. The many different sectors of economic life, represented by the variety of business corporations and trade associations, distinguish this interest-group world.

Governments Lobbying Government

These economic interests in what government does extend beyond business and labor to government itself. We described in chapter 11 the expansion during the 1960s and 1970s in federal programs providing aid for states and municipalities. Responding to these new programs and the billions of dollars distributed through them each year, state and local governments dramatically extended their Washington lobbying. They comprised four percent of all new 1983 lobby registrants before Congress. In this period, for instance, the state of Louisiana, the Kansas Corporation Commission, the city of El Paso, Texas, the county of Suffolk, New York, and the Los Angeles Rapid Transit District all registered as congressional lobbyists. Thirty states and more than 100 cities and counties have established offices or hired agents in Washington. The National Governors's Association has been especially active. Its marble building, called the Hall of the States, is just a stone's throw from the U.S. Capitol. This association maintains a staff of about 80 and sublets some 60 offices to representatives of governors, state legislatures, and associations of state administrators. Near the Hall of the States is the new headquarters of the National Association of Counties (NACO). A mile away, the National League of Cities has a new office complex, housing lobbyists for many individual municipalities. The headquarters of the U.S. Conference of Mayors is also nearby. These state and local government lobbies are now a major part of Washington interest representation.

Governments lobbying government is not confined to the states and municipalities; the federal government lobbies itself. Various agencies that have a great stake in congressional appropriations and other legislative provisions actively lobby Congress. Every cabinet department has a top congressional liaison person of assistant-secretary rank and several subordinates to assist in these efforts.

Public-Interest Groups

One of the most widely discussed developments in interest group activity in recent years is the prominent role of public interest groups. A **public-interest group** is "one that seeks a collective good, the achievement of which will not selectively or materially benefit the membership or activists of the organization."[3] The roster of public-interest groups includes environmentalists, such as Friends of the Earth, the National Wildlife Federation, and the Sierra Club. Others seek to reform the organization and conduct of American political life, the most prominent being Common Cause. Consumers Union tries to mobilize the diffuse interests of purchasers rather than producers. Foreign-policy goals such as arms control have been the focus of the Arms Control Association and the World Federalists.

Do these groups really speak for the public interest? While the concept of public interest is not simple or unambiguous, it calls attention

Serving the
public interest

to the general claims and needs of the whole population as opposed to those of special and private interests. Groups are rarely organized around the broadest and most unselfish aspirations of a society. Rather

[3] Jeffrey M. Berry, *Lobbying for the People* (Princeton, N.J.: Princeton University Press, 1977), p. 7.

SMOKING
POLLUTES
YOU AND
EVERYTHING
ELSE

AMERICAN
CANCER
SOCIETY

*The American Cancer
Society at times lobbies
as a public-interest
group.*

they grow to advance narrower objectives. Indeed, it is typically the special nature of their claims that spurs their organization. Many public interest groups, including those that take stands on environmental questions, consumer affairs, and governmental reform, argue that there are general public interests in their respective areas which are sometimes denied by the actions of special interests like private business corporations. Yet when public interest groups make their own proposals, they very often articulate another set of special interests and perspectives. Nonetheless, they encourage a competition of ideas and claims; and the values they pursue do not lead to the narrow economic benefit of their members.

The growth of public-interest groups is a product of larger changes in the composition of American society. As noted in chapter 2, there has been a recent and huge increase in the number of college-educated men and women employed in professional occupations. With this expansion has come the vast growth of a relatively new stratum of political actors: people who are well-educated, highly skilled, and attentive to issues rather than political patronage.[4] One of the ways the expanding stratum of middle-class activists has expressed itself is through public-interest groups. There are now several thousand

*Growth of public
interest groups*

[4] For an account of the expansion of one part of this new group of political activists, see James Q. Wilson, *The Amateur Democrat* (Chicago: University of Chicago Press, 1962).

An environmentalist group protests against nuclear power.

public-interest organizations operating at the local, state, and national level in the United States.[5] And this development has not been confined to the United States. Groups protesting the use of nuclear power for the generation of electricity have been active throughout Western Europe and Japan. The "green movement," expressing environmental concerns, is similarly influential in other industrialized nations. The largest environmental group in France, for example, Les Amis de la Terre (Friends of the Land) advances environmental programs and policies similar to those of Friends of the Earth and the Sierra Club in the United States.

Expanding Sector Coverage by Interest Groups

In numerical terms business-related interest groups still predominate. But extensive group organization now exists in many sectors outside the traditional ones of business and labor. For example, the social, economic, and political interests of women are represented by scores of organizations nationally and by thousands of group affiliates at the state and local levels. Education is a major activity in the United States and almost every conceivable dimension of it has formal representation.

Some groups, it should be noted, are not as heavily represented by organized interest groups; the poor and minorities are the most prominent of these. For example, while the National Association for

[5] Roger M. Williams, "The Rise of Middle Class Activism: Fighting 'City Hall,' " *Saturday Review*, March 8, 1975, pp. 12–16; Jeffrey M. Berry, *The Interest Group Society* (Boston: Little, Brown, 1984).

Underrepresented
groups

the Advancement of Colored People (NAACP) and the National Urban League are well-established and have long been active in advancing the goals of black Americans, interest-group involvement in this area is less substantial than in other sectors such as environmental and educational concerns, to say nothing of business.

Women's groups. This expression of interests is not limited to widely-publicized organizations associated with the women's movement, such as the National Organization for Women (NOW), or ERAmerica, the coalition of organizations which campaigned, unsuccessfully, for ratification of the Equal Rights Amendment. Women who work for the national government are represented by Federally Employed Women (FEW). The widows of Army, Navy, Air Force, and Marine veterans have interests in survivor benefit programs, represented by the National Association of Military Widows. For women in education there are such groups as the National Council of Administrative Women in Education and the American Association of University Women. To advance athletic programs, there is the National Association for Girls and Women in Sports. Few areas where women's interests are found in the contemporary U.S. now lack formal organization (see Table 13.2).

Table 13.2
Selected National Women's Organizations

American Association of University Women: women graduates of regionally accredited colleges, universities, and recognized foreign institutions.

ERAmerica: coalition of organizations campaigning for ratification of the Equal Rights Amendment.

Federally Employed Women (FEW): women and men who work for the federal and District of Columbia governments.

Federation of Organizations for Professional Women: women's caucuses and committees in professional associations and organizations, and people interested in equal educational and employment opportunities for women.

League of Women Voters of the United States: women and men interested in nonpartisan political action and study.

National Association of Military Widows: provides referral information to military widows on survivor benefit programs.

National Association of Women Business Owners: individuals, primarily women, who own their own businesses.

National Council of Negro Women: coalition of international organizations and individuals.

National Federation of Republican Women: volunteers for support of Republican candidates for national, state and local offices.

National Organization for Women (NOW): individuals interested in all rights for women.

National Women's Political Caucus: persons interested in greater involvement of women in politics.

Rural American Women: individuals and their affiliate organizations interested in issues relating to rural women.

Educational groups. School teachers work through the American Federation of Teachers, AFL-CIO, and the National Education Association. Private schools are represented by such groups as the Lutheran Educational Conference of North America, the National Association of Independent Schools, the National Catholic Education Association, and the Christian College Coalition. College and university interests get expressed through varied groups, among them the Association of American Colleges, the Association of American Universities, the American Council on Education, the American Association of University Professors, the Council of Graduate Schools in the United States, the Council for the Advancement of Small Colleges, the Women's College Coalition, and the National Association for Equal Opportunity in Higher Education (see Table 13.3).

INTEREST-GROUP RESOURCES

The thousands of interest groups in the American political scene vary greatly in the impact they are able to have on public policy. Some have far greater resources than others. While it is not possible to specify exactly how much influence a group will have, given its particular mix of resources, it is possible to identify the principal types of resources that groups call upon as they try to influence policy.

Size of Membership

In a democratic political system, the size of an interest group's following is and should be an important factor. Numbers matter. More

Table 13.3
Selected National Educational Organizations

American Association of School Administrators: chief school executives and other administrators at district or higher level, and teachers of school administration.
American Association of University Professors: college and university faculty and graduate students.
American Council on Education: colleges, universities, and education associations.
American Federation of Teachers, AFL-CIO: preschool through postsecondary level teachers.
American Student Association: college and university student government associations.
Association of American Universities: public and private universities with emphasis on graduate and professional education and research.
Association of Catholic Colleges and Universities: colleges, universities, and individuals interested in Catholic education.
Council for American Private Education (CAPE): national organizations serving private elementary and secondary schools.
Council for Exceptional Children: teachers, researchers, administrators, students, social workers, psychologists, and physicians who work with handicapped or gifted children.
Council for Graduate Schools in the United States: degree-granting graduate schools and graduate programs at private and public colleges and universities.
National Association for Equal Opportunity in Higher Education: predominantly black colleges and universities.
National Coalition of Public Education and Religious Liberty: coalition of groups that oppose federal aid to nonpublic schools.
National Congress of Parents and Teachers: parent-teacher associations.
National Education Association: teachers, from elementary through postsecondary level, and other educational professionals.
National Retired Teachers' Association: retired teachers.

than 17 million men and women belong to the labor unions that make up the AFL-CIO, which unquestionably adds weight to the representation AFL-CIO leaders make on behalf of various programs. Through the staff and organization of their unions, labor officials have formal ties and channels of communication to many people. But a number of factors restrict the weight of numbers. For one thing, every large group is certain to have a membership with very heterogeneous interests. AFL-CIO lobbyists claim to speak for millions of trade unionists, but in fact few pieces of legislation come before Congress where this is truly persuasive. Politicians know that unionists are divided on most political matters—much like any comparably large body of Americans. One almost never encounters the situation on a controversial question where 90 percent of the union membership is on one side and just 10 percent on the other. In the 1980 presidential election, for example, when the AFL-CIO and most member unions endorsed Democrat Jimmy Carter, unionists at large were somewhat more pro-Carter than the entire electorate, but not much more. In the 1984 presidential balloting the same sort of split occurred. Even though officials of the AFL-CIO and many of its constituent unions endorsed

AFL-CIO lobbyist talks to Senator Birch Bayh

Walter Mondale for the Democratic party's nomination early in the campaign and provided important backing for him in the nomination contest with Gary Hart and Jesse Jackson, and made a concerted effort on his behalf in the general election battle against Ronald Reagan, Mondale won only a little more than half the vote among trade unionists and their families (Table 13.4).

It is not even unusual for majorities of unionists to hold policy views *opposite* those taken by the leadership. In the 1960s and early 1970s the national union leadership generally committed itself to the goals of the civil rights movement. But majorities of the union rank and file frequently resisted the proposed changes, as did majorities of all white working-class Americans.

Table 13.4
Presidential Vote by Union Membership, 1980 and 1984 (in percent)

	1980			1984	
	Carter	Reagan	Anderson	Mondale	Reagan
Members of labor households	47	44	7	54	46
Members of households where no one belongs to a union	35	55	8	37	63

Source: Election-day surveys by CBS News and the *New York Times,* November 4, 1980, and November 6, 1984.

It is not surprising that splits develop between union leadership and the rank-and-file membership on various policy questions. Any large group attracts its members for limited objectives—in the case of the labor unions, to improve wages and working conditions. Sustained by this base, labor leaders then proceed to take stands on a broad range of important policy questions, such as race relations, taxing and spending, and foreign affairs. These positions are by-products of an institutional arrangement organized for another purpose. There is no reason to expect leaders to represent the rank and file's view directly outside of the objectives for which the group membership was developed. This does not mean that the 17,000,000 member AFL-CIO is a feeble giant. More than any other organization it is listened to when it speaks for American labor. Its membership supports an organizational structure that is often skillfully committed in election contests and policy debates. But the impact of these numbers is diluted by the geat heterogeneity of interests they entail.

Policy splits within groups

Financial Resources

Numbers are only one element determining a group's influence. Money is another critical political resource. Some groups have a lot of it, others very little. Lobbying by business corporations and trade associations—groups that are relatively weak in number of members—is often very well financed. Groups use money in a variety of ways to advance their interests, most of which are straightforward and legal. Well-financed associations of business or professional people, like the National Association of Manufacturers and the American Medical Association, employ large and politically astute staffs. They mount effective public-relations campaigns, utilizing the mass media to present their positions. In general, they use their financial resources to get their messages before legislators, other political decision-makers, and the public, to an extent quite beyond the reach of groups that lack such substantial funding.

Interests that can draw on large financial resources can also increase their access to officials, something that is troubling even when it is completely legal. One common means of increasing or protecting access is by making campaign contributions to candidates. Electioneering is very expensive, and it is becoming steadily more so, especially as the use of television expands. Candidates turn to well-financed groups for campaign contributions, and the groups often oblige. These group do not think they are buying votes and typically they are not, but they do think their contributions entitle them to get in the door and make their case the next time an issue of importance to them comes along. Or they are afraid that if they refuse an influential incumbent's request for a contribution, he or she may be unreceptive to their future appeals.

Buying access to officials

New federal campaign-finance legislation in the 1970s has encour-

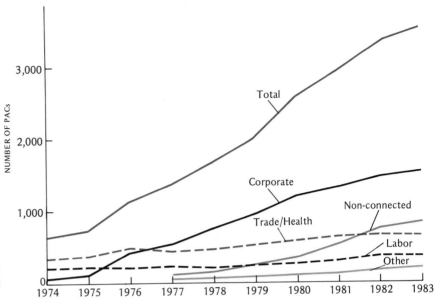

Figure 13.1
**Growth of Political
Action Committees**

Source: Federal Elections Commission Annual Report of January, 1982;

aged expansion in the number of political action committees (PACs), discussed in greater detail in chapter 15. PACs are the political campaign arms of business, labor, professional, and other interest groups, legally entitled to raise funds on a voluntary basis and to make contributions to favored candidates and parties. The number of these special-interest-group organizations grew from just 608 in 1974 to 3,525 at the beginning of 1984, according to a report issued by the Federal Elections Commission; nearly half of all PACs have been established by business corporations (see Figure 13.1). PACs are now a major vehicle for bringing private money into electoral campaigns.

Organization

There has been increasing attention in recent years to the importance of sophisticated formal organization as a group resource—such as using computers in extensive direct-mail campaigns, and building coalitions of groups to better integrate lobbying efforts. Interest groups are better organized today then ever before, and thus the disadvantages of ineffectively organized groups are greater than ever before.

Organization is an even more critical resource because American government is so fragmented and awash with contending claims and interests. Getting one's case across in this noisy, cluttered, diverse, and pluralistic setting requires planning and systematic effort. The old stereotype of the effective lobbyist as one who knows the right people and meets with them periodically to cut deals is increasingly out of touch with a political environment that puts a premium on careful organization in group dealings with a big and complex government.

Intensity of Interest

When a legislator casts a vote that a group of his constituents favors, he often hears nothing about it from them. But when he goes against some deeply felt interest, even if it is one held by only a distinct minority, the complaints are loud and persisting. Constantly bombarded, even the most principled legislator takes pains to limit criticism wherever he can without doing violence to his basic policy commitments. If an interest group has the capacity to hurt him politically, the legislator has a vested interest in placating it, especially if he can do so relatively easily. This helps explain why groups with intensely held interests often get their way on questions where a majority of the public and a majority of the legislators themselves, in their own private judgments, hold to the other side. For example, public opinion surveys have shown that two-thirds to four-fifths of the American public favors stronger gun-control legislation.[6] Yet congressional efforts to get stronger laws, opposed by groups like the National Rifle Association (NRA), have failed. This is not because the legislators doubt the polls or have been personally convinced by NRA lobbyists of the inherent wisdom of the latter's views; nor is it a result of bribery or other illicit means of persuasion. In a system where central party organization is weak and individual legislators operate largely on their own, there are strong incentives to placate interest groups. The NRA's intensity of concern, compared to the less focused involvement of most of the public, gives it a capacity to cause trouble. Congressmen are sorely tempted to appease the group unless they are strongly committed to gun control.

"Targeting" political opponents

Interest groups sometimes "target" senators and representatives whose stands on issues they find especially unsatisfactory; that is, they commit resources to defeating them in the next election. These efforts may at times contribute to their desired end, but at least as often, it seems, they backfire. Many voters resent it when an interest group wages electoral warfare on their congressman. Groups with intensively held interests gain their major successes in a different way, by convincing wavering legislators who do not have strong feelings on an issue that it just is not worth antagonizing the group on the matter.

[6] In 1981, the Gallup Organization asked a national sample: "In Massachusetts a law requires that a person who carries a gun outside his home must have a license to do so. Would you approve or disapprove of having such a law in your state?" Eighty-one percent favored such legislation, while only 17 percent disapproved (with two percent not having an opinion). Survey by the Gallup Organization, April 3–6, 1981.

Veterans march on Washington to protest the war in Vietnam.

Striking Alliances

Some groups pursue objectives that fit with prevailing views of the populace, while others cannot count on such public support. Some interests are able to call upon strong allies, while others find themselves quite isolated when they try to advance their policy goals. Even if other major resources, such as money and organization, could be equalized, a group committed to promoting more rapid economic growth would have an advantage over one that wants to extend the rights of homosexuals; the former rides the tide of favorable public opinion and has many allies, while the latter bucks public opinion and can count on little help from most other groups. The literature on interest-group activity probably places too much emphasis on the mechanical features of interest representation. The type of interest pursued is by itself very important, and groups fortunate enough to favor policies that strike a responsive chord elsewhere in the society thereby enjoy a major advantage.

TACTICS AND STRATEGIES OF INTEREST GROUPS

On every major question of American public policy, and on a great many relatively minor ones, interest groups work to persuade governmental officials to take actions consistent with what the groups think should be done. This may mean passing a law, imposing or removing a regulation, funding a program, changing the tax code, committing the country to some new objective, or countless other actions within the scope of modern government. Interest-group tactics and strategies are as diverse as the objectives for which groups intervene in public life.

Amending the Clean Air Act: A Case Study of Interest-Group Struggle

"The Clean Air Act—unquestionably the nation's most controversial environmental protection statute—is in trouble," wrote Morris Ward, a leading environmental consultant, in the summer of 1981. "That is, the Act in its current form, as passed by the Congress in 1970 and as amended in 1977, is in trouble."[7] The battle in 1981–82 over the renewal and amendment of the Clean Air Act is a recent policy dispute that prompted a classic interest-group campaign. Formidable group alignments took shape on both sides of the issue. Those contending groups made major efforts over an extended period, utilizing many of the tactics which have become staples in contemporary lobbying. And looming in the background were large questions of policy direction and compelling public interests.

The legislation. In 1970, Congress passed the Clean Air Act, which required the Environmental Protection Agency (EPA) to determine what concentrations could be safely permitted for seven major air pollutants, and then to see to it that these levels were not exceeded. The act was intended to gain major reductions in air pollution in order to promote the health of the general public, meet the special needs of such groups as the elderly and those with health problems affected by pollution, and prevent pollution damage to crops, livestock, buildings, and so on.[8]

These general objectives seem straightforward, but in fact the act is highly complex, and the detailed regulations issued by the EPA pursuant to its responsibilities under the law are even more complicated. Citizens who want to understand fully the controversies that have ensued around this statute must master such terms and acronyms as NAAQS (National Ambient Air Quality Standards), PSD (Prevention of Significant Deterioration) provisions, RACT (Reasonably Available Controlled Technology), BACT (Best Available Controlled Technology), LAER (Lowest Achievable Emission Rate), and SIP (State Implementation Plans), among others.

The complexities of environmental policy

[7] Morris A. Ward, "The Clean Air Act Controversy: Congress Confronts the Issues," *Environment*, July/August 1981, p. 6.

[8] It should be noted that air pollution control legislation goes back as far as 1955, when technical assistance was first offered to the states by the federal government in their efforts to improve air quality. The original Clean Air Act (CAA), passed in 1963 and amended in 1965 and 1966, was for the most part ineffective, since it depended solely on the voluntary cooperation of the states. The Clean Air Act (Amendments) of 1970 was the first comprehensive legislation dealing with the problem of air pollution nationally. Standards were set, and the newly constituted Environmental Protection Agency was charged with administration of the program. Amendments in 1977 established penalties for noncompliance and gave statutory force to EPA policies.

The argument. The debate over the act has not involved its general goals but rather has centered around various standards enforced to achieve the goals, such as standards for the acceptable level of auto emissions. It has also involved trade-off questions: How do you ensure environmental cleanliness without excessively obtrusive regulation? How do you protect the environment without setting back other important policy goals such as economic growth, creation of new jobs, and greater use of coal and other domestic energy resources? Many groups, including virtually all affected industries—auto, chemical, and oil companies, some trade unions, state agencies involved in implementation of the EPA standards, and others—had concluded by 1981 that the act unreasonably hampered some legitimate economic objectives and produced regulatory confusion. But many other groups—including virtually all environmentalist associations, some trade unions, government-reform groups like the League of Women Voters, and others—feared that business-led efforts to amend the act would go too far and set back the cause of a clean and healthful environment.

Business perspectives on the Clean Air Act

Business groups said they wanted "to reform the Act in certain limited ways, with a view toward boosting GNP and employment and restoring the nation's competitive position in world markets."[9] They favored such specific changes as modification of the emissions standards and deadlines affecting the auto industry, and an end to the "off-set" rule affecting the building of new plants. Under the latter, any company wanting to build in an area where the air did not meet pollution standards not only had to install the best possible pollution control equipment, but also had to buy "emission off-sets" from companies already operating in the area. That is, the incoming business had to get other companies to reduce their emissions by at least as much as the new plant would add to the overall volume of pollutants being released in the area.

Environmental group perspectives on the Clean Air Act

Environmental groups wanted to avoid any weakening of the clean air legislation. They wanted to retain the "off-set" policy. They wanted to keep strict deadlines for compliance. They feared that, in the words of Democratic Congressman Henry A. Waxman of California, chairman of the House subcommittees charged with environmental legislation, the industry-backed amendments were, cumulatively, "a blueprint for the destruction of our clean air laws."[10]

Tactics: Building coalitions. A key feature of group tactics in the clean air fight was the formation of formal coalitions. Many corporations, trade associations, labor unions, and environmental groups lobbied actively on an individual basis. But, in addition, they worked together in organized alliances for and against amending the act. On one side,

[9] Statement of the National Environmental Development Association, as printed in *Environment*, July/August 1981, p. 20.
[10] Remarks by Representative Henry A. Waxman, as quoted in the *New York Times*, June 20, 1981, p. 10.

various business and trade associations—including the Chamber of Commerce of the United States, the American Petroleum Institute, the National Coal Association, the Iron and Steel Institute, the Chemical Manufacturers' Association, the National Association of Manufacturers, the Business Roundtable, the Paper Institute, and the Edison Electric Institute—channeled much of their activity through the Clean Air Working Group. Another influential coalition was the National Environmental Development Association/Clean Air Act Project (NEDA/CAAP). Many of the major businesses which banded together in this alliance had obvious and direct stakes in applications of the legislation—oil companies like Exxon, chemical companies like du Pont, and automobile manufacturers such as General Motors. But special effort was made to enlist other organizations that didn't have such immediate interests. International Business Machines (IBM) was brought into NEDA/CAAP, a nice addition because it was so little affected by the act: Computers are a "clean" industry. The Building and Construction Trade Unions, AFL-CIO, were also included, attesting to labor-business agreement on the need for changes in the legislation.

On the other side, many environmental groups joined together to form the National Clean Air Coalition (NCAC). Represented here was the core of the environmental movement—Friends of the Earth, the Sierra Club, the National Audubon Society, the National Wildlife Federation, the Wilderness Society, and others. NCAC was also at pains to diversify its coalition, and it brought in such "disinterested" groups as the League of Women Voters and a number of trade unions, including the United Steel Workers of America and the Amalgamated Clothing and Textile Workers' Union. (See Table 13.5.)

The establishment of coalitions of interest groups on behalf of broad policy positions is by no means unique to the battle over amending the Clean Air Act. It has become a generally important part of lobbying. Just as trade associations appeared to pool the resources of individual companies, so group coalitions have developed to integrate lobbying on behalf of broad policy goals. One prominent coalition or "working group" which has operated in Washington in recent years is the Trucking Alliance. It brought together in favor of deregulation of the trucking industry such normally contending groups as Common Cause and Ralph Nader's Congress Watch on the one hand, and the National Association of Manufacturers and the American Conservative Union on the other. Another coalition is the Longshore Action Committee, which united 74 different groups, from the National Association of Manufacturers to the American Farm Bureau Federation, on behalf of legislation curtailing a federal program which compensates longshoremen, and workers in such related industries as shipbuilding and harbor construction, for on-the-job injuries. The Consumer Issues Working Group lobbied for eight years (successfully) against establishment of a federal Consumer Protection Agency. The Alaska Coalition, an alliance of environmental groups, secured

Two contending coalitions

Coalition-building: essential to lobbying

Table 13.5
Contending Groups in the Battle Over the Clean Air Act

Don't amend the Act *The National Clean Air Coalition*	*Amend the Act* *The National Environmental Development* *Association/Clean Air Act Project*
Amalgamated Clothing & Textile Workers	Allied Chemical Corporation
Americans for Democratic Action	Ashland Oil, Inc.
American Lung Association	Atlantic Richfield Company
Center for Auto Safety	Building and Construction Trades
Citizens for a Better Environment	Department, AFL-CIO
Environmental Action	Campbell Soup Company
Environmental Defense Fund	Celanese Corporation
Environmental Policy Center	Chevron U.S.A., Inc.
Friends of the Earth	Consolidation Coal Company
International Association of Machinists & Aerospace Workers	Crown Zellerbach Corporation
Izaak Walton League of America	Dow Chemical Company
League of American Bicyclists	Dravo Corporation
League of Women Voters of the United States	E. I. du Pont de Nemours & Company
Sierra Club	Exxon Company, U.S.A.
National Audubon Society	Fluor Corporation
National Consumer League	General Electric Company
National Farmers Union	General Motors Corporation
National Parks & Conservation Association	Getty Oil Corporation
National Wildlife Federation	International Business Corporation
Natural Resources Defense Council	International Paper Company
Oil, Chemical & Atomic Association	Kaiser Aluminum & Chemical Corporation
United Steelworkers of America	Mobil Oil Corporation
Wilderness Society	Occidental Petroleum Corporation
Western Organization of Resource Councils	Pennzoil Company
	Phillips Petroleum Company
	PPG Industries, Inc.
	Procter & Gamble Company
	Shell Oil Company
	Standard Oil Company (Indiana)
	Standard Oil Company (Ohio)
	Stauffer Chemical Company
	Sun Company, Inc.
	Tenneco Chemicals, Inc.
	Texaco Inc.
	Texas Oil & Gas Corporation
	Union Oil Company of California
	Westvaco
	Weyerhaeuser Company

passage of legislation to preserve from development large segments of the state of Alaska.

Various factors have contributed to the increasing recourse to carefully organized coalitions, in place of the more independent and loosely coordinated lobbying in the past. For example, power in Congress, once concentrated in the leadership and committee chairmen, was dispersed much more widely among the membership by the reforms of the late 1960s and 1970s. At the same time, congressional staff grew tremendously. Lobbyists found that they had to influence many more people to accomplish their goals. This suggested that they pool resources.[11] The use of coalitions, as in lobbying over Clean Air Act revisions, was also a step by interest groups to avoid speaking with a babble of conflicting voices. The coalition approach required groups to get their houses in order before going to Congress. Extensive interaction and compromise are necessary to hammer out reasonably united coalition positions. In the process, a whole new layer gets added to lobbying. Interest groups must spend much more time lobbying each other to build plausible coalitions and formulate common legislative approaches.

Tactics: Finding allies where you can. We tend to think of business and labor as opposing interest groups, and they often are. But as it turned out, many businesses and labor unions shared an interest in amending the Clean Air Act. Automobile manufacturers felt that the legislation created unfair burdens for their industry; so, too, did the United Auto Workers' Union. The UAW is a liberal union and usually aligns itself against the business community. But the financial troubles of auto manufacturing have meant financial troubles for auto workers, and the UAW committed itself to working with business to modify the act.

Bipartisan alliances

Most important legislative battles involve bipartisan support for proposed changes and bipartisan opposition to them. This was the case with the Clean Air Act amendments. For example, the bill containing amendments strongly backed by industry (H.R. 5252) was introduced by six members of the House of Representatives: three Democrats and three Republicans. Among them were John Dingell, a liberal Democrat from the sixteenth congressional district of Michigan, covering parts of Detroit as well as the city of Dearborn; and James T. Broyhill, a conservative Republican from the tenth congressional district of North Carolina, a largely rural district including the western Piedmont section of the state. Dingell served as chairman of the Committee on Energy and Commerce—the parent committee for environmental legislation—and Broyhill was the ranking minority member of that committee. Such bipartisan alliances on controversial measures are rare in the legislatures of most democratic countries, but they are the rule in the U.S. Congress, where party ranks are broken with abandon. Interest groups understand the importance of ad hoc legislative alliances, and they seek out "friends" on particular measures where they can find them. A liberal Democrat like Dingell would not usually be found working in tandem with a conservative Republican like Broyhill. But in this case the UAW, whose members are a big part of John Dingell's constituency, favored the same changes that industry wanted.

[11]Bill Keller, "Coalitions and Associations Transformed Strategy, Methods of Lobbying in Washington," *Congressional Quarterly*, January 23, 1982, p. 119.

Tactics: Providing information. Congressmen, required to move from one issue to another, need information and technical guidance on complex issues like the Clean Air Act revisions. Interest groups are more than happy to provide them. The Business Roundtable, for example, financed a $400,000 study of various proposed changes in the clean air legislation. The Chamber of Commerce of the United States issued detailed "suggestions for improving the Act." On the other side, the National Clean Air Coalition set forth its positions and recommendations.

Congress wanted more than technical information; it wanted policy guidance. Many congressmen, not just those notably friendly to industry, wanted to know what aspects of the act most troubled business. In the same way congressmen wanted to know which of the proposed changes especially bothered environmental groups. "You can't have everything you want: What are your priorities?" This was an important part of the information exchange between the contending groups and Congress.

The need for policy guidance

Tactics: Grassroots lobbying. During the debate on amending the Clean Air Act, interest groups made countless representations to congressmen. But they also sought to mobilize individuals and groups back home to communicate with their representatives. Environmental groups worked actively through their state and local networks. One very active business group, the U.S. Chamber of Commerce, devoted extensive resources to rallying municipal chambers of commerce around the country, to get them involved in trying to persuade their local congressmen to support amending the act.

Tactics: Public opinion. Polling is an increasingly important part of lobbying efforts. Groups vie with one another in telling legislators that they should do what the group wants because it is also what the people want. We saw in chapter 12 that the way questions are worded can affect the opinions people voice on complicated policy issues. Recognizing this, interest groups sometimes sponsor or otherwise encourage polls where questions are worded so as to prompt the desired answers. Or they emphasize only part of the answers people give—the part favorable to the group's position. The object is to get a message to legislators: "Polls are showing that big majorities of Americans want this action taken. If you don't go along, you or your party are going to pay the price for defying the will of the people."

Polls as "weapons"

Sometimes an interest group does not have an incentive to bend information from opinion surveys. Sometimes the people really do want what the group wants. And sometimes the issue is not one where politicians are likely to believe there is firm public opinion on either side, as when the questions are too narrow and technical. But more and more in big policy controversies, poll findings are being manipulated to fit in with a larger lobbying effort. This was the case in the debate over amending the Clean Air Act. Both industry and environmental groups commissioned new surveys and stressed results that seemed favorable to their respective sides. The U.S. Chamber of Commerce hired the Opinion Research Corporation (ORC) to conduct a national survey on the act in late 1981. "Most Americans support changing the nation's Clean Air Act," the Chamber argued in interpreting the ORC poll findings.

Public opinion on the Clean Air Act

Even those calling themselves active environmentalists agree on reviewing the Act periodically as new experiences are gained, according to the results of the survey. . . . The survey showed that 85 percent of the public and 78 percent of environmental activists agree that changes in the Act probably can be made so that air quality will be protected at a lower cost than now.[12]

House Democrats opposed to amending the act brought in pollster Louis Harris to assure legislators that his surveys showed Americans saying, "Keep your cotton picking hands off that environmental law."[13] In fact, as we noted in chapter 12, most Americans were not informed on the specifics of the Clean Air Act and weren't clearly committed to either side in the congressional debate. The public did not want to weaken important environmental legislation, but neither were people unreceptive to change in the law that would remove excessive regulation and unnecessary economic restrictions.

Who won? The argument over the clean air legislation had all of the ingredients of a classic *High Noon* interest-group confrontation. The stakes were large: the requirements of a growing economy on one hand and vital health and aesthetic needs on the other. Two big coalitions of interest groups went into battle—industry versus the environmentalists—each claiming to be on the side of the angels. Each used its full complement of lobbying tactics. The public was both interested and confused.

Party split on the Act   Each of the two political parties was internally divided on the question of amending the Clean Air Act. The bill that industry favored, H.R. 5252, had the strong backing of the Reagan administration. President Reagan urged amendments which "while protecting the environment, will make it possible for industry to rebuild its productive base and create more jobs." But H.R. 5252 also had the support of some key House Democrats, including John Dingell, chairman of the Energy and Commerce Committee. On the other side, opposed to the bill, was Dingell's Democratic colleague, Henry Waxman, the chair of the Subcommittee on Health and the Environment. Many Senate Republicans were also opposed to the Reagan administration and

[12] News release of the Chamber of Commerce of the United States, December 8, 1981.
[13] Testimony by Louis Harris before the Subcommittee on Health and Environment, U.S. House of Representatives, October 15, 1981.

industry position. The bill reported out by the Senate Environment and Public Works Committee made only modest changes in the Clean Air Act and was generally supported by environmentalists.

The environmentalists win

What was the final outcome of this long interest-group battle? The environmental groups won hands down. The House Energy and Commerce Committee was deadlocked, and H.R. 5252 was never reported out. No amendments of any kind passed either the House or the Senate. While environmental groups would have liked to enact changes of their own to further strengthen clean air standards, their main goal was to resist industry-backed changes that they thought weakened the legislation; in this they had complete success. Various environmental issues will continue to arise, of course, but the effort to amend the Clean Air Act in the Ninety-seventh Congress (1981–83) ended with Congress sharply divided over what to do, and thus making no changes at all.

Contrasting Types of Interest-Group Efforts

The battle over the Clean Air Act was an important one, and it revealed many facets of interest-group activities. But no case study can illustrate the whole range; in other sorts of policy matters, group objectives, competition, and tactics are different.

Narrower objectives. The clean air debate involved broad and highly visible issues. The public may not have understood the technical points being debated, but the basic controversies around the competing claims of environmental and economic objectives, were of general public concern. In contrast, many instances of interest-group intervention involve narrower issues which, though important to specific groups, do not pose questions central to the entire polity. Independent service station operators try to get Congress to pass legislation prohibiting the major oil companies from operating service stations. Dairy farmers seek to maintain a federal price support-program for milk products they cannot sell at a set price. The domestic shipbuilding industry wants to continue to receive federal subsidies initiated to make U.S. shipbuilding more competitive with foreign yards.

Sometimes the financial stake in seemingly narrow group objectives is very large. In 1978 a number of business groups came together to set priorities for changes in tax provisions affecting corporations. Meeting around a breakfast table at the Sheraton-Carlton Hotel in Washington, representatives of the major business federations settled upon an accelerated depreciation plan as their prime objective. The "10-5-3" plan, as it came to be known, referred to the length (in years) of new depreciation schedules for buildings, equipment, and vehicles, respectively. Basically, the new schedules allowed for faster tax write-offs. In 1981, having convinced the Reagan administration and congressional Democrats and Republicans to back "10-5-3," the busi-

Farmers march to Washington seeking farm subsidies.

ness coalition saw its prized provision written into the new tax legislation. Billions of tax dollars were at issue and "10-5-3" was virtually a password in the business community. But the public, and many informed observers, never saw broad questions of policy direction in the accelerated depreciation proposals. Press coverage was minimal outside of business periodicals. Few Americans knew anything at all about the "10-5-3" depreciation plan. There simply was not any public opinion on it. Only a small proportion of the efforts interest groups make to influence policy receive significant press coverage and are the subjects of relatively focused popular opinion.

No battle of the groups. On occasion, as with the 1982 clean air legislation, elaborate armies of contending groups organize on each side of an issue. Working with friendly congressmen, each of these coalitions tries to bring undecided legislators to its side. But in many other cases, most of the organization and activity takes place on one side only. For example, the business interests favoring "10-5-3" did not confront an opposing army of groups wanting to block their proposed changes. Much of the conflict leading up to enactment of "10-5-3" was within the business community itself, as different associations had different tax priorities which had to be adjusted before business could speak with a reasonably united voice. Interest-group conflict isn't uncommon, of course, but the elaborate mobilization of contending groups that happened with the Clean Air Act revisions occurs on a limited number of issues.

Lobbying the executive branch and the judiciary. In many instances, lobbying efforts center not on Congress (or a state legislature), but on executive branch departments and agencies. Earlier in American history, when the enterprise of government was less developed, the scope of policy initiatives by administrative agencies was tightly circumscribed. Today, however, government does so much and programs are of such complexity that program administration is often a central part of policy formation. Executive bureaucracies have become a main arena of interest-group activity.

Lobbying reaches the judiciary as well. As we saw in chapter 10, a primary means of group intervention in the judicial arena comes through *test cases*. The National Association for the Advancement of Colored People (NAACP) Legal Defense Fund has provided skilled attorneys and directed a long series of court challenges to racial discrimination. Similarly, the American Civil Liberties Union (ACLU) has concentrated its efforts in the courts rather than in the executive and legislative branches. In recent years, many of the newer public-interest groups, including those concerned with environmental issues, have also relied heavily on litigation: for example, by seeking court rulings to restrict the construction of nuclear power plants or to extend the scope of governmental regulation under environmental statutes.

Judicial test cases

Chrysler Corporation lobbied the executive branch to receive government guaranteed loans to bail out the company. Here, company chairman, Lee Iacocca pays back the loan.

An important Surpeme Court decision in 1982 may reduce the extent to which public-interest groups can advance policy goals through litigation. In a five-to-four decision, the Court ruled that Americans United for Separation of Church and State (an organization opposed to various governmental benefits to religion and religious denominations) had no right to sue in federal court to block the transfer of a surplus military hospital to a Christian college in Pennsylvania. The Court held that the group's 90,000 members had not been directly injured by the transfer and therefore did not have standing to bring the court challenge.[14] The more stringent the requirements the courts set for standing to sue, the harder it is for groups to mount judicial challenges to statutes they oppose.

Amicus curiae briefs

Interest groups pursue their objectives in the judicial arena in other ways, apart from initiating and supporting litigation: They "speak" to the judges and try to perusade them to adopt philosophies which the groups find attractive. Courts are a special part of the political process, and the etiquette for group attempts at persuasion is different for them than for other governmental institutions. When a group wants to convey its policy views to Congress, it sends its representatives directly to the legislators, or it may take out full-page ads in leading newspapers. Judges are not supposed to be lobbied in such ways, and for the most part they are not. To get the message through, a prime vehicle is the filing of *amicus curiae* (friend of the court) briefs. In a major case, it is not uncommon to find scores of interest groups filing *amicus* briefs on behalf of one or the other of the primary litigants. These briefs contain legal argument, but they are also a formal mechanism through which groups make known to judges their policy interpretations and preferences. The use of *amicus* briefs in important civil rights cases is discussed further in chapter 17.

GROUPS AND AMERICAN DEMOCRACY

As noted earlier, Tocqueville argued in the 1830s that Americans were unusually active in interest groups and voluntary associations. Present-day studies come to this same conclusion. Gabriel Almond and Sidney Verba found a quarter-century ago that a higher proportion of citizens belonged to voluntary associations in the United States than in Britain, West Germany, Italy, or Mexico.[15] Americans were much more likely, moreover, to have multiple group memberships. A later study by Sidney Verba and Norman Nye showed 32 percent of

Stricter requirements for standing to sue (margin note)

---

[14]*Valley Forge Christian College v. Americans United for Separation of Church and State,* 454, U.S. 464 (1982). Standing is not measured by the intensity of the litigant's interest or the fervor of his advocacy," wrote Justice William Rehnquist in the majority opinion. The important and complex legal concept of standing is discussed in chapter 10.

[15]Gabriel A. Almond and Sidney Verba, *The Civic Culture: Political Attitudes and Democracy in Five Nations* (Princeton, N.J.: Princeton University Press, 1963), pp. 301–2.

Americans as active members in community organizations, compared to 15 percent in the Netherlands, 11 percent in Japan, and 9 percent in Austria.[16] The sheer numbers of groups and the vigorous roles they play are a distinctive feature of U.S. experience. Why is this so?

Conditions for Active Group Participation

One would expect relatively free and open societies to have more extensive group participation than those with authoritarian regimes. But, as we have seen, even in established democracies like Britain, the Netherlands, West Germany, and Italy, activity lags behind that exhibited in the United States. A highly educated and affluent populace has the time, training, confidence, and other resources necessary for group organization, much more than the public of a poor country, where educational and communications resources are restricted. But, again, the United States is not alone in having the requisite education, sources of information, and economic position. Explanation for the unusually extensive group organization in America, compared to other industrial democracies, lies elsewhere.

Diversity. One factor seems to be the heterogeneity of American society. James Madison felt in 1787 that one of the virtues of a large republic like the one provided for by the Constitution was the capacity to sustain a more diverse set of groups or factions to compete against each other. American experience has borne out Madison's expectations. The United States comprises a great variety of groups—ethnic, religious, cultural, regional, and more.

Individualism. We noted at the beginning of this chapter that Tocqueville thought the strength of American individualism contributed importantly to the country's vigorous group life. One might think the opposite: that practitioners of rugged individualism would be social and political loners. Tocqueville saw that, in the United States, a nation of self-confident and assertive individuals would produce a welter of group action, as people banded together to accomplish various objectives. Passivity, or the absence of a sense of individual efficacy, are the true deterents to a vigorous associational life. "I'm important—and I can do something" spurs the formation of voluntary associations.

Decentralization. Groups organize around units where decisions get made, and governmental arrangements are a key factor determining what these units are. Centralized governmental systems, like those of

---

[16] Norman H. Nye and Sidney Verba, "Political Participation," in Fred I. Greenstein and Nelson W. Polsby, eds., *Handbook of Political Science* (Reading, Mass.: Addison-Wesley, 1975), vol. 4, pp. 24–25.

Britain and France, produce interest-group centralization. Britain has, for instance, just one national organization of farmers and one major business association. There is no counterpart in France to the fifty state AFL-CIO units, for the simple reason that there is no counterpart in France to the fifty states.

Autonomy. In many democracies, major groups are closely tied to the political parties. For example, the largest French labor organization, the Confédération Générale du Travail (CGT), has been controlled by the French Communist party. Another French labor federation—Force Ouvrière—is directed by the Socialist party. In Great Britain, the umbrella trade union federation, the Trades Union Congress (TUC), is closely tied to the Labour party. The British and French cases are quite different in one regard: In France the parties dominate the labor unions, while in Britain the reverse is true, the unions are a major force guiding the Labour party. Neither case, however, is comparable to the American situation where autonomous labor unions pursue their own interests. Many AFL-CIO officials feel closer to the Democratic party, of course, and often back its candidates, but the party and the unions are truly independent. This fits the general U.S. pattern of interest group autonomy.

Groups and Group Power

We have seen the propensity of the populace for vigorous group participation and the central role well-organized and well-financed interest groups play in governmental decision-making. What remains is to examine the central issue of group power as it relates to democratic governance. Specifically, are groups too strong? Do the maneuverings of special interests threaten the public interest? The research on these questions support a complex conclusion: Interest groups and their active involvement in political life are 1) inevitable, 2) desirable, and 3) a continuing source of problems.

Inevitable. "Liberty is to faction what air is to fire," James Madison wrote in *Federalist Paper* 10. The presence of liberty, essential and desirable, provides for factions in abundance. Madison did not want, nor think it possible, to diminish the group presence. If the U.S. were to be a free society, which he took as ordained and essential, it would have to live with the profusion of special interests, each pursuing its own goals and interests. It would be utopian to think that this country could have dynamic groups and associations without some of them acquiring resources that give them competitive advantage over others. While the United States need not adopt an "anything goes" posture before the claims of organized interests, both the active presence of interest groups and the disproportionate resources of some of them are inevitable features of American democracy.

Desirable. Many proponents of democracy find interest groups not only inevitable, but also good. Committed to popular sovereignty, democrats must applaud conditions whereby bodies of people who share political interests seek their expression and realization. Advocates of democracy may condemn certain forms of group activity, but they can hardly dispute that interest groups are the primary means through which popular sovereignty is realized. We might contrast this with totalitarian societies, where there is a continuing aversion to interest-group activity. Essential to the definition of totalitarianism, as that concept is applied to national socialism in Hitler's Germany or to Soviet communism, is the sustained effort to stamp out all forms of intermediate group life that might challenge the regime and organize people for independent political activity. On December 13, 1981, army and police in Poland began applying massive force to suppress Solidarity as an independent trade union. The mere existence of this strong interest group, independent of the regime, was a denial of the regime's exclusive claim to represent the interests of the Polish people. The presence of strong-independent interest groups imposes important limits on the power of government.

Interest groups and democracy

Democratic theory has long emphasized the essential place of a vigorous system of interest groups and other mediating structures through which the varied interests making up a society are organized and expressed.[17] Through groups, people are given meaningful identities, and the alienation of mass society is reduced.[18] Organized groups also play important roles in articulating the demands and needs of the many diverse interests within a population.[19]

Problem-causing. The operation of organized interests has long prompted concern among Americans attentive to the health of their country's democracy. In *Federalist Paper* 10 James Madison defined interest groups in a way that focused on their problem-causing possibilities:

> By a faction I understand the number of citizens, whether amounting to a majority or minority of the whole, who are united and actuated by some common impulse of passion, or of interest, adverse to the rights of other citizens, or to the permanent and aggregate interests of the community.

Their very essence aligns interest groups against the rights of other citizens and against what we today call the "public interest": "the permanent and aggregate interests of the community."

[17] For a thoughtful general statement of the essential place of interest groups in a democratic society, see Ernest Barker, *Reflections on Government* (New York: Oxford University Press, 1958).

[18] See, for example, William Kornhauser, *The Politics of Mass Society* (Glencoe, Ill.: Free Press, 1959); and Seymour Martin Lipset, *Political Man* (Garden City, N.Y.: Anchor Books, 1963), especially chaps. 1 and 2.

[19] David B. Truman, *The Governmental Process* (New York: Knopf, 1951).

Boom Town

BILL TO GIVE AWAY U.S. TIDE LANDS RESOURCES

BILL TO END U.S. REGULATION OF GAS RATES

SPECIAL TAX BENEFITS FOR OIL COMPANIES

HERBLOCK
Feb 50

Progressivism

In the early twentieth century, a political movement known as Progressivism grew up with a prime objective of purging excessive interest group influence from political parties, legislatures, and governmental administration locally and nationally. The Progressives saw American democracy dominated by a struggle between "the interests" and "the people," and they sought political reforms that would shift the balance of power from the former to the latter. The Progressives were especially troubled by what they considered the excessive power of big business interests—"the trusts"—as they had developed in such industries as oil, steel, and banking. In 1913, Woodrow Wilson, just elected president and with ties to the Progressive movement, issued a statement denouncing the role of special interests in current legislation.

Woodrow Wilson on special interests

I think that the public ought to know the extraordinary exertions being made by the lobby in Washington to gain recognition for certain alterations of the tariff bill. Washington has seldom seen so numerous, so industrious, or so insidious a lobby. . . . It is of serious interest to the country that the people at large should have no lobby and be voiceless in these matters, while great bodies of astute men seek to create an artificial opinion and to overcome the interests of the public for their private profit. . . . The Government in all its branches ought to be relieved from this intolerable burden and this constant interruption to the calm progress of debate.[20]

[20] *State Papers and Addresses by Woodrow Wilson, President of the United States* (New York: George H. Doran, 1918), pp. 9–10.

Concern over special
interests today

Americans still lament the role of pressure groups and pressure politics. Citizens have complained as much in recent years about the power of "Big Oil" as their counterparts seven and eight decades ago did about "the trusts." Lobbying is considered an often unsavory activity that carries the onus of excessive influence by big private money. There is a vivid perception of too-cozy relationships between interest groups and politicians, of wheeling and dealing behind closed doors for ends antithetical to the public interest. Three different concerns are often tangled in the general indictment of excessive group influence. One is the fear that some interests may actually come to dominate American government as a coherent power elite. A second is that groups are able to take over not the entire government but rather a great number of specific policy areas where they have special interests and get their way with little general public scrutiny or control. The third concern is about the fact that some interests are much better organized and represented than others.

Group tyranny. Madison addressed the problem of group tyranny directly, and he and the other framers of the Constitution thought they had found a satisfactory, long-term answer. We saw in chapter 5 that their answer was to so divide power, and check and balance it, that group tyranny would be impossible. A government of dispersed authority operating in a diverse and pluralistic society would be sufficient to maintain popular sovereignty and individual liberty. From the evidence (reviewed in chapters 5–10) it seems clear that the Madisonian solution has had impressive success.

Policy-making in the iron triangle. Political scientist Grant McConnell dismissed the idea of power-elite domination, observing that the American interest-group world is highly fragmented and decentralized. Political organization in the United States, he noted, has been based persistently on "small constituencies."[21] The fragmented groups of small constituencies have

> on the whole had limited ends; their tactics have been limited and often more economic than political. Where they have been openly political, they have relied upon group self-help through the exercise of well-isolated segments of public authority rather than upon action through political parties and elections.[22]

Madison wanted political organization based on small constituencies to serve as a check on group power, and today the United States has that arrangement to a degree that might surprise even its brilliant proponent.

The present problem grows out of the very success of the Madison-

[21] Grant McConnell, *Private Power and American Democracy* (New York: Knopf, 1966), p. 342.
[22] Ibid., p. 345.

ian solution. As Americans have come in recent decades to accept an enlarged mission for government, thousands of new lobbies have developed around the expansive governmental system. As the Advisory Commission on Intergovernmental Relations has noted, "Every program, every protective regulation, every tax loophole appears to have acquired its coterie of organized beneficiaries." The proliferating interest groups found the traditional dispersion of authority much to their liking. For, while the whole of government was impervious to control by any group, the many separate parts proved to be uniquely susceptible to special-interest pressures.

We saw in chapter 9 how interest groups, congressional subcommittees, and executive-agency bureaus have operated relatively closed policy systems in many discrete program areas. "Molecular government," Joseph Califano called it when he was secretary of health, education, and welfare and thus unusually well-placed to observe the problem. "Washington has become a city of political molecules," he observed, "with fragmentation of power, and often authority and responsibility, among increasingly narrow, what's-in-it-for-me interest groups and their reponsive counterparts in the executive and legislative branches."[23] National policy is too often made not for the nation but for narrow, autonomous sectors defined by special interests. The total of programs determined in each sector makes up national policy—but it is a national policy no one planned or intended.

Fragmenting power and proliferating special interests

Grant McConnell was among the first to identify this contemporary problem with interest groups. "There is a comfortable assumption," he wrote in 1966, "that interest groups will balance each other in their struggles and produce policies of moderation."[24] Unfortunately, he noted, recent American experience shows the incompleteness of this interpretation. "Repeatedly during the past half-century, relatively homogeneous groups have been effectively organized and have assumed a strong degree of power over particular areas of public policy through close collaboration with segments of government. . . ."[25]

Do special interests balance each other?

In solving the problem which Madison considered the primary one of democratic governance—preventing groups from dominating the totality of government—institutional arrangements were established which have led to a different problem: Special interests do not control the nation, but their influence over discrete policy sectors makes coherent national policy, properly responsive to the public interest, difficult to achieve.

Over- and under-representation. Criticizing the argument of some analysts that the great variety of organized groups contending with each other preserves a pluralistic balance, political scientist E. E. Schattschneider observed that "the flaw in the pluralist heaven is

---

[23] Remarks by Joseph A. Califano, Jr., before the Economic Club of Chicago, April 20, 1978.
[24] McConnell, *Private Power*, p. 362.
[25] Ibid., p. 338.

that the heavenly chorus sings with a strong upper-class accent."[26] The economically privileged enjoy greater group representation than do the poor.

There are a number of reasons why businessmen and other high-status groups have a disproportionately large place in the interest-group process. They have the financial means to sustain organized group action. This is notably the case with corporate executives, who are able to command the resources of major corporations. Also, people with large amounts of formal education have skills and training which equip them better to engage in complex political action. Economist Mancur Olson explained another facet: In certain types of small groups, an individual may find that his personal gain from achieving some collective good—a benefit for the entire group—is so substantial that it is in his interest to support an organization set up to advance it even if he has to pay all the cost of the organization effort himself. The high degree to which business interests are organized in the United States results, then, from the fact that the business community "is divided into a series of . . . 'industries,' each of which contains only a fairly small number of firms."[27] Each firm, operating through relatively compact units such as the trade associations, has a big stake in voluntarily contributing to the organized group activity because of the large individual gain it may expect.

One can probably never attain a condition where all segments of the population are equally represented by interest group efforts. Some segments simply have greater resources and incentives for group action. This does not mean that the economically disadvantaged cannot have their needs represented. What it does mean, as Schattschneider and McConnell have argued, is that adequate representation of the poor and the disadvantaged is unlikely to be achieved through the interest-group structure.

> Such protection as they have had has come from the centralized features of the political order—parties, the national government, and the presidency. . . . Many of the values Americans hold in highest esteem can only be realized through large constituencies, some indeed only by a genuinely national constituency.[28]

A free society must permit the free organization of groups and must confer on them considerable latitude in making their claims. But adequate attention to broad national interests, including the claims of people insufficiently spoken for by interest groups, requires the interventions of such primary representative institutions as political parties and the presidency. Only a *vox populi* expressed by elected representatives bound to do the people's business can counterbalance the "upper-class accents" coming from interest groups.

Disproportion between interest groups *(margin note)*

The role of political parties in representing the disadvantaged *(margin note)*

[26] E. E. Schattschneider, *The Semi-Sovereign People* (New York: Holt, 1960), p. 35.
[27] Mancur Olson, *The Logic of Collective Action* (Cambridge, Mass.: Harvard University Press, 1965), p. 34.
[28] McConnell, *Private Power*, pp. 349, 366–67.

SUMMARY

The United States displays a great variety of interest groups and, in general, a high level of group participation. While organized interests can be found in every sector touched by public policy, economic policy has prompted the greatest profusion of groups. In recent years, though, other sectors such as women's affairs, education, and environmental issues have seen a proliferation of interest groups. Public-interest groups, those that pursue collective goals that are not of immediate material benefit to their members, have also expanded greatly.

Various resources determine the extent of group influence. *Numbers* are important, as groups speaking for large constituencies can make a special claim upon political attention. But having a large constituency often means that the group also encompasses a great heterogeneity of interests, and on many issues it cannot really speak for the bulk of its members.

Money is always a critical resource: Well-financed groups can hire skilled staff, make campaign contributions, advertise, and do other things needed to gain favorable attention for their proposals. Groups speaking for *intensely held interests* have an advantage over those whose memberships, though perhaps larger, are not strongly engaged. Some interests are able to find support broadly across the society, while others must largely go it alone.

The tactics used by interest groups have been evolving. The organization of formal coalitions of groups around key policy interests is now common. It has been prompted in part by the greater dispersion of power in Congress. Groups have always been concerned with public opinion, but they now devote greater resources than previously to the measurement of opinion through polls and to efforts to demonstrate through poll data that the people are on their side.

American interest groups operate in a political environment where the parties are organizationally weak and often split internally. The groups have learned, then, to find their allies where they can across party lines. They also operate in a governmental system of divided powers; and they must concentrate on executive agencies and the judiciary as well as Congress, and on the state capitals as well as Washington.

It is always tempting to reach for a simple, focused conclusion on the role of interest groups in American democracy, like "They are too strong and threaten the public interest." But political life is too complicated for that. Groups are an *inevitable* part of democratic experience, reflecting the free choice of interests to express themselves. Groups are a *desirable* part of democratic experience, barring excessive power by government, providing people with greater representation and identification. And interest groups are a *problem-causing* side of democracy as they dominate specific policy sectors and give greater voice to some interests than others. Group power, speaking for small constituencies, must be balanced by recognition of the claims of the entire public through national institutions and electoral mandates.

14 | Voting and Elections

Free elections, with voting open to all adult citizens, as the means of choosing political leaders form the keystone of the modern democratic process. Theorist Joseph Schumpeter noted this when he defined democracy as "that institutional arrangement for arriving at political decisions in which individuals [leaders] acquire the power to decide by means of a competitive struggle for the people's vote."[1] In this chapter we will look first at the legal requirements for voting in the U.S. and at the expansion of the franchise over the nineteenth and twentieth centuries. Having the right to vote, and actually voting, are two different matters, however. We then review voter turnout, who does and does not vote, and how electoral participation in this country compares to that in other democracies. After a brief examination of the basic structural arrangements for U.S. elections, which involve a single-member district, simple-majority system, we turn to a discussion of how elections are now contested. The role of money in campaigns deserves and gets special attention. We conclude with a review of the 1984 presidential race between Republican Ronald Reagan and Democrat Walter Mondale.

EXPANDING THE FRANCHISE

Until the Civil War, the Constitution left decisions on who could vote to the states. Article I, section 2, required that "the House of Representatives shall be composed of Members chosen every second Year

---

[1] Joseph Schumpeter, *Capitalism, Socialism and Democracy* (New York: Harper and Brothers, 1942), p. 269.

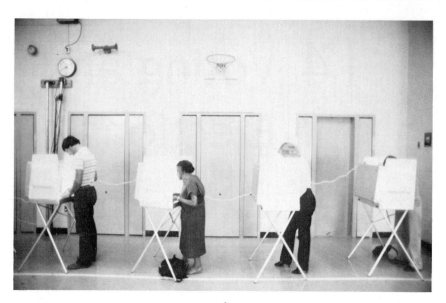

Voter registration.

by the People of the several States. . . ." But the manner in which the people would exercise this basic right was determined by the state governments. The Constitution stipulated only that the right to vote for House members must be conferred on all those who have the right to vote for "the most numerous Branch of the State Legislature." If you could vote for a state representative, you had to be permitted to vote for your national congressman.

The other principal offices of the national government were not to be chosen directly by the people at all. Members of the U.S. Senate, two from each state, were to be selected by the state legislatures (Article I, section 3); direct popular election of senators did not come until 1913, with the ratification of the Seventeenth Amendment. On the election of the president, the Constitution provided for an electoral college: "Each State shall appoint, in such Manner as the Legislature thereof may direct, a Number of Electors, equal to the whole Number of Senators and Representatives to which the State may be entitled in the Congress . . ." (Article II, section 1). The president would then be chosen by a majority in the electoral college. This basic provision remains in force, but in the 1820s and 1830s the primary role in choosing the president shifted to the entire electorate: Most states provided for quadrennial elections in which electors pledged to one presidential candidate or another were picked by popular ballot. Today people still vote for president indirectly, determining by majority vote in each state which slate of pledged electors is chosen, and hence which presidential candidate wins the state's electoral vote. If no candidate wins a majority of electoral votes nationally, the House of Representatives chooses the president, with each state casting a single vote. This latter situation, as we saw in chapter 8, has occurred only once and then only because of a flaw in the initial constitutional

Constitutional provisions for choosing leaders

language (since corrected by the Twelfth Amendment). In 1800 both Thomas Jefferson and his vice presidential running mate, Aaron Burr, got the same number of electoral votes because no distinction had been made between votes cast for president and those for vice president.

Early Economic Restrictions on Voting

At the state level, the early arguments over who should be entitled to vote centered around property ownership. When the Constitution was ratified, the idea that all adult citizens should vote, without regard to their economic position, was considered radical and was espoused by only the most extreme democrats. As a result, states commonly established property-holding and tax-paying qualifications for voting. These qualifications were fairly modest: "between one-half and three-quarters of white adult males living in the United States in 1789 were qualified to vote."[2]

Even these limitations quickly fell before the charge that they were undemocratic. By the administration of Andrew Jackson (1829–37), the franchise had been broadened in much of the United States to include virtually all white male adults. Property qualifications for voting survived into the 1840s in only several southern states and Rhode Island. Virginia did not abolish them until 1852.

Extending the Vote to Blacks

After property restrictions were removed, two large groups remained without the right to vote: all women and most black Americans. Until the Civil War, the overwhelming majority of blacks lived in the South and were slaves. President Lincoln's Emancipation Proclamation in 1863, the victory of the Union armies in 1865, and the ratification of the Thirteenth Amendment abolishing slavery in that same year were important acts in extending citizenship to blacks. But the practical achievement of many basic rights, including the right to vote, came very slowly.

The first major legal step for voting by blacks was taken in 1870 with the ratification of the Fifteenth Amendment. For the first time,

Voting and the Fifteenth Amendment

the Constitution contained a formal stipulation on who could vote: "The right of citizens of the United States to vote shall not be denied or abridged by the United States or by any State on account of race, color, or previous condition of servitude." Important though this provision was, it was effectively nullified throughout the South after the end of Reconstruction in 1876 through a variety of mechanisms. Many southern states required the payment of *poll taxes* to discourage vot-

[2]Bruce A. Campbell, *The American Electorate: Attitudes and Action* (New York: Holt, Rinehart and Winston, 1979), pp. 12–13.

The drive after 1960 to encourage blacks to vote.

ing by blacks (and by some poor whites as well), and *literacy tests* further diminished black voting.

The most formidable legal barrier was the so-called **white primary.** The Fifteenth Amendment required that *states* not deny the vote. Southern states responded by arguing that the Democratic party—which after Reconstruction was predominant throughout the region—was a private association to which this constitutional stipulation did not apply. The "private" Democratic parties of the southern states proceeded to exclude blacks from participation in their primaries, where the most important election contests occurred. Unable to vote in Democratic primaries in the one-party South, blacks were thus effectively disenfranchised by law. Not until 1944 did the United States Supreme Court strike down the white primary. In *Smith* v. *Allwright*, the Court ruled that the party primaries were part of a continuous process for choosing public officials. Since the primaries were enforced by the states, by certifying nominees chosen in them for inclusion on the ballot in the general elections, preventing blacks from voting in Democratic primaries was in fact state action in violation of the Fifteenth Amendment.[3] In 1940, only 250,000 blacks had been registered in the South; by 1946, just two years after *Smith* v. *Allwright*, the number had doubled, and by 1960 it had reached 1.4 million.

Only in the last quarter-century, however, has the right to vote been

The white primary

[3] *Smith* v. *Allwright*, 321 U.S. 649 (1944). Three years earlier, in *U.S.* v. *Classic*, 313 U.S. 299 (1941), the Supreme Court had reached the general determination that "where the primary is by law made an integral part of the election machinery," Congress has the power to regulate primary as well as general-election voter participation.

wholly guaranteed and extended to black Americans in the South. The Civil Rights Acts of 1957, 1960, 1964, and 1965, which we discuss further in chapter 17, had as their primary goal the final removal of racial discrimination in voting. Widely regarded as the most important civil rights legislation ever enacted in the United States, the 1965 law suspended literacy tests and other such devices in all states and counties where less than fifty percent of the voting-age population had been registered in 1964. It also provided for the appointment of federal examiners to register voters in these areas and to supervise the entire election process. And it required that officials in these states submit to the U.S. attorney general any election law changes which they proposed to make; the attorney general could veto the changes if he found them discriminatory. Dramatic increases in black registration and voting immediately followed the enactment of this legislation.

In 1975, the Voting Rights Act of 1965 was extended to 1982 with several additional provisions: making permanent the previously temporary ban on literacy tests, and extending coverage to "language minorities" in areas where over five percent of the voting-age population were of a single-language minority and less than fifty percent were registered or had voted in the 1972 presidential election. Hispanics were affected more than any other group. In 1982, the Voting Rights Act was again extended for another seven years. Through these actions, racial barriers to voting were at last effectively removed.

Voting rights legislation in the 1950s and 1960s

Extending the Vote to Women

The debate over women's suffrage developed at about the same time as that over black voting, but was resolved much faster. Until 1869,

Suffragette parade in Philadelphia, 1915.

women were denied the vote everywhere in the United States—everywhere in the world, for that matter. The territory of Wyoming (reflecting frontier individualism) became in 1869 the first part of the country to grant women the vote. It was followed by Colorado in 1893, Utah in 1896, and eleven other states between 1897 and 1918, until extension of the vote to women was guaranteed nationwide, with the ratification in 1920 of the Nineteenth Amendment: "The right of citizens of the United States to vote shall not be denied or abridged by the United States or by any State on account of sex."[4]

Remaining Restrictions

With the formal guarantee of voting rights to women and to blacks, the long battle to achieve universal suffrage was largely concluded. Minor debate over the age requirements for voting remained. Until 1971, the voting age in most states was set at 21. The Twenty-sixth Amendment lowered the age requirement to 18 throughout the country. No one has proposed reducing the voting age further.

Some adult residents still cannot vote. Being convicted of a felony continues to be grounds for losing the franchise. But by far the largest group excluded from balloting are resident aliens. In nineteenth-century America, aliens were often allowed to vote if they had at least begun the process of becoming citizens. The 1928 election was the first in which American citizenship was a universal prerequisite for voting. In 1984, perhaps as many as 9 million adult residents of the United States were not entitled to vote because they had not acquired citizenship.

Achieving the Vote

The enlargement of the franchise has been accompanied by a growing sense that voting is a right of national citizenship. When the Constitution was ratified, all governmental guarantees and provisions relating to the vote were the subject of state action, and there were great variations in voting requirements from one state to another. As the right to vote came to be an attribute of national citizenship, federal regulation gradually replaced that of the states on fundamental voting issues (although states continue to administer the electoral process, and administrative requirements do still vary from one state to another). *Universal* suffrage came slowly. It was not fully achieved in the eighteenth century, when American democracy was born, but rather in our own century, indeed, in the last 25 years. In assessing this slowness, we need to temper our judgment of the past by recognizing that the United States was a leader, not a follower, in extend-

---

[4] Data on the extension of the franchise to women by various states prior to passage of the Nineteenth Amendment are from *Historical Statistics of the United States: Colonial Times to 1970* (Washington, D.C.: Government Printing Office, 1971), part 2, p. 1068.

ing the vote. America was the first nation in which a mass electorate gained firm control of the processes of picking political leaders. In 1880, when only fourteen percent of adult males in the United States could not vote, the proportion was far higher elsewhere. In England about forty percent of adult males could not vote at that time.[5] Women's suffrage did not become national in the United States until 1920—but it was not provided for at all until 1945 in France, 1946 in Italy, 1952 in Greece, and 1971 in Switzerland.

PARTICIPATION IN AMERICAN ELECTIONS

As the franchise has been guaranteed to all citizens, there has been a heightening of concern over the relatively low proportion of eligible voters who actually cast ballots. According to official statistics, only fifty-three percent of voting-age residents voted in the 1980 presidential election, down one percent from 1976 and down nine percent from the turnout in the 1960 Kennedy-Nixon contest (Figure 14.1). Just over fifty-three percent of the voting-age population participated in the 1984 presidential contest.

Turnout is even lower in voting for the U.S. House of Representatives. In 1976 it dropped below the 50 percent mark for the first time in a presidential election year since the 1940s, and it was only 49 percent in 1984. In "off-year" voting for the House, without the added spur and visibility of the more publicized presidential contest, participation is lower still. Only 38 percent of the voting-age public partic-

Figure 14.1 **Percent of Voting-Age Population Voting for President since 1920**

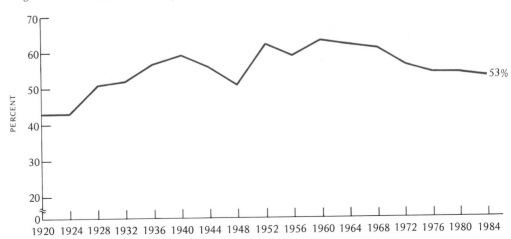

Source: 1932–76: U.S. Bureau of the Census, *Statistical Abstract of the United States, 1979,* p. 513. 1980: Idem, *Historical Statistics of the United States: Colonial Times to 1970,* 2:1073.

[5] Morton Keller, *Affairs of State* (Cambridge, Mass.: Harvard University Press, 1977), p. 523.

Figure 14.2 **Percent of Voting-Age Population Voting for U.S. House of Representatives since 1920**

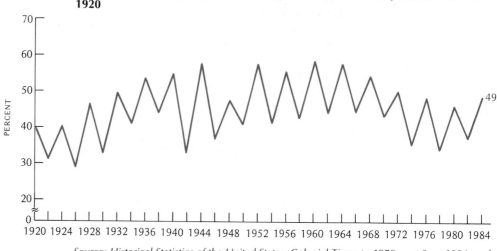

Source: *Historical Statistics of the United States: Colonial Times to 1970*, part 2, p. 1084; and *Statistical Abstract of the United States, 1984*, p. 262.

ipated in the 1982 House contests, and only 35 percent voted four years earlier (Figure 14.2).

A Confounding Decline

The country's low and somewhat declining voter participation is made more striking by its occurrence in the face of developments designed to spur voting. The drop-off in turnout of the last decade and a half has taken place at the very time the poll tax was outlawed, discrimination at polling places on the basis of race or language was prohibited, residency requirements were greatly eased, unreasonable registration dates were discarded, and many states initiated procedures to enhance participation such as mobile registrars, postcard registration, and even election-day registration.[6] Other developments associated with higher participation have also been occurring, the most notable of which is the steady increase in the amount of formal education. As data presented later in this chapter show, the strongest observed link between social characteristics of the population and inclination to vote involves education: The more of it citizens have, the higher their participation levels in elections of all types.[7] And yet as the formal education of the populace has been growing so impressively, voter turnout has been falling.

Concern has been spurred further by comparisons of turnout in the United States to that in other democracies. Although, as we will see, comparisons are more difficult to make than is sometimes supposed, the mean (or average) turnout in national elections 1945–80 was 95

[6] Curtis Gans, "The Cause: The Empty Voting Booths," *Washington Monthly*, October 1978, p. 28.

[7] See Raymond E. Wolfinger and Steven J. Rosenstone, *Who Votes?* (New Haven, Conn.: Yale Univesity Press, 1980).

percent in Australia and the Netherlands, 87 percent in West Germany, 81 percent in Norway, 79 percent in France, 77 percent in Great Britain, 76 percent in Canada, and 73 percent in Japan—while in American presidential elections during this period turnout was just 59 percent.

Is Voter Turnout a Problem?

The United States is the world's oldest democracy and a pioneer in the extension of the vote to the entire population, but it appears to have one of the lowest voter-participation rates among the world's democracies. America has taken a number of measures to spur registration and the population now seems better equipped to vote, given its high formal education, but still turnout is falling off. Has something happened to the fabric of American democracy? "Unless people begin to explore the root causes of the growing American discontent with its politics and leaders," observed Maurice Rosenblatt, president of the Committee for the Study of the American Electorate, "we will shortly have government of, for and by the few."[8] Some worry that low turnout diminishes the capacity of those not participating to represent their interests and shape policy. For example, after reviewing data suggesting that the decline in turnout between 1960 and 1976 did not take place evenly across the population but was sharpest among whites of low income and education, Howard Reiter expressed concern that this "may make federal policymakers less responsive to their [lower-status whites'] desires than they used to be. This may be especially significant for the Democratic party, which has claimed to speak for lower and working-class interests."[9] Declining and uneven voter participation may upset the proper balance of power in American democracy.

The facts on voter turnout

The level of voter participation is important to the character of the democratic process. But it is also important that we begin this examination with careful attention to the facts. One source of confusion on American voter turnout as opposed to other democracies is the lack of fully comparable statistics. The conclusion our data so obviously suggest, that voter turnout is lower here than abroad, is valid. But important qualifications on this conclusion are often overlooked. Voter turnout for the United States is regularly computed on the basis of votes as a percentage of the *voting age population;* in all other countries, turnout is calculated on votes cast as a percentage of *registered voters.* Additionally, in the United States only valid votes are counted in the total turnout, while in the other countries invalid and blank ballots are also in the total figure. These statistical dissimilarities make turnout in the United States seem lower than it actually is.

[8] Maurice Rosenblatt, "Non-Voter Study '78–'79," a report of the Committee for the Study of the American Electorate, October 1978.
[9] Howard L. Reiter, "Why Is Turnout Down?" *Public Opinion Quarterly,* Fall 1979, p. 310.

Part of the reason why data are published with one statistical convention for the United States and another elsewhere is that American registration laws result in a substantial proportion of the voting-age population not being registered in any given election. Were turnout in the United States represented as a proportion of only those actually registered, it would convey a sense of very robust participation that would be quite misleading. Most democracies have registration procedures *intended* to register virtually the entire adult citizenry; for these nations measuring turnout as a proportion of registered voters is appropriate. But as British political scientist Ivor Crewe has pointed out, "The accuracy of the turnout figures [for all countries except the United States] depends on the efficiency of the electoral registers on which they are all based. . . ."[10] In those instances where "the registers omit those unlikely to exercise their right to vote (the homeless, tenants of single rooms, immigrants), *turnout figures will be artificially inflated.*" Any situation where significant numbers of people are not counted among registered voters makes turnout appear higher than it really is; computing turnout on the basis of those registered always inflates participation rates since no registration system ever records all voting-age residents.

At the time of the 1980 U.S. presidential election, according to the Bureau of the Census, the voting-age population of the United States was about 164 million. The number of valid ballots cast for president was 86.5 million—hence the turnout figure of about 53 percent. But just 105 million Americans were registered to vote in 1980. Among those who were registered, the turnout was 82 percent, a very respectable figure.

Why were 59 million voting-age Americans unregistered? Certainly many of them did not register because they did not intend to vote. Registration and voting in the United States are part of one continuous act of electoral participation. The government does not assume the responsibility of registering people but rather requires that citizens initiate the step; millions of people who for whatever reason do not plan to vote just do not register. But among the unregistered residents are millions who are off the rolls not because of lack of interest but because by law they cannot register or vote. Perhaps as many as 9 million resident aliens of voting age in the United States don't have the citizenship required for voting. The Census figures on voting-age residents also include "institutional" populations. Those jailed for felonies are barred by law from registering and voting. Many other people who are institutionalized, like inmates of mental facilities, cannot vote. All of this means that millions of people in the United States who are of voting age are barred from registration by reason-

---

[10] Ivor Crewe, "Electoral Participation," in David Butler, Howard R. Penniman, and Austin Ranney, eds., *Democracy at the Polls: A Comparative Study of Competitive National Elections* (Washington, D.C.: American Enterprise Institute for Public Policy Research, 1981), p. 232.

able, consciously developed legal standards. By continuing to compute turnout on the basis of all those of voting age, we substantially overstate the magnitude of American nonvoting.

Voter Participation across History

If turnout is low in Amierica, it has long been that way. As we saw in Figure 14.1, participation in 1924 (as a percentage of the voting-age population) was just 43 percent, 10 percentage points lower than in 1984. And electoral participation in 1936 was essentially what it is now. Yet a very different cast has been given to participation in Roosevelt's great victory of 1936 than in the Ford-Carter, Reagan-Carter, and Reagan-Mondale contests. With the country in the midst of a great depression, which had sapped national confidence, Roosevelt came to office, told the people that they had "nothing to fear except fear itself," and proceeded to chart a bold course that rallied much of the populace to his banner. Opposition to the new initiatives was also vigorous, and the 1936 election was a spirited referendum on the New Deal. This historical account seems valid. But then why was voter participation in this buoyant referendum about the same as in recent elections in which, according to many accounts, the public has been unenthusiastic about the candidates of both parties, dissatisfied with the quality of leadership, and uneasy about the programmatic approaches the parties were offering?

There is a dimension of nonvoting in the United States unrelated to dissatisfaction with democratic performance or with the parties and their leaders. As S. M. Lipset, among others, has noted, American nonvoting is "a reflection of the stability of the system" and confidence that the next election will not produce threatening or dangerous results.[11] Elections in many countries involve contenders far more dissimilar in their programs and outlooks than are the Democrats and Republicans in the United States. The two major American political parties are middle-class alliances that share many basic ideological commitments. For a Democrat, the prospect of a Republican being elected is not usually wildly threatening, and vice versa. In Britain, the division between the leadership of the Labour and Conservative parties is much greater; in France, the gap between the Communist party and the Center-Right is greater still. Less interested or involved people are more likely to participate electorally in contests where they see the stakes to be high. As a stable democracy that has operated under the same constitutional structure for two centuries, the United States has a political system that is not so stress-filled, and many people feel they can afford the luxury of not voting.

One rebuttal to this argument is that voter turnout was much higher in the United States in the late nineteenth century than at present.

Voter turnout in nonthreatening elections

[11] Seymour Martin Lipset, *Political Man* (Garden City, N.Y.: Doubleday, 1960), p. 181.

Voter turnout historically

According to data collected by Walter Dean Burnham, voter turnout was 75 percent in the presidential election of 1892, 79 percent in 1896, and 73 percent in 1900.[12] Turnout undoubtedly was higher in the last century than in our own, but not as much higher as these statistics would suggest. Voting fraud occurred more frequently in the nineteenth century because it could be committed so easily. Stipulations on eligibility requirements were few and easily avoided. The paper ballots were printed by the political parties, not by the government. The counting of votes was often controlled by the parties and, in areas of one-party dominance, padding of the totals was commonplace. As a result, the number of votes reported in nineteenth-century elections was probably, as a routine matter, considerably larger than the number of voting-age citizens actually casting ballots. One often-cited instance of exaggeration of turnout is that of West Virginia, where the reported turnout in 1888 was actually 12,000 votes higher than the total eligible to vote!

Sources of Diminished Voter Turnout

The diminished role of political parties

When all these factors are considered, it is still clear that current voter turnout in the U.S. has dropped off over the last quarter-century. One reason involves the weakening of political parties, as we will see in chapter 15. Curtis Gans has noted that "the answer to declining participation does not lie in more sophisticated registration drives or new voting laws—although universal registration, more polling places, shorter ballots, fewer elections and better voter information would certainly marginally increase turnout." Instead, it is to be found in "more fundamental" factors, among them reversing "the decay of political and social institutions, most notably the political party. . . ."[13] As party organizations have become weaker, they have become less able to handle various of their traditional functions, including mobilizing the electorate. In times past, strong party organizations had the institutional resources needed to increase turnout. They canvassed potential voters and urged participation on behalf of party nominees. They conducted "get out the vote" drives, took people who they expected to vote for the party's candidates to and from the polls, and in general helped maintain a sense of partisan awareness and interest in the electorate. Today, in many areas of the U.S., parties do such things less vigorously than they used to.

A second factor in low voter turnout involves the scale and remoteness of the governmental process. Survey data, for example, show that large and growing segments of the population now feel that the complexity of politics and decision-making have become beyond their control. Seventy percent of those interviewed in a recent survey agreed

[12] These data have been published in *Historical Statistics of the United States: Colonial Times to 1970*, part 2, pp. 1071–72.
[13] Curtis Gans, "Non-Voter Study '78–'79," a report of the Committee for the Study of the American Electorate, December 1978, p. 6.

that government "seems so complicated that a person like me can't really understand what's going on." Modern government was seen to be big and distant. It also seemed apart from the average citizen's world, which encouraged frustration and resentment. Seventy-two percent agreed that their elected representatives in the national government "lose touch with the people pretty quickly." Another 70 percent held that "the government is pretty much run by a few big interests looking out for themselves. . . ." Sixty percent stated that "quite a few of them [people running the government] don't seem to know what they are doing."[14] In general, politics seems more out of control today than in the past.

Frustration with big government

Another contributor to voter frustration in the 1960s and 1970s was the string of bad political performances. The long and costly war in Vietnam sparked widespread protests and an even wider disillusionment with political judgment. The Watergate scandal, which resulted in the imprisonment of high governmental officials and the forced resignation of President Nixon, deeply disappointed many Americans and raised questions about the soundness of contemporary leadership. For a country that historically has had little experience with high inflation, the United States' encounter with persistent double-digit inflation in the 1970s was especially painful. It helped undermine confidence that the economy was being effectively managed. Such developments, occurring steadily for more than a decade, may well have contributed to reduced voter participation as one expression of a more general dissatisfaction with the parties and the politicians.

Poor political performance

One may expect slightly higher turnout in the 1980s than in the 1970s if political performance is seen to improve. But no big change

[14]Center for Political Studies, University of Michigan, 1980 election surveys.

is likely. The general sense of distance between the individual citizen and "big government" is likely to persist. In nineteenth-century America, most of government's work began and ended at the local level. It was easier, in such a context, for the individual voter to believe that the decision he made on election day shaped governmental action. A citizen in Bucksport, Maine, in 1840 saw a shorter and more direct link between his vote and actual governmental response than any American can today. While one may conclude that voting remains a basic check on government and recognize that collectively the millions of votes cast determine who the nation's leaders will be, the scope of modern government must detract from a sense of voter efficacy and confidence, especially among those who have little training to understand such complexity.

Who Votes?

Importance of education

People of high socioeconomic status generally vote at a much higher rate than those of low status, data analysis from massive surveys conducted by the Bureau of the Census shows. Education is especially important: it "has a very substantial effect on the probability that one will vote."[15] People with college degrees were 38 percent more likely to vote than those with fewer than five years of schooling. Income and occupation were independently much less important: Once education is held constant, income differences have little effect on rates of voter participation. Yet, the variations in rates of voting by education level are very large within all income groups.[16] Education

> imparts information about politics . . . and about a variety of skills, some of which facilitate political learning. . . . Schooling increases one's capacity for understanding and working with complex, abstract, and intangible subjects, that is, subjects like politics. . . . Learning about politics doubtless heightens interests; the more sense one can make of the political world, the more likely that one is to pay attention to it.[17]

Presumably, the increasingly complex and abstract character of politics makes education a bigger factor in determining the likelihood of voting.

An immediate stake. Another factor that comes into play is whether individuals have highly concrete interests in election outcomes. Those that do are more likely to vote. For example, farm owners, who are highly dependent on governmental decisions for their livelihood, are notably active participants. So, too, are governmental employees, who are affected by what government does just as other citizens are, but

[15] Raymond E. Wolfinger and Steven J. Rosenstone, *Who Votes?* (New Haven, Conn.: Yale University Press, 1980).
[16] Ibid., pp. 23–28.
[17] Ibid., p. 18.

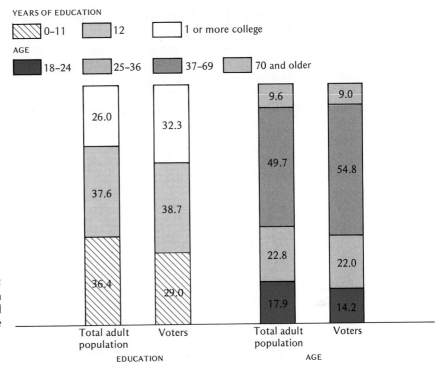

YEARS OF EDUCATION

0–11   12   1 or more college

AGE

18–24   25–36   37–69   70 and older

Figure 14.3
Age and Education Makeup of Voters and the Entire Populace

Total adult population | Voters
EDUCATION

Total adult population | Voters
AGE

Source: Wolfinger and Rosenstone, *Who Votes?*

who in addition have their wages and other conditions of employment determined by elected officials.[18]

Age. Voter turnout is lowest at the beginning of adult life, increases to reach a plateau in middle age, and then declines in old age.[19] Beyond this, the lower levels of voting by young adults are much more pronounced outside the ranks of the college-educated than for those with college training (Figure 14.3).

> In other words, the start-up costs of voting [developing a level of understanding and interest in politics] are not borne equally by all young people. The cost of entering the political system is relatively small for the educated, but for those without such skills the costs are [as a statistical expression] nearly three times as great.[20]

Partisan implications. How much do voters differ from nonvoters in political terms? Voters are generally of higher socioeconomic standing and have more formal education than nonvoters, but are their political interests and values different? If voters and nonvoters are very different politically, then the widespread nonvoting in contem-

[18] Ibid., pp. 30–35.
[19] See Lipset, *Political Man,* p. 189.
[20] Wolfinger and Rosenstone, *Who Votes?* p. 60.

porary American politics means that our electorates can be highly unrepresentative.

As a group, voters are slightly higher in Republican identification than the entire adult population by a few percentage points.[21] Modest though this difference is,

> all other political differences between voters and the general population are considerably smaller than this gap. . . . On some issues voters are a shade more liberal than the entire population; and on others they are a trifle more conservative. . . . In short, on these issues voters are virtually a carbon copy of the citizen population. Those most likely to be under-represented are people who lack opinions.[22]

The tiny differences between voters and the entire citizenry on various policy issues "suggest that on these political questions people who vote are representative of the population as a whole."[23]

Other Forms of Political Participation

Americans may turn out at the polls at a lower rate than their counterparts in other democracies, but they exercise their control over the political process through a much more extensive array of elections than any other citizenry. Over 500,000 offices are filled by election in the United States within every four-year election cycle. "No country can approach the United States in the frequency and variety of elections and thus in the amount of electoral participation in which its citizens have a right."[24] No other country chooses the lower house of its national legislature as often as every two years, as the United States does. No other country has such a broad array of offices—including judges, sheriffs, city treasurers, attorneys general—subject to election. No other country (with the exception of Switzerland) approaches the United States in the number or variety of local referenda on policy issues. The United States is almost alone in using primary elections as the vehicle for choosing party nominees; in most democratic nations party organizations pick the nominees. Ivor Crewe concludes that "the average American is entitled to do far more electing—probably by a factor of three or four—than the citizenry of any other democracy."

Frequency of American elections

This suggests a critical modification of the common observation that voter participation is low in the United States. *Turnout* in national elections is indeed low, but in other regards voter *participation* is very high. The American electorate expresses itself in more political decisions through casting ballots than the electorate of any other country.

[21] Ibid., pp. 109–110.
[22] Ibid., p. 109.
[23] Ibid., p. 111.
[24] Crewe, "Electoral Participation," in *Democracy at the Polls*, p. 232.

Table 14.1
Political Interest and Participation by Socioeconomic Position (in percent)

	Very interested in political campaigns	Contributed money to a candidate during the 1980 campaign	Attended political meetings, rallies, or other political activity
Education			
College graduate plus advanced training	55	23	19
College graduate	43	11	13
Some college	37	10	8
High school graduate	28	5	5
Less than four years of high school	26	2	6
Family income			
$50,000 or more	47	30	17
35,000–49,999	39	10	9
25,000–34,999	32	8	9
20,000–24,999	31	4	5
15,000–19,000	36	6	6
10,000–14,999	33	4	6
Under $10,000	28	2	7

Source: Center for Political Studies, University of Michigan, 1980 election surveys.

In fact, some observers suggest that the very frequency of elections in America serves to reduce the proportion turning out in any given contest: "Ho hum—another election."

Political involvement

Elections are not the only way in which people participate politically.[25] And, outside the electoral arena, Americans appear highly participatory compared to their counterparts in other countries. We noted in chapter 13 the high level of involvement in interest groups and voluntary associations in the United States. As in voting, participation in these other political activities is strongly related to socioeconomic status (Table 14.1). Only 26 percent of those with less than a high school education said in 1980 that they were "very much interested" in political campaigns, compared to 28 percent of high school graduates, 37 percent of those with some college, 43 percent of college graduates, and 55 percent of those with advanced degrees. Only 2 percent of those with little education indicated that they had made a financial contribution to a candidate, compared to 23 percent of those with the highest levels of formal training.

[25] Ronald Mason argues that political science has placed too much stress on the narrowly electoral forms of political participation. See Ronald M. Mason, "Toward A Non-Liberal Perspective on Participation," paper presented at the Midwest Political Science Association Meeting, April 1980.

THE STRUCTURE OF ELECTIONS

The arrangements under which votes are cast and tallied often exert considerable influence on election outcomes. And no set of electoral mechanics is politically neutral. For example, the *single-member district, simple-majority* electoral system used by the United States leads to results different in important regards from those encouraged by systems built around *plural-member districts* and *proportional representation*.

Translating Votes into Seats

The impact of electoral systems

Perhaps the most important single feature of an electoral system is the way it translates the votes people cast into the election of legislators and other officeholders. Consider a hypothetical example. *Votersland* is a small country with 1,000,000 registered voters and three political parties. The Liberty party is backed by 40 percent of the people, the Equality party by 30 percent, and the Brotherhood party by 30 percent. Votersland held its 1980 national election under an arrangement where the country was divided into 100 districts, each with 10,000 electors. The party winning the most votes in each had its candidate chosen as the district's congressman. Since the Equality party's 40 percent was evenly distributed across the country (as were the votes of its rivals), it had a plurality in every district. Thus the results were:

Liberty	100 seats
Equality	0 seats
Brotherhood	0 seats

As would be expected, there was a storm of protest. A party with just 40 percent of the popular vote had, in a free and open election, gained all the seats. Bowing to demands for electoral change, the legislature proceeded to rewrite the law. The new statute provided that no candidate would be declared the winner unless he received an absolute majority (50 percent or more) of the vote. If no one did, there would be a runoff election between the two candidates with the highest totals in the first round.

The 1982 elections were conducted under these new rules. The total popular vote was exactly the same as in 1980, but this time that meant no one was elected in the first round. The Liberty party had 40 percent in each district, more than its rivals but not a majority. Before the second round, the Equality and Brotherhood parties reached an arrangement whereby the one coming in third (and thus disqualified for the second round) in a district would throw its support to the party that came in second. In half the districts this was Equality, in half Brotherhood. Voters followed their leaders' wishes, and when the second-round votes were tallied, the results in half the districts were Liberty, 0 seats, Equality, 50 seats. In the other half, the final tally read Liberty 0, Brotherhood 50.

With no shift in the popular vote, representation of the Liberty backers fell from 100 to 0. Naturally, protests again erupted, and once more the rules were changed. This time the districts were abolished, and congressmen were elected on the basis of the distribution of the partisan vote nationally. Each party submitted a list of 100 candidates, with the understanding that a percentage of them would be declared elected exactly in proportion to its share of the popular vote. These new rules were tried in the 1984 elections. The popular vote was distributed as in the two previous contests. This meant that the first 40 candidates on Liberty's list were elected, the first 30 on Equality's, and the first 30 on Brotherhood's.

The Votersland example is obviously contrived, assuming such things as the popular vote being evenly distributed across an entire country, and not changing from one election to the next. But the example is fair and revealing. It shows how in perfectly free elections very different results can be obtained just by changing electoral mechanics. Variants of the three sets of rules used in the example are actually found in democratic countries around the world.

The American Electoral System

The United States conducts most of its elections under a single-member district, simple-majority, single-ballot system. Elections for seats in the U.S. House of Representatives, the Senate, state legislatures, for governorships, and for many other offices fit within this general order. It is a **single-member district** system because the area covered by the election—the entire United States in the case of House of Representatives elections, a given state for state legislative contests—is carved into a series of districts, each of which elects a single representative. In contrast, many countries employ systems with **plural-member districts**—where a single constituency chooses more than one representative. The United States has some plural-member district elections—for example, in cities where the entire council or board of alderman is chosen by voters at large rather than in single-member council or aldermanic districts. But single-member districts are the rule.

The American arrangement is a **simple-majority** and **single-ballot** system: The candidate who gets the most votes in his district is awarded the seat on the basis of a single casting of ballots. The alternative is an absolute-majority requirement, where the winner must not only get more votes than any rival but must get more than 50 percent of all ballots cast. This requires, in some instances, recourse to a second ballot or runoff election between the two highest contenders. Some *primaries*, especially in southern states, include provision for runoffs. Jesse Jackson made an issue of this provision during the

The simple-majority single-ballot system

1984 Democratic presidential contest. Like other black leaders, he saw the runoff primary as discriminatory, allowing white voters to pool their strength for the surviving white candidate against the black candidate in the second-round election. Many Democratic officials defended the runoff as essential when the first-round election has so many candidates that no one can get a majority. Primaries aside, one finds in a typical United States election (as for the House of Representatives) an arrangement where all candidates run in districts from which only one person is elected, and the candidate with the most votes in the single general-election ballot is declared the winner, whether or not he or she has an absolute majority of the votes cast.

The plural-member proportional-representation system

Some other countries operate with this single-member district, simple-majority arrangement, but they are confined largely to the English-speaking world. Britain is the political progenitor of this system. A majority of the world's democracies—including Italy, West Germany, Sweden, Israel, and Japan—count votes and award seats through some form of plural-member districts with **proportional representation** (PR). In such systems representatives are chosen from districts in which more than one candidate is elected. In Norway, for example, in 1980, 155 seats in the national legislature were spread over 20 voting constituencies; in Japan, 511 seats were allocated among 130 constituencies; and in the Netherlands, all 150 seats in the lower house of the national legislature were elected from a single constituency: the entire nation. The idea of PR is to divide seats among the contending parties in proportion to the percentage of the vote won by each of the parties. In theory, if a party receives 27 percent of the vote in a given legislative election, under PR it should get about 27 percent of the seats. The particular electoral mechanics employed under PR vary; some come closer than others to an exact link of vote and seat proportion. But the underlying idea is always the same. For PR to work, you must have plural-member districts, and you must then divide the seats among the contending parties in proportion to their percentages of the votes cast.

Which System Is Best?

What are the relative advantages and disadvantages and the partisan implications of the single-member and PR systems? The Votersland example makes evident one of the chief biases of single-member, simple-majority arrangements: They can produce big imbalances between the proportion of votes and seats won by a party. In the 1978 U.S. congressional elections, the Democrats won 54 percent of the popular vote nationally but gained 64 percent of the seats; in 1980, the proportions were 50 and 56 percent; in 1982, 55 and 62 percent; and in 1984, 50 and 58 percent.

The reason why the votes-seats ratio is not even more uneven than it is in U.S. congressional elections involves the distribution of Republican and Democratic votes around the country. Both parties have their "safe" seats: those where they enjoy a fairly comfortable majority and manage to win almost every time. In recent years the Democrats have regularly done better in House seats than in popular vote, but not so much better that the Republicans have had to cry "foul." Neither party wants to change the prevailing electoral machinery.

Is the simple-majority system unfair?

Is the single-majority system, as it operates in U.S. elections, basically unfair because it typically gives the winning party more seats than its share of the popular vote would suggest? Not necessarily. If an exact ratio of votes to seats is the goal, the U.S. arrangements are obviously flawed. But by another standard for assessing systems of representation, elections are vehicles for choosing a government by the principle of majority rule. And absolute proportionality of votes to elective office is not universally held essential to that end. In fact, sometimes proportionality makes the task of forming a coherent government much harder. A common criticism of PR is that it fractures legislatures by producing such a mix of parties that governing is difficult. The purer the form of PR, the more likely fracturing will occur. The price of the fairness of a pure system of PR may be prolonged governmental instability.[26] The Dutch PR arrangements, for example, have led to a proliferation of parties: in 1971, 14 parties secured seats in the national legislature.

What should an electoral system accomplish?

Which system is best cannot be answered, then, without attention to differing electoral goals. If elections are seen as means for gaining "an ideological census, a declaration of the voters' fundamental position on the left-right spectrum," as British political scientist David Butler puts it, there is much to be said for a pure PR arrangement, since the legislature should be a direct reflection of the proportional party preferences of the electorate. But if the goal is seen as one of choosing "viable governments" and giving such governments legitimacy, Butler suggests, the single-member system may be better. He argues that

> a clear answer may be better for the country than a mathematically exact one . . . a legislature that is a perfect mirror of what the electorate felt on one particular polling day may not be as satisfactory a basis for effective government as one that offers a cruder but more decisive reflection of majority trends.[27]

Third Parties

The single-member district, simple-majority system the United States uses for most of its electoral contests helps maintain a two-party system and penalizes third parties. In order to secure representation, a minor party must not only find considerable support in the populace but achieve more support in some districts than the established major parties. If it becomes the choice of 10 percent of voters in many dif-

[26] David Butler, "Electoral Systems," in *Democracy at the Polls*, p. 19.
[27] Ibid., pp. 22–23.

ferent districts, it wins no seats. Thus third parties are constantly vulnerable to the charge that a vote for one of them is essentially a wasted vote, since it is unlikely to join enough others to constitute a plurality of all votes cast. If the American Congress were elected on the basis of PR (without any other aspect of American society or politics being changed), the United States would almost certainly move immediately from a two-party system to a multi-party one—and the purer the form of PR employed, the greater the proliferation of parties that would result.

Third parties in Britain and the U.S.

In Great Britain, where there have been three or four important parties, the penalty that the single-member, simple-majority system imposes on those not among the top two is vividly shown. In the 1976 British national election, the Liberal party—number three in popular support at the time—received 20 percent of the vote for House of Commons candidates, but it got only 2 percent of the seats. In the 1983 elections, the new Alliance of the Liberal and Social Democratic parties garnered an impressive 26 percent of the popular vote, just 2 percentage points behind the second-place Labour party; the Alliance gained only 3 percent of the House seats, however, compared to 31 percent for Labour. Of course, the Alliance thought the system grossly unfair. In the United States, where most of the public fits comfortably behind either the Democratic or the Republican standard, the anti-third-party bias of the single-member, simple-majority system causes little concern. But in Britain, where the same system is used, there is considerable dissatisfaction because a strong alliance of two "third parties" finds itself severely penalized.

Primary Elections

Another important key feature of American electoral arrangements is the **primary election** for choosing party nominees. In no other democracy are party candidates chosen largely by rank-and-file adherents through primaries. The direct primary in the United States developed early in the twentieth century and was effectively promoted by the Progressives. They argued that leaving the choice of candidates to the party "bosses" was undemocratic, and that the fullest participation of the rank-and-file in candidate choice was desirable. American individualism provided fertile soil for this appeal. Use of primaries is now so extensive that party organizations typically have little control over candidate selection. The choice is made by party voters in election contests that are as regular and routine a part of the electoral process as are the general elections. State governments supervise all facets of the primaries, including the printing of ballots.

Open and closed primaries. Today most states use **closed primaries,** where only voters registered as party members may participate. Seven states, however, use **open primaries,** where any voter may cast a ballot, regardless of his or her party registration. The open primary has the troublesome feature of allowing supporters of the opposition to help decide who the party's nominees will be. Sometimes, these opponents understandably cast their ballots for the candidate they think will be easiest to beat in the general election. The most open of all the primaries is used in the state of Washington. A voter may cast his ballot in the Democratic primary for governor, the Republican primary for U.S. Senate, and so on, alternating as he sees fit through all of the offices.

Presidential primaries. Primaries are now widely used to pick delegates to the national parties' presidential nominating conventions. In 1984, 30 states employed primaries, although in several of these states, they applied to only one party. In several others they were only "beauty contests," meaning that they were nonbinding: they gave voters a chance to indicate their preference, without actually choosing delegates. In most states that held presidential primaries—including New York, Pennsylvania, Illinois, and California—rank-and-file voters picked the delegates directly.

Presidential caucuses. The second most common system of delegate selection in presidential nominations is the **caucus.** This has become especially popular in the Democratic party. In a typical caucus arrangement like Iowa's, rank-and-file party adherents gather in precinct meeting houses. Instead of casting ballots in the privacy of a polling booth, they publicly declare themselves for one presidential contender or another. Tallies are taken and delegates allocated. In some caucus arrangements, those favoring a candidate who does not

The Iowa caucuses begin with citizens' meetings in communities across the state.

have enough local support to win a delegate are allowed to go (after the first division) with the group supporting their second choice. The idea of the caucus is that it provides more substantial involvement than just casting a ballot: it involves spending an evening with one's neighbors and publicly declaring for a candidate. At the same time, it is like a primary in that any voter registered with the party may attend its caucuses and participate in delegate selection.

CAMPAIGNS

For those who love to campaign for elective office, or enjoy watching campaigns, the United States is a veritable horn of plenty. Nationally, the great presidential sweepstakes comes every four years; 435 House of Representatives seats are contested every biennium, as are a third of the Senate seats. At the state level, campaigns for governor, executive offices such as attorney-general, and seats in state legislatures proceed on two- and four-year cycles. County, city, and town elections—for such offices as mayor, seats on town councils, county boards of supervisors, and boards of education, and judgeships—are interspersed around the federal and state election calendars. Add to all this the primary elections that are held to choose nominees and you have the American saga: "The Endless Campaign."

Length of Campaigns

Not only the abundance, but also the duration of election contests create a political environment of almost endless campaigning. Increases in the length of campaigns are especially striking in presidential elections—for example, the 1984 presidential campaign began in earnest in 1983. Not only did prospective nominees start to make plans, but essential details of the campaign were fixed 12 to 20 months prior to the voting. Indicative of the elongated schedule, the AFL-CIO departed from its past custom and worked actively for one of the Democratic contenders in advance of the party convention. The labor movement officially endorsed Walter Mondale on October 5, 1983—13 months before election day.

"Go through fire." Walter Mondale had been an early favorite for the 1976 Democratic presidential nomination (eventually won by Jimmy Carter). But he cut short his exploratory run and withdrew from the contest, citing the bruising physical and emotional demands the long campaign would entail. "I don't think anyone should be president who is not willing to go through fire," he said. After serving four years as Carter's vice president, however, Mondale decided he was ready to go for it. His successful campaign for the 1984 Democratic nomination was one of the most arduous any candidate has ever experienced. Mondale proved he was now "willing to go through fire." Should such

"ARE YOU SURE THIS IS THE WAY IT WAS SUPPOSED TO WORK?"

willingness in fact be a requirement for the presidency? Some observers worry that many of the most able people are dissuaded from seeking high office because they are unwilling to endure the extreme rigors of prolonged campaigning. This applies not just to the presidency, but to contests for governor, seats in the U.S. Senate and House, and other important offices.

Running for Congress: a case study. The contest for the 1980 Democratic nomination for the House seat in Connecticut's 2nd congressional district is a concrete illustration of why many people are concerned. In 1979, the incumbent congressman from the 2nd district, Christopher Dodd, decided he would seek the Senate seat being vacated through the retirement of Senator Abraham Ribicoff. A number of Democrats expressed interest in succeeding Dodd in the House. One of them was Samuel Gejdenson, 31 years old, the owner of a small farm in the sparsely settled eastern Connecticut town of Bozrah. Although he had served two terms in the state legislature, Gejdenson was little known in Democratic circles and started the race with virtually no party backing. But he was willing to campaign unceasingly. With almost no money and a modest volunteer staff (his campaign manager was still in his teens) Gejdenson traveled for months around his sprawling district, attending every party function and social affair he could. The effort paid off. Gejdenson won a closely contested primary, in which one of his rivals had the party endorsement, and then went on to nip his Republican opponent in the November election.

In many ways Gejdenson's unexpected triumph is a heartening success story, showing how even in an age when campaign costs have skyrocketed, a political unknown can, through diligent pursuit and a gift for personal campaigning, win election to the U.S. Congress. But it raised a troubling question: What about other worthy individuals who have the skills and interests needed to serve in Congress, but who are unable because of the demands of their jobs or unwilling to submit to endless campaigning? "Who would drop everything else and campaign for months on end, attending every little party and social function in the district?" Gejdenson's campaign manager was asked. "Why, someone like Sam," he replied, "who didn't have much of a job and who would see getting elected to Congress the opportunity of a lifetime." Some defend the campaign trial as appropriate: a test of political zest and aptitude. Others wonder whether the campaigning side of elective office may not now loom proportionally too large.

Money and Campaigns

The number and length of campaigns in the United States, and the extent to which they now require large amounts of expensive resources such as television time for speeches and advertisements, means that American electioneering is a very expensive business. Money has become a central problem in contemporary campaigning. Without

POLLING PLACE

ELECTIONEERING PROHIBITED

On the day of any primary, general or special election, no person may, within a polling place, or in any public area within three hundred feet of such polling place do any electioneering, circulate cards or handbills of any kind, solicit signatures to any kind of petition, engage in any practice which interferes with the freedom of voters to exercise their franchise or disrupts the administration of the polling place, or conduct any exit poll or public opinion poll with voters.

No person may obstruct the doors or entries to a building in which a polling place is located or prevent free access to and from any polling place. Any sheriff, deputy sheriff, or municipal law enforcement officer shall prevent such obstruction, and may arrest any person creating such obstruction.

No person may except as provided in RCW 29.34.157, remove any ballot from the polling place before the closing of the polls or solicit any voter to show his or her ballot.

No person other than an inspector or judge of election may receive from any voter a voted ballot or deliver a blank ballot to such elector.

Any violation of this section is a misdemeanor under RCW 9A.20.010 and shall be punished under RCW 9A.20.020(3), and the person convicted may be ordered to pay the costs of prosecution.

$100.00 FINE (and cost of Prosecution) MAY BE IMPOSED FOR VIOLATION OF THE ABOVE CONDITIONS. No one but Election Officers, (R.C.W. 29.51.020) Persons voting, and One Challenger for Each Political Party allowed.

RETURN TO COUNTY AUDITOR

C 84

FORM E 305 TRICK & MURRAY SEATTLE 61500

Signs like this one prohibit any electioneering within 300 feet of a polling place.

substantial funding, parties and candidates cannot reasonably make their appeals to the electorate. Money can also become too important and be used in ways that abuse and bias popular choice. In the United States, as in other democracies, there is a continuing argument over what arrangements need be made so that the important task of communicating with voters can proceed without certain special interests that have disproportionate access to funding gaining an improper advantage.

Until the 1970s, the law governing federal campaign financing in the U.S. was the Corrupt Practices Act of 1925. It set a statutory maximum of $25,000 for total expenditures in a U.S. Senate race and $10,000 for a House campaign. These spending limits were wholly unrealistic, and they were ignored. Finance reports were supposed to be filed with the clerk of the House or the secretary of the Senate, but enforcement of this requirement, too, was lax. In a message dealing with the campaign finance legislation, President Lyndon Johnson described it as "more loophole than law."

Corrupt Practices Act of 1925

Campaign finance reform. In the early 1970s, Congress finally enacted legislation that provided for more meaningful regulation of federal elections. In 1971, Congress adopted the Federal Election Campaign Act (FECA). This law required candidates and committees to file detailed, timely reports on who was financing their campaigns and how much they were spending. It also imposed limits on how much a candidate for federal office could spend on communications media. Also enacted in 1971 was a checkoff provision allowing taxpayers to contribute $1 each from their annual federal income tax payments to a general campaign fund to be divided among eligible presidential candidates.

Two and a half years later, Congress passed sweeping amendments to the FECA. These amendments set the first spending limits for presidential candidates, covering both the pre-nomination and general election phases of the campaign. They established new expenditure limits for congressional campaigns. And they provided public funding for presidential elections: Federal matching grants would cover half the cost of the pre-nomination part of the contests and all of the cost of the general election phase, within tight spending limits. Candidates could decide not to accept federal funds, in which case they would be exempt from the spending limits. A new independent body, the Federal Election Commission (FEC), was set up to oversee this program. The six FEC commissioners are now appointed by the president to serve staggered six-year terms; no more than three can be from any one political party.

Federal Election Campaign Act and the Federal Election Commission

The campaign contribution limits provided by the 1974 legislation (as subsequently amended) are shown in Table 14.2. Under these limits, an individual may contribute no more than $1,000 to any candidate or candidate's committee in a given election, $20,000 to a party's national committee in a calendar year, $5,000 to any other political

Table 14.2
Federal Campaign Contribution Limits

Contributor:	To each candidate or candidate committee per election	To national party committees per calendar year	To any other political committee per calendar year	Total contributions to federal candidates per calendar year
Individual	$1,000	$20,000	$5,000	$25,000
Multicandidate committee*	$5,000	$15,000	$5,000	No limit
Other political committee	$1,000	$20,000	$5,000	No limit
Republican or Democratic senatorial campaign committee, or the national party committee, or a combination of both	$17,500 to U.S. Senate candidate† during the year in which candidate seeks election	Not applicable	Not applicable	Not applicable

*A multicandidate committee is any political committee with more than 50 contributors which has been registered for at least six months and, with the exception of state party committees, has made contributions to five or more federal candidates.

†Limitation applies to either candidate for nomination or candidate for election to post of U.S. senator.

Source: Federal Election Commission, *Contributions,* March 1984; idem, *Federal Election Campaign Laws,* Jan. 1984, p. 49.

committee, and no more than $25,000 in all per year. This was to prevent the wealthy from making huge contributions that might "buy" special treatment or give them undue influence. Many observers think these limits are now too low.

Funding presidential contests. American presidential elections are now conducted with public funding. In the pre-convention stage, before the parties have picked their nominees, candidates are entitled to receive federal matching funds. To qualify, they must receive contributions of at least $5,000 from people in 20 or more states, with no single contribution exceeding $250. Once these provisions are met, federal funds are made available covering 50 percent of a candidate's total expenditures up to the prescribed limits. In 1984, this meant that a candidate could receive roughly $10 million in federal funds prior to the party conventions. During the general election campaign in 1984, both Reagan and Mondale were permitted to spend just over $40 million.

Candidates not of a major party who get at least 5 percent of the vote in the current presidential election are entitled, following the election, to receive federal funding in proportion to their share of the total vote cast. Their parties also qualify for federal support in the next election. In 1980, when Carter and Reagan each received $29.4 million in federal funds for the general election campaign, independent John Anderson was granted $4.2 million. He qualified because he gained 6.6 percent of the popular vote. Anderson's independent movement would have received federal finds in 1984 if it had chosen to enter a candidate.

Funding for presidential elections

In campaign financing outside the presidency, private sources remain predominant, although 19 states provide some public subsidies for state-level contests. There has been lively debate over the desirability of making federal funds available to congressional candidates. Bills have been introduced providing for public finance in races for the House and Senate, but they have foundered on partisan wrangling. The Republican party has developed a very effective, broadly based fund-raising effort on behalf of its congressional candidates, and it sees Democratic support of public funding and tight expenditure limits as an attempt to eliminate its advantage.

Funding for congressional elections

Loopholes in spending limits. Because money is such a critical factor in campaigning, candidates, parties, and interest groups often try to get around even the most tightly drawn spending regulations. Looking for loopholes is a well-established part of the game of politics. One successful exploitation of a loophole in the legislation covering presidential campaign spending prompted a heated exchange between Gary Hart and Walter Mondale during their contest for the 1984 Democratic nomination. At issue was the independence of committees formed by persons wanting to be elected delegates to the national nominating convention. The Federal Election Commission ruled in 1980 that such delegate committees could raise funds just like any other political committee, so long as they spent the funds only for specific sorts of grass-roots activities. The FEC failed, however, to resolve the issue of the extent to which these committees could cooperate with the presidential contender the delegates favored.

Not many delegate committees were formed in 1980, so no one paid much attention to the issue. But in 1984 more than 130 of them were formed in 23 states by delegate candidates who backed Walter Mondale. They expended sizable sums, most of the funds coming from labor union political action committees. Since their expenditures did not count against Mondale's $20.2 million spending limit for pre-convention campaigning, Gary Hart and his backers protested. They charged, for example, that Mondale staff assistants had in effect been shifted from the central campaign organization to the committees, raising "serious questions . . . on whether or not this is even in violation of the laws of the United States."[28] Mondale insisted that the committees were functioning within the law. They were autonomous bodies, he said, not subject to his control. But in an effort to defuse the issue, he agreed to shut down the committees and count all of their expenditures against his legal spending limit. Some of the committees refused to suspend their operations. Wrangling over the issue continued right up to the convention. One expert on campaign finance concluded that "there always seem to be new ways, not to evade the law, but to avoid the law. The Mondale delegate committees were

Delegate committees

---

[28] *National Journal*, May 5, 1984, pp. 873, 876; Hart on NBC "Meet the Press," April 22, 1984.

used as a means of obviating the overall limit for what the Mondale campaign could spend nationally. It was a legal . . . way of operating."[29]

Independent spending. A larger issue involves the expenditure of funds in campaign-related activities by groups independent of the parties and candidates. The Supreme Court ruled in *Buckley* v. *Valeo* (1976) that Congress could not prevent those who wished to endorse or oppose a candidate's election without first consulting him from doing so. This ruling struck down a provision of the 1974 campaign finance legislation that imposed a $1,000 ceiling on such independent expenditures. As a result, if an individual or committee not involved in the campaign of a candidate (who, for the purposes of this example, we will call Congressman Smithandjones) takes out a series of newspaper advertisements urging his election, without contacting Smithandjones or anyone in his camp, that constitutes an unrestricted independent expenditure. But if, before taking out the ads, the individual talked to Smithandjones' press secretary about them, the ads would be deemed an in-kind contribution to the Smithandjones campaign. No candidate may receive more than $1,000 in in-kind contributions during any given election.

Since the late 1970s the number of groups engaging in independent spending for and against candidates has grown enormously, as has the level of their expenditures. Conservative organizations outnumber liberal ones in this area. One of the largest of the independent spenders is the National Conservative Political Action Committee (NCPAC). NCPAC got a lot of attention in the 1980 elections when four of five liberal Democratic senators whom it spent funds to defeat lost their seats. Many observers think, however, that these Democratic defeats had more to do with Ronald Reagan's coattails than with any NCPAC accomplishment. And, in fact, in 1982 congressmen targeted by NCPAC for defeat actually enjoyed an almost unbroken string of political successes. "So-called negative expenditures—such as a television advertisement that attacks a candidate's record—have brought mixed results at best and often have caused headaches for the intended beneficiary."[30]

Independent spending in U.S. elections

Are campaigns too expensive? Spending in the 1980 elections, at all levels, has been placed at $1.2 billion (Table 14.3). According to this estimate, 23 percent of the total went for the presidential contest, 20 percent for congressional races, 22 percent for state and 17 percent for local offices, with the rest for referenda, administrative and independent expenditures, and the like.[31] Still untallied, expenditures in

[29] Herbert Alexander, as quoted by Robert Pear, "Delegate Groups Continue Mondale's Pledge," *New York Times,* May 28, 1984, p. 8.
[30] Maxwell Glen, "Independent Spenders Are Gearing Up, and Reagan and GOP Stand to Benefit," *National Journal,* December 17, 1983, p. 2627.
[31] Herbert Alexander, *Financing Politics: Money, Elections, and Political Reform,* 3d ed. (Washington, D.C.: Congressional Quarterly Press, 1984), p. 9.

Table 14.3
Campaign Spending in Presidential, Congressional, and Gubernatorial
Elections since 1976 (in millions of dollars)

Year	Presidential	Congressional	Gubernatorial*
1976	158.6	125.5	not available
1978		197.3	99.7
1980	309.0†	238.9	35.9
1982		343.9	192.3

*Most states have arranged gubernatorial elections so that no contests fall in presidential election years. Thus only 13 states held gubernatorial elections in 1980, while 36 held them in 1982.

†Campaign expenditures for independent presidential candidate John B. Anderson have been included.

Source: Citizens' Research Foundation, as reprinted in Herbert E. Alexander, *Financing Politics: Money, Elections, and Political Reform,* 2d ed. (Washington, D.C.: Congressional Quarterly Press, 1980); Citizens' Research Foundation and Thad L. Beyle, "The Cost of Becoming Governor," *State Government,* Summer 1983, as reprinted in Alexander, *Financing Politics,* 3d ed., 1984.

the 1984 elections were certainly much higher; campaign spending has been climbing faster than the rate of general price increases.

This level of spending can easily bring to mind images of candidates and groups "buying" elections. But what activity is more important to a democracy than the contests for elective office? Considering that Americans spent $1.2 billion in 1982 on outboard boats and motors, $2.2 billion on hair preparations, and $11 billion on cigarettes, we may not want to begrudge the fact that they spend something over a billion dollars on national election campaigns, an essential part of the democratic process. The overall level of campaign expenditures is not the problem.

Is one party advantaged? To the extent that there is a problem, it seems to come not from the sheer amount of spending but from the possibility that some interests are better financed than others. In partisan terms, Republicans were in the past much better financed than their Democratic opponents. With its close ties to business, the GOP found it easier to secure campaign contributions. But in the long years of Democratic ascendancy following the New Deal, many groups came to see that if they wanted recognition of their interests by government, they needed to "do business" with the majority Democrats. In recent elections, Democratic House and Senate candidates have held their own with their Republican opponents. Over the course of 1981 and 1982, for example, Democratic candidates for the House of Representatives actually outspent their Republican opponents, $103.1 to $100.6 million, according to Federal Election Commission data. On the Senate side, Democratic expenditures trailed the Republicans' only slightly, $66.9 to $71.1 million. Of the ten top Senate moneyraisers, five were Democrats, five Republicans. The party split was the same in the House.

In one area the GOP has achieved an enormous financial advantage: fund-raising by party committees. In the United States, as opposed to most other democracies, the bulk of campaign funds are raised not by political parties but by individual candidates. This weakens the American parties, of course, since candidates are not dependent on them for financial sustenance. Of late, though, Republicans have placed major emphasis on party fund-raising—by the Republican National Committee (RNC), the National Republican Congressional Committee (for House of Representatives contests), and the National Republican Senatorial Committee. Through imaginative planning and heavy emphasis on new fund-raising techniques, especially direct mail, these Republican bodies have achieved extraordinary success. Their Democratic counterparts are far behind and struggling to catch up. In 1983, for example, the RNC raised more than $35 million, roughly two-and-a-half times as much as the Democratic National Committee (DNC). This total is from a great number of small contributions; the RNC had an impressive list of 1.7 million donors in its computers at the end of 1983; average contributions were in the $25 to $30 range.

This major achievement in fund-raising has given the GOP a clear institutional advantage over the Democrats in the recruitment of candidates for the House and Senate, support of such candidates, and maintenance of party unity once the elections are over. If a candidate receives little or nothing from central party bodies in the course of his campaign, he is hardly likely to be very attentive to the party once he is elected. On the other hand, if he gets critical funding from the party, as Republican House and Senate candidates now do, he is likely after the election to be reminded of and to remember this fact.

Political action committees. As a result of the 1970s campaign finance legislation the role of **political action committees** (PACs) has expanded greatly. As we saw in chapter 13, PACs are organizations formed by business corporations, trade associations, labor unions, and the like, to raise and disburse funds to advance political objectives. The emergence of corporate and labor PACs followed a long period in which such activity was restricted by law. In 1907, the Tillman Act banned corporate gifts of money to candidates for federal elective office or to any committees which supported such candidates—which does not mean, of course, that the contributions actually stopped. The ban was incorporated into the Federal Corrupt Practices Act of 1925, which extended the prohibition to cover contributions of "anything of value." The Smith-Connally Act of 1943 and the Taft-Hartley Act of 1947 banned contributions to federal-office candidates by unions from their members' dues.

The Federal Election Campaign Act of 1971 introduced an important change in this area. Specifically, it permitted the use of corporate funds and union treasury money for "the establishment, administration, and solicitation of contributions to a separate, seg-

regated fund to be used for a political purpose." These funds have
become known as PACs. Under the law, an individual can give up to
$5,000 to a PAC. By 1984, 1,536 corporate PACs were registered with
the Federal Election Commission, along with 617 trade association
PACs, 378 representing labor unions, and about 1,000 more in assorted
other categories.

PACs contributed in 1981–82 more than $87 million to candidates
in federal election campaigns. In partisan terms the distribution of
these funds was fairly even: $47 million for Democrats and $40 million for Republicans. Corporate PACs favor Republicans, not surprisingly, while labor PACs give overwhelmingly to Democrats (Table 14.4).
The big bias in overall PAC contributions is in favor of incumbents—
reflecting a desire to keep on good terms with influential lawmakers.

*PACs and campaign
contributions*

Table 14.4
PAC Contributions (1981–82) to Federal Candidates (in millions of dollars)

Type of PAC	Candidate status			Party affiliation of recipient	
	Incumbent	Challenger	Open seat	Democrat	Republican
Corporation	$21.6	$ 3.8	$ 3.9	$10.1	$19.3
Trade/member/health	17.1	2.9	2.9	9.8	13.1
Labor organization	11.9	5.8	3.2	19.7	1.2
Non-connected	5.0	3.8	2.1	5.6	5.3
Other	2.7	.3	.4	2.0	1.3
Total	58.3	16.6	12.5	47.2	40.2

Source: Federal Election Commission, release of November 29, 1983, p. 2.

PAC dollars went to incumbents over their challengers by a margin of $58 million to $17 million in 1981–82. PAC contributions to individual candidates, however, are substantially restricted. No PAC can give a candidate more than $5,000 in any election.

Campaign Techniques and Technicians

Over the last quarter-century, changes in the technology of mass communications have transformed American electioneering. The biggest single factor, of course, is the increasing use of television: Candidates can reach far more people through television news coverage, political advertisements, and televised debates than through the most vigorous traditional campaigning. Still, most candidates are unfamiliar with television at the technical level; they don't know how to buy air time, how to schedule it most advantageously, or how to develop the most effective television appeals. The more they use television, and the more dimensions the medium offers (the spread of cable networks, for instance, has opened new possibilities) the more candidates must turn to media consultants. Technological change intrudes in other areas: The application of computers to direct-mail efforts has greatly enlarged the reach of political fund-raising. As we saw in chapter 12, polling has become a large part of the apparatus of modern campaigns. Each of these developments has introduced a new group of expert technicians to candidates' inner circles.

The role of campaign technicians

The implications of this shift to technicians trouble many observers. The growing corps of campaign consultants, fund-raisers, media experts, pollsters, and others seems to emphasize the means of electioneering more than the substance of governing. One critic, Larry Sabato, thinks that

> political consultants and the new campaign technology may well be producing a whole generation of officeholders far more skilled in the art of running for office than in the art of governing. Who can forget Robert Redford as a newly elected, media-produced U.S. senator at the end of the film *The Candidate* asking pathetically, "Now what do I do?"[32]

At the presidential level, the use of campaign technicians has progressed so far that candidates of both parties have given large roles to people with little connection to the parties and little experience in the substance of political life. In 1976, Patrick Caddell served as pollster to Democratic candidate Jimmy Carter, and by all accounts had a major influence on the Carter campaign. Caddell continued to be part of Carter's inner circle of advisers after Carter moved into the White House. Pollster Richard Wirthlin had a similar place in the 1980 and 1984 Reagan campaigns, and again the polling expert became an important presidential adviser. Wirthlin continued to help shape

[32] Larry J. Sabato, *The Rise of Political Consultants* (New York: Basic Books, 1981), p. 337.

what was now administration strategy. In the first 29 months of the Reagan administration, Wirthlin met 25 times with the president and delivered over 40 public-opinion studies to officials in the White House.[33] Republican Robert Teeter and Democrat Peter Hart are other pollsters who have assumed prominent campaign and political roles.

Media advisers are also key actors in the new corps of political technicians. David Garth has been media consultant to numerous candidates, including New York Mayor John Lindsey in 1969, New Jersey Governor Brendan Byrne in 1977, and New York Governor Hugh Carey in 1978. He assisted the Mondale campaign in 1984. Gerald Rafshoon, Charles Guggenheim, Douglas Bailey, and Robert Goodman are other media consultants who have attained national prominence.

This new generation of pollsters, consultants, and managers shows a clear bias toward the fields of public relations and marketing. As a result, the talk around candidates in both parties has become increasingly dominated by matters of technique. National issues are discussed primarily as they relate to electoral strategy. A more manipulative view of politics seems the inevitable result.[34]

The 1984 Race for President

Television is still a new political medium. The Eisenhower-Stevenson presidential contest in 1952 was the first to be affected by emissions of the cathode ray tube. The 1960 campaign between Kennedy and Nixon was the first to turn heavily on the new medium. But television has become enormously influential; it is now the dominant instrument for political communication.

Television and the 1984 campaign

For better or worse, the parties are increasingly asking their prospective nominees: "But can he or she really handle television well enough?" After his defeat in the 1984 presidential balloting, Democratic nominee Walter Mondale acknowledged that he had never been comfortable in front of television cameras, and that in the future his party would have to be less tolerant of this shortcoming in its candidates. Ironically it was the television virtuosity of Ronald Reagan (born in 1911, before radio—much less television—had appeared on the scene, and the oldest president in American history) that established beyond dispute the political primacy of the new medium. Over his first term Mr. Reagan electronically entered the living rooms of millions of American families on many occasions—and a large majority of the people liked what they saw. They liked it so much, in fact, that Mr. Reagan's presidency became what Congresswoman Pat Schroeder of Colorado christened "the Teflon presidency": bad news

---

[33] Richard S. Beal and Ronald H. Hinckley, "Presidential Decisionmaking and Opinion Polls," *The Annals* 472 (March 1984):72.

[34] See Everett C. Ladd, "A Better Way to Pick Our Presidents," *Fortune*, May 5, 1980, pp. 134–35.

just would not stick to it. The President's confidence, geniality, and down-to-earth manner were magnified by television.

Still, the importance of television and Ronald Reagan's personal appeal in deciding the outcome of Campaign '84 seems to have been exaggerated. Again and again during the 1984 campaign, commentators announced that Americans supported Reagan over Mondale even though they disagreed with him on many issues, that Mr. Reagan's lead was a triumph of television-magnified personality over policy. But Reagan's appeal and the course of the campaign in fact reflected voters' underlying views on the major issues, not just matters of personal style.

Issues enter into every presidential campaign in three forms. One involves immediate, specific policy questions, like (in 1984) whether to build the MX missile, how to respond to the turbulence and insurgency in Central America, and whether income tax rates should be indexed for cost-of-living increases. A second form involves assessments of how the country is doing—what political scientists call *valence issues.* There is no partisan dispute over the desirability of peace internationally and economic prosperity domestically. Sometimes these conditons are achieved; on other occasions they are not. Incumbent presidents seeking reelection are usually rewarded when valence issues, the nature of the times, are seen as generally favorable, and they are punished when valence issues are unfavorable.

Specific policy questions and valence issues

The third form issues take in campaigns involves the public's verdict on whether the overall direction of policy leadership offered by a president or his challenger is sound. In geometry the whole is precisely equal to the sum of its parts. In politics, it is much more than, and qualitatively different from, that sum. For example, in the 1936 election many voters disagreed the Franklin Roosevelt on specific issues. And they certainly were not delighted with the way things were going in the country: unemployment averaging around 17 percent and the GNP still far below what it had been before the Depression began in 1929. Nonetheless, a large majority of Americans felt that the overall direction the Roosevelt administration was giving to national policy was right—or at least preferable to that offered by the Republicans—and FDR was reelected by a record landslide. Roosevelt was personally popular, but the new direction he gave American public policy was also popular.

The direction of policy leadership

Throughout the 1984 campaign pollsters asked the public for their views on specific policies; the results demonstrated that the majority questioned a number of steps taken by the administration. The results also showed, however, that the public approved many of Reagan's stands. There are so many specific issues—on which Americans often have relatively little information, and to which they often assign relatively little weight in presidential voting, and around which they often have ambivalent feelings and contradictory desires—that it is

hard to know the precise final tally of Reagan approvals versus Mondale approvals.

The polls left little doubt, however, that a majority thought the incumbent administration had been moving the country generally in the right direction. Ronald Reagan was first elected in 1980 in large part because voters rejected the policy direction of the Carter administration as too weak and vascillating in foreign affairs and as unsure in its handling of the domestic economy, especially the problem of persisting high inflation. Voters also endorsed Reagan's call for greater restraint in the growth of government.

The 1984 presidential race saw a highly popular incumbent run for reelection when times were generally good. Economic news for many was so upbeat that, as one observer remarked, "It might have been written by the Republican National Committee." In addition, the country generally endorsed the direction the incumbent administration had been giving to national policy over the preceding four years. In this setting, the Democrats and their presidential nominee, Walter Mondale, faced a formidable challenge. It would do them no good to curse their misfortune in having to run in circumstances so favoring their Republican opponent. But the Democrats knew they had been dealt a bad hand and that the odds were against them.

The nomination of
Geraldine Ferraro

The boldest move that Walter Mondale took in seeking to reverse the almost preordained outcome was to select congresswoman Geraldine Ferraro of Queens, New York, as his vice-presidential running mate. Ferraro had received high marks for her intelligence and political judgment, but she had served only three terms in the House of Representatives and was not widely known to voters around the country. Mondale clearly hoped that Ferraro's candidacy would widen the gender gap, which many considered a main Reagan weakness, and would give him a chance for victory.

The gender gap first appeared in American national politics early in the 1980 election campaign. Pollsters noticed that Reagan ran less well among women than among men in trial heats with President Jimmy Carter. In the November balloting Reagan ran well ahead of Carter among men, but only split the vote evenly with the president among women. Over the next four years, Reagan's presidential approval ratings were consistently weaker among the majority of American women. The sources of this gender gap have been widely analyzed and debated; it is enough here to note that many observers had concluded by the summer of 1984 that Reagan was politically vulnerable among women. And many in the Democratic party and in the women's movement felt that it was time a woman be placed on the national ticket—something no major American political party had done.

Analyzing the
gender gap

The Ferraro nomination was historic and will undoubtedly be seen as an important act in the general strengthening of women's political role. But data indicate it had little impact on the 1984 vote. The gender gap remained what it had been in the presidential election four years earlier: clear and significant, but hardly overwhelming and certaily not decisive. The CBS News/*New York Times* exit poll of November 1980 showed Reagan backed by 47 percent of women and 55 percent of men in a three-way race; this same poll in November 1984 reported Reagan receiving 57 percent of women's votes compared to 61 percent of men's. The gap seems to have been greatest between college-educated men and women, and geographically between men and women in the Northeast; it was smallest—indeed, nonexistent— among the elderly, high-school graduates, and men and women living in the South (Table 14.5). Most important is the fact that Reagan ran virtually even with Mondale among those groups of women least supportive of him, while he defeated Mondale soundly among the most pro-Republican women. The gender gap never came close to turning things around for Walter Mondale's troubled candidacy.

The Democrats' next big hope was the presidential debates. Since the first televised debates—or, as some would call them, joint press conferences— in 1960 between John F. Kennedy and Richard Nixon, the combination of massive audiences and hand-to-hand combat had

Table 14.5
The Gender Gap in Presidential Voting, 1984 (in percent)

	Reagan	Mondale
All women	57	42
All men	61	37

	Women		Men	
	Reagan	Mondale	Reagan	Mondale
By age:				
18–29	55	45	61	37
30–44	54	46	62	37
45–59	58	41	63	36
60	64	35	62	37
By region:				
Northeast	47	52	57	42
Midwest	59	41	63	35
West	57	42	62	37
South	63	36	64	36
By education:				
Less than high school	46	52	54	46
High-school graduate	60	39	61	38
With some college	58	41	63	36
College graduate	53	47	65	34

Source: Exit poll conducted by CBS News/*New York Times*, November 6, 1984.

The presidential debates

established these confrontations as a critical part of contemporary presidency campaigning. Could Mondale rescue his faltering candidacy by besting Reagan *mano a mano?* It would not be enough, Mondale adviser Patrick Caddell wrote in a memo to his principal, for Mondale to simply outpoint the president—Reagan's support was too widespread and strong for that. "The overriding objective . . . must be to 'break' Reagan—hurting him on age, on his lack of knowledge, on his grasp of issues. Mondale must not simply beat Reagan, he must take him apart."[35]

The first debate, held in Louisville, Kentucky, on October 7, 1984, went much as Mondale partisans had hoped. Mr. Reagan seemed more halting, less confident, less in command of his major themes than most observers had expected. Mr. Mondale, in contrast, was in top form. Suddenly the age issue surfaced: At 73 years, was Ronald Reagan at last showing his age? Polls indicate that the age issue never became an overriding concern of the general public, despite its domination of press commentary for a week following the first debate. But some people, including Reagan backers, were concerned.

[35] As quoted in "Campaign '84: The Inside Story," *Newsweek*, November/December 1984, p. 108.

The issue of
Reagan's age

The issue of age formed the backdrop for the second debate, held in Kansas City, Missouri, on October 21. One of the media consultants helping the President prepare for the second confrontation, Roger Ailes, raised the issue with him directly:

> "Mr. President, he said screwing up his courage, "one of those reporters might want to make a name for himself and ask you the age question." "What do you mean?" Reagan asked. He seemed surprised. "For the last 10 days, you've been pounded that you are too old for this job." The president stood silent for a moment, withdrawn into himself. Ailes was beginning to be sorry he had brought the whole thing up. Then the Reagan smile returned. "I can handle that," he said.[36]

Apparently no one but Mr. Reagan knew what his response would be until he and Mr. Mondale actually squared off: "I want you to know," Reagan said, "that I will not make age an issue of this campaign. I am not going to exploit for political purposes my opponent's youth and inexperience." The election was over.

Actually, a majority of Americans had already decided they wanted to reelect Mr. Reagan, but they needed to be reassured that he was still fully in command. They got that reassurance. On Tuesday, November 6, 1984, in the fiftieth presidential election in American history, voters returned Ronald Reagan to office for a second term by a massive popular vote margin of 59 percent to 41 percent. Walter Mondale carried the electoral votes of only his native Minnesota and the District of Columbia. In strict percentage terms Reagan's margin in 1984 fell slightly below Nixon's in 1972 and Johnson's in 1964. But Johnson and Nixon were running against candidates who were out of the mainstream of their respective parties. In contrast, Reagan confronted a centrist Democrat of ability and experience, who ran an energetic and intelligent campaign, and who was backed enthusiastically by the leaders of every major group in his party's historic alignment. Reagan's margin over Mondale of 18 percentage points was notably impressive.

Early polls indicate
final outcome

Apart from the margin of victory, perhaps the most striking feature of Campaign '84 was how early it was decided. Noting that Reagan's final vote margin was almost exactly what his margin had been in their opinion poll taken ten months earlier, the *New York Times'* editors suggested: "It's possible . . . that everything that happened in between was just a digression. The voters . . . made up their minds a long time ago."[37] The exit poll taken by the *Los Angeles Times* on November 6 confirmed this. An extraordinary 47 percent of those interviewed as they left the polls said they had reached a vote decision sometime *before* the first primaries in February, and another 21 percent had decided before September. These early deciders broke two-to-one for Reagan (Table 14.6).

[36] Ibid., p. 109.
[37] "And Still Champion," *New York Times* editorial of November 7, 1984.

Table 14.6
When Voters Decided on the 1984 Presidential Candidates (in percent)

"How long ago did you finally decide for whom you would vote?"

Today (November 6, Election Day)	4
Over the weekend	2
Last week	3
After the presidential debates two weeks ago	13
During the campaign in September	10
During the conventions in July and August	12
During the primaries from February to June	9
Before then	47

How people voted and when they decided

	Reagan	Mondale
Today (November 6, Election Day)	48	52
Over the weekend	45	55
Last week	55	45
After the presidential debates two weeks ago	43	57
During the campaign in September	53	47
During the conventions in July and August	51	49
During the primaries from February to June	62	38
Before then	63	32

Source: Exit poll conducted by the *Los Angeles Times* November 6, 1984.

SUMMARY

Universal suffrage was not achieved in the eighteenth or nineteenth centuries in the United States or any other country. Most American states dropped property qualifications for voting in the early 1800s, but many of them did not permit women to vote until ratification of the Nineteenth Amendment in 1920. Full voting participation by blacks was not realized until the civil rights legislation of the 1960s.

Today there is concern over the low and somewhat diminished level of voter turnout in the United States. Just 57 percent of voting-age residents cast ballots in the 1984 presidential election; this represented a rise of three percentage points over the 1980 voting rate, but it was still five percentage points below the turnout in 1960.

The curious way the United States expresses its rate of voter participation—as a percentage of the resident adult population, even though millions of these residents by law cannot vote—makes turnout seem lower than it really is. But it is lower than in most other democracies. This is partly because the United States has so many elections that it is hard for any one to seem a special event. The low turnout is also partly a response to a system where political stresses have been relatively manageable. The perceived cost of not voting, in short, has not been nearly as high in the United States as in most other democracies.

Voter turnout has been lower in the twentieth century than in the nineteenth, although not as much lower as statistics suggest. The weakening of political parties as institutions and the increasing distance and complexity of government have probably been major factors accounting for the drop-off in voting. Frustration bred of the experience in Vietnam and Watergate, and other political difficulties of the 1960s and 1970s, also seems to have contributed to the decline.

Two features of American electoral arrangements are especially distinguishing. One is the heavy use of primary elections to pick party nominees. The other is the reliance on the single member district, single ballot, simple majority system for translating votes into seats. This system has done much to bolster the ascendancy of the two major parties. If the U.S. instituted plural-member districts with proportional representation, it is likely that third parties would proliferate.

The number of elections held in the United States and the duration of campaigns have put a premium on political fundraising. Over the last two decades campaign costs have climbed much faster than inflation alone would have required. Television has become an increasingly important campaign resource or facility. Total election expenditures, at all levels, were placed at $1.2 billion in 1980, and as yet untallied precisely, they were higher still in 1984.

Important federal legislation covering campaign spending was enacted in 1971 and 1974. Limits were imposed on how much individuals and groups could contribute to federal candidates. Effective disclosure provisions were instituted, to be administered by the Federal Election Commission (FEC). Public funding was established for presidential elections, along with tight spending limits for candidates who accept governmental assistance.

The legislation also encouraged the formation of political action committees (PACs) by business corporations, trade associations, labor unions, and other groups, to collect and disseminate funds for political purposes. Though tightly supervised by the FEC, PACs have become the hub of current contention over money in politics. In their contributions to federal office seekers, PACs split fairly evenly between Democrats and Republicans. PACs give much more support, however, to incumbents of both parties than to challengers.

15 | Political Parties

"No America without democracy, no democracy without politics, no politics without parties, no parties without compromise and moderation."[1] Clinton Rossiter thought that most Americans would find the first of these propositions unexceptionable, but that they might take issue with the other three. "For a people that invented the modern political party, we have been strangely reluctant to take pride in our handiwork."

Political parties are in fact essential institutions in American democratic life, and the centrality of their role is sometimes insufficiently understood and appreciated. Though the Constitution does not mention parties or make any provision for them, a party system began to develop within a decade after the Constitution's ratification. Parties have been at the core of the process of representative government ever since. Every democratic country in the world has a fully formed and active party system—a condition which, if it does not necessarily prove that democracy cannot be conducted in the absence of parties, at least indicates that nowhere does it exist without them.

We will first examine the conditions and political needs that gave birth to parties in the late eighteenth and early nineteenth centuries in America. We discuss the features that distinguish the U.S. party system, compared to those of other countries. The composition of present-day Democratic and Republican coalitions, and changes occurring in partisan alignments, are then taken up. The chapter concludes with a review of recent efforts at party reform centering on the selection of presidential nominees.

---

[1] Clinton Rossiter, *Parties and Politics in America* (Ithaca, N.Y.: Cornell University Press, 1960), p. 1.

Party workers, campaign 1984.

THE BIRTH OF POLITICAL PARTIES

The American party system is the oldest in the world, fast approaching its second centennial. In the late 1790s, when parties took shape in the United States and began a struggle for control of government in popular election contests, their architects had no blueprints to follow. A new political institution was being established. Less than two hundred years later, political parties are found throughout the world.

Social Prerequisites

In the sweep of governmental experience, parties are very young institutions. They became necessary only after the revolutionary changes that gripped Western societies in the seventeenth and eighteenth centuries, and that dominated American origins: the collapse of aristocratic society; the extension of social and political egalitarianism; and the development of political ideologies, especially classical liberalism, that assigned the individual a far more elevated position than he had ever enjoyed.

Political parties are the children of egalitarianism. They appeared as a necessary institutional response to the idea of popular sovereignty, to the belief that the rank-and-file citizen should have final authority in the business of governing. In pre-egalitarian societies small groups of citizens organized to influence the affairs of state through cabals, cliques, and factions. The egalitarian revolution of the seventeenth and eighteenth centuries gave legitimacy to the idea that the entire public should be considered and consulted.

Once the notion of popular sovereignty took hold, political parties evolved rapidly. They set up organizations among the populace and linked up local units with national leadership—for example, with party officials in the legislature. They provided common political identities for elites and the rank-and-file, promoting popular cohesion for and against contrasting philosophies of government. They put flesh on the skeletal idea of representation.

Edmund Burke and the Early Argument over Parties

National interests and the need for strong parties

Parties did not emerge without a struggle. For some time after the first stirrings of egalitarianism in the seventeenth century, philosophers and politicians had trouble conceiving a permanent and legitimate role for political parties. To those like the English leader and political theorist Henry St. John, Viscount Bolingbroke, parties were "a political evil,"[2] institutions of a dangerous and untried democracy. They would represent special interests against the national interest. They would break a nation into parts, involving it in endless squabbles, blocking the pursuit of the common good.

Prior to the nineteenth century, only one theorist raised and defended the idea of political parties as essential instruments of the emerging representative government: the great British politician and philosopher Edmund Burke (1729–97). It is testimony to Burke's genius that he developed the case for a mature party system long before one came to exist. The proper question, as Burke saw it, was how the various interests in the country could be organized so as to determine policy. His answer was through political parties. "Party is a body of men united, for promoting by their joint endeavors the national interest, upon some particular principle in which they are all agreed."[3] He recognized that there would be different and competing ideas of how best to serve the national interest; all would inevitably prove futile unless their proponents organized for effective action. Once organized, political parties would become the necessary great connection between groups of citizens and governmental institutions.

[2] Henry Saint-John Bolingbroke, *A Dissertation Upon Parties*, in *The Works of Lord Bolingbroke*, vol. 2 (Philadelphia: Carey and Hart, 1841). The *Dissertation* was first published in England in 1733.
[3] Edmund Burke, *Thoughts on the Cause of the Present Discontents*, in *The Works of Edmund Burke*, vol. 2 (London: Rivington, 1815): 335. *Thoughts* was written in 1770.

In a connexion the most inconsiderable man, by adding to the weight of the whole, has his value, and his use; out of it, the greatest talents are wholly unserviceable to the publick. No man, who is not inflammed by vain-glory into enthusiasm, can flatter himself that his single, unsupported, desultory, unsystematik endeavours, are of power to defeat the subtle designs and united cabals of ambitious citizens. When bad men combine, the good must associate; else they will fall, one by one, an unpitied sacrifice in a contemptible struggle.[4]

The case for party
allegiance

Although parties as we know them did not yet exist, Burke was already what we would call a "strong party man." He believed that political figures should assess the various issues, decide which political group they would side with in order to advance a shared view of the public interest, and then give their party sustained support. Burke was not sympathetic to the argument that continuing support for a party requires a politician to subordinate the claims of his own conscience. What is incumbent upon a politician in a representative government, he insisted, is the thoughtful choice of a party whose "leading general principles in government" he can support. When an issue arises which is not of great moment, he should go along with his party, even if he happens to disagree with it. Only rarely, Burke thought, will a politician be required by deep conviction to separate himself from a party whose general goals he shares.

Development of Parties in the United States

Burke's insights into the necessary place of parties in representative governments were not readily accepted. Here in the United States, where parties first matured, James Madison did not contemplate a place for them in the constitutional order. Madison did recognize the place of interest groups or factions, but he did not foresee an essential representative role for parties. George Washington's vision also was limited to an idea of special-interest-serving factions, which he considered a necessary evil as the by-product of liberty. In his farewell address in 1796 Washington warned "in the most solemn manner against the harmful effects of the spirit of party."

Thomas Jefferson and
political parties

Thomas Jefferson had similar views, even though he was the architect of one of the world's first full-fledged parties: the Republicans, later called Democratic-Republicans, and eventually called the Democrats. The alliance Jefferson put together is the direct ancestor of the present-day Democratic party. But he considered parties troublesome enterprises, not great intruments for extending democracy. While president in 1804, Jefferson wrote William Short that

the party division in this country is certainly not among its pleasant features. To a certain degree it will always exist: and chiefly in mercantile places. In the country and those states where the Republicans have a decided superiority, party hostility has ceased to infest society.

[4]Ibid., p. 330.

Thomas Jefferson's banner slams his opponent with the phrase, "John Adams is no more."

He lamented that, while he had been quite prepared to offer his partisan opponents a few minor places in his government if they would cease to be an opposition force, they had spurned this! Even among the most prescient of Americans of the day, there was no real picture of parties as regular, necessary instruments through which the divergent views of the public are organized and expressed in an egalitarian polity.

Still, if Americans were uncertain as to the purpose of political parties, they nonetheless went ahead rapidly building them. The first stirrings of party were in the policy conflict between Hamilton and Jefferson in Washington's administration, a division which was part of a much broader argument over public policy in the new regime. As the dispute deepened, Hamilton turned to his friends in Congress, Jefferson to his—one result being that factional ties between executive and legislative leaders became much tighter. Hamilton's group took a name that raised memories of the successful fight for the Constitution: the Federalists. At this time the Jeffersonians called themselves the Republicans.

The incipient parties arose from divisions in national, rather than state, politics.[5] Thus party lines became clear in national politics before they did in state contests. The Republican party of Jefferson made its first organized efforts by endorsing candidates for Congress and for presidential electors; party tickets for state legislatures and other state offices came later.

The birth of
American parties

[5] For an excellent description, see Noble E. Cunningham, Jr., *The Jeffersonian Republicans* (Chapel Hill, N.C.: University of North Carolina Press, 1957).

By what date were Federalists and Republicans competing in a fairly sustained manner for support among a mass electorate, offering their symbols, the party labels, for the electorate to rally around? Estimates vary. One expert thinks that "we may speak of a Federalist party proper by the late months of 1793 and the early months of 1794."[6] The outlines of opposing factions in Congress were clear by then, but these dates are a bit early if one uses the criteria of constituency organization, party tickets, and the regular use of the party symbol. In 1796, for example, candidates for Congress in most states ran without any reference to party labels. But by the end of John Adams' administration in 1801, parties in the modern sense were definitely on the scene.

Early development of parties

Constituency organization first appeared in the Middle Atlantic states, especially Pennsylvania and New York. The earliest organization commonly involved "committees of correspondence": A committee of state party notables would contact influential citizens throughout the state, asking them in turn to call meetings of "our friends in your town." Republicans tended to take the initiative in introducing party machinery, but Federalists followed soon after with similar structures. Washington's leaving the presidency in 1797 was an important spur to party organization and activity, because, instead of an administration much revered and "above party," the succeeding Adams presidency was a convenient target for Jeffersonian scorn. The election of 1800 saw dramatic extensions of party organization, and diligent Republican organizational activity in support of Jefferson clearly contributed to his victory.

Early party organization

A Core Democratic Function

Political parties sprang up so quickly because they were needed to link the people to government in the first egalitarian society. They aggregated the preferences of the public for political leadership and policy choice, and converted what was incoherent and diffuse to specific, responsive public decisions. There are three distinct but closely interrelated parts to this basic function.

Representation. The potential electorate in the United States (citizens of voting age) now numbers over 150 million. It is no small task to get candidates and programs that reflect the preferences of so large and diverse a public. Effective representation is achieved when government translates popular preferences into programs, and the public concludes that government is generally responsive to its wishes. Representation, then, requires a number of things that only parties can do: building coalitions and articulating policies that meet coalitions' needs, finding popular and effective candidates to win office and implement the policies, and offering alternative candidates to

[6] William Nisbet Chambers, *Political Parties in a New Nation* (New York: Oxford University Press, 1963), p. 50.

Unlike party candidates in other Western nations who represent specific groups, the Democratic and Republican parties and their presidential candidates, here, Ronald Reagan (left) and Walter Mondale (right), often seek the support from the same groups.

those in power, so that when popular majorities are dissatisfied with governmental performance, they have somewhere to turn.

Popular control. Political parties are also necessary to enable citizens to control their government and ensure the responsiveness of public institutions. There are so many different elective offices in a country like the United States that citizens cannot consider their votes meaningful in controlling policy unless the many separate election contests are linked in some understandable fashion: for instance, balloting for the national legislature can be seen as a competition of one party against another, rather than as the unrelated competition of individuals.

Beyond this, only parties are in a position to so organize policy choices that mass publics can make judgments on them. Parties provide the "conduit or sluice by which the waters of social thought and discussion are brought to the wheels of political machinery and set to turn those wheels," as Ernest Barker once put it.[7] When they make elected officials in some sense collectively, rather than individually, responsible to the electorate, parties expand the level of meaningful popular control.

[7] Ernest Barker, *Reflections on Government* (New York: Oxford University Press, 1958, first published in 1942), p. 39.

Integration. In 1950, a committee of the American Political Science Association issued a report detailing the special responsibilities of political parties and calling for their strengthening.[8] In particular, this report stressed the parties' role in providing for "more effective formulation of general policies and programs and for better integration of all of the far-flung activities of modern government." The report noted that, because of the incredible complexity of contemporary government, it has so many different parts responsive to so many different interests that the natural centrifugal pressures are sometimes almost irresistible. Party is the one acceptable counteracting, centripetal force. Governmental integration is especially demanding in the United States, because of the extreme dispersion of authority resulting from federalism and the separation of powers. In such a system, coherence in policy simply cannot be obtained unless parties are available for bridging governmental divisions, for example, by bringing together officials in the executive and legislative branches through common partisan ties and commitments.

Parties in Nondemocratic Countries

Parties also exist in countries such as Russia and China that are in no sense representative democracies. They perform functions that even totalitarian systems find important. Political parties operate in all societies based on the premise that rank-and-file citizens need to be taken into account in the operations of government; they have come into being whenever there is need for an institution that links leadership to the general public. In a democracy, power tends to flow up over the links of party, allowing rank-and-file citizens to participate more effectively in selecting leaders and in passing judgment on their performance. In a totalitarian state such as the U.S.S.R., the flow of power is primarily, although not exclusively, downward. The single party, the totalitarian mass party, controls the institutions of government, brooking no dissent or rival political force. This type of party exists to permit a ruling elite to persuade and educate, mobilize public opinion, communicate decisions which it has taken, keep tabs on an enormously complex system, and achieve central direction over lower levels of administration.[9]

CHARACTERISTICS OF THE AMERICAN PARTY SYSTEM

Even among democracies there is considerable variety in party arrangements. A distinctively American party system evolved early in the nineteenth century; to a striking degree, it has persisted.

---

[8] *Toward a More Responsible Two-Party System,* a report of the Committee on Political Parties of the American Political Science Association (New York: Rinehart, 1950).
[9] See Maurice Duverger, *Political Parties,* 2d English ed. (London: Methuen, 1959), p. 122.

A Two-Party System

By the time Democrats and Whigs grappled for power in the 1830s, a two-party system was securely in place. In most of the major election contests, and above all in those for president, only Whigs or Democrats won. Today, Democrats and Republicans similarly dominate the contests for elective office.

Uniqueness of America's two-party system

Such a "bi-partism" is rarely encountered outside the United States. Giovanni Sartori notes that by a strict standard for inclusion into the "club" of two-party systems, including the requirement that two-party domination persist over an extended span of time, only three countries qualify: the United States, Great Britain, and New Zealand. And even Britain's inclusion must be challenged. While one of two parties, Conservative and Labour, has formed every British government in the last half-century, a third historically important party, the Liberals, has often received substantial public support. And in 1981 a new party, the Social Democrats (SDP), was formed by disaffected Labour party leaders. The alliance of the SDP and the Liberals now has the backing of about one-fourth of the British electorate. "We are seemingly approaching the paradox of having the most celebrated type of party system running out of cases."[10]

Most democracies operate with some type of multi-party system, in which at least three and often many more parties regularly draw substantial support. Even in Canada, where two parties—the Liberals and the Progressive Conservatives—have dominated federal governments, other parties have contested vigorously and often successfully for control of the provincial governments.

Why a two-party system?

As we saw in chapter 14, one reason for America's continuing attachment to this rare type of party competition is that our electoral arrangements impose severe handicaps on third-party challengers. Especially influential is the election of most candidates by the single-member district, simple-majority system. In each district one party's candidate wins the seat. The party that comes in second can argue plausibly that it is the realistic alternative for all those dissatisfied with the winner. Other parties are vulnerable to the charge that a vote for them is simply wasted. Another important reason why two parties have dominated contests for elective office throughout U.S. history is the fact of a highly consensual society distinguished by minimal ideological disagreements. As we noted in chapter 4, classical liberalism has enjoyed preeminence in American thought from the country's inception. The absence of competing ideological traditions has prevented parties representing different perspectives, such as the socialists, from finding a firm base on which to build. There has been insufficient ideological room in which to establish third and fourth parties, especially since electoral mechanics have made it hard for such challengers to operate.

[10] Sartori, *Parties and Party Systems*, p. 185.

Obstacles to
third-party
formation

The unusual success American society has enjoyed has also held back third-party challenges. The national wealth of the United States, unsurpassed by any other country for at least a century and a half, together with a high degree of social mobility and a sense that opportunity for advancement is present, have strengthened American political and economic institutions and blunted the protests that almost certainly would have been stronger otherwise. The United States has not lacked political parties bred of protest, but protest parties have found it hard to generate a broad appeal. As socialist thinker Werner Sombart remarked of the socialists' experience in America, it has "come to grief on roast beef and apple pie."[11]

Protests over racial and other ethnocultural changes have sometimes nourished third-party protests. In the 1850s the American party, popularly called the "Know-Nothings," built a politically strong appeal on anti-Catholic and anti-immigrant sentiment. In 1968, George Wallace's American Independent candidacy won 13 percent of the presidential vote on white dissatisfaction with the civil rights movement and the course of racial change. But these parties of ethnic protest have not been able to sustain themselves.

Parties of Accommodation

The extraordinary continuity evident in the persistence of a two-party system is also seen in the pragmatic cast of American party competition and the weakness of exclusive ideological appeals. The major parties of a century and a half ago were not doctrinal or even strongly programmatic, and neither are their counterparts today. "Tweedledum and Tweedledee", some have called the two big U.S. parties. In one sense this depiction is inaccurate, for there have always been important policy differences between the parties. But the differences have not had the magnitude of doctrinal fissures. Though today we talk about a more "liberal" Democratic party aligned against a more "conservative" Republican party, Democrats and Republicans share much of the American ideological inheritance. In their pursuit of majority support in a nation not sharply polarized ideologically, the two parties have had to make broad appeals, and they have attracted adherents across the political spectrum.

Heterogeneous
party coalitions

This heterogeneous character of party coalitions has encouraged the parties to practice a politics of accommodation. American parties have been "creatures of compromise . . . vast, gaudy, friendly umbrellas under which all Americans, whoever and wherever and however minded they may be, are invited to stand for the sake of being counted in the next election."[12] This contrasts sharply with the experience in

[11] Werner Sombart, "American Capitalism's Economic Rewards," in J. H. M. Laslett and S. M. Lipset, eds., *Failure of a Dream? Essays in the History of American Socialism* (Garden City, N.Y.: Anchor Books, 1974), p. 599.
[12] Rossiter, *Parties and Politics in America*, p. 11.

"ACTUALLY, THEY REMIND ME OF THE CHOICE BETWEEN THE REPUBLICANS AND DEMOCRATS THIS YEAR."

many European countries where parties have often considered it unnatural, and in a sense even undesirable, for certain social groups to find them attractive. The British Labour party, for example, really doesn't expect or want backing from the country's business establishment.

There are few places in the United States where the Democrats and Republicans do not work actively to secure the votes of virtually all identifiable interests and groups. On occasion, one party will be weak within a particular group—as the Republicans are among black Americans today. Ninety percent of black voters have regularly backed the Democrats in elections over the last 20 years, and Democrats outnumber Republicans among blacks in party identification by roughly 9 to 1. Because this condition challenges the tradition of broad-appeal accommodation politics, it is seen as a distinct liability both by the GOP and by most neutral observers, for it suggests that the GOP is not fully open to all ethnic groups in the society.

Although the major American parties have not always successfully appealed to every group, our accommodationist two-party system has unquestionably encouraged a broadening of appeals and punished failures to do so. The typical range of both Democratic and Republican support within various social groups has been between the 40 and 60 percent marks; a party's support from a given group is considered seriously weak when it falls below 40 percent.

Loose and Undemanding Alliances

Throughout U.S. history the two major parties have not required very much of either their rank-and-file supporters or the elected officials who bear their names. In this regard, American parties are the opposite of the intensely organized and disciplined Communist parties where the latter control the government, as in the Soviet Union, or where they are in seemingly permanent opposition, as in France and Italy.

Party membership. A citizen's ties to an American party are rarely formal. The Democrats and the Republicans don't have regularly enrolled, card-carrying and dues-paying members. There are no "official formalities" for admission, "no precise criteria of membership."[13] A voter becomes a Republican or a Democrat by a simple declaration, and he assumes no responsibilities when he makes that declaration. To participate in primary elections for selecting a party's candidates, a voter has at most to declare his affiliation at some specified time prior to the primary, and he may change his affiliation as he wishes. In primary elections in some states, he may even cast his vote in the selection of Republican or Democratic candidates without ever disclosing which party he prefers. These are called **open primaries.** Associating with a party is strictly and exclusively a matter of individual self-expression. "An American party," Clinton Rossiter wrote,

> is not an army, not a church, not a way of life, not even a lodge. It asks nothing of one of its adherents but his vote, a few dollars, and, if he seems willing, a few hours of his time for manning the polls, licking stamps, and ringing doorbells; and it would settle willingly for a sure vote.[14]

Undisciplined elites. Americans parties are also undemanding of the leaders who operate under their standards. The Democratic and Republican parties in the national and state government are undisciplined and lacking in internal cohesion by comparison to governmental parties in most other democracies. In the U.S. Congress, Democrats vote together against Republicans only rarely: just on organizing the House and Senate, as in the election of the Speaker of the House. Otherwise, as we saw in chapter 7, in the passage of legislation on issues large and small the parties split, with some Democrats and some Republicans voting together to form a majority, and others, the minority. In 1983, on average in contested votes, 76 percent of congressional Democrats were on one side of a question while 24 percent were on the other side. No other democracy has this degree of undiscipline among party members in the legislature.

One reason for this lack of discipline and cohesion is the unusual separation of the executive and legislature in the United States. In most democracies, as we have seen, the executive—the prime minister and the cabinet—are members of the legislature and hold office because the assembly majority supports them. In Great Britain, Prime Minister Margaret Thatcher and her cabinet are in power because the

Separation of powers and the lack of party cohesion

[13] Duverger, *Political Parties*, pp. 63–65.
[14] Rossiter, *Parties and Politics in America*, p. 25.

Conservative party has a majority in the House of Commons and that majority backs the Thatcher government. Were Conservative Members of Parliament (MPs) to cross party lines and vote with the opposition Labourites, they would be declaring "no confidence" in the Thatcher government and would remove it from office. This structure requires that party members vote together. In the American system of separation of powers, the president holds office for a fixed term independent of Congress, and Congress is elected and holds office independent of the president. A Republican member of the House of Representatives can vote against programs proposed by a Republican president as frequently as he likes without jeopardizing the government's continuation in office.

Decentralization of power

The pronounced decentralization of power in the American parties is another source of their incohesion. Congressional Republicans and Democrats hold office not because of the blessings and assistance of national party leaders, but because of the work they and their supporters have done in the districts they represent. Successful congressional candidates of both parties "did not rise through disciplined organizations," and thus "they are individualists from the beginning of their political careers. As candidates they were self-selected, self-organized, self-propelled, self-reliant. . . ."[15]

Tradition of independence

A final important source of the lack of discipline and incohesion of the Democratic and Republican governmental parties is *tradition*. In most party systems, for a member of the legislature to go against his party is to betray it. The American tradition is very different. From the earliest party experience in this country, voting independently, and not being "beholden to party bosses," have been considered virtues. Few American congressmen have ever lost their seats because they developed reputations for "flinty independence."

With power so fractured and dispersed among state and local parties and candidates, it is inevitable that officeholders will frequently cross party lines. This is true whether the spur is principle or expediency: whether the officeholder thinks good judgment requires him to vote against his party or whether good politics ordains it.

Weak Party Organizations

In American political folklore, the activities of strong party organizations or "machines" are both celebrated and condemned. Such political figures as E. H. "Boss" Crump, who headed the Democratic machine in Memphis from 1932 to 1948, and Richard Daley, who led the strong Democratic organization in Chicago for a quarter-century until his death in 1976, are among the legendary party "bosses." They dominated the machinery of their political parties and maintained strangleholds on almost all aspects of the political life of their cities.

[15] James Sundquist, "The Crisis of Competence in Our National Government," *Political Science Quarterly* (Summer 1980), p. 198.

Strong party organizations have indeed existed at various times in different parts of the U.S., especially in big cities when large numbers of immigrants were arriving. These party machines provided services to the newcomers, helping them find jobs and assisting them in bringing their problems to government agencies. In turn, the parties could count on followings which would loyally back their candidates. But muscular party organizations have been the exception in the United States, not the rule. The strong current of political individualism throughout American culture generates resentment of strong party leadership. Our very vocabulary attests to this: disciplined organizations are referred to as "machines" and their leaders depicted as undemocratic "bosses."

Distrust of strong party organizations

Mechanisms have been established to strengthen the hand of individual citizens vis-à-vis party bodies. The most dramatic case is *nominee selection*. In most democracies party leaders determine the party candidates. In the United States rank-and-file voters select the nominees through primary elections. As we saw in chapter 14, no other country approaches the United States in the degree to which rank-and-file party adherents control the nominee selection process. Primaries were established during the Progressive era early in this century. In their insistence that nominations be controlled by the voters rather than by party officials, the Progressives had great success, because they appealed to the culture's distinctive individualism. Americans insist on their individual right to determine electoral outcomes, on *their* right, not that of party machines, to control the nomination process.

Primaries and nominee selection

"Grass roots" groups in the United States carry local and national issues to the party candidates.

Party organization in
other democracies

"Let the people, not the bosses, pick the candidates" seems to most Americans a natural position. But in other democracies no comparable perspective obtains. In Japan party candidates are chosen by the party hierarchy. Choosing candidates through primary elections has no appeal to most Japanese voters. In Great Britain, France, and West Germany as well, control of nominations is thought by most voters to be properly a party organization affair. That the leadership of American party organizations does not determine nominees has meant that American parties are organizationally weaker than their counterparts in other democracies. Prospective nominees take their case directly to the voters; party officials have few sanctions over them. The Democrats and Republicans reflect durable loyalties; they have managed to hold their dominant place in electoral competition since the 1860s. Yet as organizations they are weak and undisciplined compared to most other major democratic parties.

PARTY COALITIONS

Much of the attention given to American political parties centers not on their institutional characteristics and performance, but on their standing within the electorate. Which social groups back which party? Are substantial changes in group loyalties taking place? Is one party gaining electoral strength at the expense of the other?

The New Deal
realignment

In the late 1920s and early 1930s, the existing party coalitions were transformed in what is known as the New Deal realignment. The severity of the Great Depression made large numbers of Americans receptive to new governmental initiatives. Under the leadership of President Franklin Roosevelt, the Democrats fashioned a new approach that won widespread, if far from unanimous, backing—and their ranks swelled. In 1929 the Republicans had been the national majority party; but by 1936 the Democrats had pushed them decisively into the minority. In 1929 the Republicans had spoken for an old reigning public philosophy; but by 1936 a new public philosophy was ascendent—New Deal liberalism, with its greater emphasis on government as problem-solver—and it belonged to the Democrats.

Composition of the New Deal Parties

Table 15.1 shows how various groups in American society allocated their party loyalties by 1936–37. Overall, 52 percent of the public thought of themselves as Democrats, 31 percent as Republicans, less than 2 percent as socialists, and 15 percent as independents. The differences in party loyalties and voting by economic status were quite striking. Just 39 percent of people with professional jobs were Democratic identifiers, compared to 66 percent of unskilled workers and 66 percent of the unemployed. Still, Democratic strength was impres-

Table 15.1
Party Identification and the 1936 Presidential Vote

	Party identification		1936 vote	
	Democrat	Republican	Roosevelt	Landon
Occupation				
Professionals	39	44	54	44
Managers (including businessmen)	44	38	54	45
Skilled workers	47	31	65	33
Unskilled workers	66	18	78	20
Unemployed	66	15	84	14
Region				
New England	35	38	54	43
Middle Atlantic	50	30	65	34
East North Central	46	38	59	40
West North Central	44	40	62	35
South and Southwest	78	15	83	17
Rocky Mountain States	52	30	67	32
Pacific Coast	51	31	68	30
Age				
18–20	52	29	(not eligible to vote)	
21–24	60	19	69	29
25–34	53	28	70	28
35–44	53	30	68	30
45–54	52	33	64	35
55 and older	46	40	57	41
Race, Religion, and Region				
White nonsouthern* Catholics	62	26	81	17
White nonsouthern* Protestants	31	58	52	46
White southern* Protestants	81	10	83	15
Blacks	(not available)		76	23

Source: These data are the combined results of 21 Gallup polls taken in late 1936 and 1937.

*Data on groups indicated by the asterisk are from different Gallup surveys; party identification data on Protestants and Catholics are for 1940, rather than 1936–37.

sive even among the higher economic strata, indicating Roosevelt's popularity and the breadth of the realignment over which he was presiding. In the 1936 presidential balloting, FDR was backed by majorities of professionals, businessmen, and managers.

Regional differences in party strength were massive in the 1930s. The Democrats dominated the South, reflecting an ascendancy traceable back to the Civil War. The Republicans retained their greatest strength in New England—the only part of the country where more people still called themselves Republican than Democratic. Outside the South, the Democrats were much stronger among Catholics than Protestants, as they had been for a century. Blacks had swung away from their long-standing ties to the Republicans as the party of Lincoln, but they still gave significant support to the GOP.

Regional differences

Changes in Group Loyalties

Underlying party loyalties have typically been slow to change. But by the 1980s substantial shifts in group alignments had occurred, away from those evident in the New Deal years. The vast changes that have taken place in the country in the half-century since the Great Depression have left their marks on all aspects of party makeup and competition. Tensions among the ethnic and religious groups in white America have declined greatly in recent decades; as a result, ethnic differences in party composition have diminished. Protestants still comprise a somewhat higher proportion of the Republican than of the Democratic party, but there has been a lot of movement from the days when the GOP could fairly be described as "the Protestant party." Irish Catholics are now the same proportion in both coalitions. There is only one truly dramatic ethnic difference in party composition: Blacks have become the most solidly Democratic group, and they are roughly one-fifth of the Democratic coalition. Since 1964, the GOP has had almost no following in the black community.

Changing regional alignments

In the wake of shifts in the social and economic composition of the country's geographic regions, New England and the South have changed places in their partisan ties. New England is now one of the most securely Democratic parts of the country in party identification and voting, while the South has become the most securely Republican, with the massive partisan shift of southern whites (Table 15.2). This shift mirrors a general swing in political outlook: white southerners now appear more conservative than New Englanders on most political issues.

Age Composition

Party loyalties usually change only after actual voting behavior shifts; at any point in time they reflect yesterday's, not today's, political agenda. In view of this lag, we look with special interest on the partisan attachments new voters are registering. They are not wholly cut loose from yesterday, because family socialization continues to shape them; but they are more reflective of today's commitments than are those of older voters. Does the current political generation differ from its predecessors? Perhaps. According to many of the recent polls, the Republicans are stronger among new voters than (with the exception of the very elderly) any other group.

Generational differences

Analysis of political generations came to the fore during the 1930s in the work of Karl Mannheim, Sigmund Neumann, and Rudolf Heberle. These scholars contended that people gain a frame of reference from the decisive events of the time when they first come to political consciousness—their late teens or early twenties, usually—which shapes their subsequent political commitments. Although the

Table 15.2
Party Identification and the 1984 Presidential Vote (in percent)

	Party Identification		1984	
	Democratic	Republican	Mondale	Reagan
Family Income				
Less than $10,000	48	22	55	45
$10,000–$20,000	36	30	44	56
$20,000–$30,000	33	29	39	61
$30,000–$40,000	28	31	33	67
$40,000 and more	25	35	31	69
Region				
New England	28	21	44	56
Middle Atlantic	34	30	45	55
East North Central	33	29	42	58
West North Central	31	30	42	58
Upper-South	36	30	37	63
Deep-South	37	28	39	61
Rocky Mountain States	30	37	33	67
Pacific Coast	34	33	42	58
Age				
18–24 years	32	33	41	59
25–29 years	31	34	39	61
30–39 years	33	24	43	57
40–49 years	33	28	40	60
50–59 years	36	31	38	62
60 and older	37	35	40	60
Race, Religion, and Region				
Whites outside the South	27	33	36	64
White southerners	23	37	27	73
Catholics	35	25	41	59
Blacks	81	4	91	9

Source: Election-day poll of the *Los Angeles Times,* November 6, 1984. Number of respondents: 6,758.

record is ambiguous, American partisan attachments of the last half-century show persisting effects of such generational experience. According to Gallup data, Americans who in 1951 were 50 years of age and older—and who thus came of age politically before the Great Depression and the New Deal—were markedly more Republican than all younger groups. By the late 1960s, however, the over-50 group was made up significantly of people who came of age during the Depression; a Republican tendency compared to younger groups was nowhere to be seen.[16]

In the late 1970s, some polls began showing the Republicans doing their best at the extremes of the age continuum: among those 18–24, and among the very oldest voters, who came of age before the Depression. This pattern is now seen more frequently. The NORC surveys taken in 1983 and 1984 suggest that current generational experience

[16] For supporting data, see the *Gallup Opinion Index*, June 1968.

Table 15.3
Most and Least Democratic Age Groups (in percent)

	Democrat	Republican	Independent	% Democratic minus % Republican
all ages	39	25	36	+14
ages 78 and older	31	43	26	−12
ages 62–65	48	22	30	+26
ages 30–33	43	18	39	+25
ages 22–25	31	27	42	+ 4

Source: General Social Surveys, National Opinion Research Center; composite of surveys conducted in 1983 and 1984.

is more friendly to the GOP than any other reaching back to the 1930s (Table 15.3). The Democrats do best among the generations that reached maturity in the height of the Roosevelt years, and in the late 1960s and early 1970s. The Republicans' best age groups are those who came of age politically in the Roaring Twenties and since 1975. The contrast between representatives of the Sixties generation and of the late Seventies is especially striking. According to NORC data, the Democrats' edge over the Republicans is 25 points among those 30–33 years of age, compared to just 4 points among those in their early to mid-twenties.[17]

Some surveys taken around the time of the 1984 presidential election suggested that, for the first time since the Depression, the Republicans may have even more strength than the Democrats in partisan identification among young voters. For example, a poll taken by CBS News and the *New York Times* between September 30 and October 4, 1984, found 53 percent of persons 18 to 29 years of age either clearly identifying with the GOP or leaning toward it, compared to just 37 percent for the Democrats. Whether this generational shift continues further and intensifies, or proves to be short-term, remains to be seen. It will, of course, depend on subsequent political experience.

Republican and Democratic allegiances by age

The Republicans Rebuild

In the late 1960s, poll data had shown the Democrats as a kind of "everyone party": They had more adherents than the Republicans in virtually every social group. The GOP did better in some circles than in others, especially among the well-to-do, but it rarely had a decisive edge. Because so many people had come to think of themselves as independents and, more importantly, to vote independently, the Democrats' plurality in party identification hardly gave them a secure

[17] The number of cases in each age group is sufficient so that we may be reasonably confident this large variation is not due to chance alone. In the two NORC surveys, 282 respondents were ages 30–33, while 303 were ages 22–25.

majority status. But it did fairly convey the extent of Republican weakness. The GOP touched bottom politically during the Watergate scandals.

Since the mid-1970s, however, the Republican coalition has been strengthened. In spring 1983, and again in spring 1984, NORC conducted national surveys that give us a good sense of the rebuilding that occurred since the Watergate low. The Democrats still enjoyed a substantial lead in party identification among most groups, but the GOP had regained a big lead among those with annual family incomes of $50,000 and higher, and people of British ancestry in the Northeast. The GOP also had an edge among the college-educated, among people in business and managerial jobs, and among (perhaps) residents of the West (Table 15.4).

Democratic-Republican Policy Differences

How different are rank-and-file Democrats and Republicans in their opinions on questions of government and policy? They split most sharply on matters of abstract partisanship—where party loyalties rather than policy substance are engaged. For example, Republicans and Democrats are more at odds over Ronald Reagan than they are over his programs. Terms like "liberal" and "conservative" are also evocative symbols for Republican and Democratic identifiers. Sixty percent of Republicans surveyed by NORC in 1983 called themselves conservatives, as against just 26 percent of Democrats.

Different views on the role of government

The issue of government's role in national life divides Republicans and Democrats more sharply than any other policy question. In 1983, 57 percent of Democrats felt that it is the responsibility of the government in Washington to see to it that people have help in paying for doctors and hospital bills; only 28 percent of Republicans felt this way. Differences on foreign policy disputes and on issues involving women and minorities are also evident but not as large. In all these cases, the rank-and-file reflects differences etched more distinctly at the level of party leadership.

Differences within Parties

On many social issues, such as sexual norms and abortion, and on most civil liberties matters, interparty differences are modest while those within each party by education and social status are large. For instance, legalized abortion for women who are married and don't want any more children is supported by just 32 percent and 34 percent of Democrats and Republicans, respectively, with less than high school training; it is backed by 71 percent and 62 percent of Democratic and Republican identifiers with postgraduate education. Issues like abortion are highly divisive in terms of class and culture, but the electorate does not split along partisan lines.

Table 15.4
Partisan Identification, Spring 1983–Spring 1984

	D	R	(1)−(2)
Race and Sex			
White males	34%	27%	+ 7
White females	37	29	+ 8
Black males	63	3	+60
Black females	64	7	+57
Religion			
Protestant	37	31	+ 6
Catholic	45	19	+26
Jewish	52	18	+34
Region			
Northeast	37	25	+12
Midwest	36	25	+11
West	35	35	0
South	45	21	+24
Income			
Less than $10,000	45	18	+27
$10,000–$14,999	43	21	+22
$15,000–$19,999	33	29	+ 4
$20,000–$24,999	39	24	+15
$25,000–$34,999	41	24	+17
$35,000–$49,999	36	32	+ 4
$50,000 and over	25	45	−20
Ethnicity			
Irish	39	26	+13
German, Austrian	31	33	− 2
Italian	43	21	+22
Scandinavian	34	37	− 3
East European	49	16	+33
English, Scottish, Welsh	28	37	− 9
Hispanic	53	9	+44
Black	63	5	+58
Northeast English and Scottish	18	46	−28
Occupation			
Professional, technical	32	31	+ 1
Business executive, managerial, sales	29	35	− 6
Clerical	38	28	+10
Skilled	40	20	+20
Semi-skilled and unskilled	39	22	+17
Farm	42	38	+ 4
Education			
Less than high school	49	17	+32
High school graduate	38	25	+13
Some college	34	30	+ 4
College graduate	31	38	− 7
Postgraduate education	30	32	− 2

Source: Surveys by the National Opinion Research Center, General Social Surveys, 1983 and 1984.

Figure 15.1 **Differences in Outlook within Parties**

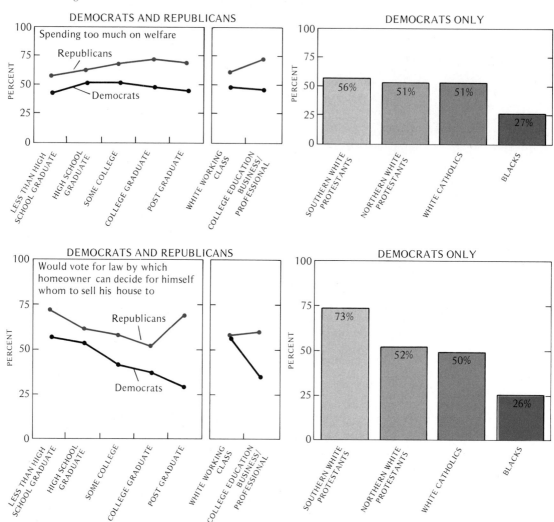

A. *Question:* Are we spending too much money on welfare, too little money, or about the right amount?

B. *Question:* Suppose there is a community-wide vote on the general housing issue. There are two possible laws to vote on (read categories A & B). Which law would you vote for? A. One law says that a homeowner can decide for himself whom to sell his house to, even if he prefers not to sell to (Negroes / Blacks) . . . B. The second law says that a homeowner cannot refuse to sell to someone because of their race or color.

The Republicans have long been described as more homogeneous than the Democrats in social makeup; this depiction still applies. The GOP also appears more homogeneous in policy outlook; educational and class groups within the party are less at odds on a number of important issues than their Democratic counterparts (Figure 15.1). The Democrats are the most unified on basic issues of the role of government—such as spending to improve the living standards of the poor. On such questions, the core of the New Deal agenda, Demo-

Figure 15.1 (continued)

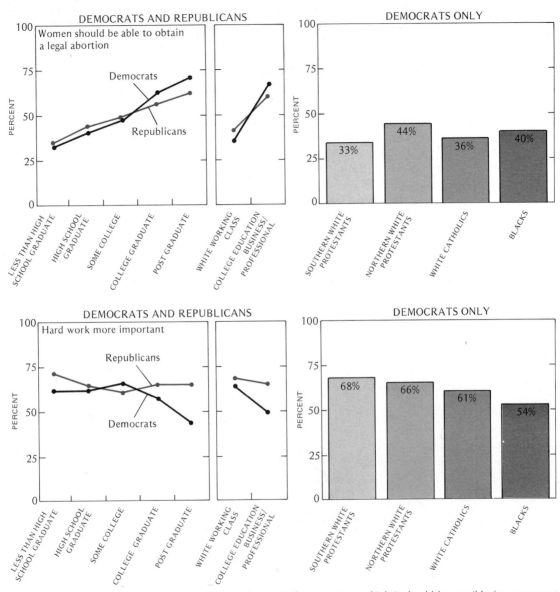

C. *Question:* Please tell me whether or not *you* think it should be possible for a pregnant woman to obtain a legal abortion if . . . she is married and doesn't want any more children.
D. *Question:* Some people say that people get ahead by their own hard work; others say that lucky breaks or help from other people are more important. Which do you think is most important?
Source: Surveys by the National Opinion Research Center, General Social Surveys. Data combined for 1980, 1982, and 1983.

cratic partisans are most sharply at odds with Republicans. On most other issues, including social and cultural questions, class differences in political outlook within the Democratic party are large and and persistent. Since the late 1960s, college-educated Democrats, and those

in professional and managerial occupations, have been more liberal
than those of lower socioeconomic status. Southern white Protestants
appear uniformly the most conservative ethnic-regional bloc; blacks
and Jews to be the most liberal.

COMPLEX CHANGES IN PARTY STRENGTH

While it is evident that substantial shifts in voter alignments have
taken place, the overall distributions of party identification still show
substantial continuity over the last half-century (Figure 15.2). The
Democrats have never lost the lead in voter loyalties they first gained
in the 1930s, although at the end of 1984 their edge was smaller than
it had been for most the period.

Are the Democrats still
the majority party?

Looking to presidential voting, one sees a different picture. The
Democrats have lost six of the last nine presidential elections, since
1952. Only once in these nine elections did they win a decisive presidential victory: in 1964, when the Republicans nominated Barry
Goldwater, a U.S. senator from Arizona who was not the first choice

Figure 15.2 **Party Identification since 1937**

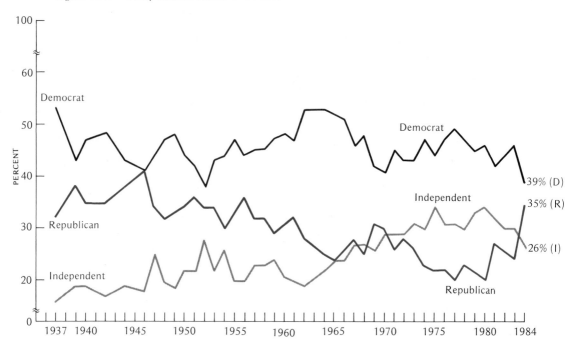

Note: Slight variation in question wording over time. In earlier years question was "Do you
consider yourself a (Republican, Democrat, Socialist, or Independent/Dem., Repub., Progressive, or Independent)? For comparison purposes, "Other," "Socialist," and "Progressive" calculated out. Figures for January–March 1971 through October–December 1979 and January–
March 1982 through January–March 1983 based on combined results of several surveys.
Source: Surveys by the Gallup Organization, latest that of Fall 1984.

even of Republicans for their party's nomination. In contrast, the GOP has gained large victories (margins of 10 percentage points or more) on five occasions: 1952, 1956, 1972, 1980, and 1984.

The pattern of presidential voting since Eisenhower clearly differs from that of the 1932–52 span; the Democrats are no longer the majority party in balloting for the presidency. Beyond this, there is a widespread sense that the United States has experienced some shift of ideological direction, that Reagan's victories in 1980 and 1984 were, at least in part, a response to changes in policy preferences among American voters.

Shifting party preferences

Still, it is equally evident that the Republicans have not established themselves as the nation's majority party. The GOP retained its majority in the U.S. Senate, which it won in 1980, in the elections of 1982 and 1984. But the Democrats have continued to hold solid majorities in the House of Representatives, governorships, and state legislatures (Table 15.5). Something has been happening that is neither a general realignment in favor of the Republicans, nor a simple persistence of the New Deal Democratic majority.

Dealignment

One dimension of the shift in voter preferences involves a long-term weakening of party loyalties, sometimes called electoral ***dealign-***

Table 15.5
Election Boxscore

	1976	1978	1980	1982	1984
House of Representatives					
Democrat	292	276	243	269	252
Republican	143	159	192	166	183
Senate					
Democrat	62	59	46	46	47
Republican	38	41	53	54	53
Governors					
Democrat	37	32	27	34	34
Republican	12	18	23	16	16
Members of State Legislatures					
Democrat	5,128	4,762	4,483	4,643	4,338
Republican	2,370	2,680	2,918	2,734	3,035
States with Both Legislative Houses and Governor of Same Party					
Democrat	29	20	17	23	18
Republican	1	4	7	4	4

Source: Public Opinion, December/January, 1983, p. 26; and *idem.,* December/January, 1985, p. 26.

ment. Some voters move across party lines, but more keep their old ties while being more willing to ignore them in individual elections.

The rise in independents

Among a number of related developments attesting to this weakening of party attachments is a growth in the proportion of Americans who think of themselves as independents, rather than as adherents of one of the political parties. Gallup surveys in the early 1950s showed the proportion of self-described independents as 18 to 20 percent; by the 1970s, the proportion had climbed to 30 to 35 percent.[18] This growth parallels large increases in actions indicating independent political behavior, such as crossing party lines and ticket-splitting. Gallup regularly asks: "For the various political offices, did you vote for all the candidates of one party, that is, a straight ticket, or did you vote for the candidates of different parties?" For the last five presidential elections the proportions saying they voted a *straight ticket* have been a fairly consistent *minority:* 37 percent in 1968, 44 percent in 1972, 41 percent in 1976, 37 percent in 1980, and 43 percent in 1984.[19]

The contemporary electorate is less anchored today than in most of American history. Whatever their future assessment of Reagan administration and Republican performance, and of the Democrats, voters are not going to recreate the extent and degree of stability in party ties that they displayed in the New Deal era. It takes little to move this electorate from one party to the other, from one election to the next.

Electoral volatility. A dealigned electorate is like an unanchored boat— it can be easily moved. American voters are highly volatile, moving this way and that over the course of a campaign and from one campaign to another. This does not mean that large numbers of voters will be in a state of flux every campaign. In 1984, for example, many Americans apparently made up their minds very early, for or against Ronald Reagan, the incumbent seeking reelection; and they stuck with their decision.[20] But the weak party loyalties characteristic of the contemporary electorate leave it inherently more volatile or changeable than electorates used to be.

In a period of dealignment, historic group attachments to parties erode rapidly, and few enduring new ones are formed in their stead. For some time it has been possible to see this process of erosion. Many

[18] The Gallup poll asked: "In politics, as of today, do you consider yourself a Republican, a Democrat, or an Independent?" The entire collection of Gallup polls, comprising more than 1,200 separate surveys reaching back into the 1930s, is contained within the archive of the Roper Center for Public Opinion Research, Storrs, Conn., and the distributions cited here are derived from scores of individual surveys within this collection.

[19] These data are from a survey taken by CBS News / *New York Times*, August 1980.

[20] The election-day poll taken by the *Los Angeles Times* in 1984 found an extraordinary 47 percent of voters stating that they had made up their minds how they would vote before the first presidential primaries in February.

of the differences in the voting of various social groups that were so evident in the New Deal era voting were scarcely evident in the 1980 and 1984 voting.[21]

Religious-group voting

The voting of religious groups is a good case in point. Throughout U.S. history, far more Protestants have been Republicans than have Catholics. The Protestant-Catholic division, a product of once-salient ethnic and cultural differences, has encompassed some of the sharpest and most persisting electoral divisions in American politics.[22] Over the last two decades, however, there has been a pronounced erosion of these voting differences (Figure 15.3). In 1960, with Democrat John Kennedy on the ticket as only the second Roman Catholic ever to be nominated for president by a major party (and the first to win the presidency), Roman Catholics were 28 percentage points less Republican than the entire electorate, while Protestants were 12 percent more Republican. By this measure, Protestants and Catholics were 40 percentage points apart in their presidential support. In 1964, Catholics were 15 percent less Republican than the national total, while Protestants were 6 percent more Republican, for an intergroup difference of 21 percentage points. Since 1964, there has been a steady decline in these differences; in 1984 Catholics were just 2 percent less Republican than the country as a whole, and Protestants were just 2 percent more Republican. This interreligious-group voting difference of just 4 percentage points, together with the spread of 6 points in 1980, is the smallest in U.S. history.

Sources of dealignment. Discussions of the progress of electoral dealignment typically emphasize two broad sources: the *sociological* and the *political-institutional.* The sociological explanation notes that an affluent, leisured, highly educated public no longer perceives the need for political parties as intermediary institutions to the degree that less-educated and less-secure publics did in the past. The political-institutional explanation stresses the deterioration of political party organizations, producing a situation where increasingly ineffective party bodies give voters scant reason to back them strongly. It also notes that other institutions, especially the national communications media and the welfare state, have assumed functions that parties once performed.

While these factors are important, another key precipitant of dealignment has received little attention: Large segments of the

[21] See Everett Ladd, "The Brittle Mandate: Electoral Dealignment and the 1980 Presidential Election," *Political Science Quarterly,* 96 (1) (Spring 1981):1–25.

[22] For data on Protestant-Catholic electoral differences historically, see Everett Ladd, *American Political Parties: Social Change and Political Response* (New York: Norton, 1970), pp. 291–94; and idem, *Transformations of the American Party System,* especially pp. 46–57, 116–24, 271–74. Richard Jensen, *The Winning of the Midwest* (Chicago: University of Chicago Press, 1971), pp. 58–88, provides some revealing data on the extent of religious differences in voting in various midwestern counties in the late nineteenth century.

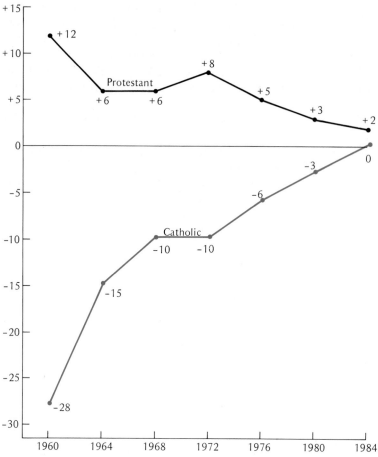

Source: Postelection surveys by the Gallup organization, latest that of November 7–10, 1980, and election-day poll of the *Los Angeles Times,* November 6, 1984.

Figure 15.3

Deviation of Protestants and Catholics from the National Voting Percentage for the Republican Presidential Candidate since 1960

American public have become so ambivalent about the proper course of public policy that they are unable to give a clear endorsement to the competing positions of the parties. Today, Democrats and Republicans offer contrasting approaches that arguably are as distinct as at any time in the past, but most voters do not feel confident about either set of partisan answers. We discussed this ambivalence in chapter 12. With regard to the role of government, many voters are of mixed minds. They do not see any alternative to government's doing a lot, but they are clearly dissatisfied with its recent performance. Not certain just what course they actually favor, many Americans have been reluctant to give strong and unequivocal support to either party.

Ambivalence and dealignment

Dealignment has weakened voters' ties to both parties; but this weakening is not neutral in partisan terms. The Democratic party had previously been the majority, and the weakening of party loyalties has diminished the strength or reliability of the Democrats' majority status. The edge still goes to the Democrats; and in lower offices, such as state and legislative seats, where there is less atten-

Dealignment and party ties

tion to the personal attributes of candidates and less likelihood of big policy issues intruding, this edge is sufficient to maintain their majority position. But in more visible offices, especially the presidency, where great policy questions demand public attention, the Democrats' margin in party identification, in its present weakened state, is easily overridden.

A Changing Political Climate

Why have the Democrats been having such a difficult time in contests that pose issues of national policy direction? Dealignment helps explain why the old Democratic majority status is less secure in offices such as the presidency, and in the Senate, but it does not explain the extent to which the Republicans have been winning.

The American public did not "swing to the right" in 1980 and 1984, and the Reagan administration did not receive a mandate from the country to implement a narrowly conservative program. But Americans announced that "something new" was needed in the country's public policies, something different from the approach to political economy that the Democratic party pioneered in the 1930s and elaborated in the ensuing decades. Without expressing certainty about the Republicans' capacity to define a successful new approach, the public has shown its substantial displeasure with the Democrats' "old-time religion."

The 1980 presidential voting. Many Democratic leaders understood this in 1980. What gave them such concern following Carter's defeat was their sense that their party was floundering intellectually and that the country had turned against its approach to governing. In July 1980, New York Democratic Senator Daniel Patrick Moynihan argued that his party had become a stale force stubbornly defending the big establishment of modern government. "There is a movement to turn Republicans into Populists, a party of the People arrayed against a Democratic Party of the State." Moynihan went on to call this role-reversal "terrifying" for the Democrats and one that might signal "the onset of the transformation of American politics." He conceded, further, that "of a sudden, the GOP has become a party of ideas."[23]

For some time, intellectuals like Moynihan had been highly critical of aspects of government performance and of the Democrats' response to these inadequacies. But concern over deficiencies in Democratic "ideas" became widespread across the party after the 1980 election. Senator Gary Hart of Colorado, who managed George McGovern's presidential campaign in 1972, and who in 1984 tried to channel the newer currents of Democratic liberalism in his own presidential bid, agreed with Moynihan that "the liberal wing of the Democratic party has run out of ideas. It has been operating on the Roosevelt momen-

Dissatisfaction with the Democrats' ideas

[23] Daniel Patrick Moynihan, "Of 'Sons' and their 'Grandsons,'" *New York Times*, July 7, 1980, p. 15.

tum of programmatic, bureaucratic solutions to the domestic agenda," even though such currents as "increased taxpayer resistance to the growth of the costs of governmental programs, inflation, the realities of international economics, and a lot of other factors . . . have been catching up with that momentum."[24]

Some Democratic leaders disagreed that their party was lacking in ideas. As former Democratic National Chairman John White put it, "the trouble is we are a party of too many ideas."[25] But behind these semantic differences was general agreement that the 1980 results reflected not just upon Jimmy Carter but upon Democratic ideas, the way the party approached the task of governing the country.

Above all, many Democrats agreed, a sense of inadequacy in their economic ideas or approach was their greatest problem. The onset of high inflation served as the focal point. Frustration with inflation could be seen across the social spectrum, but it was especially acute among the Democrats' traditional working-class and lower-middle-class constituents. And working-class voters had come by 1980 to believe, as fervently as upper-middle-class voters, that contemporary government, more than business and labor, had caused the inflationary surge. The electoral impact of this shift in class perceptions of government and the Democrats' handling of it was felt in 1980 when the party suffered its greatest losses among Americans who thought they were in trouble economically.

Public concern over inflation

"Compared to a year ago," the CBS News election-day poll asked respondents, "is your family's financial situation better today, worse today, or about the same?" Among those who thought they were better off, President Carter was preferred to Ronald Reagan by 54 percent to 38 percent, while among that third of the electorate who believed their economic position had declined, Reagan led Carter by a massive 65 percent to 25 percent. The Republican nominee made significant inroads in 1980 into the traditionally Democratic working class, splitting the blue-collar vote evenly with Carter; but most striking, he did best among blue-collar workers who thought their economic position was deteriorating. When a Republican who had long been the leader of his party's conservative wing and who ran an avowedly conservative campaign drew his greatest support from Americans, including blue-collar workers, who felt they were in trouble economically, rather than from those satisfied with their success, one sees just how far the erosion of confidence in the Democrats and their economic answers had proceeded (see Table 15.6).

Shift to the Republicans

The economy has changed much since the 1930s. Unemployment was an overwhelming problem in the Depression decade, standing at 20 percent in 1935 and nearly 15 percent just before World War II. Since the late 1960s, however, inflation has been the economic problem prompting the greatest unease. In 1984 the dollar purchased only

The changing political economy

[24] Interview conducted by the author with Senator Gary Hart, December 2, 1980.
[25] Interview conducted by the author with Democratic National Chairman John White, December 3, 1980.

Table 15.6
1980 Presidential Vote, by Perception of Financial Situation (in percent)

	Carter	Reagan	Anderson
Among all voters			
Those who thought they were better off financially than a year ago	53	37	8
Those who thought their financial position was unchanged	46	46	7
Those who thought they were worse off financially than a year ago	25	64	8
Among blue-collar workers only			
Better off	73	22	2
Unchanged	55	39	6
Worse off	30	62	5

Question: "Compared to a year ago, is your family's financial situation better today, worse today, or about the same?"

Source: CBS News election-day poll, November 4, 1980.

one-third as much as it had just sixteen years earlier. (See chapter 18 for a fuller discussion of these changes.)

Professor David Vogel argues that a resolute pragmatism distinguishes the American approach to questions of political economy. "The American public has supported whichever 'side' has offered the most effective program for promoting real economic growth." From the 1870s through the 1920s, the ascendancy of private business and its success in limiting governmental intervention ultimately rested on business' capacity "to manage successfully the transformation of America from an agrarian to a modern industrial society." The Great Depression changed that.

> Americans supported the reforms of the New Deal because they represented an effective alternative for restoring the viability of the American private sector. . . . What gave political credibility to liberal forces in America during the quarter-century following the Second World War was their ability to argue effectively that the expansion of the welfare state and the adoption of the principles of Keynesian economics were not only compatible with economic prosperity, but essential to it.[26]

In the 1970s, another shift occurred. The Democrats' approach was no longer associated with growing prosperity, and the American public became receptive to new ideas. This was the setting in 1980.

The 1982 congressional voting. In the 1982 vote for Congress, the public had its first opportunity to reaffirm or recast the tentative, some-

[26] David Vogel, "The Inadequacy of Contemporary Opposition to Business," *Daedalus,* 109 (3) (Summer 1980):47–57.

what ambiguous mandate it had extended two years earlier. The results of the 1982 balloting were viewed by some as indecisive. The Democratic party made gains, in governorships and in the House of Representatives, but it did not gain massively. The Reagan administration was told by the public to change course, but it was not repudiated: "The Center, Rediscovered" was the way the *New York Times* put it.[27] Actually, the 1982 vote was a reaffirmation of the message the electorate conveyed in 1980: The Democrats' approach to political economy was flawed, and a new Republican departure should be given a try—even though that party's capacity to govern successfully was viewed skeptically.

Especially striking as an indicator of persisting voter dissatisfaction with the Democrats' approach were the answers to the question "Which of the two political parties do you think is better able to handle the nation's economic problems?" This was asked nationally in the NBC News election-day poll, and of samples of voters in 13 states. Historically, the Democrats' margin over the Republicans had been large and persistent on this type of question. Add to that the troubled state of the economy in 1982, with the GOP in power, and one might have expected a substantial majority to prefer the Democrats. In fact, only 36 percent nationally said the Democrats were best equipped, compared to 35 percent for the Republicans, 18 percent not seeing any difference, and 10 percent not sure or not answering. Even in a Democratic state like Michigan, especially hard hit by the recession, only 38 percent said the Democrats' approach to economic problems was better—just 5 percent more than preferred the GOP's approach (see Table 15.7).

[27] *New York Times*, editorial of November 7, 1982.

Backing for the Reagan
experiment

Throughout the 1982 campaign, Americans were unhappy about the state of the economy and critical of many Reagan administration policies. On the question of whether the administration's general approach deserved endorsement or rejection, however, the 1982 verdict was to continue the Reagan experiment. A CBS News / *New York Times* poll asked, "Have you personally been helped or hurt?" Those saying "hurt" outnumbered those "helped" by better than two to one. "Apart from the impact on you personally, has the national economy been helped or hurt so far?" Again, those saying "hurt" outnumbered "helped" by a large margin, nearly two to one. On the third question, however—"Do you think the economic program eventually will help or hurt the country's economy?"—the answers revealed the intent to continue. Sixty percent said the economy would be helped, compared to just 27 percent who thought it would be hurt in the long run. While the proportions varied from one survey to another over the course of Campaign '82, in every instance where this or a comparable question was asked, a plurality said they thought the economy would be helped in the long run.

The 1984 presidential voting. If the electorate were inclined during the pain of the recession of 1982 to continue its limited mandate for a new approach to political economy, it was unlikely to vote to shift direction in 1984, once the economy had turned up and it was at least arguable that the Reagan administration's approach was working.

All during the long 1984 presidential campaign, economic news was

Table 15.7
Which Party Can Best Handle Economic Problems? (in percent)

Responses of:	Democrats best	Republicans best	No difference
All voters nationally	36	35	18
California	35	36	19
Connecticut	35	36	18
Florida	35	39	17
Illinois	35	34	19
Maryland	42	29	21
Massachusetts	46	22	22
Michigan	38	33	20
Minnesota	34	35	19
New Jersey	35	32	22
New York	35	29	22
Ohio	38	28	22
Texas	36	41	13
Virginia	35	37	16

Question: "Which of the two political parties do you think is better able to handle the nation's economic problems?"

Percentages do not add up to 100% because "no answer" and "not sure" responses have not been displayed.

Source: Election-day polls of NBC News, November 2, 1982.

about as good as an incumbent administration seeking reelection could hope for. Even interest rates, which were high by historical standards, fell during September and October. *Valence issues* (how things are going) reinforced and strengthened the public's sense that the Reagan approach to economic management was generally sound and should be continued.

Ronald Reagan's reelection victory in 1984 was the latest act in a long-playing American political drama: "As the Realignment Turns." After each election commentators ask, "Has the play opened?"—that is, did we see at least the beginning of a partisan realignment? But, in fact, the play opened a long time ago.

The time and place of the curtain raiser would almost certainly have had to be 1948 in the American South. White southerners were the strongest link in the New Deal coalition and, indeed, the most loyal supporters of the Democratic party since the Civil War. In 1948, however, they began their long march away from the Democrats. The States' Rights party of Strom Thurmond seized on white racial protest against Truman policies and carried four southern states. Democrat Harry Truman won the support of only 53 percent of white southerners. In subsequent elections over the 1950s and 1960s, regional opposition to the national Democrats' racial policies combined with the increasing attraction that a rapidly industrializing and newly prosperous South felt for the Republicans to produce a massive swing to the GOP in presidential elections. Jimmy Carter, the first bonafide southerner nominated for president by a major party since the Civil War, and clearly the beneficiary of substantial regional loyalties, was nonetheless unable in 1976 to win a majority of the vote among southern whites; he won only about one-third of this vote. Whereas 85 percent of white southerners voted for Franklin Roosevelt in 1936, only 25 percent of them backed Walter Mondale in 1984.

Over the last three decades other groups that had been mainstays of the New Deal coalition swung gradually to the Republicans. Labor unions went all out for Mondale, but the blue-collar vote went for Reagan, and the union vote (voters from households where at least one adult was a union member) gave Mondale only a modest margin. Catholics swung from their historic attachment to the Democratic party and gave Reagan a clear majority in 1984. These and other important shifts were influenced by Ronald Reagan's personal popularity, but they antedated the Reagan presidency by many years and resulted from deep-rooted social changes.

Shifting party allegiances

The group alignments evident in the 1984 presidential voting (shown in Table 15.8) represent an extraordinary shift from those of the New Deal era. Even in cases where a group is on the same partisan side as it was then, its position in the larger electoral scheme is often different. For example, black Americans gave a majority of their votes to the Democrats during the New Deal, and they did in 1984, but the Democratic share has gotten much bigger since 1964, and blacks are now a much larger component of the Democrats' electorate than ever before. A far-reaching realignment of group voting in presidential contest has occurred.

Another element we have in mind when we speak of partisan realignment is the displacement of the previous majority party and the emergence of a new majority. At the presidential level such a shift has occurred. The GOP has been victorious in four of the last five presidential elections, winning 55 percent of the total two-party vote over this span. Three of the Republican victories have been landslides: 1972, 1980, and 1984. The one election the Democrats won, in 1976, is in a sense the most graphic confirmation of the GOP's ascendancy: Jimmy Carter and the Democrats managed only the narrowest win in 1976, even though the Republican party had temporarily been decimated by the Watergate scandals.

Americans do not elect their presidents by national popular-vote majorities, of course, but by electoral vote, which are given winner-take-all to the popular-vote victor in each state. And the electoral vote maps for the last five presidential contests look even more decisively Republican than the popular vote distributions. There are 23 N^2FR^2 states: carried by Nixon in 1968 and 1972, Ford in 1976, and Reagan in 1980 and 1984. These states have 202 electoral votes—about three-fourths of the 270 electoral votes needed for a presidential victory. There are no HMC^2M states; only the District of Columbia has given its support to all of the recent Democratic nominees: Humphrey in 1968, McGovern in 1972, Carter in 1976 and 1980, and Mondale in 1984.

Along with change in group voting patterns and a new presidential majority, we associate realignment with a new mix of critical issues and a shift in the axis of conflict—a shift that has already materialized. The big act in the realignment drama of the 1970s involved a movement of voters away from the Democrats on questions of political economy—under the dual challenge of high inflation (seen as government's fault) and frustration over the extent of government's growth. This movement provides part of the backdrop for the answers a national sample gave to CBS News/*New York Times* interviewers in a poll taken from September 30 to October 4, 1984. "Which party is better able to insure a strong economy?" Fifty-four percent said the Republicans; only 27 percent said the Democrats. Confronted with such assessments, the Democrats have begun a search for new ideas, a search that almost certainly will dominate party discussion over the next four years.

Changes in group voting, in partisan ascendancy in presidential elections, and in policy cleavages sound much like great realignments in the past. But in two other regards, the present realignment differs from its predecessors, First, it is accompanied, indeed distinguished, by the continued weakening of voter loyalties to political parties in general. We discussed the progress and precipitents of dealignment earlier in this chpater. These developments are very likely to be reversed—and certainly they were not reversed in 1984.

The GOP ascendancy in presidential elections

Electoral vote since 1968

Importance of political economy

Dealignment

Table 15.8
1984 Presidential Vote by Social and Political Group (in percent)

	Reagan	Mondale
Education *		
Less than high-school education	50	49
High-school graduate	60	39
Some college	60	38
College graduate	59	40
Occupation *		
Professional/manager	62	37
White-collar worker	59	40
Blue-collar worker	53	46
Full-time student	51	48
Teacher	55	45
Unemployed	31	68
Homemaker	63	36
Military veteran	66	33
Government employee	50	48
Retired	62	37
Union household *	45	53
Income *		
Under $12,500	46	53
$12,500–24,999	57	42
$25,000–34,999	59	40
$35,000–$50,000	67	32
Over $50,000	68	31
Present financial status compared to 4 years ago **		
Better	81	19
Same	51	49
Worse	27	73
Ethnicity **		
Asian	72	28
Black	9	91
Hispanic	47	53
Whites	67	33
Religion **		
Baptist	51	49
Episcopalian	60	40
Lutheran	66	34
Methodist	65	35
Mormon	85	15
Presbyterian	68	32
Other Protestant	68	32
Catholic	59	41
Jewish	32	68
None	34	66
Party and race *		
White Democrats	31	68
Black Democrats	3	96
Region and race *		
Whites in the East	57	42
Blacks in the East	7	92

Table 15.8 (continued)

	Reagan	Mondale
Whites in the Midwest	67	32
Blacks in the Midwest	6	92
Whites in the South	72	28
Blacks in the South	9	89
Whites in the West	65	34
Age**		
18–24	59	41
25–29	61	39
30–39	57	43
40–49	59	41
50–59	62	38
60 and older	60	40
Party and race*		
White Democrats	31	68
Black Democrats	3	96
Ideology**		
Very liberal	30	70
Somewhat liberal	33	67
Middle-of-the-road	59	41
Somewhat conservative	82	18
Very conservative	81	19
Party identification**		
Very strong Democrat	7	92
Fairly strong Democrat	22	78
Independent	67	33
Fairly strong Republican	97	3
Very strong Republican	98	2
Democratic primary supporters*		
Mondale	4	96
Hart	34	65
Jackson	6	93

Source: *Data from exit poll conducted by the New York Times, November 6, 1984. **Data from exit poll conducted by the Los Angeles Times, November 6, 1984.

Throughout the country in 1984, there was an epidemic of ticket-splitting. Shrinking bands of committed partisans, and a growing proportion moved largely by the mix of personalities and policies in a given election rather than by parties, seem to be the wave of the future in American politics. The Democrats' problems with the presidency do not reflect shifts in underlying party loyalties as much as the difficulty parties have had in fashioning electoral appeals that accord with current policy expectations.

Second, the present realignment manifests a split personality: The presidency has been dominated by the Republicans in recent elections, but Congress, state legislatures, and other offices have not become GOP bastions. In the 1984 balloting, the Republicans retained control of the U.S. Senate (although they dropped two seats), but their gain of 17 seats in the House still left them trailing the Democrats 183 to 252. Among state legislatures, the GOP gained roughly 300 seats in 1984, but Democrats continued their overall ascendancy, holding over 1,300 more seats than the Republicans nationally.

Checks and balances revisited

Some observers explain the two-tier electoral system by Americans' liking for separation of powers and checks and balances. If the GOP's policy direction is to be encouraged by the election of Republican presidents, some check is useful in Congress and the state houses. Besides, many people are highly ambivalent about the role of government and other central policy issues. What better way to express these mixed feelings than by ordaining divided party control?

An incumbent's resources and realignment

Other observers stress the importance of structural factors that influence voting at the various levels. For example, as we saw in chapter 7, members of Congress now have large staffs and other resources of incumbency that are useful in advancing their reelection. Gaining high levels of name recognition and emphasizing nonpartisan service to their constituents, incumbents are now able to divorce their own electoral fortunes from those of their parties' presidential nominees. There is probably some truth to both of these explanations, but the precise mix is not known. We do know certainly that the "realignment with a split personality" is proving to be remarkably enduring.

The Republican test

Given the Republicans' control of the White House, the key to the next act in the long-playing realignment drama will likely be the public's perception of GOP performance in serving the country's social and economic well-being. Will the Republican approach ultimately be seen as *successful*, not merely *promising*? Or will it crash against deepening economic problems and social conflict? In the last analysis American voters are performance-oriented, as they have always been. A deeper, broader Republican majority will only come the old-fashioned way—the GOP will have to earn it.

PARTY REFORM

Selecting presidential nominees

From time to time, campaigns are mounted to reform various American political institutions. We saw in chapter 7, for example, the major changes that were made in congressional organization and procedures from 1965 to 1975, with the intent of correcting perceived problems. Political parties have also been affected by these recurring efforts at reform.

Party reform has often been intended to make the institution more democratic. Early in this century direct primaries were introduced to weaken party bosses and to give the rank-and-file a bigger role in what is perhaps the most important of all party functions: picking candidates for offices. Beginning in the late 1960s, the latest of the party reform attempts concentrated on changing the way presidential nominees are selected. These efforts have originated largely within the Democratic party.

The Democrats were deeply divided in 1968 between the wing that backed President Lyndon Johnson in his conduct of the Vietnam War and the large bloc in the party that bitterly opposed him on this issue. The latter felt that nominating procedures unfairly benefited the party "establishment" under Johnson, who wanted Vice President Hubert Humphrey to succeed him. (Humphrey did win the 1968 Democratic nomination but was defeated by Republican Richard Nixon in the general election.)

The McGovern-Fraser Commission

Following their tumultuous 1968 presidential convention in Chicago, the Democrats established a commission to examine possible changes in the party's presidential nomination procedures and to make recommendations for changes to be implemented prior to the next nomination contest in 1972. This Democratic commission was chaired first by Senator George McGovern of South Dakota and later by Congressman Donald Fraser of Minnesota. Officially the "Commission on Party Structure and Delegate Selection," the body was better known as the McGovern-Fraser Commission. Its report to the Democratic National Committee, *Mandate for Reform*, was presented in 1971.

The McGovern-Fraser Commission maintained that internal party democracy was the value to be promoted through reform, and that its achievement would make the party more representative of the populace and thereby stronger, more competitive, and generally better able to perform its role in the governing process. It recommended either that presidential delegates be chosen by caucuses and conventions open to all party adherents, with delegates apportioned among the contending candidates through proportional representation, or that they be selected through primaries. If a state Democratic party insisted on permitting its central committee to play a role in choosing delegates to the national convention, it had to limit the number thus selected to 10 percent of the total. Forbidden was the practice whereby "certain public or party officeholders are delegates to county, state, and national conventions by virtue of their official position." Being a major party official would no longer entitle anyone to a formal role in the party's presidential nominee selection.

Increased use of presidential primaries

These new rules led to the proliferation of presidential primaries. A later party report noted in 1978 that "while the McGovern-Fraser Commission was neutral on the question of primaries, many state parties felt that a primary offered the most protection against a challenge at the next convention."[28] There were 17 Democratic presidential primaries in 1968; the number rose to 23 by 1972 and to 30 in 1976. Less than half of all delegates to the 1968 Democratic convention had been chosen by primaries; nearly three-fourths of the 1976 Democratic delegates were thus selected. The new rules also weak-

[28] *Openness, Participation and Party Building: Reforms for a Strong Democratic Party*, Report of the Commission on Presidential Nomination and Party Structure, 1978, Morley Winograd, chairman, p. 24.

ened Democratic party organizations, as "state party organizations [took] *on more of an administrative role rather than a decision-making role in recent presidential nominations.*"[29]

The Republicans showed little enthusiasm for the kinds of changes the Democrats were imposing. But the GOP nonetheless felt the impact of some of them, like the greater reliance on primaries, which were written into state law and were applied to both parties.

The Hunt Commission

By the late 1970s, the McGovern-Fraser reform efforts were under strong criticism as actually weakening the party. Another reform commission was formed: the Commission on Presidential Nomination, chaired by Governor James B. Hunt of North Carolina. The Hunt Commission made its report to the Democratic National Committee (DNC) in early 1982, and the DNC gave final approval to its new rules for the 1984 presidential nomination process in March 1982. One important change was intended to bring party officials back again more substantially into the nomination process. The 1984 rules allocated 550 seats for *party and elected officials* as unpledged delegates. Some of these would be named by the House and Senate Democratic caucuses—with seats given to three-fifths of all congressional Democrats—and the balance would be named by state parties, giving priority to governors and big-city mayors. Unpledged delegate slots would also be reserved for each state's Democratic chair and vice-chair. Under the McGovern-Frazer rules, party leaders had to run for delegate seats like anyone else. Most of them would not run: It would be humiliating to lose, and winning might not be much better for they might anger an important group of constituents whose support they would need in their next election.

Other changes were designed to increase the chances of a decisive outcome in the search for delegates. We noted in chapter 14 that winner-take-all electoral systems encourage unambiguous electoral outcomes (clear winners and losers) while proportional representation aims at alloting seats in exact proportion to votes and thus may prevent anyone getting a majority. Hunt Commission rules led the Democrats further away from the type of proportional representation in delegate selection introduced first by the McGovern-Fraser Commission.

The 1984 rules produced their desired result—but, of course, this was not to everyone's satisfaction. The beneficiary of the rules' bias in favor of decisiveness in 1984 was Walter Mondale. His vote total in primaries and caucuses was about the same as Gary Hart's, and about twice Jesse Jackson's. But Mondale received 50 percent more delegates than Hart and five times as many as Jackson. The losers thought this was grossly unfair. The winner said he simply played by the rules. The argument over the ideal delegate-selection system seems certain to continue. Contradictory objectives are contending for recognition. No system can serve all of them.

---

[29] Ibid. Emphasis added.

SUMMARY

Political parties as we now know them first took form in the infant United States at the end of the eighteenth century. An institutional response to the new reality of political egalitarianism, they have become central institutions in all democracies, and many other countries as well. Parties are linkage institutions between the public and government. Properly organized in a democratic system, they can greatly increase voters' control over their governmental officials and public decision-making.

The American party system has a number of distinctive attributes. Almost alone in the world, it is a two-party system. For over a century, the Republicans and Democrats have won the overwhelming majority of votes and offices. The American parties are inclusive and heterogeneous, practitioners of political compromise and accommodation. They do not have members, only adherents; they exercise remarkably little discipline over their elites. Party organization is weak in the face of strong currents of political individualism. Rank-and-file voters typically select nominees through primary elections. No other democracy gives party leaders so little control over candidate selection.

The social composition of American parties is constantly changing. The Republicans have grown stronger among southerners, but they have lost ground in the Northeast. Black representation in the Democratic coalition is much larger than ever before. Whereas the Republicans long drew support disproportionately from northern Protestants, and the Democrats from Catholics, the two coalitions have now lost much of their distinctiveness in religious makeup.

For all of these and other shifts in group loyalties, the overall distributions of party identification at present are similar to what they have been over the last half-century. The Democrats still enjoy a clear margin over the Republicans. But though this edge in partisan identification is reflected in the distribution of seats in many elective offices, including state legislatures, it is certainly not evident in voting for president, which the GOP has won in six of the last nine elections. Balloting in contests where there is a clear focus on national policy direction shows major change from the patterns of the New Deal era.

In general, voter ties to both parties have weakened. *Dealignment*, the moving of voters away from strong and stable partisan loyalties, has accelerated over the past fifteen years. The electorate is now less anchored by party identifications than it used to be, and it can be shifted more easily by the issues of the time. Such issues are producing problems for the Democrats, especially as their approach to managing the economy has been questioned.

Efforts to reform the political parties have focused on making them more democratic in their internal operations. Over the last two decades, reform attempts have been concentrated within the Democratic party and have dealt with presidential nominating procedures. The 1984 Democratic rules sought to reverse a pattern begun by the party's McGovern-Fraser Commission in 1969, by modestly increasing the role of party and elected officials, and by opting for decisiveness at the expense of proportionality in the allocation of delegates.

16 | The Media

If a people are to be able to govern themselves, rather than be ruled over by others, they must have free and open access to information on the political questions they are to decide. They must have the opportunity to receive information on different perspectives, for they can hardly choose a course of action of which they are ignorant. As James Madison noted, "A people who mean to be their own governors must arm themselves with the power knowledge gives. A popular government without popular information or the means of acquiring it, is but a prologue to a farce or a tragedy, or perhaps both."[1] Recognizing this, the First Amendment to the Constitution forbade Congress from enacting any legislation curtailing the freedom of the press, and subsequent Supreme Court decisions have extended this curb to all levels of government.

Throughout this chapter, the terms "the press" and "the communications media" are used interchangeably to connote all vehicles for communicating information, including newspapers, periodicals, books, newsletters, and other forms of print media on the one hand, and radio and television (the so-called electronic press) on the other. Prominent among print media are large, mass-circulation national and metropolitan newspapers, such as the *Wall Street Journal, U.S.A. Today*, the *New York Times*, and the *Washington Post;* and popular news magazines, among them *Time, Newsweek*, and *U.S. News and World Report*. The electronic press encompasses radio and television news programming by the network giants—ABC, CBS, NBC—along with public broadcasting, and the rapidly expanding cable networks.

---

[1]James Madison, letter to W. T. Barry, August 4, 1822, in Saul K. Padover, ed., *The Complete Madison* (New York: Harper and Row, 1953), p. 331.

We begin this chapter by describing the resources of the American communications media—in particular, their capacity to reach huge audiences—and what this distribution of resources means for liberal democracy. How the press is organized in the United States and its historical evolution occupy the next two sections. The relationship of the press to major governmental insitutions, including political parties and the presidency, affects greatly the workings of the American polity, and we assess this subject in the fourth section. The chapter concludes with a discussion of the political outlook and professional norms of journalists.

COMMUNICATIONS RESOURCES AND DEMOCRACY

There is no consensus on the proper place of the press in a political system. The "founding father" of the Soviet Union, V. I. Lenin, thought that the press should be subordinate to the state. "Why should a government which is doing what it believes to be right allow itself to be criticized? It would not allow opposition by lethal weapons. Ideas are more fatal than guns."[2] In contrast, democrats insist that government should sustain the full freedom of the press. But even the firmest advocates of this democratic ideal differ on other issues surrounding this vital institution, such as how much power the press has—and should have.

The Power of the Press

It is not hard to detect the consequences of the use of power in certain instances, as when an authoritarian government uses its control of the police and armed forces to stifle opposition. But in many cases the effects are hard to measure: How much power does big business have in the United States? Organized labor? There is not even agreement on how to understand the concept of power in such instances, much less any precise measure of that power or what it achieves. We are on firmer ground when we talk not about power but about resources relevant to the exercise of power. The economic resources available to those who head certain major corporations in the United States can be described, and we can see where there is discretion in employing them and where there is not. This does not give us a definitive picture of the power or influence of American business leaders, but it does provide us with a better sense of their power potential vis-à-vis other groups. Similarly, by examining the resources available to the communications media, we gain a clearer understanding of what the debate over the power of the press involves.

Resources for political power

Let us begin with a hypothetical question. What would be the con-

[2] V. I. Lenin, quoted in Rosemary Righter, *Whose News?: Politics, the Press and the Third World* (London: Burnett Books, 1979), p. 113.

During the 1983 invasion of Grenada, the Pentagon kept journalists off that island.

Democracy and the distribution of communications resources

sequences for democracy if these two conditions obtained: (1) Government scrupulously maintained a "hands off" position with regard to the press, not using its authority to limit who communicates what to whom, but (2) certain private interests held huge and disproportionate communications resources and used these to advance their own perspectives on politics? (By communications resources we mean facilities for collecting political information and presenting it to mass audiences.) What if certain private interests owned all the television stations and used them to reach mass audiences to push their own political preferences, ignoring or misrepresenting other points of view? Could democratic government function satisfactorily in this situation? Few think that it could. Press resources matter, and even scrupulous enforcement of the First Amendment cannot solve all problems regarding these resources.

Mass Audiences

Early in American history, concerns about press resources seemed remote. The economics and technology of communications allowed new communications media, typically newspapers, to be established easily, and no one could reach very large audiences. Resources were widely dispersed. As long as government did not intervene to throttle freedom of communication, there was little to worry about. For example, in New York, the nation's largest city, the *Morning Herald* was started in 1835 with just $500 and the *Tribune* in 1841 with $3,000.[3] Anyone with a little money and writing ability could set up a newspaper and compete effectively in the dissemination of political ideas.

[3] For a general discussion of press resources prior to the Civil War, see Frank Luther Mott, *American Journalism: A History of Newspapers in the United States through 250 years, 1690 to 1940* (New York: Macmillan, 1947), pp. 215–323.

Newspapers reached at most a few thousand people, and it did not cost much to establish them.

Subsequent developments in transportation and communications changed this—making possible huge audiences and requiring great financial outlays. On an average weekday evening, about 50 million Americans tune in to the national news broadcasts of CBS, NBC, ABC, and public television. Whereas most citizens can express their views to at most a few score of their fellows, anchorman Dan Rather of CBS News reaches 15 million or more nightly. The question of how much Rather and his counterparts influence American political life has been endlessly debated with few certain conclusions. But the mere act of creating audiences of the size generated by contemporary American television news programming has encouraged the perception that vast communications power is thus imparted.

Network television audiences are unusually large, but a number of print media have also acquired huge circulations. Table 16.1 shows

Table 16.1
Paid Circulation of the Ten Largest U.S.
Daily Newspapers

Wall Street Journal	1,925,722
New York Daily News	1,544,101
USA Today	1,163,937
Los Angeles Times	1,052,637
New York Post	960,120
New York Times	905,675
Chicago Tribune	758,255
Washington Post	726,009
Chicago Sun Times	651,579
Detroit News	652,531

Source: *1983 Editor and Publisher International Yearbook* (New York: Editor and Publisher Co., 1983). The reporting date for circulation of above newspapers is September 30, 1982, with the exception of *USA Today,* which was founded only in September of 1982; we show its 1983 circulation total as reported by the *USA Today* public affairs office, Washington, D.C.

Major newspapers and magazines

the ten individual newspapers with the largest circulations. At the top of the list, with a paid circulation of nearly 2 million (and hence perhaps 4 million readers daily) is the *Wall Street Journal. USA Today* had a national circulation of about 1,200,000 in 1983. With daily paid circulations of 900,000 and 725,000, respectively, the *New York Times* and the *Washington Post* are read by very large proportions of the country's political, economic, and intellectual leaders, especially in the key New York and Washington areas.

A number of magazines have even larger circulations. (See Table 16.2.) At the top of the list among those that print primarily political

Table 16.2
Paid Circulation of Selected U.S. Magazines

News Reporting and Commentary	
Time	4,719,343
Newsweek	3,022,727
U.S. News & World Report	2,112,727
Harper's	141,934
Business	
Business Week	855,391
Fortune	700,360
Forbes	718,970
Political Opinion	
National Review	98,882
The Nation	53,817
The New Republic	97,371
The American Spectator	41,000
The Public Interest	12,000
Commentary	47,000
Other	
Readers Digest	18,299,091
TV Guide	17,275,471
National Geographic	10,469,521

Source: The *IMS 1984 Ayer Directory of Publications*, 116th ed. (Ft. Washington, Penn: IMS Press, March 1984).

news is *Time*, which sells 4.5 million copies each week and has a readership of more than 10 million. Among all magazines, the monthly *Reader's Digest* leads, with a circulation of over 18 million copies and some 40 million readers. In print and electronic journalism massive audiences have become the rule.

Financial Resources

The attainment of such huge audiences permits the great print and electronic media to generate enormous revenues, especially through the sale of advertising. In 1950 the four television networks and the 107 television stations existing in the United States had broadcast revenues of just $106 million. Thirty years later, in 1980, the three commercial networks and the 725 VHF and UHF stations enjoyed broadcasting revenues (largely from advertising) of $8.81 billion. The three networks alone had revenues of $4.57 billion in 1980.[4]

The financial resources generated by the largest communications media are used for many things, including news coverage far beyond that of any previous period. For example, CBS News now has about two hundred full-time staff members in its Washington bureau alone, including 25 on-the-air reporters. The Associated Press has about 100

Staff resources of major media

[4]*Television Fact Book*, Services Volume, 1981–82 ed. (Washington D.C.: Television Digest, 1981), pp. 59a, 60a.

reporters in Washington; the *New York Times*, 35. In all, about 1,200 reporters are assigned to the White House, and in 1983 the Washington press corps included 3,400 correspondents and editors. Such numbers make it possible for political actions to be probed and dissected to a detail unimaginable in the past.

Changing status of journalism

The great financial pressures of the major communications media permit them to support their staffs far more generously then in the past. Historically, journalists were a poorly paid professional group. At the *New York Times* in 1982, a reporter with 2 years experience earned a minumum of $37,000 a year, and leading columnists and top editors received salaries several times as great. The most dramatic salary gains have been recorded in television news. In 1983, the anchor men and women for the leading Boston television stations were paid salaries of around $500,000, while the networks' anchor people earned annual salaries in the million-dollar range. Not surprisingly, the enhanced pay of journalists and the huge audiences now open to those reporting for the leading media have increased the prestige and glamour of the journalism profession. Occupational prestige scores, which had shown journalism near the bottom compared to other professions, have over the last quarter-century recorded a sharp rise in reporters' status. And journalism school enrollments have swelled.[5]

There is no chance that the United States will return to the institutional arrangements that prevailed earlier in the country's history, when the communications resources available to any one individual or press outlet were so meager that they conferred little opportunity for undue political influence. In nineteenth-century America, the only way power over political communications could have become concentrated would have been for government to control the press. Given the technology of that time, freedom of the press was enough to assure a highly dispersed, fragmented, pluralistic press. No longer.

ORGANIZATION OF THE PRESS

Though it is not a part of the government in any democracy, the press plays an essential public-sector role, performing functions central to political life. Even when it is wholly privately owned and operated, the press has broad public responsibilities, the chief of which is seeing to it that citizens have access to the information they need to decide the issues before them.

In most democracies, a distinction is made in practice between those segments of the press that articulate particular group interests and perspectives, partisan or ideological, and those that are general-circulation vehicles of news dissemination. There is little debate over

[5] James Boylan, "News People," *Wilson Quarterly*, Special Issue, 1982, pp. 76–77.

Newstands in the United States offer a rich assortment of contending perspectives.

what public policy should be with regard to the former: Government should simply stay out of the way, allowing the journals of opinion to speak their mind freely. But with regard to general-circulation news media, there is argument in every democratic nation. How should the mass-audience press be organized to perform its broad public-sector responsibility of assuring the citizenry access to needed information?

Ownership

In the United States, there has been general agreement on one part of the answer: The press should be *privately owned and operated*, with the fewest possible governmental regulations and restraints. Democracy requires a free press, and ~edom is most securely attained when government is kept at arm's ~th. The natural interplay of market forces will ensure a variety ~eneral-circulation communications media that, in competition v ~ one another, will see to it that the news is as fully and fairly reported as is practically possible. Note that this emphasis on free markets is akin to the more general American rationale for a private business system, which emphasizes the importance of free competition in meeting consumers' needs.

The American newspapers and news magazines are private corporations, owned and operated much like other private businesses. Those wishing to establish a new paper capitalize it like those wishing to set up any other business; if they cannot maintain their news business profitably they cease to operate. Every year a number of newspapers and magazines are established while others close their doors. Newspaper births and deaths have largely balanced out in recent

The American press: a private enterprise

A Russian newstand and the official Communist Party newspaper, Pravda.

decades; there were 1,763 daily newspapers in the United States at the end of World War II, and 1,730 in 1982.[6]

In this regard, the position of the general-circulation *print media* in America is essentially the same as in other democratic countries: The print media are privately owned. The organization of radio and television in the United States differs substantially, however, from that in other democracies. The three major television networks—the Columbia Broadcasting System (CBS), the American Broadcasting Company (ABC), and the National Broadcasting Company (NBC)— together with a preponderance of local television stations, are privately owned businesses. Radio and television in Western Europe, in contrast, are for the most part managed by governmental corporations.

Radio and television ownership in the U.S.

Radio and television ownership in Europe

Throughout Europe telecommunications was seen from the beginning as a public utility to be run as a national monopoly. Telephone and telegraph systems were developed in this fashion, and when radio and television came along they were similarly organized. In France today, radio and television are run by the Office de Radiodiffusion-Télévision Française (ORTF), a government-sponsored organization set up under public ownership. Sveriges Radio, the Swedish Broadcasting Corporation, is an independent public corporation vested with sole rights of radio and television broadcasting in Sweden. In Spain, Televisión Española (TVE) is a public corporation that has been given a monopoly of broadcasting in that country. Great Britain is a partial exception to the common European pattern. The British Broadcasting Company (BBC) is a public corporation, but the Television Act of

[6]Leo Bogart, "Newspapers in Transition," *Wilson Quarterly,* Special Issue, 1982, p. 69.

1954 also provided for an Independent Television Authority. Under this legislation, private corporations are licensed to broadcast, much as radio and television stations are licensed in the United States by the Federal Communications Commission (FCC). ITV stations depend wholly on advertising revenue, just as most American television stations do.

Public radio and television

The American telecommunications industry has not always been privately controlled, and is not exclusively private today. In 1918 the American Telephone and Telegraph Company was taken over by the federal government, and remained under public control until the middle of 1919. And today, the United States has public radio and public television stations which, while small compared to the size and number of commercial networks and their affiliates, play a significant role in broadcasting. The Public Broadcasting Act of 1967 established the Corporation for Public Broadcasting (CPB). With some of the features of the British Broadcasting Company, CPB is a public corporation responsible for developing noncommercial television and radio services. It provides financial support to public radio and television station operations. Most of the funds for the Corporation for Public Broadcasting come from government—state and local as well as federal—although public radio and television stations also depend on private contributions and grants from business corporations.

Government involvement in European media

The fact that most European radio and television are managed by public corporations does not mean that, in the usual sense, they are "run by the government" or necessarily reflect the views of the politicians in power. In some European democracies, the public corporations that manage broadcasting are largely autonomous. The BBC, for example, does not operate as a mouthpiece of the political party in control of the British government at the time. Both the legal structure of the BBC and, equally important, the tradition of partisan independence preclude such governmental intrusion. In the United States, the Corporation for Public Broadcasting does not take its cues in news reporting from the president and his administration.

In some European democracies, however, there is substantial government influence over the way the public radio and television report the news. The French government shapes the news reporting of French television to a degree that would be considered unacceptable in the United States or Great Britain. The Spanish government also has great influence over the country's television news reporting.

Financing the press in the U.S. and Europe

The contrast between the United States and much of Europe is even sharper in the area of finances. Newspapers and news magazines in the United States do receive favorable postal rates. But all units of the press, print and electronic alike, depend on private resources, especially advertising, for their sustenance. They sell their product on the private market. Throughout Europe, however, there are extensive governmental subsidies. Radio and television receive much of their revenue from annual license fees that owners of radio and television sets must pay—much as motor-vehicle operators in the United States pay license fees. These fees are a type of user-directed tax. The print media also receive large and important subsidies. In Great Britain newspapers are exempted from the country's principal taxation, the value-added tax (VAT). Revenue from the sale of newspapers or from the sale of advertising is not subject to any VAT, and this confers what one observer calls "a colossal fiscal advantage, worth between five and ten percent of total [newspaper] revenue." In France the private press gets subsidized newsprint, low postal rates, and special tax privileges.[7]

Regulation

The one area where the U.S. government is significantly involved in the mass communications media is radio and television regulation. The Federal Communications Commission (FCC) licenses radio and television stations. A corporation wishing to establish a VHF or UHF television station cannot simply purchase the necessary equipment, hire staff, and begin broadcasting. The FCC must license it to operate on a particular frequency. The now rather detailed provisions of FCC licensing developed from the straightforward premise that some basic regulation of who could broadcast at what frequency was needed to prevent a hopeless scrambling of signals. There are no technical limits on the number of newspapers or news magazines that can be disseminated in a particular market; but the airwaves are a finite common property, defined by the laws of physics, rather than simply by laws of supply and demand.

FCC regulation   If the basic rationale for governmental regulation of the broadcast media is unexceptionable, the result has been to establish a governmental agency—the FCC, which is an independent regulatory commission—with substantial authority. Television stations must go before the commission every five years (every three until 1982) to renew their licenses. In practice they are rarely turned down, but there have been a few dramatic cases of denial. One was a 1969 decision in which the FCC voted 3 to 1 to refuse to renew the license of Boston's WHDH-TV, and instead to give the license to a competing applicant. The commission acted to reduce ownership concentration. WHDH was owned by a Boston newspaper that also operated two local radio stations and held controlling interest in a cable television company. Broadcasters are understandably sensitive about the possibility that the commission might deny them their license and, hence, put them out of business. The WHDH case prompted a great furor, and the FCC subsequently revised its rules so that ownership concentration would no longer be grounds for denying the renewal of a license.

[7] Anthony Smith, *The Politics of Information: Problems of Policy in Modern Media* (London: Macmillan, 1978), p. 175.

On what grounds can the FCC deny renewal? From the beginning of the broadcast industry, U.S. policy has stipulated that a license to broadcast, once conferred, is not permanent. Subsequent performance must be taken into account in determining whether renewal is to be granted. Stations are given access to a vital public resource, the airwaves. Do they use it responsibly? Are they attuned to the needs and interests of their broadcast areas? Few would argue that the FCC should automatically extend licenses regardless of what stations do on the air. But on the issue of what constitutes insufficient performance, confusion reigns. The sword rarely falls—but it is left hanging.

Federal regulation of *news* broadcasting occurs in three areas: (1) the equal-time provision, (2) the fairness doctrine, and (3) the right of rebuttal. Involved are so-called "access rights" provided through Section 315 of the Federal Communications Act of 1934 and its various amendments and interpretations. The ***equal-time*** provision stipulates that broadcasters who permit one candidate for public office to campaign on their stations must give equal opportunities to every other candidate for that office. For example, they cannot sell air-time to a Republican candidate for a U.S. Senate seat and deny the same type of time, at the same rates, to a Democratic, Libertarian, or other party candidate.

Equal-time provision

The ***fairness doctrine*** requires broadcasters who air material on controversial issues to provide reasonable time for the expression of opposing views. One recurring criticism of this requirement is that it has the *de facto* effect of limiting broadcast-media treatment of certain controversial subjects. Doris Graber argues that "the media frequently shy away from programs dealing with controversial public issues to avoid demands to air opposing views in place of revenue-producing programs."[8] Under FCC regulations, however, the media can avoid the problem of furnishing additional air-time for opposing views if they include opposing views on the issues in their regular news programming. The courts have tended to side with radio and television media if they can bring forth reasonably good evidence of "fairness" in their coverage.

Fairness doctrine

The ***right-of-rebuttal*** provisions involve the right of individuals to respond to personal attacks made over radio or television which might be held to damage their reputations. In the case of *Red Lion Broadcasting* v. *Federal Communications Commission* (1969), a liberal newsman who had written a critical book of conservative Senator Barry Goldwater brought suit because he was denied free air-time to rebut an aired attack on his book by a conservative clergyman. The latter headed a religious organization that bought and paid for the program

Right of rebuttal

---

[8] Doris A. Graber, *Mass Media and American Politics* (Washington: Congressional Quarterly Press, 1980), p. 93.

on which the book was attacked. In the *Red Lion* case, the Supreme Court granted the newsman the air-time he had demanded, free of charge, holding that maligned individuals deserve an opportunity to reply and that the public deserves the opportunity to hear opposing views.[9]

Outside of radio and television broadcasting, the press in the United States has not felt the regulatory hand of government very heavily. Most other democracies have produced more politically charged regulation. In 1983 the French government proposed a new press law prohibiting any publishing company from owning more than three nationally distributed publications dealing with politics or current affairs, and stipulating that only one of these could be a daily newspaper. The proposed legislation also provided that no publishing group could own both a national and a regional newspaper, and that no group's regional newspapers could account for more than 15 percent of total French newspaper sales.[10] If implemented, the proposed law would have its greatest impact on a newspaper owner who is an opponent of the government.

Libel Law

The application of libel laws in Great Britain and the United States provides an illustration of the comparative freedom of the American press from regulatory controls. What if a newspaper story about a political leader states things harmful to his reputation that can be demonstrated to be untrue? If he can prove in a court of law that the accounts are false, can he collect damages from the newspaper? In Britain, the answer is generally yes. Not surprisingly, the British press is reluctant to print critical materials when it is not certain that it can establish their accuracy. "British newspapers are often forced to delay publication until their evidence is watertight or until foreign newspapers and the underground press have made an item common knowledge."[11] The author of a story, the publisher, and those selling the paper or book can all be sued in Britain for defamatory libel.

New York Times v. *Sullivan*

In the United States, more than defamatory inaccuracy must be proved before a conviction for libel may be sustained. In the 1964 case of *New York Times Company* v. *Sullivan*, the Supreme Court ruled that a "public official" seeking libel damages for a matter relating to his official conduct must prove that the false statement about him had been made with "actual malice"—that is, with conscious knowledge that the statement was false or with "reckless disregard" for

[9] Graber, *Mass Media*, pp. 94–95.
[10] Paul Lewis, "France Unveils Plan to Limit Ownership of Newspapers," *New York Times*, November 20, 1983, p. 22.
[11] Max Belloff and Gillian Peole, *The Government of the United Kingdom: Political Authority in a Changing Society* (New York: Norton, 1980), pp. 336–37.

In 1984, General West-moreland (at left in right-hand photo) sued CBS, CBS commenta-tor Mike Wallace (at left in left-hand photo), and others for report-ing in a television spe-cial that the general had deceived his supe-riors as to the size of the enemy force during the Vietnam War.

whether it was or not. The Court held that, otherwise, the press or other critics would be restrained from speaking or writing for fear they could not readily demonstrate that what they had said was true. As a practical matter, it is very hard to prove that defamatory false-hoods about a public official were made with "actual malice," and the American communications media are largely free from the threat of libel action in their reporting on public officials.[12]

Similar distinctions between the legal position of the American and British press can be seen in other areas. For example, the British Offi-cial Secrets Act, passed in 1911, makes the *unauthorized receipt* of official government documents, as well as their *unauthorized publi-cation,* an offense. While the government has not used this legislation in an oppressive manner, the act is still a source of governmental restraint on the press. In contrast, in the United States, the Freedom of Information Act (1974) gives the press a strong legal base from which to force the government to release documents that they might choose to withhold. The burden is on the government to prove that some harm, as to national security, might come from release of the documents.

[12] A. E. Dick Howard, "The Press in Court," *Wilson Quarterly,* Special Issue, 1982, pp. 87–90; see also *New York Times Company v. Sullivan,* 376 U.S. 254 (1964).

Growing Centralization

The historically decentralized American press

As recently as 1960, the American communications media could be considered highly *decentralized* compared to media in most of the Western democracies. There was no national press here; newspapers, radio, and television were predominantly locally owned and managed. Whereas in Britain a few huge newspapers circulated throughout the country, in the U.S. newspapers were largely confined to their home city or town. The unsophisticated technology for printing papers, coupled with the geographic size and diversity of the country, made a national press impossible. There were only three television networks (all centered in New York City), but the majority of television and radio stations were independently owned and locally based. FCC regulations were in part responsible for this latter condition, since they provided that no corporation, the networks included, could own and operate more than seven television stations or seven AM and seven FM radio stations nationally. (In July 1984 the FCC amended this 31-year-old rule, permitting an individual or company to own as many as twelve television stations, twelve AM and twelve FM radio stations.)

Growing centralization since 1960

Over the last quarter-century, however, the local, decentralized character of the American communications media has gradually broken down. Television-station ownership is still widely dispersed. But national news reporting is handled almost exclusively by the three commercial networks, and the importance of network news and the extent of coverage have expanded greatly. Newspaper changes have been even more dramatic: New communications technology has made it possible for a newspaper whose editorial staff is located in one city to transmit information via satellite to printing plants located throughout the country. The paper is then distributed from the local plants to newsstands and subscribers just like any other local paper.

The growth of a national press

The *Wall Street Journal* was the first American newspaper to take full advantage of this new technology. The *New York Times*, perhaps the most prestigious paper in the country, began following suit in the early 1980s, although the New York City base of many of its advertising clients presented serious obstacles. New York department stores usually do not want to pay for advertising in other geographic areas. In September 1982, the Gannett chain of newspapers established *USA Today*, the first daily in American history established as a nationwide, general-circulation, general-news publication. Fifteen months after its birth, "America's newspaper," as Gannett calls it, was selling about 1.2 million copies a day all across the country. No longer could it be said that the United States lacked a national press.

These recent centralizing developments have been in addition to the long-established role of the national wire services in news reporting. Local papers draw much of their coverage from the Associated Press (AP), United Press International (UPI), the *New York Times, Washington Post,* or *Los Angeles Times* wire services.[13] The masthead may say Bangor, Maine; Tucson, Arizona; Spokane, Washington; or Savannah, Georgia; but when it comes to news of national and international politics, a few centralized reportorial organizations, with great resources, dominate the scene.

National wire services

In an age when most Americans acquire news of global developments from three television networks, from national newspapers like the *Wall Street Journal* and *USA Today,* from the wire services, or from national news magazines such as *Time* and *Newsweek,* it can no longer be claimed that the American press is sharply distinguished from that of Europe by its decentralization.[14]

EVOLUTION OF THE PRESS

The communications media in the United States today differ greatly in size, resources, organization, and modes of operation from their counterparts in earlier periods. The press evolved in the years following ratification of the Constitution with very close ties to the infant political parties. Indeed, historians often refer to newspapers in the early years as "the party press."

Newspapers and Political Parties

As the new parties took shape, politicians began starting or enlisting newspapers to help them communicate their partisan interpretations of political events to their constituents. A leading historian of American journalism, Frank Luther Mott, notes that

> as party feelings grew, a new reason for the existence of newspapers came to be recognized. Whereas nearly all newspapers heretofore had been set up as auxiliaries to printing establishments and had been looked upon merely as means which enterprising printers used to make a living, now they were more and more often founded as spokesmen of political parties. This gave a new dignity and a new color to American journalism.[15]

The early party press

The *Gazette of the United States* was established in 1789 as a semi-weekly newspaper, with the avowed intent of telling the Federalist side of things. It was to be an organ of the new government. Its founder was a Boston school teacher, John Fenno. Fenno intended "to

---

[13] The roots of the AP and UPI go back to 1848, when six New York newspapers banded together to share the costs of gathering foreign news. The major wire services now maintain huge staffs of reporters throughout the world.
[14] See Bogart, "Newspapers in Transition," p. 58.
[15] Mott, *American Journalism,* pp. 113–14.

hold up the people's own government, in a favorable point of light—and . . . by every exertion, to endear the GENERAL GOVERNMENT TO THE PEOPLE."[16] As the Republican opposition to the Federalists took shape, its leaders, especially Thomas Jefferson and James Madison, felt the need for a new paper in the capital to reflect their political point of view. Madison and Jefferson enlisted the services of Philip Freneau to edit and publish their paper, and the *National Gazette* appeared in October 1791. Other party-press ties were established around the country. The political tone of the press became so harsh, so reflective of partisan emotion, that Mott calls "the whole period of 1801–1833 . . . a kind of 'Dark Ages' of American journalism."

Another important feature of the press in the early years was its rapid assumption of a key role in American democratic life. For all their faults, early American papers succeeded in supplying common people with access to political information. The resultant growth of the press was phenomenal. At the beginning of the nineteenth century, the U.S. had about 200 little newspapers, few of which published on a daily basis. By 1835, however, the country had more than 1,200 newspapers, about 65 of which were dailies. This gave the United States more papers and a larger total circulation than any other country.[17]

Development of an Independent Popular Press

In the years after the Civil War, new printing technology greatly reduced publishing costs. New communications technology, appearing first in the telegraph, permitted news to be transmitted electronically from one part of the country to another, or from Europe to the United States, almost instantaneously. As major cities developed, they provided the population and financial base for great mass circulation dailies. The number of newspapers increased phenomenally, from about 3,500 in 1870, to roughly 7,000 in 1880, to over 12,000 in 1890. As this occurred, the controlling audience for the American press shifted from partisan groups to a mass audience. Papers gradually emerged from domination by political parties. The press came increasingly to deal with a wide variety of subjects of popular interest in addition to politics.

Joseph Pulitzer and the popular press

A key figure in the development of the mass-circulation popular press in late-nineteenth-century America was Joseph Pulitzer (after whom the well-known journalism award, the Pulitzer Prize, has been named). Pulitzer got his start as a newspaper owner in 1878, when he bought the bankrupt *St. Louis Dispatch.* Successful with that paper (which after a merger became the *Post-Dispatch*), Pulitzer moved into New York publishing in the 1880s. In 1883 he bought the *New York*

---

[16] *Gazette of the United States*, April 27, 1791, as quoted in Frank L. Mott, *Jefferson and the Press* (Baton Rouge: Louisiana State University Press, 1943), p. 15.
[17] Mott, *American Journalism*, pp. 167–68.

World and announced what he intended to do with it:

> There is room in this great and growing city for a journal that is not only cheap but bright, not only bright but large, not only large but truly democratic—dedicated to the cause of the people rather than to that of the purse potentates—devoted more to the news of the New than of the Old World—that will expose all fraud and sham, fight all public evils and abuses—that will battle for the people with earnest sincerity.[18]

The energy and flare of the *World*, and its catering to popular tastes, quickly made it enormously successful. From a circulation of 20,000 in 1883, the *World* reached 100,000 in September 1884, 250,000 in 1886, and 374,000 in 1892. It had become the largest and, carrying vast amounts of advertising, the most profitable newspaper ever published.

In the late nineteenth century and the early years of the twentieth, the search for ever larger audiences produced a flourishing of what Yellow journalism has been called "yellow journalism." Be sensational; and don't let facts slow you down—such might have been the motto of this new journalism. The battle for circulation between press lords Joseph Pulitzer and William Randolph Hearst in New York City in the 1890s displayed yellow journalism in its most rambunctious form. Perhaps the most famous story of this press battle came in 1897, when Hearst sent a leading fiction writer, Richard Harding Davis, and a distinguished illustrator, Frederic Remington, to Cuba to investigate conditions in that Spanish colony and to send back features. James Creelman, who was also a reporter for Hearst, claims that the following telegraphic exchange took place:

> HEARST, JOURNAL, NEW YORK:
> EVERYTHING IS QUIET. THERE IS NO TROUBLE HERE.
> THERE WILL BE NO WAR. WISH TO RETURN. REMINGTON.
>
> REMINGTON, HAVANA:
> PLEASE REMAIN. YOU FURNISH THE PICTURES AND I'LL
> FURNISH THE WAR. HEARST.[19]

The Rise of Professionalism

Gradually a new ethos made its way through the American press; its watchword was "professionalism." Reacting against the political distortions arising from partisan domination of the press and those resulting from the insistent sensationalism of yellow journalism, some reporters concluded that their field needed to become a profession, with its own norms and ethical standards, like law and medicine. Intellectual independence—to describe things as they are—was a key

[18] Ibid., p. 434.
[19] James Creelman, *On the Great Highway: The Wanderings and Adventures of a Special Correspondent* (Boston: Lothrop, 1901), pp. 177–78.

The Yellow Peril

William Randolph Hearst wielded enormous power through his publishing empire.

objective in this pursuit of professionalism; care, objectivity, attention to factual detail were emphasized.

Special programs were developed to teach journalists the technical tools of their profession and to instill in them professional standards. The first journalism curriculum was offered by the Wharton School of Business at the University of Pennsylvania. The first four-year program for journalism was set up in 1904 at the University of Illinois. And the first independent school of journalism was established in 1908 at the University of Missouri. In 1903 Joseph Pulitzer endowed a college of journalism at Columbia University, contributing $2 million. When the Columbia School of Journalism finally opened its doors in 1912, there were more than 30 colleges and universities offering formal training in the field. Books on the practice of journalism began to appear. And in 1910, newspaper editors in the state of Kansas adopted the first formal code of ethics for the profession.[20]

Establishment of journalism schools

Perhaps the most important change brought about by this new professionalism was the growth of journalistic independence. The press should be independent of politicians, reporting on them and their actions as fully and fairly as possible. Journalists should be independent of the control of publishers who should run the business side; the pressroom should operate according to journalistic cannons. Newsmen should write without fear or favor, subject only to their own standards of ethics and professional competency.

Journalistic independence

The idea of journalism as an autonomous profession dramatically altered the way the mass media report the news. This commitment is now a key part of the idea of "freedom of the press." The national

[20] Mott, *American Journalism*, pp. 604–5.

media organizations, such as the *New York Times* and CBS News, draw their resources largely from American business; but the norm of journalistic independence has greatly minimized business influence in reporting and editorial coverage.

Radio and Television

The first commercial radio station in the United States began operating in 1922. Over the next quarter-century this new communications medium spread like wildfire. In late 1925 more than 575 stations were on the air, in 1940 about 850, and in 1950 about 2,150. With his famous "fireside chats," broadcast throughout the country in the 1930s, Franklin Roosevelt demonstrated that radio could do more than entertain: it could be a potent political instrument.

Emergence of radio and television news

Radio journalism remained much less influential than its print counterpart. So did television, in the late 1940s and 1950s when it was establishing itself as a dominant entertainment medium. It was not until the 1960s that television news came into its own. The extension of evening television news programs from 15 minutes to 30 minutes in 1963 (for CBS News and NBC News, with ABC News following suit three years later) was a major step in the emergence of the electronic news media into the national limelight. As the networks learned that news could be more than a public service, that in an age of mass higher education there was an immense market for it, permitting the highly profitable sale of advertising, they began to devote much greater resources to news coverage.

Network news audiences

The average American spends an enormous amount of time in front of a television set—about 20 hours a week according to most studies. News broadcasts do not command as large an audience as the most successful entertainment programs, like the *M*A*S*H* special of February 28, 1983, that attracted an audience of 50 million, or the Superbowl special of January 30, 1983, which had an audience of over 40 million. Still, the network news programs command large numbers of viewers. According to A. C. Nielsen, the leading organization measuring the size of television audiences, just over 30 million households tuned in to one of the three network weekday evening news programs during the "measurement period" of November 7–20, 1983.[21] This means that Monday through Friday evening newscasts of CBS, ABC, and NBC were on average being viewed by 45–50 million people.

Public reliance on television news

Television's share of the total news audience has greatly risen over the last quarter-century. In one series of surveys, respondents were asked: "Where do you usually get your news about what's going on in the world today—from the newspapers, or radio, or television, or magazines, or talking to people, or where?" Figure 16.1 shows the

[21] Paul H. Weaver, "The New Journalism and the Old—Thoughts After Watergate," *The Public Interest*, Spring 1974, p. 72.

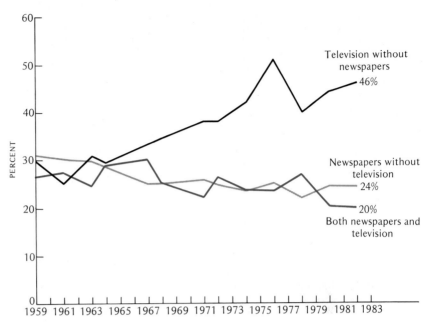

Figure 16.1
Sources of News Information

Question: Where do you usually get most of your news about what's going on in the world today—from the newspapers or radio or television or magazines?
Source: Surveys by the Roper Organization, as reported in "Trends in Attitudes Toward Television and Other Media: A Twenty-Four-Year Review" (Television Information Office occasional publication, 1983).

changing mix. In 1959, just 29 percent listed television, not newspapers, as their prime news source; by the end of 1982, the proportion had risen to 46 percent. The proportion mentioning newspapers but not television dropped from 31 to 24 percent. In all, 66 percent of respondents to the December 1982 survey cited television as a principal source of the information they receive on public affairs, while only 44 percent listed newspapers as a major news source. Evans Witt, a public-opinion polling expert for the Associated Press, cautions that these data may exaggerate the public's shift to television as a source of public affairs information. People get their news from a variety of sources and are not particularly aware of the process. They overemphasize the role of the more entertaining medium: television. This may be; still, there can be little doubt that television has become a vastly more important news source over the past quarter-century.

Americans also now indicate that they are more inclined to accept the television news version of a story than that of newspapers, radio, or magazines, in cases where these media present conflicting versions. In December 1982, 53 percent said they would tend to believe television, compared to 22 percent saying newspapers, 6 percent radio, and 8 percent magazines (Figure 16.2). Is the public asserting that "the camera cannot lie"? Certainly the public is *not* saying that it is generally happy with the way television journalism operates. A poll

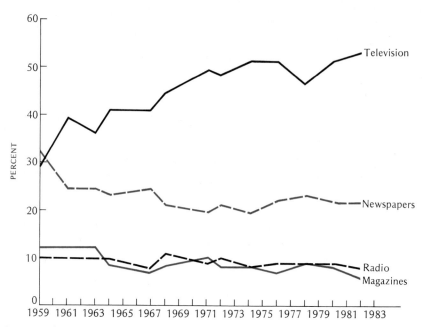

Figure 16.2
**Trustworthiness of
News Sources**

Question: If you got conflicting or different reports of the same news story from radio, television, the magazines, and the newspapers, which of the four versions would you be most inclined to believe—the one on radio or television or in magazines or newspapers?
Source: Surveys by the Roper Organization, as reported in "Trends in Attitudes Toward Television and Other Media."

taken in 1981 by ABC News found 69 percent of respondents agreeing that "network news programs too often focus on tearing things down and not enough in building up what is right and good." By a 55 to 42 percent margin, the public held that network correspondents "give too many of their own opinions and not enough of the facts." A full 40 percent did not think that overall network news does a good job of covering all sides of controversial issues (Figure 16.3). Television journalism has unquestionably won public recognition of its prominence and centrality in discussions of public affairs, but not the judgment that it has a sure grasp of how its immense responsibilities are to be exercised.

The last two centuries have seen an extraordinary evolution of the press in the United States. Through all of the changes we have seen, though, the essential democratic role of the press—of ensuring that the people have access to the information they need to decide the questions before them—remains unchanged.

THE PRESS AND GOVERNMENTAL INSTITUTIONS

The press envelops the government in the United States. Independent of those who wield governmental authority, but tied to them in a complex relationship both cooperative and adversarial, journalists

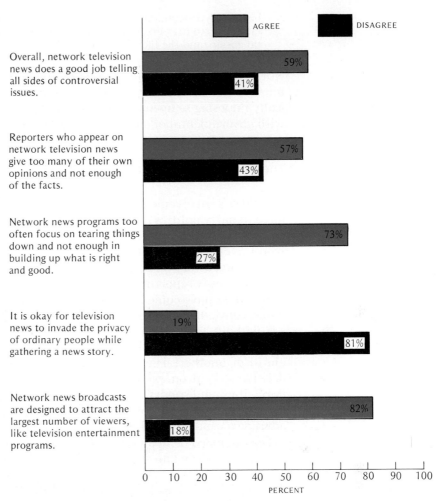

AGREE   DISAGREE

Overall, network television news does a good job telling all sides of controversial issues.

59%

41%

Reporters who appear on network television news give too many of their own opinions and not enough of the facts.

57%

43%

Network news programs too often focus on tearing things down and not enough in building up what is right and good.

73%

27%

It is okay for television news to invade the privacy of ordinary people while gathering a news story.

19%

81%

Network news broadcasts are designed to attract the largest number of viewers, like television entertainment programs.

82%

18%

Figure 16.3
Public Assessment of Network Television News

0   10   20   30   40   50   60   70   80   90   100
PERCENT

Question: I'm going to mention some things that people sometimes say about network television news and after each please tell me whether you tend to agree or disagree with it. First, do you tend to agree or disagree that . . .
Source: Survey conducted by ABC News, October 1–5, 1981.

form a critical part of government's primary audience. The president, his key aides, cabinet members, United States congressmen, and other officials interact more with the national press corps than they do with almost any other group—far more on a day-to-day basis than, say, with business and labor leaders.

The amount of contact American news reporters have with officials has long been a distinguishing feature of U.S. politics. In its openness to the press,

Interaction of press and government officials

American government differs markedly from European (even British) governments. All European journalists are immediately struck by this difference. The American reporter not only has access to official announcements and press releases; he also has the opportunity of becoming the confidante of the official and of enjoying limited but regular access to his personal thoughts, official secrets, internal departmental gossip, and the like.[22]

Not only does the U.S. press play the primary role of disseminating information on what government does, but its members are a numerically imposing segment of the *political community*, interacting closely with governmental officials as the latter do their official work.

The Press and the Political Parties

The press's involvement in the political process applies with special force to party politics and electoral campaigns. The retinue of a presidential candidate typically includes a relatively small number of aides who travel with him and, if he is thought to have any likelihood of succeeding, a very large press contingent. The press's role is not confined to simply reporting what the candidate says and does. Members of the press have come to act as "talent scouts," screening the candidates, conveying the judgment that some are promising while others are without talent. Journalists act as race-callers or handicappers telling the public how the contest is going and why one candidate is ahead of another. They function at times as self-perceived public defenders, bent on exposing what they consider to be the frailties, duplicities, and sundry inadequacies of a candidate. They even sometimes slip into the role of "assistant campaign managers," informally advising a candidate and publicly, if indirectly, promoting his cause.[23]

The press in American elections

The expanded campaign role of the national communications media is both a cause and an effect of the weakening of political parties. The extent to which the parties have introduced mechanisms for candidate selection that make voters-at-large the final judges has obviously made the press more important. The national nominating contests now center not in party committees or conventions but in mass-public-participation primaries across the country. The press has unparalleled resources for covering these contemporary campaigns; indeed, it is the only institution that can do it.

Press v. party as information source

But even if the political parties had not given up so much of their historic institutional responsibility for selecting candidates, the vast communications resources of the mass media would have severely challenged the parties. Political parties can no longer compete with the press as sources of information on candidates and the progress of electoral campaigns. Earlier in U.S. history, handbills printed by the parties and house-to-house canvassing by local party officials were

---

[22] Weaver, "New Journalism," p. 72.
[23] David S. Broder, "Political Reporters in Presidential Politics," in Charles Peters and Timothy J. Adams, eds., *Inside the System: A Washington Monthly Reader* (New York: Praeger, 1970), pp. 3–22, *passim*.

the primary sources of electoral information, but today they cannot compete with the pervasiveness, visual force, immediacy, and general audience reach of television. It is the press that brings the campaign's personalities and issues into the homes and consciousness of American voters. Political parties are now ancillary structures in the whole process of communication between candidates and elected officials on one side and voters on the other.

The Press and the President

The relationship between the press and the president is a particularly consequential one. Washington is, of course, the center of U.S. government and the hometown of the national political elite; it is consequently the center for the national press. The Washington press corps dwarfs that of any other American city, and Washington is the hub for national news reporting. Though the Washington press hardly confines itself to reporting on the president and his administration, it does give the White House vast attention, partly because the presidency is a very important office in the country and partly because presidential actions lend themselves to highly visible and focused news stories.

The contrast between press treatment of the president and Congress demonstrates this point. The executive and legislative branches are coequal in the American constitutional scheme and in practical political power as well. The presidency is one person, however, while Congress is five hundred and thirty-five. From a news standpoint,

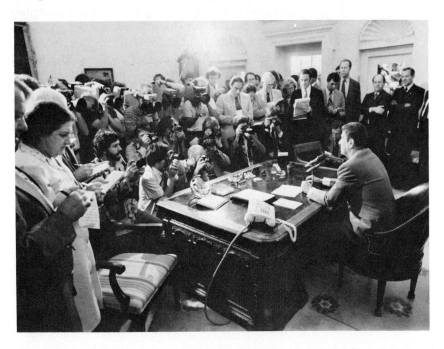

President Reagan facing the press in the White house.

reporting what happens in Congress is vastly more difficult, because of the numbers and because the story is usually less focused. As a result the press gives disproportionate attention to the president.

The extensive coverage given presidential actions and utterances, from the crucial to the trivial, has helped further elevate the presidency in contemporary American government. As television news became a more important part of the overall journalistic mix, the time-sensitive and visual properties of television made the distinctive singularity of the presidential office especially attractive, compared to the disjointed multiplicity of Congress. This bright spotlight the press has put on the presidency shows off strengths and makes the president seem larger than life; but it also illumines every weakness and alleged shortcoming. The inordinate press attention the president gets is a two-edged sword. We have seen presidents both rapidly elevated and diminished by this scrutiny. Political scientist Austin Ranney reminds us that

Press spotlight on the presidency

> no television correspondent or anchorman has ever won an Emmy or Peabody or even a promotion for a series of broadcasts focusing on what a marvelous job a president . . . is doing. Those rewards go to newspeople who expose the moral lapses, lies, and policy failures of public officials, and the president is the biggest game of all in the perennial hunt.[24]

Presidents and their aides thus have concluded that they must try to "manage" press treatment. The relationship is too important, and the consequences of negative scrutiny too great. Every modern presidency has devoted great attention—reaching well beyond the work of press secretaries—to turning the enormous powers of media coverage to the president's advantage. And still, for all the effort, no modern administration has emerged from its intricate dance with the national communications media without a sense of frustration.

Presidential "management" of the press

Tension between president and press is inevitable because the two institutions have contrasting responsibilities. Arthur Krock, for many years head of the *New York Times* Washington bureau, notes that the job of the press is to uncover the news and then get the stories to the public. The more that is reported, the better. "But the statesman has other considerations. Is it [publication of a particular account of events or intended events] premature? Will publication make the going more difficult? Will publication tend to confuse, rather than to clarify, the popular mind?"[25] A press is supposed to bring out "all the news that's fit to print," while a president is supposed to govern effectively. These contrasting objectives can never rest in perfect harmony. The amount of contemporary press coverage simply exaggerates the inherent tension.

President/press tension

[24] J. Austin Ranney, *Channels of Power: The Impact of Television on American Politics* (New York: Basic Books, 1983), p. 141.
[25] Arthur Krock, as quoted by Douglass Cater, *The Fourth Branch of Government* (New York: Vantage, 1965), p. 19.

The Press and Governmental Pluralism

In 1959, journalist and commentator Douglass Cater sought to describe the imposing role that the press had assumed in American government with an instructive title: *The Fourth Branch of Government*. News reporting is such a large and central undertaking in present-day democracy that it must be seen a formal, if extra-constitutional, "branch" of government itself.

From the standpoint of politicians, the press is both an opportunity and problem: an opportunity, because it provides them with coverage and publicity which they need to advance their candidacies and programs; a problem because press coverage may not reflect what they want brought to the public's attention. For the press, politicians are sources of exciting stories but also authors of attempts to manipulate them. From another perspective, the key element in press-politician ties is not the tensions that result but the important complementarity of their roles in American liberal democracy. James Madison and other founding fathers believed in a government of dispersed power, where no unit was too strong. The Constitution, as we have seen, has established an elaborate institutional framework to ensure the dispersion of governmental power. If this constitutional model is still sound, as many Americans believe it to be, the press, as the fourth branch of government, enlarges pluralism by further dispersing power.

Of course, the vast communications resources in the hands of an independent press are often employed in ways that governmental officials find troubling. And many neutral observers fear that in the

The fourth branch of government?

Dwayne Powell
Raleigh News and Observer
Los Angeles Times Syndicate

last 15 years or so segments of the press have become too inclined to probe for weaknesses and imperfections, thus helping to erode popular confidence in the governing process.[26] "The White House will remain in a state of siege, as the normal transactions of the political system are unearthed, magnified, and then distorted by the media."[27]

The press and the dispersion of governmental power

Still, the net effect of the extensive, autonomous, quasi-governmental powers of the American communications media seems to be to further disperse governmental power. Those inclined to believe that Madison was basically right have reason to look with some satisfaction on the part the American communications media play in contemporary governance. Those who have always felt that Madison erred by overemphasizing the advantages of fragmenting authority, to the point where coherence in policy-making and other governmental actions is hard to achieve, have reason to be concerned about the increasingly prominent political role of the press as a kind of fourth branch. For the fourth branch does make it harder for the other three to act coherently. And the more effectively it exposes their failings, the more it diminishes them in general political terms. The autonomy and centrality of the press mean that political authority, in the broadest sense, is even more dispersed and fragmented than the Madisonian constitution itself requires.

THE MEDIA, POLITICS, AND RESPONSIBILITY

Because the press plays a substantial part in political life, many are concerned with its *political outlook*—partisan and ideological. If the press is virtually a fourth branch of government, the political preferences of those who inhabit it merit attention. Those who believe that their own political preferences are underrepresented among journalists are naturally the most likely to protest against alleged press bias. For the last 25 years or so, conservatives and Republicans have more often accused the national press of bias than liberals and Democrats have. Liberal politicians who assert that the press is a hotbed of conservatism are rare, while conservative politicians who find the press a hotbed of liberalism are about as common as mosquitoes in the Everglades.

The liberal-conservative debate over the press has been a hot one at times. And it has made many members of the press defensive. We need to broaden the query into possible press biases, and answer three sets of questions.

[26] For two important survey research studies by political scientists pointing to this conclusion, see Michael Robinson, "Public Affairs Television and the Growth of Political Malaise," *American Political Science Review*, June 1976, pp. 409–32; and Arthur Miller et al., "Type-Set Politics: Impact of Newspapers on Public Confidence," *American Political Science Review*, March 1979, pp. 67–84.
[27] Richard Pious concludes his book *The American Presidency* with this lament. (New York: Basic Books, 1979), p. 417.

Possible press biases

(1) Do national journalists in the United States as a group reflect some distinctive political viewpoint? Are they, for example, more liberal or conservative in their own personal political preferences than Americans generally?

(2) If the press has a distinctive political viewpoint, does this intrude in news reporting? Journalists might have some clear political preferences personally but keep these on the sidelines in professional work?

(3) Is the issue of press liberalism/conservatism the key one? Are other aspects of the outlook of journalists more important in shaping their political role and performance than the side of the ideological or partisan spectrum on which a majority of them stand? Are there professional norms and outlooks in American journalism that impose certain biases in news reporting?

Press Liberalism

Surveys leave little doubt that the tilt among national journalists in the United States is toward values and policies generally thought of as *liberal* (in the current meaning of that word). National journalists give more backing to liberal candidates than the American public does. S. Robert Lichter and Stanley Rothman conducted a study based on in-depth interviews with 240 journalists and broadcasters at the most influential national communications media, such as the *New York Times*, the *Washington Post*, the *Wall Street Journal, Time, Newsweek, U.S. News and World Report,* and the news departments of CBS, NBC, ABC, and the Public Broadcasting System. They found that in the four presidential elections preceding their survey, these journalists had been much more supportive of the Democratic nominee than the country-at-large was. In 1972, when Republican Richard Nixon won 61 percent of the vote in the country, only 19 percent of the journalists supported him while 81 percent backed Democrat George McGovern. Four years later, Republican Gerald Ford only narrowly lost the election, winning 48 percent of the popular vote, but he was backed by just 19 percent of these leading journalists (Figure 16.4).

Lichter and Rothman found that a majority of the journalists described themselves as liberals, the stance of only about a quarter of all citizens. On a wide variety of social and cultural issues—such as affirmative-action programs for blacks and other minorities, abortion, sexual norms and conduct—the journalists were notably more liberal than the public-at-large.

Press Liberalism and Bias in Reporting

It does not follow that if newspeople are disproportionately liberal, their reporting of the news must reflect a liberal bias. As Michael Robinson points out, "press behavior—not opinion—is the key. Bias that counts must be in the copy, not just in the minds of those who

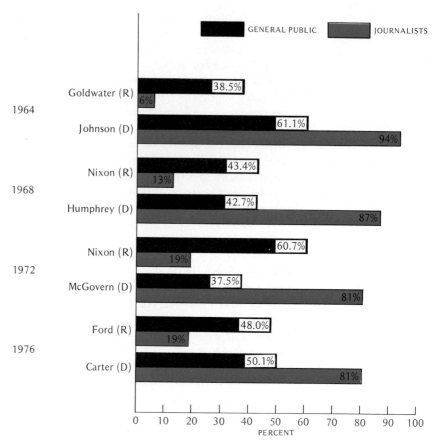

Figure 16.4
Presidential Voting Records, the American Electorate and National Journalists, 1964–76 (in percent)

Source: For a report of the Lichter and Rothman study, see S. Robert Lichter and Stanley Roth-man, "Media and Business Elites," *Public Opinion,* October / November 1981, pp. 42–46, 59–60. Data on the national vote for president may be found in *Statistical Abstract of the United States, 1982–83,* p. 472.

write it."[28] Robinson conducted a research project to find out if there were signs of liberal news bias in the press during the 1980 presidential campaign. After analyzing about 6,000 news stories, in print and electronic media alike, he did not find liberal bias. Not only did the content of stories not reflect any distinctive political leaning, but even more tellingly, the selection of stories to be covered did not betray bias.

This latter point is important and often overlooked. A story may be treated in an objective fashion, but if only a certain type of story is selected for coverage, bias could still result. As Robinson points out,

> if the press covered all business scandals objectively, but *only* covered business scandals, that agenda alone would support a theory of partisan bias. If the media always covered cost-overruns at the Pentagon but failed

[28] Michael Jay Robinson, "Just How Liberal Is the News? 1980 Revisited," *Public Opinion,* February/March 1983, p. 56. See, too, Robinson and Margaret A. Sheehan, *Over the Wire and on TV* (New York: Russell Sage Foundation, 1983).

to cover any cheating in AFDC programs, that too would be political bias, regardless of how fair the reports themselves may seem.[29]

Are reporters biased?

Even on this level, he found few signs of liberal bias during the 1980 campaign. Of course, the fact that political bias was not evident in press coverage of that campaign does not mean bias is always absent. Campaign '80 might have minimized liberal-conservative bias because the Democratic incumbent was widely seen by liberals as well as conservatives to be ineffective. Not many liberals anywhere rallied strongly to Jimmy Carter in 1980.

Others have found signs of press bias on certain issues. Stanley Rothman and Robert Lichter report that the press has greatly exaggerated the amount of opposition of informed scientists to the use of nuclear power to generate electricity. They show that a large number of scientists with knowledge about nuclear energy favor its use and do not reject it on safety grounds. The Rothman-Lichter investigation indicates, however, that press reporting portrays the scientific community as deeply split on the issue.[30]

Are reporters more receptive to liberal issues?

Some observers have concluded that the national press is especially receptive to certain kinds of issues linked to a liberal political outlook. For example, Michael Pertschuk—chairman of the Federal Trade Commission under President Carter, an ally of Ralph Nader, and a Democrat with strongly held liberal views—argues that one of the factors critical to the development of support for consumer-rights initiatives in the late 1960s and 1970s was "a newly aggressive corps of investigative and advocacy journalists, who shared the advocates' view of consumer initiatives as moral imperatives. . . ."[31] While he welcomed this development, Pertschuk himself saw the press as an ally rather than as an opponent or as what it claims to be—simply a fair-minded reporter of the news.

The press is composed of many different men and women who cover many different issues under often difficult reportorial conditions. It is not surprising that examinations of bias in press coverage have not yielded definitive conclusions as to the general rule. Few question that journalists are a quite liberal group in their personal political perspectives. But there is no comparable agreement that these personal views are often reflected in news coverage.

Political Cynicism

What is clear is that most students of the press do not consider liberal-conservative bias the big issue. Recent studies emphasize the issue

[29] Robinson, "Just How Liberal Is the News?" pp. 59–60. See, too, Robinson and Sheehan, *Over the Wire.*
[30] Stanley Rothman and S. Robert Lichter, "The Nuclear Energy Debate: Scientists, the Media and the Public," *Public Opinion,* August/September 1982, pp. 47–52.
[31] Michael Pertschuk, *Revolt Against Regulation: The Rise and Pause of the Consumer Movement* (Berkeley: University of California Press, 1982), p. 23.

of *political negativism or cynicism,* suggesting that the distinguishing bias of the press results not from its political ideology but from its professional outlook. This may encourage holding up politicians and politics as more seamy and less worthy of public support than they in fact are. Paul Weaver argues, for example, that journalists generally, and television newspeople in particular, tend to see politics as in essence "a game played by individual politicians for personal advancement, gain, or power." From this perspective, politicians are naturally inclined "to exaggerate their good qualities and to minimize their bad ones, to be deceitful, to engage in hypocrisies, to manipulate appearances." The task of the press is to expose these bad tendencies of the political world.[32] Austin Ranney makes the same argument. There is not so much "a political bias in favor of liberalism or conservatism, as a structural bias." The latter encourages a cynical and excessively manipulative view of politics.[33]

Even the most worthy official actions of political leaders are often portrayed as manipulative exercises. The Carter administration announced in 1980 a big grain deal in which China agreed to purchase between six and nine million tons of U.S.-produced wheat and corn. It was undoubtedly true that President Carter hoped the successful negotiations might help him among farmers, but the deal was hardly a campaign stunt. When CBS News aired the story, however, its tone suggested that the deal was basically an attempt at election-year manipulation. It announced the grain agreement in the last paragraph of a Campaign '80 report: "Here in Waco, a grain growing area, the President announced an agreement to sell China enormous amounts of grain—White House aides say the agreement has been in the works for a year and they deny the timing is mere campaign wizardry."[34] Although no single instance of such a slant in news reporting is likely to have much effect, constant repetition may encourage the view that most of what politicians do is mere connivance to help them get re-elected.

Michael Robinson's research supports the view that the press fosters a kind of political cynicism.

Carter and the 1980 Chinese grain deal

Has the press encouraged political cynicism?

> Events are frequently conveyed by television news through an inferential structure that often injects a negativistic, contentious, or anti-institutional bias. These biases, frequently dramatized by film portrayals of violence and aggression, evoke images of American politics and social life which are inordinately sinister and despairing.[35]

The effect of this, Robinson finds, is most substantial on viewers who approach politics without a great deal of political information or

---

[32] Paul H. Weaver, "Is Television News Biased?", *Public Interest,* Winter 1972, p. 69.
[33] Ranney, *Channels of Power,* pp. 54–55.
[34] CBS Evening News, October 22, 1980, as cited in Robinson and Sheehan, *Over the Wire,* pp. 198–200.
[35] Robinson, "Public Affairs Television," p. 430.

interest. Such viewers lack the political sophistication to reject the media depiction. As a result, they are apt to become themselves more cynical about political institutions and less confident that they can deal with such a political system.

Such findings may help us understand an important set of survey results. Public-opinion researchers have noted over the last two decades that Americans have become less confident than they were previously in the leadership of central institutions in the society, more distrustful politically, and more cynical. According to one interpretation, the public has simply reacted logically to a string of negative events and performances: the long Vietnam War and the domestic protests it engendered, the corruption of Watergate, double-digit inflation. These developments almost certainly were an important factor; but according to another view, that work like Robinson's supports, increased public cynicism may have also resulted in part from an increasing cynicism in national news reporting, especially network television.

New Professional Norms

Some students of the press think it has become more negative in its portrayal of politics because an earlier set of professional norms have weakened and a newer set have become more prominent. John Johnstone and his colleagues identify the competing normative models as the "neutral" and the "participant." In the former, "the primary journalistic sins are sensationalism—overstatements of the natural reality of events, and bias—a violation of the observer's neutrality vis-à-vis information."[36] In contrast, the "participant" press model insists that journalists should give readers the interpretative background they need to put events in a proper perspective. "In this sense, the primary journalistic value is relevance, and the cardinal sins, news suppression and superficiality." Journalists are supposed to play a more active and, to some degree, creative part in developing what is newsworthy. Johnstone and his associates found sections of the press, especially younger and more highly educated journalists, swinging toward the participant model, which invites a more critical posture.

"Neutral" and "partisan" journalism

Paul Weaver expanded on this distinction and came down harder in his evaluation. As Weaver sees it, there are two main traditions in American journalism. The one that has been dominant throughout most of the modern American experience he calls "liberal" journalism. It resembles Johnstone's "neutral" model. Liberal journalism "is characterized by a preoccupation with facts and events as such, and by an indifference to—indeed, a systematic effort to avoid—an explicitly ideological point of view."[37] In the late 1960s and 1970s, a

[36] John W. C. Johnstone et al., "The Professional Values of American Newsmen," *Public Opinion Quarterly*, Winter 1972–73, p. 523.
[37] Weaver, "The New Journalism and the Old," p. 69.

new approach emerged that Weaver calls "partisan" journalism. To the degree that it triumphs, the press finds it harder to operate as a source of reliable factual, "neutral" information for the general citizenry. It becomes more of an advocate and critic.

The "participant," "partisan" critical approach seems to have reached its high tide in the mid-1970s, after Watergate and Vietnam. Today, there appears to be a swing back to the "liberal" model. Charles B. Seib of the *Washington Post* notes that "in the old days, when a reporter let his opinions show he was quickly brought to heel by an editor," and in time was turned into "what we call an objective reporter—meaning a reporter who stuck strictly to the raw, unvarnished facts." Now, Seib maintains, while it is good that the old search for "blind objectivity" is over, "too often the new permissiveness is carried too far." The search for objectivity needs renewed emphasis.[38]

The public's commitment to fairness and objectivity

Time magazine notes that the highly critical "investigative" impulse of "participant" journalism worries many news executives. It quotes the editor of the *Oakland Tribune* as criticizing the trend of the 1960s and 1970s: "We are too hungry for blood—it sometimes seems to readers that we will not do the story unless we can do someone in." *Time* itself concludes that "the suspicious attitude among reporters leads to negativism in news coverage. The outlook of today's generation of journalists was formed during Watergate and Vietnam, when figures of authority seemed so often to be the proper adversary."[39] Work by John Immerwahr and John Doble suggests that most Americans think the press should hold to the "liberal" model. They want it to present the facts as objectively as possible. And they want it to be fair. The public believes that the general-news-dissemination segments of the press—television news and the daily papers—have an obligation not to be unduly partisan or critical, a constitutional responsibility to see to it that the populace has easy access to a balanced rendering of political happenings.[40]

What to Report: A Case Study

The debate over professional norms is not the only such issue occupying members of the press. An interesting case in 1983 that involved press handling of some missing State Department files illustrates another recurring issue in press ethics. The State Department sent a big collection of its file cabinets to the District of Columbia jail for refurbishing. Through a lapse of security at State, one drawer in one cabinet was not emptied. Prison inmates got hold of the files, which

[38] Seib's observations, discussed by James Boylan, "News People," *Wilson Quarterly,* Special Issue, 1982, pp. 82–83.
[39] "Journalism Under Fire," *Time,* December 2, 1983, p. 79.
[40] John Immerwahr and John Doble, "Freedom of the Press," *Public Opinion Quarterly,* Summer 1982, p. 185.

contained "telexes from embassies around the world, communications from CIA agents, sources in foreign embassies around the world." The classified files "dealt with Soviet missiles, the Druse in Lebanon, the border situation in Nicaragua [and the monitoring of a potential coup in the Third World]," among other things. The mistake was discovered, and most of the files were recovered and returned to the State Department. One set of files, however, was not found. The prisoner who had gotten hold of these called a reporter for a Washington television station and offered him the materials. The reporter picked them up, took them back to the station, and together with his editor perused them. The question was, Should the station put these classified materials on the air, or should it return them to the State Department without reporting on them?

The reporter who got the files, James Adams, and his editor, Betty Endicott, decided to return the materials without reporting on them. They called Senator Charles Mathias (Republican of Maryland), a member of the Foreign Relations Committee who was cleared to read such classified materials. On November 8, 1983, reporter Adams and Senator Mathias together brought the files back to State.

On what basis did Adams and Endicott reach their judgment? Endicott has stated that the key issue for her was that the documents contained no evidence that the government had lied. "If you find that the government is lying to the people, then I think you have a responsibility [to publish information revealing the lie]," she indicated. Adams has stated that "I didn't want to have a role in compromising national security. I kept asking myself the question, What good would it do?" Adams merely reported on the air that the files had been given to him and that he had returned them to the State Department. He did not divulge their substance.

This incident prompted a lively debate among journalists. Adams has stated that many news organizations called him asking for copies and refused to believe that he had not made copies before returning the documents. "You're giving gold away," they said. Staff for Jack Anderson, the syndicated columnist, were particularly insistent in prodding Adams to give them copies of the files.[41]

The deans of two major schools of journalism split on the issue. James Atwater, dean of the University of Missouri School of Journalism, the oldest in the country, supported Adams' decision. Atwater carried Adams' position one step further, stating that he would not even have read the documents prior to returning them. "I would feel like I was prying in some sense in an area I should not be involved in," he stated. "It's a complicated ethical issue." By way of contrast, the dean of the Columbia University School of Journalism, Osborn

Responsibility to publish v. national security

The ethics of press reporting

---

[41] For a thoughtful report on the State Department files and the journalistic debate over their disposition, see Jonathan Kwitny, "Returning State Department Files," *Wall Street Journal*, November 30, 1983, p. 28.

Elliott, argued that "a reporter's responsibility is to report. I can conceive of instances where the materials are indeed so sensitive as to require great care in their publication. But I would feel impelled to publish them unless I found very strong reasons internally not to."

Who is right? The story has been told of Secretary of War Stimson, in the 1930s, coming into receipt of some correspondence addressed to another political figure, material that might have proved embarrassing to the latter if Stimson had read and used it. The Secretary refused even to read the material and returned it to its rightful owner. "Gentlemen do not read other gentlemen's mail," he reportedly stated. Is such an ethic outdated, not applicable to journalists? Dean Atwater of the University of Missouri School of Journalism clearly does not think so. Or was editor Endicott right: that journalists should, in effect, read the government's mail but not report on it unless there is indication of clear governmental culpability? "Gentlemen can read other gentlemen's mail to see if the latter are lying and hence really not gentlemen." Or was Dean Elliott of Columbia University's School of Journalism on sound ground in stressing a journalistic responsibility to report everything relevant to politics, unless the gravest harm would be done? "Journalists are not 'gentlemen' at all, but rather watchdogs for the people."

The debate goes on, and its importance extends far beyond the case of these State Department files. American journalists, with unparalleled access to governmental officials, and at times inadvertent access to various private communications, have to decide where their reportorial imperatives leave off and other values—such as the right of the government to private communication—begin. In many ways, this argument is too important to be left to journalists alone, because it has important implications for the way the business of government is conducted. Wouldn't the country generally be better off if both government and the press consistently acted toward one another as gentlemen? The debate over journalistic ethics must become a debate over political ethics in the broadest sense, in a era when the press is indeed a fourth branch of government.

SUMMARY

News reporting plays an important part in democratic governance. Without ample and reliable sources of information on political officials, policies, and events, the public cannot be in a position to determine where their interests and values should lead them.

But the press—all organizations, television and newspapers included, involved in the mass dissemination of news—can never be simply a neutral source of a vital substance, a river from which citizens drink as they see fit. It is a social, economic, and political institution that gets organized in a distinctive way, that has great resources and hence potentially great power, and that is composed of men and women whose outlooks shape how they do their jobs.

In the United States the press is primarily composed of private news businesses. Newspapers and magazines are privately owned and operated in most democracies, but radio and television are commonly government enterprises. The American electronic press is, however, largely privately owned and operated. Government regulation of the print media is minimal, but the regulatory reach of government is substantial in the case of radio and television. The airwaves are a finite public resource. The Federal Communications Commission grants and renews licenses to broadcast, and it imposes such regulatory standards as the equal-time rule and the fairness doctrine.

Contemporary technology for news dissemination—including radio and TV broadcasting, cable television, and the printing of newspapers in locales around the country by satellite transmissions—has contributed to a great concentration of news resources. To reach mass audiences, large-scale organizations and extensive physical facilities are required. We have come a long way from the situation of a century-and-a-half ago when the largest news medium in the country's biggest city (New York) reached only a few thousand readers and was capitalized with a few thousand dollars. With concentration has come, inevitably, greater attention to the power of the press and greater concern over its possible biases.

Though conservatives have often charged the national media, especially television news, with having a liberal bias in their reporting, the studies that have been conducted do not substantiate this criticism. These studies do suggest, however, that journalists are now more likely to see themselves in an adversary relationship to other central institutions, including government, and to stress exposure of the latter's shortcomings and foibles. Some students of the press worry that its professional norms have contributed to the rise of an excessively cynical and manipulative view of political life.

The press and government are bound closely together in the United States. Journalists have unusually open access to government officials and they form an important part of the group with whom political figures have regular contact. Journalists are themselves part of the political community, not distant reporters on it. The press has come to play an especially extensive institutional role in the American electoral process. The news media, not the parties, are for most voters the main source of information about candidates and the shape of campaigns.

Part 5 | Public Policy

17 | Civil Liberties and Civil Rights

The American commitment to civil liberties and civil rights is given its most important formulations in the Declaration of Independence and certain amendments to the Constitution. The Declaration posits the ideal of civil rights and liberties for all citizens: "We hold these truths to be self-evident, that all men are created equal, that they are endowed by their Creator with certain unalienable rights, that among these are Life, Liberty, and the pursuit of Happiness." The Bill of Rights—the first ten amendments to the Constitution—were enacted to forbid *federal* interference with freedom of religion, speech, press, and assembly; to ensure "the right of people to be secure in their persons, houses, papers, and effects, against unreasonable searches and seizures . . ."; and to make explicit the rights of persons accused of crimes. Additional amendments enacted after the Civil War, especially the Fourteenth, were prompted by the fact that *state* governments denied blacks the most basic civil rights and liberties. The Fourteenth Amendment requires that "no State shall make or enforce any law which shall abridge the privileges or immunities of citizens of the United States; nor shall any State deprive any person of life, liberty, or property, without due process of law; nor deny to any person within its jurisdiction the equal protection of the laws." In the twentieth century, especially since 1960, the Supreme Court has interpreted the "due process" clause of the Fourteenth Amendment as enforcing upon the states all key requirements of the Bill of Rights.

Civil liberties and civil rights involve more than ringing words in great historical documents; they are a key element of contemporary public policy in the United States. In this chapter we first consider their special nature and characteristics as a policy area. Next we look at some of the important changes that have taken place in civil lib-

The historic 1963 march on Washington to protest discrimination against blacks.

erties and rights policy over the course of American history, especially the extension since World War II of the nation's guarantees of rights to the entire population. In the third section we examine the tensions currently arising in policy-making on civil rights and liberties as competing values or social objectives get set against one another. We conclude the chapter with a brief review of the governmental agencies and interest groups that are the most important actors in this sector of public policy.

THE CONSTITUTION, MAJORITY PREFERENCES, AND BASIC RIGHTS

Civil liberties and civil rights form the one major policy area where the Constitution makes detailed and explicit provisions. In other areas, it only outlines the institutional framework for decision-making. For example, on foreign policy the Constitution sets important guidelines, but these reach only to *how it is to be made,* not *what it is to be.*

The president is commander-in-chief of the armed forces; treaties do not take effect until they have secured the approval of at least two-thirds of the Senate. In the case of civil liberties and civil rights, however, the Constitution includes explicit policy statements.

Civil liberties and democratic government

Civil liberties and civil rights comprise the basic political tools and entitlements of the American people. When, for example, states deny some of their residents "the equal protection of the laws," they deny them a key element of their citizenship. Civil liberties and civil rights policies differ from those in other sectors in that they involve conditions without which democratic citizenship cannot exist. Because of this, we often assign civil liberties and civil rights issues entirely to another area: where *rights* are involved rather than legitimate *policy choices*.

Basic rights of citizenship

The idea that a right of citizenship is at issue strongly suggests that there can be only one proper course of action: that which ensures or guarantees the right. We debate what U.S. policy should be in Central America, or what government should do about the size of the federal deficit, because we assume that in these areas there is more than one valid choice. But if there is only one choice—a right to be fulfilled (even if it has at times been flagrantly denied)—the idea of policy is cast in a different light. Public policy becomes an effort to rectify present or past failings, or otherwise to ensure the proper realization of fundamental rights of American citizenship. No matter how weak its claimants are numerically, a right of citizenship must be honored.

This brings us back to the basic idea of American democracy discussed in chapter 6: democracy encompasses both *majority rule* and *minority rights*. In many areas of public policy, Americans have long believed that the preferences of the majority should be followed. But in some areas fundamental rights of individuals are engaged, whose claim must take precedence over majority wishes. Civil liberties and civil rights are often discussed in these terms.

Race relations and civil rights

Race relations provide the most dramatic and pervasive instance where the proud claim of "unalienable Rights" of every person to "Life, Liberty, and the pursuit of Happiness" is at stake. Slavery flourished in the South in America's first century. And for the next century gross categorical discrimination survived as black Americans were denied the vote and access to equal education, barred from many public facilities or segregated within them, and abused by police and the courts. Although this was the result of conscious public policy, these policies were simply wrong, morally and constitutionally.

There are many other issues in civil liberties and civil rights, however, where policy differences are such that we should submit to majoritarian resolution, where "reasonable" men and women, all committed to the constitutional system, simply disagree as to which policy is best. In these cases, conditions similar to those in other policy sectors apply: (1) A general goal may be readily articulated, but there is great uncertainty as to how that goal is best achieved; and

When should the
majority prevail?

(2) the choice is not between accepting or rejecting a fundamental right, but rather involves the relative weight to be assigned two or more competing values, all of which are worthy and consistent with national political beliefs. This is true even in the case of First Amendment questions, where the language of the Constitution seems clear and absolute: "Congress shall make no law . . . abridging the freedom of speech, or of the press. . . ." Freedom of speech is, in the American system, a fundamental right of everyone, which even large majorities may not curtail—but not every policy issue or question that arises concerning First Amendment guarantees involves an absolute and unequivocal right that must be upheld without regard to competing values or majoritarian claims.

Because issues of civil liberties and civil rights often do involve fundamental considerations of citizenship, it is tempting politically for groups and individuals to insist that a fundamental right of theirs is being denied—of speech, of the press, of the accused—rather than that an arguable policy choice is being made. For if my dispute with a policy can be construed as my dispute with a policy that denies me a basic right, I have gone a long way toward carrying the day. Our language in this policy area is replete, sometimes misleadingly so, with references to "rights"; we need to remind ourselves that the more common conditions of public policy—where reasonable people can and should differ, and majorities should carry the day—frequently apply.

SECURING BASIC RIGHTS

For a long time, problems of **civil rights** were synonymous with segregation and discrimination against black Americans. The reference is now more inclusive. It encompasses other groups in the population that have encountered *categoric discrimination:* for example, other ethnic minorities and women. Membership in groups subject to this kind of discrimination is something over which one has no control. In contrast, **civil liberties** problems typically involve the "rights of citizenship" of isolated individuals, such as persons accused of crimes, and groups made unpopular by their *beliefs*—religious, cultural, or political—rather than by attributes of birth like race or sex. Denying the right to vote to blacks is a *civil rights* issue; denying electoral participation to a small, unpopular political group is a *civil liberties* issue.

Extending Rights

All across the area of civil liberties and civil rights, one sees a clear progression or pattern of change, centered around *increasing expectations and demands,* and policy shifts that have come in response. This is especially noticeable in the years since World War II. The tim-

Women have made enormous gains in the past decades, but disagreements over what approach is needed now persist among women themselves as well as among men.

ing and magnitude of change varies from one sector to another. The political movement to advance the civil rights of black Americans was particularly strong in the 1960s; that for women's rights was more active in the late 1970s and in the 1980s. But heightened demands and important policy changes have been prominent in almost every sector of civil liberties and civil rights over the last forty years.

When it took shape as an independent nation in the eighteenth century, the United States thought of itself and was viewed by others as advanced in the extent to which it guaranteed individual rights of citizenship. Alexis de Tocqueville described America as the almost complete embodiment of individual equality and democratic governance.

> The emigrants who colonized the shores of America in the beginning of the 17th century somehow separated the democratic principle from all the principles that it has to contend with in the old communities of Europe, and transplanted it alone to the new world. It has there been able to spread in *perfect freedom* and peaceably to determine the character of the laws by influencing the manners of the country.[1]

Yet, if adherence to "the democratic principle" (by which Tocqueville certainly understood the rights of citizenship that we now call civil liberties and civil rights, as well as other aspects of social and political egalitarianism) came earlier and more substantially in

[1] Tocqueville, *Democracy in America*. Emphasis added.

Denial of rights to
blacks and women

America than in Europe, we know that it did not in fact "spread in perfect freedom." Civil liberties and civil rights that most Americans now consider absolutely fundamental were denied in Tocqueville's day, and much later. Slavery—then a flourishing institution—is, of course, the most dramatic example, but there are many others. Women were wholly disenfranchised, prohibited from voting in local, state, and federal elections. It was not until the late nineteenth century that women began to win the right to vote, and not until ratification of the Nineteenth Amendment on August 18, 1920, that the vote was fully extended to female citizens. (See chapter 14 for discussion of the extension of the suffrage in the United States over the nineteenth and twentieth centuries.)

Curbing Racial Discrimination

Changes in expectations and demands with regard to rights of citizenship have been greatly extended since the early nineteenth century. The change has been especially pronounced over the last half-century in the area of race relations. In the South, to which Negro GIs returned in 1945 and 1946, the black population was almost totally excluded from decision-making in all institutions which served the general, as opposed to solely the black, population. Nearly all public facilities in the region, including city parks and playgrounds, theaters, hotels, and restaurants, were rigidly segregated. As one small example of the pervasiveness of segregation in public facilities, the Southern Political Science Association long held its annual meeting in the tiny mountain town of Gatlinburg, in eastern Tennessee, because it was one of the very few spots in the entire South where blacks and whites (in this case, as college teachers) could meet, eat, and reside together in a resort hotel. School systems across the South were totally segregated. And blacks were almost completely disenfranchised: In the early 1940s, only 5 percent of voting-age black citizens in the South were registered voters.[2]

Violence against blacks. Perhaps the most reprehensible denial of basic citizenship rights was the vulnerability of blacks throughout much of the South to assaults on their personal safety and well-being. The Swedish social scientist Gunnar Myrdal observed in the 1940s that

> in the South the Negro's person and property are practically subject to the whim of any white person who wishes to take advantage of him or to punish him for any real or fancied wrong doing or "insult." A white man can steal from or maltreat a Negro in almost any way without fear of reprisal, because a Negro cannot claim the protection of the police or courts, and personal vengeance on the part of the offended Negro usually

[2] For further discussion of black political participation in the South, and of the changes that took place over the 1940s, 1950s, and 1960s, see Everett Ladd, *Negro Political Leadership in the South* (New York: Atheneum, 1969).

Those who protested against racial segregation were sometimes treated even more severely than those in this lunch counter sit-in.

results in organized retaliation in the form of bodily injury (including lynching), home burning or banishment. . . . Physical violence and threats against personal security do not, of course, occur to every Negro every day. . . . But violence may occur at any time, and it is the fear of it as much as violence itself which creates the injustice and the insecurity.[3]

Myrdal was not exaggerating. At least 3,275 black Americans were lynched in the South between 1882 and 1936.[4] And, as Myrdal pointed out, even if violations, intimidations, and frauds occurred only sporadically, the threat was always present.

Racial discrimination was not exclusively southern. But the denial of equal citizenship to blacks *was* far more extreme in the South than elsewhere in the country. And, as late as 1950, two-thirds of all black Americans resided in the eleven states that had seceded in 1861 to form the Confederacy.

Assertion of American values. Today, although debate goes on over the adequacy of the nation's response in civil rights, there is no doubt that extraordinary changes have occurred over the last 40 years, greatly extending the rights of black citizens. The sources of this rapid transformation are complex. Gunnar Myrdal identified one source when he pointed to the "ever-raging conflict" between the general principles of the American creed and the historic reality of American race relations—a conflict that could not persist forever. The average

[3]Gunnar Myrdal, *An American Dilemma* (New York: McGraw-Hill, 1964; first published 1944), p. 530.
[4]E. Franklin Frazier, *The Negro in the United States* (New York: Macmillan, 1957), p. 160.

American is "more of a believer and defender of the faith in humanity than the rest of the Occidentals. It is a relatively important matter to him to be true to his own ideals and to carry them out in actual life."[5]

The crucial question is not why the system of gross racial discrimination finally broke down in a rush in the 1950s and 1960s, but why this change was so slow in coming. The tensions between beliefs and practice were fundamental. A century earlier, Lincoln had seen clearly the extent and destructiveness of this contradiction. In his "House Divided" speech, delivered to the Republican state convention in Springfield, Illinois, on June 17, 1858, Lincoln cited the biblical passage "A house divided against itself cannot stand." He went on: "I believe this government cannot endure, permanently half *slave* and half *free*. I do not expect the Union to be *dissolved*—I do not expect the house to *fall*—but I *do* expect it will cease to be divided." But America's house was to remain divided for another century before the beliefs summoned action.

A "house divided" for over a century

Effects of demographic changes. Another source of change has to do with population movement. Sweeping shifts of blacks from rural to urban areas, and from the South to a more national distribution, increased the political power of black Americans. On the eve of American entry into World War I, nearly 90 percent of the black population of the United States still resided in the South; most blacks lived in rural areas and worked in agriculture. But World War I, with its

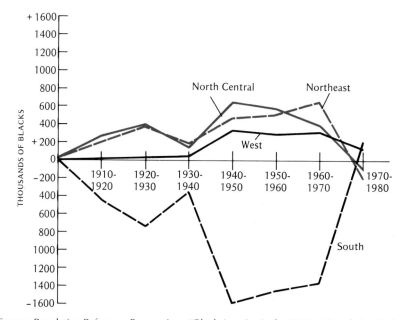

Figure 17.1

Net Migration of Blacks by Region since 1910 (in thousands)

Source: Population Reference Bureau, Inc., "Black America in the 1980s," *Population Bulletin,* vol. 37, No. 4, December 1982, p. 19. In this graph, the minus numbers, below the "zero line," indicate a net *out-migration* from the region. Positive numbers represent a net *in-migration.*

[5]Myrdal, *An American Dilemma*, p. lxx.

An example of the "Jim Crow" system.

increased demand for labor in war industries, provided large numbers of blacks with the economic opportunity to leave southern agriculture. "They began one of the most massive internal migrations in the history of the United States. . . . Three-quarters of a million Negroes moved North within a four-year period during World War I."[6] This migration continued after the war, and it expanded again during World War II. Between 1940 and 1970, the net emigration of blacks from the South into northern states was more than 4.4 million (see Figure 17.1).

Equally significant was the shift of blacks from rural areas to the cities, North and South alike. The 1960 census was the first to show a majority of southern blacks residing in urban areas. By 1980, a population that had been concentrated on farms and in small towns in the states of the old Confederacy was about evenly distributed between North and South, and overwhelmingly urban. According to the 1980 Census, only 15 percent of blacks nationally lived in rural areas, compared to 29 percent of whites. Some 57 percent of blacks, compared to just 25 percent of whites, lived in central cities.

Effects of population shifts on race relations

How did this affect race relations? The system of gross discrimination and segregation (sometimes known as "Jim Crow") had been a product of the rural South. It reflected attitudes that derived from the historical experience of slavery and the extreme vulnerability of rural blacks to intimidation and violence. The movement of large numbers of blacks to the North brought them into environments where the traditions and institutions of segregation had never been firmly established. It made black votes of increasing concern to northern politicians. The movement of blacks from rural to urban areas, South as well as North, brought them into settings where political and social

[6] Thomas Sowell, *Race and Economics* (New York: McKay, 1975), p. 49.

organization could proceed far more readily. And extralegal violence was far less pervasive among the concentrated black populations of southern cities than among the scattered populations of the rural South. Overall, the great demographic shifts of 1920–70 brought blacks into positions where political organization was easier and political influence much greater.

Sweeping changes in race relations since the 1950s

Against this backdrop, a concerted political effort was mounted in the first two decades after World War II. It went on simultaneously in five different arenas: (1) in the courts, expecially the federal courts; (2) through direct action by the civil rights movement, in marches, boycotts, sit-ins, and more; (3) within the legislative and executive branches of government, again especially at the federal level; (4) through voting and elections; and (5) in the "court" of American public opinion.

Brown v. *Board of Education of Topeka.* Many of the critical early steps were taken in the courts. Years of legal effort, led by the NAACP Legal Defense Fund, culminated in the Supreme Court's historic decision in *Brown* v. *Board of Education of Topeka* (and a series of companion cases) in 1954. (*Brown* is discussed in detail in chapter 10.) For the first time, segregated schools were declared in violation of the Equal Protection requirement of the Fourteenth Amendment. "Separate educational facilities are inherently unequal," wrote Chief Justice Earl Warren on behalf of a unanimous Court. *Brown* announced the end of "Jim Crow." It removed the aura of legitimacy and constitutionality from the entire system of racial exclusion. Although the case applied only to schools, and some recalcitrant judges tried to limit it to that arena, the Supreme Court followed up by citing *Brown* as authority for treating all official segregation as unconstitutional.[7]

Gains in education and occupational status

Direct-action protests. The early direct-action protests in the South, notably those led by a young black clergyman, Martin Luther King, Jr., played a key role. King, the son of a distinguished clergyman in Atlanta, first came to national attention in 1955 when he led a bus boycott in Montgomery, Alabama. A black woman, Rosa Parks, had been arrested in Montgomery for refusing to move to the "colored" section in the back of the bus. The boycott focused national attention not only on bus segregation in Montgomery, but on the whole pattern of segregation in public facilities across the South. It was followed by an expanding stream of direct-action protests: against discriminatory treatment by law-enforcement officials, school segregation, laws and practices which prevented blacks from eating with whites in restaurants and at lunch counters, and against almost all the forms of the old racial system.

[7]Richard Kluger, *Simple Justice: The History of Brown* v. *Board of Education and Black America's Struggle for Equality* (New York: Knopf, 1976).

Martin Luther King, Jr., was the single most influential black leader; he gave force and moral direction to the civil rights movement. Through his personal courage, eloquence as a speaker, strong commitment to nonviolence, and unflagging insistence that America honor its claim to the idea of equality, King helped shift the ground in race relations until his death at the hands of an assassin in 1968.

Table 17.1
Major Civil Rights Laws and Court Decisions, 1948–70

Year	Policy shift	Major acts, landmark cases
1948	Executive branch decrees end to discrimination against blacks in the military.	*Executive Order #9981*, issued by President Truman.
1954	"Separate but equal" doctrine struck down.	*Brown* v. *Board of Education of Topeka* (347 U.S. 483) and companion cases
1957, 1960	Acts signal the federal government to enter into a law enforcement role to protect voter rights. Actions take form of court injunctions.	*Civil Rights Act of 1957* (Public Law—PL—85-315) *Civil Rights Act of 1960* (PL 86-449)
1963	Employers required to pay equal wages to men and women for equal work.	*Equal Pay Act of 1963* (PL 88-38)
1964	Most significant policy departures in civil rights legislation since Reconstruction: guaranteeing blacks access to public accommodation, and equal employment opportunity.	*Civil Rights Act* (PL 88-352)
1964	Constitutionality of 1964 Civil Rights Act sustained.	*Heart of Atlanta Motel* v. *United States* (379 U.S. 241) *Katzenbach* v. *McClung* (379 U.S. 297)
1965	Major federal effort to guarantee voting rights to blacks.	*Voting Rights Act* (PL 89-110)
1968	Racially discriminatory housing practices made illegal. Constitutionality of 1968 fair housing policies sustained. Signals end to "officially sanctioned *de jure* racial segregation in housing," public as well as private.	*Civil Rights Act of 1968* *Jones* v. *Alfred H. Meyer Co.*

Legislation and voting. New legislation strengthened the hand of the civil rights movement (Table 17.1). Title II of the Civil Rights Act of 1964 established the substantive right not to be discriminated against in places of public accommodation. Titles III and IV authorized the Justice Department to bring suits to secure the desegregation of schools and other public facilities, upon the complaint of aggrieved parties who lacked the resources to pursue their own legal actions. The Civil Rights Acts of 1957 and 1960 were early efforts to extend the right of blacks to vote, but they had been badly watered-down to get past filibusters by southern senators. The Voting Rights Act of 1965, however, put the federal government behind the full extension and free exercise of the vote by blacks.

Public opinion and race relations. Public attitudes on racial issues became increasingly more liberal over the '50s, '60s, and '70s. When the question was first asked of a national sample in 1958, just 42 percent nationally said that if their party nominated a well-qualified black for president they would vote for him; the proportion reached 73 percent in 1969 and 85 percent in 1982 (Figure 17.2). In 1956, only 51 percent of whites said they thought white and black students should attend the same rather than separate schools; by 1982, however, 90 percent endorsed the principle of integrated education (Figure 17.3).

Public sentiment on civil rights issues is not uniform across various groups making up the population. Young adults are more supportive of racial change than older people. Americans with greater amounts

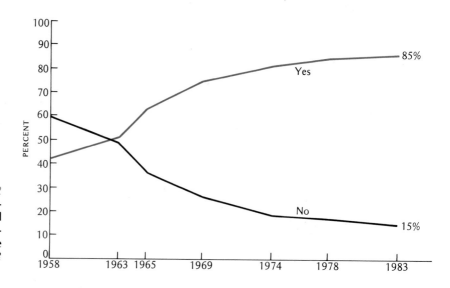

Figure 17.2
If Your Party Nominated a Well-Qualified Black Man for President, Would You Vote for Him?

The text of the question asked was essentially the same for Gallup and NORC, with minor variations.
Source: Surveys for 1958–69 were conducted by the Gallup Organization, those for 1974–1983 by the National Opinion Research Center, University of Chicago.

A meeting between Martin Luther King, Jr., and President Lyndon B. Johnson.

of formal education are more likely to endorse civil rights objectives than those with less education. And southerners are still less supportive of racial change than their fellow citizens in other parts of the country. But backing for nondiscriminatory policies has increased in all groups. For example, as we saw in chapter 3, southern racial attitudes are now much more like those elsewhere than they were in the past (Figure 3.7).

Figure 17.3 **School Integration Meets with Greater Approval**

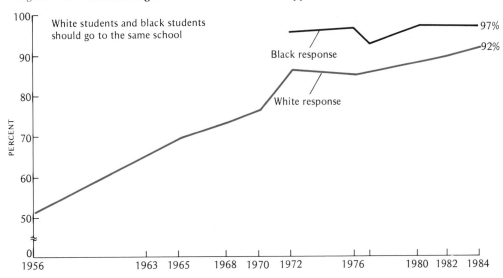

Question: Do you think white students and Negro students should go to the same schools? Question not asked for blacks by NORC until 1972.
Source: Surveys by the National Opinion Research Center, 1956–70; National Opinion Research Center, General Social Surveys, 1972, 1976, 1977, 1980, 1982, 1984.

Substantial Gains in Civil Rights

The net results of these several contributing factors are dramatic. Public accommodations throughout the country are now free of segregation. *De jure* segregation of the schools, based on law and enforced by government, has been eliminated. By the 1980s, black voter registration in the South was nearly as great proportionally as white registration (Figure 17.4). Blacks now have substantial electoral power in many cities, North and South, as the success of black candidates

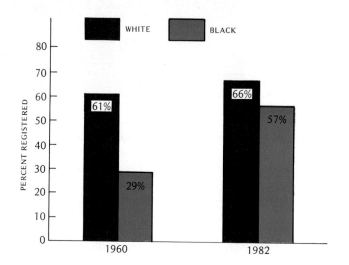

Figure 17.4
Voter Registration in the South by Race, 1960 and 1982

Source: U.S. Bureau of the Census, *Statistical Abstract of the United States, 1984,* p. 261.

attests. In 1984, a number of major U.S. cities, including Washington, Philadelphia, Chicago, Detroit, Los Angeles, and Atlanta, had black mayors. The number of blacks holding elective office climbed from just 1,500 in 1970 to over 5,000 in 1982 (Figure 17.5). Jesse Jackson's candidacy for the Democratic presidential nomination in 1984 mobilized black voters nationally and attracted about 20 percent of the total Democratic primary vote.

The proportion of blacks with at least a high school education grew from just 7 percent in 1940 to 55 percent in 1982. In 1940, the median years of school completed among black Americans age 25 and older was just 5.7, compared to 8.8 for whites. As late as 1970, the gap was almost that great. By 1982, however, it had shrunk significantly as the median for blacks climbed to 12.2 years, compared to 12.6 years for whites (Figure 17.6). Similar advances can be seen in the occupational area. Over the last decade the proportion of blacks in professional and managerial occupations increased appreciably. At the same time, blacks accounted for smaller percentages of those employed as unskilled laborers and as private household workers.

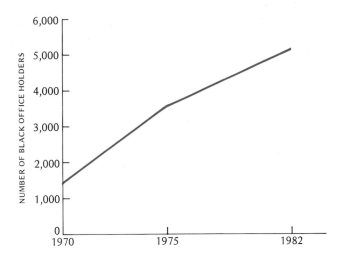

Figure 17.5
Blacks Holding Elective Office since 1970

Source: U.S. Bureau of the Census, *Statistical Abstract of the United States, 1984,* p. 261.

In two other critical areas, however, the experience of the last decade is far less encouraging. The income of black families continues to lag substantially behind that of white families: In 1982 the median income of black families was $13,598, compared to $24,603 for white families. The ratio of the incomes of the two groups has changed little over the last quarter-century. As Figure 17.7 indicates, unemployment has consistently been much higher among blacks than among whites. During the 1982 recession, unemployment in the black community surged, particularly among young black males, and this gap widened.

Figure 17.6 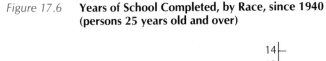 **Years of School Completed, by Race, since 1940 (persons 25 years old and over)**

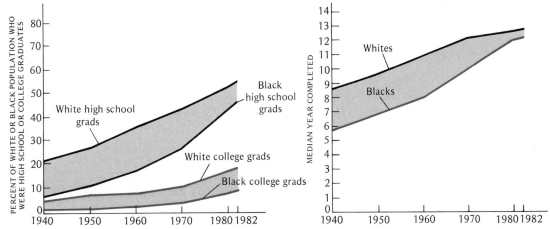

Source: Figures are based on computation of data listed in Table 223 of *Statistical Abstract of the United States, 1984,* p. 144.

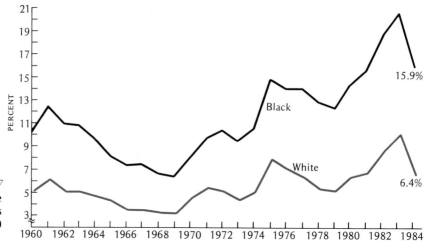

Figure 17.7
**Black and White
Unemployment Rates
since 1960**

Black data for 1960–71 are for "Blacks and other races."
Source: Population Reference Bureau, Inc., "Black America in the 1980s," *Population Bulletin,* vol. 37, no. 4, December 1982; and U.S. Department of Labor, Bureau of Labor Statistics, *Employment and Earnings,* July 1984, p. 46.

Extending the Rights of the Accused

Overall, a clear progression is evident in public policy regarding race relations since World War II, involving the extension and guarantee to black Americans of basic rights of citizenship. A similar progression can be seen in other areas involving civil rights and liberties: for example, decisions treating the constitutional protections of persons accused of crimes.

In some obvious ways, this area is very different from the civil rights issues just considered, which involved millions of law-abiding citizens who shared the common historical experience of racial discrimination, and who engaged in a range of political activities to end this legacy. The rights of the accused, in contrast, involve the claims of isolated individuals, identified as having committed crimes against society, who thus cannot express themselves in a conventional political movement. They depend largely upon the assertion of constitutional rights in courts of law. Despite such differences, the common thread of increased attention to individual rights is apparent in both areas.

The central role of the federal courts

Since World War II and especially since 1960, the U.S. Supreme Court has issued a series of opinions that together have substantially extended constitutional guarantees to persons involved in legal proceedings. A key element in these rulings is the application to the states of the full force and specificity of the Bill of Rights requirements that were originally intended to apply only to federal action.

Selective incorporation. Many Americans in the late 1780s and 1790s worried that the new national government might prove too strong and threaten individual liberty. The Bill of Rights was an important response to these concerns. It contained a set of specific prohibitions on national government action: *"Congress* shall make no law . . . ," the First Amendment begins its famous stipulation of guarantees of freedom of religion, speech, press, and assembly. By the time of the Civil War, however, the context had changed greatly. Outside the South the concern was not with federal action abridging individual liberty, but rather with denials of freedom by southern state governments. Against this backdrop the Fourteenth Amendment, ratified July 9, 1868, specified that "no *state* shall make or enforce any law which shall abridge the privileges or immunities of citizens of the United States; nor shall any state deprive any person of life, liberty, or property, without due process of law; nor deny to any person within its jurisdiction the equal protection of the laws."

Extension of guarantees under the Fourteenth Amendment

The Fourteenth Amendment was obviously intended to provide federal guarantees to black Americans against southern state denial of equality before the law. But the amendment's sweeping language has a broader reach. It does not refer just to blacks. No state government may deny *any person* "life, liberty, or property, without due process of law." The spirit is clear, but what specific requirements does it entail? Near the end of the nineteenth century, the Supreme Court began a process of **selective incorporation,** holding that specific limitations imposed on the national government by the Bill of Rights are similarly applied to state governments through the due-process clause of the Fourteenth Amendment. In *Chicago, Burlington, and Quincy Railroad Co.* v. *City of Chicago* (1897), the Court incorporated the Fifth Amendment guarantee against the taking of private property for public use without just compensation within the Fourteenth Amendment's due-process protections. Ever since that decision, as Table 17.2 shows, the Supreme Court has extended, one at a time, the range of Bill of Rights protections.

Right to counsel. In a 1938 decision *(Johnson* v. *Zerbst),* the Supreme Court ruled that the right to be represented by counsel is an absolute constitutional requirement in federal trials, under the terms of the Sixth Amendment. It wasn't until *Gideon* v. *Wainwright* in 1963, however, that the Court incorporated this guarantee of appointed counsel into the Fourteenth Amendment, making it applicable to state courts, where the bulk of criminal proceedings occur. Clarence Earl Gideon had been convicted in a Florida court of breaking and entering. Since he had no funds, he asked that the court furnish him with an attorney. The Florida judge replied:

> Mr. Gideon, I am sorry, but I cannot appoint counsel to represent you in this case. Under the laws of the state of Florida, the only time the court

Table 17.2

Major Cases Involving Selective Incorporation of the Bill of Rights into the
Fourteenth Amendment

1897	*Chicago, Burlington, and Quincy Railroad Co.* v. *Chicago*	Fifth Amendment guarantee against taking of private property for public use without just compensation
1925	*Gitlow* v. *New York*	First Amendment guarantee of freedom of speech and press
1932	*Powell* v. *Alabama*	Sixth Amendment right to employed counsel
1934	*Hamilton* v. *University of California*	First Amendment guarantee of free exercise of religion
1937	*Palko* v. *Connecticut*	Concept of "selective incorporation" articulated
1942	*Betts* v. *Brady*	Sixth Amendment guarantee of appointed counsel denied
1947	*Everson* v. *Board of Education*	First Amendment prohibition of laws respecting an establishment of religion
1948	*In re Oliver*	Sixth Amendment right to a public trial
1949	*Wolf* v. *Colorado*	Fourth Amendment guarantee against unreasonable searches and seizures, but not the exclusionary rule
1961	*Mapp* v. *Ohio*	Exclusionary rule
1962	*Robinson* v. *California*	Eighth Amendment guarantee against cruel and unusual punishment
1963	*Gideon* v. *Wainwright*	Sixth Amendment guarantee of appointed counsel
1964	*Malloy* v. *Hogan*	Fifth Amendment guarantee against compulsory self-incrimination
1965	*Pointer* v. *Texas*	Sixth Amendment right to confront opposing witnesses
1966	*Parker* v. *Gladden*	Sixth Amendment right to an impartial jury
1967	*Klopfer* v. *North Carolina*	Sixth Amendment guarantee of speedy trial
1967	*Washington* v. *Texas*	Sixth Amendment guarantee of compulsory process for obtaining witnesses
1968	*Duncan* v. *Louisiana*	Sixth Amendment guarantee of trial by jury
1969	*Benton* v. *Maryland*	Fifth Amendment guarantee against double jeopardy

can appoint [in effect, pay for] counsel to represent a defendant is when that person is charged with a capital offense. I am sorry, but I will have to deny your request to appoint counsel to defend you in this case.

If you want a lawyer, Mr. Gideon, you will have to find the funds to pay for him yourself. The Supreme Court disagreed. It accepted Gideon's claim that he was entitled to be represented by counsel, and that Florida was required to provide him with one. The Court overturned Gideon's conviction. What had been simply a right to be represented by an attorney during a trial if the defendant wanted such counsel and could afford to pay for it, became a positive obligation upon state as well as federal courts to make certain that all individuals accused of crimes be represented by attorneys. The Court concluded that

> in our adversary system of criminal justice, any person haled into court, who is too poor to hire a lawyer, cannot be assured a fair trial unless counsel is provided for him. . . . From the very beginning, our state and national constitutions and laws have laid great emphasis on procedural and substantive safeguards designed to assure fair trials before impartial tribunals in which every defendant stands equal before the law. This noble ideal cannot be realized if the poor man charged with crime has to face his accusers without a lawyer to assist him.[8]

The exclusionary rule. In *Mapp* v. *Ohio* (1961), the Court enlarged the Fourth Amendment guarantee of "the right of the people to be secure in their persons, houses, papers, and effects, against unreasonable searches and seizures . . . ," by requiring that the states do what the federal government had been required to do since 1914: exclude from criminal trials evidence that had been unconstitutionally obtained.

Mapp v. *Ohio*

Police officers in Cleveland, Ohio, had forced their way into the residence of one Dolly Mapp, searched her dwelling, and seized "certain lewd and lascivious books, pictures, and photographs. . . ." This resulted in Mapp's conviction under an Ohio obscenity statute. The Supreme Court reversed her conviction, ruling that the Fourth Amendment guarantee is enforceable against the states "by the same sanction of exclusion as is used against the federal government." Since the evidence against Dolly Mapp had been obtained in violation of her right to privacy, it could not be used in a trial as part of the government's case against her. This is known as the **exclusionary rule.** In *Mapp*, the Supreme Court put the states on notice that if they convicted people on the basis of evidence unconstitutionally obtained, they could find the convictions overturned.

The "Miranda Rules." In *Miranda* v. *Arizona* (1966), the Supreme Court ruled that no conviction, whether in federal or state court, could stand

[8] *Gideon* v. *Wainwright*, 372 U.S. 335 (1963). For an interesting account of the *Gideon* case and its implications, see Anthony Lewis, *Gideon's Trumpet* (New York: Vintage Books, 1966).

Miranda v. Arizona

if evidence introduced at the trial had been obtained by law-enforcement officers in interrogations where the accused had not been specifically advised, prior to any questioning, of his constitutional rights to remain silent and to be represented by an attorney. Ernesto A. Miranda had been convicted in a state court in Arizona of kidnapping and rape, on the basis of a confession obtained after two hours of questioning in which he was not told of his rights to counsel and to silence.

Chief Justice Earl Warren delivered the majority opinion that laid out what have come to be known as the ***"Miranda Rules."*** These rules have affected the way police officials all across the country handle the questioning of persons accused of crimes. A specific set of procedures must be followed, Warren wrote, in all cases of "custodial interrogation," which he defined as "questioning initiated by law-enforcement officers after a person has been taken into custody or otherwise deprived of his freedom of action in any significant way." Before any questioning,

> the person must be warned that he has a right to remain silent, that any statement he does make may be used as evidence against him, and that he has a right to the presence of an attorney, either retained or appointed. The defendant may waive effectuation of these rights, provided the waiver is made voluntarily, knowingly, and intelligently. If, however, he indicates in any manner and at any stage of the process that he wishes to consult with an attorney before speaking there can be no questioning. Likewise, if the individual is alone and indicates in any manner that he does not wish to be interrogated, the police may not question him.[9]

Police officers are now routinely provided with a "Miranda Card," containing a statement of the rules Warren set forth, which the officer can refer to in reading the defendant his rights.

New York v. Quarles

The Miranda requirement is now well-established. In 1984, however, the Supreme Court for the first time established a "public safety exception." A woman in Queens, New York, had hailed a police car and told the officers that a gunman had just raped her. She said that her assailant had fled into a nearby supermarket. The police entered the store, sighted a man who fitted the woman's description, chased him down an aisle and caught him. One of the officers noticed that the suspect was wearing an empty shoulder holster and asked where the gun was. The man nodded toward a pile of boxes and said, "The gun is over there." The officer had not informed the suspect of his right to remain silent before he asked about the gun, and for this reason the New York courts subsequently granted motions filed by defense attorneys to prevent the suspect's statement and the gun from being admitted as evidence. In *New York* v. *Quarles* (1984), a closely divided Supreme Court held that while the New York courts had been correct under the prevailing interpretation of the Miranda Rule, an

[9] *Miranda v. Arizona,* 384 U.S. 436 (1966).

exception had to be established. "We believe that this case presents a situation where concern for public safety must be paramount to adherence to the literal language of the prophylactic rules enunciated in Miranda," Justice William Rehnquist stated for the 5-4 majority.

COMPETING VALUES COLLIDE

One of the greatest complexities of public policy-making is the frequency with which the pursuit of one value creates problems for other worthy objectives. Would it be desirable, for instance, to increase retirement benefits paid to elderly Americans under Social Security? Of course, especially for that segment of the populace which depends on Social Security for its sustenance. Any large increase in Social Security benefits requires large tax increases, however, increases that would be resented by many taxpayers. It would cause discomforts for some as great as the comforts higher benefits would confer on others. Increasing benefits is a worthy goal, but so is keeping taxes down. There does not seem to be a single, clear-cut "right" answer; rather there is a need to compromise and adjust among competing objectives, where no one can be sure just what balance is best.

This is the situation facing the Supreme Court and the country in large areas of civil liberties and rights policy. A new plateau was reached in the 1960s, defined by greater attentiveness to individual rights than obtained previously. But on this new plateau the old need to strike appropriate balances among competing objectives has inevitably asserted itself.

The exclusionary rule revisited. We noted above that the principle of the exclusionary rule's application to the states—as a deterrent to impermissible police conduct—was established in the 1960s. This does not mean that judicial policy in this area has become a consensual matter where a straightforward provision is easily followed. As it has tried to apply the exclusionary rule, the Supreme Court has run into some thorny problems, and has found itself engulfed in a vigorous debate.

Brewer v. Williams A highly controversial case that reached the Supreme Court in 1976 and was decided the next year involved a man, Robert Williams, who was convicted by an Iowa court for the murder on Christmas Eve, 1968, of a ten-year-old girl. While being returned by police to Des Moines, Iowa, where the crime was committed, and without his attorney present, Williams was told by a detective: "I feel that you yourself are the only person that knows where this little girl's body is. . . . And, since we will be going right past the area on the way into Des Moines, I feel we should stop and locate the body, that the parents of this little girl should be entitled to a Christian burial for the little girl. . . ." No violence or compulsion was employed. After thinking about the matter for some time, Williams directed the officers to the victim's body. He was subsequently convicted of the murder.

In *Brewer* v. *Williams* (1977), a deeply divided Court set aside Williams' conviction. It held that the right to the assistance of counsel,

"guaranteed by the Sixth and Fourteenth Amendments, is indispensable to the fair administration of our adversary system of criminal justice." Williams' incriminating statements, made in response to police conduct that violated his constitutional right to counsel, should have been excluded, the Court ruled by a narrow 5-4 majority. Williams' attorney had been promised that no questioning would be attempted on the trip back to Des Moines. Yet the police officer had persisted. "The crime of which Williams was convicted," Justice Potter Stewart wrote for the majority,

> was senseless and brutal, calling for swift and energetic action by the police to apprehend the perpetrator and gather evidence with which he could be convicted. No mission of law enforcement is more important. Yet "disinterested zeal for the public good does not assure either wisdom or right in the methods it pursues." . . . The pressures on state executive and judicial officers charged with the administration of the criminal law are great, especially when the crime is murder and the victim a small child. But it is precisely the predictability of those pressures that makes imperative a resolute loyalty to the guarantees that the Constitution extends to us all.

This ruling drew strong criticism, including a bitter dissent by Chief Justice Warren Burger.

> The result in this case ought to be intolerable in any society which purports to call itself an organized society. . . . Williams is guilty of the savage murder of a small child; no member of the Court contends he is not. While in custody, and after no fewer than *five* warnings of his rights to silence and to counsel, he led police to the concealed body of his victim. The Court concedes Williams was not threatened or coerced and that he spoke and acted voluntarily and with full awareness of his constitutional rights. In the face of all this, the Court now holds that because Williams was prompted by the detective's statement—not interrogation but a statement—the jury must not be told how the police found the body.

Feelings run high, even among professional jurists in the lofty setting of the U.S. Supreme Court, when key values compete for recognition in a context where something has to give. In *Brewer* v. *Williams*, the Justices did not disagree on the high worth of both sets of contending objectives: protecting the rights of the accused and ensuring the prompt apprehension and conviction of those who commit crimes against society. But they were sharply at odds over how to balance these values in the immediate case. They disagreed on two major questions. (1) Did the police officer deny Williams his constitutional rights? The majority emphasized that the officer persisted in a kind of interrogation, even though a specific promise had been made that no questioning would take place in the absence of counsel. The minority

One view of the exclusionary rule.

stressed that a gentle appeal to the suspect's conscience is hardly equivalent to police brutality or coercion. (2) If the police did act improperly, should the evidence that resulted be excluded? Here, some justices opted for a more sweeping application of the exclusionary rule, while others felt it should not be applied to "non-egregious" police conduct—in other words, to behavior that, if technically wrong, did not threaten the "individual dignity or free will" of the suspect.

Stone v. *Powell*

The Court has continued to search for the right balance in its use of the exclusionary rule. In *Stone* v. *Powell* (1976), for example, it ruled that federal courts need not require the exclusion of evidence acquired in violation of Fourth Amendment ("unreasonable searches and seizures") guarantees, unless the prisoner could show that he was denied "a full and fair" litigation of his Fourth Amendment claim in state courts. Another exception, the so-called inevitable discovery doctrine, was issued in a case that resulted from the retrial of Robert Williams, whose first appeal we have just discussed.

Nix v. *Williams*

After the Court overturned Williams' conviction in *Brewer* v. *Williams*, the state of Iowa brought him to trial a second time in state court on the "inevitable discovery" doctrine. Williams had never been found innocent, so there was no question of double jeopardy (trying a person a second time, after he had been found not guilty). Williams' conviction had simply been set aside on the grounds that some of the evidence introduced should not have been admitted. Two hundred volunteers had been combing the area and were nearing the spot where the body was discovered, when Williams led the police to it. In the second trial, the Iowa court concluded that even without Williams' statement, the body would have been discovered anyway. In *Nix* v. *Williams* (1984), the Supreme Court accepted the state's argument. The majority opinion—written by Chief Justice Burger, author of the angry dissent in the Court's consideration of the case seven years earlier—held that the point of the "inevitable discovery" doctrine was to put the police "in the same, not a worse, position than they would have been if no police error or misconduct had occurred."

United States v. Leon

In another 1984 ruling, *United States* v. *Leon*, the Supreme Court partially adopted the "good faith" exception to the exclusionary rule. This provision follows from an argument some justices, including the chief justice, had advanced in earlier cases concerning "non-egregious" police conduct. The "good faith" exception permits the use of improperly obtained evidence as long as the police had a reasonable belief that they were acting lawfully. Writing for the majority in the *Leon* case, Justice Byron White for the present limited the application of the "good faith" exception to situations in which the police obtained a search warrant and executed a search in accord with it, only later to have the warrant found defective. The evidence obtained through such searches need not be excluded, the Court held.

Balancing conflicting values

Where the Court finds the proper balance of conflicting values or claims depends on the outlooks of the sitting justices and the national climate of opinion in which the Court is operating. In the 1980s majorities on the Burger Court are somewhat more inclined to lean toward the claims of police officials and state court decisions than the Warren Court's majorities had been in the 1960s. Still, the process of sorting out contending claims is occurring within a general structure set down in the 1960s in such decisions as *Mapp*, *Gideon*, and *Miranda*.

Other policy issues in the area of civil liberties and rights are experiencing this same sort of search for the right balance of competing objectives, within the new climate of opinion and expectations that appeared in the quarter-century after World War II.

Affirmative Action, Quotas, and Equality of Opportunity

What remedial or corrective measures should the society take to remove as quickly as possible the vestiges of racial discrimination? Part of the answer seems clear and generates little debate: Where discrimination exists in law and formal practice, it should be ended. Discriminatory legal provisions should be removed. Governmental power should be used to prevent various private groups from continuing to block black participation. But is this all that is required? If a group has been subject to a pervasive pattern of discrimination over an extended period, is it enough simply to end discrimination? Or are additional positive steps needed, at least in the short run, to extend further opportunities to the deprived group and increase its representation in various arenas of national life?

Over the last two decades programs have been developed requiring **affirmative action:** taking positive measures to undo the effects of past discrimination faster than would occur simply by stopping pres-

Affirmative action

ent discrimination. For example, if the population of a large city is 70 percent black, but blacks comprise only 20 percent of the city's police force and an even smaller proportion of ranking police officials, isn't it sound public policy to require affirmative measures to increase black police representation? Or, if blacks and Hispanics are underrepresented in the American medical professions, shouldn't medical schools actively seek to increase the numbers of their black and Hispanic students? Many people think so, and federal and state laws have mandated affirmative-action programs in education and hiring across the country.

Quotas

Much of this effort has received substantial public acceptance. Polls show, for example, that the principle of affirmative action is endorsed by large majorities. But there is disagreement on important aspects of implementation, especially on how to balance the claims of underrepresented groups with those of students and job seekers from such groups as white males that in past have had more than their proportional share. **Quotas** have been in the middle of this argument. Setting quotas means that, in order to achieve the general goal of more equitable representation that underlies affirmative action, a certain number of positions—seats in an incoming university class or new job openings—will go to applicants from groups that have endured past discrimination. Advocates of quotas defend them as practically necessary if the principle of affirmative action is to be observed. Critics insist that quotas are excessively harsh on applicants who happen to come from groups overrepresented in the past. They argue that quotas deny the important principle that people should be assessed on their individual merits, that no criteria of group membership should finally determine who is hired or admitted, and conversely who is turned down.

Regents of University of California v. *Bakke (1978)*. The efforts of the University of California at Davis Medical School to increase the number of black and Hispanic graduates produced the most publicized ruling on the use of quotas as part of affirmative action handed down to date. The Davis Medical School had developed a two-track system for applicants, with 84 of its 100 places in each year's entering class held for open competition, and the remaining 16 reserved for "disadvantaged" applicants, in practice, blacks and Mexican-Americans. This program, with its declared policy of preferential admission for ethnic minorities, was developed by personnel of the medical school without any specific outside intervention, but it was a response to general social pressure for affirmative action to hurry growth in the numbers of minority-group professionals.

Allan Bakke is a white male who applied for admission to the medical school at Davis in 1972. While employed as an engineer for a space-agency laboratory near Palo Alto, California, Bakke came in contact with medical doctors who had been studying the effects of space on the human body. He was stimulated and encouraged to become a doctor. And, after night courses in science and voluntary work in hospitals, he applied for medical school at the age of 32. Bakke's credentials for application were generally very strong. He had impressed his medical school evaluators, receiving a score of 468 out of a possible 500 in the admissions office's summary compilation of all the measures it applied. But by the time Bakke completed his application (delayed because of family illness) most of the 84 places that had been set aside for open competition had already been filled. He was rejected—even though his scores were substantially higher than those of the minority applicants subsequently admitted.

In a July 1, 1972, letter to the medical school, Bakke stated that he was not prepared to accept his rejection as legitimate:

Bakke's rebuttal

> Applicants chosen to be our doctors should be those representing the best qualifications, both academic and personal. . . . I am convinced a significant fraction . . . is judged by a separate criterion. I am referring to quotas, open or covert, for racial minorities. . . . I realize that the rationale for these quotas is that they attempt to atone for past discrimination. But instituting a new racial bias in favor of minorities is not a just solution.

Bakke went on to state that it was his belief "that admissions quotas based on race are illegal," and he indicated that he might challenge the Davis Medical School quota system in the courts.[10]

Court appeal

Still, Bakke's next step was not to sue, but rather to reapply for admission to the Davis Medical School, in the next year's class. But he was again rejected, and this time he did file suit. The California court of original jurisdiction upheld his claim; when the University of California appealed, Bakke's position was again sustained by the highest state court. In a ruling joined by six of the seven justices, the California Supreme Court held that since the University had never discriminated *against* minorities, it could not now discriminate *for* them. It said that reserving sixteen places for minorities amounted to a quota based on race. The one dissenting justice attacked the decision of the court's majority: "Two centuries of slavery and racial discrimination have left our nation an awful legacy, a largely separated society in which wealth, educational resources, employment opportunities—indeed all society's benefits—remain largely the preserve of the white-Anglo majority." It was high time that corrective measures like the preferential admissions program be instituted.

Having lost at the state level, the university carried its appeal to the U.S. Supreme Court. There, in a deeply divided opinion, Bakke's position was again sustained (and he was subsequently admitted to the Davis Medical School, graduating in 1982). The Supreme Court

---

[10]For this and other detailed information on the Bakke case, see Allan P. Sindler, *Bakke, DeFunis, and Minority Admissions: The Quest for Equal Opportunity* (New York: Longman, 1978).

Supreme Court ruling

split in an unusual way: in effect, 4, 4, and 1. The one, Justice Lewis Powell, sided with one group of four in ruling that Bakke must be admitted. But he sided with the other four in rejecting the argument that the University of California could not consider race in any way in admissions. "The state certainly has a legitimate and substantial interest in ameliorating, or eliminating where feasible, the disabling effects of identified discrimination. . . . [This interest] may be served by a properly devised admissions program involving the competitive consideration of race and ethnic origin."

Justice Powell concluded that the minority-preferential admissions program of the Davis Medical School was unconstitutional, because the way it operated violated the equal-protection clause of the Fourteenth Amendment. That program, Powell held, "involves the use of an explicit racial classification never before countenanced by this Court. It tells applicants who are not Negro, Asian, or Chicano that they are totally excluded from a specific percentage of the seats in an entering class." The Constitution does not permit this. The other four judges who voted with Powell to admit Bakke wanted to strike down the Davis plan as in violation of Title VI of the Civil Rights Act of 1964. They presumably would have gone further than Powell would have in invalidating other preferential admissions programs.

Lobbying the Court on *Bakke*

The Supreme Court was heavily lobbied in the Bakke case through the traditional judicial means of *amicus curiae* ("friend of the court") briefs (see chapter 13). Fifty-seven individuals and organizations filed *amicus* briefs, advising the Court how they construed the legal issues and requirements in this case. There were more such briefs than observers could recall in any previous instance. On Bakke's side were seven Jewish organizations, including the Anti-Defamation League of B'nai B'rith; white ethnic groups of Italian, Polish, or Ukrainian ancestry; business interests; and political conservatives. On the side of the university were briefs filed by a number of other universities, professional associations in law and medicine, civil rights groups, and minority organizations.

"Both sides are right." Especially interesting, and what in his review of the case Allan Sindler calls a "mini-*amicus* brief," is the editorial of the *New York Times* on June 19, 1977. Entitled "Reparation, American Style," the editorial covered a full half-page in tiny print. The *Times* thought the Bakke case was not only important but complex in the clash of values it presented, and that "the law, without too much difficulty, could resolve this case either way." People who are equally "wise and generous," the *Times* argued, could be found on either side.

> . . . many grow anxious on the threshold of this case. They say we must not fight evil with evil, discrimination with "reverse discrimination." They say the entire society will suffer if it compromises standards of merit in education or employment and holds back competent people to promote the fortunes of the "less qualified." They say an America only

recently liberated from official racism must require its institutions to be color-blind, to judge individuals without reference to race or ethnic origin.

Others argue, with equal passion, that there can be no remedy for inherited damage without transferring some opportunity from the advantaged majority to injured minorities. They say we cannot claim equal rights and expect to achieve them without helping minorities to exercise those rights. They say the damage will endure if policy ignores the handicaps currently inherent in some racial and ethnic status—that color must be relevant today if it is to be irrelevant tomorrow.[11]

The *Times* concluded that "both sides are right. But it is in the national interest that Mr. Bakke should lose the case."

Fullilove, et al, v. Klutznick

This controversy did not end with the *Bakke* decision. It continues to be a prominent part of the debate over civil rights policy. The Supreme Court continues to grapple with the need to reconcile competing national values and goals. In *Fullilove, et al., v. Klutznick* (1979), the Court dealt with a challenge to the constitutionality of a provision of the Public Works Employment Act of 1977, which requires that at least 10 percent of federal funds granted for local public works projects be used to procure services from minority-owned businesses. This time the Court, by a 6-3 margin, upheld the special remedial program.[12] Supreme Court justices seem to be in much the same position as the *New York Times* editorial writer: They think both sides are right, so they try to give recognition to both positions in this clash of competing values. The goal is to be "color-blind": to assign jobs and other positions without regard to group membership. But recognizing the history of past discrimination, some forms of corrective or remedial action may be appropriate in some cases.

From *de Jure* to *de Facto* Segregation

The Supreme Court ruled in *Brown* and its companion cases that governmental operation of a segregated school system violates the Fourteenth Amendment of the U.S. Constitution. That issue has been settled. *De jure* (arising out of law) segregation is no longer countenanced anywhere in the United States. But what about *de facto* segregation: the kind that results from residential patterns? For example, large sections of cities, or even entire cities, are sometimes so disproportionately black, at least among the public-school-attending population, that most black pupils attend schools that are not integrated, even though school authorities do not require or encourage this situation.

In the late 1960s, the argument over *de facto* segregation centered on the issue of busing. If urban schools located in the center of black

[11]"Reparation, American-Style," *New York Times*, June 19, 1977, p. E16.
[12]*Fullilove, et al., v. Klutznick, Secretary of Commerce, et al.*, 448 U.S. 448 (1979).

De facto segregation and busing

or white neighborhoods were to be racially integrated, it would be necessary to transport students out of their home neighborhoods. Was such busing desirable? Should it be required by law? And if required by law, how far should busing extend? Within the bounds of the city, or across an entire metropolitan area?

Federal district courts increasingly ordered busing because it seemed in many cases the only way to achieve genuine desegregation. In an important 1971 decision, *Swann* v. *Charlotte-Mecklenburg County Board of Education,* the Supreme Court reviewed one district court order, in which the Charlotte-Mecklenburg (North Carolina) Board of Education was required to bus pupils to increase integration. Considering the school authorities in default of their "affirmative obligation" to advance integration, the district court had fashioned its own busing plan, the specifics of which were worked out by a court-appointed expert.

In his opinion written for a unanimous Supreme Court, Chief Justice Burger held that the requirement of extensive busing within the school district—one key feature of which involved transporting black students, grades one through four, to outlying white schools, and transporting white students from the fifth and sixth grades into inner-city black schools—was a constitutionally defensible remedy. It was constitutional in this instance, Burger argued, because it was needed as part of the dismantling of the old system, common throughout the South, of *de jure* segregation.

Court ordered busing met with public opposition. (Federal District Judge Garrity ordered busing in Boston.)

Busing was not authorized, the chief justice maintained, to deal with *de facto* segregation. Three years after the Charlotte-Mecklenburg decision, Burger wrote the majority opinion for a sharply (5-4) divided court, overturning a district court's order of metropolitan-area-wide busing, involving the city of Detroit and the surrounding suburban school districts. There was no "substantive constitutional right," Burger held, to "any particular degree of racial balance or mixing," and the lower court's requirement of a metropolitan plan to achieve a uniform mix of black and white students throughout the area was not constitutionally authorized because it involved school districts where no official segregation had ever been shown to have occurred. The district-court ruling in this case, *Milliken* v. *Bradley*, is reviewed in chapter 10.

Is busing good public policy? Is the busing of pupils from schools in the geographic areas where they reside, so as to advance school integration, good public policy? Many experts continue to defend it. Certainly large numbers of black and white pupils will continue to attend schools largely of one race unless busing is used extensively, given prevailing residential patterns. On the other hand, court-ordered busing seems to encourage "white flight": the exodus of whites out to the suburbs. "White flight" only increases the percentage of blacks in central-city school districts, making it virtually impossible to achieve school desegregation there. The 1980 Census showed nine central cities in the United States with populations 50 percent or more black. As Table 17.3 shows, the public-school-attending populations of these cities are overwhelmingly black, such that even extensive intracity busing would do little to remove *de facto* segregation. Is metropolitan-area-wide busing needed? The Supreme Court overturned a district court's order of such busing in *Milliken v. Bradley*.

Public opinion on busing The vast majority of whites have consistently opposed busing. When, in the spring of 1983, the National Opinion Research Center asked a national sample whether "in general . . . you favor or oppose the busing of black and white school children from one district to another?" 79 percent of whites said they were against it. This same survey found 43 percent of blacks opposed to busing. The courts have struggled with this issue, and the debate over busing goes on, because there is no simple answer. Contending interests and objectives on both sides are valid ones. America has a strong national interest in seeing school integration advanced. But just how much busing should be required, in what instances? Or what are the alternatives to busing? These questions require a search for subtle balances, rather than the easy assertion of a basic "right."

Freedom of Expression

Democracy is impossible without freedom of expression—impossible if citizens are prevented from speaking and writing, meeting and

Table 17.3
Black Public School Enrollment (Grades 1–12) in U.S. Cities with Populations More than 50 Percent Black

Cities	Total population (thousands)	Percent black	Black public school enrollment as percentage of total public school enrollment
Atlanta, GA	495	67	93
Baltimore, MD	905	55	81
Birmingham, AL	301	56	76
Detroit, MI	1,514	63	91
Gary, IN	175	71	85
New Orleans, LA	593	55	97
Newark, NJ	382	58	76
Richmond, VA	249	51	85
Washington, DC	757	70	99

Source: U.S. Bureau of the Census, *Statistical Abstract of the United States, 1984,* pp. 28–30; idem, *1980 Census of Population* 1 (Washington, D.C.: Government Printing Office, 1983), chap. C.

organizing on behalf of their social aims. Although we draw many other satisfactions from free expression, we recognize its special importance to the operation of a democratic polity. Freedom of expression has always been given a high position in American law, from the First Amendment's insistence that Congress shall make no law curtailing the freedom of religion, speech, press, and assembly.

Schenck v.
United States

Despite the language of the First Amendment, the rights of free speech and other forms of expression have not been seen by most people or by American law as absolute. We recognize instances where uncurbed expression does violence to other worthy ends. Libelous and obscene speech have been held subject to restrictions. In his famous opinion in the case of *Schenck* v. *United States* (1919), Justice Oliver Wendall Holmes, Jr., offered this example of why curbs are sometimes valid: "The most stringent protection of free speech," Holmes wrote, "would not protect a man in falsely shouting fire in a theater and causing a panic." But Holmes' example is too easy. When are restrictions on *political expression* justified, and when do they have a "chilling effect" on a free society? This question has been debated in many different contexts, and the Supreme Court has struggled to provide coherent answers.

Curbs on freedom
of expression

When the United States has faced a serious threat, notably during a war, governmental authorities have generally been more willing to enact and countenance restrictions on political speech than in less threatening times. For example, during the Civil War military officials imposed curbs on speech and press under the sanction of martial law. No question of the validity of these acts was ever brought to the Supreme Court. Curbs were also enacted during World War I. The Espionage Act of 1917 penalized any circulation of false statements made with intent to interfere with military success. The Sedition Act of 1918 made it a crime to say (or do) anything that might obstruct the sale of government bonds needed to finance the war effort, or to speak or publish words intended to bring into contempt the government of the United States, or to invite resistance to its lawful acts. The legality of these two pieces of legislation, under which almost a thousand persons were convicted, was upheld in six cases decided by the Supreme Court after the war.

Dennis v. United States

In 1940, against the backdrop of the rise of fascism and communism, and the outbreak of World War II, Congress enacted the Alien Registration Act (Smith Act). It provided for punishment of anyone who "knowingly or willfully advocates . . . or teaches the duty . . . or propriety of overthrowing . . . the government of the United States . . . by force or violence. . . ." It further provided for punishment of those disseminating literature advocating such overthrow, those organizing any group "to teach, advocate or encourage" such overthrow, and those who knowingly became members of any group advocating the violent overthrow of American government. In 1948 amidst fear (some say hysteria) over domestic communism, 11 top leaders of the Communist party of the United States were indicted under the Smith Act; they were convicted in federal district court in 1949, and their conviction was subsequently upheld by the Court of Appeals and by the Supreme Court *(Dennis v. United States,* 1951).

In the majority opinion, Chief Justice Frederick Vinson observed that

"Clear and present danger"

the obvious purpose of the statute is to protect existing Government, not from change by peaceable, lawful constitutional means, but from change by violence, revolution and terrorism. That it is within the power of the Congress to protect the Government of the United States from armed rebellion is a proposition which requires little discussion. . . . We reject any principle of governmental helplessness in the face of preparation for revolution, which principle, carried to its logical conclusion, must lead to anarchy.[13]

The chief justice argued that the conviction of Eugene Dennis and the other Communist leaders represented a lawful restriction of freedom of expression under a test that the courts had applied, with varying emphases, in a number of earlier cases: the "clear and present danger" rule. A highly regarded federal judge, Learned Hand (1872–1961), expressed the rule this way in his opinion for the Court of Appeals in *Dennis:* "In each case [courts] must ask whether the gravity of the 'evil,' discounted by its improbability, justifies such invasion of free speech as is necessary to avoid the danger." Is there a compelling case that political expression in a given instance might be so intertwined with action as to threaten constitutional government? The

[13]*Dennis v. United States,* 341 U.S. 494 (1951).

*How much informa-
tion the government
should "classify" as
secret is still debated.*

Court upheld the conviction of Dennis and his associates on the ground
that there was.

Six years later, however, in *Yates* v. *United States* (1957), the Supreme
Court reversed the conviction of 14 middle-level Communist party
officials under the Smith Act. While the Court insisted that its *Yates*
ruling was consistent with that in *Dennis*, it in fact was moving to
restrict prosecution of Communist party officials. Where in 1951 a
court majority had felt that the threats posed by the party were sufficient to justify the Smith Act curtailment of its political freedom,
by 1957 a majority no longer felt that way.

Yates v. *United States*

By the 1960s, with new appointees and a changed climate of national
opinion, the Supreme Court was ready to swing more fully and consistently from the perspective that guided it in *Dennis*. It took a more
expansive view of the guarantee of the First Amendment for the right
of individual expression, and it was much less worried about the threat
of domestic communism. In *United States* v. *Robel* (1967), the Court
upheld the right of Eugene Frank Robel, an admitted member of the
Communist party, to work in a shipyard, despite a federal statute
forbidding such employment to a party member. The Court declared
the statute unconstitutional. While Congress is entitled to protect
sensitive activities from spies and saboteurs, the Court held that it
"must achieve its goal by means which have a 'less drastic' impact
on the continued vitality of First Amendment freedoms." The law, it
was ruled, was much broader than necessary to achieve its stated
purpose, since it restricted the employment opportunities of all members of the Communist party, not merely those active in the unlawful
aims of the party and thus most likely to engage in sabotage.

United States v. *Robel*

The Court moved in the 1960s to fashion a conception of the clear
and present danger rule very different from the one it offered in *Den-*

Brandenburg v. *Ohio*

nis. Brandenburg v. *Ohio* (1969) grew out of the prosecution of a Ku Klux Klan leader under Ohio's criminal syndicalism statute. A unanimous Court overturned the Klansman's conviction and declared the statute unconstitutional. Because the law purported to punish "mere advocacy" and to prevent assembly with others for such advocacy, it violated the requirement of the First and Fourteenth Amendments. The Court held that "the constitutional guarantees of free speech and free press do not permit a state to forbid or proscribe advocacy of the use of force or of law violation except *where such advocacy is directed to inciting or producing imminent lawless action and is likely to incite or produce such action*" (emphasis added). This requirement of imminency represented a fundamental shift from the Court's construction of the clear and present danger rule in *Dennis* and earlier decisions.

Obscenity and Community Standards

Political speech bears a special relationship to democratic governance. Not all forms of expression can make this claim. The Supreme Court has repeatedly ruled, for instance, that *obscene material* is *not* protected by the First Amendment. Of course, even if this is accepted, it still leaves unresolved the question of what is obscene. The Court has found it hard to fashion satisfactory formulations as to when curbs are permitted and what kinds of restrictions are valid.

Obscenity and constitutional rights

A few justices have dissented from the basic Court position that obscene and pornographic expression may be curbed; they have wanted to see all expression absolutely protected. Justice William O. Douglas (1898–1980) was prominent in this small camp. He argued that the First and Fourteenth Amendments absolutely protect obscene and non-obscene material alike. In one opinion, Douglas concluded that

> the First Amendment allows all ideas to be expressed—whether orthodox, popular, off-beat, or repulsive. I do not think it permissible to draw lines between the "good" and the "bad" and be true to the constitutional mandate to let all ideas alone. . . . The theory is that people are mature enough to pick and choose, to recognize trash when they see it, to be attracted to the literature that satisfies their deepest needs, and, hopefully, to move from plateau to plateau and finally reach the world of enduring ideas. I think this is the ideal of the Free Society written into our Constitution.[14]

As Douglas saw it, the constitutional claim of any one form of expression is equal to that of any other. "Some like Chopin, others like 'Rock and Roll.' Some are 'normal,' some are masochistic, some deviant in other respects, such as homosexual." Individuals choose as they see fit; the Constitution mandates governmental "hands off" from all curbs.

But most justices have looked for formulas that give more scope to

---

[14] Dissent by Justice William O. Douglas in *Ginzburg, et al.,* v. *United States,* 383 U.S. 492 (1966).

Regulating obscene speech

governmental officials in regulating obscene speech than they can have in the case of political speech. There have been efforts to give at least partial recognition to the contrasting ideas of different groups of people in different parts of the United States about what is unacceptably obscene or pornographic. When citizens, acting through duly constituted governmental bodies such as state legislatures or city councils, impose certain restrictions to uphold community sensibilities, the courts should not sweep these aside in the name of an absolute right of expression. Justice John Marshall Harlan (1899–1971) shared this perspective.

> The varying conditions across the country, the range of views on the need and reasons for curbing obscenity, and the traditions of local self-government in matters of public welfare all favor a far more flexible attitude in defining the bounds for the states. From my standpoint, the Fourteenth Amendment requires of a state only that it apply criteria rationally related to the accepted notion of obscenity and that it reach results not wholly out of step with current American standards.[15]

At the same time, Harlan and many other observers have been concerned lest narrow community standards censor even major works of literature and art in the name of obscenity. How is the balance to be struck?

Miller v. California

In *Miller* v. *California* (1973), the Supreme Court issued an important obscenity ruling to which it still adheres. Miller was convicted in a California court of mailing unsolicited sexually explicit material in violation of a state statute. The Supreme Court upheld his conviction, maintaining that it would be guided by three related tests in obscenity cases:

> (a) whether "the average person, applying contemporary community standards" would find that the work, taken as a whole, appeals to the prurient interest . . . (b) whether the work depicts or describes, in a patently offensive way, sexual conduct specifically defined by the applicable state law; and (c) whether the work, taken as a whole, lacks serious literary, artistic, political, or scientific value.[16]

States may curtail material that meets this obscenity test.

Men and Women in the Labor Market: The Issue of "Comparable Worth"

The movement for women's rights over the last decade has produced important changes in many areas of American society and politics. Women's rights have become an important component of civil

---

[15] The dissenting opinion of Justice Harlan in the case *A book named "John Cleland's Memoirs of a Woman of Pleasure,"* et al., v. *Attorney General of Massachusetts*, 383 U.S. 458 (1966).

[16] *Miller* v. *California*, 413 U.S. 24 (1973).

rights. The economic dimension has been especially prominent and seems certain to become more so. At issue here is ensuring nondiscrimination and equal opportunity in hiring, promoting, and compensation. With regard to the latter, especially, women's groups and others argue that a historic pattern of discrimination against women is evident in the area of compensation and that new initiatives are needed to end it.

Some of the pertinent facts are readily determined, others not so. It is apparent that women who are full-time workers on the whole make much less than their male counterparts. As Figure 17.8 indicates, the average pay of full-time female workers has been only about 60 percent that of male workers over the last decade. As more and more women take jobs outside the home, many as the prime wage-earners in their households (rather than providing supplementary earnings), and as the women's movement gives greater emphasis to the claims of equal status generally, these basic wage differences have spurred protest and action.

Several different factors contribute to the overall pay differential, and the precise weight of any one of them is not known. (1) Women have been subject to conscious, intentional wage discrimination. (2) Cultural values and norms prevailing in the past have "assigned" disproportionate numbers of higher-status jobs to male workers. (3) The recent surge of women into the labor force has produced a situation where many female workers have relatively little seniority. (4) The employment of many women has been broken by periods of child-bearing and child-rearing, which has had some cumulative impact on overall job and compensation progress. (5) Market forces deriving from the above and other factors mean that employers can in many instances hire female employees for less than they pay men. And (6)

Pay differential between men and women

Contributing factors

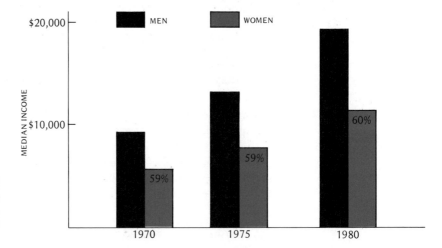

Figure 17.8
Median Money Income of Full-Time Workers, by Sex

Source: U.S. Bureau of the Census, *Statistical Abstract, 1984,* p. 469.

*Women in the work-
force—new roles.*

many of the occupational sectors where labor unions have since World War II achieved relatively high rates of compensation are occupations where women are substantially underrepresented.

Younger women in the labor force, such as those 20–24 years of age, lag much less behind their male age counterparts than is the case for older groups. This suggests that significant changes are occurring, such as the entry of more women into jobs that traditionally are higher-paying. Still, even among workers 20–24 years of age, the average pay in 1980 for female workers was only 78 percent that of male workers. Further, studies of the pay of men and women in specific occupations where comparability of skills and training is required suggest that the women still make less than the men. For example, female faculty members, at the rank of full professor, on average earn less than male full professors.[17]

Women employees and some labor unions are turning increasingly to the courts to find remedies for these pay differentials. One critical area in this litigation involves the distinction between "equal work" and "comparable work." While at first glance this might seem to be a minor semantic quibble, it is emerging as the hub of the controversy. In 1962, legislation was introduced into the U.S. House of Rep-

Comparable skills, less pay

"Equal work" versus "comparable work"

[17]"Average Faculty Salaries by Rank and Sex at Institutions," *Chronicle of Higher Education*, February 8, 1984, pp. 21–30.

resentatives to implement the Kennedy administration's commitment to equal-pay legislation. One section of the bill provided that

> no employer . . . shall discriminate . . . between employees on the basis of sex by paying wages to any employee at any rate less than the rate at which he pays wages to any employee of the opposite sex for work of comparable character on jobs the performance of which requires comparable skills, except where such payment is made pursuant to a seniority or merit increase system which does not discriminate on the basis of sex.

In hearings on this proposed legislation, debate broke out over the "comparable character" provision. Representative Katherine St. George objected to the language and offered an amendment which limited equal pay claims to those "for *equal work* on jobs, the performance of which requires *equal skills.*" She explained that her purpose was to limit wage discrimination claims to situations where men and women are paid differently for performing *the same job.*

> What we want to do in this bill is to make it exactly what it says. It is called equal pay for equal work in some of the committee hearings. There is a great difference between the word "comparable" and the word "equal." . . . The word "comparable" opens up great vistas. It gives tremendous latitude to whoever are the arbitrators in these disputes.

The House adopted the St. George amendment; the Senate, too, rejected the "comparable work" wording in favor of the "equal work" standard.

The matter did not end there, however, even though no subsequent congressional legislation has changed the "equal work" language. Job-classification procedures and standards have been sought, and in some instances applied, in which very different types of jobs are assessed as to their *intrinsic worth* or *difficulty,* compared to other types of jobs. Under these classifications, otherwise dissimilar jobs are grouped, with the stipulation that compensation should be equal for all of the different but comparable positions within a class.[18]

"Comparable worth" ruling

The issue of "comparable worth" burst forth front and center on the national political agenda following a December 1983 ruling by a federal district judge in Washington. In a suit brought by the American Federation of State, County, and Municipal Employees (AFSCME) against the state of Washington, the judge ruled that the state had failed to provide equal pay for jobs of comparable worth, as determined by classification studies. He ordered the state not only to "forthwith pay each and every individual plaintiff herein, the amount of compensation that they are entitled to receive as evaluated under [the] 'comparable worth' plan as adopted in May 1983," but to pay

---

[18] See Elaine Johansen, "From Social Doctrine to Implementation: Agenda Setting in Comparable Worth," *Policy Studies Review,* forthcoming.

back pay, commencing from September 1979. The judge appointed a "special master" to monitor compliance. If sustained upon appeal, this ruling would raise the wages and provide back pay to some 15,500 state employees in female-dominated job classifications in the state of Washington. The state had argued that the burden would be too severe because of the tremendous costs involved, a severe lack of revenue given the state's depressed economy, and the serious impact on the state's work force. Besides, the state legislature was already attempting to work out a gradual long-term solution. The court found these arguments "without merit and unpersuasive."

The immediate issue, which the Supreme Court will have to resolve, is whether the "equal pay for equal work" provision of the Equal Pay Act of 1963 can now be made to require equal pay for comparable work. This is part of a still more general issue of how society should respond to inequalities in the occupational status and compensation of women.

KEY ACTORS IN CIVIL LIBERTIES AND CIVIL RIGHTS POLICY

Certain units of the executive branch, and committtees of Congress, bear major responsibilities for policy on civil liberties and civil rights. Since World War II, the federal courts have been especially active and influential in shaping policy in this area. Outside government, a nucleus of interest groups develop policy proposals and lobby for them. These agencies and groups are the key "actors" on matters of civil liberties and rights.

The President

The president is a central figure in every sector of policy touched by federal action. In the case of civil liberties and civil rights, he sets the tone or emphasis for his administration. By appointing key executive-branch officials, especially the attorney general, he determines who will be handling specific policy initiatives. And the president submits legislation to Congress and works to secure its enactment. President Lyndon Johnson, a Democrat, had an especially ambitious agenda for new civil rights legislation in 1964 and 1965. His skillful interplay with members of Congress, notably with the Republican leadership in the Senate, was critically important in securing enactment of the 1964 Civil Rights Act and the 1965 Voting Rights Act.

The Justice Department

The head of the Department of Justice is the attorney general of the United States. He is the chief law officer of the federal government, and as such is responsible for advising the president on policy issues involving civil liberties and civil rights. One of the attorney general's chief deputies is the assistant attorney general in charge of the department's Civil Rights Division. This division is responsible for enforcing national civil rights laws, which forbid discrimination on the basis of race, national origin, religion, sex, or handicap. Civil rights laws cover voting, education, employment, housing, credit, and the use of public facilities. While the president and the attorney general intervene to set broad policy direction, the assistant attorney general for civil rights is the principal administration official in day-to-day activity in this area.

The Commission on Civil Rights

Created by the Civil Rights Act of 1957, the Commission on Civil Rights has important monitoring responsibilities for the federal government. It holds public hearings and gathers and examines information on racial, religious, sex, and age discrimination. The commission makes findings of fact, but it has no enforcement authority. Its recommendations are submitted to the president and to Congress; many of them have helped shape subsequent federal action. The commission has a small staff of about 250. Its 1984 budget was just $12 million.

Commission on Civil Rights and the Reagan administration

In 1983 the commission became embroiled in a bitter struggle, growing out of a political tug of war between the Reagan administration and its allies on the one side, and civil rights groups and congressional Democrats on the other. The immediate precipitant was President Reagan's decision in May 1983 to fire three of the six incumbent commissioners and to replace them with his own nominees. There was no question about presidential authority to do this; at issue was what political philosophy on civil rights should guide the commission. The upshot of the controversy was an agreement between the Reagan administration and congressional Democrats on new legislation reconstituting the commission. The plan, which became law in late 1983, replaced the six-member presidentially appointed commission with an eight-member panel, four of whom would be appointed by the president and four by congressional leaders. Each commissioner serves a fixed term and can be removed only for cause.

The Equal Employment Opportunity Commission

Created by the Civil Rights Act of 1964, the Equal Employment Opportunity Commission (EEOC) is charged with eliminating racial, religious, sex, and age discrimination in hiring and firing, and in other conditions of employment. With a staff of 3,200 and an 1984 budget of $154 million, the EEOC operates 48 field offices throughout the country. Each office receives charges of job discrimination under the Equal Pay Act of 1963 and the Age Discrimination in Employment Act of 1967. These charges and complaints may be against governmental or private employers, or against labor unions. Commission staff members may investigate to determine whether violations have in fact occurred. Following the investigation, they may make efforts to correct the unlawful practices through discussion and conciliation. If the latter fail, the commission may bring suit in federal district court.

Congress

The judiciary committees of both the House and Senate are the chief congressional committees with jurisdiction over civil liberties and rights policy. The House judiciary subcommittees on Civil and Constitutional Rights, and on "Courts, Civil Liberties, and the Administration of Justice, are key. In the Senate, the subcommittees on the Constitution and on the Courts have primary legislative responsibilities.

The Education and Labor Committee in the House and its counterpart, Labor and Human Resources, in the Senate, have jurisdiction over some employment-related civil rights matters. The relevant subcommittees are Employment Opportunities in the House, and Employment and Productivity in the Senate.

The Courts

In no other sector of public policy today is the judicial role as large as it is in civil liberties and rights (see chapter 10). Given the American system of government, courts are most active as political decision-makers in areas evoking basic questions of the rights of citizenship.

The courts have been active in the area of rights for those in mental hospitals (shot from One Flew Over the Cuckoo's Nest).

Because of their insulation from political accountability, the courts have been able to intervene when other units of government could not. For example, as the national consciousness shifted against racial segregation in the late 1940s and 1950s, most of the principal governmental actors were unable or disinclined to respond. Southern state governments, responsive to the white majority favoring the virtual disenfranchisement of blacks, were not going to initiate rapid policy changes. Congress was tied up, as a strong southern bloc successfully resisted major civil rights legislation, particularly through the use of the filibuster in the Senate. In this environment, the Supreme Court—with nine justices appointed for life, charged with saying what the law is with regard to rights of citizenship—was uniquely situated to effect change. Through its *Brown* ruling, the Court accomplished what no other unit of government could accomplish politically at the time.

Interest Groups

Important interest-group activity goes on in three distinct sectors touched by civil liberties and rights policy: (1) civil liberties, (2) the rights of blacks and other ethnic minorities, and (3) women's rights. With regard to civil liberties, the work of the *American Civil Liberties Union* has been especially influential. Founded in 1920, the ACLU currently employs a staff of about 330, many of whom are attorneys. The main vehicle it employs in trying to shape government policy is the "test case," where ACLU legal staff initiate a court challenge to governmental actions seen as improperly restricting civil liberties.

American Civil Liberties Union (ACLU)

The ACLU takes seriously the commitment embodied in the famous phrase often attributed (incorrectly, it turns out) to Voltaire: "I disapprove of what you say, but I will defend to the death your right to say it." Though it is generally allied with liberal political causes, the ACLU often defends the civil liberties of groups that it otherwise opposes politically. In a 1982 report, for example, the ACLU described a situation that arose when a visiting South African rugby team came to New York to play a scheduled match against an American team. Then New York Governor Hugh Carey issued an order prohibiting the game, to prevent threatened demonstrations against the team in protest of South Africa's apartheid policy. The ACLU noted that while "it of course condemns apartheid, [it] went to court to defend the South Africans' right to play, asserting that demonstrators should never be permitted to enforce a 'hecklers' veto' abridging First Amendment rights." There are numerous other examples of the ACLU's consistent opposition to restrictions on personal expression. It defended the right of the National Socialist [Nazi] party of America to march through the streets of Skokie, Illinois, where many Jews who suffered at the hands of Hitler's Nazis live, even though this cost it a serious loss of support among Jewish contributors. In Maryland the ACLU

Nazi and anti-Nazi protest—contending interests.

won a lawsuit on behalf of a school custodian fired because he was a member of the Ku Klux Klan.[19]

National Association for the Advancement of Colored People (NAACP)

The oldest civil rights organization in the United States, and one that remains among the most influential, is the *National Association for the Advancement of Colored People* (NAACP). It was founded in 1909, and now has a staff of about 130 and a national membership of roughly a half-million. The NAACP seeks the removal of racial discrimination in all areas of national life. Founded in 1939, and employing a staff of nearly 100, the *NAACP Legal Defense and Educational Fund* (LDEF) serves as the legal arm of the civil rights movement. Since the mid-1950s, the LDF has operated independently from its parent, the NAACP. Its most notable case is still *Brown* v. *Board of Education of Topeka* (1954), initiated and represented in the courts by LDEF attorneys. In recent years, the LDEF has been involved in litigation on behalf of black plaintiffs in cases of employment discrimination, voting rights, and school desegregation, among others.

National Urban League

Another highly influential civil rights organization is the *National Urban League*. It was founded in 1910, and has a staff of about 2,000 in cities across the country. The Urban League works closely with business, labor, and various civic organizations to eliminate racial discrimination, especially in the area of employment. It sponsors the Economic Development Program and the Black Executive Exchange Program. Given its ties to business, the Urban League has far greater financial resources than any other civil rights organization; it has never operated as a mass-membership group like the NAACP.

[19] The American Civil Liberties Union, "Civil Liberties in Reagan's America," October 1982 (mimeographed), pp. 23–24.

Under the leadership of Martin Luther King, Jr., the *Southern Christian Leadership Conference* (SCLC) was extraordinarily influential in mobilizing nonviolent protests against segregation throughout the South in the late 1950s and 1960s. *Operation PUSH* (People United to Serve Humanity) was founded in 1971 by Jesse Jackson and led by him until 1983 when Jackson resigned to seek the Democratic party's presidential nomination. The organization has sponsored the PUSH for Excellence Program to restore academic quality and discipline in urban schools. The *Leadership Conference on Civil Rights* was founded in 1950 as a coalition of national organizations interested in civil rights. Among its members are the Anti-Defamation League of B'nai B'rith, the Mexican-American Legal Defense and Education Fund, the National Council of La Raza, the National Council of Negro Women, the National Urban League, the NAACP Legal Defense and Educational Fund, and the AFL-CIO. The Leadership Conference has been highly influential in its congressional lobbying efforts.

Among the many groups working on behalf of women's rights, the *National Organization for Women* (NOW) is probably the best known. Founded in 1966, it has a national membership of about a quarter-million, organizations in all 50 states, and about 800 local groups. It supports "full equality for women in truly equal partnership with men." NOW has lobbied energetically for passage of the proposed Equal Rights Amendment—which in 1982 failed to secure ratification by the requisite 38 states. The amendment, which supporters will again try to enact, provides that "equal rights under the law shall not be denied or abridged by the United States or by any state on account of sex." The *National Women's Political Caucus* was established in 1971 and currently has a membership of about 60,000. The caucus says it is open to "anyone with a sincere interest in getting women more political clout." A nonpartisan organization, the caucus is organized at the local, state, and national levels to support women candidates for public office and to raise women's issues in electoral contests.

SUMMARY

Policy on civil liberties and rights differs from that in other sectors because many of its claims are presented as basic constitutional rights rather than simple group preferences. The courts try to differentiate between instances where fundamental rights of citizenship are engaged, which even large popular majorities must not infringe upon, and those where majority preferences should be respected.

The progression of public policy in any area does not follow a simple straight-line course; zigs and zags respond to the change of political leadership and events. But a clear direction is often evident. With regard to policy on civil liberties and rights, that direction involves more extensive recognition and guarantees of individual rights since World War II than obtained in earlier periods of American history. Characteristics of postindustrial society, including its affluence and high levels of education, seem linked to generally enlarged expectations concerning individuals and their entitlements.

Since World War II the system of discrimination and segregation, that had been entrenched in the South and known as "Jim Crow," has been dismantled. This is not to say that America's racial problems have been solved. But it is to say that clear and profound changes are evident in civil rights, which have promoted the principle of equality.

Other components of civil liberties and rights policy show a similar progression. Judicial guarantees of the rights of the accused have been expanded. A prime instance is the Supreme Court's extension of the range of Bill of Rights protections incorporated within the Fourteenth Amendment's due-process clause and thus made specifically binding on the states. Fourth, Fifth, and Sixth Amendment guarantees have been enforced on state courts and law-enforcement officials, as on their federal counterparts, by excluding from criminal proceedings evidence unconstitutionally obtained.

A new plateau was reached in the first quarter-century after World War II, defined by greater attentiveness to individual rights. But on this new plateau the familiar policy need to strike appropriate balances among competing objectives has asserted itself, with the Supreme Court at the center of this balancing act. The Court has in the case of the exclusionary rule tried to adjust the contending objectives of protecting the rights of the accused and ensuring the prompt apprehension and conviction of those who commit crimes.

In the controversy over affirmative action and quotas, the Court has recognized the importance of being "color-blind," more generally assigning jobs and other positions without regard to group identity or membership. But it has also recognized that the history of past discrimination cannot be ignored, and that some forms of special remedial action may be required. Many of the great contemporary arguments over civil liberties and civil rights policy stem from differences over how the claims of worthy goals and values, at times in contention one with another, are best adjusted and balanced.

18 | Political Economy

Use of governmental power to secure economic objectives comprises *political economy.* No area of public policy affects more people more immediately. Debate on management of the economy, replete with technical terms and issues, goes on constantly within the economics profession. But the debate extends far beyond, into the mainstream of American politics.

There are severe limits on what any official of American government can do to promote desired economic results. The United States does not have an economic "czar." The president has substantial authority, but so do Congress and the Federal Reserve System. Each of these important actors, whose roles we describe below, has a large measure of independence. With regard to economic policy, as in every other area of policy, power is highly dispersed.

Even more importantly, a great deal of authority over critical economic decisions does not lie within government at all, but resides in the private sector, among officials of business corporations large and small, heads of major banks and other financial institutions, labor leaders, and others. Ordinary citizens also play a large role through decisions they make, such as whether to buy homes and automobiles now or wait until a later date. How hard people work and what proportion of their incomes they save or invest have significant impact on national economic performance. Were all this not enough, many decisions important to the U.S. economy are made not by Americans at all but by foreign governments, corporations, and investors. To cite just one example, decisions made by the heads of the Organization of Petroleum-Exporting Countries (OPEC) in 1973–74 and 1979 to impose big oil price increases, and the conditions of global supply and demand that underlay OPEC's actions, were only modestly sub-

The labor force—the core of the American economy.

ject to American influence. Yet the U.S. economy suffered two serious bouts of inflation as a result of those decisions.

Politics and Economics

If policies initiated by governmental officials have only limited influence on the achievement of desired economic goals, they are far from inconsequential. They are, moreover, much more responsive to the wishes and sanctions of the general public through the political process than any other set of factors determining economic outcomes, so they are the focus of political attention and debate. Current economic performance is taken, often to a greater extent than is justified, to reflect upon the wisdom or folly of policies emanating from Washington. The electoral fate of presidents and their administrations rests in substantial part on the perceived link between their economic policies and the behavior of the national economy.

The 1984 elections were contested amidst a vigorous economic recovery. The country's **gross national product** (GNP)—the measure of the total market value of all goods and services produced in a given year—grew at a 10.1 percent rate in real terms (controlling for infla-

The 1984 economic
recovery

tion) in the first quarter of 1984 and 7.1 percent in the second quarter; although there was a slowdown in the third quarter, the overall rate for the year was vigorous, especially for an economy in the second year of a recovery. As the GNP soared, the rate of inflation declined, to the 3 to 4 percent range, depending on the measure. Job creation was at record high levels; about 105 million Americans were employed in mid-1984, compared to 99 million a year and a half earlier. In this same period unemployment dropped from over 10 percent to 7.4 percent. "To many analysts and to the Europeans," the *New York Times* concluded, "that makes the United States a remarkable job machine—the world's most remarkable."[1] The economic news was not all favorable in 1984; interest rates were high, and the federal deficit was higher than it had ever been in peacetime. But overall the economy's performance was robust. How much Reagan-administration economic policies deserved credit for this was vigorously debated; and how much developments in the economy influenced the final election outcome cannot be precisely determined. But most observers believe the link was strong.

The economy is not always booming. Just two years earlier, during the 1982 elections, the U.S. economy was deep in recession. GNP was falling in real terms, and the unemployment rate had climbed to over 10 percent for the first time since 1940. Reagan-administration policies were attacked as responsible for collapse and privation. Democrats made gains in voting for the House of Representatives and in gubernatorial races across the country. Just after the 1982 elections, the *New York Times* editorially branded the administration as a failure.

The 1982 recession

> By his own reckoning, Mr. Reagan became president for one basic reason: to restore the morale and power of America. By his own analysis, that meant above all "the rejuvenation of our economy" so that America could regain industrial strength, put all its people to work and defend its interests around the world. But the economy totters, dragging down the West and eroding American influence everywhere.[2]

Times change, and so do assessments—especially in the area of political economy, where the stakes are so high.

Disputes over Economic Theory

Presidents and other party leaders engage in a lot of *ad hoc* improvisation in their search for policies to advance such desired ends as economic growth and high employment, and to minimize such evils as inflation. But leaders are also guided by underlying economic philosophies. Although never consistently followed, these philosophies

[1] Leslie Wayne, "America's Astounding Job Machine," *New York Times*, June 17, 1984, pp. F1, 25.
[2] "The Failing Presidency," *New York Times* editorial January 9, 1983, p. E22.

are rarely absent—and economic argument goes beyond current conditions, like the recession of 1982 and the recovery of 1983–84, to a deeper dispute over which basic approach is likely to lead to the best results most of the time. The Reagan administration took office in January 1981, claiming that the Democrats' approach was flawed and that a new departure was needed. Of course, the Democrats disagreed.

The roots of the present debate over national economic policy go back more than half a century. To understand it we need to look first at how the argument was joined by the response of Franklin Roosevelt's New Deal to the challenge of the Great Depression, and how it has evolved in the face of changing economic conditions. In the second section of this chapter, we look more closely at specific developments and arguments in contemporary economic policy. We conclude with a discussion of the governmental agencies and interest groups that play key roles in the American political economy.

ECONOMIC POLICY: 1930s TO THE 1980s

Debates over economic policy often involve two entirely different questions: (1) What *goals and objectives* are to be advanced through governmental intervention? (2) How does the economy really work, and *how can a given economic objective best be achieved?* To some extent, differences over desired *ends,* and over the best *means* to attain these ends, get scrambled together in the policy debates in every nation. But the relative weight of these two dimensions varies greatly.

Economic policies in other countries

In some countries, differences over basic objectives dominate economic policy arguments. For example, in many Western democracies throughout much of this century, including France, Italy, and England, lines have been drawn between those who want more governmental control of the economy and less control by private business interests, and those who favor private ownership with reduced government influence. With the election of Socialist party leader François Mitterand as president in 1981, France took an ideological turn toward more government ownership of industries. In England, the Conservative government of Prime Minister Margaret Thatcher cut back on government ownership; its Labour party opponents vow to expand socialism when they next form the government.

America: conflicting means to a common end

In the United States, though there are differences over the goals of economic policy, the main disagreements concern how particular goals are best obtained. We want strong economic growth, high levels of employment, and low inflation—all within the general structure of a private-property-based economy. At issue are the steps the country should be taking to promote these shared objectives. Issues of economic policy often loom large in U.S. politics, but they usually encompass contending partisan claims that "we can do it better."

Americans turn to economists much as to medical doctors: We do not want them to make the patient *different*, only *well*. This "how-to-do-it" emphasis means that technical and scientific assessments of economists are often very important politically. While in the complex, highly pluralistic push-and-pull of American politics no set of economic prescriptions ever gets fully or neatly applied, politicians look to economists for general guidance on how to most effectively advance shared goals.

John Maynard Keynes and Keynesian Economics

The "how-to-do-it" prescriptions of a distinguished British economist, John Maynard Keynes (1883–1946), entered into the American debate over economic policy in the 1930s, against the backdrop of the Great Depression. The **Keynesian** approach came to dominate the thinking of professional economists in the United States and helped shape the policies of the Roosevelt administration and its successors.

What made Keynes so influential was the force of his argument that the ideas on which politicians had been leaning had ceased to fit actual economic conditions. Since the "old economics" no longer pointed government in the right direction, a "new economics" and new answers to problems of political economy were needed. In his celebrated *General Theory of Employment, Interest, and Money*, Keynes provided them.[3]

Keynesian prescriptions. Keynes offered capitalist economies a way out of the crisis they faced in the 1930s, without abandoning capitalism. He rejected the centralization and collectivization inherent in state socialism. "I come not to bury capitalism," Keynes might have said, "but to save it." A private-property-based economy, he wrote, "if it can be purged of its defects and its abuses, is the best safeguard of personal liberty in the sense that, compared with any other system, it greatly widens the field for the exercise of personal choice."[4]

What were the key elements of Keynes's primer for American and British politicians wanting tools to make their capitalist economies work better? Keynes maintained that full employment and high economic growth are best advanced by promoting *consumption* rather than *savings*. Savings tend to be hoarded rather than applied to productive investments. In contrast, the demand generated by increased consumption stimulates greater investment and promotes the best utilization of society's resources. The richer a society becomes—and by the late 1920s both Britain and the United States were, by any historical comparison, very rich societies—"the wider will tend to be

Focus on consumption and investment

---

[3] John Maynard Keynes, *The General Theory of Employment, Interest, and Money* (New York: Harcourt, Brace, 1965; first published 1936), p. 383.
[4] Ibid., p. 380.

John Maynard Keynes.

the gap between its actual and its potential production. . . ." Such a society "will have to discover much ampler opportunities for investment if the saving propensities of its wealthier members are to be compatible with the employment of its poorer members."[5]

Rather than encouraging individual thrift, then, government should help generate consumption through such means as public-works programs. "Priming the pump" was the analogy that best conveyed the idea that government spending would lead to greater activity in the private sector. These programs would put money into the hands of poorer citizens, who would then use it to buy goods. Furthermore, government spending should not be paid for by economizing in other areas. When demand lags, because people lack money to buy the things they need, government should run a deficit—that is, spend more than it takes in from taxes—to provide economic stimulus.

These increased expenditures need not even be productive in the usual sense. Keynes contended that unemployment could be reduced even "if the Treasury were to fill old bottles with bank notes, bury them at suitable depths in disused coal mines which are then filled up to the surface with town rubbish, and leave it to private enterprise . . . to dig the notes up again."[6] This remark was in part facetious, but its main message was serious. Unemployment was high and production was down because many people lacked the money required to buy necessities. If only government would pump money to those who need it, increased consumption would occur, more jobs would be cre-

"Priming the pump"

[5] Ibid., p. 31.
[6] Ibid., p. 247.

ated to produce goods to meet this demand, and investment in new plant facilities would become attractive again.

It sounded almost too good to be true. Politicians who created new social programs, especially to help those in need, and who spent for such programs more than they asked people to pay in taxes, were not being profligate or crassly buying votes; they were stimulating the economy, increasing productivity, lowering unemployment, and generally making everyone more prosperous. Many politicians were understandably happy to receive this advice. But what made Keynesianism so unassailably alluring was the fact that, in the economic context in which Keynes wrote, it was right.

Economic Conditions in the 1930s

To understand why Keynes was correct in telling the governments of Western democracies that they should forget about budget-balancing and start spending, one needs to look at the economic conditions that prevailed when *The General Theory* was written. All of the Western nations, the United States included, were experiencing in the 1930s a vast economic crisis distinguished by (1) *unemployment*, (2) *underconsumption*, and (3) *deflation*. The three went hand in hand.

Unemployment. In 1900 in the United States, the rate of **unemployment** (the number of people unemployed as a percentage of the total civilian labor force) stood at just 5 percent. It hovered around that mark for most of the ensuing three decades: 5.9 percent in 1910, 5.2

Unemployment, 1932.

percent in 1920, and just 3.2 percent in 1925. With the onset of the Depression, however, unemployment soared: It reached 8.7 percent in 1930 and by 1935 had climbed to *20.1 percent*. Even as late as 1940 it stood at 14.6 percent. Never had so many people been out of work in America. Conditions were much the same in Europe.

Massive drop in the GNP. With people unemployed, productivity, income, and consumption fell off drastically. In 1922, the GNP of the United States totaled $74.1 billion; over the next several years it rose further, reaching a high of $103.1 billion in 1929. During the Depression, however, it plummeted, bottoming out at just $55.6 billion in 1933—a drop of *nearly 50 percent from the level of just four years earlier*. We can scarcely imagine what the impact would be today if the GNP were to be cut in half in the space of a few years.

The basic productive capacities of the United States (and the other Western democracies) were as great in the mid-1930s as they had been in the late 1920s; the skills of the people, the technology, and the output possible from the factories and farms were undiminished. But, in a vicious circle, unemployment and falling income meant falling consumption, and that meant lower production, and so on, round and round.

Deflation. Today, *inflation* is so prominent a feature of American economic life that we sometimes find it hard to appreciate that throughout much of U.S. history **deflation**—falling prices—was the more common problem. In the 1920s and 1930s, because of unemployment and low consumption, prices fell dramatically. Unable to find markets for their products, manufacturers, farmers, and merchants had to cut what they were charging. According to one index, producer prices stood at 79.6 in 1920. This composite index of prices at the wholesale level fell to 50.0 in 1928, to 44.6 in 1930, and to just 33.6 in 1932. This deflationary experience was so prolonged and deep that it was not until 1948 that the composite index of wholesale prices had climbed back to its 1920 level.

Why are falling prices an economic problem? Price deflation creates a disincentive to invest in new plant facilities. The return that can be expected will lag behind current costs. Keynes noted:

> If, for any reason right or wrong, the business world *expects* that prices will fall, the processes of production tend to be inhibited. . . . The deflation which causes falling prices means impoverishment to labor and to enterprise by leading entrepreneurs to restrict production, in their endeavor to avoid losses to themselves; and is therefore disastrous to employment.[7]

---

[7] John Maynard Keynes, *A Tract on Monetary Reform*, in *The Collected Writings of John Maynard Keynes* (London: Macmillan, 1971), pp. 30, 35–36. The first edition of this work appeared in 1923.

Limited government. Keynes' call for expanded governmental management of the economy came when government was still small, with limited responsibilities. When FDR first won election in November 1932, the total budget of the national government was just $4.7 billion, or about $37 per person. Over the 1930s, under the Roosevelt administration, expenditures rose significantly, but in 1940 they were still only $9.1 billion, less than $69 a citizen. Contrast these figures to the fiscal 1984 federal budget of $845 billion, or about $3,600 per person. Keynes' call in 1936 for a broadened governmental role appeared to many to be a measured, sensible, prudent response. And it was.

In the 1930s, then, the United States and other industrial democracies found themselves with a massive economic problem. Unemployment was up, production and consumption down. The standard of living for many citizens had fallen drastically. Deflation was a prime obstacle, as it provided incentives _not_ to invest in productive plant facilities. The call for more governmental intervention, in a setting where government did relatively little, seemed excessive only to those ideologically opposed to the very idea of governmental responsibility for promoting prosperity. The triumph of Keynesianism was fundamentally empirical or practical: It read and responded better to prevailing needs than any available alternative.

The Roosevelt administration did not immediately seize upon and implement Keynesian prescriptions. Many contradictory perspectives and pressures continued to be felt. The amount of stimulus given the economy in the latter half of the 1930s was modest—much too modest, most economists now agree. Only the massive government spending made necessary by America's entry into World War II finally

Triumph of Keynesianism

Post-World War II Keynesianism

Economic depression.

ended the decade-long depression and brought unemployment down to stay. But the national leadership of the Democratic party gradually converted to the "new economics," and from World War II through the 1960s, Keynesianism exerted great influence over the American approach to issues of political economy. By 1971, even a conservative Republican president, Richard Nixon, was moved to proclaim that "now I am a Keynesian."[8]

Shifts in the Political Economy: The Post-Keynesian Era

The "new economics" spurred by John Maynard Keynes proved to be a generally successful response to the needs of one particular period and its economic conditions. But conditions change. The shifts were gradual, but by the 1970s enough had occurred to stimulate vast rethinking of economic issues and government's position in national economic life. First economists and then politicians joined in the search for another new economics.

Big government. When the New Deal expansion of government's role in the U.S. economy began, government was a modest presence. By the 1970s, it had become a major one, and it became increasingly difficult to argue that "more government" was the answer.

Table 18.1 shows the level of federal taxation from 1922 to the present. One is struck by how small the federal tax burden was in the early part of this century: just over $15 per person as late as 1932.

Table 18.1
Federal Taxation since 1922

Year	Total budget receipts (in thousands of dollars)	Per capita federal taxes
1922	4,025,901	36.58
1932	1,923,892	15.39
1940	6,879,000	52.06
1950	40,940,000	269.90
1960	92,492,000	511.93
1970	193,743,000	945.64
1980	517,100,000	2,270.97
1984 (Est.)	670,700,000	2,863.79

Source: 1922–70: Bureau of the Census, *Historical Statistics of the United States: Colonial Times to 1970*, parts 1 and 2, pp. 8, 1105–6. 1980–84: 98th Cong., 1st sess., Joint Economic Committee, *Economic Indicators*, September 1984, p. 32; Bureau of the Census, *Statistical Abstract of the United States, 1984*, p. 6.

[8] Richard Nixon, remarks made to Howard K. Smith following a nationally televised interview with Smith and three other network correspondents on January 4, 1971. Rowland Evans, Jr., and Robert D. Novak, *Nixon in the White House: The Frustration of Power* (New York: Random House, 1971), p. 372.

Table 18.2
Federal Expenditures since 1922

Year	Total federal expenditures	Per capita federal expenditures
1922	3,289,404	29.89
1932	4,659,000	37.28
1940	9,055,269	68.53
1950	39,544,037	260.70
1960	92,223,354	510.44
1970	196,587,786	959.53
1980	576,700,000	2,532.72
1982	728,375,000	3,138.20
1983	795,969,000	3,398.67
1984	845,340,000	3,609.47

Source: 1922–70: Bureau of the Census, *Historical Statistics of the United States: Colonial Times to 1970,* parts 1 and 2, pp. 8, 1114–15, 1120. 1980: idem, *Statistical Abstract of the United States, 1984,* pp. 273, 315. 1982–83: Executive Office of the President, OMB, *Budget of the U.S. Government, FY 1985,* p. 9–62; Bureau of the Census, *Government Finances in 1981–1982,* Series GF'82, no. 5.

After 1960, however, federal taxes rose sharply, from $512 per capita in 1960 to nearly $2,900 in 1984. Some of this apparent growth is illusory, accruing simply because of inflation. A 1984 dollar purchases less than a 1960 dollar. But even when inflation is controlled for, a major increase has occurred. Public opposition to tax hikes, while sometimes exaggerated, is now substantial, and some economists worry about a drag on the economy from high taxation.

Data on governmental spending show the same progression (Table 18.2). As late as 1950, total federal expenditures in the United States averaged out to just $260 per person. By 1970, however, the figure had reached almost $960 and in 1984 it stood at $3,609. Again, a significant part of this rise is not real—inflation enters the picture—but much of it *is* real. Over the last quarter-century, the rate of growth of government spending has substantially outstripped the growth of the overall economy.

The federal debt. Not surprisingly, politicians have found it easier politically to increase expenditures than taxation—especially at the national level where there are no legal requirements that the budget be balanced, and where under sluggish economic conditions there is a good case for spending beyond revenues. During the 1930s, the Roosevelt administration expended more than it collected in taxes, to provide economic stimulus. Still, over the entire decade the cumulative federal debt rose by what now appears as a modest $26.8 billion. The total debt climbed sharply during World War II, reflecting the

[margin note] Increased governmental spending

Table 18.3
Federal Debt since 1920

Year	Total (in thousands)	Per capita
1920	24,299,321	228.23
1930	16,185,310	131.51
1940	42,967,531	325.23
1943	136,696,090	999.83
1945	258,682,187	1,848.60
1950	257,357,352	1,696.67
1960	286,330,761	1,584.70
1970	370,981,707	1,811.12
1975	544,100,000	2,518.98
1980	914,300,000	4,230.00
1982	1,146,987,000	4,941.77
1983	1,381,886,000	5,900.45
1984	1,575,600,000	6,727.58

Source: 1920–70: Bureau of the Census, *Historical Statistics of the U.S.: Colonial Times to 1970*, parts 1 and 2, pp. 8, 1117–18. 1975–80: idem, *Statistical Abstract of the U.S., 1984*, pp. 6, 315. 1982–83: Executive Office of the President, OMB, *Budget of the United States Government, FY 1985*, p. 9.4.

heavy costs of the war. After 1945, however, it remained rather stable in absolute terms for the next quarter-century; as a proportion of the GNP the federal debt actually declined substantially during this period. Since 1970, though, in the face of increased expenditures, the debt has soared from $371 billion in 1970, to $544 billion in 1975, $914 billion in 1980, and $1.58 *trillion* in 1984 (Table 18.3). The latter works out to $6,728 per person. Interest on the annual deficit has become a large factor: $109.4 billion in FY 1984 alone. The federal government has run a deficit every year since 1964, regardless of whether the nation's economy was booming or in recession.

According to Keynesianism, the central government should spend more than it takes in when the economy is in recession, so as to stimulate demand, but it should tax more than it spends in periods when the economy is booming, to temper inflationary pressures and sustain even growth. This adjusting of taxing and spending levels is known as **fiscal policy.** But in recent years American politicians have found fiscal policy exceedingly hard to manage. No body of economic theory justifies the federal government's running deficits each year, as it has for two decades now. The cuts in federal income tax rates pushed by the Reagan administration in 1981 and enacted by Congress added to the size of the deficit by reducing revenues while expenditures continued to climb. But the scope and persistence of the deficit are hardly the result of any one administration's actions or any single set of economic circumstances. They are structural problems of the contemporary political economy.

Problems in
formulating
sound fiscal policy

Inflation. Unemployment was an overwhelming problem in the 1930s. Since World War II, however, it has not been as out of control, and governmental programs, notably payments to workers who have been laid off, under Unemployment Compensation, have at least somewhat cushioned the impact of being out of work. But while this happened, inflation climbed to record levels and came to dominate the public's concerns. Looking at consumer prices expressed in an index where the 1967 level is set equal to 1.00, we see that price increases were modest over the 1950s and 1960s. There was inflation, but not much. Since the late sixties, though, inflation has been formidable, moderating only since 1982. There has been a sharp decline in the dollar's purchasing power: In 1983 it would buy only one-third as much as it had just sixteen years earlier. In the early 1960s, the annual rate of increase in consumer prices averaged just one percent. Then it began climbing. Despite ups and downs, the trend from 1960 to 1980 is unmistakable: Inflationary peaks rose ever higher. Figure 18.1 shows that the valley reached in 1983–84 was lower than any had been in more than a decade. Whether this recent decline proves durable remains to be seen.

The United States is not alone in its recent encounter with persistent high inflation. Other industrial nations have had to grapple with inflationary pressures. Since 1970, Germany has had the greatest success in holding price increases down; it is the only major industrial country to have wholly avoided double-digit inflation. Great Britain has had especially high inflation. The United States has been in the middle of the pack, compared to the rest of the industrial world. Its 1983 inflation rate of 3.5 percent was lower than that of France (9.3 percent), Sweden (9.2 percent), Britain (5.3 percent), and Canada (4.5

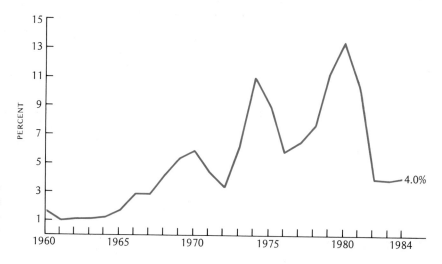

Figure 18.1
Annual Rate of Increase of Consumer Prices since 1960

Note: 1983 figure represents change from May 1982 to May 1983.
Source: Bureau of the Census, *Statistical Abstract of the United States, 1984*, p. 485; *Economic Indicators*, prepared for the Joint Economic Committee of Congress by The Council of Economic Advisers, November 1984, p. 24.

percent); but it was higher than Germany (2.6 percent) and Japan (1.8 percent).

John Maynard Keynes himself had once shown ample appreciation of the problem of inflation. In 1920 he commented on the harm high inflation can do:

Keynes on inflation

> As the inflation proceeds and the real value of the currency fluctuates wildly from month to month, all permanent relations between debtors and creditors, which form the ultimate foundation of capitalism, become so utterly disordered as to be almost meaningless; and so the process of wealth-getting degenerates into a gamble and a lottery. . . . Lenin was certainly right. There is no subtler, no surer means of overturning the existing basis of society than to debauch the currency.[9]

By the time *The General Theory* was published in 1936, Keynes had shifted his emphasis—not surprising, given the extreme deflation of the 1920s and 1930s. In recent years, though, the earlier Keynes has again made good reading. For, as Professor David Calleo has written, "this is no longer an age of underconsumption, but of inflation."[10]

Gains as well as problems. Changing conditions are often depicted in terms of the new problems they entail. Big and sometimes clumsy government efforts, political difficulties in keeping revenues in line with expenditures, and strong underlying inflationary pressures are persisting problems of the contemporary political economy, just as deflation, underconsumption, and unemployment dominated a half-century earlier. But no era, economic or otherwise, is defined simply by problems. Although discussions of the nation's economic position and performance over the last decade and a half have often been couched in the language of failings, many things have performed well.

GNP growth. Looking back on the last fifteen or so years, we see an economy that is very imperfectly described by "stagnation." The span between 1972 and 1982 was not especially good in terms of real growth in the GNP. Many key industries, including autos and steel, were going through a painful adjustment involving high domestic wage rates and intense foreign competition. The economy had to absorb massive "oil shocks" in 1973–74 and 1979: huge, rapid price hikes. Despite this, the GNP rose by $300 billion between 1972 and 1982, more than 25 percent in real terms (using the 1972 purchasing power of the dollar as the basis of comparison).[11] Remember, too, that 1982 was a year of deep recession, so this comparison understates long-term growth. If we use 1974 and 1984 as the years of comparison, the growth is about $400 billion, or nearly 33 percent.

[9] Keynes, *The Economic Consequences of the Peace* (1920), reprinted in *Collected Works*.
[10] David P. Calleo, *The Imperious Economy* (Cambridge, Mass.: Harvard University Press, 1982), p. 176.
[11] "Economic Indicators," report prepared for the Joint Economic Committee of Congress by the Council of Economic Advisers (Washington: Government Printing Office, 1984), May 1984, p. 2.

Creation of jobs. The idea that there was stagnation is contradicted even more forcefully by the national experience in job creation. The U.S. economy confronted conditions in the 1960s and 1970s that could easily have led to massively high rates of unemployment: An unprecedentedly large number of people were entering the labor force. After World War II birth rates rose dramatically and stayed high until the 1960s. By the 1970s large numbers of this "baby boom" generation were looking for jobs. Between 1946 and 1955 alone, more than 34 million people were born in the United States; by 1980 the youngest among them were 25 years old and most were in the labor force.

A second reason for the rise in the number of people seeking jobs was the jump in what economists call the "labor-force-participation rate" of women. In 1960 there were 62.4 million women in the United States 16 years of age and older; 36.5 percent of them were in the labor force—employed or actively seeking paid employment outside the home. Just 22 years later, in 1982, the female population 16 years and older totaled 92.2 million, 52.4 percent of whom were in the labor force. This translates into a total increase of 25.5 million women employed or seeking work.

These statistics tell a simple story: If the United States had not created millions of new jobs in a short span of time, the unemployment rate would have gone up like a rocket. Jobs *were* rapidly created, however—created at a rate high even by America's historical standards. Between 1973 and 1984 the United States produced about 20 million new jobs, while the industrial nations of Western Europe experienced a net loss of some 2 million jobs (Figure 18.2). Though Japan's "economic miracle" is often remarked upon, American job creation was at approximately twice the rate or proportion of Japan's over this span.

Women in the labor force

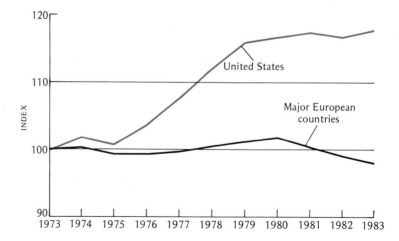

Figure 18.2
How the U.S. Stacks Up Against Europe in New Jobs

Source: Data from the Council on Foreign Relations, Inc. Figure prepared by the *New York Times,* June 17, 1984.

Figure 18.3   **National Income in the Five Wealthiest OECD Countries, 1970 and 1982**

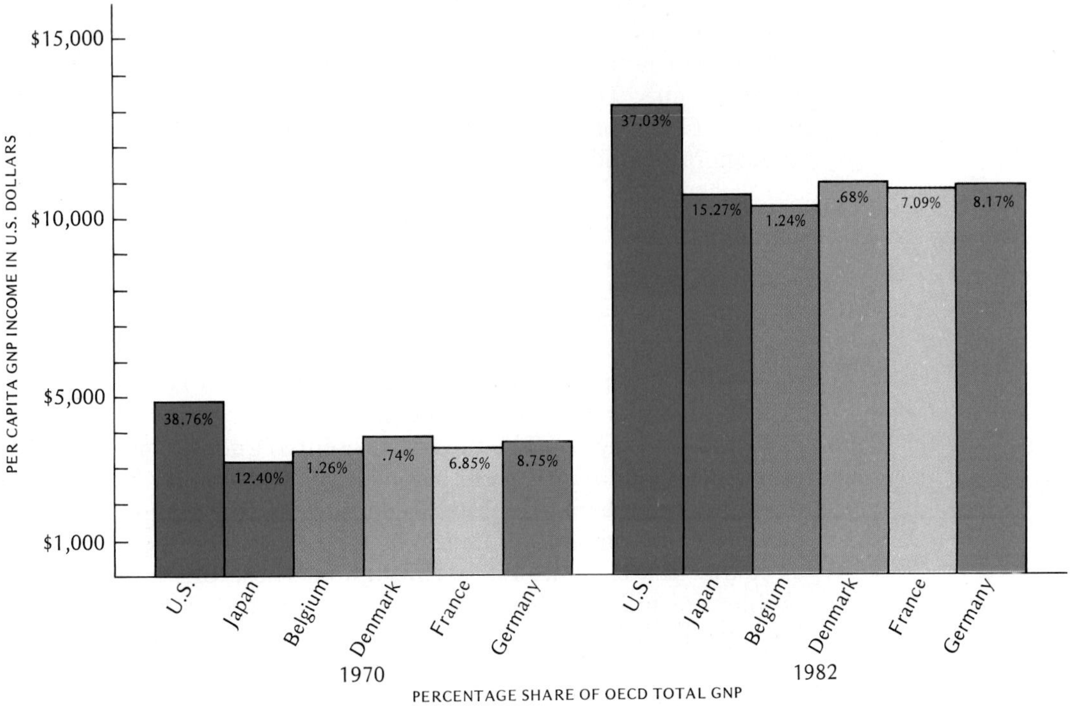

*Dollars adjusted in terms of purchasing power parity (PPP). For explanation of methodology employed in calculations see note to Table 2.3, chapter 2.
Source: Organization for Economic Cooperation and Development (OECD), *National Accounts: Main Aggregates* 1 (1953–1982):98.

Affluence. We noted in chapter 2 that the United States, a comparatively wealthy country before World War II, enjoyed a great spurt in national wealth in the first quarter-century after the war. Since the early 1970s per capita income has continued to rise in real terms. We can understand this recent performance by comparing the income growth in the United States to that in other successful industrial nations. As Figure 18.3 shows, the United States had the highest per capita income in the industrial world in 1970 and retained that position 12 years later. Its closest rivals are West Germany, France, Denmark, Japan, and tiny Luxembourg. From 1970 to 1982 Japan increased its share of the total income of all OECD countries,[12] while the United States' share declined very slightly, but on the whole income shares

[12] The countries of the Organization for Economic Cooperation and Development (OECD) are the U.S., Belgium, Denmark, France, West Germany, Greece, Ireland, Italy, Luxembourg, the Netherlands, United Kingdom, Austria, Finland, Iceland, Norway, Portugal, Spain, Sweden, Switzerland, Turkey, Canada, Japan, Australia, and New Zealand.

of the wealthy nations were stable. The United States had moved ahead proportionately.

Many factors account for recent American economic performance; achieved growth does not necessarily validate the wisdom of government policies. The point is that the movement of the United States into the new economic era is not all gloom and doom. Its adaptation of economic policy has not been notably deficient.

Public Attitudes on Political Economy

Americans seem to recognize that their nation's economy has strong features as well as weak points. But looking just at the problem side, major shifts have occurred. The level of unemployment was the litmus test of prosperity in the New Deal era; now it is the rate of inflation. Of all the problems besetting the contemporary political economy, high inflation seems to be the most resented and the most disruptive of old political loyalties and behavior. Public anxiety has paralleled movement of the inflation rate, becoming most acute in times of double-digit inflation, and diminishing somewhat when the rate fell back, as it did in 1983 and 1984. Throughout these ups and downs, the problem of inflation has remained near the top of voters' concerns. For a people who historically did not have to grapple with the problem, recent experience with steadily rising prices—eroding savings, wiping out apparent pay increases, making financial planning difficult—was terribly unsettling. Moreover, the persistence of high inflation raised questions about the capability of the national government to manage economic life effectively.

As we noted in chapter 15, recent elections have shown how much the new public concerns over the economy can disrupt traditional political calculations. The 1982 congressional elections were conducted at a time of major recession, with unemployment having climbed to over 10 percent. Double-digit unemployment dominated economic news all during the campaign, and many observers expected it to dominate the election results. It didn't. When, on election day, NBC News asked in a national poll whether it was more important to the nation's economy for the federal government to control unemployment or control inflation, the electorate split down the middle, 46 percent to 44 percent, respectively. And when voters were asked a companion question on their own financial concerns—"In terms of your own personal finances, would you rather see the federal government control inflation or unemployment?"—the results affirmed inflation's continuing centrality. By 59 to 33 percent nationally, and by solid majorities in every state surveyed—including those especially hard hit by unemployment—voters said that government's success in fighting inflation was more important to them personally.[13] Moreover, clear majorities of every occupational group (except for

Public opinion and the political economy

[13] Election-day polls by NBC News, November 2, 1982.

Figure 18.4 **Comparing Tax Burdens Borne by Families by Year and Income**

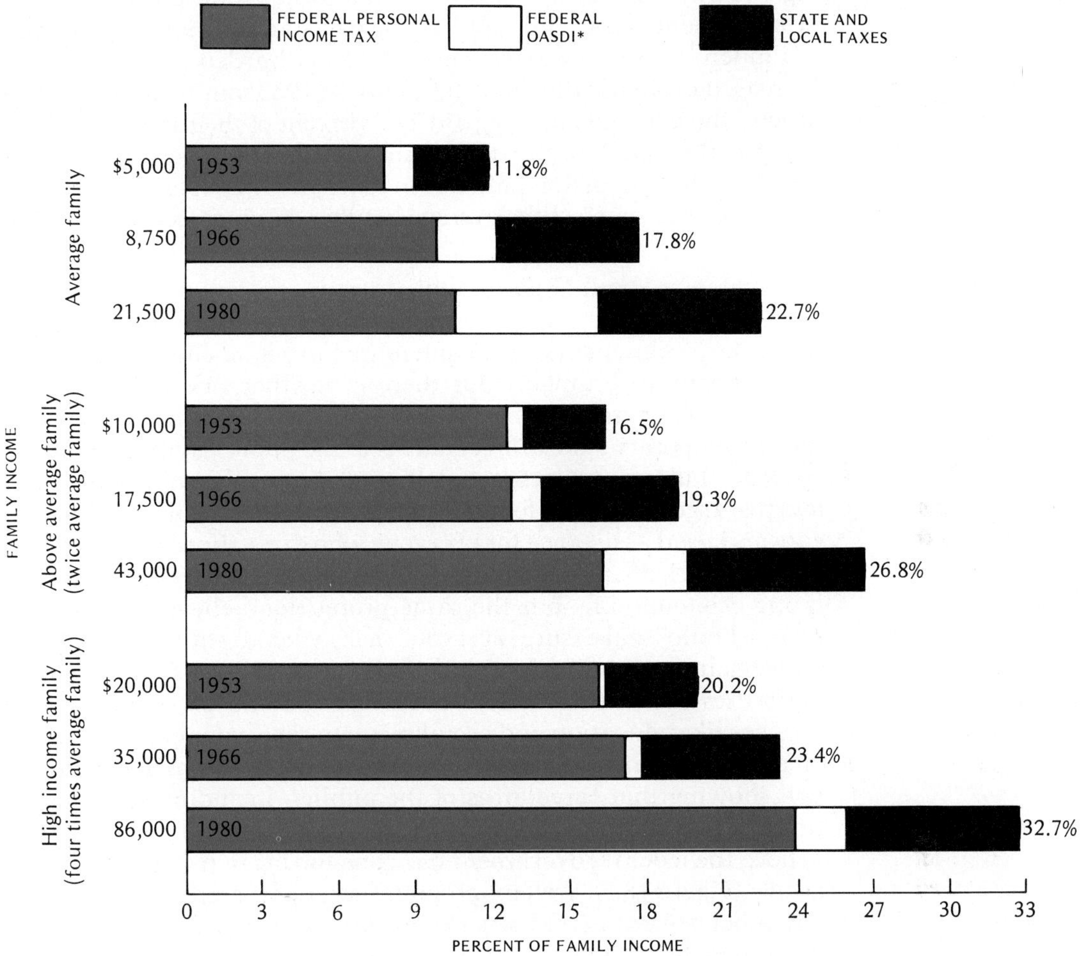

*Old Age, Survivors', and Disability Insurance taxes.
Source: Significant Features of Fiscal Federalism, 1980–81 Edition, (Washington, D.C.: Advisory Commission on Intergovernmental Relations, December 1981), p. 48.

the unemployed), of union members as well as those not in unions, and of every income group except the poor stressed inflation.

Not only has concern over inflation risen, but the public has shifted its sense of who and what are responsible for inflation. Before 1965, when Gallup interviewers asked Americans whether they thought government, business, or labor was most responsible, Republicans tended to say "labor" while Democrats answered "business." By 1968, however, large and equivalent majorities of both Democrats and Republicans said "government." In a poll taken by ABC News / *Washington Post* in January 1982, 57 percent held government responsible, while just 19 percent blamed labor and 13 percent business.[14]

[14] Survey by ABC News / *Washington Post*, January 22–30, 1982.

In the late 1960s and 1970s, governmental actions came increasingly to be seen widely as problems, not just as solutions to problems. "Government causes inflation" is one part of this. "Government taxes too much" is another part. The actual tax burden on most citizens increased dramatically after the 1950s. In 1953 families with incomes around the national average paid 11.8 percent of their income in taxes; in 1966 they paid 17.8 percent, and in 1980 22.7 percent. Incomes rose, but the proportion paid out in taxes rose much faster—and took about twice as much of the average family's earnings (see Figure 18.4).

Ambivalence about Government

All these developments have contributed to a loud chorus of criticism of American government. But there is another side to the public's response. As we saw in chapter 12, Americans are ambivalent about the contemporary state. Three-fourths of the public say that tax money spent for human services is poorly used, but at the same time three-fourths argue that the federal government should provide medical care and legal assistance for everyone who can't afford these services. Seven Americans in ten think government has gone too far in regulating economic life, but the same proportion believes that government should make sure everyone has a good standard of living. Overwhelming majorities think federal spending is too high, yet majorities just as big believe even more should be spent for basic services like education and social security. The extent of the endorsement of government is capped by a recent NBC News / Associated Press poll showing that three-fifths of the public—including solid majorities in every educational, income, and occupational group—do not believe the federal government has gone too far in trying to help poor people (Figure 18.5). Welfare programs are more deeply criticized than any other governmental service; even here, however, people do not want to go back to the levels of support provided in the past.

Political Implications

Such changing attitudes are reflected in the emphases of leaders of both parties—for example, in the assessments of Edmund G. (Jerry) Brown, Jr., a two-term Democratic governor of California (1975–83) and contender for his party's 1976 presidential nomination. "Fat government is weak government," Governor Brown argues.

> A government that gets into the business of fine-tuning [the economy] and doing what private concerns do perfectly well on their own, becomes a weak government. . . . The economic challenge before America is one of greater output, greater skill, and greater intelligence. It is *not* going to be met by a free lunch for everyone—such as tax cuts, rising credit, even higher levels of consumption than the rate we're having now. It requires investing in the infrastructure . . . equipping America to compete with

Figure 18.5   **The Government: Friend *and* Foe**

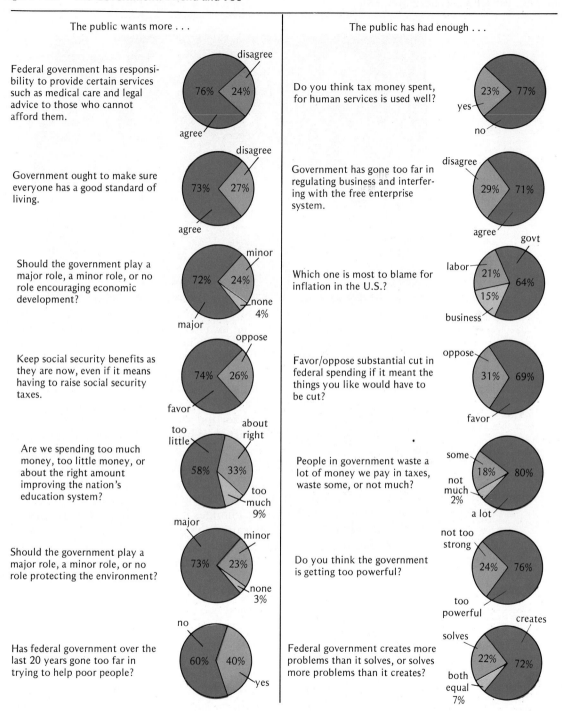

The public wants more . . .

Federal government has responsibility to provide certain services such as medical care and legal advice to those who cannot afford them.
76% agree / 24% disagree

Government ought to make sure everyone has a good standard of living.
73% agree / 27% disagree

Should the government play a major role, a minor role, or no role encouraging economic development?
72% major / 24% minor / none 4%

Keep social security benefits as they are now, even if it means having to raise social security taxes.
74% favor / 26% oppose

Are we spending too much money, too little money, or about the right amount improving the nation's education system?
58% too little / 33% about right / too much 9%

Should the government play a major role, a minor role, or no role protecting the environment?
73% major / 23% minor / none 3%

Has federal government over the last 20 years gone too far in trying to help poor people?
60% no / 40% yes

The public has had enough . . .

Do you think tax money spent, for human services is used well?
23% yes / 77% no

Government has gone too far in regulating business and interfering with the free enterprise system.
29% disagree / 71% agree

Which one is most to blame for inflation in the U.S.?
labor 21% / 15% business / 64% govt

Favor/oppose substantial cut in federal spending if it meant the things you like would have to be cut?
31% oppose / 69% favor

People in government waste a lot of money we pay in taxes, waste some, or not much?
some 18% / not much 2% / 80% a lot

Do you think the government is getting too powerful?
not too strong 24% / 76% too powerful

Federal government creates more problems than it solves, or solves more problems than it creates?
solves 22% / both equal 7% / 72% creates

Questions 1a–7a are taken from polls conducted by NBC News / Associated Press, April 1981; Research and Forecasts Company, November 1980; Roper Center / Roper Organization; November 1981; Harris, February 1982; NORC, Spring 1982; Roper Center / Roper Organization, November 1981; and NBC News / Associated Press, May 1982, respectively. Questions 1b–7b are taken from polls conducted by Roper Center / Roper Organization, November 1981; CBS News / *New York Times,* April 1981; ABC News / *Washington Post,* January 1982; NBC News / Associated Press, February 1981; CBS / University of Michigan Election Surveys, 1980; ibid.; and CBS News / *New York Times,* January 1981, respectively.

President Reagan and his economic advisers inspecting the federal budget.

people abroad who are getting lower cost capital and new tools while their wage rates are lower. We have to build on the American advantage in technology and organization management.[15]

"Big government" is no longer in, although almost no one wants to dismantle the governmental edifice already built. Economic growth is in, and both parties recognize that the terms of the debate over how best to achieve it have shifted. Which one will be the "party of prosperity"?

Criticisms of "big government"

In the New Deal era the Democrats had much more electoral success than the Republicans. Perhaps most important was their success in convincing people that they were the party of prosperity. But as we have seen, recent economic changes have affected this perception. Ronald Reagan received generally high economic marks from voters in 1984. Neither the Republicans nor the Democrats have yet established a firm contemporary hold on the title "party of prosperity."

Reagan's approach. The Reagan administration staked its claim to effective handling of the political economy on four related commitments. First, it said that the overall growth of government should be curtailed and the steady growth of federal domestic spending curbed. Second, governmental regulation of private business should be cut back. Third, federal taxes are too high and, at a minimum, their continuing growth as a proportion of personal income should be arrested. Fourth, inflation can and should be kept under control by a growing and competitive private economy, and through increases in the nation's money supply (see below) that are both steady and proportional to overall economic growth.

[15] Interview by the author with Edmund G. Brown, Jr., for *Public Opinion*, June 14, 1984.

1984 Democratic presidential candidate Walter Mondale criticizing the Reagan economic record—the large federal deficit.

The Democrats' approach. Democratic leaders insist that while big government is indeed a problem, it is the growth of military spending that is especially troublesome and that must be curbed. Second, they endorse deregulation in a number of areas of the economy but maintain that more vigorous federal regulation is needed in others, especially those involving the environment and consumer protection. Third, they argue that the Reagan-backed tax cuts were excessive and fueled an unacceptably large deficit that carries strong pressures for high interest rates and future inflation. Fourth, they believe that sustained economic growth and national prosperity will require a greater measure of intelligent federal planning and management than the Republicans favor, although management very different from that of the past.

TOOLS OF ECONOMIC POLICY

Government policies in the economic area can be sorted into three broad groups: *regulatory, monetary,* and *fiscal.* **Regulatory policy** comprises governmental standard-setting and rule-making for different sectors of the economy. Looking at developments in this area gives us a good sense of the scope of recent efforts to cut back on government's economic reach. **Monetary policy** encompasses issues of management of the nation's money supply: decisions on how much it should be expanded at any time, and such related matters as interest rates and the ease of borrowing capital. **Fiscal policy** covers governmental adjustments in taxing and spending: for example, determining whether, and by how much, overall federal spending should exceed revenues.

Regulatory Policy: The Push to Deregulate

From the time Franklin Roosevelt took office in 1933 to the early 1970s, there were two great bursts of new regulatory activity, one in the 1930s, the other beginning in the mid-1960s and extending into the early 1970s. Against this backdrop, recent developments are distinguished by efforts to cut back on governmental regulations. **Deregulation** has been the watchword of the late 1970s and the 1980s. A distinction must be made between two types of regulation: One involves the regulation of *prices* charged by businesses and the entry of firms into various industrial sectors; the other comprises regulations aimed at health, safety, and consumer protection. Since the early 1970s there has been extensive deregulation in the former area, but little in the latter.

Prices and entry. By the 1970s an enormous array of regulations setting prices and determining which firms could enter certain markets were in place—governing airlines, trucking, railroads, oil and natural gas, banks and other financial institutions. Regulations were imposed early in the development of these industries to promote orderly growth. Airlines are a good case in point: The federal Civil Aeronautics Board (CAB) determined the prices airlines could charge for tickets, and which airlines could service which routes, in an effort to achieve a stable system of air transportation linking cities large and small across the country. The industry was seen as a kind of public utility, much like telephone service and electric power. Under the CAB's rigid controls on prices and entry, the infant air industry developed impressively.

By the 1970s, however, economists and other observers felt that much of this regulation was no longer needed and that its principal continuing effect was to limit competition. In this view, governmental control over prices and entry simply preserved comfortable niches in which businesses could operate free from competitive challenge. The regulatory barriers should be removed, and free-market controls substituted. The essential element of free markets is the right to compete without permission from any governmental agency. Under open competition, firms would have greater incentive to offer better prices and services. Poorly managed firms would be driven from the market by consumer choice.

Economist Alfred Kahn played a leading role in deregulation efforts
Deregulation in the 1970s in the 1970s through both his writings and his chairmanship of the Civil Aeronautics Board when airline deregulation was rushing along.

> Whenever the government intervenes in the economy in one way or another . . . it typically confers benefits on some groups of people and, directly or indirectly, burdens on others. In so doing, it necessarily creates vested private interests in a continuation of that particular activity. The inter-

ests usually antedate the government action and provide part of the political motivation for the government's undertaking it in the first place; but the explicit intervention by the government then validates those interests, confers those benefits, and makes the beneficiaries eager to see the activity continue.[16]

The position of regulated businesses was often at odds with what a superficial reading might lead one to expect: Industries often profited from and strongly defended the control government imposed. For example, many more airlines opposed legislation deregulating that industry than favored it.

The liberal-conservative alliance. Economists do not enact national legislation. To understand how a political majority in Congress and the executive branch emerged behind deregulation, one needs to see how liberals and conservatives found reason to join forces. For conservatives, deregulation was an opportunity to "help get government off our backs." Through deregulation, market forces would be permitted to work, replacing burdensome governmental restraints, and improving productivity. But many liberal politicians, among them Senator Edward Kennedy, also enthusiastically supported deregulation of airlines, railroads, and trucking. The liberals were responding to consumer groups who had come to believe that regulations were keeping prices unnecessarily high and services poorer than they could be. To the extent that regulation was an unwarranted aid to business, liberals had every incentive to oppose it. Beyond this, as Michael Pertschuck notes, the clamor to cut back on the growth of government had grown loud by the late 1970s, and many politicians were looking for ways to show voters that they were responsive.

Rapid deregulation. With broad agreement among economists, and with liberals and conservatives making common cause, deregulation was almost irresistible. The result was a surge of well over twenty-five pieces of major new legislation and administrative rulings in this area in the late 1970s and early 1980s. What specifically has it meant?

Airline deregulation

In the airline industry, the Civil Aeronautics Board began in 1976 allowing airlines to engage in competitive pricing, and in 1978 it became much more flexible in awarding new routes. The Airline Deregulation Act of 1978 carried these developments ahead. Airlines are now free to enter and leave routes as they see fit, and to determine by themselves, subject to market pressures, what they will charge. In 1978, only 36 airlines serviced interstate markets; in 1984 more than 100 firms competed interstate. Deregulation spurred competition and decreased the market shares of the airlines that had previously been the major trunk carriers.

[16]Alfred E. Kahn, "Deregulation and Vested Interests: The Case of Airlines," in Roger G. Noll and Bruce M. Owen, *The Political Economy of Deregulation* (Washington, D.C.: American Enterprise Institute, 1983), p. 132.

In the old regulatory environment, employees, such as pilots, had been able to capture for themselves a significant part of the economic gains that accrued from technological advances, in the form of high salaries. Now, faced with competition, those carriers with large numbers of high-priced employees are struggling to adapt. Airline ticket prices under deregulation, it is generally agreed, have come to reflect much more closely actual costs of doing business. Fares in longer-haul markets and in heavily traveled routes have fallen substantially, relative to fares in short-haul and lightly traveled routes.

Rail and trucking deregulation

On the ground, the Motor Carrier Act of 1980 and the Staggers Rail Act of 1980 similarly extended trucking and rail deregulation, which had been initiated in the mid-1970s by the regulatory body with jurisdiction in the area, the Interstate Commerce Commission (ICC). While the ICC still imposes some rate and entry regulations, it now leaves much more room for market forces. Carriers can now operate in an integrated fashion across all transportation sectors. Whereas railroads had been prohibited from operating trucking companies, they are now free to do so. The old separation of ship, railroad, and truck carriers is coming to an end; firms are offering packages of transportation services which take advantage of the relative efficiencies of each of the three means.

Oil and gas deregulation

Petroleum deregulation has moved more slowly and with a lot more contention. The Natural Gas Policy Act (NGPA) of 1978 has achieved only a partial decontrol of prices. Under the NGPA, natural gas supplies were divided into various categories, with different pricing rules applied to each. "Old" gas supplies (wells tapped before the 1978 legislation went into effect) were given the lowest price. "New" gas was priced higher. "Deep" gas, drawn from wells below 15,000 feet or produced under other difficult conditions, was decontrolled altogether. This complex step-ladder pricing system was designed to remove some price controls and to give incentives for discovering new gas supplies—and in this it has had some success. Proponents of natural gas deregulation argue, though, that the NGPA leaves far too much governmental interference with the workings of the market. On the other hand, opponents maintain that consumers would have to bear big price increases if complete decontrol were rapidly obtained.[17] Consumer groups have not been convinced that natural gas deregulation is in their interest.

Is deregulation working? Results are complicated and by no means uniform. But the conclusion of most observers seems to be at least a tentative yes. Perhaps the most striking confirmation is that, after a decade of change and experimentation, almost no one advocates a return to the highly regulated environment that had previously existed.

---

[17] For an informative review of some of the principal issues in natural gas deregulation, see Henry D. Jacoby and Arthur W. Wright, "The Gordian Knot of Natural Gas Prices," in Edward J. Mitchell, ed., *The Deregulation of Natural Gas* (Washington, D.C.: American Enterprise Institute, 1983), pp. 125–48.

A foreman instructs miners on safety rules.

Health, safety, and consumer protection. Other types of governmental regulation set health and safety standards and seek to protect consumer interests. From roughly 1965 through 1975, there was an extraordinary increase in this type of regulation. For example, the Clean Water and Clean Air Acts, together with their various amendments, imposed standards and restrictions on industry relating to the emission of pollutants into the atmosphere and into the nation's lakes and rivers. In all, more than 50 major pieces of regulatory legislation were passed by Congress from the mid-1960s through the mid-1970s—including the Federal Cigarette and Labeling Advertising Act (1965), the National Traffic and Motor Vehicle Safety Act (1966), the Child Protection Act (1966), and the Flammable Fabrics Act Amendments (1967).

Earlier government regulation of business focused on a limited number of industries and was primarily concerned with prices and with the allocation of market shares. In contrast, the new legislation of the 1960s and 1970s was directed at "ameliorating the social impact of businesses, not their economic behavior."[18] As American society became wealthier in the post–World War II years, public expectations rose in such areas as environmental cleanliness and consumer protection. Various policy entrepreneurs, in Congress and in public-interest groups, responded to this new climate of opinion.

By the latter half of the 1970s, a backlash had set in against this surge of regulation. But the liberal-conservative (or Democratic-Republican) alliance evident in the campaign for airline and trucking

Changing focus of regulation in the 1960s and 1970s

[18] Michael Pertschuk, *Revolt Against Regulation* (Berkeley, Calif.: University of California Press, 1982), p. 23.

deregulation was nowhere to be seen in the environmental, consumer-protection, and health and safety areas. Instead, there was a fairly clear-cut liberal vs. conservative split. Liberals continued to defend the new regulation and often to seek its extension, while conservatives favored a rollback or at least an end to the rush to pass new laws. A political equilibrium has largely been reached, in that business and conservative interests have for the most part blocked new regulation but liberal, consumer, and environmental interests have prevented a rollback.

Fiscal and Monetary Policy: Contending Approaches among Economists

Broad changes in the economy and in thinking about how it is best managed are now reflected in five competing schools of opinion among economists. In the real world, the lines separating these positions are often blurred. Still, the five have been clearly evident in the ongoing debate over how to manage the U.S. economy through fiscal and monetary policies.

Monetarism. **Monetarism** puts a singular emphasis on controlling the money supply and the price of money (the interest rate) to secure a growing and inflation-free economy. While every economist recognizes that monetary policy is important, only monetarists make it their keystone. Monetarism now enjoys more support among professional economists than at any time in the last half-century. Its leading theorist is Milton Friedman, a Nobel Laureate in economics (1976) with a long and distinguished career at the University of Chicago.

Friedman and other monetarists start from the straightforward and, to a degree, unassailable proposition that inflation occurs as the result of "too much money chasing too few goods." For a variety of reasons—including the desire of politicians to "heat up the economy" so that they can go into election years with unemployment down and the GNP up—the money supply in the United States over the last quarter-century has been expanded in excess of what would be justified given actual increases in productivity. The inevitable result has been a reduction in the purchasing power of the dollar—inflation.

At various times when the economy has been beset by inflation, there have been short-term efforts to curtail it by sharply cutting back monetary growth. Temporary monetary tightness has indeed temporarily reduced inflation, but at substantial cost: increased unemployment and diminished productivity growth. So, after a while, expansionist policies have been resumed. What is needed, monetarists maintain, is not a lurching between overexpansion and sharp contraction, but a stable, steady growth of the money supply corresponding to and sustaining real growth. The absence of such a policy has been the main source of the country's erratic economic perfor-

Monetarist policies

mance. As a remedy, Friedman advocates legislating the monetary rule—that the money supply be expanded each year at the same annual rate as the potential growth of the country's real GNP, or at 3 to 5 percent per year. As long as this happens, any decline into recession will be modest and only temporary, and any inflationary increase in spending will burn itself out for lack of fuel.

Supply-side economics. Monetarists are usually catalogued as political conservatives because they stress the capacity of the competitive market system to allocate resources efficiently. Not all conservative private-market economists are monetarists, however. In the 1970s, a new emphasis took shape among some younger conservatives that was christened *"supply-side economics."* In contrast to monetarists, supply-siders put great weight on fiscal policy. In particular, they argue for large across-the-board tax cuts, to encourage many people (1) to work harder, since the "tax penalty" on additional earnings would be reduced; and (2) to invest more in productive enterprises, rather than trying to find economically unproductive tax shelters to escape high marginal tax rates. (The "marginal" tax rate is what a taxpayer gives the government on the last dollars he earns. In the United States, since the income tax rate climbs as one moves into higher income categories, and since some earnings can be sheltered from taxation, an individual's marginal tax rate is often much higher than the proportion of total income that he or she pays in taxes.)

Supply-side policies

Growth resulting from the immediate stimulus of a large across-the-board tax cut and from long-term encouragement of greater work efforts means there will be a much larger base of national wealth to be taxed. Paradoxically, *reduction of the tax rate* can actually culminate in an *increase in total tax revenues.* Federal expenditures would not need to be greatly reduced to compensate for the tax-rate reduction; what cuts would be needed, in the supply-side view, could be achieved by the elimination of waste and extravagance. Though their emphasis is on supply or growth-producing fiscal policies, supply-siders also endorse the monetarist goal of a modest, steady growth in the money supply.

The most controversial aspect of the supply-side diagnosis is the idea that a large cut in the tax rate would not lead to big federal deficits that would accelerate the rate of inflation. In defense, proponents of the supply-side approach argue that their position here has been misstated. "The idea that supply-side economics would provide an instant, large increase in government tax revenue by reducing tax rates was simply not true to begin with. . . ."[19] What *was* valid, in this view, was the general idea that reducing high marginal tax rates contributes to overall economic growth—benefiting everyone, including government in its need for tax revenues.

[19]Martin Anderson, "Is Supply-Side Economics Dead?" *The American Spectator,* November 1983, p. 10.

Unemployment remains a problem.

Has the Reagan administration tried and tested supply-side prescriptions? Answers to this vary. The centerpiece of the Reagan program was a substantial cut in income tax rates: a 23 percent cut over 3 years. But the overall mix of federal taxes under Reagan shows something quite different than a determined test of supply-side theory. While income tax rates were in fact reduced, other taxes rose—notably Social Security payroll taxes. In addition, much of the reduction in income tax rates merely offset the effects of "bracket creep," which occurs as inflation pushes people into higher income tax brackets. Nonetheless, the Reagan administration has been guided by a mix of supply-side and monetarist ideas. Supply-siders hail the strength of the 1983–84 recovery, and the low rate of inflation, as at least partial confirmation of the validity of their approach. Supply-side economics has been propounded by a number of economists and politicians. Among them are Arthur Laffer of the University of Southern California, social commentator George Gilder, and Congressman Jack Kemp (Republican of New York).

The old-time religion. Neither monetarism nor the supply-side approach is the old "mainstream" economics of American conservatives. Herbert Stein, who served as chairman of the Council of Economic Advisers under Richard Nixon (1972–74), has labeled the traditional conservative approach to economic policy ***"the old-time religion"*** and is one of its most effective spokesmen. The established economic approach of Republican conservatives emphasizes governmental austerity: an effort to curb the perceived profligacy of the Democrats.

It stresses a tight money supply, the importance of balanced federal budgets, restraint in federal spending, and a willingness to endure some slowing down of the economy to wring inflation out of the system.

Traditional conservative economics

In the 1980s, politicians emphasizing the prudence and austerity of the "old-time religion" are not hard to find, in spite of the attention monetarism and supply-side economics have received. The massive federal deficits of 1983 and 1984, for example, prompted some congressional conservatives to work to close the budgetary gap, by both reducing expenditures and increasing taxes. While President Reagan opposed any major tax hike, influential GOP senators like Robert Dole (Kansas), chairman of the Senate Finance Committee, and Pete Domenici (New Mexico), chairman of the Senate Budget Committee, pushed for increases. Even within a conservative Republican administration, important differences over economic policy were evident, stemming from the contrasting perspectives of supply-siders, for whom the very idea of a tax increase is anathema; monetarists, who are primarily concerned with the failure of the Federal Reserve to follow their prescription for slow, steady monetary growth; and traditional conservatives who feel that large budget deficits carry unacceptable threats to the long-term health of the economy.

Industrial policy. The three positions we have described thus far are basically the province of conservatives. The other two main approaches that vie for attention in the 1980s have liberals as their proponents. One goes under the label ***industrial policy.*** This approach blends an emphasis on stimulating economic growth—which liberals and conservatives alike can agree on—with an enlarged role for government in promoting the conditions for growth. Tensions in American society will rise, proponents of an industrial policy approach argue, unless ways are found to strengthen America's competitive position in the world economy, especially vis-à-vis Japan. Government must take the lead here, generally in finding new means of promoting growth.

How are productivity gains and more rapid growth to be achieved? The answer, according to economists such as Lester Thurow of MIT and industry analyst Robert Reich of the Harvard Business School, is in part to copy those nations like Japan which have been doing especially well of late. The Japanese government has provided major support for the development of industries with high growth potential—sometimes called "sunrise industries." Thurow gives as an example of this encouragement Japan's great success in robotics: the use of robots to assist in manufacturing.

> The problem for the robotics industry [in Japan] was that the seller couldn't get economies of scale to sell a lot of robots so he could sell them cheaply. Buyers wanted only one or two. So JDB [the Japanese Development Bank] stepped in and financed a short-term leasing company.

They didn't subsidize anyone, but they bought the robots, guaranteed producers a market of so many robots a year, and then leased the robots to industry. Now if robots had been a failure, the leasing company would have taken a bath. But they were a great success, and the Japanese conquered robots before the rest of us got started. [Today] they have 14,000; we have 4,000.[20]

New industrial policy

In the United States, the federal government needs to step in, industrial policy proponents insist, with new programs to encourage productivity gains and economic growth along the lines of the Japanese model. As one such means, Thurow advocates a kind of National Science Foundation for American industry, providing funding for the development and introduction of important new technologies. He also favors "industrial triage" as the companion approach to "sunset industries." Just as "sunrise industries" need economic encouragement from government, so industries in decline need to be put out of business faster so that the economy can adapt to new opportunities.

The Japanese are currently doing this in the aluminum industry, forcing reductions in the business. The Japanese Development Bank plays a role by buying obsolete facilities, then tearing them down. They don't get full value but they get something. Something similar should be done for [American firms like] International Harvester so that they get out of the tractor business and into trucks, which they do well.[21]

Keynesian economics revisited. While having lost the kind of intellectual and political preeminence they enjoyed from the late 1930s to the 1960s, Keynesians and the economic policies they favor still figure prominently in America's economic debates, as the fifth major school of opinion. At the core of Keynesianism are two basic elements: expansionism and the welfare state. Full employment is a central goal, one that both requires and makes possible high and rapid growth of the GNP. To ensure growth, government must manage the level of demand: When demand is insufficient, government should provide economic stimulus, by spending more than it takes in; conversely, when demand is excessive, the government should put the brakes on through fiscal policy.

A rapidly growing economy provides, Keynesians maintain, a "growth dividend": additional revenues that can be expended to enlarge social programs. As in earlier decades, the Keynesian emphasis now includes an expansive, growing federal responsibility for public welfare through antipoverty programs, Social Security, Medicare, and more. Keynesian economists such as Paul Samuelson of MIT and James Tobin of Yale remain strong advocates of an expanding welfare state.

[20]Interview by the author with Lester Thurow, *Public Opinion*, August / September 1983, pp. 7, 58.
[21]Ibid.

THE ECONOMIC POLICY-MAKERS

The development and execution of economic policy for the United States falls disproportionately on certain units of the federal government: the president and his White House advisers; the Federal Reserve System; the Treasury Department; and, within Congress, the appropriations, finance, and budget committees. A number of organized groups and interests in the private sector are also influential.

The President

In 1928, Republican Herbert Hoover was elected president by a massive majority (58.1 percent to 40.8 percent) over his Democratic opponent, Alfred E. Smith. Considered part of the "progressive" wing of the Republican party, Hoover was hailed for his achievements in business, government, and humanitarian assistance. Just four years later, however, Hoover lay buried under an electoral landslide that brought to power Franklin Roosevelt and big Democratic majorities in both houses of Congress. What had so drastically changed Hoover's fortunes was the Great Depression.

Republican policies were hardly the sole cause of the worldwide economic collapse, and Hoover's own responsibility for the Depression was more limited still. Few experts would argue that the Depression would have occured with any less severity had Al Smith and the Democrats taken office in 1929. But Hoover became president, and his administration was the Depression's main political victim. Again and again since the 1930s, we have seen presidential popularity substantially affected by how the economy is doing.

All U.S. politicians want to see their country as prosperous as possible, and believe sincerely that the policies they espouse will contribute to that end in the long run. Elections are not held "in the long run," however, and political leaders also pursue short-term policies to encourage an upbeat economy for the next election campaign. The result, political scientist Edward Tufte has found, is

Economics and the electoral cycle

> an electoral rhythm to the national economic performance of many capitalist democracies. . . . In the United States, the electoral, economic cycle from 1948 to 1976 (other than the Eisenhower years) has consisted of . . . a four-year presidential cycle in the unemployment rate, with downturns in unemployment in the months before the presidential election and upturns in the unemployment rate usually beginning from 12 to 18 months after the election.[22]

Tufte notes, too, that personal income tends to grow faster in election years than in years without elections. He concludes that "these pat-

---

[22] Edward R. Tufte, *Political Control of the Economy* (Princeton, N.J.: Princeton University Press, 1978), pp. 26–27.

terns are consistent with the character of the economic tools available to control real disposable income and unemployment.... Further, the greater the electoral stakes, the greater the economic stimulation. In particular, those years when incumbent presidents sought re-election enjoyed the most favorable short-run economic conditions."[23]

Monetary policy and the Federal Reserve

Monetary policy can have the greatest impact on short-term economic performance. The president has, however, little direct control over monetary policy. That authority resides largely in a unit of the national government that has been given substantial formal independence from both president and Congress: the *Federal Reserve System.* A president's influence over monetary decisions must come indirectly, then, from persuading and/or pressuring the Federal Reserve to take steps he favors.

The Federal Reserve System

The U.S. Constitution confers upon Congress the power "to coin money" and to "regulate the value thereof" (Article I, section 8). For all practical purposes, however, this authority has been delegated to the **Federal Reserve.** "The Fed" is the central bank of the United States. Every major democracy has a central bank, because each needs a publicly controlled financial institution capable of conducting its monetary affairs.

Established in 1913, the Federal Reserve combines centralization and decentralization, and private as well as public involvement, in the U.S. central bank. The system has four main elements: (1) the Board of Governors, which has its headquarters in Washington; (2) the Federal Open Market Committee; (3) twelve Federal Reserve banks, together with their 25 branches and other facilities located throughout the United States; and (4) all of the member commercial banks, including all national banks and those state-chartered banks that have elected to join the system (see Figure 18.6).

The Board of Governors. **The Board of Governors** is at the apex of the system. Its seven members are appointed for long (14-year) staggered terms, to insulate them from political pressure. Terms of board members are also so arranged that one expires every two years, which means that no president, even if he served eight years in office, could appoint more than four members. These provisions prevent a president from exerting the kind of control over the Federal Reserve that he can over the Cabinet departments. The chairman and vice chairman of the Federal Reserve Board are named by the president for four-year terms. The position of chairman—occupied since 1978 by Paul Volker—has become enormously influential in policy-making.

The Board of Governors and its chairman have broad policy-mak-

---

[23] Ibid., pp. 12, 27.

Figure 18.6 **Organization of the Federal Reserve System**

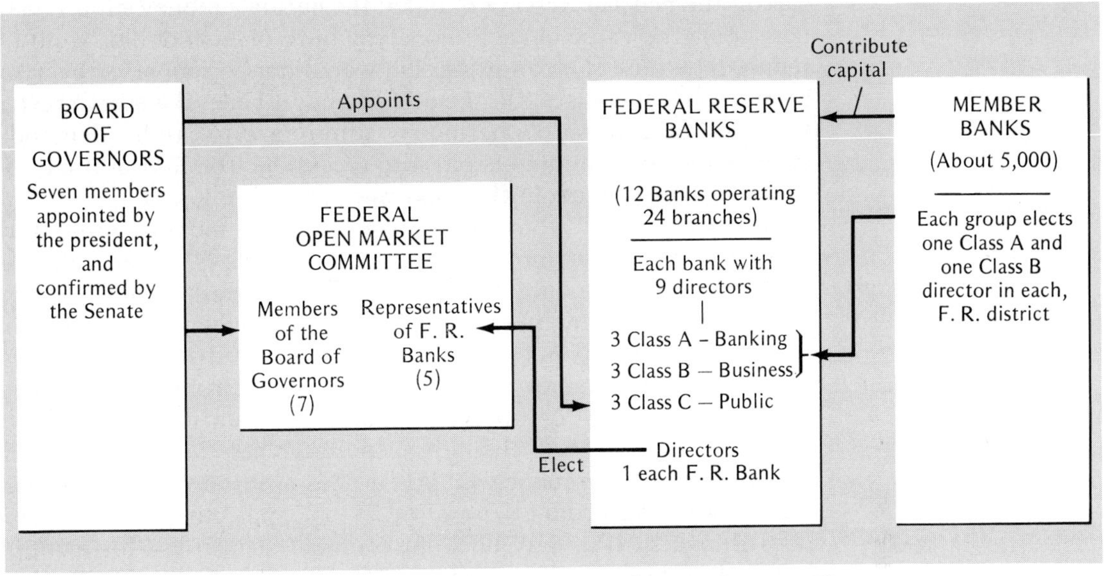

Source: Board of Governors, *The Federal Reserve System*, p. 50.

The discount rate

ing and supervisory authority. They establish the reserve requirements for member banks, which help determine how much money the latter will have available for loans and thus expand or contract available credit. They review and approve ***discount-rate*** actions of the Federal Reserve banks. The discount rate is the rate of interest charged to member banks when they borrow from the Reserve banks. The higher the discount rate, the higher the interest rates banks will have to charge their customers for home mortgages, car loans, and the like. In addition, the Board of Governors conducts examinations of the Federal Reserve banks, requires reports from them, supervises the issue and retirement of Federal Reserve notes (the nation's paper money), and exercises jurisdiction over the admission of state banks into the Federal Reserve System. If the board finds malperformance or illegal behavior, it can issue "cease and desist orders" and suspend member banks from further use of the credit facilities of the Federal Reserve.

Federal Open-Market Committee. Closely linked to the work of the Federal Reserve Board is that of the ***Federal Open-Market Committee*** (FOMC). Each of the seven board members is also a member of the FOMC, which includes, as well, five representatives of the Reserve banks (elected annually). The "open-market operations" are the prime vehicles used by the Fed to determine the size of the nation's money supply.

The basic rules in money-supply regulation are simple enough. Too rapid an expansion of the money supply contributes to an overheating of the economy and to inflation. To take an extreme hypothetical case, if the Federal Reserve doubled the nation's money supply in the next year, the value of each monetary unit, of each dollar, would be reduced, because such an expansion would not be supported by actual productivity increases. On the other hand, if Federal Reserve restrictions on the growth of the money supply are too tight, demand is curbed and the economy is put into recession. The task of the FOMC interventions is to avoid these extremes.

Money-supply regulation

This is easier said than done. Regulating the money supply of the United States is enormously complicated. There is no general agreement on how the money supply is understood and calculated, given current economic realities. Gone are the days when money was simply the coins or paper currency people carried in their pockets. Today, the majority of "money" takes the form of electronic bytes of information within the computers of financial institutions: the balances of various personal and business accounts. When the Federal Reserve acts to increase the money supply, it does not literally run the printing presses and produce more pieces of paper currency. Rather, it does things such as buy back government securities—for example, bonds that the federal government issued to help finance the national debt. When the Fed buys back bonds, it pays for them by checks drawn on its accounts, and these checks are in turn deposited into various bank accounts around the country. The money supply is thus increased because these banks can lend more money.

The Federal Reserve banks. The Federal Reserve Board and the FOMC are agencies of the federal government. This is not the case for the twelve **Federal Reserve banks** and their branches, often called "quasi-public" banks, for they reflect an interesting blend of private ownership and public control. Each Reserve bank is owned by the member commercial banks in its district. Upon joining the Federal Reserve System, commercial banks are required to purchase shares of stock in the Reserve bank which serves their area. Reserve banks are incorporated institutions with their own boards of directors. But despite their private ownership, Reserve banks are fundamentally public institutions. They are not motivated by profits as private businesses must be. All of their earnings, after operating expenses have been met, are paid into the U.S. Treasury. These central banks are supposed to promote the growth and well-being of the economy as a whole.

The Reserve banks are sometimes referred to as "bankers' banks," meaning that they perform functions for commercial banks much as the latter do for the general public. Just as commercial banks receive deposits from the public and make loans to the public, so the Reserve banks receive deposits and extend loans to commercial banks. The Reserve banks also have a third main function which commercial banks no longer perform (although they once did): issuing currency. Congress has provided that the Reserve banks alone put into circulation the country's paper money. Look at a one-dollar bill; right above the portrait of Washington you will see imprinted "Federal Reserve Note."

Political pressures on the Fed. Monetary policy is critically important, and the Federal Reserve makes it. This puts the Fed in a political storm center. For example, if the Fed has been restricting the growth of the money supply in an effort to check inflation, the demand for available money is likely to be very high. This means interest rates are likely to be high. If home mortgages are at annual rates of 17 percent interest, and automobile loans are at 14 percent, large numbers of people who need such loans to make their purchases are not going to be able to afford them. The housing and automobile industries are especially vulnerable to high interest rates, so naturally they press for lower rates. We have noted that an attempt was made to insulate the Fed from such pressures, and that this was partly successful. But only partly so. No institution like the Federal Reserve can operate in a democratic nation in disregard of the policy demands made on it.

The executive branch and the Federal Reserve

Given the pressure, the position of the president and his administration becomes critical. When the president strongly backs the Fed in its current approach to monetary policy, this usually gives it enough support to persist. Without the president's backing, however, the Fed is terribly vulnerable, given the other pressures almost certain to be placed on it. Thus we have a situation where, in formal institutional terms, the Fed is separate from the president and his administration but where, in a practical sense, it is sensitive to the suggestions for monetary policy that emanate from the White House. The president and the Federal Reserve need each other. The Fed needs the president's political backing and sustenance. And the monetary policies which the Fed conducts are extremely important to national economic performance, on which the success of any administration hinges.

Presidential elections and the Federal Reserve

Signals coming from the president in the first years of his term are much more likely to encourage the Federal Reserve to pursue a restrictive, inflation-checking approach to currency expansion than those received in the months preceding the next presidential election. No party wants to run for re-election in an economic environment where productivity is down and unemployment up. Signals sent to the Fed from the White House, when thoughts there turn to the next presidential election, have tended to encourage the expansion of the money supply.[24] This may be changing. The nation's experience with high inflation during the 1970s has produced a climate of great sensitivity about anything that looks as though it might encourage a renewal of inflation.

[24] Robert J. Shapiro, "Politics and the Federal Reserve," *The Public Interest*, Winter 1982, p. 119.

The Council of Economic Advisers

Recognizing the president's need for more economic expertise in the White House, the Employment Act of 1946 established the **Council of Economic Advisers** (CEA). The council consists of three members appointed by the president, with confirmation by the Senate. The president designates one of the three as chairman. For the last three decades, the chairman of the CEA has been a key figure in federal economic policy. He is one of a small group of high-level economic officials who interact regularly with the president, advising him on what economic issues need his attention and what his options are. Other members of this informal economic policy committee are the secretary of the Treasury and the director of the Office of Management and Budget (OMB). The Council of Economic Advisers does not make and execute policy; rather, it advises the president.[25]

The Treasury Department

Established in 1789, the **Treasury** is one of the original executive departments. Today it is by far the most influential Cabinet department in economic policy. We discussed its functions in chapter 9. The Treasury is in the middle of economic planning and policy management. Its secretary serves with the head of the OMB and the chairman of the Council of Economic Advisers in what has developed over successive administrations to be an informal economic central committee. One of the secretary's principal associates, the undersecretary for monetary affairs, is the administration's chief liaison person with the Federal Reserve Board of Governors and the FOMC. The government's agency for tax administration, the Internal Revenue Service, is located within the Treasury Department. So, too, is the Office of the Comptroller of the Currency; the comptroller shares with the Federal Reserve broad responsibilities for supervising and regulating commercial banks.

Office of Management and Budget

Located in the Executive Office of the President, the **Office of Management and Budget** (OMB) was established in 1970 as a successor to the old Bureau of the Budget. Among its various activities, the OMB assists the president in preparing the budget he submits each year to

---

[25] For a thoughtful discussion of the advisory responsibilities of the Council of Economic Advisers, and its interaction with other units of the executive branch, see Herbert Stein, "The Chief Executive as Chief Economist," in William Fellner, ed., *Essays in Contemporary Economic Problems* (Washington, D.C.: American Enterprise Institute, 1981), pp. 53–78.

Congress and, more generally, in formulating a fiscal program for the U.S. government. It is also responsible for overseeing executive branch expenditures.

The OMB operates from the premise that the executive budget cannot be left to the separate acts of the various departments and agencies. It is concerned with the budget's overall impact. It adjusts the "wish lists" of all the executive agencies, producing a reasonably unified budget that reflects at least in part the administration's fiscal policy judgments and objectives. It then presents this budget before Congress. When the Reagan administration was pushing its ambitious program of budget reductions in 1981 and 1982, OMB director David Stockman played the pivotal role.

The Departments of Commerce, Labor, and Agriculture

Commerce Department

No other executive agencies rival the Treasury, the OMB, and the Federal Reserve in the conduct of U.S. economic policy. Others do play substantial parts, however. The **Commerce Department** is supposed to encourage international trade and economic development. To these ends it administers programs designed to block unfair foreign trade competition, compiles social and economic data needed for business and governmental planning, assists in the development of the U.S. merchant marine, makes grants for the increased use of scientific and technological resources, grants patents and registers trademarks, and encourages the growth of minority-run businesses. In any administration, the secretary of commerce is the principal liaison person to U.S. industry.

Department of Labor

The **Department of Labor** is, in effect, the labor counterpart to Commerce. It is the administration's primary link with the American labor movement. It administers a variety of federal labor laws, including those dealing with worker safety, minimum wage and overtime pay, freedom from employment discrimination, and unemployment insurance. The Department also has responsibilities for protecting workers' pension rights. Through its Bureau of Labor Statistics (BLS), it serves as the key source of employment-related data. The BLS's consumer price index (CPI) is the most widely used measure of inflation. The CPI measures the average change in prices over time in a fixed "market basket" of goods and services bought either by urban workers or by all urban consumers.

Department of Agriculture

The **Department of Agriculture** (USDA) does for farming many of the things Commerce and Labor do for the industrial sector. It is supposed to help maintain and improve the income of farmers, and to develop and expand their markets at home and abroad. It operates environmental programs to protect soil, water, forests, and other natural resources. The USDA's research programs have been important in extending scientific advances to agriculture.

Congress

The American system of separation of powers requires that **Congress** and the executive branch share authority and work together in complex joint efforts to formulate public policy. Congress has a say in every area of fiscal and regulatory policy. Within Congress, the *Appropriations Committees* of both the Senate and the House, and their many subcommittees, play major roles in determining how much money is appropriated for various agencies and programs. Tax legislation is the province of the *Ways and Means Committee* of the House and the *Finance Committee* of the Senate. Historically, these four major committees have been the main arms of Congress in economic policy-making.

Congress and the budget process

In the early 1970s, however, Congress sought to strengthen its fiscal performance. One particular problem stemmed from the piecemeal way in which it developed the budget. Committees responsible for policy in various substantive areas, like defense and education, worked on programs, and the appropriations subcommittees provided funding needed to pay for them. But Congress was able to handle the budget only as "the sum of its parts." Fitting the pieces together to form the *Budget of the United States,* conforming to coherent national fiscal policy, had become almost impossible. Besides, more and more congressmen felt that they needed their own sources of economic information, to balance the capabilities of the executive branch. To meet these needs, the Congressional Budget Act of 1974 was passed, setting up House and Senate Budget committees and the Congressional Budget Office (CBO). These new congressional agencies are described in chapter 7.

Business Groups

Many **business groups** concern themselves only with specific government actions. Shoe manufacturers, for example, seek government help in keeping out foreign competition. Some groups, though, make claims for economic policies that they deem essential to the overall health of the nation's economy. While much of business lobbying is conducted on behalf of a great variety of special interests, some is designed to advance business perspectives on what the general interest requires. The latter include such matters as interest rates, inflation, economic productivity, and growth.

U.S. Chamber of Commerce

Among the most important business organizations influencing general economic policy is the *Chamber of Commerce of the United States.* With over 4,000 organization members—including local, state, and regional Chambers of Commerce, more then 150,000 individual business members, and an active Washington staff of over 400—the U.S. Chamber has achieved a great deal of influence. In its own words, the chamber eschews "the role of a 'special pleader' on behalf of a particular industry or geographical area," and similarly avoids taking stands "on such matters as prices, rates or charges for particular commodities or products or services of an industry. . . ." Instead, it lobbies to cut federal spending, reduce taxes, and promote deregulation. The chamber's economic program encompasses virtually every area of governmental action.

Another group with broad policy concerns is the *Business Roundtable*. If the U.S. Chamber is built on numbers, with tens of thousands of members in communities throughout the country, the Roundtable applies the muscle of a select few. Its membership is limited to some 200 chief executive officers (CEOs) of the largest business corporations in the United States. The current roster includes the heads of AT&T, Prudential-Bache, Chase Manhatten Bank, Exxon, du Pont, IBM, U.S. Steel, Proctor & Gamble, General Electric, and other business giants.

Selective in its membership, the Business Roundtable concentrates on a few big-impact issues. Rather than relying on a staff of professional lobbyists, the CEOs of the Roundtable personally get into the fray. The Roundtable provides selective, highly personal intervention on major national economic questions by the heads of the country's largest and most powerful corporations. The CEOs who make up the Business Roundtable rarely have difficulty getting an audience with

The Business Roundtable

Some labor groups strongly advocate buying only American made goods.

the president, the heads of Cabinet departments, the chairman of the Federal Reserve Board, or key members of Congress.

Business often seems to have its greatest impact on economic policy not through traditional lobbying efforts, but rather as it defines a "climate of opinion" on the effects of governmental actions. For example, the chairman and governors of the Federal Reserve are constantly exposed to the professional assessments of the financial community. The latter "grade" the Fed much as music critics rate the performance of symphony orchestras. Business needs and interests enter into such assessments, of course, but more is involved: One group of finance professionals is looking at the work of another. Business constitutes a large part of the audience from whom governmental officials get daily cues and evaluations as they conduct national economic policy.

Labor Groups

There are fewer labor unions now in the 1980s than there were two decades ago, and these unions enroll a significantly smaller portion of the total labor force. Still, the American labor movement remains an important actor in economic policy-making. The key unit of organized labor is the national leadership of the American Federation of Labor–Congress of Industrial Organizations (AFL-CIO). The AFL-CIO is a federation of various national unions, such as the Auto Workers, the American Federation of Teachers, the Garment Workers, the Steel Workers, the Machinists, and the Amalgamated Meat Cutters. In all, just over 100 separate national unions are affiliated with the AFL-CIO; the federation has nearly 14 million dues-paying members.

AFL-CIO

From its Washington headquarters, housed in a large marble building just two blocks from the White House, the AFL-CIO takes positions on a wide assortment of policy questions. Like the U.S. Chamber, the AFL-CIO offers its own version of national economic policy. Its effective organization throughout much of the country, its staff resources, and its close ties to important segments of the Democratic party give the AFL-CIO a great deal of access and influence—although the very closeness of its links to the Democrats have made it something of an outsider when Republicans control the federal executive.

SUMMARY

Political economy involves the uses of governmental power to effect economic goals. The areas of economic policies attempted by American government include *regulation* of the private economy; controls over the supply of money and credit, which is the field of *monetary policy;* and efforts to adjust levels of taxation and expenditures, which is *fiscal policy.*

Committed to the general ideal of a growing private-property-based, individual-serving economy, Americans have not engaged much in debates over basic ends; questions of what are the best means, of *"how to do it,"* have predominated. Prompted by the conditions of the Great Depression, leaders and citizens alike swung to a new view of what arrangements of the political economy would best effectuate growing prosperity. A much-expanded role for government figured prominently in the new perspective. *John Maynard Keynes*, a distinguished English economist, offered prescriptions that proved enormously influential and that, in the incomplete and imperfect way of democratic politics, came to underlay the claim of the Democrats as the "party of prosperity."

By the late 1960s, however, a new set of economic conditions had begun to disrupt the Keynesian view of the world. *Inflation* had replaced *deflation* as the predominant challenge to sustained economic prosperity. Excessive growth of government and excessive governmental intervention in economic life—as in the area of *regulation*—appeared to require new responses. The mainstream of economic thinking shifted. This shift is evident in the work of professional economists and, as well, in the outlook and expectations of the general public.

At present, the Republican and Democratic parties find themselves in a contest to claim the title of "party of prosperity" that had been won by the Democrats in the New Deal era. The Reagan administration received high marks in 1983 and 1984, given the vigorous economic recovery, but longer-term experience will be needed to determine whether the changed economic conditions will produce a permanent Republican advantage in the area of political economy.

Shifts in the economy and in thinking about how it is best managed are now reflected in the debates among five schools of professional economic opinion. *Monetarists* put a singular emphasis on controlling the money supply and the price of money (interest rates) to secure a growing, inflation-free economy. *Supply-siders* emphasize the importance of fiscal policy, especially the stimulation of work incentives and economic growth through large cuts in the marginal tax rates: what proportion taxpayers give the government of the last dollars they earn. *"Old-time religion"* economists stress tight money, balanced budgets, and restraints on federal spending.

Advocates of *industrial policy* share the traditional liberal view that a large measure of governmental intervention in the economy is desirable; but they want government to pursue new means of stimulating economic growth, borrowing on the successes Japan has had. *Keynesians* continue to emphasize fiscal policy answers to achieve the economic expansion that can sustain an enlargement of social welfare programs.

Among the governmental agencies that play key roles in formulating and executing economic policy, the *Federal Reserve System* is especially important. "The Fed" is the central bank of the United States. Its *Federal Open Market Committee* is charged with taking actions that determine the size and rate of expansion of the nation's money supply.

19 | Public Welfare

"We the People of the United States," the Preamble to the Constitution proclaims, establish the Constitution to achieve a number of vital objectives, among them to "promote the general welfare." Although public-welfare programs have been greatly expanded only over the last half-century, the idea that government exists to promote public-welfare is as old as the American federal union. In contemporary American politics, the term "welfare state" is subject to contrasting interpretations, and for some it carries the image of government spending excessively for certain welfare programs. But neutrally and factually, the United States is a welfare state—a nation where government by common consent does a great many things to extend the well-being of the people.

Discussions of welfare policy are made unnecessarily confusing by a failure to distinguish between two meanings of the term. *Welfare policies* are sometimes understood as limited to assisting persons in economic need. But *welfare* also encompasses a broader range of governmental programs to enhance the security and betterment of the entire populace. The framers of the Constitution clearly had the second meaning in mind when they wrote the Preamble. And, more recently, Americans have supported the idea of government providing a comprehensive range of social services—such as the Social Security system, which provides benefits for all economic groups.[1]

Public Opinion and Welfare

The politics of public welfare, as programs benefiting the poor, differs from the politics of welfare programs whose beneficiaries are the great

[1] Charles E. Gilbert, "Welfare Policy," in Fred I. Greenstein and Nelson W. Polsby, eds., *Handbook of Political Science* 6 (Redding, Mass.: Addison-Wesley, 1975), pp. 111–12.

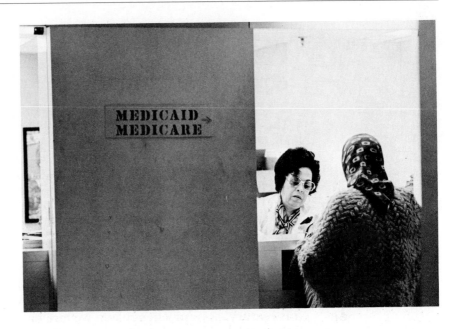

majority of citizens. But even when we look only at the first sector, we encounter confusion as to what the public thinks and expects. Americans in recent years are supposed to have been in an antigovernment mood, frustrated by the rising costs of welfare programs for the needy. Public opinion polls have shown repeatedly that large majorities resent the growth of "welfare." At the same time, though, equally large majorities have declared themselves firmly committed to increasing governmental efforts to "help the poor." Cut "welfare"—but do more to aid the poor.

Pollster Louis Harris asked a sample of Americans nationally, "If you had to choose, would you rather see increased spending for [READ LIST] or no further increases in this area by the federal government?" Note the huge differences in this one survey between helping "the poor" and helping "people on welfare."[2]

	Increase spending	Oppose increase	Not sure
On helping the poor	62%	31%	7%
For people on welfare	22%	69%	9%

Daniel Yankelovich found the same sharp split in a national survey his organization conducted. "There's a lot of talk these days about cutting back on government spending. How do you feel—would you like to see the government spend more money, less money, or just

[2] Surveys by Louis Harris and Associates, December 17–21, 1972; and Yankelovich, Skelly and White, January 1976.

about what they are spending now on":

	More	Less	Same	Not sure
Help for the poor	51%	15%	30%	5%
Welfare	18%	47%	31%	5%

These polls capture a fundamental contradiction in popular beliefs and expectations. Over the last half-century, the American public has shown itself troubled by much of what "welfare" has come to connote, but at the same time it is committed to governmental help for those in need. This is not a minor semantic distinction but rather a matter of deep-seated philosophy.

THE AMERICAN APPROACH TO WELFARE

As nations become wealthier and thus better able to finance welfare programs, these programs increase. In every Western democracy in this century, government's role in welfare has steadily expanded (as indicated by major real increases in public-welfare spending). Expenditures for welfare programs were low when the absolute need for such programs was greatest—and have reached their highest historic levels precisely when absolute need is the least severe. This does not diminish the importance of current efforts or the need for spending; but welfare spending is in significant measure "the art of the possible."

To take just one example, total social-welfare expenditures by local, state, and federal governments in the United States were $6.5 billion in 1935, in the face of overwhelming need resulting from the Great Depression. This averaged about $51 per person. In contrast, total governmental spending in 1984 was roughly $620 billion for all public welfare programs, or approximately $2,700 per capita. Even when the effects of inflation are taken into account, the increase is enormous. It has resulted not so much from the efforts of individual political leaders and parties as from the changing capacities and expectations made possible by modern industrial development. Other countries show the same progression, starting from different bases.

Two Approaches to Welfare

Despite similarities, each country approaches welfare issues in its own distinctive manner, reflecting its history and values. Two hypothetical contrasting national philosophies on welfare policy help us see the range and importance of these variations.

Country A has long shown a strong preference for a collectivist rather than individualistic approach. The majority of its citizens concluded from their country's historical experience that individual efforts were insufficient in the absence of major governmental efforts to extend economic security and well-being. Centralized governmental welfare programs in health, unemployment insurance, and pensions for the aged were developed in the late nineteenth century and, with strong public backing, were expanded in the twentieth century. The public sees governmental intervention as a desirable response to community needs. National values also strongly support governmental efforts to reduce economic inequality: redistributing wealth through progressive taxation and public-benefits programs.

Country B prefers an individualistic approach. Its public has concluded from national experience that great opportunities for advancement are present if individual effort is made to realize them. The public strongly backs equality of opportunity. But it rejects equality of result—where government redistributes income and other values to minimize differences in socioeconomic status. It finds governmental intervention often more problem-causing than helpful. It wants to see individual citizens given the widest freedom to make their own way and to enjoy what they earn.

The American approach

Few observers would confuse the United States with the model of Country A. As we noted elsewhere (especially chapter 4), American political ideology enshrined many of the central assumptions of classical liberalism, and it is notably attentive to assertions of individual rights and interests. Political philosophies representing collectivist goals have foundered on America's singular individualism. Citizens believe that their society gives unusual opportunities to the individual and have been less inclined than their counterparts in many other countries to back collective action through the state. The American idea of equality aims at equal opportunity, not equal results.

Still, it would be a mistake to see the United States as a pure embodiment of Country B. Americans have not been hostile to government. Two types of governmental action in the welfare area have found fertile soil in the United States: (1) to provide a general climate where individual interests and pursuits can be more fully realized; and (2) to help people who through no lack of effort find themselves in need. Modern United States welfare policies have been shaped by the public's insistence that the policies extend social and political individualism rather than restrict it.

"Helping the Poor" versus "Welfare"

What about the distinction the polls show? Americans back governmental efforts to help the needy but are uncomfortable with "welfare." A summer 1983 survey by ABC News and the *Washington Post*[3] found 67 percent of the public wanting to increase government spending for the poor, compared to just 6 percent who favored cutting it, and 26 percent who wanted to keep spending at the current

[3] Survey by ABC News/*Washington Post*, July 28-August 1, 1983.

level. American egalitarianism stresses giving individuals an equal opportunity to compete. We back the claims of deserving individuals who find themselves in need: the ill, the elderly, those unable to find work, children whose families cannot provide for them. We support job-training programs, programs that extend access to college education through government grants and loans, and more.

What about individuals who are able-bodied but unwilling to make the effort to support themselves and their families? An ideology that emphasizes individual responsibility, and insists that American society offers unusual opportunities to those who try, is much less sympathetic. "The opportunity is there; I make the effort; you should too if you are not too old, too young, or too infirm." Many Americans, sympathetic to programs that extend opportunity to those whom they see as the deserving poor, are unhappy about "welfare." In the informal shorthand of American politics, "welfare" has come to connote the avoidance of individual responsibility and effort.

Belief in the importance of individual effort depends, of course, on the belief that society offers great opportunities for advancement to those willing and able to work for it. "Do you agree or disagree that it is true in this country that if you work hard, eventually you will get ahead?" When asked this question in 1983, the American public answered by a margin of 2 to 1 that hard work is rewarded.[4] Majorities of the lowest income groups as well as of the highest gave this assessment.

American ambivalence about welfare. Americans believe that government should help the deserving poor but able individuals should help themselves. They also believe that existing welfare programs reach large numbers who really need them but are, at the same time, exploited by those unwilling to do what they can for themselves. This mix of values and assessments generates ambivalence about the practical operations of welfare programs. In a question posed by interviewers from NORC in the spring of 1984, respondents were asked to locate themselves on a five-point scale (Figure 19.1). By picking point 1, a respondent was indicating strong agreement that "the government in Washington should do everything possible to improve the standard of living of all poor Americans"; by selecting point 5, he was agreeing strongly that "it is not the government's responsibility and each person should take care of himself." The midpoint on the scale was identified as "I agree with both answers." By far the largest proportion—49 percent of all respondents—put themselves at the midpoint. The contradiction here results from the pull of contending social and political values.

Americans have tried to reconcile these contrasting perspectives. One result is the judgment that welfare programs should require those able to work to do so, as a condition for receiving public assistance;

[4] Poll by ABC News/*Washington Post*, November 3–7, 1983.

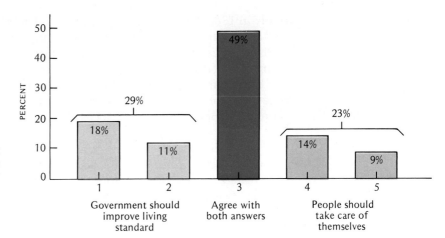

Figure 19.1
Ambivalence About Government's Role in Welfare Policy

Question: "I'd like to talk with you about issues some people tell us are important. Some people think that the government in Washington should do everything possible to improve the standard of living of all poor Americans; they are at Point 1. Other people think it is not the government's responsibility, and that each person should take care of himself; they are at Point 5." Where would you place yourself on this scale, or haven't you made up your mind on this?"
Source: Survey by National Opinion Research Center, General Social Survey, Spring 1984.

this is sometimes called "workfare." Whenever administrators have sought to implement such a rule, they have encountered serious practical difficulties. Jobs that able-bodied welfare recipients are trained to perform may not be available in significant numbers, in the right geographic areas. But Americans continue to endorse this requirement. Another response is to provide *in-kind benefits* rather than cash payments. People in need are given government-supported medical care, subsidized housing, and food stamps rather than simply bigger welfare checks. The idea is that need will be more directly targeted, and recipients will be less likely to be discouraged from learning to help themselves. In 1980, local, state, and national governments in the United States expended $61.3 billion in means-tested welfare benefits: benefits available only to persons meeting certain standards of financial need. Of this total, $42.4 billion were in-kind, while only $18.9 billion were cash payments.[5]

Extending Individual Security and Opportunity

The strong commitments in American ideology to individual responsibility, and equality of opportunity rather than results, have slowed the development of the "welfare state" here. When the U.S. Congress first passed comprehensive Social Security legislation in 1935, most European countries had long since enacted similar programs: Ger-

[5] Timothy M. Smeeding, "Alternate Methods for Valuing Selected In-Kind Transfer Benefits and Measuring their Effect on Poverty," *Technical Paper* 50 (Washington, D.C.: U.S. Bureau of the Census, 1982), p. 2.

many in 1889, England in 1908, and Sweden in 1913. And throughout the twentieth century, U.S. governmental expenditures for public-welfare programs have been a significantly smaller proportion of the country's GNP than comparable programs have been of the GNPs of the European democracies. Despite this overall experience, in some areas American spending for public welfare is proportionally greater than in Europe. Education is a case in point.

Education. In the latter half of the nineteenth century, primary and secondary education became free, public, and virtually universal in the United States—long before it was thus extended in any other country. Government-assisted mass higher education also came sooner to the United States; today a higher proportion of Americans are enrolled in colleges and universities, most with substantial government assistance, than in other wealthy nations such as West Germany, France, Britain, or Japan. America's educational expenditures, on a per capita basis, have consistently surpassed those of other industrial nations.

Is education a public-welfare program? It is closely linked to the idea of public welfare. Through public schools the authority and resources of government are used to make generally available a resource considered essential to personal opportunity and national well-being. Why are Americans less inclined than citizens of other industrial nations to support many governmental welfare initiatives, yet so supportive of programs in education? Public education historically has been an attractive value in the United States because of its close link to individual opportunity. Through access to education, people obtain the means of developing their talents and moving ahead socially and economically. Public spending for education extends the opportunity for individual initiative.

Social Security. During the 1930s, partly as a result of the Great Depression and partly as a more gradual response to new needs attendant upon industrialization and urbanization, many Americans came to feel that expanded governmental welfare efforts were needed and would complement individual efforts. Passage of the Social Security Act in 1935, with such key provisions as Old Age and Survivors Insurance, and Unemployment Compensation, became possible as a result of this shift in public thinking. When Gallup asked a cross-section of Americans nationally in November 1936 whether they favored "the compulsory Old Age Insurance plan, starting in January, which requires employers and workers to make equal contributions to worker's pensions?", 68 percent said they did.[6] From this high base, support grew rapidly.

[6] Michael E. Schiltz, "Public Attitudes toward Social Security, 1935–1965," *Research Report 33* of the Social Security Administration (Washington, D.C.: Government Printing Office, 1970), p. 18.

In recent years, Social Security taxes have risen dramatically, because benefit levels have been raised and the proportion of currently employed workers paying into the system has declined relative to the proportion currently drawing benefits. In light of this, questions have been raised as to whether public support might erode. But it has not. The increases in Social Security benefits have been substantial, but few Americans describe them as too high: only 16 percent according to a 1981 poll. What is even more striking, given the sharp rise in employee payroll taxes for the program, is that most people do not claim that Social Security *taxes* are too high. During the debate in the early 1980s over what changes should be made to solve the growing financial problems of the Social Security system, polls repeatedly asked the public which way they wanted to go to bring receipts and expenditures into balance: raising taxes or reducing benefits. The response was always the same: If a choice must be made, raise taxes rather than cut benefits (Figure 19.2).

These responses attest to the prophetic character of President Franklin Roosevelt's observations at the time Social Security was enacted. Responding to the argument that the Social Security tax was relatively regressive compared to the graduated income tax, because many working-class families paid in the same amount as those in high-income brackets, the president observed:

Social Security versus "welfare"

> I guess you're right on the economics, but those taxes [payroll deductions] were never a problem of economics. They are politics all the way through. We put those payroll contributions there so as to give the contributors a legal, moral, and political right to collect their pensions and their unemployment benefits. With those taxes in there, no damn politician can ever scrap my Social Security program.[7]

Social Security was not "welfare." Its benefits were to be bought and paid for by individuals to provide for their economic security and well-being.

Social Security has never operated like a private annuity or pension program, where the benefits derived are a direct function of contributions made; but Roosevelt's initial idea of setting the system up on the theme of individuals' earning future benefits through regular payroll deductions, was a shrewd reading of American values. Workers *wanted* to "pay their share." In 1938 Gallup asked whether the Social Security law should be changed so that *employers* pay the whole amount. The idea might have seemed attractive; the prestige of American business was low after the Great Depression, and what workers would not want to be freed from having to make payments and have employers foot the whole bill? But only 15 percent of those surveyed favored changing the law to eliminate the tax on individual workers.

[7] Quoted in Arthur M. Schlesinger, Jr., *The Coming of the New Deal* (Boston: Houghton Mifflin, 1958), pp. 308–9.

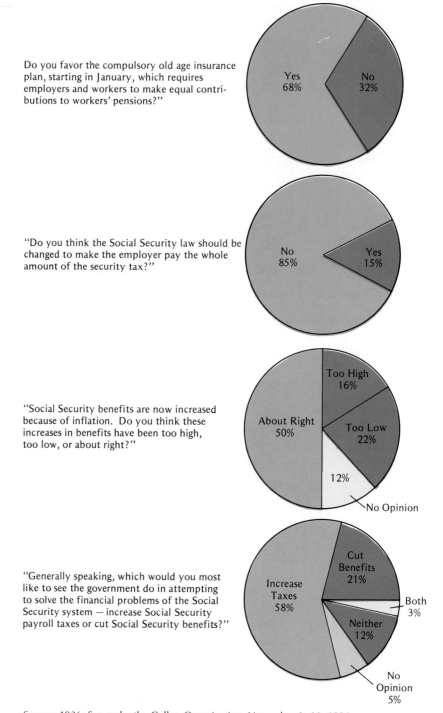

Do you favor the compulsory old age insurance plan, starting in January, which requires employers and workers to make equal contributions to workers' pensions?"

Yes 68%
No 32%

"Do you think the Social Security law should be changed to make the employer pay the whole amount of the security tax?"

No 85%
Yes 15%

"Social Security benefits are now increased because of inflation. Do you think these increases in benefits have been too high, too low, or about right?"

Too High 16%
Too Low 22%
About Right 50%
12%
No Opinion

"Generally speaking, which would you most like to see the government do in attempting to solve the financial problems of the Social Security system — increase Social Security payroll taxes or cut Social Security benefits?"

Cut Benefits 21%
Increase Taxes 58%
Both 3%
Neither 12%
No Opinion 5%

Figure 19.2
Public Attitudes toward Social Security

Source: 1936: Survey by the Gallup Organization, November 6–11, 1936.
1938: Survey by the Gallup Organization, December 30, 1937–January 4, 1938.
1981: Survey by CBS News / New York Times, June 28–July 1, 1981.
1983: Survey by ABC News / Washington Post, January 18–22, 1983.

Support for Social
Security

Social Security is now a broadly supported program for which most Americans are prepared to make sacrifices (in the form of higher payroll taxes) so that a rise in benefits can be sustained. It is seen as essential in providing a measure of security for individuals, such that they can look forward to a retirement income at least sufficient for a basic standard of living. The health-care components of Social Security, added in 1965 as medical benefits for the elderly (Medicare) and the needy (Medicaid), have found the same high measure of public backing that the Old Age Pension and Assistance programs attained earlier. The possibility of being denied adequate health care because one lacked the money to pay for it, or of finding one's retirement savings wiped out through catastrophic illness, seems incompatible with the sense most Americans now have of their needs and entitlements.

Minority versus Majority Welfare

Public welfare connotes two different kinds of programs: (1) means-tested programs, such as Aid for Families with Dependent Children (AFDC) and Medicaid, targeted to help the poor; and (2) those for which no means tests are applied, like the Old Age, Survivors', and Disability Insurance (OASDI) and the Medicare components of Social Security, which in effect apply to the entire population.

Two types of public
welfare policies

At first glance, the politics of these two components of welfare would seem to be entirely different. In the first case, a majority who are not poor are asked to assist a minority who are. The majority pay, but only a distinct minority of the total population draw direct material benefits. In contrast, the second set of welfare programs, like OASDI and Medicare (and public education), ask the majority to support measures to help themselves. All who contribute to OASDI can expect to collect benefits. We might expect the latter programs to have easier sledding politically than the first set.

This is not the case. While spending for welfare programs for the benefit of the majority of the population has expanded greatly over the last twenty years, the *rate of increase* of all means-tested benefits has been as great. There has been much discussion about the impact of Reagan-administration policy changes on this relationship, and some argue that recent cuts have fallen disproportionately on the poor. From the early 1960s through the early 1980s, though, the contrasting political dynamics of majoritarian and minoritarian beneficiary programs did not produce less growth among the latter. We will review the available data pertinent to this issue in greater detail later in the chapter. One reason is that U.S. public opinion tends to apply one set of standards to both sectors. If a program is seen to enlarge the opportunity for constructive individualism, it gets support. This is true of programs to help the "deserving poor" as well as those conferring benefits on the many. The decisive consideration often seems to be whether a program squares with the country's special mix of liberal individualism—a standard not inherently stacked against persons in economic need.

Federalism and Public Welfare

Another distinctive aspect of the American approach to welfare policy involves the extent to which states and municipalities participate in financing and managing welfare programs. Federalism is enormously important in the American welfare system. Prior to the Great Depression, the national government had a modest role in public welfare; veterans' benefits were the one big program. But when the nationwide Depression crisis brought Washington into the welfare picture in a big way, nationally inspired and funded programs were frequently grafted onto an existing system of state-centered management. A few key public-welfare programs are funded and administered exclusively through national agencies—notably, OASDI and Medicare—but many of the most important programs are federal-state partnerships: Medicaid, AFDC, Food Stamps, and Unemployment Compensation. Public-welfare programs throughout much of Europe are run by national agencies with centralized standards and uniform benefits, but the American programs are often decentralized and vary substantially from state to state.

Aid to Families with Dependent Children is a case in point. AFDC is a means-tested program developed to provide assistance for children

The food stamp program is a joint federal and state venture.

Aid to Families with
Dependent Children

whose parents were unable to provide properly for them. In 1950 it was expanded to give support to adults in such families, as well as to their dependent children. Today, a large proportion of AFDC recipient families are female-headed: the father either is not present or is not providing support. AFDC is administered at the state level, subject to some federal regulations, with funding provided jointly by Washington and the states. There are large variations in benefits from one state to another. Individual states have the authority to set benefit levels, and they have made different choices. The average monthly payment per family in 1983 ranged from $464 in California to just $92 in Mississippi. (Alaska, where benefits appear even higher, is not comparable because prices are so much higher there.) Whether such differences should be permitted or, instead, uniform benefits provided across the country has been hotly debated. AFDC is an extreme case. In other programs, such as Food Stamps, national benefit levels *have* been applied.

WELFARE PROGRAMS AND POLICIES

Welfare programs in which the federal government participates may be distinguished by several different dimensions: (1) whether benefits are targeted just to the poor or to the general population; (2) whether programs are run exclusively by the national government or have state participation; (3) among the latter, whether the state role extends to financing the program, administering it, or both. Table 19.1 provides information on these dimensions for eight of the largest U.S. welfare programs. It does not include all federal welfare programs; even some large ones have been omitted—such as housing subsidies, and educational assistance for needy or disadvantaged students. But these eight programs are the core of U.S. public welfare efforts and account for a very large slice of all welfare spending—about $360 billion in 1984.

Eight core welfare
programs

Four of these eight programs are targeted to persons in financial need: federal Supplemental Security Income (SSI); Medicaid; Aid to Families with Dependent Children (AFDC); and Food Stamps. Two programs serve the general population without regard to economic status: Old Age, Survivors', and Disability Insurance (OASDI); and Medicare. The two remaining programs, Veterans' Benefits and Unemployment Compensation, are not located effectively by this distinction. Most veterans' benefits do not have means tests, but some do. One has to have served in the country's armed services (or in certain instances be a member of a veteran's family) to qualify. Unemployment Compensation does not have any means test; yet it has an obvious economic requirement: one must be out of work to qualify.

Attesting to the federalized character of American welfare programs, only three of the eight programs described in Table 19.1 are

Table 19.1
Major Public-Welfare Programs

Program and program costs (1984)	Key legislation	Tax source	Funding	Administration	Function
1. Old Age, Survivors Disability Insurance (OASDI); $179 billion	Social Security Act of 1935, extensively amended	Payroll tax with shares paid by employers and employees	Federal; trust funds set up in U.S. Treasury.	Federal: HHS/Social Security Adm.	National pension system for the retired, the bereaved, the orphaned, and the disabled.
2. Federal Supplemental Security Income (SSI); $8.6 billion	Social Security Amendments of 1972	General revenue	Federal; states are "encouraged to provided optional supplements."	Federal: Social Security Adm.	Assistance to the aged poor. Need, the sole criterion, is established by a means test.
3. Medicare; $61 billion	Social Security Amendments of 1965	For *Part A* of program, basic health insurance: payroll tax, shares paid by employers and employees. For *Part B*, supplementary medical care, general revenue and premiums paid by beneficiaries.	*(Part A)* Federal; Hospital insurance trust fund is repository for payroll tax revenues. *(Part B)* Federal and client funded.	Federal: HHS/Health Care Financing Adm.	Health insurance for the aged. (Part A) Basic inpatient hospital services, and post-hospital care for persons 65 and older. (Part B) Payment of 80% of patient's costs for physicians and various medical specialists, regardless of where services are performed.
4. Medicaid; $38 billion	Social Security Admendments of 1965	General revenue	Federal matching grants provided to states according to state per-capita income.	Federal and State. *Federal:* HHS/Health Care Financing Adm. *State:* basic provider of health care—according to federal standards—to those who qualify. State may set ceiling on benefits and may exercise options on choice of physicians and facilities.	Health care to the poor through payments to health-care providers—hospitals, doctors, nursing facilities, rural health clinics.

Program	Legislative basis	Source of funds	Financing	Administration	Purpose
5. Aid to Families with Dependent Children (AFDC); $15 billion	Social Security Act of 1935, amended over 100 times	General revenue	Federal government reimburses states for about half of benefit costs.	States. Set criteria for eligibility and benefit level "within broad federal rules."	Financial assistance for poor families, pegged to the care of dependent children.
6. Food Stamp Program; $11 billion	Food Stamp Act of 1964	General revenue	Federal, except for state share of administrative expenses.	Jointly federal, state, and local. *Federal:* USDA/Consumer Services, Family Nutrition program. *State and local:* welfare agencies.	"Help lower-income Americans maintain a nutritious diet."
7. Unemployment Compensation; $21 billion	Social Security Act of 1935; extensively amended	Payroll tax on employers	State tax on employers funds regular benefits; state and federal taxes (in equal portions) on employers funds extended benefits.	Federal by U.S. Employment and Training Adm. (Dept. of Labor), and state by employment security agency of each state. Each state administers its Unemployment Compensation program according to a "certified state plan." States provide benefits schedule (benefit ceilings, duration, etc.), following federal guidelines. States collect employer taxes and disburse benefits "payable under the laws of individual states."	Unemployment insurance for persons temporarily unable to find a job.
8. Veterans' benefits; $26 billion	Many statutes, including Serviceman's Readjustment Act of 1944—GI Bill of Rights	General revenue	Federal	Federal through Veterans Administration.	Benefits for U.S. war veterans and dependents, including: compensation for loss due to disabilities or death resulting from military service; pensions for the disabled; education benefits, home loan guarantees; burial expenses; medical services and care.

financed and operated exclusively by the national government: OASDI, Medicare, and Veterans' Benefits. The other five involve some form of joint federal-state financing or management.

The Social Security Administration administers SSI. Uniform national eligibility standards are imposed. But there is state financial participation. Congress required all states to supplement the federal minimums in the SSI program to the extent necessary so that persons who had previously been receiving state-administered assistance at higher levels would not suffer a reduction of benefits in the shift to a federally administered program. These mandatory supplements are strictly transitional. But the states are also encouraged under SSI to provide optional supplements above the federal minimums. The federal government pays all costs of administering the supplements when the states opt to have the Social Security Administration handle all the paperwork.

States' role in welfare programs

Medicaid uses a combination of federal and state funds in providing medical assistance to the poor. About half of the program costs are borne by Washington. The states are required to provide health benefits, according to federal standards, to all who qualify for public assistance, but the states set the benefit levels and administer the program. ***AFDC*** involves a federal-state mix similar to that of Medicaid. The national government reimburses the states for about half of the total benefit costs. The states administer the program and set criteria for eligibility, as well as benefit levels, subject to a variety of federal requirements. The ***Food Stamp*** program is totally federally funded, and uniform eligibility standards are required of all states. At the same time, state welfare agencies actually administer the program.

Under ***Unemployment Compensation*** the states collect from employers (all those employing eight or more workers) according to a federally determined wage base, but they must place these tax receipts in the federally administered Unemployment Trust Fund (where separate accounts are maintained for each state). The federal government shares in the costs of extended benefits. When a state is overdrawn, as happens quite often in periods of high unemployment, it can borrow from the federal government to assure a continuation of prescribed benefits. Unemployment Compensation is managed by the states subject to federal standards.

Spending on Welfare

Whether the United States is spending more or less than it should for social-welfare programs is a matter on which party and interest-group leaders, social scientists, and others disagree. Differing political values determine "How much is enough?" But it is clear what expenditures are and how they have changed over the last few decades. The rate of increase in welfare expenditures has by any measure been substantial.

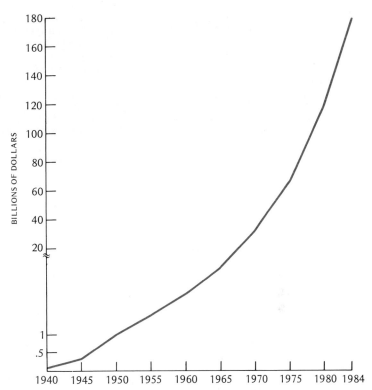

Figure 19.3
**Benefits Paid under
Social Security (OASDI)
since 1940**

Source: 1937–55: U.S. Bureau of the Census, *Historical Statistics: Colonial Times to 1970,* part 1, p. 347. *1960–80:* Idem, *Statistical Abstract, 1984,* p. 379. *1984 estimate:* Executive Office of the President, OMB, *Budget of the United States Government, Fiscal Year 1985,* p. 5–115.

Figure 19.3 shows that in 1950 OASDI disbursed about $1 billion; just over four decades later, in 1984, expenditures were $179.2 billion. Obviously, the increase is enormous. But how much of it is simply a product of inflation, and how much is real? How have expenditures changed in comparison to the overall performance of the economy? Does welfare now claim a larger or smaller proportion of overall public outlays?

Looking at Table 19.2 in answer to these questions, if spending is expressed in 1980 purchasing power (constant 1980 dollars), all social-welfare expenditures by government—local, state, and national—have climbed from just under $74 billion in 1950 to just over $492 billion in 1980. Included in these totals are expenditures for Social Security, education, help for the poor, medical care, and veterans' benefits. Real per-capita welfare spending increased by more than 400 percent over this 30-year span. Veterans' benefits were the one area where inflation-controlled expenditures were lower in 1980 than they had been three decades before. There were unusually heavy benefit requirements in the years immediately following World War II.

Social-welfare spending has also been increasing at a rate much greater than the overall economy. In 1950 government welfare expenditures were only 8 percent of the GNP; 30 years later the proportion

Growth of welfare
spending

Table 19.2
Social-Welfare Spending under Public Programs, 1950–80
(in constant 1980 dollars)

FY	Total spending (in millions of dollars)	Per capita spending					
		All programs	Social insurance	Public aid	Veterans' programs	Education	All health and medical care
1950	$ 73,650.3	$ 479.75	$101.23	$ 51.13	$138.93	$136.70	$ 62.80
1960	129,940.9	711.77	262.72	56.01	73.62	240.47	87.36
1970	281,945.5	1,354.46	507.27	153.60	83.64	473.95	235.12
1980	492,231.7	2,140.08	994.15	314.15	92.50	524.10	437.81

"Total spending" excludes expenditures within foreign countries for OASDI and Civil Service retirement benefits, veterans' programs, and education. "All programs" includes housing, not shown separately here. "All health and medical care" combines health and medical care with medical services provided in connection with social insurance, public aid, veterans', and vocational rehabilitation programs.

Source: Social Security Bulletin, 46 (8), August 1983.

had more than doubled, to just under 19 percent. As the country got wealthier, welfare spending by government became a bigger proportion of the total. This increase was especially pronounced at the federal level, where welfare spending was just 3.7 percent of the GNP in 1950 but rose to 11.5 percent of the GNP in 1980.[8] Social-welfare spending has claimed a steadily increasing share of government's expenditures. In 1950, just 26 percent of all federal spending went for social welfare; 30 years later, the proportion had climbed to 54 percent.

The big jump in welfare spending reflects increases in both the number of beneficiaries and the amount of benefits provided to individual recipients. The most dramatic increase in the former has come in the Social Security program. In 1960 14.8 million people received benefits under OASDI; twenty-two years later the number was 35.8 million. Some of this increase resulted from policy changes expanding coverage. Another large part resulted from demographic shifts: the simple expansion of the number of older people.

A "Reagan Revolution"?

In response to the steep climb in welfare spending, the leaders of both parties and the general public began to feel that checks had to be imposed. Around 1975, as a result of this new bipartisan consensus, welfare expenditures began to level off. As a proportion of all federal spending, welfare spending actually dropped between 1975 and 1980.

This was the setting when Ronald Reagan assumed the presidency in January 1981. He had campaigned on the theme that the national government had become too big and too intrusive, and that the rate

[8] *Social Security Bulletin,* 46 (8), August 1983.

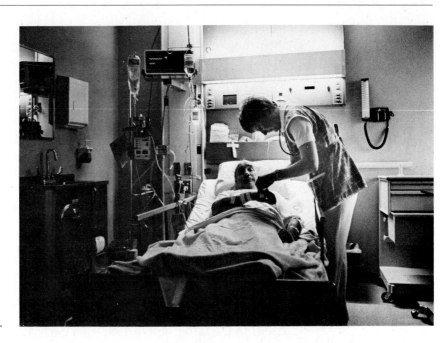

Medicare.

of domestic welfare spending had been climbing far too precipi-
tously. Once in office, the Reagan administration sought to cut back
on some components of domestic welfare programs.[9] But the result
has been only a modest overall extension of the leveling-off trend that
began during the Carter years. This belies the ringing rhetoric on the
"Reagan revolution" in domestic welfare spending. "All in all," writes
economist John Weicher after a careful review of the data, "both the
budget and the program changes turn out to be smaller than much of
the public discussion would suggest...."[10]

Social Security and Medicare. Early in 1981, the Reagan administration proposed changes in future Social Security benefits that, if
implemented, would have reduced the rate of future cost increases.
But when floated, these proposals generated furious attacks from
interest groups representing the elderly and some leaders in both
parties, and the administration quickly backed away from them. The
president subsequently charged a bipartisan commission with the task
of proposing changes to meet the immediate financial problems of
Social Security. The commission was successful in the sense that its
limited proposals secured legislative enactment and produced additional revenue.[11] But only the most modest cuts were made in pro-

[9] For an early effort to assess the impacts of Reagan-administration program changes
more analytically and dispassionately, see John L. Palmer and Isabel V. Sawhill, eds.,
The Reagan Experiment (Washington, D.C.: Urban Institute Press, 1982).
[10] John C. Weicher, "The Safety Net after Three Years," in *Maintaining the Safety Net*
(Washington, D.C.: American Enterprise Institute, 1984), p. 17.
[11] See "Report of the National Commission on Social Security Reform," Alan Green-
span, chairman (Washington, D.C.: Government Printing Office, January 1983).

jected future increases in program costs, and expenditures continued their rapid climb. In 1980, $119 billion were paid out through OASDI; in fiscal year 1984, $179 billion—an increase of $60 billion, or 50 percent, in the space of four years. The progression is the same in Medicare. In fiscal year 1980, Medicare expenditures were about $36 billion; four years later, they had risen by more than $24 billion, or roughly 70 percent.

Social Security and Medicare are what is known as "entitlement programs." This means that outlays expand automatically with inflation and with the growth of eligible populations. Congress does not appropriate a fixed sum of money, but rather all that is needed to cover all who are entitled to specified benefits. Finding the political agreement needed to change the entitlement formulas—to reduce the amount benefits increase or to cut back on eligibility—is exceedingly difficult. These programs receive strong, widespread public support.

"Entitlement programs"

Unemployment Compensation. The Reagan administration did not try to cut Unemployment Compensation. The main factor producing year-to-year variations in unemployment costs is the unemployment rate itself: In the latter half of 1982, and early 1983, when unemployment climbed to over 10 percent, program costs naturally soared. They declined in 1984, as the unemployment rate dropped to about 7 percent. Even so, expenditures for unemployment compensation were $21 billion in 1984, compared to $12 billion in 1980.

Helping the poor. Federal spending for the poor during the Reagan years has been the subject of vigorous debate. Democrats have accused the administration of unfairness and insensitivity to the needy, while the administration has argued that it has maintained, even strengthened, the "safety net." "Safety net" refers to assistance programs providing for the poor, which are supposed to prevent anyone from falling too far economically. What do the data show has actually happened? Federal spending for low-income benefit programs totaled $50.1 billion in 1980, and it rose to $67.5 in 1984, a gain of 34 percent (Table 19.3). This rise is less than that for Social Security and Medicare, but it hardly suggests that low-income assistance has been demolished. Even controlling for the effects of inflation, federal spending for the poor increased modestly during Reagan's first term.[12]

Spending for the poor is increasing more slowly now than it did over the preceding two decades. Whether this is a positive or negative accomplishment is arguable. In one area, subsidized housing construction, the administration succeeded in getting changes greater than the data in Table 19.3 suggest; it managed to stop almost all new subsidized construction. Current spending also reflects interest

[12]Weicher, "The Safety Net after Three Years," pp. 8–13.

Table 19.3

Federal Spending for Benefit Programs for Low-Income Persons, 1980 and 1984 (billions of dollars)

	1980	1984
Aid to Families with Dependent Children (AFDC)	7.3	8.1
Supplemental Security Income (SSI)	6.4	8.6
Housing assistance	5.4	10.0
Food and nutrition assistance (including Food Stamps)	13.9	17.6
Medicaid	14.0	20.2
Total	50.1	67.5

Source: Budget of the United States Government, FY 1985, pp. 5-120, 121. The figures for AFDC and Medicaid do not include the state government shares, which are about 50 percent of the total costs of these programs.

and subsidy payments on *past* long-term bonds and contracts, so it does not reveal the full magnitude of a reduction that will be evident in future budgets. Moreover, these basic budgetary data do not clearly reflect major administration efforts to direct benefits more precisely to low-income people and to cut assistance to persons above the poverty line. For example, the income limit for receiving food stamps has been reduced from 60 percent to just 30 percent above the poverty line. The administration argues that help for those who are most needy has been increased more than overall spending suggests, because assistance is now better targeted. Critics charge that important segments of the working poor have suffered. Overall, though, the level of welfare spending that has resulted from the Reagan efforts represents only modest reductions from what was established during the preceding Democratic administration.

Boundaries for change. At every stage in American history, needs dictated by the socioeconomic setting, together with expectations of the populace, have established basic levels of governmental action. Politicians operate within the boundaries set; their actions can be very important but are usually less than partisan rhetoric suggests. Ronald Reagan came to office seeking to reduce the rate of increase of domestic welfare spending and, as we discuss in the next chapter, to increase the effort in national defense. By the end of his first term he could claim some success in both pursuits. But, as Figure 19.4 shows, the Reagan shifts were within boundaries established by national needs, resources, and expectations. Federal spending was actually a greater proportion of the GNP at the end of Reagan's first term than when he took office. Health and income-security spending stayed constant, as a proportion of both the GNP and total federal spending. Defense spending rose, but it remained within the boundaries of recent U.S. commitments.

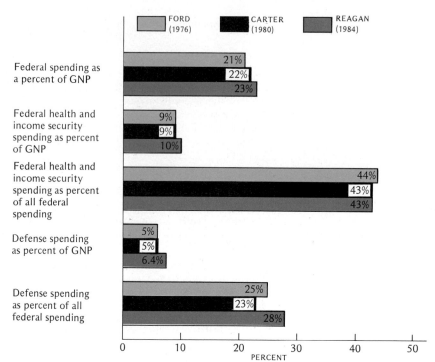

Source: Economic Indicators, prepared for the Joint Economic Committee of Congress by the Council of Economic Advisers, May 1984, pp. 32–33.

Figure 19.4
Government Spending under Ford, Carter, and Reagan

"How to Do It"?

Over the last half-century, Democrats have given stronger backing than Republicans to the expansion of government welfare programs. They can be credited with, or blamed for, the overall design and levels of American public welfare. Today, the parties remain divided philosophically over how much government should be doing in the welfare area—with the Democrats still inclined to turn more to the government and the Republicans more to private-sector solutions. While important, this partisan split is often overshadowed by complex "how to do it" issues that arise in the administration of the national welfare system.

Restraining medical costs. Many Republicans and Democrats agree that mechanisms must be found to restrict the escalating growth of medical costs, without denying people the medical care they need. Expenditure increases under Medicare and Medicaid are so substantial that liberals and conservatives alike worry they will crowd out other programs. Since there are political limits on how much taxes can be raised, the rapid escalation of medical costs will be borne by relative reductions in other areas of welfare spending. David Swoap, who served as under secretary in the Department of Health and Human

Services in the Reagan administration, has argued that

> any real solution [to the problems of Medicare and Medicaid] must affect our entire health-care delivery system and must attack the primary reason costs are out of control: a health-care industry in this country immune from the forces of the marketplace. Government and insurance coverage insulates consumers and providers from the true cost of care; an open-ended reimbursement system rewards excessive admissions, excessive services and inefficient use of high technology; and a mass of regulations stifles the entrepreneurship and innovation the industry so badly needs to cut waste and create efficiency.[13]

Swoap is a Republican and a conservative; many who are Democrats and liberals make virtually identical assessments.

Assisting the needy without discouraging work. How does one go about setting benefits for the poor so that they will be sufficiently generous, but at the same time will not encourage people to stop work and "go on welfare"? Over the last quarter-century, this question has been endlessly debated and various reforms proposed—with results that are to almost no one's satisfaction.

One of the most comprehensive and innovative reform proposals was made during the Nixon administration, under the initiative of presidential adviser Daniel P. Moynihan. Known as the Family Assistance Plan (FAP), it was designed to replace AFDC and provide a basic income for all families, where the head of the household was working as well as where that individual was unemployed, and single-parent

Family Assistance Plan

[13]David B. Swoap, "Medicare Crisis Is Only a Symptom," *Wall Street Journal*, January 3, 1984, p. 30.

and two-parent families alike. It would have established a national minimum income below which no family would fall. All FAP recipients who were able to work would be required to do so, or enter job training programs. Their earnings would be offset against their FAP benefits, but in such a way that, as their job income rose, they would be better off overall than if they were receiving FAP benefits only. Family Assistance was supposed to help reduce the "notch" problem: A family whose income falls below a specific level qualifies for certain cash welfare benefits and for a great variety of in-kind assistance, such as subsidized housing, free medical care, and food stamps. Families with incomes just above the qualifying levels are sometimes worse off than many families who are on welfare and who receive the full mix of cash and in-kind assistance. FAP would help these families just above the "notch" (the working poor) by giving them additional assistance.

But Family Assistance had its own deficiencies, as Moynihan himself subsequently acknowledged.

> The Administration might seriously have hoped that Family Assistance would, subtly but powerfully, so alter incentive structures that the incidence of female-dependent families would decline, but conservatives could point out that under FAP, no less than under AFDC, any low-income family with an employed head could substantially increase the "cash flow" through its various pockets and pocketbooks by the simple expedient of breaking up and putting the women and children on welfare. Reform indeed![14]

Measuring Poverty and "Income"

Not only is it hard to figure out how to achieve various goals that we bring to welfare programs, it is difficult even to describe accurately the needs to be met and the extent of the contributions that existing programs make. *Poverty* in a country like the United States, as we have seen, involves relative as well as absolute deprivation. People are poor when their incomes are well below the average, even when their living standards do not involve absolute privation. When children are growing up, they draw their sense of what is an acceptable standard of living from what they see around them. If they are denied what is available to most of their friends, they are likely to think of themselves as deprived.

The "relative" dimension of poverty

Attempts to measure the number of people below the poverty level in the United States, while of some merit in assessing social need and performance, founder on this "relative" dimension of poverty. According to widely used Bureau of the Census calculations, 35.3 million Americans, out of a population of some 236 million, were "below

[14]Daniel P. Moynihan, *The Politics of a Guaranteed Income: The Nixon Administration and the Family Assistance Plan* (New York: Random House, 1973), p. 446.

the poverty line" in 1983. About 24 million of them were whites, 9.9 million blacks, 4.3 million of Hispanic background.[15] These statistics are a mixture of absolute and relative criteria relating to poverty. Relative criteria simply cannot be excluded entirely, yet there can be no agreement on precisely how they should be included. Poverty exists in the United States. Part of it involves absolute deprivation; another very large part stems simply from the fact that some have much less than others.

We need the best possible information on income distribution and standards of living if we are to assess the adequacy of existing welfare programs. Since, however, the claim is made that poverty is a quantifiable condition, the statistics that go into the poverty calculations have become political footballs. Should they show a sharp decline in the number described as poor, advocates of programs to help the poor fear that others would draw the conclusion that somehow "the problem was being solved" and that national efforts could be relaxed.

One result of the political sensitivity surrounding poverty statistics is a reluctance to change the way they are computed, even when it is apparent that the formula has become grossly inadequate. Today the prime deficiency of the poverty statistics is their failure to include in-kind transfer benefits. As we noted earlier in this chapter, in-kind transfers involve such benefits as subsidized housing, food stamps, and the provision of medical care. A Bureau of the Census study of 1982 documents the fact that since the early to mid-1960s, as overall public-welfare expenditures have climbed in the United States, the growth has been far greater among in-kind benefits than cash payments.[16] In 1965 two-thirds of all the major means-tested welfare benefits conferred in the United States were in the form of cash; in-kind benefits amounted to one-third, or less than $2 billion. By 1980, however, the proportions were completely reversed: Nearly 70 percent of all means-tested welfare benefits were of the in-kind variety—about $42.5 billion worth (Table 19.4).

Measuring welfare benefits

These data have important implications for the adequacy of statistics on income and poverty, because most of the widely used income statistics *exclude in-kind benefits entirely.* Poverty and income statistics in the United States are based on *money income only:* cash received from employment, Social Security, public assistance and welfare, interest, property. Computing *income* exclusively in terms of *money income* mattered little prior to the 1960s because for most people, and the poor in particular, in-kind transfers were not substantial. But as in-kind transfers have expanded greatly over the last two decades, income statistics have become increasingly flawed. A variety of pro-

Money income v. in-kind benefits

[15] Bureau of the Census, Population Division.
[16] Thanks to this important study conducted in 1982 at the Bureau of the Census, we now have a much better sense of this statistical deficiency. The study was done under the direction of Timothy M. Smeeding: *Alternate Methods for Valuing Selected In-Kind Transfer Benefits and Measuring Their Effect on Poverty,* Technical Paper #50 (Washington, D.C.: Government Printing Office, 1982).

Table 19.4
Major Transfer Benefits since 1965 (market value of benefits in billions of dollars)

Type of benefit	1965	1970	1975	1980
Major in-kind transfers (means-tested and non-means-tested)* Total food, housing and medical care	$2.166	$15.014	$36.685	$72.527
Major means-tested transfer benefits only				
Cash public assistance	4.025	8.864	16.312	18.863
In-kind benefits	1.954	8.628	22.197	42.436
Percent of total means-tested benefits which are in-kind	32.7	49.3	57.5	69.2

*Means-tested income-transfer programs are those which benefit only families with low enough incomes and resources (assets) to qualify. Non-means-tested benefits have no income or resource test.

Source: Timothy M. Smeeding, *Alternate Methods for Valuing Selected In-Kind Transfer Benefits and Measuring Their Effect on Poverty*, (Washington, D.C.: Government Printing Office, 1982), p. 3.

grams have been enacted to deal with the problem of poverty. To set up these programs and then to exclude two-thirds of the benefits they confer from the official measures of the incidence of poverty makes something of a mockery of statistical effort.

The reason why the exclusion has been allowed to persist is apparent, however. It does not involve the fact that calculating the value of in-kind benefits is excessively complex; the 1982 Census study provides impressive evidence that sound estimates can be made. Rather, poverty statistics have continued to be computed the old way because a shift to include in-kind assistance might be seen to change the incidence of poverty. Table 19.5 shows how the numbers change with different formulas for assessing the value of in-kind transfers.

Why exclude in-kind benefits?

The Census study employed three different calculations of the value of in-kind benefits received by the poor. The *market value* of in-kind

Table 19.5
How Many Americans Were below the Poverty Line in 1980?

	Present government calculations		New census measures					
			Market value		Recipient or cash equivalent value		Poverty budget share value	
	Number (in thousands)	%	Number	%	Number	%	Number	%
All ages	23,623	11.1	13,634	6.4	17,318	8.2	18,866	8.9
Elderly (65 or older)	4,097	14.7	1,251	4.5	2,242	8.0	3,019	10.8

Source: Smeeding, *Alternate Methods for Valuing Selected In-Kind Transfer Benefits*, pp. ix–x.

Three kinds of
calculations

transfers is equal to their purchase price in the private market—for example, what one would have to pay for medical care received under the Medicaid program. The *recipient or cash-equivalent value* is the amount of cash which would make the recipient just as well off as the in-kind transfer; the latter reflects the recipient's own assessments of the value of the benefits conferred through the in-kind transfers. The *poverty-budget share-value* limits the value of food, housing, or medical transfers to the proportions spent on these items by persons at or near the poverty line in 1960–61, when in-kind transfers were minimal. This third measure assumes that in-kind benefits in excess of these amounts are not relevant for determining poverty status—since an excess of one type of good (like medical care) does not make up for a lack of another (like housing).

There are sound bases for all three calculations. The key point here, though, is that all three recognize that in-kind transfers confer substantial real benefits that are part of total income. If the major in-kind transfers are counted and assessed by the market-value calculation, the number of Americans below the poverty line in 1980 is seen to shrink by about 10 million persons. The number of elderly Americans below the poverty line that year drops from just over 4 million to 1.25 million.

It should be noted that the distortion resulting from omitting in-kind transfers is not limited to income data on the poor. The Census study did not attempt to measure all of the in-kind benefits received by middle- and upper-income families, but it did document that these are enormous. Even the highly incomplete Census calculations showed $167.4 billion in non-means-tested, in-kind transfers in 1980. For example, many companies pay all or part of the health insurance premiums of their employees, thus conferring substantial in-kind medical benefits. By excluding in-kind transfers, income statistics for all groups of Americans are made seriously incomplete.

THE MAKERS OF WELFARE POLICY

The President

As with other policy areas, discussion of the key actors in welfare policy must begin with the president. He sets the tone of his administration's approach to various welfare issues. In his budgetary decisions, reflected in the annual budget he presents to Congress and tries to implement through the Office of Management and Budget, the president gains his greatest leverage over federal welfare programs.

When a strong president seeks a shift of direction in U.S. welfare policies and when the national climate of opinion supports him—as with Franklin Roosevelt during his first administration, Lyndon Johnson during his first three years as president, and Ronald Reagan early in his presidency—the chief executive plays a decisive role. But

"Yes, You Remembered Me"

The Forgotten Man

F.D.R.

the images of FDR boldly crafting the new welfare approaches of the New Deal, of LBJ bringing the "Great Society" to fruition through his War on Poverty and the Medicare and Medicaid extensions to Social Security, can be misleading. These are instances of unusual presidential initiatives, in times unusually receptive to change. More often, the president appears less the bold innovator than the captive of a complex set of political interests and pressures.

The president's role in welfare policy

A president's authority and capacity for independent policy initiatives are weaker in the area of public welfare than in foreign and defense policy (which we discuss in the next chapter), and weaker than in the field of economic policy (discussed in the last chapter). The multiplicity and strength of contending interests with immediate and continuing stakes in what government does in the area of welfare policy are unrivaled in any other broad policy area. Economic developments like inflation and unemployment deeply affect the entire population, but they seem more abstract; interest-group involvement is oriented more to end results and less to immediate details. Presidents are judged by those ultimate results—for example, whether unemployment is kept low and inflation under control—but they have room to maneuver among means. In contrast, any proposal for a shift of benefits under Social Security or Medicare provokes intense interest group response. Governmental policy-making in foreign affairs and political economy revolves exclusively around the actions of the national government. Not so with welfare policies. The states play a big part, in partnership with Washington; this adds to the mix of interests that must be satisfied before substantial change can be achieved.

The Department of Health and Human Services

Created in 1953, the Department of Health, Education, and Welfare (HEW) was redesignated in 1979 as **Health and Human Services** (HHS). At that time Education was established as a separate department. HHS describes itself as "the Cabinet-level department of the federal Executive Branch most concerned with people and most involved with the nation's human concerns." It doesn't exaggerate when it asserts that "in one way or another—whether it is mailing out Social Security checks or making health services more widely available—HHS touches the lives of more Americans than any other federal agency."[17] HHS is the principal welfare agency of the national government (Figure 19.5).

Budget data alone give a good indication of the scope of HHS-administered programs. In 1973, the department (then HEW) became the largest in the federal government, surpassing Defense in total expenditures. Its 1984 budget of $296 billion was easily the largest, even with its education component now separate.

Within HHS the biggest unit is the Social Security Administration (SSA), created in 1946 as a successor to the original Social Security Board. SSA's 1984 outlays of just over $200 billion would make it the second largest department in the U.S. government (exceeded only by Defense) were it free-standing. Under the direction of a commissioner, the Social Security Administration is responsible for managing the contributory social-insurance program covering pensions for retired workers, benefits for those disabled, and cash payments made to surviving members of workers' families. By one measure, it is among the most "efficient" of all federal agencies: It takes a relatively small staff to dispose of a very large amount of money. SSA is a medium-size federal agency, with only 88,000 employees. Its tasks are highly routinized: dispensing Social Security checks and resolving questions of eligibility.

The budget of the Social Security Administration would be even more imposing if SSA had financial and management responsibilities for all of the basic Social Security programs. Medicare and Medicaid have been transferred, however, to another unit of HHS, the Health Care Financing Administration (HCFA). HCFA was created in 1977. Wholly a program of the federal government, Medicare is directly administered by HCFA. Medicaid, in contrast, is a joint federal- and state-financed program administered by state welfare agencies. HCFA

Social Security Administration

Health Care Financing Administration

---

[17] This description of HHS is taken from its description in the *United States Government Manual, 1983/84*, p. 266.

Figure 19.5 **Department of Health and Human Services**

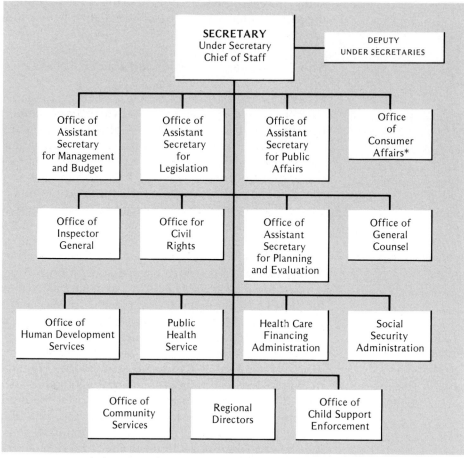

*Located administratively in HHS, but reports to the president.
Source: The United States Government Manual, 1984–85, p. 831.

processes federal grants to the states. Total budget outlays of the Health Care Financing Administration in 1984 were about $86 billion.

Public Health Service

Another important agency within the Department of Health and Human Services is the Public Health Service (PHS). It began a long time ago, through an act of Congress of July 1798 which authorized hospitals to provide care for American merchant seamen. The Public Health Service Act of 1944 gave the PHS its present institutional form, although its responsibilities have since been substantially expanded. Among its principal units are the Alcohol, Drug Abuse, and Mental Health Administration; the Centers for Disease Control; the Food and Drug Administration; the Health Resources and Services Administration; and the National Institutes of Health. The latter conduct and support biomedical research into various diseases, including cancer, heart and lung diseases, arthritis, allergies, and infectious diseases. The 1984 budget of the National Institutes of Health was about $4 billion—making it the largest federal government sponsor of academic research. Total 1984 spending of the Public Health Service was $8.3 billion.

The Department of Agriculture

The ***Department of Agriculture*** (USDA) is hardly a mainline welfare agency. Its natural counterpart is not the Department of Health and Human Services, but the Labor and Commerce departments. Nonetheless, through its Food and Nutrition Service (FNS), established in 1969, the Department of Agriculture is one of the principal providers of support for needy Americans. With a 1984 budget of about $17 billion (out of Agriculture's total budget of $35 billion), it operates a number of food-related welfare programs—the largest of which is Food Stamps. The Food Stamp program provides food coupons to needy persons to increase their resources for food purchases. Entirely funded through FNS, and with uniform eligibility standards required of all states, Food Stamps are actually administered by state and local welfare agencies. Other FNS programs are the National School Lunch Program, the Child Care Food Program, the Special Milk Program for Children, and the Special Supplemental Food Program for Women, Infants, and Children.

Food and Nutrition Service

The Department of Housing and Urban Development

With a 1984 budget of about $16 billion, the ***Department of Housing and Urban Development*** (HUD) has a number of housing-related responsibilities; the biggest involves housing assistance for the needy.

A downtown area rebuilt with federal grants from HUD.

Together with state agencies, HUD provides partial financing for low-rent public housing projects owned, managed, and administered by local housing authorities. Income standards for occupancy are set by the local agencies, subject to HUD guidelines. Rental charges cannot exceed 25 percent of the net monthly money income of recipients.

HUD funding also subsidizes rentals by low-income families in the private sector. Under *rent-supplement plans*, the difference between the "fair market rent" of a dwelling and the rent charged to the tenant is paid to the owner by the government. Under *interest-reduction programs*, the amount of interest paid on a mortgage by the owner of a property is reduced, with the requirement that the subsequent savings be passed along to low-income tenants through lower rent charges.

HUD administers the Community Development Block Grants (CDBG). These grants go largely to medium-size and large cities for community development, including neighborhood revitalization and increased community services. Together, the housing subsidies and the Community Development Block Grants account for well over 80 percent of all HUD spending.

The Department of Education

The **Department of Education** administers two large programs of educational assistance for low-income persons. One, aimed at the primary and secondary school population, supports compensatory education for the disadvantaged. Its 1984 budget was about $3.4 billion. The department also assists needy students in higher education. Key programs here are the Basic and Supplemental Educational Opportunity Grants (Pell Grants), which are restricted to students from low-income families attending institutions of higher education. As grants, these funds need not be repaid. The department also administers a program of guaranteed loans for students from middle-income as well as low-income families. These loans are interest-free while the student is enrolled in undergraduate or graduate education and need not be repaid during this period; the loans must be repaid over a ten-year span after graduation. In 1984, federal expenditures for higher-education grants and loans totaled about $7 billion.

The Veterans Administration

The **Veterans Administration** (VA) was established in its present form as an independent executive-branch agency in 1930, with the consolidation of several federal bureaus then handling veterans' affairs. Operating with FY 1984 outlays of almost $26 billion, the VA is a major federal welfare agency. Its beneficiaries are, of course, veterans of U.S. military service: for some programs, all veterans; for others, veterans of particular wars, needy veterans, those who suffered disabilities as a result of their military service, and surviving family members of veterans who lost their lives while performing military duties.

The largest VA programs are those covering disability compensation and pensions based on financial need. These programs expended about $14 billion in 1984. The next largest group provides medical benefits for veterans. The VA's Department of Medicine and Surgery operates 172 medical centers, 225 clinics, and 99 nursing homes, as well as other facilities. VA-provided medical benefits cost about $8 billion in FY 1984. Life insurance, subsidized loans for housing, and education assistance are also provided by the VA.

ACTION

The purpose of the federal voluntary action agency, ACTION, is to mobilize Americans for voluntary service. Created in 1971 as an independent agency, its principal projects are VISTA (Volunteers in Service to America) and the Foster Grandparent Program. Its total 1984 budget was just $130 million. VISTA was set up to provide opportunities for volunteers to share their skills in locally sponsored projects involving drug abuse, resettlement of refugees in the United States, and distribution of emergency food and shelter, among others. Foster Grandparents are low-income people of at least 60 years of age who receive small stipends for their service. They work with retarded and handicapped children, in daycare centers, in homes for disadvantaged children, in literacy programs, and so on.

Congress

Hundreds of pieces of original legislation and subsequent amendments provide the statutory base for federal welfare policies. Congress' work in this area extends more deeply into the details of policy than it does in the other major areas we discuss in chapters 17, 18, and 20. We have noted that the independent role of the courts in policy formation has been enormous in civil liberties and civil rights, and that the Federal Reserve system has broad responsibilities for the details of policy in the political economy. And we will see in the next chapter that the president's range of discretion in specifying foreign policy is still very great, despite the congressional reassertion of the 1970s that we discussed in chapter 7. In the area of welfare policy—on Social Security, Medicare and Medicaid, Food Stamps, Unemployment Compensation, veterans' benefits—Congress is at the center of policy specification. No executive agency has the degree of independence in the area of welfare that the Federal Reserve has on monetary matters. Constituency interests are immediate and intense, and an elaborate network of interest groups lobby Congress on the full range of minute policy details. Congressional oversight of the executive bureaus that administer the various welfare programs is close and continuing.

For a legislature noted for its dispersion of responsibility among committees with overlapping jurisdiction, Congress' organization in public welfare seems reasonably coherent and straightforward. The big issue for the main Social Security programs is how to find the money to pay for them. Because of this, the *taxation* committees of Congress—*Finance* in the Senate, *Ways and Means* in the House—have become especially important. Within Finance, the Health, and the Social Security and Income Maintenance Programs subcommittees are the key ones. Their counterparts in Ways and Means are the Health, and the Social Security subcommittees. As in every other policy area, the House and Senate *Appropriations* committees play critical roles in developing federal welfare policy by setting expenditures levels. Though the responsibilities given the new *Budget* committees have cut somewhat into the independence of Appropriations—through procedures intended to make sure that individual funding commitments relate to comprehensive budget targets—the Appropriations committees and their subcommittees are still enormously influential.

Jurisdiction over legislation determining the substance of many human resources programs rests in the Senate with the *Labor and Human Resources* Committee. Its subcommittees on Aging; Alcoholism and Drug Abuse; Education, Arts and Humanities; Family and Human Services; and the Handicapped all have important program responsibilities. On the House side, the key committee is *Education and Labor.* Subcommittees for Health and Safety, and Human Resources, together with three different ones for education, handle most of the legislative business. Federal housing programs fall under the Housing and Urban Affairs Subcommittee of the *Banking, Housing and Urban Affairs* Committee in the Senate. In the House, the Housing and Community Development Subcommittee of the *Banking, Finance and Urban Affairs* Committee plays the comparable role. Food Stamps and related nutrition programs come under the *Agriculture* committees of both houses of Congress. The Senate Subcommittee on Agriculture, Nutrition, and Forestry; and the House Subcommittee on Domestic Marketing, Consumer Relations, and Nutrition are the key ones. Both the House and Senate have committees on *Veterans' Affairs.* The one in the Senate does not operate through subcommittees. The one in the House does, and its main subcommittees are Compensation, Pension, and Insurance; Education, Training, and Employment; and Hospitals and Health Care.

Interest Groups

As befits programs costing hundreds of billions of dollars annually and prescribing benefits for virtually every citizen, public welfare receives massive interest-group attention. Most of the big "omnibus" interest groups, like the AFL-CIO and the Chambers of Commerce of the United States, are active in big welfare-policy debates, such as those over the Reagan reductions. But much of the lobbying effort in the welfare area involves highly focused efforts by smaller and more specialized groups to influence program detail.

Groups of citizens express their interests in many different ways.

Interest-group networks

There is a group network in each policy area. For example, for retirement benefits, the key groups are the American Association of Retired Persons (AARP) and the National Council of Senior Citizens. Medical programs for the elderly are the concern of the Coalition for Health Funding, the American Association of Homes for the Aging, the American Health Care Association, the Blue Cross and Blue Shield Associations, the Federation of American Hospitals, and the Committee for National Health Insurance. Among the groups that have special interest in programs for the poor are the American Public Welfare Association, which is made up of federal, state, and local welfare agencies; the Food Research and Action Center, which seeks to extend federal food assistance; and the Children's Defense League, which is active across the range of welfare issues, though its efforts are targeted at children's needs.

The area of special health problems and needs has its own mix of interest groups. The use of potentially harmful chemicals as food additives, and a variety of problems relating to nutrition, occupy the attention of the health research group of Ralph Nader's Public Citizen Inc., Planned Parenthood, Zero Population Growth, and the Center for Population Options are among the groups interested in family planning policies. The Mental Health Law Project and the National Mental Health Association lobby nationally for programs in this area, as do the Association for Retarded Citizens, the American Council of the Blind, and the National Association of the Deaf—for their respective concerns.

In the housing area, the National Housing Rehabilitation Association monitors federal rehabilitation efforts. The National Association of Home Builders represents the construction industry. The National

Council on Aging lobbies for housing subsidies for the elderly. The National Association of Housing Cooperatives backs governmental assistance to housing cooperatives open to low- and moderate-income families. The veterans' benefits area is highly organized. The American Legion National Organization and the American Veterans of World War II, Korea, and Vietnam (AMVets) were both chartered by Congress and charged with assisting veterans in making claims for benefits. The Legion and the AMVets do broad-focus lobbying. Other more specialized groups like the Disabled American Veterans are active in specific areas.

All these areas are characterized by very close interaction and ties among the interested groups, the responsible congressional subcommittees, and the relevant executive agency bureaus, of the sort we described in chapters 7 and 9. In its broad outlines, American welfare policy reflects national opinion and values. But the details of various programs emerge from bureau and subcommittee adjustments of group demands in a series of highly specialized policy systems.

SUMMARY

Welfare policy is sometimes taken to include only governmental efforts to help the needy. But the majority of public-welfare programs, including Social Security and Medicare, are directed to all economic groups, not just the poor. The main impetus for the expansion of welfare spending in the United States and every other industrial democracy over the last half-century is the heightened expectations of citizens for greater protection and security. Present-day affluence means that most people expect more consumer goods than preceding generations did; it also means they expect more help from government, such as the assurance through Social Security and Medicare of basic retirement income and health care.

American ideology puts special emphasis on individual responsibility and insists that American society offers unusual opportunities to those who apply themselves. Because of this, the United States has been less inclined than other industrial democracies to back collective governmental efforts at promoting public welfare. But two types of government action have found strong support in the United States: to create a climate where individual opportunity is expanded and individual interests are more fully realized; and to help people who through no lack of individual effort find themselves in need. Public education is a collective welfare program whose primary function is to extend individual opportunity, and education has received more governmental support in the U.S. than in any other country.

Federalism exerts major influence on American welfare programs. Though some of the big programs are funded and administered exclusively through national agencies—veterans' benefits, Social Security, and Medicare—many others involve partnership of the federal and state governments. This is true of Medicaid, AFDC, Food Stamps, and Unemployment Compensation. In most other democracies public-welfare programs are run by national agencies which impose uniform standards and benefits, but in the United States their administration is often decentralized and their provisions vary from state to state.

Since the New Deal, the rate of welfare spending has risen rapidly in the United States, far faster than the overall economy has expanded. Thus welfare expenditures have accounted for a steadily expanding share of the nation's GNP. Between 1950 and 1980, for instance, all social welfare expenditures by local, state, and national government climbed from about $74 billion to $492 billion (expressed in dollars of 1980 purchasing power).

In response to this steep rise, many leaders in both parties, and the general public, swung to the view that some curbs should be imposed. As a result, the *rate of increase* of welfare expenditures was reduced. At the federal level, the Reagan administration has pushed for reduction further than a majority of Democratic leaders want or support, and a major political battle has been joined. The net result of this partisan struggle has been some significant slowing of the overall rise—although welfare spending is still rising in real terms.

Not all pressing issues in the area of public welfare involve sharp partisan conflict. In many instances the key question is how to accomplish goals that leaders of both parties want but do not know how to accomplish. There is general agreement that expenditure increases in the health-care programs, Medicare and Medicaid, are out of control and threaten to crowd out spending in other important areas. There is also agreement that the existing levels of real health benefits to individuals should not be reduced. The search, then, transcending party ideology, is for changes in the health-care delivery system that can achieve discipline over cost escalation without cutting benefits. It is as difficult as it sounds.

20 | Foreign and Defense Policy

From its beginnings the United States has been part of an international community; as such it is strongly affected by developments beyond its shores. Before independence, the thirteen colonies found their future being shaped by decisions made in England, decisions they often resented. And American independence from Britain was greatly helped along by military aid that France, then Britain's major rival, gave to the United States. Foreign trade and commerce also were vital to eighteenth-century America and remain so today. As a result, the United States since 1776 has had to devise ways of dealing with the world outside—to formulate and implement foreign and defense policy. Never in U.S. history has it been possible to ignore the rest of the world; the only issue has been how America interacts with it.

Foreign and defense policy comprises the agreements, alliances, and other programs that nations devise for dealing with the international community. A country formulates its particular foreign policy in a setting determined by its own needs, resources, values and aspirations, and political institutions. We will look first at aspects of the setting for American foreign policy. Next we will review U.S. foreign and defense policies in the modern era: the years since World War II. Finally we will discuss the governmental institutions and interest groups that play key roles in the foreign policy and defense spheres.

The Goals of Foreign Policy

The United States shares with all nations some basic needs and objectives with respect to foreign policy. Perhaps the most funda-

The 1983 U.S. invasion of Grenada sought to protect U.S. citizens on the island and to prevent the establishment of another Communist base in the Caribbean.

mental of these is the need to preserve territorial integrity and national sovereignty. In times past, this meant protecting one's borders from invasion by foreign troops. But in the present age of nuclear weapons and guided missiles, the United States could sustain damage of devastating proportions without foreign soldiers even approaching its shores. Questions of national defense become vastly more complex and troubling. Preserving national sovereignty is not only a military matter. Alliances are formed, treaties negotiated, and foreign policy conducted to maintain national sovereignty *without* war. Often when a country does go to war, it is because other elements of its foreign policy have been unable to accomplish the most basic and enduring objective: guaranteeing its security. A related foreign policy objective is to protect citizens and their property in all their lawful relations with foreign states—as when Americans travel abroad or engage in foreign commerce.

Advancing national economic interests

Advancing national economic interests is another common goal. The increasing interdependence of the contemporary world economy has made this goal loom even larger than in the past. Many national economies now depend heavily on petroleum imports, for example, and maintaining an adequate supply at acceptable prices is for them a critical foreign policy requirement. The level of international trade and restraints on trade, rates of foreign currency exchange, the interests of domestic producers confronted with foreign competition and of domestic producers seeking foreign markets—all these and more such interests make persisting claims on the foreign policy of America and other nations.

Extending democracy. Each nation has its own special mix of institutions, values, needs, and resources that determine how it goes about trying to meet common objectives. Each country has, as well, certain objectives which are uniquely its own or which it may share with only a few other states. These sometimes derive from important national ideological commitments. For example, from this country's earliest days, many Americans have believed not only that democratic government serves them well but that its growth should be encouraged elsewhere. Similarly, promoting human rights and individual liberty in other nations has long been an important goal of American foreign policy. For example, the Carter administration stressed, as a prerequisite for receiving U.S. foreign aid, that countries show a greater commitment to the human rights of their own citizens. Similarly, many members of Congress have insisted in recent years that increased American aid to El Salvador be based on that nation's improving its record on human rights. The election of José Napoleón Duarte, a committed democrat, to the Salvadoran presidency in 1984 encouraged Congress to expand foreign assistance to his troubled land. Disagreement among Americans has come not so much in the articulation of the goal of encouraging human rights abroad as in the search for appropriate means for advancing it. What are the ethically acceptable and practically useful measures for achieving the country's philosophic commitment to enlarging the scope of freedom and democratic government?

World leadership. At every point in modern history, a few nations have been thrust by their economic resources and military power into a world leadership role. Especially since World War II, the United States has been one such country, and the exercise of leadership has been one end of American foreign policy. But what to some are the noble ends of a nation's claims to leadership are to others the unacceptable impulses to "imperialism." Consider the long and costly U.S. involvement in the fighting in Vietnam. Were American actions there a laudable effort to exercise free-world leadership in containing communism and upholding the right of South Vietnam to national independence? Or was Vietnam a poor use of American power, a case where the motives were good but the chosen means disastrous? Or was it yet something else, the inappropriate meddling, for selfish ends, in the affairs of others? Debate over these contrasting interpretations went on throughout the Vietnam War and continues today. The U.S. presence in the Middle East is an expression of its claims and responsibilities for world leadership. But it, too, remains controversial, and public opinion changes depending on the policy of the day. Most Americans applauded the Camp David Accord, which resulted when President Carter brought Egypt's President Anwar Sadat and Israel's Prime Minister Menachem Begin to the negotiating table. But for many, President Reagan's sending an American peacekeeping force of 1,600

Marines to Lebanon in September 1982 prompted great concern, especially after the October 23 terrorist attack on the Marine compound at Beirut Airport killed more than 220 Americans. Still, like Great Britain in the nineteenth and early twentieth centuries and the Soviet Union today, America is now committed to world leadership.

Democracies and foreign affairs. Reviewing foreign policy in *Democracy in America,* Alexis de Tocqueville praised the course the United States followed in its first half-century after independence. It had, rather effectively, held to the position laid down by George Washington in his Farewell Address: Washington counseled his countrymen to take advantage of "our [geographically] detached and distant situation." "Why quit," the president had asked, "our own to stand upon foreign ground? Why, by interweaving our destiny with that of any part of Europe, entangle our peace and prosperity in the toils of European ambition, rivalship, interest, humor, or caprice?" Tocqueville thought Washington was right for the time, but he wondered what would happen when more was required of American policy than avoiding "entangling alliances."

"As for myself," Tocqueville wrote, "I do not hesitate to say that it is especially in the conduct of their foreign relations that democracies appear to me decidedly inferior to other governments." Problems will arise, he argued, because

Tocqueville on foreign policy

> foreign politics demand scarcely any of those qualities which are peculiar to a democracy; they require, on the contrary, the perfect use of almost all those in which it is deficient. Democracy is favorable to the increase of the internal resources of a state; it diffuses wealth and comfort, promotes public spirit, and fortifies the respect for law in all classes of society: All these are advantages which have only an indirect influence on the relations which one people bears to another. But a democracy can only with great difficulty regulate the details of an important undertaking, persevere in a fixed design, and work out its execution in spite of serious obstacles. It cannot combine its measures with secrecy or await their consequences with patience.[1]

Special constraints on democratic governments

In our own time, politicians and scholars have often reached the similar conclusion that democracies face special problems in foreign affairs. One basic theme keeps recurring: Stable authoritarian governments, despite their many social, economic, and political weaknesses, can ignore divergent interests, set a coherent course of foreign policy action, pour resources disproportionately into the means (notably military) for advancing foreign objectives, indulge in whatever secrecy is needed, and persevere in a foreign policy over long periods of time. Given their contrasting commitments and organization, democracies find it hard to respond with comparable coherence, persistence, and dispatch. Among contemporary leaders sharing

[1] Tocqueville, *Democracy in America,* pp. 243–45.

Tocqueville's concern is Henry Kissinger, who left teaching political science at Harvard to become national security adviser under Richard Nixon and then secretary of state under Nixon and Gerald Ford. Kissinger believes that the U.S.S.R. has been able to concentrate its resources in such a way as to make it a formidable adversary of the otherwise much stronger industrial democracies.[2]

The democracies before World War II

Perhaps the most vivid memory of many twentieth-century students of foreign affairs comes from the experience leading up to World War II. The industrial democracies of that time—including the United States, Great Britain, and France—had resources that outstripped those of the dictatorships aligned against them. But the democracies found it hard to act coherently in employing their social and economic strengths to meet the challenge. It seemed that so many of the things that made the democracies vastly preferable places in which to live— their openness, freedom for debate and dissent, responsiveness to popular demands for consumer spending rather than preparations for war, ease with which governments were changed, and possibility of debate within government over what actions should be pursued— made it hard for them to handle the single-minded ruthlessness of Hitler's Germany.

The experience of the 1930s may indeed be an extreme case. But, even so, was it not a tragic example of *a recurring problem that free and open societies confront* in conducting foreign relations with countries that are not free and not open? Democracy demands freedom and openness; if these characteristics impose problems, the problems must be borne. No political system can optimize every objective. Still, the question does remind us that differences in type of government do affect the conduct of foreign policy. Democratic government imposes some special constraints. One of the most important results from the fact that democracy opens up the process of developing and executing foreign policy (as it does domestic policy) to active political debate and competition. Administrations change regularly through free elections; this virtually mandates periodic shifts in foreign policy. The oscillations which result from the American electoral cycle frequently disconcert and frustrate other nations that must do business with us, even other democracies that are themselves subject to the same processes and that understand that it is a necessary part of democratic governance.

FOREIGN AND DEFENSE POLICY SINCE WORLD WAR II

Our study of the American party system and other political institutions has revealed long periods of continuity, interrupted on occasion by some fundamental change that initiates a new course. Foreign pol-

[2] Henry Kissinger, "The Footsteps of History," in *For the Record* (Boston: Little, Brown, 1981), p. 264.

icy can be similarly marked off into a few periods. World War II was a great watershed; U.S. policy after the war has been significantly different than it was before.

Emergence as a World Power

The most important factors changing the course of U.S. foreign policy after World War II involve *national power*—specifically, the major increases in U.S. power and the sharp decline in the position of the three principal international powers of the prewar era: Germany, France, and Great Britain. The bases of American influence in international affairs were not all suddenly erected in the 1940s. After the Civil War, the United States rapidly industrialized; by 1900 its industrial economy was the world's largest. These productive capabilities did not automatically mandate an expanded international role, but they were an important resource for it. For one thing, American productivity could be harnessed for military production. World War I demonstrated the impact this could have; the United States became the "factory" or principal supplier of the allied war effort. But World War II was a greater turning point. The industrial capacity of this country was revitalized and extended by the successful war effort, while the principal European nations were devastated by aerial bombing and combat on the ground. The end of the war saw a much greater disproportion between U.S. and European economic strength.

In 1946, the major European states were grappling with political problems resulting from their having been ravaged by two major wars in just three decades. Quite apart from their economic capacity, their

President Truman (middle), Josef Stalin of the U.S.S.R. (left uniformed) and Britain's prime minister Winston Churchill meet after World War II.

resolve to sustain world leadership had weakened. All of the European nations needed desperately to turn inward and reconstruct their own societies. While large, the American losses in World War II did not begin to approach those of the European powers. With its economy now dominant and its political will sustained, the United States was thrust into the power vacuum left by the European collapse.

The guiding approach to U.S. foreign policy prior to World War II has often been called **isolationist.** This term is misleading, however. As we noted at the beginning of this chapter, America was never truly isolated from world affairs. **Unilateralist** is a more accurate description. George Washington thought we could and should avoid getting drawn into the European system of alliances, and for a long time American foreign policy adhered to this plan. The United States occasionally intervened internationally, but for the most part it did so selectively and without assuming responsibility for maintaining a worldwide balance of power. For example, throughout the nineteenth century, following the proclamation by President James Monroe in 1823 of what we know as the Monroe Doctrine—asserting special U.S.

America's historic commitment to unilateralism

Prior to World War II, those who wanted to keep the U.S. out of "Europe's war" had much support as this Madison Square Garden rally suggests.

interests in its own hemisphere and warning European powers not to try to extend their colonial systems in the American continents—the United States intervened selectively in Latin American affairs. Given the technology of the nineteenth and early twentieth centuries, the physical distance of the United States from Europe permitted it to "go it alone." But more than anything else, American unilateralism was sustained by the vast commitment Great Britain made to maintaining a world balance of power. "During most of the nineteenth century and early twentieth century," political scientist John Spanier writes,

> the United States was able to preserve its historical isolation from "power politics" thanks to the balance of power on the European continent maintained by Britain to protect its own security. No one state or coalition of states was able to conquer most of Europe, organize its vast resources in manpower and industrial strength, and then use these to menace the United States. Britain's opposition to any state's seeking such hegemony therefore made it possible for the United States to remain what today is called "non-aligned."[3]

After World War II, however, Britain was no longer able to play this role. Among the Western democracies, only the United States could sustain a new balance in the postwar world.

The new course of American foreign policy after World War II, then, was not simply a position taken by leaders who happened to be in power at the time. It reflected the structural position the United States had assumed in the international community. While much has happened since 1946 to affect it—for example, the revival of the European and Japanese economies—the position of the United States has not changed fundamentally. Through eight postwar administrations and kaleidoscopic shifts in international problems and crises, powerful continuities are evident in American foreign and defense policy.

Shift in American policy after World War II

Containment

The words "balance of power" have a ring of nineteenth-century Europe, conjuring up a picture of nations forming elaborate alliance systems to prevent their opponents from getting too strong and threatening their interests. The words also suggest a kind of international amorality: "power politics" rather than a commitment to moral purposes. Yet, early efforts to maintain a balance of power were by no means without large moral objectives. When Great Britain maintained the European balance for a century after Napoleon's defeat at Waterloo in 1812, it provided the basis for an extended period of peace.

After World War II, the United States set about performing, in its own way, the balance-of-power role that had been Britain's. Ameri-

[3] John Spanier, *American Foreign Policy since World War II*, 9th ed. (New York: Holt, Rinehart and Winston, 1983), p. 3.

Containment

ca's effort was called **containment.** The United States was "containing" the Soviet Union and communist expansion. If one had to pick a date for the beginning of U.S. containment policy, February 21, 1947, would be a good choice. On that date the first secretary of the British embassy in Washington handed American officials two notes from his government, one concerning Greece, the other Turkey. They both stated that Britain could no longer meet its traditional responsibilities in those two countries. Since Greece and Turkey were on the verge of collapse, Britain's decision meant that a Soviet breakthrough in the area could be stopped only by a major American commitment.

The Truman Doctrine

American leaders felt that they had to act. President Harry Truman appeared before a joint session of Congress on March 12, 1947, to announce a major departure from historic American foreign policy. Setting forth what came to be known as the Truman Doctrine, the president argued that the United States must be "willing to help free peoples to maintain their institutions and their national integrity against aggressive movements that seek to impose upon them totalitarian regimes." Elaborating further, Truman asserted that "it must be the policy of the United States to support free peoples who are resisting attempted subjugation by armed minorities or by outside pressure." To meet the immediate need, he urged Congress to appropriate $400 million for economic and military assistance to Greece and Turkey. He also asked authorization to send both American civilian and military personnel to help those two countries rebuild their domestic economies and strengthen their armies.

President Truman urging Congress to appropriate money for economic and military aid to Greece and Turkey.

America's view of the
Soviet Union

The intellectual case for the new containment policy was made impressively by George Kennan, then a State Department official and its leading Soviet expert. Kennan argued that "the main element of any United States policy toward the Soviet Union must be that of a long-term, patient but firm and vigilant containment of Russian expansive tendencies." To block Soviet thrusts, counterforce must be applied "at a series of constantly shifting geographical and political points, corresponding to the shifts and maneuvers of Soviet policy. . . ."[4] Kennan maintained that the Soviets would push ahead wherever they saw an opening, or accommodate to resistance when it was effectively offered. Against this, only the measured application of Western unity and strength could succeed. The U.S. should have no illusions that the U.S.S.R. would somehow give up on its ultimate policy of "cautious, persistent pressure toward the disruption and weakening of all rival influence and rival power." But if the United States applied a policy of containment firmly and patiently, Kennan concluded, it would not only successfully hold the line; it would also create the conditions for "either the break-up or the gradual mellowing of Soviet power." Over the four decades since Kennan wrote, his vision of containment has provided the foundation for American policy.

The Marshall Plan and NATO

In the wake of World War II, misery was widespread throughout devastated Europe. On humanitarian grounds alone, there was a strong case for a program of American assistance. But America's preference for a democratic Europe, and its security needs in the area, also demanded action. Democratic governments able to resist communist advances could hardly survive in the absence of rapid economic recovery. The most important U.S. response was the initiation of a recovery program commonly known as the Marshall Plan. It was first set forth in 1947 and named for the man who announced it, Secretary of State George C. Marshall. Through the Marshall Plan, the United States gave West European nations over $12 billion dollars—more than half of which went to Britain, France, and West Germany. The effort was extraordinarily successful; by 1950, Europe was already exceeding its prewar levels of production.

The birth of NATO

As the economic program proceeded, so did the promotion of a military alliance, spurred by Soviet actions. In February 1948, the Soviets engineered the overthrow of an independent democratic government in Czechoslovakia, putting that country under communist domination. In July 1948, the Soviets imposed a blockade on Berlin, seeking to drive the Western powers out of that city. In response

[4]George Kennan, "The Sources of Soviet Conduct," *Foreign Affairs*, July 1947, pp. 575–76. Because Kennan was at the time an official of the Truman administration, he signed the piece simply "by X."

In response to the 1948 Soviet blockade on Berlin, the U.S. airlifted supplies to Berlin.

to such military acts, the United States and the democracies of Western Europe established a military alliance, the North Atlantic Treaty Organization (NATO). The North Atlantic Treaty was signed in April 1949, and ratified by the U.S. Senate three months later.

Strong Rhetoric, Cautious Policy

At times in the late 1940s and 1950s, some American political leaders sounded a call for something more than simply "containing" Soviet expansion. In the 1952 presidential campaign, the out-of-power Republicans attacked the Democrats on the issue of containment, arguing that it conceded the initiative to the Soviet Union. As John Foster Dulles—then the leading Republican foreign policy spokesman—saw it, containment aimed only at preserving the status quo and thus was "negative, futile, and immoral." The objective of American foreign policy, Dulles argued, should be not to coexist indefinitely with a communist threat but rather to eliminate the threat. American power should be committed to a rollback of Soviet power.

In fact, however, the Republican administration of Dwight Eisenhower, elected in 1952, continued for the most part the basic approach developed in 1947–49. The Korean War was concluded with a peace agreement that left in place the situation that prevailed before North Korea's 1950 attack on South Korea: A communist regime allied with the Soviet Union remained in power north of the 38th parallel, while a noncommunist regime, allied to the United States, existed in the South. More importantly, the Eisenhower administration did almost nothing to challenge Soviet control in Eastern Europe, not even in

Cautious containment in Korea and Eastern Europe

the face of the brutal use of Soviet military power in crushing the October–November 1956 revolt in Hungary against that country's Soviet-dominated regime. The United States stuck to a cautious policy of containment even though its rhetoric at times suggested an anticommunist crusade.

Public opinion on U.S. foreign policy

One reason for this was that the American people never wanted a crusade. The public was frustrated by the Soviet Union's behavior, as in stifling national independence in Eastern Europe, but it resisted measures that would lead to war. Reviewing public opinion on recent U.S. foreign policy, political scientist William Schneider concluded that the public wanted "boldness and self-assertion from the nation's leaders" but not actions increasing the risk of war.[5] This posture seems to have characterized American opinion since World War II.

Vietnam: The Misapplication of Containment

Though a great power with far-reaching international interests, the United States was far from omnipotent. American power had to be carefully and selectively applied, distinguishing between cases vital to national security and cases not so, and taking into account the human and material costs that would be incurred in any intervention. These strictures on costs were observed fairly carefully until the mid-1960s, when the administration of Lyndon Johnson committed a half-million American soldiers to a land war 9,000 miles from the continental United States, in an area (Indochina) which was undeveloped economically, without resources that mattered to the industrial world, and which lacked strategic location. Lasting longer than any other military conflict in U.S. history, the Vietnam War claimed the lives of some 50,000 American soldiers, as well as hundreds of thousands of Vietnamese, and it drained billions of dollars in economic and military resources. The United States did not start this war; it did not seek to subjugate anyone, but rather sought to prevent the regime in North Vietnam from toppling the regime in the South.

Division and protest

But the question of costs had not been carefully considered. Even with the best motives, democracies cannot fight ten-year wars in which they are party to great destruction in areas remote from their immediate national interests. In the United States, the Vietnam War sparked bitter domestic divisions, including massive protests on American college and university campuses. It created a domestic political situation that preoccupied and crippled two presidencies, Lyndon Johnson's and Richard Nixon's. Begun to attest to the strength of American resolve in containing communist aggression, the Vietnam War shook that resolve more fundamentally than any other event since World War II.

[5] William Schneider, "Conservatism, Not Interventionism: Trends in Foreign Policy Opinion, 1974–1982," in Kenneth Dye, et al., *Eagle Defiant: United States Foreign Policy in the 1980s* (Boston: Little Brown, 1983), p. 34.

Even now, more then a decade after the United States withdrew from Indochina, the debate continues over why we intervened and what the lessons of the war for future American policy actually are. The only issue on which there is something approaching consensus is that the United States should *not* have become involved militarily. When a poll conducted by CBS News and the *New York Times* in January 1983 asked, "Looking back, do you think the U.S. did the right thing in getting into the fighting in Vietnam, or should we have stayed out?" 77 percent felt the country had erred. Only 14 percent still believed that the U.S. had done the right thing overall in getting into the fighting, while 9 percent had no opinion.[6] American public opinion was not always this way. When a Gallup poll in April 1967 asked, "Do you think the United States made a mistake sending troops to fight in Vietnam?" only 37 percent said the decision had been in error, while 50 percent believed it had been the right one and 13 percent were unsure.[7] Many Americans supported the objectives for which the country intervened; but as the war went on, more and more concluded that its costs were excessive.

The debate over American involvement in Vietnam has been a three-way rather than a two-way division. Two separate questions were at issue: (1) whether the objectives and view of the world that led American officials to bring the country into the war were sound; and (2) whether the immediate action and strategy were appropriate. The position defended by Lyndon Johnson's administration held that the long-standing policy of containment was correct, and that the U.S. military intervention in Vietnam was a necessary application of it. A second position objected both to the general vision and to the specific action. For those who held this view, containment was a flawed idea. It relied too much on the use of American military power, and it was too inclined to fix responsibility for international tensions on the Soviet Union and to overlook U.S. responsibility. The American engagement in Vietnam represented a bad application of a bad general policy. But from the beginning of heavy U.S. involvement in Vietnam, some held a third position: the containment policy was generally sound, but Vietnam was a misapplication of it because the human and material costs were excessive. It was just such a calculation that had led the United States not to intervene in Hungary in 1956 and Czechoslovakia in 1968, when Soviet troops crushed popular independence movements in those countries. The numbers holding to this third position grew as the Vietnam War continued. In 1976, Norman Podhoretz, the editor of *Commentary* magazine, summed up the case that one may strongly criticize the means without disparaging the intended end:

> Vietnam was the wrong war in the wrong place at the wrong time. . . .
> When we were losing we said we were winning, and in a desperate effort

[6] Survey taken by CBS News/*New York Times*, January 16–19, 1983.
[7] Gallup poll of April 19–24, 1967.

The horror of the Vietnam War ended with a frantic flight from Saigon.

to win, we applied military force in ways that were at once brutal and inhibited and that inspired widespread repugnance at home. But wrong as the war the United States fought in Vietnam was in all these respects, it was not wrong in the purposes for which it was fought. Those purposes were to check the spread of Communism in a country which, though not free, still enjoyed more liberty then any Communist regime allows (and certainly more then it has enjoyed since falling to the Communists). . . .[8]

Political reaction to Vietnam

As the war dragged, large segments of the public grew weary of struggle, and confused and disillusioned by it. One result for a time was a turning inward, an insistence on greater prudence and caution in American foreign policy, and a reduced willingness to support a costly military establishment. Political leaders took steps that they hoped would prevent any future repetition of the Vietnam debacle. In 1974 Congress passed the War Powers Resolution, curbing the president's authority, as commander-in-chief, to commit American forces to battle (see chapter 7). The Carter administration came into office in 1977 intent on scaling back the country's role as "global policeman" and on re-emphasizing the moral dimensions of American international leadership through moral persuasion on behalf of human rights.

[8] Norman Podhoretz, "Making the World Safe for Communism," *Commentary*, April 1976, p. 40; idem, *Why We Were in Vietnam* (New York: Simon and Schuster, 1982).

It is not that the Carter administration ever really abandoned the overriding objective of containment, but, as Robert Osgood has noted,

> The new Administration set out to implement it in a manner congenial to American geopolitical retrenchment and moral resurgence—by downplaying the "inordinate fear of communism" that had led the country "to embrace any dictator who joined us in our fear" . . . aligning the United States with the forces of black majority rule in southern Africa; and concentrating on the transcendent "global questions" of justice, equity, and human rights . . . preventing nuclear proliferation, curbing the arms trade, and promoting the rights of the individual against cruelty and oppression.[9]

Reassertion

De-emphasizing the military aspects of containment fitted the American mood after the disappointment and disillusionment of Vietnam. But it did not lead to the results its proponents had hoped for. The Soviet Union asserted itself aggressively in a number of areas. The invasion of Afghanistan by Soviet soldiers in late 1979 indicated to many Americans that a de-emphasis by this country on the application of its military power would not encourage comparable restraint on the Soviets' part. The invasion of Afghanistan followed closely on the heels of the seizure by Iranians of the U.S. embassy and staff in Teheran, Iran, which added to a sense of frustration over national weakness. American public opinion soon reflected a new assertiveness. By the spring of 1980, the National Opinion Research Center found in its national survey of American attitudes that 60 percent of the public believed the United States was spending too little for defense, while just 12 percent thought defense spending was too high and 28 percent thought it was at about the right level.[10]

The Carter administration shifted its emphasis. In a speech at the U.S. Naval Academy in June 1978, the president reaffirmed the country's long-standing commitment to containment, charging that the Soviet Union had exploited *détente* to cover "a continuing aggressive struggle for political advantage and increased influence in a variety of ways." More importantly, the Carter administration took such concrete steps as urging substantial increases in defense spending and a modernization of nuclear forces based in Western Europe for that region's defense. In his January 1980 State of the Union Address, the president announced an extension of American military commitments, in what came to be known as the Carter Doctrine: "An attempt by any outside force to gain control of the Persian Gulf region [important in the flow of petroleum to the U.S., Europe, and Japan] will be regarded as an assault on the vital interests of the United States of

The Carter Doctrine

[9] Robert E. Osgood, "The Revitalization of Containment," *Foreign Affairs* 60 (3), 1982, p. 469.
[10] National Opinion Research Center, *General Social Survey*, Spring 1980.

Russian soldiers and equipment in Afghanistan, ongoing challenge to U.S. containment policy.

America, and such an assault will be repelled by any means necessary, including military force."

New efforts to contain Soviet expansion

The post-Vietnam reaction in U.S. foreign policy had been greatly tempered. When the Reagan administration took office in January 1981, it placed even more emphasis on strengthening American military forces and containing the Soviet Union. As Robert Osgood noted, "The dominant theme of President Reagan's foreign policy, to which all major policies were subordinated, was revitalizing the containment of Soviet expansion."[11] Much has happened since 1947 to alter the practical implementation of containment, including a major increase in Soviet military strength. Reacting to perceived mistakes of his predecessor, each postwar president has imposed his own style and substance upon the practical working-out of the idea of containment. Following Vietnam, its central assumptions were questioned more vigorously than ever before. But now, in the 1980s, U.S. policy is still guided by the basic approach which the Truman administration developed just after World War II. Moreover, the U.S. public continues to support the main assumptions of the containment policy, as seen in Figure 20.1.

Policy Differences

Important policy differences have also persisted. One major source of conflict is the basic tension that inheres to the foreign policy goals and perspectives most Americans hold. As we noted in chapter 12,

[11] Osgood, "Revitalization," p. 472.

Figure 20.1
**A. Commitment to
Containment**

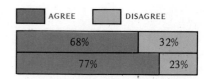

October 1981
(ABC/*Washington Post*)
November 1983
(*Los Angeles Times*)

Question: Now I'm going to read a few statements, and for each, I'd like you to tell me whether you tend to agree with that statement or disagree with it, or if, perhaps, you have no opinion about it. . . . The United States should take all steps, including the use of force, to prevent the spread of communism (October 1981, ABC News / *Washington Post*). Do you agree or disagree with the following statement: The U.S. government should take all steps necessary—including the use of military force—to prevent the spread of communism? (Nov. 12–17, 1983, *Los Angeles Times*)
Source: Surveys by ABC News / *Washington Post*, October 14–18, 1981, and by the *Los Angeles Times*, Nov. 12–17, 1983.

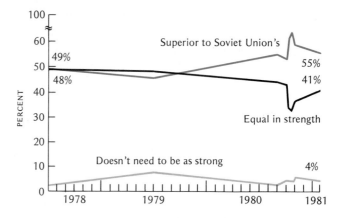

Question: Do you think the military strength of the United States should be superior to the Soviet Union, should be about equal in strength, or doesn't the United States need to be (exactly) as strong as the Soviet Union?
Source: Surveys by CBS News / *New York Times*, latest that of January 26–29, 1981.

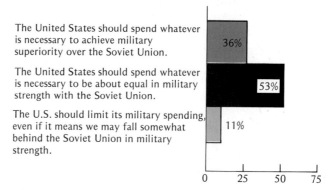

The United States should spend whatever is necessary to achieve military superiority over the Soviet Union.

The United States should spend whatever is necessary to be about equal in military strength with the Soviet Union.

The U.S. should limit its military spending, even if it means we may fall somewhat behind the Soviet Union in military strength.

Question: Which of these three statements comes closest to your own views?
Source: ABC / *Washington Post*, November 3–7, 1983.

Figure 20.1 (continued)
B. Support for U.S. World Role

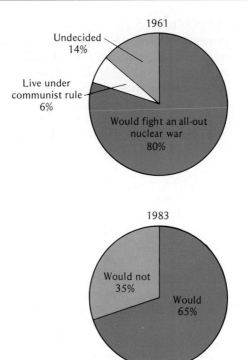

Question: Suppose you had to make the decision between fighting an all-out nuclear war or living under Communist rule—how would you decide?
Source: Survey by the Gallup Organization, October 19–24, 1961.

Question: Would you be willing to risk the destruction of the United States rather than be dominated by the Russians, or not?
Source: Survey by the *New York Times*, November 18–22, 1983.

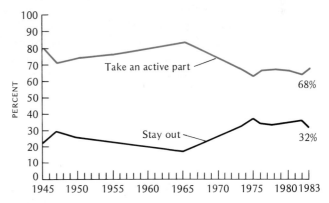

Question: Do you think it would be best for the future of this country if we take an active part in world affairs, or if we (stay / stayed) out of world affairs?
Source: Surveys by the Gallup Organization, October 1945 and August 1947; National Opinion Research Center, January 1950 through June 1965; National Opinion Research Center, General Social Surveys, spring 1973 through spring 1978; Louis Harris and Associates, November 1980; National Opinion Research Center, General Social Surveys, spring 1982 and spring 1983.

the public is deeply committed to peace. It favors steps to reduce international tensions, control the arms race, lessen the chance of nuclear war. It wants the United States to find ways through which its competition with the Soviet Union is confined to peaceful processes rather than military actions. Yet the public is highly suspicious of the Soviet Union. It thinks that country will take advantage of American weakness. It backs high levels of military spending because it doesn't want the United States to be inferior militarily to the U.S.S.R. It wants American strength counterpoised against Soviet expansion.

The shifting search for balance. These two perspectives can be reconciled to some degree, but they always coexist uneasily. How is the right balance to be struck between making every effort to ease tensions and making every effort to apply firm containment? Emphasize the first, and the result is widespread criticism of American foreign and defense policy as too weak. Emphasize the second, and policy comes under attack for increasing the risk of war. Even within a given administration, these tensions are evident: The Carter administration took office stressing measures to downplay the military side of the country's response to international challenges; it left office emphasizing a stronger military posture. Many Americans, including leaders of both parties, want to combine commitments to peaceful accommodation with firm military resistance to aggression.

Liberal versus conservative internationalists. Foreign policy divisions in the United States involve more than a persisting reactive search for the proper balance of competing, widely shared goals or impulses. Especially among party elites and segments of the public that pay the most attention to foreign affairs, the contemporary liberal-conservative division is evident. It was deepened by the bitterness and distrust of the Vietnam War years. William Schneider identified both sides in this policy conflict as internationalists, because both accept the idea that the United States must be actively involved in world affairs. Liberal internationalists, Schneider noted, stress economic and humanitarian issues over security issues and containing Soviet expansion. "They . . . regard the common problems facing all of humanity as more urgent than the ideological differences between East and West." In contrast, conservative internationalists see Soviet (or Soviet-encouraged) expansionism as the main threat to the world community. They stress military preparedness and the importance of clearly signaling Western resolve.[12]

This debate involves contrasting views of the essential character of the Soviet Union as a political system and of the psychology of its leaders. With or without acknowledging it, American foreign policymakers play psychologist to the Soviet leadership. What are those

[12] Schneider, "Conservatism," p. 40.

The question of
"Soviet psychology"
leaders really like? What are their motivations? What kinds of American actions in the international sphere are most likely to advance world peace and discourage Soviet expansion? As vice president from 1953 to 1961, and then as president from 1969 to 1974, Richard Nixon had extensive contact with Soviet officials. From this he developed a reading of Soviet psychology that he applied fairly consistently in shaping his policy approach. "The basic rule of Soviet behavior was laid down years ago by Lenin," Nixon writes. "Probe with bayonets. If you encounter steel, withdraw. If you encounter mush, continue. . . . Ruling out force is considered an act of virtue in the West: The Soviets and other potential aggressors consider it a sign of weakness. Ruling out American use of force provokes the use of force against us."[13] Conservative internationalists generally would agree with these assessments.

Contrast Nixon's views with those of Cyrus Vance, secretary of state under President Jimmy Carter. Vance recorded in a book what he had written to Soviet Foreign Minister Andrei Gromyko after the Soviet invasion of Afghanistan in late 1979:

> The relationship between our two countries was the most critical factor in determining whether the world would live in peace, and the series of events culminating in Soviet actions in Afghanistan had brought us to a fork in the road. I said that it was vital that both of us give sober consideration to the implications of the current situation for each side's interest in the maintenance of world peace. I went on to say that despite the differing political convictions of our countries, and because of the inherent competitive interest between us, we had sought to establish common rules of behavior that would reduce the risk of conflict. This, I said, would not be possible unless both of us recognize the need to act with restraint in troubled areas. . . . I closed by saying that if there was restraint on both sides and respect for the independence and territorial integrity of the states in the region, our respective interests need not lead to confrontation, and requested that he indicate to us Soviet intentions in both Afghanistan and the region.[14]

Liberal internationalists like Vance are more confident that there is a mutuality of interests that can be recognized and acted upon by the U.S. and the U.S.S.R.

Military Balance: How Much Is Enough?

There is widespread agreement that American military forces are a necessary instrument of the nation's foreign policy. But there is disagreement on the issue of, militarily, how much is enough. If the object of a strong American defense is to convince the Soviet Union not to take certain aggressive acts, how much military capability is required? This complicated question involves objective facts on the relative

[13] Richard M. Nixon, *The Real War* (New York: Warner Books, 1980), pp. 2, 4, 293–94.
[14] Cyrus Vance, *Hard Choices* (New York: Simon and Schuster, 1983), pp. 138, 394–95.

Soviet missile on display during May Day parade.

capabilities of Soviet and American weaponry, facts not easily determined. It also involves issues of what Soviet reactions are likely to be, based upon their perceptions of American preparedness. And it is made even more complicated because America's defense capabilities are determined not just by numbers and types of weapons, but also by the country's political readiness to employ its military strength in various circumstances. ". . . [M]ilitary capabilities reveal nothing about resolve. Resolve is a function of leadership, a people's traditions and expectations, and their perceptions of what is at stake."[15]

U.S. military expenditures. America is spending more today for military purposes in absolute dollar terms than at any other time in its history. By itself this finding does not tell us very much. The United States is also spending much more today for education, Social Security, various welfare programs, protecting the environment, preventing crime, and so on, than ever before. Because of the substantial inflation since World War II, a dollar had only one-fourth the purchasing power in 1984 that it had in 1945. We need to examine expenditures in constant dollar terms, adjusting for inflation to show actual purchasing power. When this is done, we see that the level of U.S. military spending increased in the 1960s and then, following the Vietnam War, declined sharply. By 1976, the United States was spending *less* in real terms than it spent in the early 1960s. Since 1978, however, the level of real military spending has increased substantially (see Figure 20.2).

[15] Richard Ned Labow, "Misconceptions in American Strategic Assessment," *Political Science Quarterly*, Summer 1983, p. 206.

Figure 20.2 **U.S. Defense Spending since 1965 (constant 1972 dollars)**

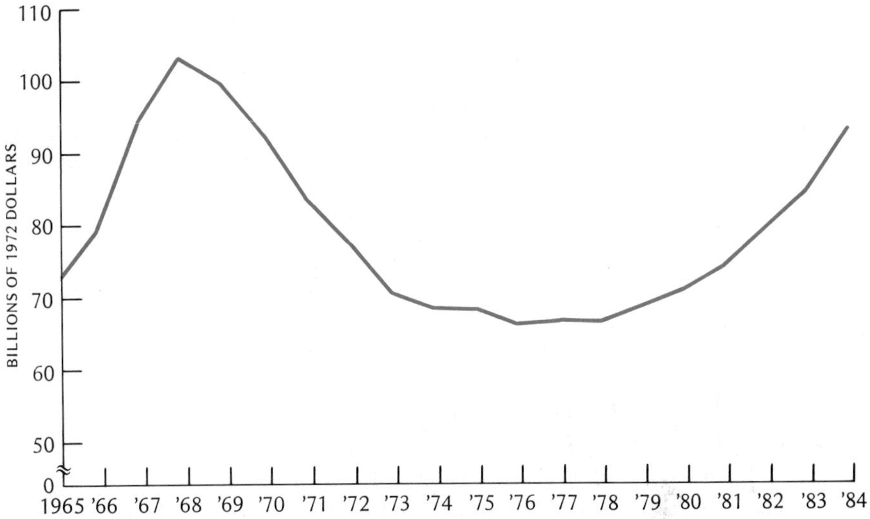

Source: Executive Office of the President, OMB, *Budget of the United States Government, FY 1985*, p. (9–61).

Defense spending as a proportion of the GNP

In the last full year of World War II (1944), roughly one-third of the total American GNP and three-fourths of all federal government expenditures were assigned to the military effort. In the demobilization that followed the war, there was a vast reduction in these proportions: In 1950, just 4 percent of the GNP and 27 percent of the federal budget went for military purposes. The proportions then rose sharply, spurred in part by the Korean War, and reached their postwar highs of 9 percent of the GNP and 49 percent of the federal budget in 1955. During the 1970s, reflecting the national frustration with the war in Vietnam, they fell sharply: The military's share of the GNP dropped from 8 percent in 1970 to 5 percent in 1979. Having claimed nearly half of the federal budget in the 1950s, defense spending accounted for less than a fourth by the end of the 1970s. Most recently, under the defense buildup begun late in the Carter administration and accelerated under Reagan, this decline has reversed: In 1984, defense spending was 6.4 percent of the American GNP and 27 percent of all federal expenditures.

U.S.-U.S.S.R. expenditures. Defense efforts are not made in a vacuum. How do the United States and the Soviet Union compare in the extent of their efforts? This comparison is critical, but not easily made. The Soviet Union does not share its defense data with the United States. Intelligence efforts yield some of the needed information, but not all of it and not all reliably. The problem of comparison is compounded by the difficulty of translating Soviet expenditures into terms resembling those used in the West. The American and Soviet economies are fundamentally different. As the International Institute for Strategic Studies points out:

> Soviet pricing practices are quite different from those in the West. Objectives are set in real terms with no requirement for money prices to coincide with the real costs of goods and services. The ruble [the Russian currency] cost of the defense effort may thus not reflect the real cost of alternate production forgone. . . . If ruble estimates are then converted into dollars to facilitate international comparison, the difficulties are compounded, because the exchange rate chosen should relate the purchasing power of a ruble in the Soviet Union to that of a dollar in the U.S.A. The official exchange rate is considered inadequate for this purpose, and there is no consensus on an alternative.[16]

Western experts have sought to meet these problems by estimating how much it would cost to *produce and man the equivalent of the Soviet defense effort in the United States*. Even this is fraught with difficulties, though, because if it were confronted with the American price structure, the Soviet Union might well resort to a pattern of spending different from its present one. For example, the Soviet Union might well not maintain as large an army as it does if it had to pay its soldiers the wages the United States must pay.

Problems in comparing U.S./U.S.S.R. spending

We know that Soviet defense spending has been rising significantly over the last two decades and that the Soviet Union is now spending somewhat more than the United States—although we don't know precisely how much more. A study done by the Library of Congress for the Senate Armed Services Committee in 1976 concluded that "the quantitative military balance since 1965 had shifted substantially in favor of the Soviet Union."[17] The Defense Department concluded in 1983 that Soviet defense outlays were 30 percent greater than those of the United States.[18]

NATO versus the Warsaw Pact. A more complete comparison requires consideration of the military expenditures not only of the U.S. and the U.S.S.R. but of their principal allies. This shows the Soviet side in a weaker relative position. Figure 20.3 compares the expenditures of all the countries in NATO to those of the Warsaw Pact nations— which include the U.S.S.R. and the East European countries bound to it. Outside of what the Soviet Union itself spends, Warsaw Pact expenditures are modest. But other NATO countries make quite substantial military expenditures. Using overall figures, we see the West roughly equal to the Soviet bloc rather than trailing it. NATO spending exceeded that of the Warsaw Pact by about $10 billion in 1972, fell behind in the mid-1970s, then pulled ahead again in 1982. The Warsaw Pact countries expend a much higher proportion of their total

---

[16]*The Military Balance 1982–1983* (London: International Institute for Strategic Studies, 1982), pp. 12–13.
[17]Congressional Quarterly, *U.S. Defense Policy* (Washington, D.C.: Congressional Quarterly, 1983), p. 13.
[18]*Defense Budget, FY 1984* (Washington, D.C.: Department of Defense, 1983), p. 7.

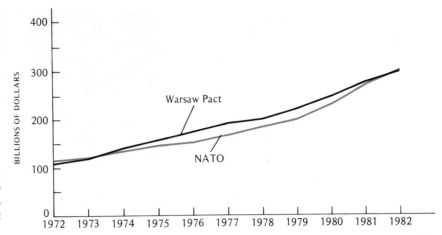

Figure 20.3
NATO and Warsaw Pact Military Expenditures since 1972

Source: World Military Expenditures and Arms Transfers, 1972–1982 (Washington, D.C.: U.S. Arms Control and Disarmament Agency, 1984), p. 14.

GNP on the military, but since their economies are smaller than those of the NATO states, even their higher proportional commitment still leaves them at a rough parity.

What Weapons Are Needed?

Paralleling the argument over how big the U.S. defense commitment should be is another over what new weapons would best contribute, in the most cost-effective way, to national security. The issue of new ballistic missiles illustrates this debate. In the early 1980s, America's intercontinental ballistic missiles (ICBMs) consisted largely of 1,000 "Minuteman" missiles which were products of the technology of the late 1950s and 1960s. More and more experts had come to feel that this system was too vulnerable, given the great technological advances and numerical increases in Soviet ICBMs. As McGeorge Bundy, national security adviser under President Kennedy, observed in 1978:

> Our Minuteman force was developed in the late 1950s as a solid-fuel, quick-reaction, hard-site system essentially invulnerable to the first strike capabilities of any other nation. It was an excellent system in its time, a pathbreaker for the missile age. . . . Nonetheless it is certain that we would not today design or build a system with any such vulnerability as that which faces Minuteman, and it is no longer plausible that our best course is to leave it as it is. . . .[19]

Development of a replacement for Minuteman had actually begun in the late 1960s, and was designated "MX"—"M" denoted missile and "X" experimental or not yet designated. By the early 1970s, the

[19] McGeorge Bundy, "Stability and Strategic Arms Control," *International Security,* Winter 1978, p. 11.

*American MX missile
under development.*

Air Force had outlined its basic requirements for the new missile. The MX needed to carry more re-entry vehicles (for warheads) than the existing ICBMs, and this meant it would have to be able to lift a heavier "payload." Greater accuracy was also required. Finally, the new missile needed to be housed in such a way as to solve what many defense experts considered the most urgent threat: the danger that existing U.S. missiles could be destroyed in their silos by Soviet ICBMs.

Commission on
Strategic Forces

When Jimmy Carter became president, he initiated an examination of whether development of the MX was necessary and, if it was, what form it should take. By mid-1979, he had concluded that the MX was needed. He insisted that "acknowledged inferiority" in the American ICBM force would be "destabilizing," and might encourage the Soviet Union to strike. But the argument over the MX continued, especially over how the missile should be based to reduce its vulnerability. It was still unresolved when Ronald Reagan took office.[20] Against the backdrop of a decade of unresolved debate, Reagan appointed in January 1983 a "Commission on Strategic Forces" to "examine the future of our ICBM forces and to recommend basing alternatives." The commission brought together two former secretaries of state and four for-

[20] For a useful examination of the MX debate, see Paul N. Stockton, "Defense Policy: Arms Development and Arms Control: The Strange Case of the MX Missile," in Allen P. Sindler, ed., *American Politics and Public Policy* (Washington, D.C.: Congressional Quarterly Press, 1982), pp. 225–53.

mer secretaries of defense, representing administrations from Richard Nixon through Jimmy Carter. Its makeup reflected the desperate search for bipartisan support for some plan. The chair of the commission was Brent Scowcroft, who had been national security adviser under President Ford. The Scowcroft commission urged that the MX be deployed. It asserted that the best arrangement for basing the missile, given all considerations including cost, was to put it in the old Minuteman silos. To get the benefit of modernization without escalating the arms race, the commission recommended that 154 existing ICBMs, of the oldest varieties, be retired and replaced by 100 new MXs.[21] A narrow bipartisan majority in Congress was in support of the Scowcroft plan. In 1984 this slim majority held up through repeated challenges to building the MX, especially by Democrats in the House of Representatives.

The saga of the MX has elements common to many contemporary weapons debates. Even when there is considerable agreement on a broad objective, there may be intense disagreement over how the objective is to be carried out. Moreover, the saga shows what long spans of time may be required to implement costly and technically complex decisions. Contrasting goals and interests—for example, achieving arms control with the Soviet Union, and maintaining American defense capabilities in the face of continuing technological change—were present in the MX debate as in other such weapons policy decisions.

"North-South" Issues

American foreign policy since World War II has been occupied primarily with East-West relations—involving relations with the Soviet Union and related defense and security issues. But the U.S. and the U.S.S.R., and their immediate allies, make up only a small part of the world's population. For most people outside the industrial West and the Soviet orbit—for most countries of the Third World—the problem of poverty and its effects is of the most compelling importance. However the conflict between the West and the communist bloc is explained and justified, it so absorbs attention and, through the arms race, economic resources that it greatly restricts efforts to combat world poverty.

Huge population increases

Because the more developed countries are located disproportionately in temperate parts of the Northern Hemisphere, while the less developed countries lie largely to the South, questions of international economic development are now referred to as "North-South" issues. North-South issues reach beyond the immediate needs of the less-developed countries and involve every nation. In 1983, the planet's population was nearly five billion, up almost two billion since 1960. While the more-developed countries have curbed rapid popu-

[21] *Report of the President's Commission on Strategic Forces*, April 1983, p. 18.

lation growth, the less-developed regions have not. Mexico's population alone increased by 25 million in the last 15 years, India's by 200 million. The implications of this population growth—political, economic, environmental,—are enormous.

Economic assistance

The United States government is currently spending about $5 billion a year in assistance to Third World countries to alleviate poverty and promote economic growth. In 1984, $1 billion went in the form of food assistance. About $1.8 billion were expended through the U.S. Agency for International Development (AID) in bilateral development programs in some 60 countries. The United States also contributes to the World Bank, and three regional banks for Latin America, Asia, and Africa. These institutions make loans for economic development in Third World countries through direct contributions of the United States and other developed countries, and by borrowing in world capital markets backed by "collectible capital": a means by which contributing governments guarantee loan repayments. In 1984 the United States contributed $1.5 billion directly and guaranteed another $3 billion in loans through the collectible capital provision.

Debt burdens
and repayment

Yet, while this level of assistance is substantial, experts believe it is not nearly enough. The economic plight of many developing countries is compounded by their accumulation of a staggering debt to industrial nations like the United States, West Germany, and France, to the point where debt repayment and interest exceed the amount of all new assistance. For example, in 1983 the developing countries were net exporters of capital; their interest payments totaled $52 billion (on all loans to all countries), while their new loans from all sources like the World Bank amounted to just $35 billion. Richard Feinberg of the Overseas Development Council, a research facility that examines problems of developing countries, argues that there is doubt both that some of these Third-World nations can in simple economic terms squeeze enough capital from their economies to service their debts, and that they can pay the domestic political costs of doing so.[22] In May 1984 the presidents of Mexico, Colombia, Brazil, and Argentina issued a joint statement that their capacity to handle their debt burdens was strained to the breaking point: "We do not accept seeing ourselves forced into a situation of insolvency and continuous economic crisis. Our nations cannot indefinitely accept these hazards."

Some Third World countries have circulated draft proposals calling for rescheduling of their debt repayments. Common to these proposals is a grace period, of perhaps 5 years, during which these countries would make no debt payments—giving them time to get back on their feet economically. Western experts who do not accept this solution agree that some major steps must be taken. They suggest, for example, that interests rates might be reduced to the actual cost of the funds being loaned, with the Western banks foregoing their

[22]As cited by Christopher Madison, "Economic Focus," *National Journal*, 23 (June 9, 1984):1145.

normal margin of profit. Whatever steps are taken, the problem of Third World debt will remain a large one. And it reflects an even bigger problem: the gap between the financial resources of rich and poor countries.

East-West conflict and third-world countries

The economic difficulties of the Third World, exacerbated by rapidly expanding populations, are made even more difficult to solve by their being caught up in East-West conflict. Conditions in Central America are a good case in point. Sometimes, in the debate over what U.S. policy in that troubled region should be, the argument is joined as to whether the region's problems are primarily in the form of domestic poverty and injustice, or instead are caused by Soviet, Cuban, and Nicaraguan-backed efforts to undermine established governments through force of arms. But in fact both sides have a point, and the interaction of these two realities compounds the overall problem. Oppressive poverty creates dissatisfactions that can be exploited by outside forces, and the conflict that results, as in El Salvador, makes it harder, not easier, to address some of the underlying economic problems. It is tempting to conclude simply that Third World countries should be disengaged from the conflict of East and West. But the real issue is how that disengagement can be achieved.

FOREIGN- AND DEFENSE-POLICY-MAKERS

Each American policy system has its own distinctive mix of governmental agencies and interest groups. Foreign policy has one special ingredient that separates it from every other policy area: It is the only one in which *foreign governments* are active participants. The United States has established alliances with various foreign countries, the most important of which is NATO. These governments affect aspects of American foreign and defense policy, because the alliances require a common approach and shared responsibilities. Our allies are not the only nations that try to shape American foreign relations. Because the United States plays such a large role in world affairs, what it does or does not do is often of great consequence to many nations, friend and foe alike. And because of the openness of America's democratic decision-making, the world has learned that there are many avenues to influence. Foreign governments have become sophisticated actors in the complex process of American foreign policy formation.

The President: Chief Foreign-Policy-Maker

In no other area of U.S. public policy does the scope of the president's formal authority or the extent of his day-to-day influence approach what it is in the foreign and defense sphere. First, the grant of power given him by the Constitution is greater in foreign policy than elsewhere. Second, there is a special practical need for the president to represent the United States in dealing with other countries and in response to international challenges. Third, while the president must share the foreign policy stage with other actors, the contending agency and group pressures he encounters are less formidable than in any sector of domestic policy.

Constitutional authority in foreign policy

The president's constitutional authority has been described in chapter 8. With regard to American international relations, the grant is especially impressive. The first presidential power explicitly stated by the Constitution makes him "Commander-in-Chief of the Army and Navy of the United States . . ." (Article II, section 2). This section also gives the president authority to make treaties with foreign countries (although the concurrence of the Senate by two-thirds vote is required), and confers upon him authority to appoint the entire American foreign policy establishment, including the heads of what are now the departments of State and Defense, and all U.S. ambassadors to foreign countries.

Still, the president's role would not be as large as it is were the practical necessities of foreign-policy-making not so favorable to presidential assertions. In debates over government's role in managing the economy, or over new social-welfare proposals, the president can hardly claim to embody the needs and interests of the United States. As the popularly elected head of the executive branch, he has a claim to substantial influence. But each of his domestic policy initiatives is only one effort among many; the president can never hope to be more than *primus inter pares*, first among equals. When a foreign crisis occurs, however, or negotiations proceed on an arms limitation treaty, a president can and often does plausibly claim to articulate transcending national interests. Critics of his approach usually grant him greater room to maneuver than they would on any domestic issue.

The power to act in military crises

The contemporary importance of the American military establishment in the country's foreign relations has made the president's constitutional position as commander-in-chief unusually influential. Congress has taken steps over the last decade to reassert its authority in questions of war and peace, but when a military crisis ensues the president alone has a mandate to act with the dispatch and force national security requires. President Kennedy acted forcefully, imposing a military blockade on Cuba, during the missile crisis of 1962, when the Soviet Union placed offensive missiles in Cuba, just 90 miles from the U.S. mainland. And President Reagan sent U.S. troops to the Carribean island of Grenada in October 1983 to prevent the establishment of a Soviet-bloc military base on the island and to protect 1,000 Americans, mostly students, who were in residence there. Much less stands between the president and decisive action in foreign policy than elsewhere. Executive agencies and Congress play key roles, but they typically lack the capacity to block determined presidential initiatives as they can in the domestic-policy spheres. Interest groups try to shape foreign policy, but they are far

President Kennedy (second from right) meeting with the National Security Council on U.S. Air Force reconnaissance photographs of Soviet launch cites in Cuba (below).

less numerous or muscular than their counterparts in the fields of social welfare or economic management. In part the idea of a "national interest," as distinct from contending group interests, is in reality more imposing in foreign policy than anywhere else.

The National Security Council

The most important institutional change made since World War II to provide the president with more assistance in discharging his foreign policy responsibilities was the creation of the National Security Council (NSC). Established by the National Security Act of 1947, the NSC is charged with advising the president "with respect to the integration of domestic, foreign, and military policies relating to the national security." Its membership includes the president as chairman, the vice president, and the secretaries of state and defense. The director of the Central Intelligence Agency and the chairman of the Joint Chiefs of Staff are statutory advisers to the NSC. Heads of other international agencies, such as the United States Information Agency and the Agency for International Development, also participate at times in council activities. So does the president's personal staff; one of these staff positions—the assistant for national security affairs—has become exceptionally prominent, as described below.

How its members participate, and how the council operates generally, are strictly at the president's discretion. The NSC's deliberations and decisions are only advisory to him. Every president since Truman has, however, chosen to make the NSC an important instrument of presidential foreign policy management. As political scientists Charles Kegley, Jr., and Eugene Wittkopf have noted, presidents turn to the council for help in tackling persisting problems confronting presidential leadership in foreign policy: "acquiring information; identifying issues; coping with crisis; making decisions; coordinating actions; and assuring agency performance in accordance with presidential wishes."[23]

NSC as presidential adviser

Since 1961, in John Kennedy's presidency, the National Security Council has been less important as a formal mechanism than as the locus of an enlarged corps of presidential advisers. The impetus for expanding the number and influence of the president's personal foreign policy staff has been basically the same as for augmenting the role of his domestic assistants. The executive establishment has grown so large that if a president confines himself to making the big decisions, then leaves their implementation to the departmental bureaucracies, he is apt to lose effective control over his administration's policy. Key to the expanded role of the NSC staff was the elevation of the president's special assistant for national security affairs, who directs the staff of the NSC. From McGeorge Bundy, Kennedy's national security adviser, through Henry Kissinger (appointed by Richard Nixon), Zbigniew Brzezinski (Jimmy Carter), and William Clark and Robert McFarlane (Ronald Reagan), the national security adviser has played a major part in managing foreign policy; at times his influence has rivaled and even surpassed that of the secretary of state. The security adviser and his NSC staff have been "the president's men" in White House management of American foreign relations.

The national security adviser

[23]Charles W. Kegley, Jr., and Eugene R. Wittkopf, *American Foreign Policy: Pattern and Process* (New York: St. Martin's Press, 1982), p. 329.

Under Kennedy, the NSC staff moved to fill what the president believed was a persisting deficiency of the State Department. As Theodore Sorensen, one of Kennedy's top aides, put it:

> The President was discouraged with the State Department almost as soon as he took office. He felt that it too often seemed to have a built-in inertia which deadened initiative and that its tendency toward excessive delay obscured determination. It spoke with too many voices and too little vigor. It was never clear to the President . . . who was in charge, who was clearly delegated to do what, and why his own policy line seemed consistently to be altered or evaded [at the State Department].[24]

Bundy and his NSC staff became Kennedy's personal foreign policy team.

Under Richard Nixon and his national security adviser, Henry Kissinger, many of the characteristic developments of the Kennedy era were extended further. Providing personal assistance to the president, the NSC staff was enlarged and its day-to-day managerial authority increased. It was the White House, far more than the established departmental bureaucracies of State and Defense, that was shaping, down to considerable detail, U.S. activities in the foreign sphere. Kissinger initially put together a staff of 28 professionals, but the staff grew to 52 by the middle of 1971. Kissinger and his assistants came to manage an elaborate committee system that brought the various departments and agencies involved in U.S. foreign and defense policy under their direct supervision.

The NSC and the State Department

When Henry Kissinger became secretary of state and gave up the post of national security adviser, influence shifted back to the State Department. But the underlying *raison d'être* for a strong assistant for national security affairs and his White House bureaucracy—modern presidents' belief that they need personal staff machinery for managing America's far-flung foreign commitments—has proved to be enduring. In campaigning for the presidency, Jimmy Carter criticized Kissinger and his "Lone Ranger" style as national security adviser. Carter promised to downgrade the NSC staff and return the management of foreign policy to the regular executive departments, especially State. By the end of the Carter presidency, however, security assistant Zbigniew Brzezinski had emerged as the president's principal foreign policy adviser, and a dominant White House role in managing U.S. foreign initiatives was again asserted. The Reagan presidency followed a similar course. At the outset, there was a clear intent to downplay the role of the national security adviser. But again, as the Reagan presidency progressed the management responsibilities of the White House–based NSC staff were expanded—though not to anything approaching what they had been under Kissinger.

[24] Theodore Sorensen, *Kennedy* (New York: Harper and Row, 1965), p. 287.

The Department of State

Among the many departments and agencies of the "foreign affairs government" of the United States, the Department of State bears the broadest formal responsibilities. Its work includes representing the United States in roughly 50 different international organizations, conducting bilateral negotiations on matters large and small with other countries, and formulating policy recommendations in virtually every facet of U.S. foreign relations. To discharge these responsibilities, the department operated (as of April 1983) a network of nearly 300 posts throught the world—including 136 embassies, 12 missions, 67 consulates general, and 31 consulates.[25] Extensive though this seems, the State Department is actually quite small compared to most of the other departmental bureaucracies of the executive branch. It has a staff of roughly 24,000 worldwide, as against over 147,000 for Health and Human Services, and an annual budget (in FY 1984) of about $2.6 billion. Figure 20.4 shows the State Department's principal operating units.

Related agencies   Three other agencies involved in foreign affairs are loosely attached to the State Department: the Arms Control and Disarmament Agency (ACDA), which conducts research on arms control and disarmament policy and negotiates on these subjects with other countries; the United States Information Agency (USIA), which handles cultural and informational activities directed at overseas audiences; and the International Development Cooperation Agency (IDCA), which is responsible for coordinating U.S. economic assistance to developing countries. The Agency for International Development (AID) is the principal operating arm of the IDCA, administering the country's major bilateral aid programs.

The Department of Defense

The Department of Defense (DOD) has the biggest payroll in the United States, with more than two million men and woman on active duty in the armed forces and about one million civilian employees (Figure 20.5). The DOD expended about $221 billion in 1984. Even the physical dimensions of the DOD's headquarters seem to affirm symbolically the department's massive governmental presense. The Pentagon "is one of the largest office buildings in the world, covering, under one roof, 17½ miles of corridors running into and around 83 acres of offices, drafting rooms ... restaurants, auditoriums, dispensaries, banks, a shopping center, a printing plant, and even its own fire department."[26] Even so, the DOD has long since outgrown the building.

[25] For detailed information on the internal organization of the Department of State, see the *United States Government Manual, 1984/85* (Washington, D.C.: Government Printing Office, 1984), p. 383.
[26] C. W. Borklund, *The Department of Defense* (New York: Praeger, 1968), pp. 95–97.

Figure 20.4 **Department of State**

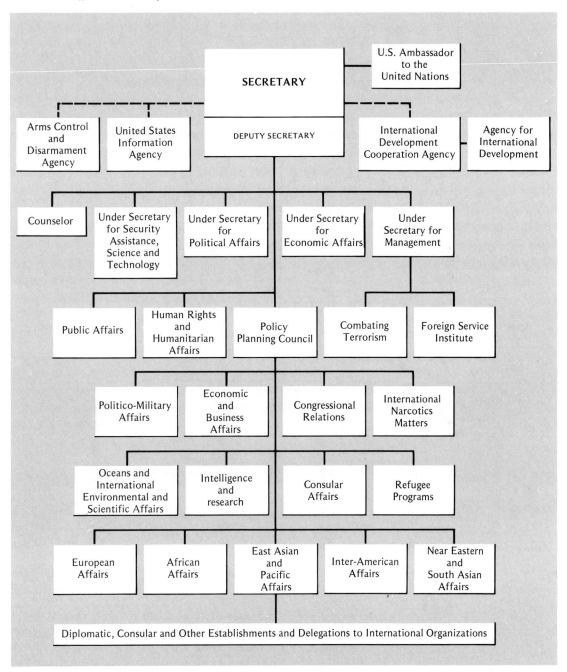

Source: United States Government Manual 1984–85, p. 836.

Figure 20.5   **Department of Defense**

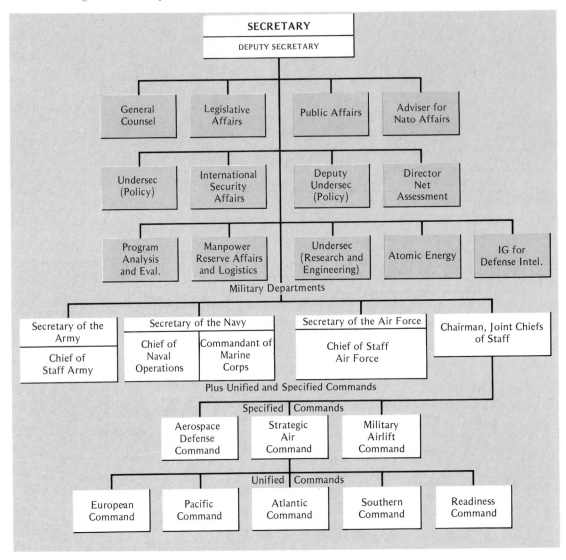

Source: The United States Government Manual 1984–85, p. 824.

Critics worry about the overall role of the Defense Department in American public policy. The sheer number of employees dependent upon the department for their livelihood is itself a source of influence. The total includes not only active-duty military personnel and regular civilian employees, but also millions of other workers indirectly employed through DOD expenditures for weapons, construction, and more. In 1984, the department spent over $64 billion for weapons procurement, $25 billion for research and development, and $4 billion for military construction. Many business corporations and other private organizations are heavily dependent upon DOD decisions. The foreign affairs role of the department is not simply a product of its economic muscle. It also results from the fact that American military power is a primary instrument of the country's foreign policy and international leadership. Adam Yarmolinsky, who served as deputy assistant secretary of defense for international security affairs under Kennedy and Johnson, argued that the central place of military calculations in U.S. foreign policy extends well beyond the intervention of military officials themselves.

> Civilians like [secretaries of state] Dean Acheson, [John Foster] Dulles, and Dean Rusk did not speak lines written for them by the Joint Chiefs or by secretaries of defense. They spoke their convictions in the language most likely to pursuade Congress and the public. They framed their proposals in such a way as to justify open support by military men. It is fair to say that if American foreign policy became partially militarized, the blame should not be laid primarily on the military establishment, but on presidents, civilian policymakers, the Congress, and the American people—and on the situation in which they found themselves.[27]

The joint chiefs of staff

Within each military service, the senior officer is responsible for advising his civilian secretary (the secretaries of the Army, Navy, and Air Force) on military issues and for maintaining the effectiveness of the armed forces under his authority. These military officials—the chief of staff of the Army, the chief of staff of the Air Force, the chief of naval operations, and the commandant of the Marine Corps—constitute collectively the joint chiefs of staff (JCS). The chairman of the JCS is appointed by the president, subject to Senate confirmation, from among the officers of one of the military departments. Drawing on its own staff of some 400 officers, and the ideas and recommendations developed by each branch of the armed forces, the JCS advises the secretary of defense and the president on all military matters relating to national security, such as what weapons systems are needed, military assistance to countries allied to the United States, and plans for industrial mobilization. The service chiefs have not been reluctant to take their views on national security directly to influential members of Congress.

Intelligence Services

The beginnings of a major U.S. effort in foreign intelligence may be traced to the Japanese bombing of Pearl Harbor. The success of that attack revealed gross deficiencies in the country's intelligence gath-

---

[27] Adam Yarmolinsky, *The Military Establishment: Its Impact on American Society* (New York: Harper and Row, 1971), p. 37.

ering and spurred a new emphasis. Today, the United States has a vast and complex network of intelligence agencies that play a large part in foreign affairs. "Intelligence" covers many different activities. While the first image is often that of the spy or covert operator—whether Ian Fleming's daring "007" or John Le Carré's introspective "Smiley"—most intelligence work is highly technical and done far from enemy lines. Whether they are monitoring Russian newspapers and magazines, or analyzing photographs taken by reconnaissance satellites, intelligence agency staffers are usually very different from the stereotypical spy. Popular folklore has it that American intelligence activity is centered in the Central Intelligence Agency (CIA). This is inaccurate. The CIA is an important part of the intelligence community, but it is by no means the largest, either in staff or in budget.

DOD intelligence agencies. The Defense Department does more in the intelligence-gathering area than any other executive agency. Units of the DOD expend over 80 percent of the total intelligence budget. According to data assembled a decade ago by Victor Marchetti and John Marks—former CIA and State Department staff officers—the largest of the DOD intelligence units, Air Force Intelligence, accounted for nearly half of all U.S. intelligence expenditures.[28] Including the National Reconnaissance Office, Air Force Intelligence is responsible for the extremely costly and highly effective surveillance carried out through orbiting satellites. With their sophisticated photographic and electronic equipment, the reconnaissance satellites have become the most basic U.S. source of technical intelligence data.

The National Security Agency (NSA), also in the DOD, is the second largest in the U.S. intelligence community in total budget. It handles "signal intelligence" and "cryptology": code-breaking and code-making. Utilizing highly advanced technology, including elaborate computer systems, the NSA intercepts and interprets messages sent by other countries; it also tries to ensure the security of messages sent by the United States. It does technical work for codes used by the CIA, the FBI, the military services, the State Department, and other federal agencies.

The Central Intelligence Agency. Only about 10 percent of the staff involved in U.S. intelligence activities is in the employ of the Central Intelligence Agency. When the CIA was established in 1947 as the successor to the World War II Office of Strategic Services (OSS), it was intended to integrate many separate pieces of national intelligence-gathering. Over the ensuing years, its coordinating function has diminished. The CIA carries on its major activities within three operating units: the directorates of Intelligence, Science and Technology,

[28] Victor Marchetti and John D. Marks, *The CIA and the Cult of Intelligence* (New York: Knopf, 1974).

and Operations. The first two are devoted principally to intelligence-processing and assessment, and the third to clandestine activities abroad.

The preponderance of intelligence-gathering conducted under CIA auspices involves the straightforward compilation of available information from already-published sources throughout the world. Much of the CIA's expertise is devoted to selecting, translating, interpreting, and assessing this vast accumulation of data. Experts have questioned the quality of the CIA's foreign evaluations. The agency has done its share to contribute to this lack of confidence—as, for example, in 1976, when it dramatically reversed its assessment of the rate of the Soviet Union's military buildup, saying, in effect, that it had been wrong in its calculations of the preceding years, and that the U.S.S.R. was in fact strengthening its military capabilities much faster than had been thought.

Spying and covert operations. It is not, however, the foreign data assessments as much as the clandestine activities that have gotten the CIA into political trouble in the United States and made it a source of public conern. *Clandestine activities* include two different activities: spying of the type that must be done with agents rather than satellites or electronic equipment; and covert operations conducted for or against foreign governments. The CIA's notably unsuccessful orchestration of the "Bay of Pigs" invasion by anti-Castro Cuban exiles in 1961, and the agency's intervention in Iran on behalf of the Shah prior to his downfall in 1979, are much-debated examples of covert operations.

Many Americans have ambivalent feelings about foreign intelligence-gathering. On the one hand, they grant its necessity, given world conditions—and as long as it is carried out through such "antiseptic" technology as reconnaissance satellites, their political objections are moderate. But when it extends to clandestine activites, especially operations against foreign governments, objections mount. Too much of such activity seems undemocratic—but too little seems incautious—imperiling the country's defenses against foreign adversaries.

In the mid-1970s, Congress sought to exert greater control over covert interventions and to reduce their scope. The Hughes-Ryan Amendment to the 1974 Foreign Assistance Act required that the president certify to Congress that he had approved any covert intervention as "important to the national interests of the United States." Congress was to be informed in a "timely manner." In practice, this meant informing House and Senate committees on foreign affairs and foreign relations, appropriations, armed services, and intelligence—so that as many as 200 members of Congress and their staffs could be knowledgeable about impending *secret* operations in foreign countries. By 1980, the pendulum had swung back; the Hughes-Ryan Amendment was repealed, and congressional oversight in the intelli-

Public opinion on covert intelligence operations

Congressional oversight in intelligence operations

gence area was restricted in response to the feeling that in the previous six years the United States had gone too far and had put a "straitjacket" on its covert capabilities. Under the Reagan administration and CIA Director William Casey, the CIA resumed covert operations. Its support in 1983 and 1984 of Nicaraguan rebels brought the agency back into the limelight and prompted renewed criticism. In particular, CIA participation in the mining of Nicaraguan ports to put pressure on the Sandinista government led to charges that the agency was not keeping Congress properly informed about its covert operations, and to a debate over whether the mining was justified. In April 1984, Congress passed a non-binding resolution that no U.S. funds should be used to mine Nicaraguan waters, after administration officials said the mining operation had been stopped.

The director of Central Intelligence is not only the head of the Central Intelligence Agency; he also has general responsibility for coordinating the entire U.S. intelligence community. His limited authority over all intelligence expenditures adds muscle to this role. He is responsible to the National Security Council, and through the NSC to the president.

Other Executive Agencies with Foreign-Policy Responsibilities

The departments of state and defense, the intelligence agencies, and the National Security Council exist primarily to manage American foreign and defense policy. Though they are not as exclusively involved, a number of other executive agencies play substantial parts. The *Treasury Department* is heavily involved in international monetary policy, centering around the position of the U.S. dollar compared to foreign currencies. Treasury also administers multilateral economic assistance, including U.S. contributions through the International Monetary Fund, the International Bank for Reconstruction and Development (World Bank), the Inter-American Development Bank, the Asian Development Bank, and the African Development Fund. The *Commerce Department* participates in international affairs through its role in promoting U.S. commerce abroad. At times this brings it into conflict with other agencies, as when Commerce wants to encourage the sale of "high tech" equipment whose foreign sale the DOD wants to block. The *Office of the United States Trade Representative*, in the Executive Office of the President, directs U.S. participation in trade negotiations with foreign countries. The *Department of Agriculture* has been thrust into a significant foreign policy role by the exceptional productivity of American agriculture. On such issues as grain sales to the Soviet Union, the secretary of agriculture is an influential participant. The department's *Foreign Agriculture Service* administers the Food for Peace program, through which the United States each year channels about a billion dollars of food assistance for humanitarian purposes.

Congress

As with every other component of public policy, foreign-policy-making in the United States is shaped by the checks and balances and separation of powers imbedded in the Constitution. The president is the country's chief foreign-policy-maker, but Congress has great resources to resist him, and its concurrence is necessary if his policies are to succeed. The president negotiates treaties with foreign countries, but Senate approval of those treaties (by two-thirds vote) is required. The president is commander-in-chief of the armed forces, but Congress appropriates the funds needed to pay the troops and build new weapons. When president and Congress generally agree on foreign policy, their interaction does not command much attention. But in periods of sharp disagreement, separation of powers often leads to some incoherence in foreign policy, especially since Congress itself is often divided. The Vietnam War saw president and Congress frequently at odds; so today do questions of U.S. involvement in Central America. Measures such as the War Powers Resolution (see chapter 7) reflect not just a reassertion of congressional authority in foreign affairs but the presence of deep splits over means and ends of U.S. foreign relations.

A few congressional committees and their various subcommittees occupy key positions in the foreign and defense sphere: in the House of Representatives, the appropriations, armed services, and foreign affairs committees; and in the Senate, appropriations, armed services, and foreign relations. The chairmen of these committees, especially of the Senate armed services and foreign relations committees, are often figures of considerable influence in American foreign-policy-making.

Interest Groups

Many of the biggest controversies in U.S. foreign and defense policy grow out of issues where broad national interests, rather than particular group interests, are involved. The benefits thought to accrue from a particular policy are widely distributed across the entire population; the perceived costs are also widely shared. The issue of what response the United States should make to the ferment in Central America is case in point. President Reagan and his advisers argue that the United States should do more militarily to resist communist advances in the region. Many Democrats, including Walter Mondale, Gary Hart, and Jesse Jackson (who were the main contenders for the 1984 Democratic presidential nomination), want to restrict U.S. military activity while emphasizing economic assistance and other cooperative ventures in the region. Both sides insist that the benefits that will accrue from their approach will be general—for example, that the United States will be more secure and better regarded. In such foreign policy disputes, contending interest groups are distinguished by their broad ideological perspectives on what the national interest is and how it is to be served.

Foreign-policy
interest groups

The *Committee on the Present Danger* (CPD) is a foreign-policy interest group committed to strengthening American defense. Founded in 1976, it includes various public figures and foreign-policy intellectuals who believe that Soviet intentions, together with the rapid Soviet military buildup of the last two decades, pose a serious challenge to American security. In the popular idiom, CPD leaders are "hawks" and "hardliners." On the other side, groups such as the National Committee for a Sane Nuclear Policy, Ground Zero, and the Union of Concerned Scientists insist that emphasis on strengthening U.S. military capacity only makes for a more unstable and frightening "balance of terror," increasing the likelihood of war. They stress negotiations to reduce Soviet and U.S. armaments, especially nuclear arms control. Such groups are often called "doves."

Many interest groups, including those whose primary concerns fall outside the foreign and defense sphere, from time to time compete in the ideological battle over the direction of U.S. policy. The AFL-CIO is immediately concerned with the wages and other conditions of employment of American workers. But throughout the years since World War II, AFL-CIO leadership has been highly suspicious of Soviet intentions and supportive of a strong U.S. military presence. Conversely, Common Cause, a public-interest group with a broad agenda of governmental and social reform domestically, has consistently opposed new weapons development. Groups of a generally liberal bent, such as the American Civil Liberties Union and Americans for Democratic Action, often line up against conservative groups like Americans for Conservative Action and the Conservative Caucus on foreign and defense issues.

Concentrated benefits. On other foreign policy and defense issues, the concerns are not general ones of national direction but rather involve specific group interests. Such areas of particular interest-group activity center on (1) issues of American trade and commerce with foreign countries; (2) arguments over particular weapons systems and who will build them; and (3) issues touching on ethnic concerns.

Trade. The world economy has become so interdependent that virtually all sectors of American industry and labor are affected by developments abroad. Inevitably, claims are made on U.S. trade policies. In recent years, for example, the auto industry and the United Automobile Workers of America (UAW) have pushed for import restrictions on Japanese-produced cars, which have gained a large slice of domestic sales. Here, as in so many instances of protectionist demands, trade unions and industry have made a common cause.

Soviet freighter picks up U.S. grain.

Automobile producers are worried about Japanese sales; so too is the UAW, whose workers have lost jobs as the sales of domestic producers have declined.

Organizations representing American farmers, such as the American Farm Bureau Federation and the National Grange, have lobbied energetically for increased sales of U.S. farm products abroad. Sometimes their commitment to increasing sales has brought them into direct conflict with administration policy. The most dramatic recent instance involved U.S. grain sales to the Soviet Union. Following the Soviet invasion of Afghanistan in late 1979, the Carter administration abrogated an agreement which gave the U.S.S.R. the right to purchase U.S. grain. This step may have been sound given broad national interests, but it was very costly to some American farmers, who lost sales to grain producers in other countries and saw their incomes drop when the domestic market became glutted. The farm lobby opposed the Carter grain embargo, and eventually succeeded in getting the Reagan administration to repeal it. It also insisted on a new agreement with the Soviet Union to guarantee that grain sales would not be halted in the next Soviet-U.S. confrontation. The five-year agreement signed by the United States and the U.S.S.R. in the summer of 1983 was in large measure the Reagan administration's response to the farmers' demands.

Weapons. There is continuing argument over how much the United States should spend militarily. But much of the defense lobbying is done by business corporations on behalf of the particular equipment they produce, by unions representing workers in defense industries, and by the cities and states where defense contractors are located. As we saw earlier, the dispute over general defense needs is further complicated by a great deal of particularistic economic interests.

Ethnic group conflicts. As a "nation of nations," the United States has long seen its politics occupied by competing ethnic claims and conflict. This is true in foreign as well as domestic policy. Americans of various ethnic backgrounds often have special interests in matters affecting their mother countries. America's emergence into a far more active role in world affairs in this century naturally enlarged the scope of ethnic-group influence on the country's foreign policy. "As long as the United States remained largely isolated from the conflicts of Europe," Senator Charles Mathias wrote, "ethnic pressures had limited foreign policy impact. . . . After World War I, however, and to a far greater extent after World War II, when the United States acquired world responsibility, ethnic politics took on a new significance."[29]

Since its founding in 1948, the State of Israel has received unstinting support from American Jews, with the American-Israel Public Affairs Committee (AIPAC) especially effective. Founded in 1951, AIPAC has on its executive committee the presidents of virtually all the major U.S. Jewish organizations. A number of factors—from the influential position of American Jews in the country's social and political life, to the widespread sympathy most Americans feel toward Israel as a small, beleaguered democracy—have helped give AIPAC a strong voice in the shaping of U.S. policy in the Middle East.[30]

The work of AIPAC and other Jewish groups on behalf of Israel does not stand alone in the field of ethnic lobbying. As political scientists Thomas Franck and Edward Weisband note, "There are, from time to time, very active Greek, Irish, Chicano, Hungaro-Romanian, Chinese, and other lobbies. Efforts are also underway to mobilize black Americans into an Afro-American lobby which, potentially, could be the most powerful of all."[31] Greek-Americans, working through the American Hellenic Educational Progressive Association (AHEPA) and the American Hellenic Institute Public Affairs Committee (AHIPAC) have had considerable influence on U.S. policies toward Greece and Greece's historic enemy, Turkey. A particularly strong effort by the Greek organizations led Congress to punish Turkey for its invasion of Cyprus in 1974. There being no strong counter-group of Turkish extraction, an embargo was imposed on weapons sales and military assistance to Turkey—against the advice of the president and most

[29]Charles McC. Mathias, Jr., "Ethnic Groups and Foreign Policy," *Foreign Affairs,* Summer 1981, p. 981.
[30]Thomas M. Franck and Edward Weisband, *Foreign Policy by Congress* (New York: Oxford University Press, 1979), p. 186. For a valuable overview of the impact of ethnic attachments on U.S. foreign policy in the twentieth century, see Louis Gerson, *The Hyphenate in Recent American Politics and Diplomacy* (Lawrence, Ks.: University of Kansas Press, 1964).
[31]Franck and Weisband, *Foreign Policy*, p. 187.

congressional leaders of both parties, who thought it would harm Turkish participation in NATO.

Government–interest group interactions. In foreign affairs as on domestic issues, any picture that shows a helpless government being muscled by interest groups is highly misleading. Groups make demands, but often they do so in conjunction with some governmental officials, and even at the officials' behest, to influence other officials. A complete picture shows some groups and parts of the government aligned against other groups and other parts of government in unending battles over policy. The fight in 1977 and 1978 over Senate ratification of the Panama Canal treaties provides a case in point. Recognizing that it faced a major uphill battle to get the necessary 67 senators to vote for ratification of the treaties, the Carter administration took the lead in assembling an impressive coalition of supporting interest groups, ranging from the AFL-CIO to the U.S. Chamber of Commerce. At the same time, senators opposed to ratification worked closely with similarly inclined groups, including the American Legion, the Veterans of Foreign Wars, the American Conservative Union, and the National Conservative Political Action Committee. In this case the administration coalition prevailed: the treaties were ratified, returning the Canal Zone to Panamanian sovereignty.

Lobbying by foreign governments. As noted earlier, two conditions together encourage an enormous amount of lobbying by foreign governments to influence American foreign policy. First, decisions made in the United States matter to many other countries. Second, the United States is a democracy where power is widely dispersed. There are multiple points of entry for any group—foreign or domestic—that wants to affect policy. If a foreign government is unhappy with the president's approach, it may hope to influence public opinion, Congress, or even some executive agencies to help turn those policies around.

Foreign-government lobbying takes all forms, some massive and well-orchestrated, others small and even naive. The Cuban leader Fidel Castro's efforts with the Presidential Commission on Central American Issues is an example of the latter. In the summer of 1983, President Reagan appointed a bipartisan commission to review the situation in Central America and to chart a course for U.S. policy there. Shortly after his appointment to the commission, John Silber, the president of Boston University, reported that he had received a letter and suggestions from Castro, along with a copy of a book Castro had written. Silber assumed that the Cuban dictator had sent similar messages to the other commissioners.[32] Apparently Castro succeeded only in amusing the commission.

---

[32] Interview with John Silber, *Christian Science Monitor,* September 8, 1983, p. 18.

Foreign citizens have big stakes in U.S. policy. Here, West Germans protest the deployment of American Pershing II missiles.

One common approach by foreign governments involves hiring Washington lawyers and public relations firms to conduct lobbying campaigns. The Foreign Agents Registration Act of 1938 (FARA) requires that every agent who engages in political activity in the interest of a foreign government or agency must register with the Justice Department. Foreign diplomats, persons engaged in bona fide commercial activities, and those in international philanthropy or scientific and artistic pursuits are exempted. In 1983, more than 650 agents were registered under FARA. Many of the lawyers and other lobbyists hired by foreign governments are political figures who have held prominent positions in previous administrations. For example, in recent years former Secretary of Defense Clark Clifford has been retained by Algeria; former Attorney General Richard Kleindienst by Algeria; and former Senate Foreign Relations Committee Chairman J. William Fulbright by Saudi Arabia.

Foreign governments also lobby directly through their embassies. And they deal with Congress as well as with executive agencies like the State Department. In many ways, they behave just like well-financed domestic interest groups. The United States government itself engages in lobbying in foreign countries where such activity is possible, but not on the scale that some foreign governments do in the United States.

SUMMARY

At every point in American history, the country has found itself affected by developments beyond its shores. The demands of foreign and defense policy have been unavoidable; the only question has been what policy should be. American foreign policy is conducted within the special constraints of democratic government—which means that it must be open, subject to political competition, and responsive to public opinion. Some observers, from Tocqueville on, have felt that from a purely tactical standpoint democracies are thus put at some disadvantage in their relations with authoritarian governments. The latter can set a course of foreign policy action, commit resources disproportionately to its attainment, be as secretive as is necessary, and persevere in the policy over long periods of time.

The basic approach of the United States to foreign affairs shifted after World War II. The major European powers of the prewar world—Britain, France, and Germany—had been devastated, and they needed to turn inward to reconstruct their own societies. No Western nation besides the United States had the resources to maintain an international balance of power, counterbalancing the Soviet Union, which emerged in 1945 as the dominant power on the Eurasian land mass.

The name attached to the American balance-of-power effort is *containment:* containing the Soviet Union and communist expansion. Pursuing this policy, the United States assisted in the rapid postwar reconstruction of the European democracies, assumed leadership of various military alliances including NATO, maintained a large defense establishment, and committed U.S. troops in response to communist-bloc expansion, as in the invasion of South Korea. Yet while it engaged in these ambitous undertakings, the United States' implementation of containment was on the whole cautious and restrained. American public opinion never supported a crusading stance against the U.S.S.R.

The one major exception in a record of generally cautious and prudent balance-of-power politics came in Vietnam, when the United States committed a half-million troops to a prolonged military effort to block the communist takeover of South Vietnam. As the war proceeded, growing proportions of the American public concluded that the human and material costs of the conflict were excessive. Domestic divisions resulting from the war dominated U.S. politics from the mid-1960s through the mid-1970s.

Among political leaders three different interpretations found substantial support: (1) that the postwar containment policy is sound, and the Vietnam intervention was a necessary if painful application of it; (2) that containment is flawed as a basic policy approach, and Vietnam was a bad application of a bad policy; and (3) that the rationale for containment is sound, but the massive U.S. intervention in Vietnam was ill-conceived.

There is little disagreement in the United States on the need to maintain a strong defense, but there is disagreement on how much is enough, and on what weapons systems are required given considerations of cost and security. U.S. military spending declined significantly during the 1970s, partly as a result of widespread dissatisfaction with the U.S. role in Vietnam. This decline is evident when military expenditures are calculated with controls for the effect of inflation, and when they are expressed as proportions of the GNP and all federal spending. It is also evident when U.S. military spending is compared to that of the U.S.S.R.

Since the late 1970s, however, the pendulum has swung the other way. Concern prompted by the perception of U.S. weakness compared to the U.S.S.R. led to new bipartisan efforts to expand real defense spending. The Reagan administration has strongly supported a defense buildup, and has received the support of Congress for much of what it has proposed.

The National Security Act of 1947 established the National Security Council (NSC) as a key advisory body assisting the president in the conduct of American foreign and defense policy. Besides the president, NSC membership includes the vice president and the secretaries of state and defense. The director of Central Intelligence and the chairman of the joint Chiefs of Staff are statutory advisers to the NSC. The assistant to the president for national security affairs manages the NSC staff and operates as an influential presidential adviser in foreign-policy-making.

Appendix One | The Declaration of Independence

When in the course of human events, it becomes necessary for one people to dissolve the political bands which have connected them with another, and to assume among the Powers of the earth, the separate and equal station to which the Laws of Nature and of Nature's God entitle them, a decent respect to the opinions of mankind requires that they should declare the causes which impel them to the separation.

We hold these truths to be self-evident, that all men are created equal, that they are endowed by their Creator with certain unalienable rights, that among these are Life, Liberty, and the pursuit of Happiness. That to secure these rights, Governments are instituted among Men, deriving their just powers from the consent of the governed. That whenever any Form of Government becomes destructive of these ends, it is the Right of the People to alter or to abolish it, and to institute new Government, laying its foundation on such principles and organizing its powers in such form, as to them shall seem most likely to effect their Safety and Happiness. Prudence, indeed, will dictate that Governments long established should not be changed for light and transient causes; and accordingly all experience hath shown, that mankind are more disposed to suffer, while evils are sufferable, than to right themselves by abolishing the forms to which they are accustomed. But when a long train of abuses and usurpations, pursuing invariably the same Object evinces a design to reduce them under absolute Despotism, it is their right, it is their duty, to throw off such Government, and to provide new Guards for their future security.—Such has been the patient sufferance of these Colonies; and such is now the necessity which constrains them to alter their former Systems of Government. The history of the present King of Great Britain is a history of repeated injuries and usurpations, all having in direct object the establishment of an absolute Tyranny over these States. To prove this, let Facts be submitted to a candid world.

He has refused his Assent to Laws, the most wholesome and necessary for the public good.

He has forbidden his Governors to pass Laws of immediate and pressing importance, unless suspended in their operation till his Assent should be obtained; and when so suspended, he has utterly neglected to attend to them.

He has refused to pass other Laws for the accommodation of large districts of people, unless those people would relinquish the right of Representation in the Legislature, a right inestimable to them and formidable to tyrants only.

He has called together legislative bodies at places unusual, uncomfortable, and distant from the depository of their public Records, for the sole purpose of fatiguing them into compliance with his measures.

He has dissolved Representative Houses repeatedly, for opposing with manly firmness his invasions on the rights of the people.

He has refused for a long time, after such dissolutions, to cause others to be elected; whereby the Legislative powers, incapable of Annihilation, have returned to the People at large for their exercise; the State remaining in the mean time exposed to all dangers of invasion from without, and convulsions within.

He has endeavoured to prevent the population of these States; for that purpose obstructing the Laws of Naturalization of Foreigners; refusing to pass others to encourage their migrations hither, and raising the conditions of new Appropriations of Lands.

He has obstructed the Administration of Justice, by refusing his Asent to Laws for establishing Judiciary powers.

He has made Judges dependent on his Will alone, for the tenure of their offices, and the amount and payment of their salaries.

He has erected a multitude of New Offices, and sent hither swarms of Officers to harass our People, and eat out their substance.

He has kept among us, in times of peace, Standing Armies without the Consent of our legislature.

He has affected to render the Military independent of and superior to the Civil Power.

He has combined with others to subject us to a jurisdiction foreign to our constitution, and unacknowledged by our laws; giving his Assent to their Acts of pretended Legislation:

For quartering large bodies of armed troops among us:

For protecting them, by a mock Trial, from Punishment for any Murders which they should commit on the Inhabitants of these States:

For cutting off our Trade with all parts of the world:

For imposing taxes on us without our Consent:

For depriving us of many cases, of the benefits of Trial by jury:

For transporting us beyond Seas to be tried for pretended offences:

For abolishing the free System of English Laws in a neighbouring Province, establishing therein an Arbitrary government, and enlarging its Boundaries so as to render it at once an example and fit instrument for introducing the same absolute rule into these Colonies:

For taking away our Charters, abolishing our most valuable Laws, and altering fundamentally the Forms of our Governments:

For suspending our own Legislatures, and declaring themselves invested with Power to legislate for us in all cases whatsoever.

He has abdicated Government here, by declaring us out of his Protection and waging War against us.

He has plundered our seas, ravaged our Coasts, burnt our towns, and destroyed the lives of our people.

He is at this time transporting large armies of foreign mercenaries to compleat the works of death, desolation, and tyranny, already begun with circumstances of Cruelty & perfidy scarcely paralleled in the most barbarous ages, and totally unworthy the Head of a civilized nation.

He has constrained our fellow Citizens taken Captive on the high Seas to bear Arms against their Country, to become the executioners of their friends and Brethren, or to fall themselves by their Hands.

He has excited domestic insurrections amongst us, and has endeavoured to bring on the inhabitants of our frontiers, the merciless Indian Savages, whose known rule of warfare, is an undistinguished destruction of all ages, sexes, and conditions.

In every stage of these Oppressions We have Petitioned for Redress in the most humble terms: Our repeated Petitions have been answered only by repeated injury. A Prince, whose character is thus marked by every act which may define a Tyrant, is unfit to be the ruler of a free people.

Nor have We been wanting in attention to our British brethren. We have warned them from time to time of attempts by their legislature to extend an unwarrantable jurisdiction over us. We have reminded them of the circumstances of our emigration and settlement here. We have appealed to their native justice and magnanimity, and we have conjured them by the ties of our common kindred to disavow these usurpations, which, would inevitably interrupt our connections and correspondence. They too must have been deaf to the voice of justice and of consanguinity. We must, therefore, acquiesce in the necessity, which denounces our Separation, and hold them, as we hold the rest of mankind, Enemies in War, in Peace Friends.

WE, THEREFORE, the Representatives of the UNITED STATES OF AMERICA, in General Congress, Assembled, appealing to the Supreme Judge of the world for the rectitude of our intentions, do, in the Name, and by Authority of the good People of these Colonies, solemnly publish and declare, That these United Colonies are, and of Right ought to be FREE AND INDEPENDENT STATES; that they are Absolved from all Allegiance to the British Crown, and that all political connection between them and the State of Great Britain, is and ought to be totally dissolved; and that as Free and Independent States, they have full Power to levy War, conclude Peace, contract Alliances, establish Commerce, and to do all other Acts and Things which Independent States may of right do. And for the support of this Declaration, with a firm reliance on the Protection of Divine Providence, we mutually pledge to each other our Lives, our Fortunes, and our sacred Honor.

The foregoing Declaration was, by order of Congress, engrossed, and signed by the following members:

John Hancock

NEW HAMPSHIRE
Josiah Bartlett
William Whipple
Matthew Thornton

MASSACHUSETTS BAY
Samuel Adams
John Adams
Robert Treat Paine
Elbridge Gerry

RHODE ISLAND
Stephen Hopkins
William Ellery

CONNECTICUT
Roger Sherman
Samuel Huntington
William Williams
Oliver Wolcott

NEW YORK
William Floyd
Philip Livingston
Francis Lewis
Lewis Morris

NEW JERSEY
Richard Stockton
John Witherspoon
Francis Hopkinson
John Hart
Abraham Clark

PENNSYLVANIA
Robert Morris
Benjamin Rush
Benjamin Franklin
John Morton
George Clymer

James Smith
George Taylor
James Wilson
George Ross

DELAWARE
Caesar Rodney
George Read
Thomas M'Kean

MARYLAND
Samuel Chase
William Paca
Thomas Stone
Charles Carroll,
of Carrollton

VIRGINIA
George Wythe
Richard Henry Lee

Thomas Jefferson
Benjamin Harrison
Thomas Nelson, Jr.
Francis Lightfoot Lee
Carter Braxton

NORTH CAROLINA
William Hooper
Joseph Hewes
John Penn

SOUTH CAROLINA
Edward Rutledge
Thomas Heyward, Jr.

Thomas Lynch, Jr.
Arthur Middleton

GEORGIA
Button Gwinnett
Lyman Hall
George Walton

Resolved, That copies of the Declaration be sent to the several assemblies, conventions, and committees, or councils of safety, and to the several commanding officers of the continental troops; that it be proclaimed in each of the United States, at the head of the army.

Appendix Two

The Constitution of the United States

We the People of the United States, in order to form a more perfect Union, establish Justice, insure domestic Tranquility, provide for the common defence, promote the general Welfare, and secure the Blessings of Liberty to ourselves and our Posterity, do ordain and establish this Constitution for the United States of America.

ARTICLE I.

Section 1. All legislative Powers herein granted shall be vested in a Congress of the United States, which shall consist of a Senate and House of Representatives.

Section 2. The House of Representatives shall be composed of Members chosen every second Year by the People of the several States, and the Electors in each State shall have the Qualifications requisite for Electors of the most numerous Branch of the State Legislature.

No Person shall be a Representative who shall not have attained to the Age of twenty five Years, and been seven Years a Citizen of the United States, and who shall not, when elected, be an Inhabitant of that State in which he shall be chosen.

Representatives and direct Taxes shall be apportioned among the several States which may be included within this Union, according to their respective Numbers, which snall be determined by adding to the whole Number of free Persons, including those bound to Service for a Term of Years, and excluding Indians not taxed, three fifths of all other Persons. The actual Enumeration shall be made within three Years after the first Meeting of the Congress of the United States, and within every subsequent Term of ten Years, in such Manner as they shall by Law direct. The Number of Representatives shall not exceed one for every thirty Thousand, but each State shall have at Least one Representative; and until such enumeration shall be made, the State of New Hampshire shall be entitled to chuse three, Massachusetts eight,

Rhode-Island and Providence Plantations one, Connecticut five, New-York six, New Jersey four, Pennsylvania eight, Delaware one, Maryland six, Virginia ten, North Carolina five, South Carolina five, and Georgia three.

When vacancies happen in the Representation from any State, the Executive Authority thereof shall issue Writs of Election to fill such Vacancies.

The House of Representatives shall chuse their Speaker and other Officers; and shall have the sole Power of Impeachment.

Section 3. The Senate of the United States shall be composed of two Senators from each State, chosen by the Legislature thereof, for six Years; and each Senator shall have one Vote.

Immediately after they shall be assembled in Consequence of the first Election, they shall be divided as equally as may be into three Classes. The Seats of the Senators of the first Class shall be vacated at the Expiration of the second Year, of the second Clas at the Expiration of the fourth Year, and of the third Class at the Expiration of the sixth Year, so that one third may be chosen every second Year; and if Vacancies happen by Resignation, or otherwise, during the Recess of the Legislature of any State, the Executive thereof may make temporary Appointments until the next Meeting of the Legislature, which shall then fill such Vacancies.

No Person shall be a Senator who shall not have attained to the Age of thirty Years, and been nine Years a Citizen of the United States, and who shall not, when elected, be an Inhabitant of that State for which he shall be chosen.

The Vice President of the United States shall be President of the Senate, but shall have no Vote, unless they be equally divided.

The Senate shall chuse their other Officers, and also a President pro tempore, in the Absence of the Vice President, or when he shall exercise the Office of President of the United States.

The Senate shall have the sole Power to try all Impeachments. When sitting for that Purpose, they shall be on Oath or Affirmation. When the President of the United States is tried, the Chief Justice shall preside: And no Person shall be convicted without the Concurrence of two thirds of the Members present.

Judgment in Cases of Impeachment shall not extend further than to removal from Office, and disqualification to hold and enjoy any Office of honor, Trust or Profit under the United States: but the Party convicted shall nevertheless be liable and subject to Indictment, Trial, Judgment and Punishment, according to Law.

Section 4. The Times, Places and Manner of holding Elections for Senators and Representatives, shall be prescribed in each State by the Legislature thereof, but the Congress may at any time by Law make or alter such Regulations, except as to the Places of chusing Senators.

The Congress shall assemble at least once in every Year, and such Meeting shall be on the first Monday in December, unless they shall by Law appoint a different Day.

Section 5. Each House shall be the Judge of the Elections, Returns and Qualifications of its own Members, and a Majority of each shall constitute a Quorum to do Business; but a smaller Number may adjourn from day to day, and may be authorized to compel the Attendance of absent Members, in such Manner, and under such Penalties as each House may provide.

Each House may determine the Rules of its Proceedings, punish its Members for disorderly Behaviour, and, with the Concurrence of two thirds, expel a Member.

Each House shall keep a Journal of its Proceedings, and from time to time publish the same, excepting such Parts as may in their Judgment require Secrecy; and the Yeas and Nays of the Members of either House on any question shall, at the Desire of one fifth of those Present, be entered on the Journal.

Neither House, during the Session of Congress, shall, without the Consent of the other, adjourn for more than three days, nor to any other Place than that in which the two Houses shall be sitting.

Section 6. The Senators and Representatives shall receive a Compensation for their Services, to be ascertained by Law, and paid out of the Treasury of the United States. They shall in all Cases, except Treason, Felony and Breach of the Peace, be privileged from Arrest during their Attendance at the Session of their respective Houses, and in going to and returning from the same; and for any Speech or Debate in either House, they shall not be questioned in any other Place.

No Senator or Representative shall, during the Time for which he was elected, be appointed to any civil Office under the Authority of the United States, which shall have been created, or the Emoluments whereof shall have been encreased during such time; and no Person holding any Office under the United States, shall be a Member of either House during his Continuance in Office.

Section 7. All Bills for raising Revenue shall originate in the House of Representatives; but the Senate may propose or concur with Amendments as on other Bills.

Every Bill which shall have passed the House of Representatives and the Senate shall, before it becomes a Law, be presented to the President of the United States; If he approve he shall sign it, but if not he shall return it, with his Objections to that House in which it shall have originated, who shall enter the Objections at large on their Journal, and proceed to reconsider it. If after such Reconsideration two thirds of that House shall agree to pass the Bill, it shall be sent, together with the Objections, to the other House, by which it shall likewise be reconsidered, and if approved by two thirds of that House, it shall become a Law. But in all such Cases the Votes of both Houses shall be determined by yeas and Nays, and the Names of the Persons voting for and against the Bill shall be entered on the Journal of each House respectively. If any Bill shall not be returned by the President within ten Days (Sundays excepted) after it shall have been presented to him, the Same shall be a Law, in like Manner as if he had signed it, unless the Congress by their Adjournment prevent its Return, in which Case it shall not be a Law.

Every Order, Resolution, or Vote to which the Concurrence of the Senate and House of Representatives may be necessary (except on a question of Adjournment) shall be presented to the President of the United States; and before the Same shall take Effect, shall be approved by him, or being disapproved by him, shall be repassed by two thirds of the Senate and House or Representatives, according to the Rules and Limitations prescribed in the Case of a Bill.

Section 8. The Congress shall have Power To lay and collect Taxes, Duties, Imposts and Excises, to pay the Debts and provide for the common Defence and general Welfare of the United States; but all Duties, Imposts and Excises shall be uniform throughout the United States.

To borrow Money on the credit of the United States;

To regulate Commerce with foreign Nations, and among the several States, and with the Indian Tribes;

To establish an uniform Rule of Naturalization, and uniform Laws on the subject of Bankruptcies throughout the United States;

To coin Money, regulate the Value thereof, and of foreign Coin, and fix the Standard of Weights and Measures;

To provide for the Punishment of counterfeiting the Securities and current Coin of the United States;

To establish Post Offices and Post Roads;

To promote the Progress of Science and useful Arts, by securing for limited Times to Authors and Inventors the exclusive Right to their respective Writings and Discoveries;

To constitute Tribunals inferior to the supreme Court;

To define and punish Piracies and Felonies committed on the high Seas, and Offences against the Law of Nations;

To declare War, grant Letters of Marque and Reprisal, and make Rules concerning Captures on Land and Water;

To raise and support Armies, but no Appropriation of Money to that Use shall be for a longer Term than two Years;

To provide and maintain a Navy;

To make Rules for the Government and Regulation of the land and naval Forces;

To provide for calling forth the Militia to execute the Laws of the Union, suppress Insurrections and repel Invasions;

To provide for organizing, arming, and disciplining, the Militia, and for governing such Part of them as may be employed in the Service of the United States, reserving to the States respectively, the Appointment of the Officers, and the Authority of training the Militia according to the discipline prescribed by Congress;

To exercise exclusive Legislation in all Cases whatsoever, over such District (not exceeding ten Miles square) as may, by Cession of particular States, and the Acceptance of Congress, become the Seat of the Government of the United States, and to exercise like Authority over all Places purchased by the Consent of the Legislature of the State in which the Same shall be, for the Erection of Forts, Magazines, Arsenals, dock-Yards, and other needful Buildings;—And

To make all Laws which shall be necessary and proper for carrying into Execution the foregoing Powers, and all other Powers vested by this Constitution in the Government of the United States, or in any Department or Officer thereof.

Section 9. The Migration or Importation of such Persons as any of the States now existing shall think proper to admit, shall not be prohibited by the Congress prior to the Year one thousand eight hundred and eight, but a Tax or duty may be imposed on such Importation, not exceeding ten dollars for each Person.

The Privilege of the Writ of Habeas Corpus shall not be suspended, unless when in Cases of Rebellion or Invasion the public Safety may require it.

No Bill of Attainder or ex post facto Law shall be passed.

No Capitation, or other direct, Tax shall be laid, unless in Proportion to the Census or Enumeration herein before directed to be taken.

No Tax or Duty shall be laid on Articles exported from any State.

No Preference shall be given by any Regulation of Commerce or Revenue to the Ports of one State over those of another; nor shall Vessels bound to, or from, one State, be obliged to enter, clear, or pay Duties in another.

No Money shall be drawn from the Treasury, but in Consequence of Appropriations made by Law, and a regular Statement and Account of the Receipts and Expenditures of all public Money shall be published from time to time.

No Title of Nobility shall be granted by the United States: And no Person holding any Office of Profit or trust under them, shall, without the Consent of the Congress, accept of any present, Emolument, Office, or Title, of any kind whatever, from any King, Prince, or foreign State.

Section 10. No State shall enter into any Treaty, Alliance, or Confederation; grant Letters of Marque and Reprisal; coin Money; emit Bills of Credit; make any Thing but gold and silver Coin a Tender in Payment of Debts; pass any Bill of Attainder, ex post facto Law, or Law impairing the Obligation of Contracts, or grant any Title of Nobility.

No State shall, without the Consent of the Congress, lay any Imposts or Duties on Imports or Exports, except what may be absolutely necessary for executing its inspection Laws: and the net Produce of all Duties and Imposts, laid by any State on Imports or Exports, shall be for the Use of the Treasury of the United States; and all such Laws shall be subject to the Revision and Controul of the Congress.

No State shall, without the Consent of Congress, lay any Duty of Tonnage, keep Troops, or Ships of War in time of Peace, enter into any Agreement or Compact with another State, or with a foreign Power, or engage in War, unless actually invaded, or in such imminent Danger as will not admit of delay.

ARTICLE II.

Section 1. The executive Power shall be vested in a President of the United States of America. He shall hold his Office during the term of four Years, and, together with the Vice President, chosen for the same Term, be elected, as follows

Each State shall appoint, in such Manner as the Legislature thereof may direct, a Number of Electors, equal to the whole Number of Senators and Representatives to which the State may be entitled in the Congress: but no Senator or Representative, or Person holding an Office of Trust or Profit under the United States, shall be appointed an Elector.

The Electors shall meet in their respective States, and vote by Ballot for two Persons, of whom one at least shall not be an Inhabitant of the same State with themselves. and they shall make a List of all the Persons voted for, and of the Number of Votes for each; which List they shall sign and certify, and transmit sealed to the Seat of the Government of the United States, directed to the President of the Senate. The President of the Senate shall, in the Presence of the Senate and House of Representatives, open all the Certificates, and the Votes shall then be counted. The Person having the greatest Number of Votes shall be the President, if such Number be a Majority of the whole Number of electors appointed; and if there be more than one who have such Majority, and have an equal Number of Votes, then the House of Representatives shall immediately chuse by Ballot one of them for President; and if no Person have a Majority, then for the five highest on the List the said House shall in like Manner chuse the President. But in chusing the President, the Votes shall be taken by States, the Representation from each State having one Vote; A quorum for this Purpose shall consist of a Member or Members from two thirds of the States, and a Majority all the States shall be necessary to a Choice. In every Case, after the Choice of the President, the Person having the greatest Number of Votes of the Electors shall be the Vice President. But if there should remain two or more who have equal Votes, the Senate shall chuse from them by Ballot the Vice President.

The Congress may determine the Time of chusing the Electors, and the Day on which they shall give their Votes; which Day shall be the same throughout the United States.

No Person except a natural born Citizen, or a Citizen of the United States, at the time of the Adoption of this Constitution, shall be eligible to the Office of President, neither shall any Person be eligible to that Office who shall not have attained to the Age of thirty five Years, and been fourteen Years a Resident within the United States.

In Case of the Removal of the President from Office, or of his Death, Resignation, or Inability to discharge the Powers and Duties of the said Office, the Same shall devolve on the Vice President, and the Congress may by Law provide for the Case of Removal, Death, Resignation or Inability, both of the President and Vice President, declaring what Officer shall then act as President, and such Officer shall act accordingly, until the Diability be removed, or a President shall be elected.

The President shall, at stated Times, receive for his Services, a Compensation, which shall neither be encreased or diminished during the Period for which he shall have been elected, and he shall not receive within that Period any other Emolument from the United States, or any of them.

Before he enters on the Execution of his Office, he shall take the following Oath or Affirmation:—"I do solemnly swear (or affirm) that I will faithfully execute the Office of President of the United States, and will to the best of my Ability, preserve, protect and defend the Constitution of the United States."

Section 2. The President shall be Commander in Chief of the Army and Navy of the United States, and of the Militia of the several States, when called into the actual Service of the United States; he may require the Opinion, in writing, of the principal Officer in each of the executive Departments, upon any Subject relating to the Duties of their respective Offices, and he shall have Power to grant Reprieves and Pardons for Offences against the United States, except in Cases of Impeachment.

He shall have Power, by and with the Advice and Consent of the Senate, to make Treaties, provided two thirds of the Senators present concur; and he shall nominate, and by and with the Advice and Consent of the Senate, shall appoint Ambassadors, other public Ministers and Consuls, Judges of the supreme Court, and all other officers of the United States, whose Appointments are not herein otherwise provided for, and which shall be established by Law; but the Congress may by Law vest the Appointment of such inferior Officers, as they think proper, in the President alone, in the Courts of Law, or in the Heads of Departments.

The President shall have Power to fill up all Vacancies that may happen during the Recess of the Senate, by granting Commissions which shall expire at the End of their next Session.

Section 3. He shall from time to time give to the Congress Information of the State of the Union, and recommend to their Consideration such Measures as he shall judge necessary and expedient; he may, on extraordinary Occasions, convene both Houses, or either of them, and in Case of Disagreement between them, with Respect to the Time of Adjournment, he may adjourn them to such Time as he shall think proper; he shall receive Ambassadors and other public Ministers; he shall take Care that the Laws be faithfully executed, and shall Commission all the Officers of the United States.

Section 4. The President, Vice President and all civil Officers of the United States, shall be removed from Office on Impeachment for, and Conviction of, Treason, Bribery, or other high Crimes and Misdemeanors.

ARTICLE III.

Section 1. The judicial Power of the United States, shall be vested in one supreme Court, and in such inferior Courts as the Congress may from time to time ordain and establish. The Judges, both of the supreme and inferior Courts, shall hold their Offices during good Behaviour, and shall, at stated Times, receive for their Services, a Compensation, which shall not be diminished during their Continuance in Office.

Section 2. The judicial Power shall extend to all Cases, in Law and Equity, arising under this Constitution, the Laws of the United States, and Treaties made, or which shall be made, under their Authority;—to all Cases affecting Ambassadors, other public Ministers and Consuls;—to all Cases of admiralty and maritime Jurisdiction;—to Controversies to which the United States shall be a Party;—to Controversies between two or more States;—between a State and Citizens of another State;—between Citizens of different States,—between Citizens of the same State claiming Lands under Grants of different States, and between a State, or the Citizens thereof, and foreign States, Citizens or Subjects.

In all cases affecting Ambassadors, other public Ministers and Consuls, and those in which a State shall be Party, the supreme Court shall have original Jurisdiction. In all the other Cases before mentioned, the supreme Court shall have appellate Jurisdiction, both as to Law and Fact, with such Exceptions, and under such Regulations as the Congress shall make.

The Trial of all Crimes, except in Cases of Impeachment, shall be by Jury; and such Trial shall be held in the State where the said Crimes shall have been committed; but when not committed within any State, the Trial shall be at such Place or Places as the Congress may by Law have directed.

Section 3. Treason against the United States, shall consist only in levying War against them, or in adhering to their Enemies, giving them Aid and Comfort. No Person shall be convicted of Treason unless on the Testimony of two Witnesses to the same overt Act, or on Confession in open Court.

The Congress shall have Power to declare the Punishment of Treason, but no Attainder of Treason shall work Corruption of Blood, or Forfeiture except during the Life of the Person attainted.

ARTICLE IV.

Section 1. Full Faith and Credit shall be given in each State to the public Acts, Records, and judicial Proceedings of every other State. And the Congess may by general Laws prescribe the Manner in which such Acts, Records and Proceedings shall be proved, and the Effect thereof.

Section 2. The Citizens of each State shall be entitled to all Privileges and Immunities of Citizens in the several States.

A Person charged in any State with Treason, Felony, or other Crime, who shall flee from Justice, and be found in another State, shall on Demand of the executive Authority of the State from which he fled, be delivered up, to be removed to the State having Jurisdiction of the Crime.

No Person held to Service or Labour in one State, under the Laws thereof, escaping into another, shall, in Consequence of any Law or Regulation therein, be discharged from such Service or Labour, but shall be delivered up on Claim of the Party to whom such Service or Labour may be due.

Section 3. New States may be admitted by the Congress into this Union; but no new State shall be formed or erected within the Jurisdiction of any other State; nor any State be formed by the Junction of two or more States, or Parts of States, without the consent of the Legislatures of the States concerned as well as of the Congress.

The Congress shall have Power to dispose of and make all neeedful Rules and Regulations respecting the Territory or other Property belonging to the United States; and nothing in this Constitution shall be so construed as to Prejudice any Claims of the United States, or of any particular States.

Section 4. The United States shall guarantee to every State in this Union a Republican Form of Government, and shall protect each of them against Invasion; and on Application of the Legislature, or of the Executive (when the Legislature cannot be convened) against domestic Violence.

ARTICLE V.

The Congress, whenever two thirds of both Houses shall deem it necessary, shall propose Amendments to this Constitution, or, on the Application of the Legislatures of two thirds of the several States shall call a Convention for proposing Amendments, which, in either Case, shall be valid to all Intents and Purposes, as Part of this Constitution, when ratified by the Legislatures of three fourths of the several States, or by Conventions in three fourths thereof, as the one or the other Mode of Ratification may be proposed by the Congress; Provided that no Amendment which may be made prior to the Year One thousand eight hundred and eight shall in any Manner affect the first and fourth Clauses in the Ninth Section of the first Article; and that no State, without its Consent, shall be deprived of it's equal Suffrage in the Senate.

ARTICLE VI.

All Debts contracted and Engagements entered into, before the Adoption of this Constitution, shall be as valid against the United States under this Constitution, as under the Confederation.

This Constitution, and the Laws of the United States which shall be made in Pursuance thereof; and all Treaties made, or which shall be made, under the Authority of the United States, shall be the supreme Law of the Land; and the Judges in every State shall be bound thereby, any Thing in the Constitution or Laws of any State to the Contrary notwithstanding.

The Senators and Representatives before mentioned, and the Members of the several State Legislatures, and all executive and judicial Officers, both of the United States and of the several States, shall be bound by Oath or Affirmation, to support this Constitution; but no religious Test shall ever be required as a Qualification to any Office or public Trust under the United States.

ARTICLE VII.

The Ratification of the Conventions of nine States, shall be sufficient for the Establishment of this Constitution between the States so ratifying the Same.

Done in Convention by the Unanimous Consent of the States present the Seventeenth Day of September in the Year of our Lord one thousand seven hundred and Eighty seven and of the Independence of the United States of America the Twelfth. In witness thereof We have hereunto subscribed our Names,

G⁰: WASHINGTON—Presidᵗ and deputy from Virginia

New Hampshire { John Langdon
Nicholas Gilman

Massachusetts { Nathaniel Gorham
Rufus King

Connecticut { Wᵐ Samˡ Johnson
Roger Sherman

New York { Alexander Hamilton

New Jersey { Wil: Livingston
David A. Brearley.
Wᵐ Paterson.
Jona: Dayton

Pennsylvania { B. Franklin
Thomas Mifflin
Robᵗ Morris
Geo. Clymer
Thoˢ. FitzSimons
Jared Ingersoll
James Wilson
Gouv Morris

Delaware { Geo: Read
Gunning Bed-
ford jun
John Dickinson
Richard Bassett
Jaco: Broom

Maryland { James McHenry
Dan of Sᵗ Thoˢ
Jenifer
Danˡ Carroll

Virginia { John Blair—
James Madison Jr.

North Carolina { Wᵐ. Blount
Richᵈ Dobbs
Spaight.
Hu Williamson

South Carolina { J. Rutledge
Charles Cotesworth
Pinckney
Charles Pinckney
Pierce Butler.

Georgia { William Few
Abr Baldwin

Amendments to the Constitution

Articles in addition to, and Amendment of the Constitution of the United States of America, proposed by Congress, and ratified by the Legislatures of the several States, pursuant to the fifth Article of the original Constitution.

AMENDMENT 1.

Congress shall make no law respecting an establishment of religion, or prohibiting the free exercise thereof; or abridging the freedom of speech, or of the press; or the right of the people peaceably to assemble, and to petition the Government for a redress of grievances.

AMENDMENT 2.

A well regulated Militia, being necessary to the security of a free State, the right of the people to keep and bear Arms, shall not be infringed.

AMENDMENT 3.

No Soldier shall, in time of peace be quartered in any house, without the consent of the Owner, nor in time of war, but in a manner to be prescribed by law.

AMENDMENT 4.

The right of the people to be secure in their persons, houses, papers, and effects, against unreasonable searches and seizures, shall not be violated, and no Warrants shall issue, but upon probable cause, supported by Oath or affirmation, and particularly describing the place to be searched, and the persons or things to be seized.

AMENDMENT 5.

No person shall be held to answer for a capital, or otherwise infamous crime, unless on a presentment or indictment of a Grand Jury, except in cases arising in the land or naval forces, or in the Militia, when in actual service in time of War or public danger; nor shall any person be subject for the same offence to be twice put in jeopardy of life or limb; nor shall be compelled in any criminal case to be a witness against himself, nor be deprived of life, liberty, or property, without due process of law; nor shall private property be taken for public use, without just compensation.

AMENDMENT 6.

In all criminal prosecutions, the accused shall enjoy the right to a speedy and public trial, by an impartial jury of the State and district wherein the crime shall have been committed, which district shall have been previously ascertained by law, and to be informed of the nature and cause of the accusation; to be confronted with the witnesses against him; to have compulsory process for obtaining witnesses in his favor, and to have the Assistance of Counsel for his defence.

AMENDMENT 7.

In Suits at common law, where the value in controversy shall exceed twenty dollars, the right of trial by jury shall be preserved, and no fact tried by a jury, shall be otherwise re-examined in any Court of the United States, than according to the rules of the common law.

AMENDMENT 8.

Excessive bail shall not be required, nor excessive fines imposed, nor cruel and unusual punishments inflicted.

AMENDMENT 9.

The enumeration in the Constitution, of certain rights, shall not be construed to deny or disparage others retained by the people.

AMENDMENT 10.

The powers not delegated to the United States by the Constitution, nor prohibited by it to the States, are reserved to the States respectively, or to the people. [Amendments 1–10 **(The Bill of Rights)** ratified, 1791]

AMENDMENT 11.

The Judicial power of the United States shall not be construed to extend to any suit in law or equity, commenced or prosecuted against one of the United States by Citizens of another State, or by Citizens or Subjects of any Foreign State. [ratified, 1795]

AMENDMENT 12.

The Electors shall meet in their respective states, and vote by ballot for President and Vice-President, one of whom, at least, shall not be an inhabitant of the same state with themselves; they shall name in their ballots the person voted for as President, and in distinct ballots the person voted for as Vice-President, and they shall make distinct lists of all persons voted for as President, and of all persons voted for as Vice-President, and of the number of votes for each, which lists they shall sign and certify, and transmit sealed to the seat of the government of the United States, directed to the President of the Senate;—The President of the Senate shall, in the presence of the Senate and House of Representatives, open all the certificates and the votes shall then be counted;—The person having the greatest number of votes for President, shall be the President, if such number be a majority of the whole number of Electors appointed; and if no person have such majority, then from the persons having the highest numbers not exceeding three on the list of those voted for as President, the House of Representatives shall choose immediately, by ballot, the President. But in choosing the President, the votes shall be taken by states, the representation from each state having one vote: a quorum for this purpose shall consist of a member or members from two-thirds of the states, and a majority of all the states shall be necessary to a choice. And if the House of of Representatives shall not choose a President whenever the right of choice shall devolve upon them, before the fourth day of March next following, then the Vice-President shall act as President, as in the case of the death or other constitutional disability of the President.—The person having the greatest number of votes as Vice-President, shall be the Vice-President, if such number be a majority of the whole number of Electors appointed, and if no person have a majority, then from the two highest numbers on the list, the Senate shall choose the Vice-President; a quorum for the purpose shall consist of two-thirds of the whole number of Senators, and a majority of the whole number shall be necessary to a choice. But no person constitutionally ineligible to the office of President shall be eligible to that of Vice-President of the United States. [ratified, 1804]

AMENDMENT 13.

Section 1. Neither slavery not involuntary servitude, except as a punishment for crime whereof the party shall have been duly convicted, shall exist within the United States, or any place subject to their jurisdiction.

Section 2. Congress shall have power to enforce this article by appropriate legislation. [ratified, 1865]

AMENDMENT 14.

Section 1. All persons born or naturalized in the United States, and subject to the jurisdiction thereof, are citizens of the United States and of the State wherein they reside. No State shall make or enforce any law which shall abridge the privileges or immunities of citizens of the United States; nor shall any State deprive any person of life, liberty, or property, without due process of law; not deny to any person within its jurisdiction the equal protection of the laws.

Section 2. Representatives shall be apportioned among the several States according to their respective numbers, counting the whole number of persons in each State, excluding Indians not taxed. But when the right to vote at any election for the choice of electors for President and Vice President of the United States, Representatives in Congress, the Executive and Judicial officers of a State, or the members of the Legislature thereof, is denied to any of the male inhabitants of such State, being twenty-one years of age, and citizens of the United States, or in any way abridged, except for participation in rebellion, or other crime, the basis of representation therein shall be reduced in the proportion which the number of such male citizens shall bear to the whole number of male citizens twenty-one years of age in such State.

Section 3. No person shall be a Senator or Representative in Congress, or elector of President and Vice President, or hold any office, civil or military, under the United States, or under any State, who, having previously taken an oath, as a member of Congress, or as an officer of the United States, or as a member of any State legislature, or as an executive or judicial officer of any State, to support the Constitution of the United States, shall have engaged in insurrection or rebellion against the same, or given aid or comfort to the enemies thereof. But Congress may by a vote of two-thirds of each House, remove such disability.

Section 4. The validity of the public debt of the United States, authorized by law, including debts incurred for payment of pensions and bounties for services in suppressing insurrection or rebellion, shall not be questioned. But neither the United States nor any State shall assume or pay any debt or obligation incurred in aid of insurrection or rebellion against the United States, or any claim for the loss or emancipation of any slave; but all such debts, obligations and claims shall be held illegal and void.

Section 5. The Congress shall have power to enforce, by appropriate legislation, the provisions of this article. [ratified, 1868]

AMENDMENT 15.

Section 1. The right of citizens of the United States to vote shall not be denied or abridged by the United States or by any State on account of race, color, or previous condition of servitude.

Section 2. The Congress shall have power to enforce this article by appropriate legislation. [ratified, 1870]

AMENDMENT 16.

The Congress shall have power to lay and collect taxes on incomes, from whatever source derived, without apportionment among the several States, and without regard to any census or enumeration. [ratified, 1913]

Amendment 17.

The Senate of the United States shall be composed of two senators from each State, elected by the people thereof, for six years; and each Senator shall have one vote. The electors in each State shall have the qualifications requisite for electors of the most numerous branch of the State legislature.

When vacancies happen in the representation of any State in the Senate, the executive authority of such State shall issue writs of election to fill such vacancies: *Provided,* That the legislature of any State may empower the executive thereof to make temporary appointments until the people fill the vacancies by election as the legislature may direct.

This amendment shall not be so construed as to affect the election or term of any senator chosen before it becomes valid as part of the Constitution. [ratified, 1913]

Amendment 18.

After one year from the ratification of this article, the manufacture, sale, or transportation of intoxicating liquors within, the importation thereof into, or the exportation thereof from the United States and all territory subject to the jurisdiction thereof for beverage purposes is hereby prohibited.

The Congress and the several States shall have concurrent power to enforce this article by appropriate legislation.

This article shall be inoperative unless it shall have been ratified as an amendment to the Constitution by the legislatures of the several States, as provided in the Constitution, within seven years from the date of the submission thereof to the States by Congress. [ratified, 1919]

Amendment 19.

The right of citizens of the United States to vote shall not be denied or abridged by the United States or by any State on account of sex.

The Congress shall have power by appropriate legislation to enforce the provisions of this article. [ratified, 1920]

Amendment 20.

Section 1. The terms of the President and Vice-President shall end at noon on the twentieth day of January, and the terms of Senators and Representatives at noon on the third day of January, of the years in which such terms would have ended if this article had not been ratified; and the terms of their successors shall then begin.

Section 2. The Congress shall assemble at least once in every year, and such meeting shall begin at noon on the third day of January, unless they shall by law appoint a different day.

Section 3. If, at the time fixed for the beginning of the term of the President, the President-elect shall have died, the Vice-President-elect shall become President. If a President shall not have been chosen before the time fixed for the beginning of his term, or if the President-elect shall have failed to qualify, then the Vice-President-elect shall act as President until a President shall have qualified; and the Congress may by law provide for the case wherein neither a President-elect nor a Vice-President-elect shall have qualified, declaring who shall then act as President, or the manner in which one who is to act shall be selected, and such person shall act accordingly until a President or Vice-President shall have qualified.

Section 4. The Congress may by law provide for the case of the death of any of the persons from whom the House of Representatives may choose a President whenever the right of choice shall have devolved upon them, and for the case of the death of any of the persons from whom the Senate may choose a Vice-President whenever the right of choice shall have devolved upon them.

Section 5. Sections 1 and 2 shall take effect on the 15th day of October following the ratification of this article.

Section 6. This article shall be inoperative unless it shall have been ratified as an amendment to the Constitution by the legislatures of three-fourths of the several States within seven years from the date of its submission. [ratified, 1933]

Amendment 21.

Section 1. The eighteenth article of amendment to the Constitution of the United States is hereby repealed.

Section 2. The transportation or importation into any State, Territory or possession of the United States for delivery or use therein of intoxicating liquors, in violation of the laws thereof, is hereby prohibited.

Section 3. This article shall be inoperative unless it shall have been ratified as an amendment to the Constitution by convention in the several States, as provided in the Constitution, within seven years from the date of the submission thereof to the States by the Congress. [ratified, 1933]

Amendment 22.

Section 1. No person shall be elected to the office of the President more than twice, and no person who has held the office of President, or acted as President, for more than two years of a term to which some other person was elected President shall be elected to the office of the President more than once. But this Article shall not apply to any person holding the office of President when this Article was proposed by the Congress, and shall not prevent any person who may be holding the office of President, or acting as President, during the term within which this Article becomes operative from holding the office of President or acting as President during the remainder of such term.

Section 2. This article shall be inoperative unless it shall have been ratified as an amendment to the Constitution by the legislatures of three-fourths of the several States within seven years from the date of its submission to the States by the Congress. [ratified, 1951]

Amendment 23.

Section 1. The District constituting the seat of government of the United States shall appoint in such manner as the Congress may direct:

A number of electors of President and Vice-President equal to the whole number of Senators and Representatives in Congress to which the District would be entitled if it were a State, but in no event more than the least populous State; they shall be in addition to those appointed by the States, but they shall be considered, for the purposes of the election of President and Vice-President, to be electors appointed by a State; and they shall meet in the District and perform such duties as provided by the twelfth article of amendment.

Section 2. The Congress shall have the power to enforce this article by appropriate legislation. [ratified, 1961]

Amendment 24.

Section 1. The right of citizens of the United States to vote in any primary or other election for President or Vice President, for electors for President or Vice President, or for Senator or Representative in Congress, shall not be denied or abridged by the United States or any State by reason of failure to pay any poll tax or other tax.

Section 2. The Congress shall have power to enforce this article by appropriate legislation. [ratified, 1964]

Amendment 25.

Section 1. In case of the removal of the President from office or of his death or resignation, the Vice President shall become President.

Section 2. Whenever there is a vacancy in the office of Vice President, the President shall nominate a Vice President who shall take office upon confirmation by a majority vote of both Houses of Congress.

Section 3. Whenever the President transmits to the President pro tempore of the Senate and the Speaker of the House of Representatives his written declaration that he is unable to discharge the powers and duties of his office, and until he transmits to them a written declaration to the contrary, such powers and duties shall be discharged by the Vice President as Acting President.

Section 4. Whenever the Vice President and a majority of either the principal officers of the executive departments or of such other body as Congress may by law provide, transmit to the President pro tempore of the Senate and the Speaker of the House of Representatives their written declaration that the President is unable to discharge the powers and duties of his office, the Vice President shall immediately assume the powers and duties of the office as Acting President.

Thereafter, when the President transmits to the President pro tempore of the Senate and the Speaker of the House of Representatives his written declaration that no inability exists, he shall resume the powers and duties of his office unless the Vice President and a majority of either the principal officers of the executive departments or of such other body as Congress may by law provide, transmit within four days to the President pro tempore of the Senate and the Speaker of the House of Representatives their written declaration that the President is unable to discharge the powers and duties of his office. Thereupon Congress shall decide the issue, assembling within forty-eight hours for that purpose if not in session. If the Congress, within twenty-one days after receipt of the latter written declaration, or, if Congress is not in session, within twenty-one days after Congress is required to assemble, determines by two-thirds vote of both Houses that the President is unable to discharge the powers and duties of his office, the Vice President shall continue to discharge the same as Acting President; otherwise, the President shall resume the powers and duties of his office. [ratified, 1967]

Amendment 26.

Section 1. The right of citizens of the United States, who are eighteen years of age or older, to vote shall not be denied or abridged by the United States or by any State on account of age.

Section 2. The Congress shall have power to enforce this article by appropriate legislation. [ratified, 1971]

Glossary

This glossary is intended to serve as a learning aid. Short definitions are given for all **boldface terms** in the text and other terms common to discussions of American government and politics. These may help you focus on particular terms, but for a full explanation, it is best to consult the text discussion. Some listings in the glossary reflect ideas in the text, though are not necessarily named as such. Text chapter and page references accompany each entry in the glossary.

activists Persons highly involved in politics, for example, by running for public office, working in campaigns, contributing time and money to political causes, etc. *[Ch. 6, pp. 103–6; Ch. 13, pp. 357–59]*

affirmative action A plan or program involving active efforts to overcome past discrimination based on race, ethnicity, or sex, through recruiting more students from the groups that have been discriminated against in the past or by extending employment opportunities to members of these groups. *[Ch. 17, p. 532]*

affluent society A society where national wealth is such that most people are decisively removed from concerns over having enough food, or adequate clothing and shelter. The economic advances in the United States after World War II left much of the country's population clearly beyond subsistence concerns. *[Ch. 2, p. 28]*

amendment Formal changes made in the language of a constitution, or of a piece of legislation. The Constitution of the United States has been amended 26 times since the basic document was ratified in 1789. *[Ch. 5, p. 86; Ch. 6, p. 99; Ch. 11, p. 277]*

American exceptionalism The idea, shared by many Americans since the eighteenth century, that their country possessed unique resources, opportunity, and promise. Sociologist Daniel Bell describes the idea: "Having a common political faith from the start, [America] would escape the ideological vicissitudes and divisive passions of the European polity, and, being entirely a middle-class society . . . it would not become 'decadent' as had every other society in history." *[Ch. 5, p. 74]*

amicus curiae (briefs) This Latin term means literally "friend of the court." Individuals or groups, not direct parties to a law suit, sometimes seek to influence the court's judgment by filing a brief—a written argument—setting forth the issues in the case as the group sees them. *[Ch. 13, p. 378; Ch. 17, p. 535]*

anti-federalists Americans who were against adoption of the new Constitution in 1787 and 1788, on the grounds that it established too strong a central government, one which would threaten individual and states' rights. Among the leading anti-federalists were George Mason, Richard Henry Lee, and Patrick Henry of Virginia, and George Clinton and Robert Yates of New York. *[Ch. 5, p. 85]*

appeal A formal legal proceeding in which a party losing a case in a lower court requests a higher court to review aspects of the decision. More specifically, the term refers to cases that may be brought to the U.S. Supreme Court—the country's highest court of appeals—as a matter of right; this includes cases where legislation is declared unconstitutional. Such cases must be heard by the Supreme Court "on appeal." *[Ch. 10, p. 260]*

appellate jurisdiction Judicial authority to review lower court decisions. The Supreme Court and the federal circuit courts of appeal have appellate jurisdiction, and all states have appeals courts to review decisions of lower state courts. *[Ch. 10, p. 259]*

appropriations bills Measures enacted by legislatures granting funds for governmental programs and agencies. Appropriations committees of the House and Senate of the U.S. Congress have the responsibility of drafting appropriations bills for the federal government. *[Ch. 7, p. 148]*

aristocracy The hereditary ruling class in societies built on the premise of ascribing or determining social position by birth. *[Ch. 4, pp. 65, 67; Ch. 5, p. 83]*

Articles of Confederation The first constitution of the United States, agreed to by the thirteen original states as the basis for their joint government. Drafted in 1776, the Articles were not ratified by all the states until 1781; they were replaced in 1789 by the United States Constitution. *[Ch. 5, p. 76]*

balance of power In international relations, a relationship where opposing alliances of countries are sufficiently equal that no nation or bloc is able to impose itself on the others. Countries have sometimes sought to maintain an international balance or equilibrium—as Great Britain did in the nineteenth and early twentieth centuries. *[Ch. 20, p. 639]*

bicameralism Refers to a two-house legislature, in contrast to unicameralism, where there is only one house to a legislature. The United States Congress is bicameral, composed of the Senate and House of Representatives, and every American state legislature is bicameral with the exception of Nebraska, which is unicameral. *[Ch. 7, p. 119]*

bilateral aid Foreign economic or military assistance given directly by one government to another. In contrast, multilateral assistance is contributed by a number of countries to some international body, like the United Nations or the World Bank, which then distributes the assistance to less developed nations. *[Ch. 20, p. 664]*

bill of attainder An act of a legislature declaring the guilt of an individual or a group and prescribing punishment without judicial proceedings. Sections 9 and 10 of Article I of the U.S. Constitution forbid Congress and the state legislatures from enacting bills of attainder. *[Ch. 11, pp. 279]*

Bill of Rights The first ten amendments to the U.S. Constitution, ratified in 1791, guaranteeing freedom of speech, assembly, religion, and specifying rights of persons accused of crimes. *[Ch. 5, p. 86]*

bipartism A party system where competition for elective office is largely between two contending parties. The United States, where the Democrats and the Republicans dominate government at all levels, is a prime case of bipartism. *[Ch. 15, p. 437]*

block grants Grants to state and local governments for services in broad program areas. Block grants may be used at the discretion of state and local officials, as long as certain general requirements set by the federal government are met. *[Ch. 11, p. 296]*

boycott An organized effort to achieve a social, economic, or political objective by refusing to deal with a person, organization, or nation seen as the offending party. Civil rights groups have urged their supporters to boycott products of corporations they consider unsupportive of civil rights objectives, such as equal employment opportunity. *[Ch. 17, p. 518]*

bureaucracy Literally, rule by bureaus or by groups of appointed officials. The term now connotes an administrative system—governmental or private—that carries out policy through standardized procedures and is based on a specialization of duties. This term also sometimes connotes excessive growth and red tape in administrative agencies. *[Ch. 2, p. 27; Ch. 9, p. 211]*

bureaus The major working units of governmental departments or agencies. Bureaus like the Public Health Service of the federal Department of Health and Human Services and the Bureau of Indian Affairs of the Department of the Interior have primary program responsibilities in their respective areas. *[Ch. 9, p. 211]*

cabinet The heads (secretaries) of the thirteen executive departments granted senior status for the breadth and importance of their program responsibilities form an informal group known as the president's cabinet. In parliamentary systems, cabinets have formal statutory responsibilities: the cabinet is collectively the government. *[Ch. 9, p. 205; Ch. 7, p. 119]*

calendar In a legislature, a schedule containing all bills to be considered. In the House of Representatives, when a committee reports out a bill, it is placed on one of five calendars: *union*, for appropriations and revenue legislation; *House*, for nonfiscal public bills; *consent*, for noncontroversial measures; *private*, for legislative measures dealing with specific individuals or groups; and *discharge*, for petitions to remove committees from their jurisdiction over a legislative measure. *[Ch. 7, p. 123]*

capitalism An economic philosophy or type of economy based on private property, in which prices are set in the market place on the basis of supply and demand. *[Ch. 4, p. 60; Ch. 18, p. 558]*

categorical grants Grant funds made available by the federal government to state or local governments for a specifically described category of services. Grants to the states for highway construction are an early, and still important, case of categorical grants-in-aid. *[Ch. 11, p. 295]*

caucus A legislative caucus is the meeting of all members of a political party in a legislature to pick party leaders or decide the party's position on proposed legislation. A nominating caucus, on the other hand, is a meeting of party officials or members to select candidates for an upcoming election. *[Ch. 7, p. 139; Ch. 14, p. 409]*

censorship Governmental restraint on speech or other forms of expression. Supreme Court rulings have distinguished between censorship in the case of political speech (justified in only the most extreme circumstances) and that of certain forms of nonpolitical expression, such as material that might be deemed pornographic (where some forms of censorship can be more readily defended). *[Ch. 17, p. 543]*

certiorari, writ of An order issued by an appeals court to a lower court to transmit the records of a case for review. Most of the cases heard by the U.S. Supreme Court reach it through *writs of certiorari*, authorized by the Judiciary Act of 1925. When at least four of the nine justices conclude a case should be reviewed, *certiorari* is granted. *[Ch. 10, p. 259]*

checks and balances In the American system, the constitutional grant of authority to the executive, legislative, and judicial branches such that each can limit actions of the other. Examples include the president's authority to veto legislation passed by Congress and the Supreme Court's power to invalidate acts of both the executive and legislative branches on grounds of their unconstitutionality. *[Ch. 5, p. 83]*

civil liberties The rights of individuals to the freedoms of expression specified in the First Amendment, and to protection when they are accused of crimes. Civil liberties problems typically involve persons made unpopular by their individual beliefs or actions—rather than by attributes of birth like race or sex. *[Ch. 17, pp. 510–11]*

civil rights For a long time synonymous with the claims of black Americans for nondiscrimination and equal treatment under the laws, civil rights is now seen to encompass all groups in the population that have encountered categoric discrimination, such as other ethnic minorities and women. Membership in groups subject to this kind of discrimination is

something over which individuals have no control. *[Ch. 17, pp. 510–11]*

civil service Civilian employees of government who gain their employment through the nonpolitical standards and tests of a merit system. A civil service took shape in the United States following legislative reforms of the late nineteenth century that were designed to end the "spoils system," under which most government workers were political appointees. *[Ch. 9, pp. 226, 230]*

class-action suits A lawsuit brought by an individual or group on behalf of all individuals who share a similar grievance. The famous school desegregation case, *Brown v. Board of Education of Topeka, Kansas* (1954), is an example; it was brought not just on behalf of Linda Brown but for all black students in the Topeka public schools. *[Ch. 10, p. 261]*

class conflict Political conflict organized around the contending interests of social classes—such as "capitalists," or business class, and "proletariats," or working class. The term connotes strong tensions or fundamental disagreements among the main economic groups making up the society. *[Ch. 2, p. 33; Ch. 4, p. 72]*

classical liberalism A broad political ideology that developed in Europe in the seventeenth and eighteenth centuries, brought to the United States by the early settlers, and still the dominant cluster of underlying American political beliefs. A strong individualism is central to classical liberalism, including an emphasis on individual rights, political liberty, private property, and a minimum of restraint by government. *[Ch. 4, p. 63]*

"clear and present danger" First propounded by Supreme Court Justice Oliver Wendell Holmes, Jr. in *Schenck v. United States* (1919), this test has been variously applied by the Court to determine the permissible boundaries under which speech may be restricted: "The question in every case is whether the words used are used in such circumstances and are of such a nature as to create a clear and present danger that they bring about the substantive evils that Congress has a right to prevent." *[Ch. 17, pp. 540–42]*

closed primaries Elections in which rank-and-file party members choose the party's nominees, with the requirement that party adherence must be avowed before they can participate. For example, only declared Democrats can vote in a closed Democratic primary. *[Ch. 14, p. 408]*

cloture A parliamentary procedure used to end debate in a legislative body which, like the U.S. Senate, provides in its general rules for unlimited debate. Senate Rule 22 provides that if a petition to end debate on a measure is approved by three-fifths of the Senate (60 senators), no senator may thereafter speak on it for more than one hour. Cloture is necessary because the right to extended debate is sometimes used by legislative minorities to "talk a bill to death." See filibuster. *[Ch. 7, p. 121]*

coalition The coming together of various parties, groups, or political interests to advance shared political objectives. Each of the two major political parties in the United States is a heterogeneous coalition of political interests united to win governmental power *[Ch. 15, pp. 434, 443]*

coattails The capacity of a popular candidate at the head of a party's slate to draw votes for other party candidates on the same ballot. For example, the strong backing for Ronald Reagan in his run for reelection as president in 1984 brought some votes to Republican candidates for Congress and for state and local office that they otherwise would not have had. Many observers think the "coattails effect" is generally weaker now than in the past, because more voters are inclined to split their tickets. *[Ch. 15, pp. 465–66]*

cold war The prolonged rivalry and conflict in the years since World War II between the Western democracies and the Communist countries; it is called "cold" because the conflict typically has not extended to the battlefield, has not involved open or "hot" warfare. *[Ch. 20, p. 642]*

commerce clause Article I, Section 8 of the Constitution gives Congress the power "to regulate commerce with foreign nations, and among the several states, and with Indian tribes." Historically, much federal government intervention in domestic economic affairs has been justified on the grounds that the regulation of some facet of interstate commerce was involved. *[Ch. 5, p. 30]*

"Committees of Correspondence" When political parties took shape in the United States in the 1790s, one of the first steps was the establishment of "Corresponding Committees" in support of candidates. These committees were usually appointed for the purpose of helping to elect a favored candidate. Through them, like-minded people in various communities around a state kept in contact and formed a political network. *[Ch. 15, p. 434]*

comparable worth A doctrine or policy perspective advanced with the support of women's groups and some trade unions to remedy inequities in the compensation levels for jobs held disproportionately by women. The doctrine of comparable worth holds that employers should be forbidden from paying employees of one sex at a rate less than that paid employees of the opposite sex for work of "comparable character" on jobs which require "comparable skills." It thus differs significantly from the idea of *"equal* pay for *equal* work," which holds only that men and women must not be paid differently for performing the same job. *[Ch. 17, pp. 543–47]*

concurrent jurisdiction Authority granted to two or more courts to adjudicate cases involving the same subject matter. The term commonly refers to areas where federal and state courts may hear the same kind of case. *[Ch. 10, p. 258]*

confederation An association of independent states, in which the latter agree to confer certain limited authority upon a central government while retaining their full individual sovereignty. The first Constitution of the United States, the Articles of Confederation, provided for such a system; the thirteen states possessed virtually all governmental power, having simply joined together in what the Articles called a "firm league of friendship." *[Ch. 11, p. 273]*

conference committees Special joint committees of the U.S. Congress formed to resolve conflicts in the form of legislation passed by the House and Senate. Since a bill must be passed by both houses in exactly the same form for it to become law, conference committees are essential elements in the legislative process. *[Ch. 7, p. 125]*

conservative As used in the contemporary United States, a political philosophy that seeks to limit the role of government in domestic affairs and/or to encourage traditional social values and relationships. In foreign affairs, the term connotes an inclination to favor high levels of defense spending and a "hard-line" foreign policy toward the Soviet Union. *[Ch. 15, p. 438; Ch. 20, p. 650]*

constant dollars The price of goods and services expressed in dollars adjusted to account for the effects of inflation—that is, dollars of constant purchasing power. Unless constant dollar adjustments are made, comparisons of expenditures at one point in time to those at another may be very deceiving. *[Ch. 20, p. 653]*

Constitution A fundamental law that prescribes the framework of government and the nature and extent of governmental authority. The American Constitution treats only the most basic institutional arrangements and powers, and the basic rights of citizenship, leaving it to simple legislation to specify the program details. *[Ch. 5, p. 73]*

containment policy American foreign policy since World War II, aimed at maintaining an international balance of power and curbing the Soviet or Communist expansion. *[Ch. 20, p. 639]*

Court-packing plan The famous attempt by President Franklin Roosevelt in 1937 to secure congressional approval of legislation permitting the president to nominate a new Supreme Court justice for every sitting justice on the Court who, upon reaching 70 years of age, did not retire. Congress rejected Roosevelt's proposal. *[Ch. 8, pp. 163, 164]*

dealignment The weakening of voters' loyalties to the political parties, expressed in larger proportions of the electorate calling themselves independents and alternating in their support of one party's candidates and the other's. *[Ch. 15, p. 453]*

***de facto* segregation** Racial segregation in schools resulting not from public policy or design but from the fact of racial concentrations in residence. Thus, if pupils attend schools in their neighborhoods, and the neighborhoods are virtually all black, or all white, school segregation will in fact occur. *[Ch. 17, p. 536]*

deficit The amount by which governmental expenditures exceed revenues. *[Ch. 18, p. 565]*

deflation An economic condition in which the price of goods and services falls—as opposed to *inflation*, which is a rise in the price level. In the 1920s and the 1930s in the United States, there was a dramatic decline in prices, which discouraged investment in new factories and other productive facilities, as businessmen saw the prospect of falling returns on their investment. *[Ch. 18, p. 561]*

***de jure* segregation** Racial segregation based on the law or the formal policies of governmental agencies. Up until the school desegregation decisions of the 1950s, laws throughout the South provided for separate school systems for black and white pupils. *[Ch. 17, p. 522]*

democracy Derived from the Greek words *demos* (the people) and *kratos* (authority), democracy is a system of government in which ultimate political power rests with the public at large. The American idea of democracy blends rule by the people with an emphasis on the recognition of basic rights of minorities which even strong popular majorities may not infringe. *[Ch. 6, p. 94]*

depression A severe economic slump including high unemployment, a reduced production of goods and services, and a falling national income. The worst of these economic crises in the U.S., known as the Great Depression, began with the stock market crash in 1929 and persisted throughout the 1930s. *[Ch. 18, pp. 560–63]*

deregulation The political movement in the United States in the 1970s and 1980s to reduce the level of governmental regulation, especially of prices and the entry of firms into various markets. Deregulation has proceeded furthest in such industries as trucking, airlines, and banking. *[Ch. 18, p. 576]*

détente A description of efforts to reduce tensions between countries whose contending interests and philosophies leave them antagonistic; specifically, the emphasis on limited cooperation between the United States and the Soviet Union in an effort to reduce the likelihood of overt conflict between the superpowers. *[Ch. 20, p. 646]*

direct-action protests Civil rights marches, sit-ins, boycotts, and other nonviolent actions aimed at overturning segregation and gross discrimination, especially in the American South in the 1950s and 1960s. *[Ch. 17, p. 518]*

direct primary An election in which rank-and-file members of a political party vote to determine who the party's nominees will be. Direct primaries were advanced by the Progressives in the early nineteenth century to weaken the hold of party "bosses" on nominee selection. *[Ch. 6, p. 101]*

discharge petition A legislative procedure, used in the House of Representatives, whereby a committee with jurisdiction over a bill may be relieved of its jurisdiction by majority vote of the entire House. The procedure is used when a committee is seeking to kill a bill by holding on to it and not reporting it out for House action. *[Ch. 7, p. 123]*

discount rate The rate of interest Federal Reserve Banks charge commercial banks for the money the latter borrow from the Fed; the higher the discount rate, the higher the rate of interest commercial banks must in turn charge their customers. *[Ch. 18, p. 587]*

dissenting opinion When judges of appeals courts disagree with a decision of their court's majority, they may express their formal written disagreement. Strong, cogent dissenting opinions by Supreme Court justices have often had lasting influence in helping to reshape thinking on an issue. *[Ch. 10, p. 242]*

district courts (federal) The courts where most cases originating in the federal system are first tried. Federal district courts have "original jurisdiction," as the workhorse trial courts. *[Ch. 10, p. 254]*

double jeopardy The Fifth Amendment to the U.S. Constitution provides that no person shall be "subject for the same offense to be twice put in jeopardy of life or limb"; that is, a person tried for a crime and found innocent shall not be again put on trial for that same offense. The Fifth Amendment originally applied just to cases in federal court, but in 1969 the Supreme Court held the protection against double jeopardy binding on the states through the due process clause of the Fourteenth Amendment. *[Ch. 5, p. 87]*

dual federalism A nineteenth-century philosophy of federal government/state government relations which presupposed a very clear line of demarcation between the two. Each was assigned a large measure of independence for governmental actions in its own sphere, but the states were seen as having the larger sphere of action. *[Ch. 11, p. 282]*

due process The Fifth and Fourteenth Amendments to the Constitution provide that the national and state governments, respectively, shall not arbitrarily deny any person his life, liberty, or property. The idea of due process has always connoted adherence to proper procedures of action established in law, and at times the Supreme Court has additionally interpreted the term as requiring both the reasonableness of governmental actions and limits on the scope of those actions. *[Ch. 11, p. 279]*

egalitarianism A political-philosophic position that stresses the value of social equality. The "egalitarian revolution" which began in the West in the seventeenth and eighteenth centuries rejected the rigid social hierarchy and inequality inherent in the then-existing aristocratic societies. *[Ch. 4, pp. 67–70; Ch. 15, p. 430]*

electoral college Americans do not vote directly for the candidates for president and vice-president, but rather for slates of electors in each state pledged to one candidate or the other. Each state has a number of electoral votes equal to the number of representatives it has in Congress—its two senators plus however many members of the House of Representatives it has. The candidates receiving a majority of the electoral votes (at least 270) are declared elected president and vice-president. *[Ch. 8, p. 160]*

electoral volatility As party loyalties have weakened over the last quarter-century, more and more voters have moved back and forth from one party to the other depending on immediate events and the personal appeals of contending candidates. *[Ch. 15, p. 454]*

electronic press Refers to the fact that the electronic media of communication—radio and television—have become primary sources of political information for many Americans. The press is no longer confined to newspapers and news magazines. *[Ch. 16, p. 470]*

elites Groups of persons who possess disproportionately large amounts of some scarce value—money, social prestige, political power, etc. Political elites exert extensive influence over political decision-making. *[Ch. 6, p. 105]*

entitlement programs Government programs requiring the payment of benefits to all individuals who meet the established eligibility requirements set forth in the legislation. Thus expenditures for an entitlement program such as Social Security are determined not by annual appropriations limits established by Congress, but rather by what is required to give all those eligible for benefits the level of monetary payments the law prescribes. *[Ch. 19, p. 614]*

equal employment opportunity The policy that racial, religious, sex, and age discrimination must be barred in hiring and firing employees and setting other conditions of their employment. At the federal level, the Equal Employment Opportunity Commission is charged with enforcing relevant federal statutes. [Ch. 17, p. 548]

Equal Rights Amendment (ERA) A proposed amendment to the U.S. Constitution, which did not receive the approval of a sufficient number of states for ratification in its first submission, providing that "equality of rights under the law shall not be denied or abridged by the United States or by any state on account of sex." [Ch. 17, p. 552]

equal time rule A provision of Section 315 of the Federal Communications Act of 1934 that requires that broadcasters who permit one candidate for public office to campaign on their stations must give equal opportunity to every other candidate for that office. They cannot sell airtime to a Democratic candidate for the House of Representatives, for example, and deny the same type of time at the same rates to a Republican candidate. [Ch. 16, p. 480]

equality of opportunity The political-philosophic position that insists a society should take all reasonable steps to assure its citizens an equal chance to pursue successfully life, liberty, and happiness, but that it should recognize the legitimacy of different levels of actual attainment. [Ch. 17, p. 532]

equality of result The position that a society should seek to achieve a condition where each citizen has approximately equal resources— where, for example, salaries are relatively equal. The varieties of socialism seek some measure of equality of result. [Ch. 19, p. 599]

establishment clause The First Amendment to the U.S. Constitution provides that "Congress shall make no law respecting an establishment of religion. . . ." It was enacted initially to prevent the creation of an of-

ficial church or religion in the United States. [Ch. 6, pp. 98–99]

exclusionary rule A legal position developed by the Supreme Court requiring that evidence or statements unlawfully obtained may not be used in court proceedings against individuals accused of crimes. [Ch. 17, p. 527]

exclusive jurisdiction The assignment to one court only of jurisdiction over a certain category of cases. For example, cases arising from alleged violation of state criminal statutes originate exclusively in the designated trial courts of the state. [Ch. 10, p. 258]

ex post facto law Article I, sections 9 and 10 of the Constitution forbid the national and state governments from enacting any subsequent legislation that makes illegal an act that was legal at the time it was committed or that changes the penalty for a crime after its commission. The latin words mean simply "after the fact." [Ch. 11, p. 279]

factions A term used variously in the eighteenth century to refer to what we would now call interest groups, or to loosely organized cliques of like-minded political leaders—in the sense of a "faction" in a state legislature. [Ch. 5, p. 84; Ch. 13, p. 355]

fairness doctrine Section 315 of the Federal Communications Act of 1934 requires radio and television broadcasters who air material on controversial issues to provide reasonable time for the expression of opposing viewpoints. [Ch. 16, p. 480]

Federal Reserve System The central bank of the United States, including the Board of Governors and the Federal Reserve Banks located throughout the United States, with broad powers to regulate the money supply and interest rates. [Ch. 18, p. 586]

federalism A system of government, found in the United States and a number of other countries including Canada, Switzerland, and India, in which power is constitutionally divided between a central government and governments of the constituent states or provinces. *[Ch. 11, p. 273]*

Federalist Papers Eighty-five essays authored by John Jay, James Madison, and Alexander Hamilton, published in New York newspapers in late 1787 and early 1788, defending the newly proposed U.S. Constitution and urging its ratification. *[Ch. 5, pp. 84–85]*

federalists Initially, those who favored ratification of the U.S. Constitution establishing a federal system of government in place of the previous confederal form. Later, a political party whose most prominent leaders were Alexander Hamilton and John Adams, which had its principal supporters among mercantile and other business interests in the Northeast. The Federalist party disappeared early in the nineteenth century. *[Ch. 5, p. 85; Ch. 15, p. 433]*

filibuster An attempt in the U.S. Senate to defeat a bill by taking advantage of the unlimited debate provisions of Senate rules and talking indefinitely on it, preventing action on other legislative business. *[Ch. 7, p. 121]*

fiscal policy Governmental efforts to maintain a prospering economy by varying taxation and expenditure levels. For example, if government increases expenditures well beyond tax revenues, its fiscal policy is providing economic stimulus. *[Ch. 18, p. 565]*

fiscal year (FY) The twelve-month span in which financial accounting is made. The accounting year of the federal government runs from October 1 to September 30. "FY '85" refers to the fiscal year ending September 30, 1985. *[Ch. 18, pp. 563–65]*

"fourth branch of government" Refers to the prominent position of the press in government and politics in democracies like the United States—such that the press is seen figuratively as a branch of the government itself. *[Ch. 16, p. 495]*

franchise The right to vote. *[Ch. 14, pp. 387–88, 392]*

Frostbelt Refers to the older industrial states of the Northeast and Midwest that have experienced at times painful adjustments with the movement of people and jobs to more newly industrializing (and warmer) states South and West. *[Ch. 3, p. 46]*

full faith and credit Article IV, Section 1 of the U.S. Constitution requires that "full faith and credit shall be given in each state to the public acts, records, and judicial proceedings of every other state." *[Ch. 11, p. 281]*

gerrymandering Drawing legislative district lines to obtain partisan political advantage. Some legislative districts have truly bizarre shapes, reflecting a party's efforts to carve the constituency to its advantage. *[Ch. 7, p. 119]*

grants-in-aid Funds appropriated by Congress to state and local governments for various programs administered by state agencies under federal standards: health, welfare, and highway construction programs are important ones built on federal grants-in-aid. *[Ch. 11, p. 291]*

gross national product (GNP) A statistical measure of the total value of goods and services produced in a country in a particular period. Changes in the gross national product of the United States from one year to another are primary indicators of the rate of economic growth. *[Ch. 18, p. 555]*

habeas corpus (writ of) An order of a court requiring officials who have custody of a prisoner to bring the prisoner to court and justify his detention. *[Ch. 5, p. 87]*

"hawks" and "doves" Ornithological references to foreign policy positions; "hawks" are those taking a "hard line" to foreign adversaries, while foreign policy "doves" are more inclined to offer olive branches. *[Ch. 20, p. 672]*

ideology A set of political beliefs and values that are constrained or linked together. Political ideologies prescribe answers to such questions as how government should be organized, what roles it should play, how a nation's economy should be managed, the distribution of resources among groups making up the populace, etc. *[Ch. 4, p. 62]*

impeachment The bringing of formal charges of misconduct in office against a public official; the president of the United States and other federal officers may be impeached for "high crimes and misdemeanors" by the House of Representatives, following which a trial on the impeachment charges is held in the Senate. *[Ch. 8, p. 166]*

impoundment The president's holding back funds which Congress appropriated for various stated purposes. Richard Nixon's ambitious use of impoundment in the late 1960s and early 1970s provoked a major confrontation with Congress and led to the passage of important new legislation restricting the president's use of this tool. *[Ch. 7, p. 147]*

independent regulatory commissions Agencies charged with regulation of American economic life, including interstate commerce, banking, and financial affairs, communications, and labor relations. The independent regulatory commissions were set up with the idea that they should be insulated from regular presidential leadership and political direction; commissioners are appointed for long (five years or more), staggered terms, and may be dismissed by the president only for "inefficiency, neglect of duty, or malfeasance in office." *[Ch. 9, p. 209]*

individualism A political and social philosophy that places special emphasis on the rights of individuals and on individual freedom and initiative as the basis for social action. *[Ch. 4, pp. 63, 70]*

industrial policy An approach to economic policy in the contemporary United States which blends an emphasis on stimulating economic growth with an enlarged role for government, especially in promoting the conditions for growth. Advocates of industrial policy look to Japan for ideas of a new government-business partnership to stimulate growth industries. *[Ch. 18, p. 583]*

inflation Increases in the price of goods and services. Bouts of "double-digit inflation"—annual increases in consumer prices of 10% or more—in the United States in the 1970s prompted a strong public demand for corrective actions by government. *[Ch. 18, pp. 566, 511]*

initiative An electoral procedure through which citizens may propose legislation or constitutional amendments by petitions signed by a requisite number of voters—usually in the range of 5–15% of the total in a state. Propositions receiving the requisite number of signatures are placed on the ballot for decision by majority vote in the next election. *[Ch. 6, p. 101]*

in-kind benefits Benefits in the form of goods and services, rather than cash. For example, welfare programs in the United States often provide beneficiaries with hospital and doctor's care, subsidized housing, food stamps, and other noncash assistance. *[Ch. 19, p. 601]*

interest group A body of people acting in an organized fashion to advance shared political interests. *[Ch. 13, p. 351]*

iron triangle Refers to the close interaction that often occurs in policy formation in the United States among the executive branch bureau with immediate responsibility for a policy area, the legislative subcommittee that supervises the agency and policy, and the interest groups with immediate stakes in the area. It is the relatively closed nature of these bureau–subcommittee–interest group relationships that led to their depiction as iron-hard. *[Ch. 9, pp. 216–17; Ch. 13, p. 383]*

isolationism A description often given, somewhat erroneously, to American foreign policy prior to World War II, suggesting that the U.S. somehow sought to isolate itself from the rest of the world. In fact, American foreign policy was typically based on the premise that the country should intervene in world affairs as its interests dictate, but that its intervention should *not* be through an established system of alliances. *[Ch. 20, p. 630]*

"Jim Crow" laws The name applied to a body of laws enacted in southern states for a century after the Civil War providing for the segregation of blacks and their exclusion from full participation in social, economic, and political life. *[Ch. 17, p. 518]*

joint committees Legislative committees composed of members of both houses in bicameral legislatures. *[Ch. 7, p. 125]*

judicial activism The broadening intervention of higher courts, especially the federal courts, in policy formation and execution. Advocates of judicial activism endorse this expanded role, arguing that greater juridical protection of individual rights is needed. *[Ch. 10, pp. 250–51]*

judicial review The power of courts, such as the U.S. Supreme Court, to review acts of the legislative and executive branches and, ultimately, to invalidate them if they are held to be in violation of constitutional requirements. *[Ch. 10, p. 237]*

judicial self-restraint A position arguing that judges should grant great leeway to the decisions and actions of popularly elected legislatures and executives, except when such actions are in patent contradiction of constitutional standards. *[Ch. 10, p. 253]*

jurisdiction The authority of a court to hear and decide a category of cases. *[Ch. 10, p. 258]*

justiciability The issue of whether courts are institutionally suited to providing remedies in a particular type of case. Is there something that a court can do for a plaintiff if the plaintiff is in the legal right? Does the subject lend itself to resolution by a court of law? *[Ch. 10, p. 262]*

Keynesian economics Economic perspectives and understanding that owe an intellectual debt to the pioneering work of British economist John Maynard Keynes (1883–1946). Present-day Keynesians remain committed to the use of fiscal policy to promote economic growth, and to an expanding welfare state. *[Ch. 18, pp. 558–60]*

legislative apportionment The distribution of legislative seats among the states or, more generally, among any set of constituent governmental units. *[Ch. 10, p. 245]*

legislative oversight The attempt by Congress (or by a state legislature) to surpervise the executive branch as it administers the laws the legislature has enacted. *[Ch. 7, p. 151]*

legislative veto The president or some executive branch agency is granted authority to act in a given policy or administrative area, but with the stipulation that the subsequent resolution of one or both houses of Congress may overturn the executive action. The constitutionality of the legislative veto under the American system of separation of powers is now under challenge. *[Ch. 7, p. 152]*

libel Publication of a story harmful to the reputation of an individual that can be demonstrated to be untrue. In the United States, before libel may be established in the case of a public official against some news medium, not only defamatory inaccuracy but also malicious intent must be demonstrated. *[Ch. 16, p. 481]*

liberal In contemporary American usage, a position which favors a more expansive use of government in economic management and the promotion of public welfare. Historically, the term refers to classical liberalism—a doctrine developed in Europe in the seventeenth and eighteenth centuries and brought to the U.S. by early settlers, emphasizing individual rights, private property, and limited government. *[Ch. 4, p. 63]*

libertarian A political doctrine emphasizing individual liberty as the primary value society should promote and insisting that governmental restraints on individual action be kept to a minimum. *[Ch. 6, p. 109]*

lobbying Refers to the various efforts by interest group officials to influence governmental decisions, especially legislative votes. The term "lobby" was first used in seventeenth-century England, when a large anteroom near the House of Commons was referred to as "the lobby," and those who approached members of Parliament trying to influence them were lobbying. *[Ch. 13, p. 351]*

machine The American aversion to strong party organizations has led to the use of a number of pejorative terms to refer to them. Strong organizations are "machines," and their efforts at political influence are "machine politics." The nefarious chaps who head these political machines are the party "bosses." *[Ch. 15, pp. 441–42]*

majority leader Usually, the chief spokesman and ranking official of the majority party in a legislature. In the American House of Representatives, however, the Speaker is in fact the leader of the majority party, and the person designated majority leader is in fact his principal deputy and floor lieutenant. *[Ch. 7, p. 131]*

mandamus, writ of A court order requiring an individual, corporation, or government official to perform a specified act—fulfilling a contract, meeting his or her clear ministerial responsibilities, etc. *[Ch. 10, p. 238]*

manifest destiny The idea, widely shared by eighteenth- and nineteenth-century Americans, that the country was justified in expanding territorially, because of a special virtue and mission of the American people different from anything known previously. *[Ch. 5, pp. 75–76]*

Marxism An economic and political philosophy derived from the writings of the nineteenth-century German theorist Karl Marx, proclaimed by modern-day Communist countries and movements as their theoretical underpinnings. *[Ch. 6, p. 106]*

the melting pot The idea of America as a land where people of diverse backgrounds come together to form one nation; the achievement of strong American national unity out of diverse backgrounds. *[Ch. 4, p. 64]*

merit system Often used interchangeably with "civil service," a merit system is, specifically, a set of procedures for hiring, promoting, and dismissing government employees on the basis of their professional or technical performance, rather than political preference. *[Ch. 9, p. 225]*

military-industrial complex A term first used by President Dwight Eisenhower, referring to the growth in post–World War II America of a big permanent defense establishment and a large array of business corporations heavily dependent upon defense contracts. *[Ch. 20, pp. 664, 667]*

minority leader The leader of the minority party in a legislative body. *[ch. 7, p. 133]*

"Miranda Rules" A specific set of procedures that the Supreme Court has required law enforcement officials to follow in questioning persons accused of crimes—including the explicit warning to the accused that he has a right to remain silent, that any statement he may make may be used as evidence against him, and that he has the right to the presence of an attorney during any interrogation. *[Ch. 17, pp. 527–28]*

"molecular government" A description of the policy process in the United States as one broken down into a series of relatively small, separate and distinct environments where policies affecting a particular collection of groups or interests are worked out. *[Ch. 13, p. 384]*

monetarism A school in economic thought which places strong emphasis on controlling the money supply and the price of money (the interest rate) to secure a growing and inflation-free economy. *[Ch. 18, p. 580]*

monetary policy Encompasses issues of management of the country's money supply: decisions on how much it should be expanded at any time, and such related matters as interest rates and the ease of borrowing capital. *[Ch. 18, pp. 575, 586]*

"necessary and proper" clause The final clause of Article I, Section 8 of the U.S. Constitution gives Congress the authority to enact all laws "necessary and proper" to the carrying out of the specific powers and responsibilities previously enumerated. Because it is so expansive a grant of authority, it is sometimes known as the "elastic" clause. *[Ch. 7, p. 118; Ch. 11, p. 278]*

neutral competence The ideal that civil servants would be seen by their political superiors, and would so see their roles, as sources of policy expertise and administrative skills serving any lawfully constituted government, whatever its political leanings. *[Ch. 9, p. 231]*

the New Deal The administration in the 1930s of Democratic president Franklin D. Roosevelt and the new programs of economic management and public welfare that this administration developed. *[Ch. 15, p. 443]*

New Deal realignment The pronounced shift in the standing of the political parties, in which the Democrats replaced the Republicans as the new majority party, on the basis of new policy commitments that secured broad approval. *[Ch. 15, p. 443]*

North Atlantic Treaty Organization (NATO) An alliance of the United States, Canada, and a number of European nations, established under the North Atlantic Treaty of 1949, as a collective defense to balance the Soviet Union and its East European satellites. *[Ch. 20, p. 641]*

nullification The extreme States' Rights doctrine, espoused by various political leaders including John C. Calhoun, holding that the states retain the right to review actions and laws of the central government and, if need be, to declare them "null and void." *[Ch. 11, p. 281]*

oligarchy A system of government in which political power is held and exercised by a small elite group, whose position is based on military power, wealth, and/or social position. *[Ch. 6, p. 94]*

open primary A system of primary elections for choosing party nominees which permits voters to decide on election day which party primary they will participate in without expressing any affiliation with that party. *[Ch. 14, pp. 408–9]*

opinion of the court The majority opinion handed down by a court of law in a particular case. *[Ch. 10, p. 242]*

original jurisdiction Authority to adjudicate a case at its inception. The federal district courts are the primary courts of original jurisdiction in the federal system; trial courts in every state have this same responsibility. *[Ch. 10, pp. 258–59]*

parliamentary government A system of government where authority is vested in the legislature and in a cabinet elected by and responsible to that legislature. At present, the British, Canadian, West German, and Italian governments are examples of the parliamentary form. *[Ch. 7, pp. 118–19]*

participatory democracy An ideal of democratic government which emphasizes the importance of maximum direct participation in governmental affairs and decision-making by individual citizens. *[Ch. 6, p. 100]*

party identification Voters' feelings of attachment to or loyalty for a political party. In the United States, where few people hold any formal party membership, the Republican and Democratic parties are seen to be composed of people who simply think of themselves as Republicans or Democrats. *[Ch. 15, pp. 443–46]*

party platforms Statements of values and programs developed by Democratic and Republican party leaders and delegates at their national nominating conventions. *[Ch. 15, pp. 457–61]*

party press Early in American history, most newspapers had avowed ties to one political party or the other and, indeed, depended on subsidies from the parties—printing contracts and the like. Far from espousing the ideals of objectivity or neutrality, newspapers saw themselves as spokesmen for the contending parties. *[Ch. 16, p. 484]*

patronage The granting of jobs, contracts, and other political favors by the party in power. *[Ch. 9, pp. 219, 225–27]*

Pentagon The huge five-sided office building in Arlington, Virginia, across the Potomac River from Washington, D.C., which is the headquarters of the Department of Defense. *[Ch. 20, pp. 664, 667]*

per capita GNP The total dollar value of the country's production of goods and services in a given period of time, divided by the number of people in the country; that is, the level of national economic output expressed on a per-person basis. *[Ch. 18, pp. 555–56, 563–65]*

plaintiff The person who initiates a law suit in civil law; in criminal law, it is the government that formally brings charges and is known as the prosecution. *[Ch. 10, 242–45]*

pluralism The concept referring to a society as composed of diverse interests and groups which compete to achieve their social and political objectives and share in the exercise of political power—as opposed to a condition of society where one group or set of interests possesses disproportionate political power, to the exclusion of other groups' interests. *[Ch. 6, pp. 107–8; Ch. 11, p. 303]*

plurality The winning of an election with more votes than any other candidate or party but not necessarily with an absolute majority of the total vote; if three candidates contend and one wins 40%, the second 35%, and the third 25%, the first wins a plurality but not a majority of the vote. In most but not all elections in the U.S., a simple plurality of the vote is sufficient to win. *[Ch. 15, pp. 447–48]*

plural-member district A legislative district from which two or more representatives are elected; in the United States, the preponderance of legislative districts are of the *single-member* variety. *[Ch. 14, p. 405]*

political action committees (PACs) Organizations formed by business corporations, labor unions, trade associations, ideological groups, and the like to raise and disperse funds for political objectives—including making contributions to candidates for electoral office. The activities of PACs are formally sanctioned and tightly regulated in federal campaign finance legislation. *[Ch. 6, p. 109; Ch. 14, pp. 418–19]*

political culture The general attitudes and values of a people which bear on the conduct of government and politics. *[Ch. 1, pp. 4–5]*

political socialization The introduction of young people to a country's political norms and values—through the family, the press, the schools, etc. *[Ch. 4, p. 62]*

polity Generally, a term meaning "political system"; specifically, a term meaning a type of democratic government with constitutional protection of minority rights. *[Preface; Ch. 6, p. 94]*

poll tax A tax that must be paid in order to vote. Widely used earlier in American history, poll taxes are now held to be unconstitutional. *[Ch. 14, pp. 389–90]*

popular sovereignty The concept which holds that ultimate political authority resides with the general public; synonymous with "government by the people," the idea of popular sovereignty is at the core of democracy. *[Ch. 6, p. 97]*

postindustrial Term referring to socioeconomic conditions which have recently appeared in the United States and a few other economically advanced countries, where the dominant occupational center has moved from manufacturing to the service sector, and where high levels of education and advanced technology contribute to new clusters of political interests as well as to a new dynamic for further economic development. *[Ch. 2, p. 17]*

power elite A group or cluster of political interests held to exercise disproportionate power; a term introduced by sociologist C. Wright Mills. *[Ch. 6, pp. 105–6]*

power of the purse The historic authority of democratic legislatures to control governmental finance by the requirement that no monies may be expanded without explicit legislative appropriation; Article I, Section 9 of the U.S. Constitution grants the Congress the power of the purse. *[Ch. 7, p. 147]*

president pro tempore The presiding officer of the U.S. Senate in the absence of the vice-president; position conferred on the senator from the majority party who has the greatest seniority in the Senate. *[Ch. 7, pp. 131–34]*

presidential primary Election held for choosing delegates to the Republican or Democratic party's national presidential nominating convention; developed early in the nineteenth century to open up delegate selection to the rank and file of party adherents. *[Ch. 14, p. 409]*

primary election An election held before the general election, in which rank-and-file voters select candidates for the Democratic and Republican party slates; primaries began replacing party organizational bodies—such as state central committees and state conventions—as the instruments of nominee selection early in the twentieth century. [Ch. 14, p. 408]

probability sampling Public opinion polls now rely on select respondents through statistical approaches designed to give every individual an equal or known chance of being included in the sample. [Ch. 12, pp. 330–31]

progressive taxation Based on the principle that the tax rate should increase as the amount of income increases; the federal income tax is a progressive tax, whereas state sales taxes typically provide for the same rate or percentage of taxation regardless of income. [Ch. 19, p. 603]

progressivism A political movement that developed in the United States early in the twentieth century, especially strong in the urban, professional middle classes, which sought governmental reforms to weaken "party bosses" and special interests and to reduce corruption. [Ch. 6, pp. 100–101]

project grants Federal grants-in-aid developed in the 1960s and 1970s to provide variable grants to state and local governments and to nonprofit human services organizations for such projects as bilingual education, control of juvenile delinquency, and assistance for the handicapped. [Ch. 11, p. 295]

proportional representation (PR) Electoral systems based on multi-member districts, where seats are divided among the contending parties in proportion to their percentages of the votes cast. [Ch. 14, p. 406]

public-interest group An interest group that seeks collective goods, the achievement of which will not materially benefit the group's members or activists; contrasts with more conventional interest groups based on immediate economic interests; includes groups with environmental objectives, civil liberties goals, etc. [Ch. 13, p. 357]

quota sampling A means of selecting respondents in public opinion polls in which quotas of respondents are drawn to match known group distributions in the population—so many men and women, so many young people, so many manual workers, etc. In the U.S., quota sampling has largely been replaced by probability sampling. [Ch. 12, pp. 330–31]

quotas The setting of numerical targets for admitting minority-group students or hiring minority employees, with the intent of increasing the representation of groups historically subject to discrimination. [Ch. 17, p. 533]

random-digit dialing A means of selecting respondents in telephone surveys that applies the theory of probability sampling. [Ch. 12, pp. 330–31]

ranking member The legislator with the greatest seniority on a particular committee of any member of his political party; in Congress the ranking majority party member on a committee typically becomes the committee chairman. [Ch. 7, pp. 127–28, 131–32]

ratification The formal approval of a constitution or compact or amendments thereto. Amendments to the U.S. Constitution require ratification by extraordinary majorities, including three-fourths of all the states. [Ch. 5, p. 85]

realignment A major shift in the partisan support of the social groups making up a society and in the lines of conflict over public policy. [Ch. 15, pp. 443–44]

reapportionment The redrawing of legislative district lines to reflect changed conditions, typically, in the U.S., to reflect population shifts following each decennial census. [Ch. 10, pp. 245–47]

reconciliation A legislative procedure in the U.S. Congress through which a resolution passed by both houses reconciles the specific appropriations for individual programs and agencies with an overall budget ceiling that Congress has set. *[Ch. 7, p. 150]*

referendum An electoral procedure widely used in American state and local governments where rank-and-file voters may approve or disapprove a legislative act; the legislature refers a policy matter or constitutional amendment to the electorate for final action. *[Ch. 6, p. 101]*

regressive taxation Forms of taxation where the tax burden falls disproportionately on low-income persons; the application of sales taxes to food and other necessities, which is done in a few states, is an example of highly regressive taxation. *[Ch. 19, p. 601]*

representative democracy A democratic system in which the public chooses representatives, including legislators, who are charged with working out the details of legislation and policy—as opposed to direct democracy in which the public expresses itself directly on specific policy questions. *[Ch. 5, pp. 90–91]*

republicanism A philosophy of government which holds that institutions and policies should reflect popular wishes, rather than being the province of some elite such as a hereditary aristocracy. *[Ch. 6, p. 97]*

research and development (R&D) Expenditures for scientific research and technological development required for the development of new products, weaponry, medical advances, etc. *[Ch. 2, p. 21]*

revenue-sharing A form of federal grants-in-aid in which federal funds are made available to state and local governments to be used largely at the latter's discretion—subject only to the requirement that they may not be used for programs which discriminate on the basis of race, national origin, sex, age, religion, or physical handicap. *[Ch. 11, p. 297]*

right of rebuttal A provision of Section 315 of the Federal Communications Act of 1934 which involves the right of individuals to respond to personal attacks made on them over radio or television which might be held to damage their reputations. *[Ch. 16, pp. 480–81]*

roll-call vote (or record vote) The vote by a legislature in which the roll of all members of the body is called, or now in which the vote of each member is recorded electronically. *[Ch. 7, pp. 131–32]*

rule A set of provisions issued by the Rules Committee of the House of Representatives which stipulate the conditions under which a bill is debated on the House floor—whether and how subsequent amendments may be introduced, the time limit for debate, etc. *[Ch. 7, pp. 122–23]*

sampling error Refers to the extent to which the results in a sample of respondents in a public opinion survey can be expected to differ from the results that would be obtained if everyone in the population had been interviewed. *[Ch. 12, pp. 330–31]*

secession The extreme states' rights position which argued that the American states retained sovereignty and could leave the government established by the Constitution if they so chose; finally rejected at Appomattox Court House in 1865. *[Ch. 11, p. 282]*

segregation The separation of whites and blacks in public facilities; established by law throughout the states of the American South after the Civil War and survived largely intact up until the 1950s and 1960s. *[Ch. 17, p. 514]*

select and special committees In Congress, committees established to investigate special problems and to report on them to the parent chamber—e.g., the House Select Committee on Aging—and those established to perform special functions for one party or the other in Congress, such as the Republican Senatorial Campaign Committee. *[Ch. 7, p. 125]*

selective incorporation A series of rulings by the U.S. Supreme Court that the various specific guarantees of the first ten amendments to the Constitution, which applied initially only to the federal government, be applied as well against state infringement through the due process clause of the Fourteenth Amendment—that no state may deny any person "life, liberty, or property, without due process of law." *[Ch. 17, p. 525]*

Senatorial courtesy The unwritten agreement among senators whereby they will not agree to a president's appointment of various officials, especially federal district court judges, if these nominations are not acceptable to the senator or senators of the president's party from the state where the office is located. *[Ch. 10, p. 265]*

senior executive service (SES) Established by the 1978 Civil Service Reform Act, the SES includes about 8500 executives in the three highest General Service (GS) grades of federal employment and in the top levels of the Executive Schedule; an effort to develop in the U.S. a cadre of skilled, experienced career officials trusted and relied upon by succeeding administrations with contrasting political goals. *[Ch. 9, p. 231]*

seniority Custom long observed in the U.S. Congress whereby many leadership positions, especially committee and subcommittee chairmanships, are assigned on the basis of length of service in Congress or on a particular committee. *[Ch. 7, p. 144]*

separate but equal doctrine A doctrine proclaimed by the Supreme Court in *Plessy v. Ferguson* (1896), permitting segregated facilities for blacks in various states on the pretense that these facilities are equal to those available to whites. "Separate but equal" was overturned by the Supreme Court in a series of decisions in the 1940s and 1950s, especially *Brown v. Board of Education of Topeka* (1954). *[Ch. 10, p. 243]*

separation of powers A central principle of American government whereby governmental power is constitutionally divided among the executive, legislative, and judicial branches. *[Ch. 5, p. 83]*

single-member districts Legislative districts from which only a single legislator is chosen, typically by plurality vote. Seats in the U.S. Congress, and in state legislatures, are apportioned on the single-member district basis. *[Ch. 14, p. 405]*

Speaker The chief presiding officer of the U.S. House of Representatives, who is also the leader of the majority party in the House and elected by that majority; second in line of presidential succession, after the vice-president. *[Ch. 7, pp. 131, 139]*

split-ticket voting Ballots cast in which voters support candidates of one party for certain offices while backing the other party's candidates in other contests on the same ballot; split-ticket voting has become increasingly common over the last quarter-century. *[Ch. 15, p. 454]*

spoils system Awarding government jobs to political supporters of the winning party; widely followed in the U.S. until the development of merit civil service systems in the late nineteenth and early twentieth centuries. *[Ch. 9, pp. 225–26]*

"spreading the action" A series of steps taken in the U.S. Congress in the late 1960s and 1970s to strengthen the position of individual representatives—increasing their staffs, enlarging the number of subcommittees, extending subcommittee independence, etc. *[Ch. 7, p. 128]*

standing To bring suit, an individual must show that he has sutained or been threatened with real injury; merely having an interest in a matter is not sufficient to establish standing to sue. *[Ch. 10, p. 260]*

standing committees The permanently established committees responsible for legislation in the various major substantive areas—such as the foreign relations, judiciary, and appropriations committees in the U.S. Congress. *[Ch. 7, p. 125]*

states' rights In the most general sense, those rights and powers reserved to the states in the American federal system; more specifically, the various arguments made historically which emphasize the claims of states against various federal actions. *[Ch. 11, pp. 281–82]*

straight-ticket voting Casting a ballot in which one supports a party's nominees for all of the offices being voted upon. *[Ch. 15, p. 454]*

suffrage The right to vote; gradually extended in the United States in the nineteenth and twentieth centuries, so that now the suffrage extends to virtually all citizens 18 years of age and older. *[Ch. 10, p. 247; Ch. 14, pp. 391–93]*

Sunbelt Refers to the warm-weather states of the South and West that have received substantial in-migrations and economic development over the last quarter-century. *[Ch. 3, p. 46]*

supply-side economics An approach to questions of political economy in the United States which emphasizes the importance of tax cuts and other measures designed to encourage greater individual initiative, investment, and overall economic growth,

especially by reducing high marginal tax rates. *[Ch. 18, p. 581]*

supremacy doctrine Article VI of the U.S. Constitution provides that the Constitution and laws enacted by the national government under it are the supreme law of the land, to which state legislation and actions must submit. *[Ch. 10, pp. 235–36; Ch. 11, p. 278]*

third parties In the United States, where two parties have historically dominated electoral contests, all other minor parties. *[Ch. 14, p. 407–408; Ch. 15, p. 437]*

"Tweedledum and Tweedledee" Refers to the argument that the two major political parties in the U.S. are pretty much alike in their policy commitments; a literary illusion to creations of Lewis Carroll in his *Through the Looking Glass:*

Some say compared to Bononcini
That Mynheer Handel's but a ninny;
Others aver that he to Handel
Is scarcely fit to hold a candle.
Strange all this difference should be
'Twixt tweedle-dum and tweedle-dee.
[Ch. 6, p. 109; Ch. 15, p. 438]

unanimous consent A time-saving procedure used in Congress and other legislative bodies in the adoption of noncontroversial legislation, motions, etc.; "without objection," regular procedures, including roll-call votes, are dispensed with when such noncontroversial measures are being considered. *[Ch. 7, p. 122]*

unemployment compensation Benefits for unemployed workers, first established in the United States at the national level by the Social Security Act of 1936. *[Ch. 19, pp. 609–10]*

unicameralism Legislative power resting with one house or chamber, rather than with two (which is bicameralism). Of the fifty state legislatures in the United States, only one, Nebraska's, is unicameral, but the majority of local government legislatures—county boards and town councils—are unicameral. *[Ch. 7, p. 119; Ch. 11, 278]*

unilateralism The dominant approach in U.S. foreign policy until World War II, in which the United States elected to "go it alone" in the sense of avoiding a system of regular alliances with foreign countries. *[Ch. 20, p. 638]*

unitary government A centralized government, like Great Britain's, in which local governments exercise only those powers assigned to them by the national government—in contrast to the federal system employed in the United States where power is constitutionally divided between the national and state governments. *[Ch. 11, p. 273]*

veto The power of a political executive, such as the president, to kill a piece of legislation by refusing to sign it; the president's veto of bills may be overridden by Congress by a two-thirds vote. *[Ch. 5, p. 84]*

welfare state A concept referring to the role of government as a basic provider of individual economic security and well-being; the complex array of social programs developed in many modern societies, in the case of the United States beginning with the New Deal. *[Ch. 19, pp. 596–605]*

whip An assistant floor leader in a legislature, whose responsibilities include trying to persuade his party's legislators to hold to the position the leadership has determined. *[Ch. 7, Fig. 7.3]*

white primary To continue to exclude blacks from meaningful electoral participation, even following passage of the Fifteenth Amendment, which forbids states from denying the right to vote on the grounds of race, southern states took the position that primaries were not in fact Fifteenth Amendment-covered elections but rather the instruments of parties as private organizations. The "private" Democratic parties of the South then forbade black participation. The white primary was declared unconstitutional by the Supreme Court in *Smith v. Allright* (1944) *[Ch. 14, p. 390]*

yellow journalism Refers to the sensationalism which came to flourish in the American press in the late nineteenth century as publishers such as William Randolph Hearst sought to expand greatly their readership with a stream of color and titillation. *[Ch. 16, p. 486]*

Photograph Credits

Index